HOLLAND
BELGIUM
& LUXEMBOURG

THE ROUGH GUIDE

THE ROUGH GUIDES

OTHER AVAILABLE ROUGH GUIDES

EUROPE • ITALY • VENICE • TUSCANY & UMBRIA • SICILY • GREECE
CRETE • FRANCE • PARIS • PROVENCE • BRITTANY & NORMANDY
PYRENEES • PORTUGAL • SPAIN • BARCELONA • SCANDINAVIA
IRELAND • AMSTERDAM • GERMANY • BERLIN • CZECHOSLOVAKIA
HUNGARY • POLAND • EASTERN EUROPE • YUGOSLAVIA • ISRAEL
TURKEY • NEPAL • HONG KONG • EGYPT • WEST AFRICA • KENYA
TUNISIA • MOROCCO • ZIMBABWE & BOTSWANA • USA • FLORIDA
CALIFORNIA & WEST COAST USA • SAN FRANCISCO • NEW YORK
CANADA • MEXICO • PERU • BRAZIL • GUATEMALA & BELIZE
MEDITERRANEAN WILDLIFE • WOMEN TRAVEL
NOTHING VENTURED

FORTHCOMING
BULGARIA • THAILAND • WORLD MUSIC

ROUGH GUIDE CREDITS

Series Editor: Mark Ellingham
Editorial: Martin Dunford, John Fisher, Jack Holland, Jonathan Buckley, Greg Ward
Production: Susanne Hillen, Kate Berens, Andy Hilliard, Vivien Antwi
Typesetting: Gail Jammy
Series Design: Andrew Oliver

Special **thanks** to Michael Baert and the Belgian Tourist Office, Rudi Boersma at Netherlands Railways, Marcel Balthus and the Netherlands Board of Tourism, Belgian National Railways, the Luxembourg Tourist Office and (as ever) Odette Taminiau of the VVV in Amsterdam, all of whose help was invaluable in the preparation of this guide. Thanks also to Bridget Bouch, Cathy Rees, Emma Rose Rees, Mog Greenwood; to Kate Berens for lightning proofreading, Gail Jammy for equally rapid page make-up and Rachel Papworth for eleventh-hour information.

The publishers and authors have done their best to ensure the accuracy and currency of all the information in *Holland, Belgium and Luxembourg: The Rough Guide;* however, they can accept no responsibility for any loss, injury, or inconvenience sustained by any traveller as a result of information or advice contained in the guide.

First published by Harrap Columbus, Chelsea House, 26 Market Square, Bromley, Kent BR1 1NA and reprinted 1991.
This 1992 reprint published by Rough Guides Ltd, 149 Kennington Lane, London SE11 4EZ.
Distributed by Penguin Books, 27 Wrights Lane, London W8 5TZ.

Typeset in Linotron Univers and Century Old Style
Printed in the UK by Cox & Wyman Ltd, Reading, Berks.

Illustrations in Part One and Part Three by Ed Briant; Basics illustration by David Loftus; Contexts illustration by Sally Davies.

528pp
includes index

A catalogue record for this book is available from the British Library.

ISBN 1-85828-003-6 (previously published by Harrap Columbus under ISBN 0-7471-0111-6)

HOLLAND BELGIUM & LUXEMBOURG

THE ROUGH GUIDE

Written and researched by

**MARTIN DUNFORD,
JACK HOLLAND and PHIL LEE**

with additional research by
Nicola Baxter, Ros Belford, Laura P. Valtorta
and Sara and Jon Henley

Edited by

Martin Dunford and Jack Holland

THE ROUGH GUIDES

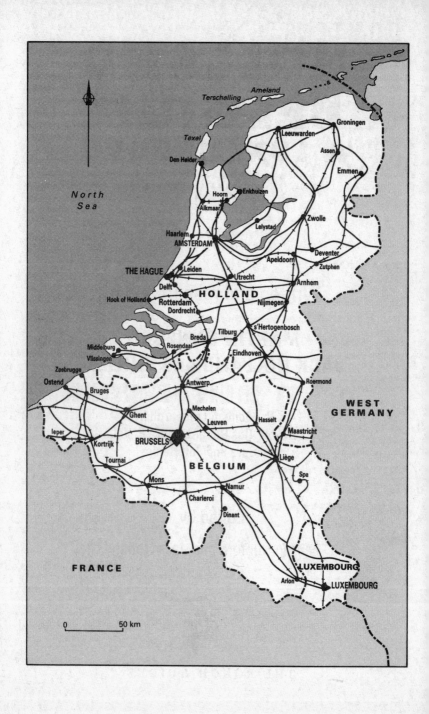

CONTENTS

INTRODUCTION

olland, **Belgium** and **Luxembourg** together make up one of the most densely populated regions of Europe. Historically, all three nations have been closely entwined, sharing the same history of colonial oppression and subsequent independence until 1830, when Belgium and Luxembourg became separate states. As a result, there are cultural similarities which run very deep: in language – Dutch is spoken in both Holland and northern Belgium, French in southern Belgium and Luxembourg; in cuisine – southern Belgium's long and honourable tradition of good food influencing the rich dishes of Luxembourg to the east; even in architecture – compare the gabled facades of northern Belgium to those of provincial Holland. The landscape also ignores frontiers, the plains of northern Belgium merging into the flat southern provinces of Holland. Sometimes, travelling around, you would hardly know you had crossed a border: formalities are few, and there's often little obvious change apart from car registration plates and currency – and between Belgium and Luxembourg even that remains the same.

Within this homogeneity, however, regional differences remain, especially in Belgium, which clearly divides between the north – Flanders – a flat Flemish-speaking region that's home to most of its historic towns, and the hillier French-speaking southern region of Wallonia. Holland is a less obviously divided state, its unifying factor being water, the presence of which is reflected almost everywhere – in the food (plenty of fish), the look of the towns (charmingly cut by canals), and the landscape, the reclaimed polder areas enjoying slender protection from the open sea by means of dykes. In spite of this there are discernible regions. Though only three hours away by train, Friesland – and especially its offshore islands – can seem a world away from Amsterdam and the other Randstad cities, a feeling reinforced by the attitudes of the locals, who look on the capital as a kind of faraway "sin city" that impinges little on their everyday lives.

Despite these distinctions, few travellers stray far beyond the major centres of Bruges, Brussels and Amsterdam, most treating the Low Countries as a sort of weekend-away destination for the work-weary. Certainly few really know – or care to know – the region, which is a shame as there is plenty to discover. The Belgian (and Luxembourg) Ardennes offer some of the wildest, most untamed **scenery** in this part of Europe, fast-flowing rivers and steep gorges sitting beneath green hills and towering crags high enough for some of Europe's most northerly ski resorts. Belgium and Holland also hold some of Europe's most historic **cities** – places like Bruges, Ghent, Antwerp, Leiden, Haarlem and Maastricht, to name only the most memorable – all of which have superbly preserved city centres, while maintaining a lively and relevant cultural life. Of the **capitals**, Belgium has in **Brussels** one of Europe's most cosmopolitan and happening cities, despite its relatively dour reputation; **Amsterdam**, with its delicate balance of seediness and culture, and perhaps the world's most beautifully preserved city centre, needs no introduction; while **Luxembourg** more than compensates for a lack of sights with a marvellously spectacular location.

Among things to do and see, you can enjoy the well-displayed fruits of the region's long and distinguished **artistic tradition** in some wonderful galleries. Outside the urban centres, **cycling** is not surprisingly a big activity, both in the low landscapes of north Belgium and Holland and – to a greater degree if anything – in the hills of the Ardennes. **Hiking**, too, is second to none, in the Belgian Ardennes and in Luxembourg, while in northern Holland at low tide people go *wadlopen* or **mud-walking** across the dank mud flats to the Frisian islands.

Climate and when to go

All three countries enjoy a temperate **climate**, with warm, if fairly mild, summers and cold winters. Generally speaking, temperatures rise the further south you go, with Belgium a couple of degrees warmer than Holland for much of the year. To the east, also, temperatures begin to dip, as the more severe climate of continental Europe begins to assert itself. In all three countries, rain is a possibility all year round.

Holland's climate is influenced by the ubiquitous proximity of water, and in winter city centre canals can make the streets alongside brutally cold – though the western, maritime side of the country is in general warmer than the eastern provinces. **Belgium** enjoys a fairly standard temperate climate, slightly warmer than Holland on the whole, though growing colder the further east you go – something emphasised by the increase in altitude with the Ardennes. In **Luxembourg** temperatures are that little bit more extreme, with sometimes fairly harsh winters that almost always bring snow. In both countries you can expect more rain in the Ardennes and upland regions.

As regards **clothing**, you should take whatever you would wear at the same time of year in Britain – heavy coats, hats and gloves in winter, lighter clothes and warm sweaters for the evening in summer, with some kind of rain protection all year round.

AVERAGE DAILY TEMPERATURES (C)			
	Holland	**Belgium**	**Luxembourg**
January	2	1	0
February	2	4	1
March	5	7	7
April	8	11	11
May	12	13	13
June	15	18	17
July	17	19	19
August	17	18	16
September	15	17	15
October	11	12	9
November	6	7	4
December	3	3	2

PART ONE

THE
BASICS

GETTING THERE

The wide range of options available – by plane, train or coach – to reach Holland, Belgium or Luxembourg means deciding between a low-cost but time-consuming ferry crossing and a swift but more expensive flight. Whichever alternative you opt for, you'll find a variety of competitive fares.

BY PLANE

Flying to any of the major airports in the Low Countries – Schipol (for Amsterdam), Brussels, Antwerp or Maastricht – represents a considerable saving in time compared to the ferry connections: Schipol, for example, is just fifty minutes' flying time from London.

Fares tend to be slightly more expensive to destinations other than Schipol or Brussels: the large number of flights passing through both these cities has led to a mass of cheap tickets, and it's reasonably easy to find a return fare from London for around £70; a standard, unrestricted ticket will cost well over £100. To find the current bargains, study the ads in the Sunday travel sections of the quality newspapers (*The Observer* especially) or, if you live in London, the back pages of the listings magazine *Time Out* or the *Evening Standard*.

Alternatively, go to a **discount flight agent** such as *STA Travel, Campus Travel* or *Council Travel* (addresses below), who specialise in youth flights and, if you're under 26 or a student, can offer savings on the price of a flight; they also offer ordinary discounted tickets.

It's also worth trying the **national scheduled airlines** – *British Airways, Sabena* and *Luxair* – since their fares can be competitive with the cheaper operators. The best deal you'll get with a scheduled airline is with an APEX or Super PEX ticket: these cost around £100 return (£160 upward for Luxembourg) and have to be booked fourteen days in advance; you have to spend one Saturday night abroad, and have no option to change your flight. To gain more flexibility you'll need to buy a standard return – which can prove more than twice as expensive. The **smaller operators**, such as *British Midland, Air UK* and *Air Europe*, sometimes work out cheaper.

If you don't live in London, bear in mind that there's a plethora of flights leaving from various **UK regional airports**, especially to Benelux capital cities, and that these can be good value alternatives, particularly if you use the smaller operators. Their APEX fares average £125 return, but bargains can be found as low as £65. The larger, national carriers tend to be prohibitively expensive. It's also worth considering a **package deal** if you want to stay in one city and have your accommodation arrangements organised beforehand; these can be surprisingly good value (see below for more details).

BY TRAIN

TO HOLLAND

British Rail operates combined **boat-train** services from London to Amsterdam (Centraal Station). Two daily departures run from Liverpool Street via Harwich to the Hook of Holland, passing through Rotterdam, The Hague, Leiden and Haarlem before reaching Amsterdam; return fares are £56 for a five-day excursion, £71 otherwise. There are four daily departures from London Victoria via Dover and Ostend in Belgium; five-day excursions cost £53, longer stays as much as £99, depending on the sailing and the time of year. Total journey times are the same on both routes (10–12hr), and tickets are valid for two months. Basically, the choice of route really depends on how long you want to spend on the water. If you opt to travel at night, cabin supplements start at around £10 per person. Tickets for these services (and to all other destinations in the Low Countries) can be bought from any

AIRLINE ADDRESSES AND ROUTES

Aer Lingus 223 Regent St, London W1 (☎081/569 5555). Birmingham to Brussels, Manchester to Schipol

Air Europe 52 Grosvenor Gdns, London SW1 (☎0345/ 444737). London (Gatwick) to Rotterdam, Antwerp and Brussels.

Air UK Stansted Airport (☎0345/666777). London (Heathrow), Aberdeen, Edinburgh, Glasgow, Humberside, Leeds, Newcastle and Teeside to Schipol; Stansted to Brussels.

Birmingham European Airways Birmingham Airport (☎021/782 0711). Birmingham to Schipol.

British Airways 421 Oxford St, London W1 (☎081/897 4000). London (Heathrow), Aberdeen, Belfast, Birmingham, Edinburgh, Glasgow, Manchester and Newcastle to Schipol; London (Heathrow) to Brussels, Antwerp and Luxembourg, Manchester to Brussels.

British Midland (☎071/581 0864). London (Heathrow) and East Midlands to Schipol; Birmingham to Brussels.

Dan Air c/o Davies & Newman, 21 Coxpur St, London SW1. (☎0293/820222). Manchester (including a £42 one-way student/under 26 fare), Newcastle and Teeside to Schipol.

Europe Express (☎0345/444737). London (Gatwick) to Rotterdam.

Flexair (☎0800/289447). London (City Airport) to Rotterdam.

KLM 8 Hanover St, London W1 (☎081/750 9000). London (Heathrow), Birmingham, Manchester and Newcastle to Schipol.

London City Airways (☎071/511 4200). London (City Airport) to Schipol.

Luxair Terminal 2, Heathrow Airport, London (☎081/745 4254). London (Heathrow) to Luxembourg.

Netherlines 8 Hanover St, London W1. (☎081/750 9000). Birmingham, Luton, Southampton, Bristol, Manchester and Teeside to Schipol.

NLM 8 Hanover St, London W1. (☎081/750 9000). London (Gatwick and Heathrow) to Eindhoven and Rotterdam, London (Gatwick) to Maastricht.

Region Airways c/o Routair Ltd., Southend Airport (☎0702/541353). Southend to Rotterdam and Brussels.

Sabena 36 Piccadilly, London W1 (☎081/780 1444). London (Heathrow), Birmingham, Manchester and Southend to Brussels, London (Heathrow) to Antwerp.

Suckling Airways Ipswich Airport (☎0473/729091). Manchester to Schipol via Cambridge.

Transavia (☎0293/38181). London (Gatwick) to Schipol.

DISCOUNT FLIGHT AGENTS

Campus Travel 52 Grosvenor Gardens, London SW1 (☎071/730 3402).

Council Travel 28a Poland St, London W1 (☎071/437 7767).

STA Travel 86 Old Brompton Rd, London SW7 and 117 Euston Rd, London N1 (☎071/937 9921).

Travel Cuts 295 Regent St, London W1 (☎071/255 1944).

British Rail ticket office, many high street travel agents or *Eurotrain* (see below).

To travel to any city in Holland, there's a flat fare from London of £38.50 single, £71 return if you travel via the Hook. Travelling via Ostend individual fares apply unless you opt for a five-day excursion fare for £53.

RAIL ENQUIRIES

British Rail European Enquiries ☎071/834 2345

Eurotrain 52 Grosvenor Gardens, London SW1 (☎071/730 3402)

TO BELGIUM AND LUXEMBOURG

To Belgium: services run three times a day from London Victoria via Dover and Ostend, stopping at Bruges and Ghent before reaching Brussels. There's an option of ferry or jetfoil services across the channel: journey times to Brussels are 8–10 hours by boat, 6 hours by jetfoil; fares are £48 for a five-day excursion ticket, £57.50 otherwise. Jetfoil supplements are £6 each way.

To Luxembourg: take either the jetfoil or ferry options detailed above and change at Brussels' Midi Station; the train arrives in Luxembourg 2 hours 30 minutes later. Fares are £62 for a five-day excursion, £73 otherwise.

TAKING YOUR BIKE

Most people who take their bikes to the Low Countries go by **train**. Take your bike along with you to the station at least an hour before departure and register it with *British Rail*. It's then loaded on to the train for you and delivered to the station at which you intend to arrive . . . but there's no guarantee it will turn up when you do. In practice, bikes can arrive anything up to 48 hours later – and you should plan accordingly.

Taking your bike on the **ferry** presents few problems. Bicycles travel free on *P&O* and *Sealink*, and for £2–7 on Olau Lines, depending on the sailing and the season. Simply turn up with your machine and secure it in the designated area.

Taking your bike on a **plane** is equally straightforward – provided you can let the airline know at least a week in advance. Contact them directly to make a cargo booking for your bike, then take your machine with you when you travel. At the airport you'll need to detach the wheels and fold down the handlebars. The bike will be included in your luggage allowance (usually 20kg); if the total exceeds that, you'll need to pay for the difference. For more on cycling, see p.22.

YOUTH FARES

Fares can be cut drastically for those **under 26**. BIJ (youth) tickets are available from *Eurotrain*, 52 Grosvenor Gardens, London SW1 (☎071/730 3402), plus branches nationwide, or most other student/youth travel agents. These cost £46 (return) to Amsterdam, £47.50 to Brussels, £64 to Luxembourg; tickets are valid for two months and you can stop off en route as many times as you wish. It is, of course, possible to buy a BIJ ticket to any destination on the rail network in any of the three countries.

Another cash-saving possibility for those under 26 (and resident in Europe for six months) is the **InterRail pass**, currently costing £155 from any major UK railway station or student/youth travel agents, which is valid for one month's travel on all European (and Moroccan) railways, and gives half-price discounts on British trains and some cross-channel and North Sea ferries. This could cut costs significantly if the Low Countries form part of your European travels (see also the Benelux Tourrail card in "Low Countries Connections" below). A variation on the standard card that also gives reductions on ferries is the **InterRail Flexicard** (£145), which provides the same benefits as the *InterRail* pass but is valid for any ten days within a month.

BY COACH

Travelling by long-distance **coach** is a good option if you're over 26, since fares are roughly the same as for under-26 rail travel. Choices are between coach and hovercraft (via Dover–Calais) and the slower coach and ferry (normally overnight via Dover–Zeebrugge).

COACH FARES

Destination	Eurolines	Hoverspeed
Amsterdam	12hr/£46	11hr/£46
Rotterdam	11hr/£46	9hr/£46
The Hague	11hr 30min/£46	9hr 30min/£46
Brussels	11hr/£43	8hr/£43
Bruges	6hr/£43	
Antwerp	9hr 30min/£43	7hr 30min/£43
Ghent	6hr 30min/£43	

Eurolines, operated by *National Express* offer four daily departures from London's Victoria coach station to **Amsterdam** in summer, via Breda, Rotterdam and The Hague or Breda and Utrecht (one service leaving in the morning, the other overnight). They also run coaches once daily overnight to **Brussels**, via Antwerp. *Eurolines* also act as agents for *Hoverspeed* who offer similar services, but with faster hovercraft crossings. Their twice daily London–Brussels service runs through Bruges and Ghent (daily morning service) or Lille and Mons (daily afternoon service). Tickets for all services are bookable through most travel agents or *British Rail* travel centres, and there's an eight percent reduction for under-25s and students.

COACH COMPANIES

Hoverspeed City Sprint (☎081/554 7061).
National Express/Eurolines (☎071/730 0202), plus agents nationwide.

FERRY DETAILS

Routes and prices

Destination	Operator	Frequency	Duration	One-way Fares	
				Car, 2 adults, 2 kids	Foot passenger
HOLLAND					
Harwich–Hook of Holland	*Sealink*	2 daily	6hr 45min (day) 8hr 45min (night)	£84–132	£26
Sheerness–Vlissingen	*Olau Lines*	2 daily	7hr (day) 8hr 30min (night)	£97–117	£22.50
Hull–Rotterdam	*North Sea Ferries*	1 daily	14hr	£164–179	£38.50
BELGIUM					
Dover–Zeebrugge	*P&O*	6 daily	4hr 30min	£65–117	£19
Dover–Ostend	*P&O*	6–8 daily	4hr	£65–117	£19
Felixtowe–Zeebrugge	*P&O*	2 daily	5hr 45min (day) 8hr (night)	£77–124	£19
FRANCE					
Ramsgate–Dunkerque	*Sally Line*	2hr 30min	5 daily	£56–104	£16

Discount tickets

Sealink: 2-day (53hr) foot passenger return excursions for £32; inclusive vehicle plus 5 passengers 5-day returns.

P&O: 60-hour returns for the price of a single; 5-day save 25 percent off standard fare.

Olau: 2-day foot passenger returns for 15 percent more than a standard return; various off-peak and combination tickets.

Ferry Companies

North Sea Ferries, King George Dock, Hedon Road, Hull HU9 5QA (☎0482/77177).

Olau Lines Sheerness, Kent MW12 1SN (☎0795/666666).

Sealink PO Box 29, London SW1V 1JX (☎0233/47047).

P&O Russell Street, Dover, Kent CT16 1QB (☎0304/203388). 127 Regent Street, London W1R 8LB (☎01/734 4431).

Sally Line Argyle Centre, York St, Ramsgate, Kent CT11 9DS (☎0843/595522); 81 Piccadilly, London W1V 9HF (☎01/464 1123).

BY CAR: TAKING THE FERRY

Until the Channel Tunnel opens, you can only take your car to the continent by **ferry**. Below is a list of the routes that take you into the Low Countries.

High street **travel agents** have various fares and brochures on offer; it's worth shopping around for the most competitive deals. Prices vary with the month, day and even hour that you're travelling, how long you're staying, the size of your car, and the different ferry companies are always offering special fares to outdo their competitors. In particular, since the price structures tend to be geared around one-way rather than return travel, you don't necessarily have to cross over and back from the same port.

ROUTES AND FARES

The **most direct ferry crossings into Holland** are via Harwich to the Hook of Holland, and from Sheerness to Vlissingen. It takes approximately one hour to drive from the Hook to Amsterdam; from Vlissingen it takes roughly two and a half hours.

If you're **heading for Belgium**, or want to spend less time crossing the water, consider instead sailing either from Dover to Zeebrugge or Ostend or, if you live in the Midlands or north of England, from Felixstowe to Zeebrugge. A further option from the north of England is the Hull–Rotterdam service, which leaves you just an hour or so's drive from Amsterdam.

If you're just going for a **weekend break**, check out the short-period excursion fares offered by all the companies; usually 53 hour or five day returns which can cost the same as a single. If you have kids, *Sealink* have the best deals: on day crossings children under fourteen may travel free, and at night go for fifty percent discount; other companies tend to give a fifty percent discount across the board. All also carry **children** under four free. Note that for those **under 26**, or a **student**, *Eurotrain* can knock a few pounds off ferry tickets.

Booking ahead is strongly recommended for motorists; indeed it's essential in high season. Passengers/cyclists can normally just turn up and board, at any time of year.

HITCHING

It's relatively easy to get lifts once in Holland or Belgium, so **hitching** can be a good way of cutting costs. Bear in mind though, that since drivers have been made to account for unauthorised passengers, it's no longer possible to travel over for free in a truck-driver's cab. To make sure of a lift on arrival, talk to as many people as you can on the ferry and do your best to cajole them into picking you up on the other side of customs.

FROM EIRE

There are no direct **ferry links** from Ireland to the Dutch or Belgian coasts, but if you are a student or under 26, **flights to Amsterdam and Brussels** direct from Dublin, Cork or Shannon can be had from IR£170 return through *USIT* (Aston Quay, O'Connell Bridge, Dublin 2; ☎0001/778117; and other branches countrywide). **Flights to Luxembourg** via London (for students under 32 only) cost UK£44 each way. For non-students and those over 26, fares start at around the same price but escalate quickly: book well in advance for bargains. *USIT* also offer flights from Belfast to Amsterdam (£106 for students/under-26s, £137 otherwise) and Brussels (£155/184). Their office at *Belfast Student Travel*, 13b College Street, Belfast, BT1 6ET (☎0232/324073), has details.

FROM AUSTRALIA AND NEW ZEALAND

Cheapest option is to fly to London, for which there are plenty of good deals, and pick up a connection from there. Reckon on paying around AUS$1750 return from Sydney, NZ$2040 from Auckland. **STA**, 1a Lee St, Railway Square, Sydney 2000 (☎2/212 1255), and in New Zealand, **STS**, 10 High St, PO Box 4156, Auckland (☎9/339 723) are the best operators – see the phone book for other branches in other cities.

PACKAGES

Don't be put off by the idea of going on a **package**: most consist of no more than travel and accommodation and can work out an easy way of cutting costs and hassle – especially if you live

PACKAGE HOLIDAY COMPANIES

Amsterdam/Belgian Travel Service 54 Ebury Street, London SW1W 0LU (☎071/730 3422). Amsterdam and various Belgian cities. Inexpensive.

Anglo Dutch Sports 30a Foxgrove Rd, Beckenham, Kent (☎081/650 2347). Specialists in cycling holidays, with a wide and flexible range of destinations.

Cresta (W.H. Smith Travel), W.H. Smith Travel Agencies (☎0345/056511). Amsterdam, Brussels and Bruges: uses more upmarket hotels.

Olau Short Breaks Olau Line Ferries, Sheerness, Kent ME12 1SN (☎0795/662233). An interesting variety of short holidays, including cycling tours (bike supplied).

Thomson First Floor, Greater London House, Hampstead Road, London NW1 7SD (☎071/387 6510). Amsterdam and Brussels: often the cheapest.

Time Off 2a Chester Close, London SW1X 7BQ (☎071/235 8070). Amsterdam, The Hague, Brussels, Bruges and Luxembourg.

Travelscene 94 Baker Street, London W1M 2HD (☎071/935 1025); 22a Cheapside, Bradford BD1 4JA (☎0274/392911). Amsterdam, Brussels, Bruges, Ghent and Luxembourg. Good for regional flight departures.

Travel Young 38 Store Street, London WC1E 7BZ (☎071/580 6762). Specialists in youth and student travel, offering deals with multi-bedded hostel accommodation as well as good value arrangements on regular double rooms.

some distance from London, since many operators offer a good-value range of regional flight departures. Depending on the type of hotel you opt for (anything from budget to five-star are available with most companies), city breaks in Amsterdam, Brussels, Luxembourg and most other cities start at £70 per person for return coach and hovercraft travel and two nights' accommodation in a one-star hotel with breakfast, or a little over £100 if you fly. A travel agent can advise further on the best deals available, or you can contact one of the **operators** listed above.

LOW COUNTRIES CONNECTIONS

Both Holland and Belgium have an extensive **rail network**, and connections between the two countries are good, with hourly trains linking south Holland (Roosendaal) to Brussels (via Antwerp), and connecting Maastricht in Holland to Brussels via Liège. Trains to Luxembourg from Brussels pass either though Liège or Namur; from Holland they pass through Brussels or Maastricht and Liège. There are no border formalities when travelling by train.

If you're planning to travel across the whole Low Countries region by train, it's worth considering a **Benelux Tourrail** card. This enables you to travel on all Dutch, Belgian and Luxembourg railways for five out of a specified seventeen days and costs £43.50 (£31 if you're under 26). It's available from any rail station in Holland, Belgium or Luxembourg, or in England from NS, the Dutch Railways office, at 25–28 Buckingham Gate, London SW1E 6LD (℡071/630 1735).

Most **bus stations** in the Low Countries are next to train stations. Bus services often complement train routes, and are more useful for local hops than long-distance journeys. In Luxembourg the bus network is much more extensive than the train – with a Benelux Tourrail card you can travel free on the buses run by Luxembourg railways.

Road connections are fast, usually with no border formalities to slow you down. If you're taking your own car you'll need a green card from your insurance company, but not an international driving licence. **Car hire** costs are broadly comparable with the UK: prices for the smallest vehicle (inclusive of collision damage waiver and insurance) start at £160 per week in Holland, £170 in Belgium and £133 in Luxembourg. Of the international rental companies, *Hertz* tend to be the cheapest: you may be able to make some small savings by going to local operators.

Plane connections might be worth considering as an alternative to a long train trip. The Amsterdam–Brussels route is served by *Sabena* and *NLM*: there are roughly eight flights daily and the cheapest PEX return fares, only bookable once in Holland or Belgium, are £71; a single booked from outside these countries will cost £69. The Amsterdam–Luxembourg route is operated by *Netherlines* and *Luxair*: a PEX return, again only bookable in the countries concerned, costs £114; there's a special under-25 fare of £44 one-way, £88 return, only bookable the day before you travel. An ordinary, unrestricted single costs £111.

CAR HIRE COMPANIES

Avis ℡081/848 8733
Budget ℡0800/181 181
Europcar ℡081/950 5050
Hertz ℡081/679 1799

RED TAPE AND VISAS

Citizens of Britain, Eire, Australia, Canada or the USA need only a valid passport to stay three months in Holland, Belgium or Luxembourg. A one-year British Visitor's Passport, obtainable from post offices, is also valid for the same period. On arrival, make sure you have enough money to convince officials you can support yourself. Poorer-looking visitors are often checked, and if you can't flash a few travellers' cheques or notes you may not be allowed in.

For longer stays, you officially need an **extension visa**. These are obtainable in advance from the relevant embassy in your own country. In reality, if you hold a European Community passport restrictions are fairly loose – they're not always date-stamped when entering the country – though if you are definitely planning to stay and work it's probably best to get a stamp anyway.

Non-EC nationals, however, should always have their documents in order. **Residence permits** are preferably obtained from outside the particular country and are issued for a maximum term of one year – upon proof of income from sources other than employment in that country, and sometimes not even then. **Work permits** for non-EC nationals are even harder to get; your prospective employer must apply locally while you simultaneously apply at home; both parties must await its issuance (by no means automatic) before proceeding.

CUSTOMS

For residents of EC countries the **duty-free allowance** is 300 cigarettes if bought tax-paid in the EC, 200 if bought duty-free or outside the EC. These allowances are doubled for those living outside the EC. Wherever you've arrived from you're allowed one litre of duty-free spirits (don't bother utilising your five-litre wine allowance – it's cheaper to buy it locally). Allowances are the same when returning to Britain and in all cases apply only to those over the age of 17.

British **customs officials** tend to assume that anyone youthful-looking coming directly from Holland, in particular, is a potential dope fiend or pornographer – strip searches and unpleasantness are frequent, particularly at airports. Those with drugs, pornography or flick knives can expect a hard time and most likely arrest.

NETHERLANDS EMBASSIES AND CONSULATES

Great Britain 38 Hyde Park Gate, London SW7 (☎071/585 5040).

Eire 160 Merrion Road, Dublin 4 (☎01/693 444).

Belgium Wetensehschapsstraat 35/ Rue De Le Science 35, 1040 Brussels (☎02/2230 3020).

Luxembourg 5 rue C M Spoor, L-2546 Luxembourg (☎275 70).

Australia 130 Empire Circus, Yarralumla, Canberra A.C.T. 2600 (☎62/733 111).

New Zealand Investment House, 10th Floor, Balance and Featherstone Street, Wellington (☎04/738 652).

Canada 3rd Floor, 275 Slater Street, Ottowa, Ontario ONT K1P 5H9 (☎613/237 5030).

USA 4200 Linnean Avenue N.W., Washington D.C. 20008 3896 (☎202/244 5300); 1 Rockefeller Plaza, 11th Floor, New York NY 10020 2094 (☎212/246 1429).

Denmark Toldbodgade 95, 1253 Copenhagen K (☎01/156 293).

Norway Oscargate 29, 0352 Oslo 3 (☎02/60 21 93).

Sweden Gotgatan 16A, 11646 Stockholm (☎08/247180).

BELGIAN EMBASSIES AND CONSULATES

Great Britain 103 Eaton Square, London SW1 (☎071/235 5422).

Eire Shrewsbury House, 2 Shrewsbury Rd, Ballsbridge, Dublin 4 (☎01/69 20 82).

Netherlands Lange Vijverberg 12, 2513 AC, The Hague (☎070/64 49 10); Drentestr. 11, 1083 HK, Amsterdam (☎020/42 97 63).

Luxembourg 4 rue de Girondins 4, Residence Champagne, L. 1626, Luxembourg (☎44 27 46).

Canada The Sandringham, 85 Range Rd, Suite 601–604, Ottawa, Ontario, K1N 8J6 (☎613/236 7267).

USA 3330 Garfield St N.W., Washington DC, 20008 (☎202/333 6900).

Australia 19 Arkana St, Yarralumla, A.C.T. 2600 Canberra (☎062/73 25 01).

New Zealand 1 Willeston St, Wellington (☎04/ 72 95 58).

Denmark Øster Allé 7, 2100 Copenhagen Ø (☎01/ 26 03 88).

Norway Drammensveien 103c, 0273 Oslo 2 (☎02/ 55 22 15).

Sweden 13a Villegatan, Fack 10268, Stockholm (☎08/11 88 58).

LUXEMBOURG EMBASSIES AND CONSULATES

Great Britain and Eire 27 Wilton Crescent, London SW1X 8SD (☎071/235 6963).

Netherlands Nassaulaan 8, NL 2514 JS, The Hague (☎070/60 75 16).

Belgium Avenue de Cortenbergh 75, B 1040 Brussels (☎02/733 9977).

USA and Canada 2200 Massachusetts Avenue N.W., Washington D.C. 20008 (☎202/265 4171).

INFORMATION AND MAPS

Before you leave, a wealth of information can be picked up from each of the Benelux countries, tourist offices in London. Each offers glossy leaflets on the various regions, maps, useful accommodation lists and other general bumph.

The national rail networks also have London offices that can supply timetables, route maps and details of special deals. See "Getting Around" in the appropriate country sections for

details. All of the **maps** listed below are available from *Stanfords*, 12–14 Long Acre, London WC2E 9LP (☎071/836 1321).

HOLLAND

The **Netherlands Board of Tourism** (the NBT) has a mass of information on the country, with useful leaflets on the main tourist attractions, annual events and accommodation. They produce booklets detailing the country's campsites, hotels, where to find private rooms, as well as special interest leaflets on cycling and watersports, and publish a reasonable map of the country for 50p. The NBT also issues the *Holland Leisure Card*, which, for about £7.50, entitles you to (among other things) hefty discounts on domestic Dutch flights, car rental excursions and a variety of entrance charges in Holland – a bargain if you're planning to stay for any length of time.

Once in Holland, head for the **VVV**. Just about every town (and most large villages) has a VVV office, usually in the centre or by the train station. In addition to handing out basic maps (often for free) and English info on the main sights, the VVV keeps lists of local accommodation options, and, for a small fee, will book rooms for you – useful if

NETHERLANDS BOARD OF TOURISM OFFICES

Britain and Eire 25–28 Buckingham Gate, London SW1E 6LD (☎071/630 0451).

Australia Suite 302, 5 Elizabeth Street, Sydney, NSW 2000 (☎2/27 69 21).

Canada 25 Adelaide St. East, Suite 710, Toronto, Ontario. M5C 1Y2 (☎416/363 1577).

Sweden Styrmansgatan 8, 114 54 Stockholm (☎08/782 9925).

USA 355 Lexington Avenue, 21st Floor, New York, NY 10017 (☎212/370 7367);

225 N. Michigan Avenue, Suite 326, Chicago, IL 60601 (☎312/819 0300); 605 Market Street, Room 401, San Francisco, CA 94105 (☎415/543 6772).

West Germany Laurenplatz 1–3, 500-Köln-1 (☎221/23 62 62).

you want to avoid a long walk only to find a full hotel. Most VVV offices also keep information on neighbouring towns, which can be a great help for forward planning. Opening hours vary, and are detailed – along with phone numbers – in the text.

MAPS

For travelling purposes, the best road **map** of Holland is that published by Kümmerly and Frey (£4.95). For more detailed **regional maps**, aside from the NBT's own plan, the Dutch motoring organisation ANWB publish an excellent 1:100,000 series that covers the whole country (£3.95 each). Though our city maps should be adequate for most purposes, the best large-scale alternative are the *Falk Plans* (£4.95), most of which have gazetteers.

BELGIUM AND LUXEMBOURG

The **Belgian Tourist Office** offer a similarly comprehensive service, stocking free booklets detailing hotels and campsites across the country,

as well as a series of regional booklets packed with useful information. They also offer a free map, complete with basic city plans.

In Belgium there are tourist offices in all but the smallest villages. They often have free maps and, in the larger towns, offer an accommodation booking service: in smaller towns you won't find a booking service, though offices will often phone ahead and make a reservation for you; in both cases, this will be done without charge.

Branches of the **Luxembourg Tourist Office** abroad publish free booklets of hotel and restaurant listings, with reliable prices and gradings, and publish the usual array of bumph and maps. Ask also for their annually updated "Tourist Information" booklet, detailing everything from the opening times of all the country's major tourist sights to where to go ballooning. In Luxembourg itself even the very smallest town will have a tourist office of some description, with maps of the immediate area and details of accommodation, which they can sometimes book for you.

BELGIAN TOURIST OFFICES

Great Britain Premier House, 2 Gayton Rd, Harrow, Middlesex HA1 2XU (☎081/861 3300).

Holland Herengracht 435, 1017 BR Amsterdam (☎020/25 12 51).

Italy Piazza Velasca 5, 1-20122 Milan (☎02/86 05 66).

Sweden Markvadsgatan 16, S-104 32 Stockholm (☎08/34 15 75).

Denmark Vester Farimagsgade 7–9, 1606 Copenhagen V (☎01/12 30 27).

Germany Berliner Allee 47, D4000 Düsseldorf 1 (☎0211/32 60 08).

USA 745 Fifth Ave., New York NY 10151 (☎212/758 8130).

LUXEMBOURG TOURIST OFFICES

UK 36–37 Piccadilly, London W1V 9PA (☎071/434 2800).

Holland Nassaulaan 8, Postbus 18660, 2502 ER, The Hague (☎70/649041).

Luxembourg Bureau du Tourisme Luxembourgeois, 104 Avenue Louise, Boite 1, B-1050, Brussels (☎02/646 0370).

MAPS

The Belgian Tourist Office gives out a decent free map of the country that incorporates basic city plans – something you'll also find in the offices' *Belgium Historic Cities* brochure. Otherwise, the best value **general road map** of Belgium (and Luxembourg) is the 1:350,000 Michelin map, which costs £2.65; the 1:300,000 Kümmerly and Frey map (£4.95) covers the same area. The most useful **regional maps** are those of Flanders, the Ardennes and Wallonia, published by *Geocart* at £4.95 each.

HEALTH AND INSURANCE

As fellow members of the European Community, both Britain and Eire have reciprocal health agreements with Holland, Belgium and Luxembourg.

These provide for free medical advice and treatment on presentation of **certificate E111** – though in practice many doctors and pharmacists charge, and it's up to you to be reimbursed by the DHS once you're home: make sure you get receipts for all prescriptions and/or treatment. To get an E111, fill in a form at any post office, and you'll be issued with a certificate immediately. Without an E111 you won't be turned away from a doctor or hospital, but will almost certainly have to contribute towards treatment.

For non-EC citizens **travel insurance** is essential, and it's a wise additional protection for everyone, since policies cover your cash and possessions as well as the cost of medicines, medical and dental treatment. Among British insurance companies, *Endsleigh* are about the cheapest. Premiums cost about £11 a fortnight, available from youth/student travel offices, or direct from 97–107 Southampton Row, London WC1 (☎071/580 4311). You'll need to keep all medical bills to reclaim costs and report the incident to the police should you have something stolen – see "Police and Trouble" below.

Minor ailments can be remedied at **chemists** (*Drogisterij* in Dutch, *Pharmacie* in French), which supply toiletries, non-prescription drugs, tampons, condoms and the like. In Holland, an *Apotheek* or pharmacy (usually open Mon–Fri 9.30am–5.30 or 6pm) is where you go to get a prescription filled. To get a prescription or **consult a doctor**, ask at the local tourist office: if you're in a large city, British embassies and legations keep a list of local English-speaking doctors.

POLICE AND TROUBLE

There's little reason why you need ever come into contact with the police forces of Holland, Belgium or Luxembourg: this is an area of Europe that's relatively free of street crime. Even in Brussels, Amsterdam and the larger cities you shouldn't have too many problems, though it's obviously as well to be on your guard against petty theft: secure your things in a locker when staying in hostel accommodation, and never leave any valuables in a tent or car. If you're on a bike, **make sure it is well locked up – bike theft and resale is one of the major industries in most cities.**

As far as **personal safety** goes, it's normally possible to walk anywhere in the centres of the larger cities at any time of day, though women should obviously be wary of badly lit or empty streets; public transport, even late at night, isn't usually a problem.

If you are unlucky enough to have **something stolen**, report it immediately to the nearest police station. Get them to write a statement detailing what has been lost for your insurance claim when you get home, and remember to make a note of the report number – or, better still, ask for a copy of the statement itself.

Should you find yourself in trouble, or simply need **assistance of a legal or social nature**, there are a couple of organisations in Holland that might be able to help. **JAC** give free confidential help to young people, especially foreign nationals, on work, alien status, drugs and accommodation matters. There's also **MAIC**, who similarly specialise in legal advice, though not just for young people; and they will also help on other matters. Both organisations have offices in the larger cities; some of them are listed in the text.

In Belgium, the Catholic church has traditionally been the main provider of social care and support. However there's also **Infor-Jeunes/Info Jeugd**, a nationwide information organisation similar to JAC. In large cities, **S.O.S. Jeune** have a 24-hour emergency number listed in the phone book or available from the operator.

Holland – specifically Amsterdam – is where **drugs** are most visible. Though it is legal to possess up to 28 grams of cannabis for your own consumption, the liberal attitude towards its being smoked exists only the capital, with very small scenes in the larger cities. In Belgium and Luxembourg the possession and use of any drugs is illegal, and in the current conservative climate, would be guaranteed to get you into trouble.

MONEY AND BANKS

The currency of Holland is the guilder, that of Belgium the franc; Luxembourg's currency is also the franc, and it's on a par with the Belgian franc. However, whereas Belgian francs are always accepted in Luxembourg, Luxembourg francs are rarely taken as legal tender in Belgium.

TRAVELLERS' CHEQUES

The best way of carrying the bulk of your money is in **travellers' cheques**, available from most high street banks (whether or not you have an account) for a usual fee of one percent of the amount ordered. An alternative is the **Eurocheque** book and card, issued on request by most British banks to account holders, which can be used to get cash in the majority of European banks and bureaux de change. This works out slightly more expensive than travellers' cheques, but can be more convenient. Bear in mind that you always need your passport as well as the Eurocheque card to obtain cash at Benelux banks.

PLASTIC MONEY

Visa, Access (*Eurocard*), *Diners Club* and *American Express* cards can be used in most banks and bureaux de change – if you're prepared to withdraw a minimum of the equivalent of (very roughly) £100. Credit cards are less popular than you might expect, although most mainstream shops, hotels and restaurants will take at least one brand. Check before you commit yourself to spending. Eurocheques are the most commonly used form of payment after cash.

EXCHANGING MONEY

Exchanging money is rarely problematic and seldom expensive. Banks offer the best exchange rates, but commissions vary and it's worth shopping around. Best bet out of banking hours are the exchange offices found at railway stations, which open late and at weekends: otherwise numerous bureaux de change, hostels, hotels, campsites, tourist offices, airports, ferry terminals and ferries offer rates that range from decent to diabolical. See the "Costs, Money and Banks" sections for each country for more details on opening hours and the various ways of changing money.

COMMUNICATIONS: POST AND PHONE

You can have letters sent **poste restante** to any post office in Holland (main offices only in Belgium and Luxembourg) by addressing them "Poste Restante" followed by the name of the town and country. When picking up mail take your passport, and make sure they check under middle names and initials, as letters often get misfiled.

Phone boxes are plentiful and almost invariably work; most are similar to the new-style British machines, and English instructions are normally posted inside. To make a direct call to Britain, dial the country code, wait for the tone and then omit the first 0 in the area code. To reverse the charges, phone the operator (they all speak English) and ask to make a "collect call".

Post office opening hours and other details are given under each individual country's section on "Communications". Postal charges are not particularly high, but the cost of stamps and postcards can soon take a chunk out of the daily budget.

DIALLING CODES TO BRITAIN

from **Holland** ☎09 44
from **Belgium** ☎00 44
from **Luxembourg** ☎00 44

GAY LIFE

As you'd expect, it's in Holland's **cities** that gay life is most visible and enjoyable. **Amsterdam** is probably the best city in Europe in which to be gay – attitudes are tolerant, bars are excellent and plentiful, and support groups and facilities are unequalled; see p.83 for listings. Elsewhere in Holland, while the scene isn't anything like as extensive, it's always well-organised: Rotterdam, The Hague, Nijmegen and Groningen each have an enjoyable nightlife, and all cities of any size have a branch of *COC*, the national organisation for gay men and women, which can offer help, information, and usually a coffee bar. Their national HQ is at Rozenstraat 8, Amsterdam (☎020/23 11 92). You'll also find addresses for each city in the "Listings" sections.

Gay life in **Belgium and Luxembourg** isn't so upfront. Brussels and Antwerp are the main centres, but both sit very firmly in Amsterdam's shadow – and most gay travellers overlook what is by and large a far less "international" scene in these two countries. The Belgian national organisation for gay men and women is *FWH*, Dambruggestraat 204, Antwerp (☎03/233 25 02). The legal **age of consent** for gay men is 16 in Holland and Belgium, 18 in Luxembourg.

WOMEN

Of all the Low Countries' cities **Amsterdam** has the most impressive feminist infrastructure: support groups, health centres, and businesses are run by and for women, and there's a good range of bars and discos, a few exclusively for women. Once outside the capital you'll frequently be reminded just how parochial Holland is – attitudes and behaviour acceptable in Amsterdam will be frowned on elsewhere, especially in the Catholic south. Many towns in Holland have a *Vrouwenhuis* or women's centre, a meeting place that organises various activities, discussion groups and events exclusively for women. These are often the best place to meet local women and make feminist connections; sadly, many have closed in recent years: where still applicable, addresses are given in the Guide.

Belgium, with the strong influence of the Catholic church, has a less liberal tradition: women are still scarce in the upper echelons of business and government, abortion is still illegal (though an estimated 15,000 abortions a year are carried out in feminist clinics), and tax laws discriminate against two-career families. Belgian feminist organisations seem to be operated mainly by lesbians, and, perhaps a result, the women's movements in Holland and France have been comparatively more successful in involving women from a broader spectrum of backgrounds.

By and large, nowhere in the Low Countries is **unsafe** for women travelling alone – the seedier areas of the big cities may feel threatening, but with common sense and circumspection you shouldn't have anything to worry about.

The native **lesbian scene** is smaller and more subdued than the gay one. Many politically active lesbians move within tight circles, and it takes time to for foreign visitors to find out what's happening. Good places to begin are the women-only cafés listed in the text.

BUSINESS HOURS AND PUBLIC HOLIDAYS

The Benelux weekend fades painlessly into the working week with many shops staying closed on Monday morning, even in major cities. **Opening hours** tend to be from 9am to 5.30 or 6pm, with many shops open until later in the evening, especially on Thursday and Friday in summer: larger supermarkets stay open till 8pm, Monday to Friday. Things shut down a little earlier on Saturday, and only die-hard money makers open up shop on a Sunday. Most towns have a **market day**, usually midweek (and sometimes Saturday morning), and this is often the liveliest day to be in a town, particularly when the stalls fill the central square or *markt*; very occasionally you'll see elderly women wearing bona fide peasant costume. Though the tradition has died out in all but the smallest towns and villages, some shops close for the **half-day** on Wednesday or Thursday afternoon.

Though closed on Christmas, New Year's and Boxing days, and on Mondays, all state-run museums adopt Sunday hours on the following **public holidays**, when most shops and banks are closed.

PUBLIC HOLIDAYS

HOLLAND

New Year's Day

Good Friday (many shops open)

Easter Sunday and Monday

April 30 (Queen's Birthday, many shops open)

August 15 (Ascension Day)

Whit Sunday and Monday

Dec 5 (early closing for St Nicholas' birthday)

Christmas Day

December 26

BELGIUM

New Year's Day

Easter Monday

Labour Day (May 1)

Ascension Day

All Saints' Day (November 1)

Armistice Day (November 11)

King's Birthday (November 15)

Christmas Day

LUXEMBOURG

New Year's Day

Easter Monday

May Day (May 1)

Ascension Day

Whit Monday

National Day (June 23)

Assumption Day

All Saints Day (November 1)

Christmas Day

Boxing Day

- THE NORTH AND THE FRISIAN ISLANDS
- NORTH HOLLAND
- AMSTERDAM
- OVERIJSSEL, FLEVOLAND AND GELDERLAND
- SOUTH HOLLAND AND UTRECHT
- THE SOUTH
- WEST GERMANY
- BELGIUM

0   50 km

Introduction

Holland, or (to give the country its proper name) The Netherlands, is a country partly reclaimed from the waters of the North Sea, an artificially created land, around half of which lies at or below sea level. Land reclamation has been the dominant motif of its history, the result a country of resonant and unique images – flat, fertile landscapes punctured by windmills and church spires; ornately gabled terraces flanking peaceful canals; huge, open skies; and mile up on mile of grassy dune, backing onto wide stretches of pristine sandy beach.

A leading colonial power, its mercantile fleets once challenged the best in the world for supremacy and its standard of living (for the majority at least) was second to none. These days Holland is one of the most developed countries in the world, small and urban, with the highest population density in Europe, its fourteen million or so inhabitants concentrated into an area about the size of southern England. It's an international, well-integrated place; everyone speaks English, communications and infrastructure are genuinely efficient, and its companies – Philips, Unilever, Shell – are at the forefront of the new, free-trading Europe. Politically, also, the Dutch government's policies (despite something of an Eighties backlash) are those of consensus: among Europe's – and the world's – most liberal, with relaxed laws regarding soft drugs, and forward-thinking attitudes on social issues. The crime rate, too, though on the increase, is relatively low.

■ Where to go

If you say you're going to Holland, everyone will immediately assume you're going to Amsterdam. Indeed for such a small and accessible country, Holland is, apart from Amsterdam, relatively unknown territory. Some people may confess to a brief visit to Rotterdam or The Hague, but for most people Amsterdam basically *is* Holland – there's nothing remotely worth seeing outside the capital, so if you're not going there, why go at all?

It's an attitude exacerbated by the chauvinism of Amsterdammers themselves, many of whom rarely set foot outside the limits of their own city. It's true that in many ways the rest of Holland can seem terribly dull after the bright lights of the capital, but to write off the rest of the country would be to miss much, especially considering the size of the place and the efficiency of its transport systems, which make everywhere easily accessible.

Although throughout the guide we use the name Holland to mean the whole country, in fact it actually only refers to two of The Netherlands' **twelve provinces** – **North** and **South Holland**, in the west of the country. These for the most part are unrelentingly flat territory, much of it reclaimed land that has since become home to a grouping of towns known collectively as the **Randstad** (literally "rim town") – a circular urban sprawl that holds the country's largest cities and the majority of its population. Travelling here is easy, with trains and buses cheap and efficient and language no problem; at times, you barely feel abroad at all. Amsterdam is rightly the main focus: there's no other city which has its vitality and cosmopolitanism – or, indeed, its features of interest. But the other Randstad towns are worth a visit too – places like **Haarlem**, **Leiden** and **Delft** with their old canal-girded centres; the gritty port city of **Rotterdam**; the dignified architecture and stately air of **The Hague**, home of the government and the Dutch royals. Not to mention the **bulbfields** which spread all around – in spring, justifiably, the one thing that never fails to draw tourists out of Amsterdam.

Outside of the Randstad life moves slower, and although you're never far from civilisation, travelling is marginally more time-consuming and the incidence of English-speakers more sporadic. The **islands** of the north, most of them off the coast of the province of **Friesland**, are prime holiday territory for the Dutch, though they retain a rather untamed air, sparsely settled after the crowded Randstad cities. The rest of Friesland, too, along with the adjoining provinces of **Groningen** and **Drenthe**, can feel rather cut off, its inhabitants speaking a dialect of Dutch not spoken elsewhere in the country. Which isn't to say it's dull: Friesland's capital, **Leeuwarden**, is a likeable city, and neighbouring **Groningen** is one of the country's busiest cultural centres, lent verve by its large resident student population. To the south, the provinces of **Overijssel** and **Gelderland**, at least in their eastern portions, herald Holland's first few bumps, the landscape undulating into heathy moorland around the towns of **Arnhem** and **Apeldoorn**, and another lively student city, **Nijmegen**. Further south still lie the predominantly Catholic provinces of

Limburg, **North Brabant** and **Zeeland**. The latter is well-named – literally "Sealand", made up of a series of low-lying islands connected by road and protected from the encroaching waters of the North Sea by one of Holland's most ambitious projects, the Delta Plan. Heading east, **North Brabant** is gently rolling heath and farmland, centring on the historic cities of **Breda** and **Den Bosch**, and, not least, the modern manufacturing hub of **Eindhoven**, home to the electronics giant Philips. Lastly, **Limburg** occupies the slim scythe of land that reaches down between the Belgian and German borders, perhaps the least Dutch of all Holland's provinces – its landscape, in the south at least, genuinely hilly, and with as cosmopolitan a capital in **Maastricht** as they come.

Getting Around

Getting around is never a problem in Holland: it's a small country, distances are short, and the longest journey you'll ever make – say from Amsterdam to Maastricht – takes under three hours by train or car. Public transport in and around towns and cities, too, is efficient and cheap, buses (and sometimes trams) running on an easy-to-understand ticketing system that covers the whole country. The two networks link up together neatly – bus terminals almost everywhere situated next door to the train station.

■ Trains

The best way of travelling around Holland is to take the **train**. The system, run by *Nederlanse Spoorwegen* or *NS* (*Netherlands Railways*), is one of the best in Europe: trains are fast, modern and frequent, fares relatively low, and the network of lines extremely comprehensive. They're also normally very punctual. **Ordinary fares** are calcu-

lated by the kilometre, diminishing proportionately the further you travel. *NS* publish a booklet detailing costs and distances, so it's easy enough to work out broadly how much a ticket will cost. As a rough guide, reckon on spending about f12 to travel 50km or so; returns are simply double the price of a single, and first-class fares cost about fifty percent on top. With any ticket, you're also free to stop off anywhere en route and continue your journey later that day. For a one-way ticket ask for an "enkele reis"; a return is a "retour".

Of a number of ways of saving money on these rates, the **dagretour**, or day return, is the most commonly used, valid for 24 hours and costing around ten percent less than an ordinary single. A **weekend return**, travelling on Saturday and returning Sunday, costs the price of a dagretour plus f2.50. If you're visiting some specific attraction on a day out from somewhere by train, consider also buying a **dagtochtkaart** – a special ticket which includes the price of admission to selected sights (say Enkhuizen's Zuider Zee Museum or the Hoge Veluwe Park) with the price of a return ticket, usually saving a good deal. There are 75 possible excursions in all, though most are only possible between May and September: ask for the booklet *Er Op Uit!*, which has full details.

If you're going to be travelling extensively by train, consider buying a **rail pass**. There are a number of different kinds of pass: a one-day rover ticket which entitles the holder to one day's unlimited travel anywhere in Holland for £15.50 (second-class); a three- or seven-day rover, giving unlimited travel for £22.50 or £33.50 respectively; or a Holland Rail Pass, which entitles you to three consecutive days' unlimited travel within a fifteen-day period for £24. Optional **extras** issued in conjunction with the rover tickets are public transport link cards (f1.50–6), which allow the additional free use of town and country buses and trams all over the country. Consider also the **Benelux Tourrail Card**, valid for any five days within a specified seventeen on all three national rail networks as well as country buses in Luxembourg. Costs are £28.50 if you're under 26, £40 if not. In addition to these are various deals and passes for teenagers up to 18 years of age, available in summer, as well as arrangements for families and groups of people travelling together.

Everywhere buses stop outside railway stations, but if you don't wish to take a bus, *NS* have devised a **treintaxi** scheme, whereby for f5

a head in thirty towns across the country, excluding Amsterdam, The Hague, Rotterdam and Utrecht, a taxi will take you anywhere within the city limits, even if you're travelling alone – though drivers are supposed to wait ten minutes for other passengers. Vouchers for *treintaxis* must be purchased when you buy your rail ticket.

Stations aren't the run-down slums you often find in Britain, but bright, well-equipped places, with copious information and facilities that – even in some of the smaller towns – include a

coffee shop and restaurant, florist and newspaper/bookshop, and often a GWK bureau de change. The food in the restaurants, incidentally, is usually good, filling and reasonably priced.

Netherlands Railways publish mounds of **information** annually on the various services, passes, fares and suchlike – most of it in English. They also produce a free condensed timetable detailing inter-city services, and a full timetable (*spoorboekje*), available in advance either from the *Netherlands Railways* office in London, or from any Dutch railway station (f6.50). You can also buy rover tickets before you leave from *Netherlands Railways*; their office is at 25–28 Buckingham Gate, London SW1E 6LD (☎071/630 1735).

■ Buses

Supplementing the train network are **buses** – run by local companies but again ruthlessly efficient, spanning out to cover the local surroundings from ranks of bus stops almost always located bang next to the railway station, cutting walking time to a minimum. Ticketing is simple, organised on a system that covers the whole country. You need buy just one kind of ticket wherever you are, a *strippenkaart*. The country is divided into zones: the driver will cancel one strip on your *strippen-kaart* for your journey plus one for each of the zones you travel through (on city trams and metro systems it's up to you to cancel it yourself (see the *Amsterdam* chapter). In the larger towns and cities you'll find you only need to use two zones for the centre. You can buy 6- or 10-strip *strippen-kaarts* from bus drivers, or the better value 15-strip (f9.05) or 45-strip (f25.85) *strippenkaarts* in advance from railway stations, tobacconists and local public transport offices.

■ Driving and hitching

Driving around Holland is much as you would expect – painless and quick. The country has a uniformly good and comprehensive road network, most of the major towns linked by some kind of motorway or dual carriageway, and the excellence of the public transport system means things rarely get too congested, even on the outskirts of the major cities. **Rules of the road** are much as in any other mainland European country: you drive on the right; speed-limits are 50kph in built-up areas, 80kph outside, 120kph on motorways. Drivers and front-seat passengers are required by law to wear seatbelts, and crackdowns on drunken driving are severe. There are no toll roads, but some of the bridges and tunnels exact tolls – usually around f4–5 for a private car. Petrol isn't particularly cheap, at a little under f2 a litre, but again the distances mean this isn't much of a factor anyway.

In order to drive in Holland you need an ordinary full British **driver's licence**, and, if you bring your own car, a green card of insurance – though you can obtain last-minute insurance cover at border exchange offices. If you **break down**, the Dutch automobile organisation, the ANWB, offers reciprocal repair and breakdown services to AA/RAC members; their nationwide number is ☎06/0888, and there are special roadside telephones on motorways. If you're not an AA or RAC member, you can either pay for this service, or, for a f75 fee, become a temporary (one month) member.

Car hire is fairly expensive: reckon on paying upwards of f700 for a small car for a week, with unlimited mileage, or around f60 a day plus 60c per kilometre – though obviously there are much cheaper weekend deals available.

Hitching is feasible throughout the country: the Dutch are usually well disposed towards giving lifts, and the dense population and road network mean that it's unusual to get stuck anywhere. Bear in mind, though, that motorways are hard to avoid, and that it's only legal to hitch on sliproads.

■ Cycling

If you're not especially pushed for time, **cycling** is *the* way to see the country. Holland's largely flat landscape makes travelling by bike an almost effortless pursuit, and the short distances involved make it possible to see most of the country this way, using the nationwide system of well-signposted cycle paths – which often divert away from the main roads into the countryside. The 1:100,000 ANWB maps show all the cycle paths and are perfectly adequate for touring. Ask also for the NBT booklet, *Cycling in Holland*, which details a number of suggested routes and has other advice for cyclists.

The NBT, in association with regional VVV offices, also organise **cycling package holidays** all over the country, which include bicycle, accommodation, maps and other information and can be booked in the UK through *Anglo-Dutch Sports*, 30a Foxgrove Road, Beckenham, Kent BR3 2BD (☎081/650 2347). See *Basics* for more details.

Most people, however, either **bring their own bike** (in which case see the prices and conditions under "Getting There"), or **hire one**. Bikes can be hired from all main train stations for f7 a day or f28 per week plus a f50 deposit (f200 in larger centres); if you have a valid train ticket, it costs just f4.25 a day. You'll also need some form of ID. The snag is that cycles must be returned to the station from which they were hired, making onward hops by hired bike impossible. Failing

CYCLING TERMS	
Tyre	*Band*
Puncture	*Lek*
Brake	*Rem*
Chain	*Keting*
Wheel	*Wiel*
Pedal	*Trapper*
Pump	*Pomp*
Handlebars	*Stuur*
Broken	*Kapot*

that, most bike shops hire out bicycles, usually for around the same amount as railway stations, though they may be more flexible on deposits – some accept a passport in lieu of cash; otherwise again expect to have to leave f50–200. Wherever you hire your bike from, in summer it can be a good idea to book a machine in advance.

It is possible take your **bike on trains**, but it isn't encouraged, and a ticket costs f7–16, depending on the day and time of year. Be warned that space is limited and you're not allowed to load your machine on at all during the rush hour – between 6.30am and 9am and 4.30pm and 6pm. Bear in mind when cycling in Holland that you should never, ever, leave your bike **unlocked**, even for a few minutes. In the larger cities especially used bikes are big business, machines the prey of thiefs armed with bolt-croppers.

Sleeping

Accommodation is not particularly cheap in Holland, though a wide network of official and unofficial youth hostels, and generally well-equipped campsites, can help to cut costs. Wherever you stay, you should book during the summer and over holiday periods like Easter, when places can run short.

■ Hotels and private rooms

All **hotels** in Holland are graded on a star system, up to five stars. One-star and no star hotels are rare, and prices for two-star establishments start at around f75 for a double room without private bath or shower; count on paying upwards of f85 if you want your own facilities. Three-star hotels cost about f120–150; for four- and five-star places you'll pay f200–300, which won't always include breakfast. In cheaper places prices usually include a reasonable breakfast, though not always; be sure to check first as some hotels use this as a sneaky way of adding f10 or so to your bill.

During the summer, in all parts of the country but especially in Amsterdam and the major tourist centres, it's a good idea to **book a room** in advance. You can do this most easily by phoning the hotel direct – we've listed phone numbers throughout the guide, and English is almost always spoken so there should be no language problem. You can also make reservations through the *Netherlands Reservation Centre* (NRC), PO Box 404, 2260 AK Leidschendam (Mon–Fri 8am–8pm, Ssat 8am–2pm; ☎070/20 25 00), which can book hotel rooms, apartments and bungalows all over the country. Reservations are confirmed in writing and the service is free. In Holland itself, you can make advance reservations in person through VVV offices, for a fee of f3.50 per person.

One way of cutting costs is, wherever possible, to use **private accommodation** – rooms in private homes that are let out to visitors on a bed and breakfast basis; they're sometimes known as pensions. Prices are usually quoted per person and are normally around f30; breakfast usually costs about f5 on top. You have to go through the VVV to find private rooms: they will either give you a list to follow up independently or will insist they book the accommodation themselves and levy the appropriate booking fee. Bear in mind, also, that not all VVVs offer private accommodation; generally you'll find it only in the larger towns and tourist centres.

■ Hostels, sleep-ins, student rooms

There are about 45 official **youth hostels** in Holland, all within the IYHF and open to members for a little under f20 per person per night, including breakfast. Accommodation is usually in dormitories, though some hostels have single and double-bedded rooms. Meals are often available – about f14 for a filling dinner – and in some hostels there are kitchens where you can self-cater. It is possible for non-members to stay in official hostels, though they'll pay more; given the price of membership, it's worth joining even if you're only going to be doing a little hostelling.

To join before you leave Britain, contact the YHA head office at 14 Southampton Street, London WC2 (☎01/836 8542); membership currently costs £4 a year for those under 21, £7 otherwise. Whether you're a member or not, you should book in advance if possible during the summer months by contacting the hostels direct, as some places get crammed. For a full list of Dutch hostels, contact the *Nederlandse Jeugdherberg Central (NJHC)*, Prof. Tulplein 4, 1018 GX Amsterdam (☎020/551 3155), or consult the IYHF guide to European youth hostels (£5.95).

In addition to official hostels, the larger cities – particularly Amsterdam – often have a number of **unofficial hostels** touting dormitory accommodation (and invariably double and triple-bedded rooms too) at broadly similar prices, though inevitably standards are sometimes not as high or as reliable as the official IYHF places. We've detailed possibilities in the guide. In some cities you may also come across something known as a **Sleep-in** – dormitory accommodation run by the local council that's often cheaper than regular hostels and normally only open during the summer. Locations vary from year to year; again, we've tried to give some indication of locations in the guide, but for the most current information contact the VVV. The same goes for **student accommodation**, which is sporadically open to travellers during the summer holidays in some university towns. We've detailed definite possibilities in the guide, but the VVV usually has up-to-date information.

■ Campsites and cabins

Camping is a serious option in Holland: there are plenty of sites, most are very well equipped, and they represent a good saving on other forms of accommodation. Prices vary greatly, mainly depending on the number of facilities available, but you can generally expect to pay around f5 per person, plus another f5–10 for a tent, and another f5 or so if you have a car or motorcycle. Everywhere the VVV will have details of the nearest site, though we've given indications throughout the text. There's also a free NBT list of selected sites, and the ANWB publish an annual list of Dutch campsites (f16.50), available from bookshops in Holland itself or in advance from

the ANWB direct, at Wassenaarseweg 220, The Hague (☎070/314 7147).

Some sites also have **cabins**, known as *trekkershutten* – spartanly furnished affairs that can house a maximum of four people for around f44 a night. Again, both the NBT and ANWB can provide a list of these, the latter for f2.50, though you should normally book – either by phoning the site direct or through the *Netherlands Reservations Centre* (address and phone number above).

Costs, Money and Banks

Though by a slim margin the least expensive country in the Benelux region, costs in Holland are never cheap, and British visitors will find price levels for most things the same or slightly higher than at home.

If you come for a short time and stay in one place, sleep in youth hostels or camp, and eat out rarely, you can get by on around £10–15 a day; staying in hotels, travelling around the country, eating out most evenings and doing some socialising, expect to spend at least £25 a day.

■ Money and banks

Dutch **currency** is the guilder, written as "f" or "Dfl", and made up of 100 cents ("c"). It comes in **coins** worth 5c, tiny fiddly 10c pieces, 25c, f1, f2.50 and f5; denominations of **notes** are f5 (though these are being phased out), f10, f25, f50, f100, and – rarely – f250 and f500. At time of writing the exchange rate was very slightly under f3 to one pound sterling. Dutch banknotes are currently undergoing a process of **redesign**: the f25 note was the first to be changed, and others are to follow, although the overall attractiveness of the currency doesn't seem to be greatly improved.

Many shops and restaurants accept the major **credit cards** – Visa, *Access (Eurocard)*, *American Express* and *Diners Club* – and, subject to a roughly f300 minimum, *GWK* offices and many banks give (pricey) cash advances on all cards.

As ever, **banks** are the best place to change travellers' cheques and cash. Their hours are Monday–Friday 9am–4pm. In the larger cities, Amsterdam for example, some banks are also open Thursday 7–9pm and occasionally on Saturday mornings, though changing money at odd times is never a problem, as the nationwide network of *De Grenswisselkantoren (GWK)* exchange offices, usually at railway stations, are open very late hours every day – sometimes (as in Amsterdam) even 24 hours. At these you can change money or travellers' cheques, obtain cash advances on all the major credit cards, even arrange travel insurance. You can also change money at most VVV offices, though the rates will be less favourable, as it will at numerous bureaux de change dotted about the larger cities – *Change Express* are just one national change office. Hotels, hostels and campsites will also often change money, though you should only use them when desperate – they often give rip-off rates. Basically, when stuck, you're best off using *GWK*.

Communications

In a country as small as Holland, essential communications – post and phones – are easy and efficient, whether sending a postcard or phoning the other end of the country.

■ Post

Dutch **post offices** are plentiful and easy to use, usually open Monday–Friday 8.30am–5pm and often on Saturday from 8.30am–noon. Be sure to join the right queue, though, if you only want stamps (*postzegelen*), as post offices handle numerous other services. Broadly, the charges are 55c for postcards within Europe, 75c outside, 75c for letters up to 20g within Europe, f1 outside. Post boxes are everywhere, though make sure you use the correct slot, marked "Overige". If you're receiving mail rather than sending it, poste restante is available at main post offices countrywide; to collect items, you need your passport.

■ Phones

The Dutch **phone system** is similarly straightforward. The green-trim telephone boxes are like the newer British ones and others throughout Europe: you deposit the money before making a call and a digital display tells you the amount of credit remaining. The slots take 25c, f1 and f2.50 coins; only wholly unused coins are returned. Phone boxes taking only phonecards are becoming more common, and a card is a good way to avoid queueing and convenient for calling abroad. They're available from post offices and railway stations – f5 for the equivalent of twenty local calls.

If you are calling home, in the larger cities it might be better to use a post office (in Amsterdam it's known as the "Telehouse"), where you can make your call from a booth and settle up afterwards. They're usually open until at least 8pm, sometimes later (24 hours in Amsterdam); the discount rate on international calls is in effect between 8am and 8pm. You can also, obviously, make calls from hotels, though expect this to be much more expensive than anywhere else.

INTERNATIONAL DIALLING CODES

Great Britain ☎09 44
Ireland ☎09 353
Australia ☎09 61
New Zealand ☎09 64
USA and Canada ☎09 1

USEFUL NUMBERS

Operator calls ☎06 01 04
Directory enquiries ☎008 (daily 8am–10pm). Outside these times dial ☎06 899 11 33, though this is expensive.
International directory enquiries ☎06 04 18
Emergencies ☎06 11
Fire, ☎21 21 21

Police ☎22 22 22
Ambulance ☎555 5555
Collect calls ☎06 04 10. Or for calls to the UK: ☎06 022 9944; to the USA and Canada ☎06 022 9111; to Australia ☎06 022 0061. These numbers connect directly to national operators and usually provide a quicker service.

■ Media

There's no problem finding **British newspapers** in Holland. They're widely available, on the same day of publication in the Randstad towns, the day after elsewhere, for around f3; current issues of magazines, too, can be found pretty much all over. If you can't find one, railway station bookstalls are always a good bet, though most newsagents in the larger cities will stock at least a few overseas newspapers and magazines.

Of the **Dutch press**, the right-leaning downmarket *De Telegraaf* is one of the most widely read papers, as is the centre-right but less scandal-ridden *Algemeeen Dagsblad*. *De Volkskrant* is a centre-left daily not unlike Britain's *Guardian*; *NRC Handelsblad* is a relatively uncommitted paper supposedly favoured by the country's intellectuals.

British TV and radio stations can also be picked up in Holland. BBC Radio 4 is found on 1500m longwave, and the World Service on 463m medium wave and shortwave frequencies between 75m and 49m at intervals throughout the day and night. If you're staying somewhere with cable TV, it's possible to tune into BBC1 and BBC2 at most times during the day, and a flick through the stations might also turn up any number of cable and satellite options: Superchannel – an at times dreadfully amateurish mix of videos, soaps and movies; MTV – 24-hour pop videos; CNN, which gives 24-hour American news coverage; or Eurosport – up-to-the-minute footage of contests like the women's world curling championships or European Handball league. None of it's a great disaster if missed. For the rest, there's the Dutch TV channels, which regularly run American and British programmes and films with Dutch subtitles. In some parts of the country, mainly the south, you've also got the programmes of the Belgian and German networks to choose from.

Food and Drink

Holland is – quite rightly – not renowned for its cuisine, but although much is unimaginative, it's rarely unpleasant. The country has a good supply of non-European restaurants, especially Indonesian and Chinese; Dutch food holds one or two surprises; and if you're selective prices are rarely high enough to break the bank. Drinking, too, is easily affordable, Dutch beer – and bars – being one of the real pleasures of the country.

■ Food

Dutch food tends to be higher in protein content than in variety: steak, chicken and fish, along with filling soups and stews, are staple fare, usually served up in enormous quantities. It can, however, at its best, be excellent, some restaurants offering increasingly adventurous crossovers with French cuisine at good value prices, especially *eetcafés* and bars.

Breakfast

In all but the very cheapest hostels or most expensive hotels **breakfast** (*ontbijt*) will be included in the price of the room. Though usually nothing fancy, it's always very filling: rolls, cheese, ham, hard-boiled eggs, jam and honey or peanut butter are the principal ingredients. If you don't have a hotel breakfast, many bars and cafés serve at least rolls and sandwiches.

The **coffee** is normally good and strong, served with a little tub of *koffiemelk* (evaporated milk); ordinary milk is rarely used. If you want coffee with warm milk, ask for a *koffie verkeerd*. Most bars also serve cappuccino and espresso coffees, although bear in mind that many stop serving coffee altogether around 11pm. **Tea** generally comes with lemon if anything – if you want milk you have to ask for it. **Chocolate** (*chocomel*) is also popular, served hot or cold: for a real treat drink it hot with a layer of fresh whipped cream (*slagroom*) on top. Some coffee shops also sell aniseed-flavoured warm milk or *anijsmelk*.

Snacks, cakes, cheeses

For the rest of the day, eating cheaply and well, particularly on your feet, is no real problem, although those on the tightest of budgets may find themselves dependent on the dubious delights of **Dutch fast food**. This has its own peculiarities. Chips – *frites* – are the most common standby (*vlaamse* or "Flemish" *frites* are the best), either sprinkled with salt or smothered with huge gobs of mayonnaise (*fritesaus*) or, alternatively, curry, goulash or tomato sauce; if you don't want your chips rendered completely unrecognisable, say so. Often chips are complemented with *kroketten* – spiced minced meat covered with breadcrumbs and deep fried – or *fricandel*, a frankfurter-like sausage. All these are available over the counter at evil-smelling fast-food places (*Febo* is the most common chain), or, for a guilder or so, from heated glass compartments outside.

Tastier, and good both as a snack and a full lunch, are the **fish specialities** sold in street kiosks: salted raw herrings, smoked eel, mackerel in a roll (*gerookte paling*), mussels and various kinds of deep-fried fish; tip your head back and dangle the fish into your mouth, Dutch-style. Look out for "green" or *maatje* herring, eaten raw with onions in early summer. A nationwide chain of fish restaurants, *Noordzee*, serve up well-priced fish-based rolls and sandwiches as well as good value fish lunches.

Another fast snack you'll see everywhere is **shoarma** – kebabs basically, sold in numerous Turkish restaurants and takeaways; a shoarma in pitta will set you back about f5 on average. Other street foods include **pancakes**, sweet or spicy, also widely available at sit-down restaurants; **waffles**, doused with maple syrup; and **poffertjes**, shell-shaped dough balls served with masses of melted butter and icing sugar – an extremely filling snack. Try also **oliebollen**, greasy doughnuts sometimes filled with fruit (often apple) or custard (a *berliner*) and traditionally served at New Year. Dutch **cakes and biscuits** are always good, and filling, best eaten in a *banketbakkerij* with a small serving area; or buy a bag and eat them on the hoof. Apart from the ubiquitous *appelgebak* – wedges of apple and cinnamon tart – things to try include *spekulaas*, a cinammon biscuit with gingerbread texture; *stroopwafels*, butter wafers sandwiched together with runny syrup; *amandelkoek*, cakes with a biscuity outside and melt-in-the-mouth almond paste inside. In Limburge you should also sample *Limburgse Vla* – a pie with various fruit fillings.

As for the kind of food you can expect to encounter in bars, there are **sandwiches and rolls** (*boterham* and *broodjes*) – often open-faced, and varying from a slice of tired cheese on old bread to something so embellished it's almost a complete meal – as well as more substantial fare. A sandwich made with French bread is known as a *stokbrood*. In the winter, *erwtensoep* (aka *snert*) is available in most bars, and at about f5.50 a shot makes a great buy for lunch: thick pea soup filled with smoked sausage and served with a portion of smoked bacon on *pumpernickel*. Or there's an *uitsmijter* (literally, "bouncer"): one, two, or three fried eggs on buttered bread, topped with a choice of ham, cheese or roast beef – at about f8, another good budget lunch.

Holland's **cheeses** have an unjustified reputation abroad for being bland. This is because they tend to export the lower quality products and keep the best for themselves. In fact, Dutch cheese can be delicious, although there isn't the variety you get in, say, France or Britain. Most are based on the same soft creamy *Goudas*, and differences in taste come with the varying stages of maturity – *jong*, *belegen*, or *oud*. *Jong* cheese has a mild flavour, *belegen* is much tastier, while *oud* can be pungent and strong, with a flaky texture not unlike parmesan. Among the other cheeses you'll find, best known is the round red *Edam*, made principally for export and not eaten much by the Dutch; *Leidse*, simply Gouda with cumin seeds; *Maasdammer*, strong, creamy, and full of holes; and Dutch-made *Emmentals* and *Gruyères*. The best way to eat cheese here is the way the Dutch do it, in thin slices (cut with a cheese slice or *kaasschaaf*) rather than in large hunks.

Sit-down eating

Sit-down eating is possible at many different sorts of establishment. The majority of **bars** serve food, everything from sandwiches to a full menu, in which case they may be known as an **eetcafé**. These type of places tend to be open all day, serving both lunch and dinner. Full-blown **restaurants**, on the other hand, tend to open in the evening only, usually from around 5.30 or 6pm until around 11pm. Bear in mind everywhere, especially in the smaller provincial towns, that the Dutch tend to eat early, usually around 7.30 or 8pm, and that after about 10pm you'll find many restaurant kitchens closed.

If you're on a budget, stick to **dagschotels** (dish of the day) wherever possible, for which you pay around f15, bottom-line, for a meat or fish dish heavily garnished with potatoes and other vegetables and salad. Otherwise, meat dishes go for f15–25; fish is generally high-quality but rarely especially cheap at f20–25 and up, on average. The three-course **tourist menu**, which you'll see touted at some mainstream restaurants, is – at f19–20 or so – reasonable value, but the food is often extremely dull. Surprisingly enough, **railway station restaurants** are a good standby: every station has one, and they serve full meals, in huge portions, for f10–15.

Vegetarian food isn't a problem in Holland. Many *eetcafés* and restaurants have at least one meat-free menu item, and you'll find a few vegetarian restaurants in most towns, offering full-course set meals for f10–15. Bear in mind, though, that vegetarian restaurants often close early.

DUTCH FOOD AND DRINK TERMS

Basics

Boter	Butter	Nagerechten	Desserts
Brood	Bread	Peper	Pepper
Broodje	Sandwich/roll	Pindakaas	Peanut butter
Dranken	Drinks	Sla/salade	Salad
Eieren	Eggs	Smeerkaas	Cheese spread
Groenten	Vegetables	Stokbrood	French bread
Gerst	Semolina; the type of grain used in Algerian *couscous*, popular in vegetarian restaurants	Suiker	Sugar
		Vis	Fish
		Vlees	Meat
		Voorgerechten	Starters, hors d'oeuvres
Honing	Honey		
Hoofdgerechten	Main courses	Vruchten	Fruit
Kaas	Cheese	Warm	Hot
Koud	Cold	Zout	Salt

Starters and Snacks

Erwtensoep/snert	Thick pea soup with bacon or sausage	Uitsmijter	Ham or cheese with eggs on bread
Huzarensalade	Egg salad	Koffietafel	A light midday meal of cold meats, cheese, bread, and perhaps soup
Patates/Frites	Chips		
Soep	Soup		

Meat and Poultry

Biefstuk (hollandse)	Steak	Kalfsvlees	Veal
Biefstuk (duitse)	Hamburger	Karbonade	Chop
Eend	Duck	Kip	Chicken
Fricandeau	Roast pork	Kroket	Spiced minced meat in breadcrumbs
Fricandel	A frankfurter-like sausage		
Gehakt	Minced meat	Lamsvlees	Lamb
Ham	Ham	Lever	Liver
Hutspot	Beef stew with vegetables	Rookvlees	Smoked beef
		Spek	Bacon
Kalkoen	Turkey	Worst	Sausages

Fish

Garnalen	Prawns	Mosselen	Mussels	Schelvis	Shellfish
Haring	Herring	Haringsalade	Herring salad	Forel	Trout
Kabeljauw	Cod	Paling	Eel	Tong	Sole
Makreel	Mackerel	Schol	Plaice	Zalm	Salmon

Terms

Doorbakken	Well-done	Gerookt	Smoked
Gebakken	Fried/baked	Gestoofd	Stewed
Gebraden	Roast	Half doorbakken	Medium
Gekookt	Boiled	Hollandse saus	Hollandaise (a milk and egg sauce)
Gegrild	Grilled		
Geraspt	Grated	Rood	Rare

Vegetables

Aardappelen	Potatoes	*Champignons*	Mushrooms	*Rijst*	Rice
Boerenkool	Mashed potato and cabbage	*Erwten*	Peas	*Sla*	Salad, lettuce
		Knoflook	Garlic	*Uien*	Onions
Bloemkool	Cauliflower	*Komkommer*	Cucumber	*Wortelen*	Carrots
Bonen	Beans	*Prei*	Leek	*Zuurkool*	Sauerkraut

Indonesian Dishes and Terms

Ajam	Chicken	*Nasi Goreng*	Fried rice with meat/chicken and vegetables
Bami	Noodles with meat/ chicken and vegetables	*Nasi Rames*	*Rijsttafel* on a single plate
Daging	Beef	*Pedis*	Hot and spicy
Gado gado	Vegetables in peanut sauce	*Pisang*	Banana
		Rijsttafel	Collection of different spicy dishes served with plain rice
Goreng	Fried		
Ikan	Fish	*Sambal*	Hot, chilli-based sauce
Katjang	Peanut	*Satesaus*	Peanut sauce to accompany meat grilled on skewers
Kroepoek	Prawn crackers		
Loempia	Spring rolls	*Seroendeng*	Spicy fried, shredded coconut
Nasi	Rice	*Tauge*	Bean sprouts

Sweets and Desserts

Appelgebak	Apple tart or cake	*Pannekoeken*	Pancakes
Drop	Dutch licorice, available in zoet (sweet) or zout (salted) varieties – the latter an acquired taste	*Pepernoten*	Dutch ginger nuts
		Poffertjes	Small pancakes, fritters
		(Slag) room	(Whipped) cream
Gebak	Pastry	*Speculaas*	Spice & honey-flavoured biscuit
Ijs	Ice cream	*Stroopwafels*	Waffles
Koekjes	Biscuits	*Taai-taai*	Dutch honey cake
Oliebollen	Doughnuts	*Vla*	Custard

Fruits and Nuts

Aardbei	Strawberry	*Citroen*	Lemon	*Kokosnoot*	Coconut
Amandel	Almond	*Druiven*	Grape	*Peer*	Pear
Appel	Apple	*Hazelnoot*	Hazelnut	*Perzik*	Peach
Appelmoes	Apple purée	*Framboos*	Raspberry	*Pinda*	Peanut
		Kers	Cherry	*Pruim*	Plum/prune

Drinks

Bessenjenever	Blackcurrant gin	*Pils*	Dutch beer	*Sinaasappelsap*	Orange juice
Citroenjenever	Lemon gin	*Proost* !	Cheers!	*Tomatensap*	Tomato juice
Droog	Dry	*Thee*	Tea	*Chocomel*	Chocolate milk
Frisdranken	Soft drinks	*Vruchtensap*	Fruit juice		
Jenever	Dutch gin	*Wijn*	Wine	*Anijsmelk*	Aniseed- flavoured warm milk
Karnemelk	Buttermilk	*(wit/rood/rose)*	(white/red/ rosé)		
Koffie	Coffee				
Kopstoot	Beer with a jenever chaser	*Zoet*	Sweet	*Koffie verkeerd*	Coffee with warm milk
		Vieux	Dutch brandy		
Melk	Milk			*Met slagroom*	With whipped cream
Met ijs	With ice	*Appelsap*	Apple juice		

Of foreign cuisines, **Italian** food is ubiquitous and a good cheap standby: pizzas and pasta dishes start at a fairly uniform f10–11 in all but the ritziest places. **Chinese** restaurants are also common, as are (increasingly) **Spanish** and **Tex-Mex** eateries, all of which serve well-priced, filling food. **Indonesian** restaurants, too, are widespread, and are normally well worth checking out. You can eat à la carte – *Nasi Goreng* and *Bami Goreng* (rice or noodles with meat) are good basic dishes, though there are normally more exciting things on the menu, some very spicy; chicken or beef in peanut sauce (*sate*) is always available. Failing that, if you're hungry order a *rijstaffel*: boiled rice and/or noodles served with a huge number of spicy side dishes and hot *sambal* sauce on the side. Eaten with the spoon in the right hand, fork in the left, and with dry white or rosé wine, or beer, this doesn't come cheap, but it's delicious and is normally more than enough for two; indeed that's the usual way to order it – reckon on paying about f60–70 for two people.

■ Drinking

Most **drinking** is done either in the cosy environs of a **brown café** (*bruin kroeg*) – so named because of the colour of the walls, often stained by years of tobacco smoke – or in more modern-looking **designer bars**, minimally furnished and usually catering to a younger crowd. Most bars open until around 1am during the week, 2am at weekends, though some don't bother to open until lunchtime, a few not until around 4pm. There is a further drinking establishment you may come across, though they're no longer all that common – *proeflokaalen* or **tasting houses**, originally the sampling houses of small distillers, now small, old-fashioned bars that only serve spirits and close up around 8pm. Bear in mind that many cafés are a good source of budget **food**, when they're sometimes designated *eetcafés*. Most bars offer sandwiches and soup, or at least hard-boiled eggs from the bar.

Beer

Other than in tasting houses, the most commonly consumed beverage is **beer**. This is usually served in small (just under half-pint) measures; ask for "een pils" – "may I have?" is "mag ik?"; as in "mag ik een pils?". Much of your beer will be frothing head; requests to have it poured

English-style meet with various responses, but it's worth trying. Prices are fairly standard: you don't pay much over the odds for sitting outside or drinking in a swanky bar or club; reckon on paying f2–2.50 a glass pretty much everywhere. Some bars, particularly those popular with the local English community, serve beer in larger measures, roughly approximate to a pint, for which you can expect to pay f5–6. Beer is much cheaper bought from a supermarket, most brands retailing at a little over f1 for a half-litre bottle (just under a pint).

The most commonly seen names are *Heineken*, *Amstel*, *Oranjeboom* and *Grolsch*, all of which you can find more or less nationwide. *Grolsch* is reputedly the strongest. Expect them to be stronger and more distinctive than the watery approximations brewed under licence in Britain. In the southern provinces of North Brabant and Limburg you'll also find a number of locally brewed beers – *Bavaria* from Brabant, *De Ridder*, *Leeuw*, *Gulpen* and *Brand* (the latter the country's oldest brewer) from Limburg, all of which are well worth trying.

You will also, of course, especially in the south of the country, come across plenty of the better-known **Belgian brands**, like *Stella Artois* and the darker *De Koninck*, available on tap, and bottled beers like *Duvel*, *Trappiste* and the cherry-flavoured *Kriek*. There are also a number of beers which are **seasonally available**: *Bokbier*, similar to an English mild, is widespread in autumn; white beers (*witbieren*) like *Hoegaarden*, *Dentergems* and *Raaf* are available in summer, often served with a slice of a lemon – very refreshing. See "Belgium and Luxembourg", "Eating and Drinking".

Wine and Spirits

Wine is reasonably priced – expect to pay around f6 or so for an average bottle of French white or red. As for **spirits**, the indigenous drink is **jenever**, or Dutch gin – not unlike British gin, but a bit weaker and oilier, made from molasses and flavoured with juniper berries: it's served in small glasses and is traditionally drunk straight, often knocked back in one gulp with much hearty back-slapping. There are a number of varieties: *Oud* (old) is smooth and mellow, *Jong* (young) packs more of a punch – though neither are extremely alcoholic. *Zeer oude* is very old jenever. The older jenevers are a little more expensive but are stronger and less oily. In a bar, ask for a *borreltje* (straight jenever) or a *bittertje* (with angostura); if you've a sweeter tooth, try a *bessenjenever* – blackcurrant-flavoured gin; for a glass of beer with a jenever chaser, ask for a *kopstoot*. A glass of jenever in a bar will cost you around f2.50; in a supermarket bottles sell for around f14. Imported spirits are considerably more expensive.

Other drinks you'll see include numerous Dutch **liqueurs**, notably *advocaat* or eggnog, the sweet blue *curacao* and luminous green *pisang ambo*, as well as an assortment of luridly coloured **fruit brandies** best left for experimentation at the end of an evening. There's also the Dutch-produced brandy, *Vieux*, which tastes as if it's made from prunes but is in fact grape-based, and various regional firewaters, such as *elske* from Maastricht – made from the leaves, berries and bark of alder bushes.

Galleries, Museums and Churches

Holland is strong on museums and galleries: most towns have at least a small collection of Dutch art worth looking at, as well as several other museums on a variety of subjects.

■ Galleries and museums

There are a number of **different kinds of museum** you'll come across time and again: a Rijksmuseum is a state-run museum, housing a national collection on a specific theme; a Stedelijk or Gemeente museum is run by the local town council and can vary from a small but quality collection of art to dusty arrays of local archaeological finds; a *tentoonstelling* is a temporary exhibition, usually of contemporary art. **Opening times** are fairly uniform across the country – generally Tuesday to Saturday 10am to 5pm, Sun 1pm or 2pm to 5pm; entry prices for the more ordinary collections are normally around f2–5, children half-price. Many museums offer at least some English information, even if it's just a returnable leaflet.

If you're intending to visit more than a handful of museums (and this is easily done in Amsterdam alone), it's worth investing in a **Museumcard**. Available from the VVV, or direct from museums, this currently costs f25 if you're under 26, f40 otherwise; it's valid for a year and grants free access to all state and municipally-run museums and galleries throughout the country – in practice by far the majority. Considering it costs over f15 alone just to visit Amsterdam's Rijksmuseum and Van Gogh museum, it's a purchase worth making. Where museumcards aren't accepted, we've said so in the text.

One alternative to the museumcard is the Cultureel Jongeren Paspoort or **CJP**, which if you're under 35 years of age gets you reductions in museums and on theatre, film and concert tickets for f25 – though bear in mind that the discounts vary wildly and in many cases are not that substantial. CJPs are valid across Holland and are available from the Uitburo in Amsterdam. There is also the **Holland Leisure Card**, available before you leave for Holland through the NBT, purchase of which includes a museumcard among other benefits – details on p.31.

■ Churches

Dutch **churches** are normally rather austere – stripped bare after the Reformation, their spartan white paint-work emphasising the effect of their often soaring Gothic lines. Organs are often the only embellishment, great ornate affairs that put out a terrific – and awesome – noise, and only in the Catholic south of the country will you find the occasional church that still retains anything of the mystery of pre-Calvinist rituals. Opening times for visitors vary enormously, though northern churches do usually have set times when visits are possible – assuming, of course, that there's something inside worth seeing. Falling attendances, however, also mean that you'll see churches that have been pragmatically turned over to other purposes – exhibition halls, concert halls, even apartments. In the south, unless there's something of special interest, you may find visits confined to services.

Festivals and Annual Events

Holland has few national annual events, and aside from the carnivals that are celebrated in the southern part of the country, and a sprinkling of religious-orientated celebrations, most annual shindigs are arts- or music-based affairs, confined to a particular town or city. In addition there are also markets and folkloric events, rather bogusly sustained for tourists, that take place during summer only, the Alkmaar cheese market being one of the most famous examples.

FESTIVALS DIARY

January
Mid-Jan Leiden Jazz Week.
End Jan Rotterdam Film Festival.

February
Mid-Feb West Frisian Flora exhibition, Bovenkarspel.
Third week of Feb Carnivals in Maastricht and in other southern towns.

March
End March–end May Keukenhof Gardens, Lisse, displays in the bulbfields and hothouses.
End March–end May Frans Roozen Nursery, Vogelenzang, displays in gardens and hothouses.
Sunday closest to March 15 Amsterdam: *Stille Ommegang* procession through the city streets to the St Nicolaaskerk.

April
April–Oct Amsterdam: city illuminations on bridges and buildings.
April–Oct Amsterdam: Tramline Museum, trams from Amsterdam South to Amstelveen and back.
Second Sunday in April Rotterdam Marathon.
April–Sept Alkmaar Cheese Market on Friday mornings.
April 22–24 Groningen: avant-garde jazz festival.
April 28 Flower Parade from Haarlem to Noordwijk.
April 30 Amsterdam: *Koninginnedag* (Queen's Birthday), celebrated by a fair on Dam Square, street markets and fireworks in the evening.

May
Early May Amsterdam Marathon.
End May Breda: traditional jazz festival, with open-air concerts and street parades.
May 30 Scheveningen: "Flag Day" to mark the opening of the Dutch herring season.

June
June 1–30 Holland Festival. Amsterdam, Rotterdam, The Hague: international arts festival.
June 1–21 Amsterdam: Summer Festival of modern theatre, music, dance and mime.
June 8 Geleen: Pink Pop Festival.
Early June Bolsward: Frisian "eleven cities" cycle race, using bicycles instead of the traditional ice skates.

Early June Apeldoorn: "Jazz in the Woods" festival.
Mid-June Scheveningen: International Kite Festival.
Mid-June to mid-July Middleburg: International Festival of new avant-garde music.
End June–end Aug Schagen: West Frisian Folk Market, preceded by processions, etc, on Thursday mornings.
Last week Amsterdam: Festival van Verleiding, theatre productions and other events to celebrate Gay Pride Week.

July
Early July Drenthe Four-Day Cycle Event.
July 1–Sept 30 The Hague: International Rose Exhibition.
July–end Aug Hoorn: Traditional market, with folk dancing and old crafts, Wednesday mornings.
July–end Aug Purmerend: cheeese market, Thursday mornings.
Early July The Hague: North Sea Jazz Festival.
End July Nijmegen Four-Day Cycle Event.

August
Early Aug Sneek Week: international sailing event.
Mid-Aug Scheveningen: International Firework festival, two displays each evening.
Mid-Aug Brabant Four-Day Cycle Event, starting in Tilburg.
End Aug Zandvoort: International Grand Prix motor-racing event.

September
Mid-Sept Amsterdam: Boulevard of Broken Dreams Arts Festival.

October
Mid-Oct Maastricht: Jazz festival.

November
Mid-Nov Throughout the country: arrival of St Nicholas.

December
Dec 6 Pakjesavond. Though it tends to be a private affair, this is the day Dutch kids receive their Christmas presents. If you're here on that day and have Dutch friends, it's worth knowing that it's traditional to give a present together with a rude poem you have written caricaturing the recipient.

Most festivals, as you might expect, take place in summer. Contact the local VVV for up-to-date details – and remember that wherever you might be staying, huge swathes of the country are no more than a short train ride away.

Of the country's **annual cultural events**, the *Holland Festival*, held in June in Amsterdam, Rotterdam and The Hague, is probably the most diverse, with theatre, opera and classical music by mainly Dutch performers. The Hague's *North Sea Jazz Festival* in July probably has more prestige, and attracts a host of big names. There's more jazz on offer in June with Apeldoorn's *Jazz in the Woods* binge; check out also the Europe-renowned *Pink Pop Festival*, held in Geleen just north of Maastricht early the same month, which attracts top level performers.

Outside summer, **other annual events** include, of course, the **bulbfields** – at their best between March and May. There are a number of places you can visit in the bulbfield areas of North and South Holland, notably the dazzling Keukenhof Gardens and – for a taste of the industry in action – the Aalsmeer flower auction. If you're around in February, a number of towns in Holland's southern provinces host pre-lenten **carnivals**, notably Maastricht; while an event to look out for also in February (though really any time when the weather is cold enough) is the **Elfstedentocht** – Friesland's uniquely exiting, and gruelling, canal skating race between the province's eleven towns.

Directory

ADDRESSES These are written, for example, as Haarlemmerstraat 15 III, which means the third-floor apartment at number 15 Haarlemmerstraat. The ground floor is indicated by h/s (huis) after the number. The figures 1e or 2e before a street name are an abbreviation for Eerste and Tweede respectively – first and second streets of the same name. Dutch zip codes can be found in the directory kept at post offices or by taking the number in purple on a large-scale Falkplan and putting "10" in front (note that complete codes have a two-letter indicator as well).

AIRPORT TAX Not charged when leaving The Netherlands.

BIKE HIRE See p.22.

BRING Toiletries, film and English-language books, all of which are expensive in Holland. Also antihistamine cream if you react badly to mosquitoes – it can be hard to find in Holland.

CAR PROBLEMS See p.22.

CONTRACEPTIVES Condoms are available from *drogisterij* or – in Amsterdam – the *Condomerie* (p.82). But to get the pill you need a doctor's prescription – see p.12.

DISABLED VISITORS Though public transportation systems tend to have no facilities for disabled passengers, many major museums, concert halls, theatres, churches and public buildings are accessible to visitors in wheelchairs. VVV offices, themselves accessible, can provide lists of those that have ramps and lifts, or where staff are trained to escort disabled visitors. *Netherlands Railways* offer a comprehensive service for disabled travellers, including a timetable in Braille, free escort service and assistance at all stations. Get more details by calling ☎030/33 12 53 (Mon–Fri 8.30am–4pm), or from The Netherlands Board of Tourism leaflet, *Holland for the Handicapped*, which also describes hotel and camping facilities throughout the country. There is also a desk in the Schipol Arrivals Hall (North), open 6am to 11pm, to help disabled people through the airport. Last but not least, paper currency has dots in the corner to indicate its value to the visually impaired.

ELECTRIC CURRENT 220v AC – effectively the same as British; American apparatus requires a transformer; both will need new plugs or an adaptor.

EMERGENCIES Phone ☎06 11. Or, in lesser emergencies: **Police** ☎22 22 22; **Ambulance** ☎55 55 555; **Fire** ☎21 21 21.

FLOWERS It doesn't take long to notice the Dutch enthusiasm for flowers and plants of all kinds: windows are often festooned with blooms and greenery, and shops and markets sell sprays and bunches for next to nothing. Flowers are grown year-round, though obviously spring is the best time to come if this is your interest, when the bulbfields (and glasshouses) of North and South Holland are dense with colour – tulips, hyacinths and narcissi are the main blooms. Later in the year there are rhododendrons, and, in Friesland and Groningen, fields of yellow rape; in summer roses appear, while the autumn sees late chrysanthemums. For more on Holland's flowers, pick up the NBT's *Flowers* booklet, and turn to p.113 for the best of the bulbfields. Buying bulbs is easiest by placing an order with a specialist company, who will handle the packing and legal paperwork for you.

ISIC CARDS Student ID won't help you gain reduced admission to very much at all, and certainly not museums; for this you need a museumcard or CJP (see p.31).

LEFT LUGGAGE At all railway stations. Where there is no actual office, there will always be lockers, charging either f1 or f2 – depending on size – for 24 hours.

MOSQUITOES These thrive in Holland's watery environment, and bite their worst at campsites. An antihistamine cream such as *Phenergan* is the best antidote.

SHOPPING Two stores you'll see all over Holland are *Vroom & Dressman* and *HEMA* – department stores that are useful for stocking up on basic supplies such as toiletries, etc. Of the two, *HEMA* is the cheaper, a sort of Dutch Woolworths, many branches of which also have a cheap restaurant that makes a good place for a cheap if unexciting budget lunch. Among **things to buy to take home**, cheese is an obvious

choice – it's better and there's more variety than at home. Flowers (see above) are also dirt cheap everywhere. You might also try *drop* or Dutch licorice, which comes in myriad different varieties including with salt, without salt, or with honey. As for books, most good bookshops stock at least a few English paperbacks, though at higher prices than in Britain; look out also for branches of *De Slegte*, a countrywide chain (with a couple of branches in Belgium) that sells secondhand and discounted books, a good proportion of which will be in English; we've listed addresses in the guide.

TIME One hour ahead of Britain, six hours ahead of Eastern Standard Time.

TIPPING Don't bother, since restaurants, hotels, taxis, etc, must include a fifteen percent service charge by law. Only if you're somewhere *really* flash is it considered proper to round up the bill to the nearest guilder. In public loos, it's normal to leave about 25c.

TRAVEL AGENTS *NBBS* are the nationwide student/youth travel organisation and the best source of *BIJ* tickets, discount flights for anyone, etc. They have branches in all the main Dutch cities – see our listings for addresses.

WAR CEMETERIES Though it saw less action than either Belgium or Luxembourg, there was fierce fighting in parts of Holland during the last war, notably at Arnhem, where several thousand British and Polish servicemen are remembered at the Oosterbeek cemetery. There are other military cemeteries in the east and south of the country, not least at Margraten, where around 8000 US soldiers are buried.

WINDMILLS The best place to see windmills is at Kinderdijk near Dordrecht; they're also still very much part of the landscape in the polderlands north of Amsterdam. Some, too, have been moved and reassembled out of harm's way in the open-air museums at Zaanse Schans (Zaandam) and the Netherlands Open-Air Museum just outside Arnhem.

CHAPTER ONE

AMSTERDAM

Amsterdam is a compact, instantly likeable capital: appealing to look at, pleasant to walk around, and with an enticing mix of the provincial and the cosmopolitan. The city has a welcoming attitude towards visitors, and a uniquely youthful orientation, shaped by the liberal counter-culture of the last two decades. It's hard not to feel drawn in by the buzz of open-air summer events, by the intimacy of the clubs and bars, or by the Dutch facility with languages – English, for example, is spoken almost everywhere.

The city's layout is determined by a cobweb of canals radiating out from a medieval core, which, along with planned seventeenth-century extensions further out, provide elegant backdrops for living or wandering. The conventional sights are for the most part low-key – the **Anne Frank House** being a notable exception – but Amsterdam has developed a world-class group of museums and galleries. The **Van Gogh Museum** is, for many, reason enough in itself to visit the city; add to it the **Rijksmuseum**, with its collections of medieval and seventeenth-century Dutch paintings, the contemporary and experimental **Stedelijk**, plus hundreds of smaller galleries, and the international quality of the art is evident.

But it's Amsterdam's **population and politics** that constitute its most enduring characteristics. Notorious during the 1960s and 1970s as the heart of radical, "liberated" Europe, the city mellowed only marginally during the Eighties, and despite the inevitable late-Eighties yuppification retains a resilient laid-back feel. The authorities are trying to play down the counter-culture label and boost Amsterdam's economy by cultivating a businesslike image for the city and a more conventional reputation for the arts. Sporadic battles erupt over urban development plans, as Amsterdam's inhabitants, perennially short on low-cost housing, object to the construction of yet another high-rise hotel or prestige opera house. But it's a tension that keeps the city on its toes. Overall, the keynote is tolerance, or *gezelligheid* as Amsterdammers say. Though untranslatable, the term conjures up a sense of laid-back intimacy; put simply, Amsterdam is a city that's as congenial a place to hang out in as you'll find.

Amsterdam has responded to its youth culture with a social and sensible attitude to soft drugs. Entertainment has a similarly innovative edge, exemplified by **multi-media complexes** like the *Melkweg*, whose offerings are at the forefront of contemporary film, dance, drama and music. There are some great **coffee shops**, serving cannabis products and soft drinks instead of alcohol, and the more conventional **bars** range from the traditional, bare-floored *brown cafés* to new-wave designer haunts. The city's **club** scene is by contrast relatively subdued, with its venues modest by London standards, and the emphasis more on dancing than posing.

If you intend spending any time in Amsterdam, or want to find out about it in greater detail, get hold of a copy of *The Rough Guide to Amsterdam*, (Harrap Columbus, £5.95).

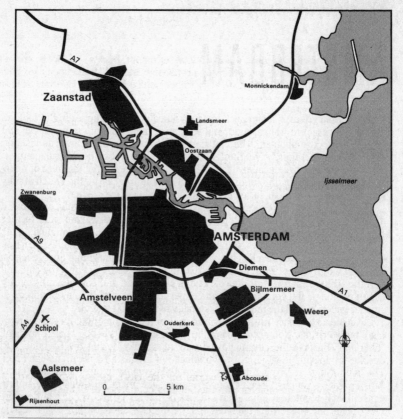

Arrival, information and getting around

Amsterdam has only one international airport, **Schipol**. This is connected by train with Amsterdam's **Centraal Station**, a fast service leaving every fifteen minutes during the day, every hour at night; the journey takes twenty minutes and costs f4.40 one way. Amsterdam has a number of suburban **train stations**, but all major internal and international traffic is handled by **Amsterdam Centraal**. Arriving here leaves you at the hub of all bus and tram routes and just five minutes' walk from Dam Square. Almost all **buses** arrive at **Centraal Station** too, except for Hoverspeed's *City Sprint* service, which calls at **Stadionplein**, before terminating at **Leidseplein**, linked to the city centre by trams #1, #2 and #5.

Getting around the city

By European capital standards Amsterdam is small, its public transport excellent, and most of the things you might conceivably want to see can be found in the city's compact centre: **getting around** couldn't be easier.

The telephone code for Amsterdam is ☎020

Apart from walking, **trams** – and, to a lesser extent, **buses** – offer the easiest transport alternative: the system is comprehensive and not at all expensive. Your first stop should be the main *GVB* (city transit) office in front of Centraal Station (next door to the *VVV*; Mon–Fri 7am–10.30pm, Sat & Sun 8am–10.30pm) where you can pick up a free route map and an English guide to the **ticketing** system.

This needs explaining. *Dagkaarten* (**day tickets**) are valid for as many days as you need – prices currently start at f8.85 for one day, going up to f17.25 for four, and f2.75 for each additional day. Or you can buy a *strippenkaart*. These are valid nationwide and work on a zonal arrangement whereby you cancel two strips for one zone, three strips for two and so on, when you board the tram or bus (the driver will do it for you on a bus; on trams you're trusted to do it yourself). The most practical *strippenkaart* has fifteen strips (currently f9.05), and can be purchased ahead of time at any *GVB* office (the others are in the Scheepvaarthuis at the corner of Prins Hendrikkade and Binnenkant, and there is sometimes a portacabin parked outside the Stadsschouwburg on Leidseplein), post office, selected tobacconists, or at railway station ticket counters. There's also a forty-strip card available for f25.85 – useful if you intend to travel further afield. Otherwise two-, three-, and ten-strip tickets are available from the driver – though they work out considerably more expensive. You'll rarely need to travel outside the central zone, so most of the time cancelling two strips is sufficient. Additional people can travel on the same *strippenkaart* by cancelling the requisite number of strips. Also, don't forget that the stamp made on the *strippenkaart* is timed and valid for an hour: you don't need to cancel it again if you change trams or buses within that time. If caught without a ticket, you're liable for a f26 fine, due on the spot, so it pays to be honest.

The *strippenkaart* system also works on the city's **metro**, which starts at Centraal Station and connects with the building complexes of Bijlmermeer to the east. It's clean, modern and punctual, although it can be a bit hairy at night, and apart from a couple of stops in the eastern reaches of the centre, most of the stations are in the suburbs and used mainly by commuters.

All of the above services stop running around 12.30am, when a wide network of **night buses** rolls into action, roughly hourly until 4am from Centraal Station to most parts of the city; the *GVB* offers a leaflet detailing all the routes.

Taxis are plentiful but expensive, and found in ranks on main city squares (Stationsplein, Dam Square, Leidseplein, etc.) or by phoning ☎77 77 77 – you can't hail them. Taxis aside, it's generally unwise to travel **by car**: parking is either difficult or expensive, and even if you have brought your own car it won't make any difference to the zealous traffic police, who will clamp you or tow you away whatever the registration plate says. Reclaiming a car from the pound costs at least f250; a clamp is cheaper – you're only charged for the excess meter time – but you have to present yourself personally at the nearest clamp office to get it removed. If you get caught and don't know what to do, call ☎27 58 66.

Another possibility, and a practical one, is to go native and opt for a **bicycle**: the city's well-defined network of bicycle lanes (*fietspaden*) means that this can be a remarkably safe way of getting around. If you haven't brought your own, it's possible to **hire a bike** from Centraal Station (f7 a day, f28 a week plus f200 deposit), or from a number of similarly priced bike hire firms scattered around

Bus route

Tram route

Metro route

Zone boundary

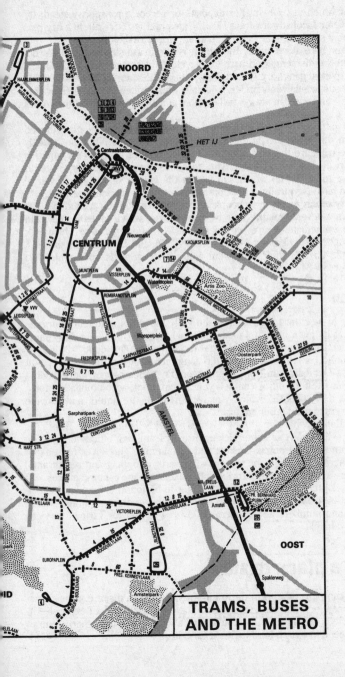

**TRAMS, BUSES
AND THE METRO**

town, most of which ask for smaller deposits or accept a passport instead: try *Rent-a-Bike*, Pieter Jacobsdwarsstraat 17, off Damstraat (☎25 50 29), f9 a day plus f50 deposit and a passport – they also do tandems for f25 a day.

Lock up your bike at *all times*. Bike theft is rife in Amsterdam, and it's not unusual to see the dismembered parts of bicycles still chained to their railings, victims of sharp-eyed gangs armed with bolt cutters who roam the streets hawking their prizes at suspiciously low prices. Ironically, this is often the cheapest way to pick up a bike – and you can always sell it (often at a profit) when the time comes to go home.

One way of getting orientated is to take a **canal trip** on one of the glass-topped boats that jam the major canals during the summer season. While not exactly riveting, these trips are the best way to see canal houses, and have a soporific charm if you're feeling lazy. Of the many to choose from, *P.Kooij* (☎23 38 10) runs hour-long tours for f8, which leave from the corner of Rokin and Lange Brugsteeg and have (atypically) a live commentary that's just about bearable.

As far as **city tours** go, plenty of people are willing to guide you around by road: the *GVB* offers a seventy-minute tour by *tourist tram*, which takes in the main sights of the immediate centre; or operators like *Lindbergh* (the cheapest), Damrak 26 (☎22 27 66), *Keytours*, Dam 19 (☎24 73 10), and *Holland International*, Damrak 7 (☎22 25 50), offer three-hour tours with stop-offs and, again, live commentary for f30–34.

Information

The first place to head for information is the *VVV*, the nationwide tourist organisation, either at its main branch outside Centraal Station (June–Aug daily 9am–11pm, Sept–Oct daily 9am–9pm, mid-Oct–May Mon–Fri 9am–6pm; ☎26 64 44, office hours only), or at Leidsestraat 106 (summer Mon–Sat 9am–11pm, Sun 9am–9pm, Sept–Oct daily 9am–9pm, winter Mon–Fri 10.30am–5pm, Sat 10.30am–9pm, closed Sun). Either office can sell you a map, book accommodation for a f3.50 fee (plus a f4 "deposit" which you reclaim from the hotel), and provide informed answers to most other enquiries.

For information on what's on, the *VVV* issues a weekly listings guide, *What's On In Amsterdam*, which you can either pick up directly from their offices for f1.50, or obtain free from selected hotels, hostels and restaurants. This gives reasonably complete, if uncritical, listings for museums, the arts, shopping and restaurants. Otherwise there's rather a dearth of critical, English-language listings sources.

Of the many Dutch-language monthly freebies to be found in bars and restaurants, the best is *Agenda*, whose listings have a more youthful slant and whose addresses, phone numbers and numerous advertisements for various services could prove invaluable.

Finding a place to stay

Unless you're camping, **accommodation** in Amsterdam is a major expense: even hostels are pricey for what you get, and hotels are among the most expensive in Europe. The city's size means that you'll inevitably end up somewhere central, but you'll still need to search hard to find a bargain.

At peak periods throughout the year (July–Aug, Christmas) it's advisable to book ahead of time – rooms can be swallowed up alarmingly quickly, especially during the summer and you may find it difficult to find somewhere to stay. The *VVV* will make advance bookings and book rooms on the spot for a f3.50 fee, or sell you a comprehensive accommodation list for f1.

Note: all tram line directions given below are from the Centraal Station.

Hostels

Most hostels expect you to provide your own sleeping bag (bed linen is often available for a small fee), set a nightly curfew, and, for security reasons, lock guests out of the dormitories for a short period each day.

Official youth hostels

Vondel Park, Zandpad 5 (☎83 17 44). For facilities, the better of the two official hostels. It has a bar, restaurant, TV rooms and kitchen for guests' use, and is well-located for the summer events in the park. Rates f18 per person, including use of secure lockers, f5 extra for non-YHA member. f35–50 for double rooms. Curfew 2am. Tram #1, #2, #5.

Stadsdoelen, Kloveniersburgwal 97 (☎24 68 32). Nearer to the station (on the edge of the Red Light district) and with slightly more inviting dorms. Although no double rooms, prices and curfew the same. Restaurant serves good value, though very basic, food. Tram #4, #9, #16, #24, #25.

Other hostels

Amstel, Steiger 5, De Ruijterkade (☎26 42 47). The only survivor of a number of barge hotels which used to be moored behind Centraal Station – now closed due to fire risks. This was always the largest and best-known, and still makes for a cheap and central place to stay. Prices range from f25 per person in a four-bed dormitory to f36 per person in a double room with private shower and toilet. All private rooms have phone and TV; all prices include breakfast.

Bob's Youth Hostel, N. Z. Voorburgwal 92 (☎23 00 63). An old favourite of backpackers, this has small, clean dorms for f18 per person including breakfast in the ground floor coffee shop; the curfew 3.30am. A short walk from Centraal Station.

Eben Haezer, Bloemstraat 179 (☎24 47 17). Don't be put off: though you may be given a booklet on Jesus, and the slogans on the walls may not be the ones you'd put up on yours, this Christian youth hostel isn't evangelical, but simply provides neat, clean dormitories for rock bottom prices – f14 per person including bed linen and a hearty breakfast. Curfew 1am on weekends; age limit 35 – though this is negotiable. Tram #13, #14, #17.

International Student Centre, Keizersgracht 15 (☎25 13 64). Terrific location close to the station, with dorm beds for f19, doubles for f75 and up, and a good mixture of triples and four-bedded rooms from f25 per person. Spotless rooms, too; breakfast is extra.

Kabul, Warmeosstraat 38–42 (☎23 71 58). Doesn't really justify its higher (f25) dorm rates, but the doubles are quite reasonable at f55–75, and triples and four-bedded rooms are also available. There's no lockout or curfew, it's an easy walk from the station, and the late-opening Kabul bar next door has regular live bands. Breakfast f6 extra. Wheelchair access.

Sleep-In, 's-Gravesandestraat 51 (☎94 74 44). A little way out of the centre but easily the city's cheapest accommodation with beds at f11 per person. Dorms are enormous, facilities minimal, but the atmosphere is great, and there are regular weekly films and musical and theatre performances. Also, around 600 beds mean you're unlikely to be turned away. No curfew, but open June to mid-Sept only. Weesperplein metro station or tram #6.

Hotels

Amsterdam's **hotels** start at around f60 for a double, absolute minimum, and although a filling Dutch breakfast is normally included at all but the most expensive places, many middle-range hotels give the barest value for the money. There are exceptions, but don't be afraid to ask to see the room first – and to refuse it if you don't like it.

The **prices** quoted are for the cheapest rooms (usually with a shared bath) in high season, and include breakfast unless otherwise stated; most places have cheaper off-season prices.

Inexpensive to moderate (under f100)

Acro, Jan Luykenstraat 44 (☎66 20 526). Excellent, modern hotel which has been completely refurbished with stylish rooms and a plush bar and self-service restaurant. Doubles from f105 (slightly more if you stay only one night) but well worth the money. Tram #2, #3, #5, #12.

De Admiraal, Herengracht 563 (☎26 21 50). Friendly hotel just off Rembrandtsplein. Doubles from f85. Tram #84.

Adolesce, Nieuwe Keizersgracht 26 (☎26 39 59). Nicely situated just off the Amstel, with a choice of doubles at f80. Curfew 2am. Bus #31, #150.

Bema, Concertgebouwplein 19b (☎79 13 96). Very small but a friendly place, handy for concerts and museums. Doubles f85.

Beursstraat, Beursstraat 9 (☎26 37 01). Nestling behind Berlage's Stock Exchange, a basic but cheap hotel with doubles from f60, not including breakfast. A short walk from Centraal Station.

Brian, Singel 69 (☎24 46 61). Cheap at f30 per person including breakfast, and with equally inexpensive triple and quadruple rooms available too. But if you're looking for something peaceful, this ain't the place. Tram #1, #2, #5, #13, #17.

Centralpark West, Roemer Visscherstraat 27 (☎85 22 85). With large, nicely furnished rooms, the *Centralpark West* is particularly good value. Popular with gay clientele: from f90 for a double. Tram #2, #3, #5, #12.

Clemens, Raadhuisstraat 39 (☎24 60 89). One of a number of inexpensive hotels that are situated in the Art Nouveau crescent of the Utrecht Building. Clean, neat and good value for money, with doubles for around f75. As Raadhuisstraat is one of the city's busiest streets, you should ask for a room at the back. Tram #13, #14, #17.

Continental, Damrak 40–41 (☎22 33 63). Though on the noisy tourist drag of Damrak, a clean and friendly hotel with doubles for f90 and up, breakfast f6.50. A short walk from Centraal Station.

Crown, O.Z. Voorburgwal 21 (☎26 96 64). Friendly budget hotel in the red light area. Doubles at f80–90, breakfast f5.

Pension Kitty, Plantage Middenlaan 40 (☎22 68 19). A little bit out from the centre, but decent-sized rooms for around f75 a double, including as much breakfast as you can eat. Good value. Tram #9, get off at the zoo.

Prinsenhof, Prinsengracht 810 (☎23 17 72). Tastefully decorated hotel with doubles from around f90. Best rooms at the back. Pleasant enough, if a bit tight with the showers, which are often kept locked. Tram #4.

Ronnie, Raadhuisstraat 41 (☎24 28 21). Recently taken over by the American cousins of the *Clemens'* owners, and with equally good prices and facilities. Friendly and helpful, with doubles from f80 including breakfast. Three-, four-, and five-person rooms, too. Tram #13, #14, #17.

Seven Bridges, Reguliersgracht 31 (☎23 13 29). One of the city's most beautiful and best-value hotels both inside and out, with doubles starting at f95. Tram #4.

Westertoren, Raadhuisstraat 35 (☎24 46 39). Welcoming and clean, with doubles from f75. Very good value for the this price-range, with breakfast served in your room. Tram #14.

Moderate to expensive (over f150)

Acca, Van de Veldestraat 3a (☎66 25 262). *The* place to go if you've got money to burn: an intimate luxury hotel with double rooms starting at around f250. Tram #2, #3, #5, #12.

Agora, Singel 462 (☎27 22 00). Nicely located, small, amicable hotel near the flower market, with doubles from f125, three- and four-bedded rooms for proportionately less. Tram #1, #2, #5.

Canal House, Keizersgracht 148 (☎22 51 82). Magnificently restored seventeenth-century building, centrally located on a principal *grachten*. American family-run with a friendly bar and cosy rooms. f175–200. Tram #13, #14, #17.

Estherea, Singel 305–307 (☎24 51 46). Pleasant middle-of-the-road hotel in a converted canal house, with doubles at f155–230. Tram #1, #2.

Toren, Keizersgracht 164 (☎22 60 33). Fine example of a seventeenth-century.canal house and once the home of a Dutch prime minister. Doubles from f115. Tram #13, #14, #17.

Weichmann, Prinsengracht 328–330 (☎26 89 62). A modern, comfortable hotel in two restored canal houses run by an engaging Dutch-American couple – excellent value for the price. Doubles from f105, triples and quads also available from f200–225. Tram #13, #14, #17.

Camping

There are several **campsites** in Amsterdam, most of which are easily accessible by public transport or by car. The *VVV* directs most visitors to the "youth campsites" of *Vliegenbos* and *Zeeburg*, open April to September, while grown-ups and those with caravans or campers are advised to use one of the other sites.

Amsterdamse Bos, Kleine Noorddijk 1, Amstelveen (☎41 68 68). Many facilities but a pretty long way out. Open April–Nov, and charges f10.35 for one person alone, inclusive of showers, car or campervan per person, and f6.60 if you're travelling in a group of two or more people. Yellow bus #171 or #172 and a short walk.

Amsterdam Ijsclub, Ijsbaanpad 45 (☎62 09 16). Vast campsite situated near the Olympic Stadium: aside from *Vliegenbos*, the closest to the city centre. Camping shop and canteen. Rates f4.25 per person, f3 per tent, parking f2.50. Trams #16 or #24, night bus #73 or #74.

Gaasper Camping, Loosdrechtdreef 7 (☎96 73 26). Amsterdam's newest campsite, just the other side of the Bijlmermeer housing complex, f4.50 per person, f3–f4 per tent, plus a charge for showers (f1.25). Metro to Gaasperplas station and a three-minute walk; night bus #75.

Vliegenbos, Meeuwenlaan 138 (☎36 88 55). A relaxed and friendly site, just a ten-minute bus ride from the station. Facilities include a general shop and bike hire. Costs f4.50 a night per person without car, f5.75 if you're over 30; f7.50 with car, f6.50 with motorbike. Hot showers f1.25. Bus #32, from Centraal Station, night bus #77.

Zeeburg, Zuider Ijdijk 34a (☎94 44 30). Slightly better equipped than the *Vliegenbos*, in that it has a bar. But more difficult to get to and a little more expensive: f5.50 per person plus f1 per tent, f2.50 per car, f1 per shower, f2 per motorbike. Tram #3 or #10 to Muiderpoort Station, then bus #37, then a ten-minute walk; also served by night bus #76.

The City

Amsterdam is a small city: its centre is compact, its buildings restrained, and, although the concentric canal system can initially be confusing, finding your bearings is straightforward. The centre of the city – along with the main canals, the area in which you'll spend most of your time – is the old **medieval core**, which fans south from Centraal Station, taking in the main artery of Damrak, Dam Square and Rokin. This, Amsterdam's commercial heart, boasts the best of its bustling street life, and is home to shops, many bars and restaurants and, not least, the infamous **Red Light district**. The area is bordered by the Singel, first of the **big canals**, on the far side of which curl Herengracht, Keizersgracht and Prinsengracht. These canals are part of a major seventeenth-century urban extension and, with the radial streets of Leidsestraat, Vijzelstraat and Utrechtsestraat, create Amsterdam's distinctive cobweb shape.

Further out, the **Jordaan** grew up as a slum and immigrant quarter and remains the traditional heart of working-class Amsterdam, though these days there is a firm yuppie edge to the area. On the other side of town, the **Jodenhoek** was, as its name suggests, once home to the city's Jewish community. Now it's probably Amsterdam's most visibly changed district, and, since the construction of the Muziektheater and metro, the principal source of squabbles over the city's future.

Across the Singelgracht, which marks the outer limit of today's centre, lie the largely residential districts of **Amsterdam South**, **West** and **East**, in themselves not of great interest, though with attractions (principally the main museums) that could tempt you out that way.

Stationsplein, Damrak and the Red Light District

This is the heart of the city and where you'll almost certainly arrive. It's a small area, but a varied one, ranging from the vigour of Stationsplein – the city's major traffic junction and home of the *VVV* (tourist) office – to the strategic tourist trap of Damrak and the studied (though real enough) sleaze of the Red Light district, not surprisingly one of Amsterdam's biggest tourist attractions.

Stationsplein and down Damrak

The neo-Renaissance **Centraal Station** is an imposing prelude to the city. When built late in the last century, this was a controversial structure, as it obscured the views of the port that brought Amsterdam its wealth. Since then, however, shipping has moved out to more spacious dock areas to the west and east, and the station is now one of Amsterdam's most resonant landmarks and a natural focal point for urban life. Stand here and all of Amsterdam, with its faintly oriental skyline of spires and cupolas, lies before you.

Stationsplein, immediately outside, is a messy open space, but come summer there's no livelier part of the city, as street performers compete for attention with the careening trams that converge dangerously from all sides. It's without a doubt a promising place to arrive, and with that in mind the municipal authorities are cleaning up the area's image, notably in the southeastern corner, where the once-notorious Zeedijk is being developed (see p.45).

Just down the street from Zeedijk, the dome of the **St. Nicolaaskerk** catches the eye: despite a dilapidated exterior, it's the city's foremost Catholic church, having replaced the clandestine Amstelkring (see p.68) in 1887. Even if you manage to coordinate your visit with the limited open hours (April–Oct Tues–Fri 11am–4pm, Sat 2–4pm), you'll find that there's not much of note inside – except, on the high altar, the crown of Austro-Hungarian Emperor Maximilian, very much a symbol of the city and one you'll see again and again (on top of the Westerkerk and on much of the city's official literature).

Above all, though, Stationsplein acts as a filter for Amsterdam's newcomers, and from here **Damrak**, an unenticing avenue lined by tacky, over-priced restaurants and the bobbing canal boats of Amsterdam's considerable tourist industry, storms south into the heart of the city. Just past the boats is the Stock Exchange, or **Beurs** (sometimes known as the "Beurs van Berlage"), designed at the turn of the century by the leading light of the Dutch modern movement, H. P. Berlage. With its various styles from Romanesque to neo-Renaissance interwoven with a minimum of ornamentation, it is something of a seminal work. Slip inside the entrance on Beursplein and look at the main hall, where exposed ironwork and shallow-arched arcades combine to give a real sense of space. Today it's no longer used as an exchange; the Beurs often hosts visiting theatre groups and exhibitions.

During the prewar years, the **De Bijenkorf** department store building, facing the Beurs and extending as far as Dam Square, was a successful Jewish concern – so much so that during the occupation the authorities, fearing altercations with the Jewish staff, forbade German soldiers from shopping on the ground floor.

Around the Red Light District

Had you turned left off Damrak before the Beurs, you would have found yourself in the **RED LIGHT DISTRICT**, bordered by the oldest street in the city, Warmoesstraat, and stretching across two canals which marked the edge of medieval Amsterdam. The **prostitution** here is sadly, but perhaps inevitably, one of the real sights of the city – and one of its most distinctive draws. The upfront nature of the porno industry here makes Soho seem tame by comparison.

Two canals form the backbone of the area: **Oude Zijds Voorburgwal** and **Oude Zijds Achterburgwal**. These, and the narrow connecting passages, are, most evenings of the year, thronged with people here to discover just how shocking it all is. The nasty edge to the district is, oddly enough, sharper during the daytime, when the pimps hang out in shifty gangs and drug addicts wait anxiously, assessing the chances of scoring their next hit.

Narrow **Warmoesstraat** itself is seedy and uninviting, and a little way up stands the **Oude Kerk**, its precincts offering a reverential peace after the excesses of the Red Light district – though even here some of the houses have the familiar *Kamer te huur* sign and window seat. There's been a church on this site since the late thirteenth century, even before the Dam was built, but most of the present building dates from the fourteenth century.

Having been stripped bare during the Reformation and recently very thoroughly restored, the Oude Kerk is nowadays a survivor rather than an architectural masterpiece. Its handful of interesting features include – apart from a few faded vault paintings – some beautifully carved misericords in the choir, and the memorial tablet of Rembrandt's wife, Saskia van Uylenburg, who is buried here. It costs a guilder to get in and, in summer, another to ascend the tower. (Summer Mon–Sat 11am–5pm; winter Mon–Sat 1–3pm; ring vestry bell for attention; tower June–Sept Mon & Thurs 2–5pm, Tues & Wed 11am–2pm.)

There's little else to stop for along Oude Zijds; only the clandestine **Amstelkring**, at the Zeedijk end of O. Z. Voorburgwal, is of real interest, once the principal Catholic place of worship in the city and now a museum (see p.68). Just past here, **Zeedijk** itself, though much cleaned up, provides evidence of more urban blight; until recently, you had to run the gauntlet of Surinamese heroin dealers trying to fast-talk you into a quick sale while idle groups of police-

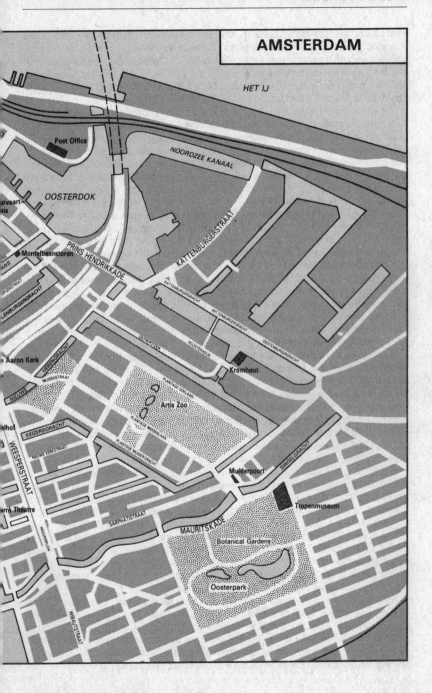

AMSTERDAM

HET IJ

Post Office

NOORDZEE KANAAL

OOSTERDOK

KATTENBURGERSTRAAT

ovaart-
ais

PRINS HENDRIKKADE

Montelbaanstoren

KATTENBURGERGRACHT

WITTENBURGERGRACHT

OOSTENBURGERGRACHT

ENBURGERGRACHT

ENTREPOTDOK

HOOGTEKADIJK

HERENGRACHT

Aaron Kerk

Kromhout

MUIDERSTRAAT

PLANTAGE DOKLAAN

NIEUWE

Artis Zoo

PLANTAGE MIDDENLAAN

KEIZERSGRACHT

lhof

PLANTAGE MUIDERGRACHT

NIEUWE KERK STRAAT

WEESPERSTRAAT

Muiderpoort

SINGELGRACHT

Tropenmuseum

rré Theatre

WEESPERPLEIN

SARPHATISTRAAT

MAURITSKADE

Botanical Gardens

Oosterpark

WIBAUTSTRAAT

men looked on. The police claim to have the area under control now – part of the city-wide push to polish up Amsterdam's tarnished reputation as a tourist centre – and certainly this narrow street is considerably less intimidating than it once was. But for the moment there's a long way to go: Zeedijk is still terribly dilapidated, and the heroin dealers – albeit much depleted in number – are creeping back to shoot up in doorways and hustle passers-by for small change.

For the moment, then, the best thing to do is hurry through. Zeedijk opens out on to **Nieuwmarkt** and the top end of **Gelderskade**, which together form the hub of Amsterdam's tiny Chinese quarter. As its name suggests, Nieuwmarkt was once one of Amsterdam's most important markets, first for fish, later for the cloth traders from the adjacent Jewish quarter, and nowadays for antiques on Sunday. During the last war it was surrounded by barbed wire behind which Jews were penned while awaiting deportation. The main focus of the square, the turreted **Waag**, or old **St Antoniespoort**, has played a variety of roles over the years. Originally part of the fortifications that encircled Amsterdam before the seventeenth-century expansion, it later became the civic weighing-house, and for a time was used by a number of the city's guilds, including the Surgeons' – the young Rembrandt's *Anatomy Lesson of Dr. Tulp* was based on the activities here.

Kloveniersburgwal, which leads south from Nieuwmarkt, was the outer of the three eastern canals of sixteenth-century Amsterdam. Although not among the more attractive waterways, it does boast, on the left, one of the city's most impressive canal houses. Built for the Trip family in 1662, and large enough to house the Rijksmuseum collection for most of the nineteenth century, the **Trippenhuis** is a huge overblown mansion, its Corinthian pilasters and grand frieze providing a suitable reflection of the owners' importance.

Further up the canal, on the corner of Oude Hoogstraat, the red-brick former headquarters of the **Dutch East India Company** is a monumental building, built in 1606 shortly after the founding of the company. It was from here that the Dutch organised and regulated the trading interests in the Far East which made the country so profitable in the seventeenth century. Under the greedy auspices of the East India Company, the Netherlands (especially its most prosperous provinces, Holland and Zeeland) exploited the natural resources of the group of islands now known as Indonesia for several centuries, satisfying the whims of Amsterdam's burghers with shiploads of spices, textiles and exotic woods.

For all that, the building itself is of little interest, occupied these days by offices. It's better to continue on towards the southern end of Kloveniersburgwal, to where the **Oudmannhuispoort** passage leads through to O. Z. Achterburgwal. This was once part of an almshouse for elderly men, but is now filled with second-hand bookstalls and a group of buildings serving Amsterdam University. On O. Z. Achterburgwal you look across to the pretty **Huis op de Drie Grachten**, "House on the Three Canals", on the corner of Grimburgwal, which runs alongside more university buildings. A little way down O. Z. Voorburgwal on the right, through an ornate gateway, is the **Agnietenkapel**, also owned by the university and containing exhibitions on academic life through the ages.

At the corner a passage cuts through to **Nes**, a long, narrow street, once home to the philosopher Spinoza; or you can make your way back up Oude Zijds past the **Galerie Mokum**, named after the old Jewish nickname for the city, now in general use. From here it's just a few yards to Rokin and, beyond, Kalverstraat. Alternatively, sink into one of the terrace seats of *'t Gasthuys* café, a popular student haunt and excellent for either a quick drink or a full lunch.

Dam Square to Muntplein

Dam Square gives the city its name: in the thirteenth century the river Amstel was dammed here, and the small fishing village that grew around it became known as "Amstelredam". Boats could sail right into the square and unload their imported grain in the middle of the rapidly growing town, and the later building of Amsterdam's principal church, the Nieuwe Kerk, along with the Royal Palace, formally marked Dam Square as Amsterdam's centre.

Though robbed a little of its dignity by the trams that scuttle across it, the square is still the hub of the city. At its centre there's a **War Memorial**, an unsightly stone tusk filled with soil from each of The Netherlands' eleven provinces and Indonesia. It serves as a gathering place for the square's milling tourists who seem to be wondering if, among the musicians and drug pushers, they've really found the heart of liberated Amsterdam.

Across the square, the **Royal Palace** (July–Aug 12.30–4pm; Sept–June guided tours Wed 1.30pm; f2.50, no museumcards) seems neither Dutch nor palatial – understandably so since it was originally built from imported stone as the city's town hall. At the time of its construction in the mid-seventeenth century, it was the largest town hall in Europe, supported by 13,659 wooden piles driven into the Dam's sandy soil. Inside, the *Citizen's Hall* proclaims the pride and confidence of the Golden Age, with the enthroned figure of Amsterdam looking down at the world and heavens at her feet, the whole sumptuously inlaid in brass and marble. A good-natured and witty symbolism pervades the building: cocks fight above the entrance to the *Court of Petty Affairs*, while Apollo, god of the sun and the arts, brings harmony to the disputes. On a more sober note, death sentences were pronounced at the *High Court of Justice* at the front of the building, and the condemned immediately executed on a scaffold outside.

The building received its royal monicker in 1808 when Napoleon's brother Louis commandeered it as the one building fit for an installed king. Lonely and isolated, Louis briefly ruled from here, until forced to acquiesce to Napoleon's autocratic demands. Upon his abdication in 1810 he left behind a sizeable amount of Empire furniture, most of which is exhibited in the rooms he converted.

Vying for importance with the Palace is the **Nieuwe Kerk** (daily 11am–4pm, Sun noon–2pm and 4–5pm) – despite its name, a fifteenth-century structure rebuilt several times after fires. Though impressive from the outside, the Nieuwe Kerk has long since lost out in rivalries with the Oude Kerk and the Royal Palace (it was forbidden a tower in case it outshone the new town hall), and is now used only for exhibitions, organ concerts and state occasions; Queen Beatrix was crowned here in 1980. The interior is neat and orderly, its sheer Gothic lines only slightly weighed down by seventeenth-century fixtures such as the massive pulpit and organ. Of the catalogue of household names from Dutch history, Admiral de Ruyter, seventeenth-century Holland's most valiant naval hero, lies in an opulent tomb in the choir, and the poet Vondel, a sort of Dutch Shakespeare, is commemorated by a small urn near the entrance.

Heading south from Dam Square, Damrak Street turns into the broad sweep of Rokin, which follows the old course of the Amstel River. Lined with grandiose nineteenth-century mansions – Amsterdam's Sotheby's is here, and, further down, the elaborate fin de siècle interior of the *Maison de Bonneterie* clothes store – Rokin gives trams running to and from Dam Square their single chance to accelerate in the city; cross with care.

Café

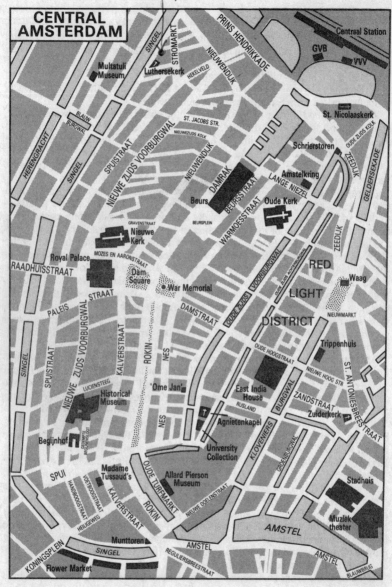

Running parallel with Rokin, **Kalverstraat** has been a commercial centre since it hosted a cattle market in medieval times; now it has declined into a standard European shopping mall, an uninspired strip of monotonous clothes shops differentiated only by the varying strains of disco music they pump out. About halfway down the street, a lopsided and frivolous gateway forms an unexpected entrance to the former municipal orphanage that's now the **Amsterdam Historical Museum** (see p.69). The main way in is by the eye-catching Civil Guard Gallery, just around the corner off Sint Luciensteeg, which leads on to Gedempte Beginesloot and the **Begijnhof** (p.52).

Kalverstraat comes to an ignoble end in a stretch of ice-cream parlours and fast-food outlets before reaching **Muntplein**. Originally a mint and part of the old city walls, the **Munttoren** was topped with a spire by Hendrik de Keyser in 1620 and is possibly the most famous of the towers dotting the city, a landmark perfectly designed for postcards when framed by the flowers of the nearby floating Bloemenmarkt (flower market). From here, Reguliersbreestraat turns left toward the gay bars and loud restaurants of Rembrandtsplein, while Vijzelstraat heads straight out to the edge of the Amsterdam crescent.

Nieuwe Zijds Voorburgwal to Spui

Nieuwe Zijds begins with a bottleneck of trams swinging down from the Centraal Station, and one of the first buildings you see is the **Holiday Inn**, built on the site of an old tenement building called **Wyers**. The 1985 clearance of squatters from Wyers ranks among the most infamous of the decade's anti-squatting campaigns, having involved much protest and some violence throughout the city. The squatters had occupied the building in an attempt to prevent another slice of the city from being handed over to a profit-hungry multinational and converted from residential use. Although widely supported by the people of Amsterdam, they were no match for the economic muscle of the American company, and it wasn't long before the riot police were sent in; construction of the hotel soon followed.

The fate of the **Luthersekerk**, directly west from here on Kattengat, hasn't been much better. With its copper-green dome, (which gives this area the label of *Koepelkwartier* or Dome Neighbourhood), it's been deconsecrated and acquired as a conference centre for the luxury Sonesta Hotel nearby. It's still possible, however, to look inside during the Sunday morning classical concerts. To the east, **Spuistraat** begins at a fork in N. Z. Voorburgwal, with a small red-light area edging around the St Dominicus Kerk. These are the red lights the tourists miss, and the business here has the seamy feel of the real thing.

Things only improve as you move south and approach the Nieuwe Kerk: there's a medieval eccentricity to the streets here, and all seediness vanishes as designer clothes shops appear in the old workshops clustered around the church. Walk down the wonderfully named *Zwarte Handsteeg* (Black Hand Alley) and you're back on Nieuwe Zijds. Just across the road, the former **Post Office** building manages to hold its own against the Nieuwe Kerk and Royal Palace. Built in 1899, its whimsical embellishments continue the town's tradition of sticking towers on things – here, as everywhere, purely for the hell of it.

Both Spuistraat and Nieuwe Zijds culminate in **Spui**, a chic corner of town with a mixture of bookshops and packed bars centred around a small, rather cloying statue of a young boy – known as *'t Lieverdje* (Little Darling) – which was a gift to the city from a large cigarette company. Twenty years ago this was the scene of a series of demonstrations organised by the Provos, a left-wing group that grew out of the original squatters' movement. With the alternative culture then at its most militant, the Provos labelled 't Lieverdje a monument to tomorrow's addiction to capitalism and turned up in force every Saturday evening to preach to the Spui's assembled drinkers. When the police arrived to break up these small "happenings", they did little to endear themselves to the public – and much to gain sympathy for the Provos.

Spui's main attraction, though, is neither obvious nor signposted. Perhaps those who run the **Begijnhof** want it this way: enclosed on three sides, this small court of buildings is an enclave of tranquillity at once typically Dutch and totally removed from the surrounding streets. Most of the houses are seventeenth–century, but one, number 34, dates from 1475 – the oldest house in Amsterdam, and one built before the city forbade the construction of houses in wood, an essential precaution against fire. *Hofjes* (little courtyards) are found all over the Low Countries. Built by rich individuals or city councils for the poor and elderly, the houses usually turn inwards around a small court, their backs to the outside world. This sense of retreat suited the women who, without taking full vows, led a religious life in the *hofjes*, which often had their own chapel. Here the order was known as *Begijns*, and such was its standing in the city community that it was allowed to quietly continue its tradition of worship even after Catholicism was suppressed in 1587. Mass was inconspicuously celebrated in the concealed **Catholic Church**: the plain and unadorned **English Reformed Church,** which takes up one side of the Begijnhof, was handed over to Amsterdam's English community when the Begijns were deprived of their main place of worship and, like the *hofje* itself, it's a model of prim simplicity. Inside are several old English memorial plaques, and pulpit panels designed by the young Piet Mondrian.

The Main *Grachten*: from Raadhuisstraat to the Amstel

It's hard to pick out any particular points to head for along the **three main canals**. Most of the houses have been turned into offices or hotels, and there's little of specific interest apart from museums. Rather, the appeal lies in wandering along selected stretches and admiring the gables while taking in the calm of the tree-lined canals, unusual in the centre of a modern European capital. For shops, bars, restaurants and the like, explore the streets connecting the canals.

In the city's expansion in the seventeenth century, the three main waterways, Herengracht, Keizersgracht and Prinsengracht, were set aside for the residences and offices of the richer and more influential Amsterdam merchants, while the radial canals were left for more modest artisans' homes. Even the richest burgher had to conform to a set of stylistic rules when building his house, and taxes were levied according to the width of the properties. This produced the loose conformity you see today: tall, narrow residences, with individualism restricted to heavy decorative gables and sometimes a gablestone to denote name and occupation.

West to Vijzelstraat

Of the three canals, **Herengracht** ("Gentlemen's Canal") was the first to be dug, and so attracted the wealthiest merchants and the biggest, most ostentatious houses. The others, **Keizersgracht** ("Emperor's Canal") and especially **Prinsengracht** ("Prince's Canal"), ended up with noticeably smaller houses – though both still hold some of the most sought-after properties in the city. Today, Herengracht remains the city's grandest stretch of water, especially between Leidsestraat and Vijzelstraat, but you may find the older and less pretentious houses and warehouses of Prinsengracht more appealing.

One of the most imposing facades along **Herengracht** is the **Bijbels Museum**, which occupies a four-gabled, seventeenth-century stone house frilled with tendrils, carved fruit and scrollwork.

Further along, **number 380** is even more ornate, an exact copy of a Loire château – stone again, with a main gable embellished with reclining figures, and a bay window stuck with cherubs, mythical characters, and an abundance of acanthus leaves.

The one mansion you'll notice in your wanderings along **Keizersgracht** is that used in part by the experimental *Shaffy Theatre* group (see p.77) – the **Felix Meritis building** at Keizersgracht 324, a heavy neoclassical monolith built in the late eighteenth century to house the artistic and scientific activities of the society of the same name. It used to be headquarters of the Dutch Communist Party; they sold it to the council who now lease it to the theatre – though recently there has been speculation over its closure.

On the corner of Keizersgracht and Leidsestraat, the designer department store, *Metz & Co.*, with its corner dome by Gerrit Rietveld, has a top-floor restaurant and tearoom with one of the best views of the city. **Leidsestraat** itself is a long, slender passage across the main canals chiefly given over to airline offices and tourist boards, and to the trams that crash along the narrow thoroughfare, dangerously scattering passers-by. At its southern end the street broadens into **Leidseplein**, hub of Amsterdam's nightlife but by day a none-too-attractive open space littered with sandwich boards touting the surrounding American burger joints. There's probably a greater concentration of bars, restaurants and clubs here than anywhere else in the city, and the streets extend off the square in a bright jumble of jutting signs and neon lights; around the corner, in a converted dairy, lurks the famous *Melkweg* (p.78). As for the square itself, on summer nights especially it can ignite with an almost carnival-like vibrancy, drinkers spilling out of cafés to see sword-swallowers and fire-eaters do their tricks, while the restaurants join in enthusiastically, placing their tables outside so you can eat without missing the fun. On a good night Leidseplein is Amsterdam at its carefree, exuberant best.

On the far corner, the **Stadsschouwburg** is the city's prime performance space after the Muziektheater, while behind, and architecturally much more impressive, is the fairy-castle **American Hotel**. Even if you're not thirsty it's worth a peek inside, the leaded stained glass, shallow brick arches, chandeliers and carefully coordinated furnishings as fine an example of the complete stylistic vision of Art Nouveau as you'll find.

Walking east from here, **Weteringschans**, and, running parallel, **Lijnbaansgracht**, ring the modern city centre. On the right the **Rijksmuseum** (p.65) looms large across the canal; left, Spiegelgracht and, further on, Nieuwe Spiegelstraat lead into the **Spiegelkwartier**, the focus of the Amsterdam antique trade. It's a small area, but there are around fifty dealers here – none, as you might expect, particularly inexpensive.

Kerkstraat, a narrow street featuring an odd mixture of gay bookshops and art galleries, leads east from here to connect with **Vijzelstraat** at the **ABN Bank Building**, through which the street actually runs. Looking towards Muntplein, the oversized **Nederlandsche Handelsmaatschapij Building** (now also owned by *ABN*) is another bank building totally unsympathetic with its surroundings. Though a much worthier work architecturally than the later ABN bank, it would look more at home in downtown Manhattan than on the banks of a Dutch canal.

In the other direction, Vijzelstraat becomes the filled-in **Vijzelgracht**, which culminates in a roundabout at **Weteringplantsoen**, and, on its southern side, one of Amsterdam's saddest spots. It was here, on April 3, 1945, that twenty people were shot by the Nazis – an example, in the last few weeks of their power, to anyone who might consider opposing them. An excerpt from a poem by Sjoerd on the wall recalls the incident with carefully levelled restraint:

> *When to the will of tyrants,*
> *A nation's head is bowed,*
> *It loses more than life and goods —*
> *Its very light goes out.*

In a wholly different vein, the **Heineken Brewery** (☎70 79 11) opposite, runs daily tours at 10am and 2pm. At a guilder a head these are a must: just be sure to arrive early, since tickets for both tours go on sale 9.30am and are normally gone by 9.45am. Though the brewery recently stopped production, and is in the process of being turned into a museum, it's still interesting to explore the old plant. Afterwards, you are given snacks and free beer, and the atmosphere is convivial – as you'd imagine when there are 200 people downing as much free beer as they can drink. Whether you have just one, or drink yourself into a stupor, it's a diverting way to get a lunchtime aperitif.

Rembrandtsplein and its environs

Towards the Amstel, the area cornered by Herengracht's eastern reaches is dominated by **Rembrandtsplein**, a dishevelled bit of greenery fringed with cafés and their terraces. This claims to be a centre of city nightlife, though the square's crowded restaurants are today firmly tourist-targeted; you should expect to pay inflated prices. Rembrandt's pigeon-spattered statue stands in the middle, his back wisely turned against the square's worst excesses, which include live (but deadly) outdoor music. Of the cafés, only the bar of the **Schiller Hotel** at number 26 stands out, with an original Art Deco interior reminiscent of a great ocean liner.

The streets leading north from Rembrandtsplein to the Amstel river are more exciting, containing many of the city's mainstream **gay bars** – accessible to all, and less costly than their upstart neighbours. **Amstelstraat** is the main thoroughfare east, crossing the river at the **Blauwbrug** (Blue Bridge), and affording views across of the new and unimaginative **Muziektheater** and **Town Hall** complex. Heading west, **Reguliersbreestraat** links Rembrandtsplein to Muntplein and, among slot-machine arcades and sex shops, houses the **Tuschinski**, the city's most famous cinema, with an interior that's a wonderful example of the Art Deco excesses of the 1920s. Expressionist paintings, coloured marbles, Persian carpets add to a general air of all-pervasive decadence. You can obviously see all this if you're here to watch a film (the Tuschinski shows all the most popular general releases); if you're not, guided tours are laid on during July and August on Sunday and Monday mornings at 10.30am (f5 per person).

To the south of Rembrandtsplein, **Thorbeckeplein** scores points for having a thinner concentration of clog and card shops, but is hardly a fitting memorial for Rudolf Thorbecke, a politician whose liberal reforms of the late nineteenth century furthered the city tradition of open-minded tolerance, and whose statue stands a short way from the topless bars and sex shows. **Reguliersgracht** flows south from here, a broad canal of distinctive steep bridges that was to have been filled in at the beginning of the century, but was saved when public outcry rose against the destruction of one of the city's more alluring stretches of water. The three great *grachten* nearby don't contain houses quite as grand as those to the west, but a handful of buildings can be visited: the **Van Loon House** at Keizersgracht 672 and the **Willet-Holthuysen House** at Herengracht 605 are both worthwhile examples of the seventeenth-century patrician canal house, and, best of all, the **Six Collection** at Amstel 218 contains an easily absorbed group of paintings in a remarkably unspoiled mansion – though the current Baron Six, who lives there, discourages visitors. For details of all three, see pp. 71, 71, and 70 respectively.

As the canals approach the Amstel, their houses become increasingly residential: even **Kerkstraat** is tamed of its bars and clubs, turning east of Reguliersgracht into a pleasant if unremarkable neighbourhood that lies beside the **Amstelveld**, a small square-cum-football pitch that few visitors happen upon. The **Amstelkerk**, a seventeenth-century graffiti-covered wooden church with a nineteenth-century Gothic interior, marks the corner, and a Monday **flower market** here adds a splash of colour. **Utrechtsestraat**, the other artery that flows to and from Rembrandtsplein, is probably Amsterdam's most up-and-coming strip and contains most of the area's commercial activity, much of it in the shape of mid- to upper-bracket restaurants. It ends in the concrete wasteland of **Frederiksplein** – more a glorified tram stop than a square, presided over by the massive glass box of the **Netherlands Bank**. Leading off Frederiksplein, Sarphatistraat crosses the wide and windy reaches of the **Amstel River**, whose eastern side is stacked with chunky buildings such as the **Carré Theatre**, built as a circus in the early 1900s, but now more often a space for music and drama. Just beyond, the **Magere Brug**, (Skinny Bridge) is (inexplicably) focus of much attention in the tourist brochures, and hence the most famous of the city's swinging bridges. More worthy of a serious look is the **Amstel Hof**, a large and forbidding former *hofje* that was one of a number of charitable institutions built east of the Amstel after a seventeenth-century decision to extend the major canals eastward towards the new harbour and shipbuilding quarter. Takers for the new land were few, and the city had no option but to offer it to charities at discount prices.

West from the Dam

Unlike the Jodenhoek, the area west of Amsterdam's immediate centre is one of the city's most untouched neighbourhoods – and one of its loveliest. The Prinsengracht here has a gentle beauty quite unlike its grander rivals, and holds the Anne Frank House as a specific draw; and the Jordaan, just beyond, with its narrow waterways spotted with tiny shops and bars, is as good (and as pretty) a place for idle strolling as you'll find.

The Westerkerk and the Anne Frank House
From behind the Royal Palace, **Raadhuisstraat** leads west across Herengracht and curves around the elegant nineteenth-century Art Nouveau **Utrecht Building** towards **Westermarkt**. Here, at Westermarkt 6, the seventeenth-century French philosopher René Descartes lived for a short time, happy that the business-oriented character of the city left him able to work and think without being disturbed. As he wrote at the time, "Everybody except me is in business and so absorbed by profit-making I could spend my entire life here without being noticed by a soul".

It's the **Westerkerk** (daily 10am–4pm, closed Sun), though, which dominates the square, its tower – without question Amsterdam's finest – soaring graciously above the gables of Prinsengracht. The church was designed by Hendrik de Keyser (architect also of the Zuiderkerk and Noorderkerk) as part of the general seventeenth-century enlargement of the city, and was completed in 1631. But while this is probably Amsterdam's most visually appealing church from the outside, there's little within of special note. Rembrandt, who was living nearby when he died, is commemorated by a small memorial in the north aisle. His pauper's grave can no longer be located; indeed, there's a possibility that he's not here at all, since many of the bodies were moved to a cemetery when underground heating was installed. The memorial is, however, close to where Rembrandt's son Titus is buried. During recent excavations, bones have been unearthed which could be those of Titus and even Rembrandt – something which has made the church authorities very excited about the resultant tourist possibilities. The church tower is open between June 1 and September 15, on Tuesday, Wednesday, Friday and Saturday from 2 to 5pm (guided tour only).

Directly outside the church stands a small, simple statue of **Anne Frank** by the Dutch sculptor Mari Andriessen – a careful and evocative site, since it was just a few steps from here, at Prinsengracht 263, that the young diarist used to listen to the Westertoren bells until they were taken away to be melted down for the Nazi war effort. The story of Anne Frank, her family and friends is well known. Anne's father, Otto, was a well-to-do Jewish businessman who ran a successful spice-trading business and lived in the southern part of the city. The Franks went into hiding in July 1942, along with a Jewish business partner and his family, separated from the eyes of the outside world by a bookcase that doubled as a door. As far as everyone else was concerned, they had fled to Switzerland.

One day in the summer of 1944 the Franks were betrayed by a Dutch collaborator: the Gestapo arrived and forced open the bookcase, whereupon the occupants of the annexe were all arrested and quickly sent to Westerbork – the northern Netherlands German labour camp where all Dutch Jews were processed before being moved to Belsen or Auschwitz. Of the eight who had been in the annexe, only Otto Frank survived; Anne and her sister died of typhus within a short time of each other in Belsen, just one week before the German surrender.

Anne Frank's diary was among the few things left behind in the annexe. It was retrieved by one of the people who had helped the Franks and handed to Anne's father on his return from Auschwitz; he later decided to publish it. Since its appearance in 1947, it has been constantly in print, translated into 54 languages and has sold thirteen million copies worldwide. In 1957 the *Anne Frank Foundation* set up the **Anne Frank House** (July–Aug Mon–Sat 9am–7pm, Sun 10am–7pm; Sept–June Mon–Sat 9am–5pm, Sun 10am–5pm; closed Yom Kippur – Oct 9; f5, no museumcards; ☎26 45 33), one of the most deservedly popular tourist attractions in town; bearing this in mind, the best time to visit is early morning before the crowds arrive.

The rooms the Franks lived in for two years are left much the same as they were during the war, even down to the movie star pin-ups in Anne's bedroom and the marks on the wall recording the children's heights. A number of other rooms offer background detail on the war and occupation, one offering a video biography of Anne, from her frustrated hopes in hiding in the annexe up to her death in 1945, another detailing the gruesome atrocities of Nazism, as well as giving some up-to-date examples of fascism and anti-semitism in Europe which draw pertinent parallels with the war years. Anne Frank was only one of 100,000 Dutch Jews who died during that time, but this, her final home, provides one of the most enduring testaments to the horrors of Nazism.

The Jordaan and around

Across the Prinsengracht, on the northern side of Rozengracht, **THE JORDAAN** is a likeable and easily explored area of narrow canals, narrower streets and simple, architecturally varied houses. The name is said to come from the French *jardin*, and many of the streets are named after flowers. Falling outside the seventeenth-century concentric-canal plan, the area was not subject to municipal controls, which led to its becoming a centre of property speculation, developing as a series of canals and streets that followed the original polder ditches and rough paths. In contrast to the splendour of the three main *grachten*, the Jordaan became Amsterdam's slum quarter, home of artisans, tradespeople, and Jewish or Huguenot refugees who had fled here to escape religious persecution at home. Though tolerated, the immigrants remained distinct minorities and were treated as such, living in what were often cramped and unsanitary quarters. Later, after much rebuilding, the Jordaan became the inner-city enclave of Amsterdam's growing industrial working class – which, in spite of increasing gentrification, it to some extent remains. The last couple of decades have seen the Jordaan gain a reputation as the home of young "alternative" Amsterdam, but there's a core population of residents, especially in the northern reaches, who retain long-standing roots in the district.

Other than a handful of bars and restaurants, some posh clothes shops and the odd outdoor market, there's nothing very specific to see (though it's a wonderful neighbourhood for a wander) apart from its *hofjes* – seventeenth-century almshouses for the city's elderly population. There were – and are – *hofjes* all over the city (most famously the Begijnhof, p.52), but there's a concentration in the Jordaan, and if you're passing through, it is worth looking in on a courtyard or two; many of them have real charm. Bear in mind, though, that most are still lived in, and be discreet.

Of those that warrant a specific visit, the **Van Bienen Hofje**, opposite the Noordermarkt at Prinsengracht 89–133, is the grandest, built in 1804, according to the entrance tablet, "for the relief and shelter of those in need". A little way down the canal at Prinsengracht 157–171, **Zon's Hofje** has a leafier, more gentle beauty; and, back in the main grid of the Jordaan, the **Claes Claesz Hofje** on 1e Egelantierdwarsstraat, a much earlier almshouse (built in 1616 for poor widows), is now noisily occupied by students of the Amsterdam Conservatory of Music. For more on *hofjes* – and an account of one of the country's most famous, the Frans Hals Museum in Haarlem – see p.90.

More general wanderings start on **Rozengracht**, the filled-in canal where, at number 184, Rembrandt once lived – though the house itself has long since disappeared and only a plaque marks the spot. Though not the Jordaan proper, the area south of this street is a likeable one, centring on the pretty Lauriergracht and including, at Elandsgracht 109, the **De Looier indoor antique market** – where a leisurely browse may unearth a bargain (see p.82). North of Rozengracht the Jordaan's streets and canals run off diagonally, bordering Prinsengracht. The main street of the district is **Westerstraat** (where there's a Monday general market), which runs down to join Prinsengracht at **Noordermarkt** and Hendrik de Keyser's **Noorderkerk**. This church, finished in 1623, is probably the architect's least successful creation in Amsterdam; nor is the square particularly attractive, part car park, part children's playground. It's the site of a Monday antiques market and the regular Saturday morning *Boerenmarkt* (farmers' market) during summer months. The next street over, **Lindengracht**, is home to another Saturday market, this time general. If you're interested in shopping, also check out **Tweede Anjelierdwarsstraat** and **Tweede Tuindwarsstraat** – two streets which hold the bulk of the Jordaan's ever-increasing trendy stores and clothing shops, and some of its liveliest bars and cafés for restorative sipping.

Brouwersgracht, just beyond, is one of Amsterdam's most picturesque and most photographed canals, marking what is in effect the northern boundary of the Jordaan and the beginning of a district loosely known as the **SHIPPING QUARTER**, which centres on the long arteries of **Haarlemmerstraat** and **Haarlemmerdijk**. In the seventeenth century this district was at the cutting edge of Amsterdam's trade: the warehouses along Brouwersgracht provided storage space for the spoils brought back from the high seas, and the building on Haarlemmerstraat at Herenmarkt, the **West Indies House**, was home of the Dutch West Indies Company, who administered much of the business. Today it's a good area for cheap restaurants and off-beat shops: the warehouses have been largely taken over and converted into spacious apartments, and the West Indies Company Building has a courtyard containing an overstated statue of Peter Stuyvesant, governor of New Amsterdam (later named New York), and a swanky restaurant named after the seventeenth-century Dutch naval hero Piet Heijn.

At the far end of Haarlemmerdijk, the **Haarlemmerpoort** is an oversized and very un-Amsterdam–like former gateway to the city. Beyond this you can either walk on to the **Westerpark**, one of the city's smaller and more enticing parks, or duck under the railway lines to the **WESTERN ISLANDS** district, where ships were once unloaded and where there are now rows of gaunt warehouses – an atmospheric area, still largely deserted. Across the Westerkanaal on Zaanstraat and Spaarndammerplantsoen, the **Eigen Haard** housing project is probably the most central example you'll see of the Amsterdam School of architecture that flourished in the early part of this century. Designed by Michael de Klerk, the project attempted to alleviate the previously appalling housing conditions of the city's poor, with rounded corners, turrets, and bulging windows and balconies lending individuality to what would otherwise be very plain brick residences.

The Jodenhoek and Eastern Islands

Though there's hardly any visible evidence today, from the sixteenth century onward Amsterdam was the home of Jews escaping persecution throughout Europe. Under the terms of the Union of Utrecht, Jews enjoyed a tolerance and freedom unknown elsewhere, and they arrived in the city to practise the crafts of diamond processing, sugar refining and tobacco production – effectively the only trades open to them since the city's guilds excluded Jews from following any of the traditional crafts. This largely impoverished Jewish community lived in one of the least desirable stretches of the city, the old dock areas around Jodenbreestraat, which became known as the **JODENHOEK**. The docks moved east to Kattenburg, Wittenburg and Oostenburg – the **EASTERN ISLANDS**. By the early years of this century Jewish life was commercially and culturally an integral part of the city, the growing demand for diamonds making Jewish expertise invaluable and bringing wealth to the community for the first time.

In the 1930s the community's numbers swelled with Jews who had fled persecution in Germany. In May 1940, however, the Nazis invaded, sealing off the Jodenhoek as a ghetto. Jews were not allowed to use public transport or own a telephone, and were placed under a curfew. Round-ups and deportations continued until the last days of the war: out of a total of 80,000 Jews in the city, 75,000 were murdered in concentration camps.

After the war the Jodenhoek lay deserted: those who had lived here were dead or deported, and their few possessions were quickly looted. As the need fo ood and raw materials grew in postwar shortages, the houses were slowly dismantled and destroyed, a destruction finalised in the 1970s with the completion of the metro that links the city centre to the outer suburbs.

The Jodenhoek: Jodenbreestraat to Plantage Middenlaan

Nieuwmarkt signals the beginning of what was the Jodenhoek, and **St Antoniesbreestraat** leads to its heart, an uncomfortably modernised street whose original old houses were demolished to widen the road for the heavy traffic that the Nieuwmarkt redevelopment (see below) would bring. The decorative landmark of Hendrik de Keyser's **Zuiderkerk** is similarly surrounded by new development: undergoing a major reconstruction, its tower is irregularly open in summer months, and is the best place for an overview of this part of town.

St Antoniesbreestraat runs into **Jodenbreestraat**, once the Jodenhoek's principal market and centre of Jewish activity. After the shipbuilding industry moved further east, this area (the small islands of Uilenburg and Marken) became the site of the worst living conditions in the city: it wasn't until 1911 that the area was declared a health hazard and redeveloped. Jodenbreestraat itself was modernised and widened in the 1970s and it lost much of its character as a result: only when you reach the **Rembrandt House** at number 6 (Mon–Fri 10am–5pm, Sun 1–5pm; f3.50) do you find any continuity with the past. Rembrandt bought the house at the height of his fame and popularity, living here for over twenty years and spending a fortune on furnishings – an expense that helped lead to his bankruptcy. The house itself is disappointing – mostly a reconstruction and with no artefacts from Rembrandt's life on exhibit – but you can view a great variety of the artist's engravings here. The biblical illustrations attract the most attention, though the studies of tramps and vagabonds are more accessible; a good accompanying exhibit explains Rembrandt's engraving techniques.

Jodenbreestraat runs parallel to its sibling development, the new **Muziektheater and Town Hall** on **Waterlooplein**, whose building occasioned the biggest public dispute the city had seen since the Nieuwmarkt was dug up in the 1970s to make way for the metro. The Waterlooplein, a marshy, insanitary area that rapidly became known as the poorest patch of the city, was the first neighbourhood settled by the Jews. By the late nineteenth century, things had become so bad that the canals crossing the area were filled in and the shanty houses razed; the street markets then shifted here from St Antoniesbreestraat and Jodenbreestraat. The Waterlooplein quickly became Amsterdam's largest and liveliest market, and a link between the Jewish community and the predominantly Gentile one across the Amstel. During the war it became infamous again, this time as a site for Nazi round-ups; in the 1950s it regained some of its vibrancy when the city's flea market was established here. Later, when the council announced the building of a massive new opera complex that would all but fill the square, opposition was widespread. People believed that it should be turned into a residential area at best, a popular performance space at least – anything but an elitist opera house. Attempts to prevent the building failed, but since opening in 1986 the Muziektheater has successfully established itself with visitors and performers alike, and the **flea market** has come back after being moved for a few years to nearby Valkenburgstraat.

Just behind the Muziektheater, on the corner of Mr Visserplein, is the **Mozes en Aaron Kerk**, originally a small (clandestine) Catholic church that was rebuilt in rather glum neoclassical style in the mid-nineteenth century. The area around Mr Visserplein, today a busy and dangerous junction for traffic speeding towards the IJ tunnel, has the most tangible mementoes of the Jewish community. The brown and bulky **Portuguese Synagogue** (Mon–Fri 10am–noon, 1–4pm; Sun 10am–1pm; free) was completed in 1675 by Sephardic Jews who had moved to Amsterdam from Spain and Portugal to escape the Inquisition, and who prospered here in the seventeenth and eighteenth centuries. When it was completed the Portuguese Synagogue was the largest in the world: today the Sephardic community has dwindled to thirty or forty.

Across the way from the Portuguese Synagogue the **Jewish Historical Museum** is cleverly housed in a complex of High German synagogues that date from the late seventeenth century. For many years after the war the buildings lay in ruins, and it's only recently that the museum has moved in. In addition to photos and mementoes from the holocaust, the museum gives a broad introduction to Jewish beliefs and life. For opening hours and a full description, see p.70.

Between the museum and the Portuguese Synagogue is **J. D. Meijerplein**, where a small statue marks the spot on which, in February 1941, 400 young Jewish men were arrested and taken to eventual execution at Mauthausen, in reprisal for the killing of a Nazi sympathiser in a street fight between members of the Jewish resistance and the Dutch Nazi party. The arrests sparked off the "February Strike", a general strike led by transport workers and dockers and organised by the outlawed Communist party in protest against the deportations and treatment of the Jews. Although broken by mass arrests after only two days, it was a demonstration of solidarity with the Jews that was unique in occupied Europe and unusual in The Netherlands, where the majority of people had done little to prevent or protest the actions of the SS.

Leaving Mr Visserplein via Muiderstraat, with the prim **Hortus Botanicus** (botanical gardens) to the right (see p.69), you reach another sad relic of the war at Plantage Middenlaan 24. The **Hollandse Schouwburg**, a predominantly Jewish theatre before 1940, was the main assembly point for Dutch Jews prior to their deportation to Germany. Inside, there was no daylight and families were packed in for days in conditions that foreshadowed the camps. The house across the street, now a teacher training college, was used as a day nursery. Some, possibly hundreds, managed to escape through here and a plaque outside extols the memory of those "who saved the children".

Prins Hendrikkade and the Eastern Islands

The broad boulevard that fronts the grey waters of the Oosterdok is **Prins Hendrikkade**, a continuation of the road that leads to Stationsplein in the west and goes on deep into the docks of eastern Amsterdam. In the seventeenth century merchant vessels packed the harbour, carrying the goods that created the city's enormous wealth: today Prins Hendrikkade is a major artery for cars flowing north via the IJ tunnel, and the only ships docked here belong to the police or navy. But the road is lined with buildings that point to its nautical past. The first of these, the squat **Schrierstoren**, was traditionally the place where, in the Middle Ages, tearful women saw their husbands off to sea (the name could be translated as "weepers' tower") – though this is probably more romantic invention than fact. A sixteenth-century inlaid stone records the emotional leave-takings, while another, much more recent, tablet recalls the departure of Henry Hudson from here in 1609 – the voyage on which he inadvertently discovered Manhattan. A little further along, the **Scheepvaarthuis** at Prins Hendrikkade 8 is covered inside and out with bas reliefs and other decoration relating the city's maritime history; it's also embellished with slender turrets and expressionistic masonry characteristic of the Amsterdam School of architecture.

Further along still, the wide **Oude Schans** was the main entrance to the old shipbuilding quarter, and the **Montelbaanstoren** tower that stands about half-way down was built in 1512 to protect the merchant fleet. A century later, when the city felt more secure and could afford such luxuries, it was topped with a decorative spire by Hendrik de Keyser, the architect who did much to create Amsterdam's prickly skyline.

The chief pillar of the wealth of the city in the sixteenth century was the **Dutch East India Company**. Its expeditions established links with India, Sri Lanka and the Indonesian islands, and later China and Japan, using the Dutch Republic's large fleet of vessels to rob the Portuguese and Spanish of their trade and the undefended islanders of their wood and spices. Dutch expansionism wasn't purely mercantile: not only had the East India Company been given a trading monopoly in all lands east of the Cape of Good Hope, but also unlimited military, judicial and political powers in the countries it administered. Behind the satisfied smiles of the comfortable burghers of the Golden Age was a slavery and exploitation nightmare.

The twin warehouses where the East India Company began its operations still stand at Prins Hendrikkade 176, but a better picture of the might of Dutch naval power can be found in the **Maritime Museum** on Kattenburgerplein, housed in a fortress-like former arsenal of the seventeenth century (p.70).

As the wealth from the colonies poured in, the old dock area to the southeast around Uilenburg was no longer able to cope, and the East India Company financed a major reclamation of, and expansion into, the marshland to the east of the existing waterfront, forming the three islands of **Kattenburg**, **Wittenburg**, and **Oostenburg**. A shipbuilding industry developed, and in time the Eastern Islands became the home of a large community working in the shipfitting and dockyard industries. The nineteenth century brought the construction of iron ships, and at a wharf at Hoogte Kadijk 147 an old shipyard is now the **Kromhout Museum** (p.70). The museum still patches up ancient boats and offers a slide show that's a useful introduction to the area's history.

In time, the shipyards of the Eastern Islands declined, the working-class neighbourhood shrank, and today there's not much to show of a once-lively community. The **Oosterkerk**, across the water from the Kromhout, now functions as a social and exhibition centre, part of an attempt to give back this area some of its former identity. South of the Kromhout, it's worth wandering through to the **Entrepot Dok**, a line of old warehouses, each bearing the name of a destination above its door. Recreated as hi-tech offices and apartments, and with weird gurglings coming from the **Artis Zoo** across the way, it seems an odd sort of end for the Eastern Islands' rich maritime tradition.

Keep going down Oostenburgergracht and you'll reach **"De Gooyer"**, a windmill that dates from 1814. Once mills were all over Amsterdam, pumping water and grinding grain; today only this old corn mill remains, now converted into a shop, though its sails still turn on the first Saturday of the month – wind permitting.

The Outer Limits: South, West and East

Amsterdam is a small city and its residential outer neighbourhoods can be easily reached from the city centre. Of them, the **South** holds most interest, with all the major museums, the Vondelpark (a must on summer Sundays), the raucous "De Pijp" quarter and the 1930s architecture of the New South more than justifying the tram ride. As for the other districts, you'll find a good deal less reason for making the effort. The **West** is nothing special, aside from the occasional odd park and one lively immigrant quarter; nor is the **East**, although this does have one conceivable target in the Tropical Museum.

The Old South

During the nineteenth century, unable to hold its mushrooming population within the limits of its canals, Amsterdam began to expand, spreading into the neighbourhoods beyond the Singelgracht which now make up the district known as the **OLD SOUTH**. This large and disparate area includes the leafy residential quarters immediately south of Leidseplein as well as the working-class enclaves further east. **The Vondelpark** lies at the centre of the former, today the city's most enticing park. Named after the seventeenth-century poet Joost van der Vondel, and funded by local residents, it was landscaped in the latter part of the last century in the English style, with a bandstand and an emphasis on nature rather than on formal gardens. Today it's a regular forum for drama and other performance arts in the summer, and at weekends young Amsterdam flocks here to meet friends, laze by the lake, buy trinkets from the flea markets in the area or listen to music – though the live bands that once formed the main focus here were recently banned due to pressure from local residents; it's not certain whether they'll return.

The area to the southeast of the park is one of Amsterdam's better-heeled residential districts, with designer shops and delis along chic **P. C. Hooftstraat** and **Van Baerlestraat**, and some of the city's fancier hotels (and plenty of its cheaper ones, too) on their connecting streets. But what this area really means to the visitor is **museums**, a number of which – the **Rijksmuseum**, **Van Gogh** and **Stedelijk** (pp 65, 67 and 68) – are imposingly grouped around the grassy wedge of **Museumplein**. This fans back as far as the Concertgebouw at its southern end, and is a bare and rather windswept open space.

At the bottom end of Museumplein, on sleek Van Baerlestraat, is the **Concertgebouw**, completed in 1883 and renowned for its marvellous acoustics and its famed – and much recorded – resident orchestra. The Old South isn't all culture, however, and by no means is it all wealthy either. Walking east from Museumplein, across Hobbemakade, you enter the busy heart of the Old South, known as **"De Pijp"** (The Pipe) after its long, sombre canyons of brick tenements that went up in the nineteenth century as the city grew out of its canal-girded centre. The population here is dense and overcrowded, much of it made up of immigrants, and De Pijp has always been one of the city's closest-knit communities – and one of its liveliest. Recently, it has been forced to absorb some of the worst residue of Amsterdam's heroin-dealing trouble spots (those which have been "cleaned up" elsewhere by the police), and you'll see groups of policemen hanging around keeping a sharp eye out for any illicit trading. But it's still a cheerful area, its hub the long slim thoroughfare of **Albert Cuypstraat**, whose daily general market – which stretches for about a mile between Ferdinand Bolstraat and Van Woustraat – is the largest in the city.

The New South

Aside from the small but pretty **Sarphatipark**, a few blocks south of the Albert Cuyp, there's little else to detain you in the Old South, and you'd be better off either walking or catching a tram down into the **NEW SOUTH** – a real contrast to its neighbour and the first properly planned extension to the city since the concentric canals of the seventeenth century. The Dutch architect H. P. Berlage was responsible for the overall plan, but he died before it could be started and the design was largely carried out in the 1930s by two prominent architects of the Amsterdam School, Michael de Klerk and Piet Kramer. Cutbacks in the city's subsidy led them to tone down the more imaginative aspects of the scheme, and most of the buildings are markedly more sober than previous Amsterdam School works (such as the Scheepvarthuis on Prins Hendrikade; p.61). But otherwise they followed Berlage faithfully, sticking to the architect's plan of wide boulevards and crooked side streets, and adding the odd splash of individuality to corners, windows and balconies.

Nowdays the New South is one of Amsterdam's most sought-after addresses. **Apollolaan**, **Stadionweg** and, a little way east, **Churchilllaan**, are home to luxury hotels and some of the city's most sumptuous properties, huge idiosyncratic mansions set back from the street behind trees and generous gardens. **Beethovenstraat**, main street of the New South, is a fashionable shopping boulevard, with high-priced, slightly staid stôres catering for the wealthy residents.

The area achieved a brief period of notoriety in 1969, when John Lennon and Yoko Ono staged their week-long **Bed-In** for peace in the Amsterdam Hilton on Apollolaan. The press came from all over; fans crowded outside, hanging on the couple's anti-war proclamations, and the episode was seen as the beginning of John and Yoko's subsequent campaign for peace worldwide. At the opposite end of Beethovenstraat, dense trees and shrubs of the **Beatrixpark** flank the antiseptic surroundings of the adjacent **RAI exhibition centre**: a complex of trade and conference centres built a few years back as part of the city's plan to attract more business people – along with their considerable expense accounts. It's of little general appeal (though one hall does sporadically host concerts), but if you're at a loose end you may find one of its many exhibitions interesting. The **Olympic Stadium**, built for the 1928 games, is a useful landmark; just north of it is the **Haarlemmermeer Station**, terminus of the summer museum tram which runs several times a day to the Amsterdamse Bos further south, technically outside the city limits in Amstelveen.

The **Amsterdamse Bos** is the city's largest open space, a 2000-acre woodland park planted during the 1930s in a mammoth project to utilise the wasted energies of the city's unemployed. If it's out of season or you're not into old trams, take one of the buses (#170, #171, #172) which run directly from Stationsplein. Once there, the best way to get around is to hire a bicycle (March–Oct) from the main entrance on Van Nijenrodeeweg and follow the 27 miles of path. It's also possible to hire canoes, canal bikes and motor boats. The Bosmuseum, a few kilometres along the Bosbaan from the main entrance, has maps and basic information.

The West

Of all Amsterdam's outer central districts, Amsterdam **WEST** is probably the least appealing, primarily a residential area with only a couple of nondescript parks as possible destinations. There's the **OLD WEST**, whose busy Turkish and Middle Eastern immigrant-based streetlife can be worth checking out if you find yourself in the vicinity: **Kinkerstraat** is a good place to bargain-hunt if you're not after anything fancy, and there's also the vigorous **ten Katestraat market**, about halfway down the street on the right. But outside of this zone, in the districts of Bos en Lommer and Overtoomse Veld, there's little other than the large – but on the whole mediocre – **Rembrandtpark** to draw you out this far.

The East

A cupolaed box splattered with graffiti and topped with a crudely carved pediment, the sturdy **Muiderpoort** marks the boundary between Amsterdam's centre and the beginning of Amsterdam **EAST**. Across the canal the gabled and turreted **Royal Tropen Institute** has a marble-and-stucco entrance hall which you can peek into, though the only part open to visitors is the excellent Tropenmuseum around the corner (see p.71).

Behind the Tropen Institute, the **Oosterpark** is a peaceful oblong of green, and a gentle introduction to the area, which extends south and east, a solidly working-class district for the most part, particularly on the far side of Linnaeusstraat. There's a high immigrant presence, and housing is still relatively poor, though there's ambitious urban renewal going on, and many of the ageing terraced houses have been torn down to make way for new and better-equipped public housing. As in the Old South, there's an underlying drug problem here, but while you're unlikely to need (or want) to come out here, it's by no means a forbidding district. Two things which may make you decide to visit (apart from the Zeeburg campsite, p.43) are the **Dapperstraat market** – a kind of Eastern equivalent to the Albert Cuyp – and, at the end of tram routes #3 and #10, the **Flevopark**, dull in itself but giving access to the Ijsselmeer and Dutch countryside right out of Ruisdael.

Amsterdam's Museums

If you're visiting more than a couple of museums it's advisable to buy a **museum-card**. Available from the *VVV* (f25 if you're under 26, f40 otherwise), it's valid for a year and grants free entry to all state and municipally run museums, not only in Amsterdam but throughout the country. You need a passport photo to get one, but considering it costs f15 to visit the Rijksmuseum and the Stedelijk alone, it's a bargain if you intend to visit more than a couple of museums; where museumcards *aren't* accepted we've said so. An alternative is the **Cultureel Jongeren Paspoort** or **CJP**, which for f25 gets you reductions in museums, and on theatre, concert and *filmhuis* tickets – though these can vary greatly, and are often not that substantial. Valid throughout the country and in Belgium, it's available only to those under 35 and can be bought from the *Uitburo* in the Stadsschouwburg on Leidseplein. Incidentally, **entry-prices for kids** are usually half that of the adult admission.

Opening times, particularly of state-run museums, tend to follow a pattern: closed on Monday, open from 10am to 5pm Tuesday to Saturday and from 1 to 5pm on Sunday and public holidays. Almost all the museums offer at least basic **information** in English or a written English guide.

The Rijksmuseum

Stadhouderskade 42. Tues–Sat 10am–5pm, Sun 1–5pm; f6.50. Tram #7, #10, #16, #24, #25. For more on Dutch art and artists, see Contexts.

The **RIJKSMUSEUM** is the one museum you shouldn't leave Amsterdam without visiting, if only briefly. Its **seventeenth-century Dutch paintings** constitute far and away the best collection to be found anywhere, with twenty or so Rembrandts alone, as well as copious arrays of works by Steen, Hals, Vermeer and many other Dutch artists of the era – all engagingly displayed with the layperson in mind. There are, too, representative displays of all other pre-twentieth–century periods of Dutch and Flemish painting, along with treasures in the **medieval art** and **Asiatic** sections that are not to be missed. To do justice to the place demands repeated visits; if time is limited, it's best to be content with the core paintings and a few selective forays into other sections.

Paintings of the fifteenth to seventeenth centuries

From the first floor shop, the eastern wing runs chronologically through the Rijksmuseum's collection of Low Countries painting. After works from the early **netherlandish period** begin the classic paintings of the **DUTCH GOLDEN AGE**: portraits by Hals and Rembrandt, landscapes by Jan van Goyen and Jacob van Ruisdael, the riotous scenes of Jan Steen and the peaceful interiors of Vermeer and Pieter de Hooch. First, though, are some early seventeenth-century works, including **Frans Hals'** expansive *Isaac Massa and His Wife* and more sensational paintings such as **Dirck van Baburen's** *Prometheus in Chains* – a work from the Utrecht School, which used Caravaggio's paintings as its model.

Beyond this are the works of **Rembrandt** and some of his better-known pupils. Perhaps the most striking is the *Portrait of Maria Trip*, but look, too, at Ferdinand Bol's *Portrait of Elizabeth Bas*, Govert Flinck's *Rembrandt as a Shepherd* – interesting if only for its subject – and the *Portrait of Abraham Potter* by **Carel Fabritius**, this last a restrained, skilful work painted by one of Rembrandt's most talented (and shortest-lived) students.

The next rooms take you into the latter half of the seventeenth century, and include the carousing peasants paintings of **Jan Steen**. Steen's *Morning Toilet* is full of associations, referring either to pleasures just had or about to be taken, while his *Feast of St Nicholas*, with its squabbling children, makes the festival a celebration of pure greed – much like the drunken gluttony of the *Merry Family* nearby. And the out-of-control ugliness of *After the Drinking Bout* leaves no room for doubt about what Steen thought of all this ribaldry.

It's in the last few rooms, though, that the Dutch interior really comes into its own, with a gentle moralising that grows ever more subtle. **Vermeer's** *The Letter* reveals a tension between servant and mistress – the lute on the woman's lap was a well-known sexual symbol of the time – and the symbolism in the use of a map behind the *Young Woman Reading a Letter* hints at the far-flung places her loved one is writing from. The paintings of **Pieter de Hooch** are less symbolic, more exercises in lighting, but they're as good a visual guide to the everyday life and habits of the seventeenth-century Dutch bourgeoisie as you'll find.

Mingling with these interior scenes are more paintings by **Hals** and **Rembrandt** – later works, for the most part, from the painters' mature periods. Hals weighs in with a handful of portraits, including the boisterous *Merry Toper*, while Rembrandt – here at his most private and expressive best – is represented by a portrait of his first wife *Saskia*, a couple of his mother, and a touching depiction of his cowled son, *Titus*.

A small room off to the side of the last one offers an introduction to the **GALLERY OF HONOUR** and one of the Rijksmuseum's great treasures – Rembrandt's *The Night Watch*, the most famous and most valuable of all the artist's pictures, recently restored after being slashed by a vandal in 1975. The painting is a so-called Civil Guard portrait, named after the bands of militia that got together in the sixteenth century to defend the home front during the wars with the Spanish. They later grew into social clubs for local dignitaries – most of whom would commission a group portrait as a mark of prestige. This, of the Guards of the Kloveniersdoelen in Amsterdam, was erroneously tagged *The Night Watch* in the nineteenth century – a result both of the romanticism of the age and the fact that for years the painting was covered in soot. Though not as subtle as much of the artist's later work, it's an adept piece, full of movement and carefully arranged – these paintings were collections of individual portraits as much as group pictures, and part of the problem in creating one was to include each individual face while simultaneously producing a coherent group scene. The sponsors paid for a prominent position in the painting, and the artist had also to reflect this.

Elsewhere, the Gallery of Honour houses the large-scale works from the museum's collection of Dutch paintings. Some of these are notable only for their size – the selection of naval battles particularly – but a number do stand out, and would in any museum. Two of Rembrandt's better-known pupils crop up here: **Nicholas Maes**, with one of his typically intimate scenes in *Dreaming*, and **Ferdinand Bol**, both in his *Regents of the Nieuwe Zijds Workhouse* and the elegantly composed *Venus and Adonis*. The dashing *Self-portrait* is his too, a rich and successful character leaning on a sleeping cupid. By way of contrast, Rembrandt himself follows with a late *Self-portrait*, caught in mid-shrug as the Apostle Paul, a self-aware and defeated old man. Opposite, *The Stallmeesters* is an example of one of his later commissions and, as do so many of Rembrandt's later works, it demonstrates his ability to capture a staggering range of subtle expressions. Nearby is *The Jewish Bride*, one of his last pictures, finished in 1665.

Later Dutch painting

To pick up chronologically where the Gallery of Honour left off, it's necessary to move down to the ground floor, where the **eighteenth- and nineteenth-century DUTCH PAINTINGS** collection begins with the work of **Cornelis Troost**, whose eighteenth-century comic scenes earned him the dubiously deserved title of the "Dutch Hogarth". More enduring are the later pictures, notably the pastels of Pierre-Paul Prud'hon and **Jan Ekels'** *The Writer* – small and simple, the lighting and attention to detail imitative of Vermeer.

After this, rooms follow each other haphazardly, with sundry landscapes and portraiture from the lesser nineteenth-century artists. **Jongkind** is best of the bunch, his murky *River Landscape in France* typical of the Impressionism that was developing in the nineteenth century. The chief proponents of Dutch Impressionism originated from or worked in The Hague, and the handy label of the **Hague School** covers a variety of styles and painters who shared a clarity and sensitivity in their depiction of the Dutch landscape. Of the major Hague School painters, the Rijksmuseum is strongest on the work of the **Maris Brothers** and **Jan Weissenbruch**, whose land- and seascapes, such as *View near the Geestbrug*, hark back to the compositional techniques of van Ruisdael.

While members of the Hague School were creating gentle landscapes, a younger generation of Impressionist painters working in Amsterdam – the **Amsterdam School** – was using a darker palette to capture city scenes. By far the most important picture from this turn-of-the-century group is **G. H. Breitner's** *Singelbrug near Paleisstraat in Amsterdam*, a random moment in the street recorded and framed with photographic dispassion.

Other collections

The collection of **Medieval and Renaissance applied art** on the first floor is perhaps the most impressive other section, filled with jewellery, religious art, woodcarving and statuary from the Low Countries and northern Europe. There's a massive collection of **fine art** from later centuries, including galleries stuffed from floor to ceiling with **delftware**, furniture, ceramics and textiles from the sixteenth century on: its mostly dull stuff, with only the **dolls' houses** providing diversion.

The **Dutch history section** focuses on the naval might that brought Holland its wealth with fearsome **model ships** and galleries filled with relics of Holland's naval and colonial past. Holland's colonial connection with the East means that Asian art can be found in most of the museums' collections, but the **Asian collection** proper holds its most prized treasures: chiefly graceful paintings, ceramics and lacquerwork and jewellery.

Rijksmuseum Vincent van Gogh

Paulus Potterstraat 7. Tram #2, #3, #5, #12, #16. Tues–Sat 10am–5pm, Sun 1–5pm; f10.

Vincent van Gogh is arguably the most popular, most reproduced and most talked-about of all modern artists, so it's not surprising that the **RIJKSMUSEUM VINCENT VAN GOGH**, opened in 1973 and comprising the extensive collection of the artist's art-dealer brother Theo, is Amsterdam's top tourist attraction. During the recent celebrations of the hundredth anniversary of his death, the museum was packed for several weeks. Housed in an angular building designed by the aged Gerritt Rietveld, it's a gentle and unassuming introduction to the man and his art – and one which, due both to the quality of the collection and the building, succeeds superbly well.

The first works go back to the artist's **early years** in southern Holland, where he was born: these are dark and sombre for the most part, like the haunting, flickering light of *The Potato Eaters* – one of van Gogh's best-known paintings. Across the hall, the sobriety of these early works is easily transposed on to the Parisian urban landscape, particularly in his *View of Paris:* but before long, under the sway of fellow painters and, after the bleak countryside of North Brabant and the sheer colour of the city itself, his approach began to change. This is most noticeable in the views of Montmartre windmills, a couple of self-portraits, and the pictures from Asnières just outside Paris.

In February 1888, van Gogh moved to **Arles**, inviting Gauguin to join him a little while later. With the change of scenery came a heightened interest in colour, and the predominance of yellow as a recurring motif: it's represented most vividly in *The Yellow House*. A canvas from the artist's *Sunflowers* series is justly one of his most lauded works, intensely, almost obsessively, rendered in the deepest oranges, golds and ochres he could find.

At the asylum in **St Remy**, where van Gogh committed himself after snipping off part of his ear and offering it to a local prostitute, nature took a more abstract form in his work – trees bent into cruel, sinister shapes, skies coloured purple and yellow, as in the *Garden of St Paul's Hospital*. Van Gogh is at his most expressionistic here, the paint applied thickly, often with a palette knife, especially in the final, tortured paintings done at **Auvers**, including *Undergrowth*, *The Reaper*, or *Wheatfield with Crows*, in which the fields swirl and writhe under black, moving skies. It was only a few weeks after completing this last painting that van Gogh shot and fatally wounded himself.

On the second floor, the museum shows a revolving selection from its vast stock of van Gogh's **drawings**, notebooks and letters, and also affords space to relevant temporary exhibitions. The top floor is used as a **temporary exhibition space** year round, usually showing works loaned from other galleries that illustrate the artistic influences on van Gogh, or his own influence on other artists.

Stedelijk Museum

Paulus Potterstraat 13. Tram #2, #3, #5, #12, #16. Daily 11am–5pm; f7.

Despite its reputation as Amsterdam's number one venue for modern art, the **STEDELIJK** can be a bit disappointing. True, its temporary exhibitions are often of world renown, and worth catching if you happen to be in town, but the museum is primarily devoted to displays of **contemporary art on loan**. Should you want to see something of its extensive permanent collection (impressively complete from the nineteenth century onwards) you'll need to be here in the summer, when the museum's holdings are shown through much of July and August.

Of the museum's **permanent collection**, there's always a good (rotating) smattering hanging on the **first floor**. Briefly, and broadly, this starts off with drawings by Picasso, Matisse and their contemporaries, and moves on to paintings by major Impressionists – Manet, Monet, Bonnard – and Post-Impressionists: Ensor, van Gogh, and Cezanne. Further on, Mondrian holds sway, from the early, muddy-coloured abstractions to the cool, boldly coloured rectangular blocks for which he's most famous. Similarly, Kasimir Malevich is well represented, his dense attempts at Cubism leading to the dynamism and, again, bold, primary tones of his "Suprematist" paintings. You may also find a good stock of Marc Chagall's paintings (the museum owns a wide selection), and a number of pictures by American Abstract Expressionists Mark Rothko, Ellsworth Kelly, and Barnett Newman. Jean Dubuffet, too, with his swipes at the art establishment, may well have a profile, and you might catch Matisse's large cut-out, *The Parakeet and the Mermaid*.

Two additional large-scale attractions are on the ground floor – Karel Appel's *Bar* in the foyer, installed for the opening of the Stedelijk in the 1950s, and the same artist's wild daubings in the museum's restaurant. Look out, too, for Ed Kienholz's model of his local bar in Los Angeles, the *Beanery* (1965), housed in the basement of the museum.

Other museums

Amstelkring Museum

O.Z. Voorburgwal 40. Tram #4, #9, #16, #24, #25. Mon–Sat 10am–5pm, Sun 1–5pm; f3.50.

In the seventeenth century, Catholics had to confine their worship to the privacy of their own homes – an arrangement which led to the growth of so-called clandestine Catholic churches throughout the city. Known as "Our Dear Lord in the Attic", this is the only one left; it occupies the loft of a wealthy merchant's house, together with those of two smaller houses behind it. The **church** is delightful and the **house** itself has been left beautifully untouched, its original furnishings (reminiscent of interiors by Vermeer or de Hooch) making the Amstelkring a tranquil and still relatively undiscovered escape from the excesses of the nearby Red Light district. One of the city's best and least demanding small museums.

Amsterdam Historical Museum

Kalverstraat 92. Tram #1, #2, #4, #5, #9, #14, #16, #24, #25. Daily 11am–5pm; f3.50; guided tours on Wed and Sat at 3pm.

Housed in the restored seventeenth-century buildings of the Civic Orphanage, Amsterdam's Historical Museum attempts to survey the city's development with artefacts, paintings and documents from the thirteenth century onwards. Much is centred around the "Golden Age" of the seventeenth century: a large group of paintings portrays the city in its heyday and the good art collection shows how the wealthy bourgeoisie decorated their homes. Sadly, most of the rest of the museum is poorly documented and lacks continuity. Still, it's worth seeing for the nineteenth-century paintings and photos and, more notably, the play-it-yourself **carillon** and the **Regents' Chamber**, unchanged since the Regents dispensed civic charity there 300 years ago. Directly outside the museum, the glassed-in **Civic Guard Gallery** draws passers-by with free glimpses of the large company portraits – there's a selection from the earliest of the 1540s to the lighter affairs of the seventeenth century.

Anne Frank House

Prinsengracht 263. Tram #13, #14, #17. July–Aug Mon–Sat 9am–7pm, Sun 10am–7pm; Sept–June Mon–Sat 9am–5pm, Sun 10am–5pm; f5, children f3; no museumcards.

See p.56.

Fodor Museum

Keizersgracht 609. Tram #16, #24, #25. Daily 11am–5pm; admission varies with exhibition, but normally f1. Phone ☎24 99 19 for exhibition details.

Rotating exhibitions of works by contemporary Amsterdam artists. There's an annual summer exhibition of art bought by the city council, and the museum arranges exchanges with other European capitals. Information printed in English is rare, but the museum's monthly magazine should help you keep in touch.

Hortus Botanicus

Plantage Middenlaan 2. Tram #7, #9, #14. April–Sept Mon–Fri 9am–5pm, Sat & Sun 11am–5pm; f5.

Pocket-sized botanical gardens whose 6000 plant species make a wonderfully relaxed break from the rest of central Amsterdam. Worth wandering in for the sticky pleasures of the hothouses, its terrapins, and for the world's oldest (and probably largest) potted plant. Stop off for coffee and cakes in the orangery.

Jewish Historical Museum

J.D. Meijerplein. Metro to Waterlooplein, Tram #9, #14. Daily, except Yom Kippur, 11am–5pm; f5.

Housed in a former Ashkenazi synagogue complex in the old Jewish quarter of Amsterdam, the Jewish Museum is one of the most modern and impressive in western Europe; it won the 1988 European Museum of the Year award. Four synagogues, built during the seventeenth and eighteenth centuries, have been restored and linked together as a centre for the study of the history of the Jewish community that's designed to be of interest to all.

Kromhout Shipyard Museum

Hoogte Kadijk 147. Bus #22, #28. Mon–Fri 10am–4pm; f2.50 (includes guided tour), no museumcards.

The Kromhout shipyard was one of the few survivors of the decline in shipbuilding during the nineteenth century. It struggled along producing engines and iron ships until it closed in 1969 and was saved from demolition by being turned into a combination of industrial monument, operating shipyard, and museum. Money is still tight, which means that little shipbuilding or restoring is going on at the moment, but the enthusiastic staff and good explanatory background material make this an up-and-coming place, and a useful adjunct to the Maritime Museum nearby.

Maritime Museum

Kattenburgerplein 1. Bus #22, #28. Tues–Sat 10am–5pm, Sun 1–5pm; f5, children f3.

A well-presented display of the country's maritime past in an endless collection of maps, navigational equipment and weapons, though most impressive are the large and intricate **models** of sailing ships and men-of-war that date from the same period as the original vessels.

Rembrandt House

Jodenbreestraat 4–6. Metro to Nieuwmarkt. Mon–Sat 10am–5pm, Sun 1–5pm; f2.
See p.59.

Resistance Museum

Lekstraat 63. Tram #4, #12, #25. Tues–Fri 10am–5pm; Sat–Sun 1–5pm; f3.50.

Strikingly installed in a former synagogue, the Resistance Museum charts the rise of the resistance from the German invasion of The Netherlands in May 1940 to the country's liberation in 1945. The museum has a fascinating collection of contemporary material – photos, illegal newsletters, anti-Jewish propaganda and deportation orders. The English guide to the exhibition, available for f1.50, is essential.

The Six Collection

Amstel 218. Tram #4. Apply first (with passport) at the Rijksmuseum for a note of introduction. This is essential; the house is still lived in and is extremely protective of its privacy. You most definitely won't get in without the letter. Open May 1–Oct 30 Mon–Fri 10am–noon and 2–4pm; Nov 1–April 30 Mon–Fri 10am–noon; Closed public holidays; free.

The Six Collection is deliberately underplayed in the city's tourist brochures, in part because only those with a little knowledge of Dutch art will find it rewarding, and, more importantly, because the current Baron Six, descendent of the seventeenth-century collector and burgomaster, still lives in the elaborately furnished canal house and doesn't encourage visitors – worth bearing in mind if you do come. **Rembrandt** was a friend of the burgomaster and his *Portrait of Jan Six* is the collection's greatest treasure. Painted in 1654, it's a brilliant work, the impressionistic treatment of the hands subtly focusing attention on the subject's face. The collection – which contains work by Hals, Cuyp and Terbosch – is well-explained by the staff, and the whole group of paintings is a must if you have any interest in seventeenth-century painting.

Tropenmuseum

Linnaeusstraat 2. Tram #3, #6, #9, #10. Mon–Fri 10am–5pm, Sat–Sun noon–5pm; f6.

As part of the old Colonial Institute (now the less controversially titled Tropical Institute), this museum used to display only artefacts from the Dutch colonies. Since the 1950s, however, when Indonesia was granted independence, it has collected applied arts from all over, and its holdings now cover the world. It makes for an impressively unstuffy exposition of the contemporary life and problems of the developing world – both urban, covering the ever-expanding slum dwellings of cities such as Bombay, and rural, examining such issues as the dangerous wholesale destruction of the world's tropical rainforests. The best sections are those devoted to Africa, India and (not surprisingly) Indonesia, but it's really all worth seeing, even if you have little interest in ethnography. Also look in on the bookshop, which has a good selection of books on Third World subjects.

Canal House museums

Willet-Holthuysen Museum

Herengracht 605. Tram #4, #9, #14. Daily 11am–4pm; f1.75.

Splendidly decorated in Rococo style, this is more museum than home, containing Abraham Willet's collection of glass and ceramics. But, save for the basement kitchen, a well-equipped replica of a seventeenth-century kitchen, it's very much look-don't-touch territory. Out back there's an immaculate eighteenth-century garden – worth the price of the admission alone.

Van Loon Museum

Keizersgracht 672. Tram #4, #9, #14. Mon only, 10am–5pm; f5.

Less grand and more likeable than the nearby Willet-Holthuysen, with a pleasantly down-at-heel interior of peeling stucco and shabby paintwork. Built in 1672, the house's first tenant was the artist Ferdinand Bol; fortunately he didn't suffer the fate of many subsequent owners who seem to have been cursed with a series of bankruptcies and scandals for over two hundred years. The van Loon family bought the house in 1884, bringing with them a collection of family portraits and homely bits and pieces that stretch from 1580 to 1949.

Two other museums housed in buildings that offer a flavour of seventeenth-century Dutch interiors are the Amstelkring (p.68) and the Six Collection (p.70).

Eating

Amsterdam may not be the culinary capital of Europe, but there's a good supply of ethnic restaurants, especially Indonesian and Chinese, and the prices (by big-city standards) are hard to beat. And there are *eetcafés* and bars which serve increasingly adventurous food, quite cheaply, in a relaxed and unpretentious setting.

Dutch food tends to be higher in protein content than on imagination: steak, chicken and fish, along with filling soups and stews, are staple fare. Where possible, stick to *dagschotels* (dish of the day), a meat and two vegetable combination for which you pay around f15, bottom-line, for what tend to be enormous portions. The three-course *tourist menu*, which the authorities push at several of the city's more mainstream restaurants, is – at f19–20 or so – no great bargain, and usually extremely dull.

A wide selection of **vegetarian** restaurants offer full-course set meals for around f10 to f12. Another cheap standby is **Italian** food: pizzas and pasta dishes start at a fairly uniform f10–11 in all but the ritziest places. **Chinese** restaurants are also common, as are (increasingly) **Spanish**, and there are a handful of **Tex-Mex** eateries, all of which serve well-priced, filling food.

But Amsterdam's real speciality is its **Indonesian** restaurants. You can eat à la carte; *Nasi Goreng* and *Bami Goreng* (rice or noodles with meat) are ubiquitous dishes, and chicken or beef in peanut sauce (*sate*) is available everywhere too. Or order a *rijstaffel*: boiled rice and/or noodles served with a number of spicy side dishes and hot *sambal* sauce on the side.

For good-value eating, the **bar listings** on p.74 are also worth checking: many serve food, and at lunchtime it's possible to fill up extremely cheaply with a bowl of soup or a french bread sandwich. The Dutch eat out early – rarely later than 9pm – and in both restaurants and bars, kitchens are normally closed by 11pm at the latest; vegetarian restaurants tend to shut their doors even earlier.

Mensas

These are Amsterdam's student caféterias, and as such are not frequented so much for the quality of the food as for the prices which at around f7.50 for a full meal can hardly be beaten. The food itself isn't bad, filling enough if not especially tasty.

Atrium, O. Z. Voorburgwal 237 (☎525 3999). Open Mon–Fri noon–2pm and 5–7pm, all year round.

De Weesper, Weesperstraat 5 (☎22 40 36). Open Mon–Fri 5–7.25pm, year-round.

Dutch and fish restaurants

Albatros, Westerstraat 264 (☎27 99 32). Family-run restaurant serving some mouthwateringly imaginative fish dishes – though, at f30 up, for no mean cost. A place to splash out and linger over a meal.

De Bak, Prinsengracht 193 (☎25 79 72). Good portions for moderate prices, though lately somewhat of a tourist hangout and with a menu that seems to have shrunk down to spare ribs and not much else. See also *De Bak*'s sister restaurant, *Sing Singel*, below.

Claes Claesz, Egelantiersstraat 24–26 (☎25 53 06). Exceptionally friendly Jordaan restaurant that attracts a good mixed crowd and serves excellent Dutch food, though not at all cheaply. Reckon on f25 and up for a main course. Live music most nights.

Haesje Claes, N. Z. Voorburgwal 320 (☎24 99 98). Dutch cuisine at its best. Extremely popular; go as early as you can manage.

Keuken van 1870, Spuistraat 4 (☎24 89 65). Basic, traditional Dutch cooking – a good deal if money's short.

Moeder's Pot, Vinkenstraat 119 (☎23 76 43). Ultra-cheap Dutch food. Recommended.

Noordzee, Kalverstraat 122 (☎23 73 37). Central Amsterdam branch of a chain that specialises in cheap fish lunches, sandwiches and take away fish 'n' chips. Meals for under f10, sandwiches f3–f5.

Vegetarian restaurants

De Bast, Huidenstraat 19 (☎24 97 47). Pleasant and tasty food, though the ambience is a bit clinical and service can be slow. Good lunch specials.

Egg Cream, St. Jacobstraat 19 (☎23 05 75). Amsterdam's most famous vegetarian restaurant, cheap and atmospheric, though the food isn't always exclusively veggie. Set meals f8–f12. Bear in mind the early closing time of 8pm.

Klaver Koning, Koningstraat 29 (☎26 10 85). Excellent upmarket vegetarian restaurant, with decent wine and a refreshingly un-ascetic atmosphere. But not cheap.

Sisters, Nes 102 (☎26 39 70). A busy vegetarian restaurant serving *dagschotels* and other main courses for around f16, as well as plenty of snack-type items. Open until 10pm.

Ethnic restaurants

Aphrodite, Lange Leidsedwarsstraat 91 (☎22 73 82). Refined Greek cooking in a street where you certainly wouldn't expect it. Fair prices too.

Bojo, Lange Leidsedwarsstraat 51 (☎22 74 34). Possibly the best-value – if not the best – Indonesian place in town, and open until 6am. Expect to wait for a table, though – we weren't the first to discover it. Highly recommended.

Burger's Patio, 2e Tuindwarsstraat 12 (☎23 68 54). Moderately priced, young and convivial Italian restaurant. Despite the name, not a burger in sight.

Casa di David, Singel 426 (☎24 50 93). Solid-value Italian place with a sister self-service restaurant at Kalverstraat 180.

Filoxenia, Berenstraat 8 (☎24 42 92). Small, friendly, reasonably priced Greek restaurant.

Intermezzo, Herenstraat 28 (☎26 01 67). Good French-Dutch cooking at above-average prices, but worth every penny.

Jaya, 1e Anjeliersdwarsstraat 18 (☎24 01 22). One of the smallest and finest of the city's Indonesian restaurants, with classical music as an accompaniment to your food. Bookings advised.

De Kikker, Egelantiersstraat 130 (☎27 91 98). Two-tier, top quality French restaurant that has a downstairs *eetcafé* with dagschotels for around f23. Upstairs is only really accessible for the well-dressed, wealthy, committed gourmet.

Koh-I-Noor, Westermarkt 29 (☎23 31 33). One of the city's better Indian restaurants, and not overpriced.

La Cacerola, Weteringstraat 41 (☎26 53 97). Small and secluded Spanish eatery, with likeable if eccentric service.

Lana Thai, Warmoesstraat 10 (☎24 21 79). The best Thai restaurant in town, with seating overlooking the water of Damrak. Quality food, chic surroundings and fair prices. Closed Tues.

Mamma Mia, 2e Leliedwarsstraat 13 (☎25 82 38). Good selection of pizzas, from f12, in a pleasant family atmosphere.

Mughal, Rokin 107 (☎24 24 16). Above-average and centrally located restaurant serving Pakistani food.

Nieuwe Lange Muur, Berenstraat 28 (☎25 89 53). Friendly, cheap takeaway with a couple of tables. Chinese, Vietnamese, Indonesian dishes.

Oshima, Prinsengracht 411 (☎25 09 96). Amsterdam's first centrally located and reasonably priced Japanese restaurant. Sushi a speciality, from f12.50; main courses f25 plus. In summer the restaurant can get a bit sticky; book early if you don't want to sit on Tatami.

Pizzeria Mimo, Lange Leidsedwarsstraat 37 (☎22 79 35). Perhaps the best of the dozens of Italian restaurants along this street.

Rias Altas, Westermarkt 25 (☎24 25 10). Food in abundance, masterfully cooked and genially served. Good starters, fine house wine, full meals f19–20. Arguably the city's best Spanish restaurant. Its sister restaurant is **Centra**, Lange Niezel 29.

Rose's Cantina, Reguliersdwarsstraat 38 (☎25 97 97). In the heart of trendy Amsterdam, this qualifies as possibly the city's most crowded restaurant. No bookings, and you'll almost definitely have to wait, but it's no hardship to sit at the bar nursing a cocktail and watching the would-be cool bunch – the margaritas should carry a public health warning. The Tex-Mex food is good too, from around f16.

Rum Runners, Prinsengracht 277 (☎27 40 79). Caribbean-style bar/restaurant situated in the old Westerkerk hall. Expensive cocktails but well-priced if not always devastatingly tasty food. Summer terrace and live South American music Wed–Sun evening.

The Tandoor, Leidseplein 19 (☎23 44 15). Doesn't live up to its excellent reputation, but the tandoori dishes are very tasty.

Tempo Doeloe, Utrechtsestraat 75 (☎25 67 18). Reliable place close by Rembrandtsplein. As with all Indonesian restaurants, be guided by the waiter when choosing a *rijstaffel* – some of the dishes are very hot indeed.

Het Tuinhuysch, Wolvenstraat 16 (☎ 23 91 56). Wonderful, delicate French cooking at fairly gentle prices; set menu f29.

Warung Span Macaranda, Gerard Doustraat 39 (☎73 01 29). Surinamese/Javanese *eetcafé*. Cheap and cheerful; closed on Wednesdays.

Drinking

There are two kinds of Amsterdam **bar**. The traditional, old-style bar or **brown café** (*bruin kroeg*), so named because of the dingy colour of their nicotine-stained walls, and the slick, self-consciously modern **designer bar**, as un-brown as possible and geared to a largely young crowd. Most bars open until around 1am during the week, 2am at weekends, though some don't open until lunchtime, or even about 4pm; reckon on paying roughly f2.50 for a small beer.

You can also use bars as a source for **budget eating**: many (often designated *eetcafés*) offer a complete menu, and most will make you a sandwich or bowl of soup; at the very least you can snack on hard-boiled eggs from the counter for a guilder or so each.

Inner Centre bars

Blincker, St Barberenstraat 7–9. Squeezed between the top end of Nes and O. Z. Voorburgwal, this hi-tech bar, all exposed steel and hanging plants, is more comfortable than it looks. Arrive early if you want a seat – there's a direct entrance from the *Frascati Theatre* next door, and performances let out around 10pm.

Cul de Sac, O. Z. Voorburgwal 99. Down a long alley in what used to be a seventeenth-century spice warehouse, this is a handy retreat from the Red Light district. Small, quiet and friendly.

De Drie Fleschjes, Gravenstraat 18. Tasting-house for spirits and liqueurs, which would originally have been made on the premises. No beer, and no seats either; its clients tend to be well-heeled or well-soused (often both).

De Engelbewaarder, Kloveniersburgwal 59. Once the meeting place of Amsterdam's book-ish types, this is still known as the "literary café". Relaxed and informal, it has live jazz on Sunday evenings.

Flying Dutchman, Martelaarsgracht 13. Principal watering-hole of Amsterdam's British expatriate community and not a word of Dutch is to be heard. Usually packed with stoned regulars crowding in to use the pool table or dartboards, or simply to cash in on the Dutchman's reasonably priced large-size beers.

Frascati, Nes 59. Theatre bar, elegantly brown with mirrors and a pink marble bar, popular with a young media-type crowd. Good, too, for both lunchtime and informal evening eating, with a full meal for around f15, snacks and soups for much less. Recommended.

't Gasthuys, Grimburgwal 7. Convivial brown café packed during the school year with students from the university across the canal. Features include good food and summer seat-ing outside by the water.

Harry's American Bar, Spuistraat 285. One of a number of would-be sophisticated hang-outs at the top end of Spuistraat, Harry's is primarily a haunt for Amsterdam's more elderly *bon vivants*, with easy listening jazz and an unhealthily wide selection of cocktails.

Luxembourg, Spui 22–24. The latest watering-hole of Amsterdam's advertising and media brigade – striped shirts and bow ties abound. It's crowded too. If you can get in, it's actually a very elegant bar with a good (though pricey) selection of snacks. Overlooks the Singel at the back.

De Pieter, St Pieterspoortsteeg 29. Opens at 10pm, and plays host to bands on Wed nights, a disco on Sat, and blaring music the rest of the week. Dark, very noisy, with a wildly eclectic crowd.

De Pilsener Club, Begijnensteeg 4. More like someone's front room than a bar – indeed all drinks mysteriously appear from a back room. Photographs on the wall record generations of sociable drinking.

De Pilsery, Gravenstraat 10. Roomy bar behind the Nieuwe Kerk that has a comfortable back room and plays good jazz. Above all, though, you drink here for the bar's authentic nineteenth-century surroundings – little changed, right down to the cash register.

Scheltema, N. Z. Voorburgwal 242. Journalists' bar, now only frequented by more senior newshounds and their occasionally famous interviewees, since all the newspapers that had their headquarters along here moved to the suburbs. Faded turn-of-the-century feel, with a reading table and meals for under f20.

La Strada, N. Z. Voorburgwal 93–95. Exceptionally trendy bar whose interior changes monthly as aspiring – and not always inspiring – local artists are given free reign with the decor. Occasional fully fledged exhibitions, poetry readings, live music on Sat. Good food too – pasta dishes start at f15.

Waterloo, Zwanenburgwal 15. This hyper-designer bar under the Muziektheater features a TV screen broadcasting continuous (silent) music videos in the floor – and a good view. It's also a sleek restaurant.

Wynand Fockink, Pijlsteeg 31. Ancient tasting-house about the size of a large cupboard. Closes 8pm.

Outer Central bars

Aas van Bokalen, Keizersgracht 335. Unpretentious local bar, with good food from f17. Great collection of Motown tapes. Very small, so go either early or late.

Chris, Bloemstraat 42. Proud of itself for being the Jordaan's (and Amsterdam's) oldest bar, dating from the early seventeenth century. Comfortable and homely.

H'88, Herengracht 88. Part of a student complex, this place stays open until 6am, by which time it's strictly diehard drinkers' territory.

Land van Walem, Keizersgracht 449. Walem is one of Amsterdam's nouveau-chic cafés: cool, light, and vehemently non-brown. Clientele are stylish in taste and dress, food a kind of hybrid French-Dutch with full meals going for around f20; there's a wide selection of newspapers and magazines that includes some in English. Usually packed.

Morlang, Keizersgracht 451. Bar/restaurant of the new wave yuppie variety (much like *Walem* next door), serving good food for around f15. Live music Tues.

Nol, Westerstraat 109. Probably the epitome of the jolly Jordaan singing bar, a luridly lit dive popular with jovial Jordaan gangsters and ordinary Amsterdammers alike. Open late.

Paris Brest, Prinsengracht 375. Next door to Van Puffelen (see below) and owned by the same man, Paris Brest is the designer alternative: all chrome and glass and black leather filofaxes. A very reasonable set menu at f29.

De Prins, Prinsengracht 124. Boisterous student bar, with a wide range of drinks and a well-priced menu that includes fondues. In a great part of town.

Schiller, Rembrandtsplein 26. Art Deco bar of the upstairs hotel, authentic in both feel and decor, and though it's suffered something of a decline of late, offering a genteel escape from the tackiness of most of the rest of Rembrandtsplein. Meals – French-Dutch – go for around f20.

De Tuin, 2e Tuindwarsstraat 13. The Jordaan has some marvellously unpretentious bars, and this is one of the best: agreeably unkempt and filled with locals.

Coffee shops and tearooms

There are two types of Amsterdam **coffee shops**: those whose principle business is the buying, selling and consuming of dope, and the more traditional places that sell neither dope nor alcohol but do serve sandwiches or a light menu for lower prices than in a fully fledged restaurant; some offer pastries or chocolates.

The so-called **"smoking" coffee shops** are easy to identify: pumping out varieties of acid house or hard rock, brightly lit, with starkly modern furniture and an accent on healthy food, they're about as far from the cosy Dutch *brown café* as it's possible to get. Smoking dope is the primary pastime (all sell a range of hash and grass), and most also have video screens, (loud) music, and a selection of games from baccarat to pool; they're open roughly from late morning/midday until around midnight. For more on dope see p.13.

The growth of "smoking" coffee shops has made "straight" places increasingly defensive, and all of the coffee shops listed as **"non-smoking"** go to great lengths to emphasise that they don't sell dope, and that its consumption on the premises is strictly forbidden; some are even considering calling themselves "tearooms" to avoid confusion. Again, if you're not sure, ask.

"Smoking"

The Bulldog, Leidseplein 13–17; O. Z. Voorburgwal 90; O. Z. Voorburgwal 132; Hekelveld 7. The biggest and most famous of the coffee-shop chains, and a long way from its pokey Red Light district/dive origins. The main Leidseplein branch (the "Palace"), housed in a former police station, has a large cocktail bar, coffee shop, juice bar, and souvenir shop. It's large and brash, not at all the place for a quiet smoke, though the dope they sell (packaged up in neat little brand-labelled bags) is reliably good.

Extase, Oude Hoogstraat 2. Part of a chain run that is considerably less chi-chi than the big cheeses.

Fancy Free, Martelaarsgracht 4; Haarlemmerstraat 64. Slick, pink, plush and commercial, very much in *The Bulldog* mould.

Goa, Kloveniersburgwal 42. A member of the *Extase* chain (see above).

Pie in the Sky, 2e Laurierdwarsstraat 64. Beautiful canal-corner setting, great for outside summer lounging.

Prix d'Ami, Haringpakkersteeg 3; Nieuwendijk 239. Super-entrepreneurial Amsterdam chain, but with little of the character of its rivals.

Rusland, Rusland 16. One of the first Amsterdam coffee shops, and a cramped and vibrant place that's a favourite with both dope fans and tea addicts (43 different kinds). A little worse for a recent extension, but still a cut above the rest.

"Non-smoking"

Bâton, Herengracht 82. Convivial coffee shop with a huge array of sandwiches. Handy for cheap lunches in a central location.

J.G. Beune, Haarlemmerdijk 156. Age-old chocolatier with a tearoom attached.

Café Panini, Vijzelgracht 3–5. Coffee shop-cum-restaurant that features good sandwiches and, in the evening, pasta dishes.

De Eenhorn, Warmoesstraat 16. Raw brick walls, oak beams, paintings and classical music. A stark contrast to the surrounding Red Light district.

Granny, 1e van der Helststraat 45. Just off the Albert Cuyp market, with terrific *appelgebak* and *koffie verkeerd*.

Lindsay's Teashop, Kalverstraat 185. An attempt to recreate a little piece of England in the unlikely location of the basement of the American Discount Book Centre. The food, though, is fine: real English cream teas, with homemade pies and trifles. And it's a refreshing escape from the Kalverstraat shopping mafia.

Studio 2, Singel 504. Pleasantly situated, airy coffee shop that sells a delicious selection of rolls and sandwiches. Recommended.

Nightlife

Amsterdam is not a major cultural centre, by any standards. Its performance spaces are small for the most part, and the city is not a regular stop on the touring circuits of major companies. Rather, it's a gathering spot for fringe performances, and buzzes with places offering a wide – and often inventive – range of affordable entertainment.

The city has a great many **multi-media centres;** programmes everywhere can be varied and unpredictable, so always check "what's on" listings carefully. As far as live music goes, **rock, jazz, salsa** and **Latin American** music, are well-represented in a number of small bars and clubs. The Concertgebouw assures Amsterdam a high ranking in the **classical music** stakes, and the city has pulled itself up into the big leagues for **dance and opera** with the building of the new Muziektheater on the Amstel. As for **theatre**, a number of companies perform regularly in English, and at **cinemas**, foreign-language films are rarely shown without English subtitles.

The largest of Amsterdam's **festivals** is the annual **Holland Festival**, a prestigious and international, if slightly highbrow, series of opera, music, theatre, and dance performances held throughout the city. The **Summer Festival** (*Zomerfestijn*), based at the *Shaffy Theatre* during the first two weeks of July, is quite different, presenting the latest in non-mainstream developments in the arts at smaller outlets all over town – and with events that are deliberately accessible to non-Dutch-speakers.

Information and tickets

Your first stop should be the *Uitburo*, in the Stadsschouwburg on the corner of Marnixstraat and Leidseplein (Mon–Sat 10am–6pm, Thurs until 9pm; ☎21 12 11), which offers advice on anything remotely cultural, sells tickets, and is the best source of the major **listings magazines**. **Tickets** for most performances can be bought at the Uitburo and *VVV* offices (fees f2 and f2.50 respectively), or can be reserved by phone from the *VVV*. You can also book seats, again free of charge, through the *National Bookings Centre* (☎070 20 25 00)

Concert halls and multi-media centres

Carré Theatre, Amstel 115–125 (☎22 52 25). Hosts all kinds of top international acts: anything from the Peking Circus to rap and Russian folk dance.

Jaap Eden Hall, Radioweg 64 (☎94 98 94). Large concert hall in the east of the city which occasionally stages big-name gigs. Heavy metal bands a favourite. Prices f15–f40; tram #9.

Meervaart, Osdorpplein 205 (☎10 73 93). A modern multi-media centre on the outskirts of town (tram 1, bus #19, #23) with a varied programme of international music, film, theatre, and dance. Film tickets f8, other events f5–f20.

Melkweg, Lijnbaansgracht 234a (☎24 17 77). Probably Amsterdam's most famous entertainment venue, and these days one of the city's prime arts centres. Its theatre space serves as an outlet for small, inventive international groups, virtually all of which perform in English, and the concert hall plays host to a broad range of bands. Other features include a fine monthly film programme, weekend discos, a tearoom selling dope, and a bar and restaurant. General admission is f4 plus f3 membership (valid one month); otherwise, concerts begin around 10.30pm and admission ranges from f7.50–f25. Those visiting more than once should buy a *reductiekaart* (f5) – valid for three months and giving a worthwhile discount on admission. The *Melkweg* is closed on Mondays.

Stadsschouwburg, Leidseplein 26 (☎25 04 35). Somewhat overshadowed by the Muziektheater but still a significant stager of opera and dance. Tickets f10–f25.

Live music

Akhnaton, Bakkerstraat 12 (☎24 33 96). Three-storey youth centre with live music at the weekends – hip-hop's a recent speciality. Starts around 10pm, admission around f5. Currently under renovation and due to reopen in September 1990.

Maloe Melo, Lijnbaansgracht 160 (☎25 33 00). Describes itself as a blues club, though its tiny stage just as often reverberates to rockabilly and rock 'n' roll. Nightly from around 10.30pm.

Paradiso, Weteringschans 6–8 (☎26 45 21). A converted church that features bands ranging from the up-and-coming to well-known names on the brink of stardom. Also hosts classical concerts, lectures and debates. Entrance f10–f25, plus f3 for a month's membership. The bands usually get started at 10.30pm.

PH 31, Prins Hendriklaan 31 (☎73 68 50). Amply amplified hard-core punk and new wave bands from 11pm every night in a bare, whitewashed room smack in the middle of the posh Vondelpark neighbourhood. Sun night jazz and blues sessions from 8.30pm. Tram #2.

Café Alto, Korte Leidsedwarsstraat 115 (☎26 32 49). Legendary little jazz bar just off Leidseplein. Quality modern jazz every night from 10pm until about 2.30am. Big on atmosphere, though slightly cramped.

Bimhuis, Oude Schans 73–77 (☎23 33 73). Excellent jazz auditorium and ultra-modern bar. Concerts Thurs–Sat at 9pm (f7.50–f15), free jazz sessions Mon & Tues at 10.30pm. Live music in the bar, Sun afternoons at 4pm, also free.

Cab Kaye's, Beulingstraat 9 (☎23 35 94). Jazz pianist Cab Kaye's bar offers piano music weekend nights 10pm–2am. Slightly middle-aged, though with an intimate atmosphere that attracts after-hours musicians.

Joseph Lamm Jazz Club, Van Diemenstraat 8 (☎22 80 86). Traditional jazz centre which encourages dancing. Live music Fri & Sat 9pm–3am, f5; jam sessions Sun 8pm–2am, free.

Latin Club, O. Z. Voorburgwal 254 (☎24 22 70). Salsa/cocktail bar with occasional live bands and a tape selection imported from South America; 2pm–2am (weekends until 3am).

Rum Runners, Prinsengracht 277 (☎27 40 79). Trendy Caribbean restaurant and cocktail bar in the former hall of the Westerkerk. Live (mainly laid-back Latin American) bands Sun at 2pm and 7.30pm, Wed at 7.30pm.

Soeterijn, Linnaeusstraat (☎56 88 00). Part of the Tropenmuseum, this theatre specialises in the drama, dance, film, and music of developing countries. Admission f5–f15; political and ethnic films, f7.50; ethnic dance and theatre, much of it in English, f15. Tram #9, #10, #14.

The String, Nes 98 (☎25 90 15). Folk every evening.

Contemporary and classical

Concertgebouw, Van Baerlestraat 98 (☎71 83 45). Under its new conductor, Ricardo Schailly, the *Concertgebouw* is one of the most dynamic orchestras in the world and after a recent facelift is looking and sounding better than ever. Free lunchtime concerts Sept–May (doors open 12.15pm, arrive early), and swing/jazz nights from time to time; f15–f50.

Ijsbreker, Weesperzijde 23 (☎668 18 05). Large, varied programme of international modern, chamber and experimental music. Out of the town centre near the Amstel, a great place to spend a summer afternoon; f12.50; Tram #3, #6, #7, #10.

Muziektheater, Amstel 3 (☎25 54 55). Via the Netherlands Opera, which is resident here, Amsterdam's fullest opera programme. Tickets f15–f50 and, except for weekends, go quickly.

Villa Baranka, Prins Hendrikkade 140 (☎27 64 80). New arts forum which aims to create a "salon" in a six-storey building and which stages (mainly classical) theatre and music, poetry readings, and art workshops. Performances both afternoons and evenings, but mainly confined to the weekends; f10–f20.

Discos and clubs

Technically, you have to be a member to **get in** some clubs (those that call themselves "societies"), though in practice this can either be waived or inexpensively arranged at the door. Most clubs open around 10pm and close up around 4am or slightly later, but there's no point in arriving before midnight. On the whole – unless stated otherwise – music is basic Top 40 fodder, drink prices normally 50 percent or so more than what you pay in a bar.

Bebop, Amstelstraat 24 (☎25 01 11). A massive and spectacular disco celebrating the USA, set off by a laser and light system that descends over the dance floor. Open 11am–4pm Thurs (free), Fri (f5), & Sat (f10), and with occasional live music.

Havana Club, Reguliersdwarsstraat 17–19 (☎20 67 88). Recently opened and already very popular with a mixed clientele (gay, yuppie, art crowd). Early disco on weekdays, 8pm–1am (Fri & Sat until 2am), Sun 5pm–1am.

Mazzo, Rozengracht 114 (☎26 75 00). One of the city's hippest discos. Angular bar, video screens and a sharp, image-obsessed crowd. Live music Tues & Wed. Open every night 11pm–4/5am, admission f5 (includes free drink).

Odeon, Singel 460 (☎24 97 11). Two dance floors, (the upstairs one only open weekends) and a stylishly elegant interior, play host to an invariably yuppie gang. Open throughout the week, 10pm–5/6am, admission f7.50 on weekends, other times f5.

Oxshoofd, Herengracht 114 (☎22 76 85). Broad selection of music, plus late-closing restaurant. Open all week midnight–6/7am, admission f5 (including f2.50 drink voucher).

(Op de schaal van) Richter 36, Reguliersdwarsstraat 36 (☎26 15 75). This small, split-level club, supposed to resemble a building after an earthquake, draws in one of the city's most conspicuously chic crowds. Fairly flexible door policy, and host to a TV chat show. Open throughout the week 11pm–5am, admission f5.

The Roxy, Singel 465 (☎20 03 54). Housed in an old cinema with varied music – wildest night right now is Friday, Acid House night. Good place to get invited to parties. Wed–Sun 11pm–5am. Admission f10, though the door policy is highly selective, and members only are admitted when it's crowded.

Film

The Dutch use subtitles for foreign films (most of which are in English) which means that language isn't a problem. If you want to be sure, look out for the words *Nederlands Gesproken* printed next to the title in the listings; this indicates it's been dubbed into Dutch. Tickets go for about f13, though *Alfa*, *Bellevue*, *Cinerama* and *De Uitkijk* have considerably reduced prices Monday to Thursday. One cinema – the extravagantly Art Deco *Tuschinski*, Reguliersbreestraat 26 – is worth visiting no matter what's showing; screen one tends to be especially interesting.

   Programmes change Thursday: most bars and cafés have a weekly film schedule pinned up; otherwise check the usual listings sources, principally the what's-on supplement of Wednesday's *Het Parool* and *Uitkrant*'s *Filmagenda* section.

Theatre

Surprisingly, for a city that functions so much in English, there are only two English-language theatre groups: the *American Repertory Theater* (*ART*), which has an office at Kerkstraat 4 (☎25 94 95) and concentrates on contemporary work; and the *English Speaking Theatre of Amsterdam* (*ESTA*), Leidsestraat 106 (☎22 97 42), which stages more varied productions and emphasises modern British drama. Neither has its own theatre, but you can catch both at venues all over town. There are also regular English-language productions and performances by touring groups at the theatres listed below and at multi-media centres. For details of annual festivals, see p.31.

Shops

You'll find much of what's available in Amsterdam's shops at home – and often more cheaply. Where Amsterdam scores, however, is in some excellent, unusual **speciality shops** (designer clocks, rubber stamps, Indonesian arts, condoms, to name just a few), a handful of good **markets**, and its shopping convenience – the city's centre concentrates most of what's interesting within its tight borders.

Shopping areas and opening hours

There are few specific **shopping areas**. But broadly, **Nieuwendijk**, **Kalverstraat**, and **Leidsestraat** are where you'll find mass-market clothes and mainstream department stores; **Rokin**, running parallel, is more pricey; the

Jordaan, west of the centre, is home to more specialised, more adventurous clothes shops; while to the south, **P.C. Hooftstraat, Van Baerlestraat**, and **Beethovenstraat** play host to designer clothiers, upmarket ceramics stores, confectioners and delicatessens. There's also the **Spiegelkwaartier**, centre of Amsterdam's antique trade, which cuts through the main canals near the Rijksmuseum. Many of the most interesting, and more specialised shops are scattered among the small streets which connect the main canals.

As for **hours**, most shops take Monday morning off, and open from 9.30am to 6 or 6.30pm the rest of the week except Sunday; they stay open late on Thursday and close early Wednesday afternoon. Larger shops will accept **payment** by a major credit card (*American Express, Visa, Access*, etc.), but never by travellers' cheque.

Department stores

De Bijenkorf, Damrak 90. Dominating the northern corner of Dam Square, this is the city's top shop, a huge bustling place that has an indisputably wide range and little of the snobbishness of a place like Harrods – or even *Metz* (see below).

HEMA, Nieuwendijk 174; Reguliersbreestraat 10. A kind of Dutch Woolworth's, but of a better quality: good for stocking up on toiletries and other essentials, and occasional designer delights.

Metz & Co., Keizersgracht 455 . By far the city's swishest store, with the accent on Liberty prints, stylish ceramics and designer furniture. If your funds won't stretch quite that far, settle for a cup of coffee in the top floor Rietveld restaurant, which affords great views over the canals.

Vroom & Dreesman, Kalverstraat 201–221 & 212–224. The main Amsterdam branch of the middle-ground nationwide chain. Again, useful for essentials.

Books, magazines and card shops

Though prices are upped, virtually all Amsterdam bookshops stock at least a small selection of **English-language books**, and in the city centre it's possible to pick up most English **newspapers** the day they come out; English-language **magazines**, too, are available from newsstands and bookshops.

A la Carte, Spui 23. Travel guides and maps.

Allert de Lange, Damrak 62. Perhaps Amsterdam's best bookshop, with a great stock of Penguins, a marvellous travel section, and an informed staff.

Art Unlimited, Keizersgracht 510. Enormous card and poster shop. Good for communiqués home that don't involve windmills.

Athenaeum, Spui 14–16. Excellent all-round bookshop, with a more adventurous stock than W.H. Smith's.

Bruna. A nationwide chain, and a safe bet for popular paperbacks and mainstream newspapers and magazines. Branches all over town; for the nearest, look in the phone book under *Bruna*.

Cards for Days, Huidenstraat 26. A good bet for silly cards.

The English Bookshop, Lauriergracht 71. Exclusively English-language bookshop with a small but quirky collection of titles, many of which you won't find elsewhere.

Paper Moon, Singel 417. Well-stocked card shop.

W.H. Smith, Kalverstraat 152. Dutch branch of the UK high-street chain – a predictable selection but strong on travel and language, and with a useful ordering service. Prices are sometimes cheaper than in regular Dutch bookshops.

Cheap and secondhand clothes

Amsterdam has a fair array of one-off, individually run places, youth-orientated clothes shops and/or **second-hand clothing** stores in the Jordaan, on Nieuwe Hoogstraat (a handful), or along the narrow streets that connect the major canals west of the city centre. The Waterlooplein flea market (see below) is also an excellent hunting ground for second-hand clothes.

Bop Street, 1e Bloemdwarsstraat 14. 1950s clothes and memorabilia.

Empathy, Berenstraat 16. Vintage clothes. On the expensive side, but some very nice stuff.

The End, Nieuwe Hoogstraat 26. Unspectacular but inexpensive.

Jojo, Huidenstraat 23. Particularly good for trench coats and Fifties jackets.

Lady Day, Hartenstraat 9. Good-quality second-hand clothes at reasonable prices.

Puck, Nieuwe Hoogstraat 1. Vintage second-hand clothes.

Zipper, Huidenstraat 7; Nieuwe Hoogstraat 10. Mainly used-clothes selected for style and quality – or so it says on the door. Prices start high.

Markets

Amsterdam's markets are more diverting than its shops. There's a fine central **flea market** on Waterlooplein, vibrant **street markets** such as the Albert Cuyp, emphasising food and cheap clothing, and smaller **weekly markets** devoted to everything from stamps to flowers.

Albert Cuyp, Mon–Sat 9am–4.30pm. Amsterdam's best-known – and best – general market.

Bloemenmarkt, on the Singel between Muntplein and Koningsplein. Mon–Sat 9am–4.30pm. Plants and flowers, pots and bulbs, sold from stalls on floating barges. Very reasonable.

Boerenmarkt (Noordermarkt). Sat 10am–1pm. Organic produce, handicrafts, chickens, pets and exotic birds.

"De Looier", Elandsgracht Mon–Thurs 11am–5pm, Sat 9am–5pm. Indoor antiques stalls, selling a wide variety of goods.

Nieuwmarkt, May–Sept Sun 10am–5pm. Good-quality antiques.

Noordermarkt, Mon 7.30am–1.30pm. More junk than antiques.

Waterlooplein Mon–Sat 10am–4pm. New and second-hand clothes, antiques, junk, books and bikes. Amsterdam's best and most enjoyable browse.

Miscellaneous and ethnic

Perhaps more than any other place in Europe, Amsterdam is a great source for shops devoted to one particular product or interest. What follows is a selection of favourites:

Condomerie Het Gulden Vlies, Warmoesstraat 141. Condoms of every shape, size and flavour imaginable. All in the best possible taste.

Electric Lady, 2e Leliedwarsstraat 4. Pungently 1970s collection of psychedelia of all kinds, most of it luminous.

Flying Objects, 2e Tuindwarsstraat 8. Beautiful kites at sky-high prices.

The Head Shop, Kloveniersburgwal 39. What it says.

Jacob Hooij, Kloveniersburgwal 12. Homeopathic chemist with an ancient interior and a huge stock of *drop* – Dutch licorice.

Donald E. Jongejans, Noorderkerkstraat 18. Hundreds of spectacle frames, none of them new, some of them very ancient. Supplied the specs for Bertolucci's *The Last Emperor*.

't Klompenhuisje, Nieuwe Hoogstraat 9a. Amsterdam's best and brightest array of clogs.

Posthumus, St. Luciensteeg 15. Posh stationery, cards and, best of all, a choice of hundreds of rubber stamps.

't Winkeltje, Prinsengracht 228. Jumble of cheap glassware and crockery, candlesticks, antique tin toys, kitsch souvenirs, old apothecaries jars and flasks. Perfect for browsing.

Listings

Airline Offices *Aer Lingus*, Heiligweg 14 (☎23 95 89); *Air UK* (☎74 77 47); *British Airways*, Stadhouderskade 4 (☎85 22 11); *British Midland* Strawinskylaan 1535 (☎06 022 24 26); *Canadian Pacific*, Stadhouderskade 2 (☎85 17 21); *KLM*, Leidseplein 1 (☎64 93 633); *NLM City Hopper*, Schipol Airport (☎64 92 227); *Pan Am*, Leidseplein 29 (☎26 20 21); *Qantas*, Stadhouderskade 6 (☎83 80 810); *Transavia*, Schipol Airport (☎60 46 518); *TWA*, Singel 540-4 (☎26 22 27).

Baby-sitters *Babysit Centrale Kriterion*, 2e Rozendwarsstraat 24 (☎24 58 48). Long-established agency with a high reputation, using students at least 18 years old. Inexpensive 24-hour service: f5–10 per hour, plus an administrative charge depending on the time of day. Book sitters between 5.30–7pm.

Banks and Exchanges Amsterdam **banks** usually offer the best deal for changing money. Hours are Monday to Friday, 9am to 4pm, with a few banks open on Thursday 7 to 9pm or Saturday morning; all are closed on public holidays. At other times you'll need to go to one of the many **bureaux de change** scattered around town. The most useful of these are *GWK* in the Centraal Station (Mon–Sat 7am–10.45pm, Sun 8am–10.45pm) and *Change Express* Leidsestraat 106, Damrak 17 & 86, Kalverstraat 150 (open daily until midnight).

Car Hire *Budget*, Overtoom 121 (☎12 60 66) or *Europcar*, Overtoom 51–53 (☎83 21 23) are slightly less expensive than *Hertz* and *Avis*, but the cheapest are such local operators as *Diks*, Gen. Vetterstraat 51–55 (☎17 85 05); van Ostadestraat 278–280 (☎66 23 366), whose prices start at around f47 a day plus a charge per kilometre over 100km.

Car Parks *Parking Prinsengracht*, Prinsengracht 540–2 (☎25 98 52) f3 per hour, around f20 per day. Others: *De Bijenkorf*, on Beursplein, and *Europarking*, at Marnixstraat 250. There are also underground garages under the Muziektheater and Museumplein.

Churches Services in English at the *English Reformed Church*, Begijnhof (☎24 96 65), Sun at 10.30am; the *Anglican Church*, Groenburgwal 42 (☎24 88 77), Sun at 10.30am and 7.30pm; English Catholic Mass at the church of *St John and Ursula*, Begijnhof (☎22 19 18), on Sun at 12.15pm, May–Aug. For details of other religious services, consult the *VVV*.

Consulates/Embassies *UK*, General Koningslaan 44 (☎76 43 43); *USA*, Museumplein 19 (☎66 45 661).

Cycle Tours *Yellow Bike* N. Z. Voorburgwal 66 (☎20 69 40) run 20km bike tours around the city, starting from Centraal Station: f25, bike supplied, tours leave daily at 9am, 1pm and 7pm.

Gay and Lesbian Amsterdam's **gay scene** focuses around the bars of Kerkstraat-Reguliersdwarstraat, Amstel and Amstelstraat, and Warmoesstraat. Among the best-known gay bars are: *Amstel Taverne*, Amstel 54; *Chez Manfred*, Halvemaansteeg 10; *Eagle*, Warmoesstraat 86; *Open*, Amstelstraat 5. **Women only/lesbian bars** include: *Het Bruine Paard*, Prinsengracht 44; *Saarein*, Elandstraat 119; and *VivrelaVie*, Amstelstraat 7. For more information on gay and lesbian matters, contact COC, Rozenstraat 8 (☎26 86 00).

Launderettes *The Clean Brothers* is the best, at Jakob Van Lennepkade 179, Westerstraat 26 and Rozengracht 59 (daily until 9pm). Other launderettes at: Warmoesstraat 30, Oude Doelenstraat 12 and Herenstraat 24. Otherwise look under *Wassalons* in the Yellow Pages.

Left Luggage Centraal Station. Mon–Fri 5am–1am, Sat–Sun 6am–1am; f1.25 per item, bikes f1.65, lockers f1.50 for 30 hours.

Police Station Headquarters: Elandsgracht 117 (☎559 91 11): other central stations include Lijnbaansgracht (☎559 23 10); Warmoesstraat 44-46 (☎559 22 10).

Post Office Main office is at Singel 250, (Mon–Fri 8.30am–6pm, Thurs 8.30am–8.30pm, Saturday 9am–noon). Other central post offices include Keizersgracht 757; Kerkstraat 169; in *Vroom & Dreesman* at Kalverstraat 201; and at Stadhouderskade 41.

Telephones Easiest place to make calls is the **Telehouse**, Raadhuisstraat 46–50 (24hrs). A discount rate on international calls is in effect between 8pm and 8am.

Telephone Helplines In English: *AIDS Helpline*, (☎06 32 12 120) Mon–Fri 2–10pm; *Legal Hotline* (☎548 2611); *Mental and Social problems* (☎16 16 66); *Tram, Bus, and Metro Information* (☎27 27 27).

Travel Agents *NBBS* at Dam 17 (☎20 50 71), Leidsestraat 53 (☎38 17 36) and Ceinturbaan 294 (☎79 93 37), is the Amsterdam branch of the nationwide student/youth travel organisation and the best source of *BIJ* tickets, discount flights for anyone, etc. Also worth checking out are: *Nouvelles Frontières*, van Baerlestraat 3 (☎66 44 131); *Budget Bus*, Rokin 10 (☎27 51 51); *Budget Air*, Rokin 34 (☎27 12 51); *Magic Plane*, Rokin 38 (☎26 48 44).

Women's Contacts Amsterdam has an impressive feminist infrastructure: support groups, health centres, businesses run by and for women, and there's a good range of bars and discos, a few exclusively for women. Best starting point to find out what's going on in the city is the *Vrouwenhuis*, Nieuwe Herengracht 95 (☎25 20 66; open most days at varying times), an organising centre for women's activities/cultural events. *Villa Baranka*, Prins Hendrikkade 140 (☎27 64 80) is a cross-cultural art studio with performance art, literature and poetry readings by and for women., and *Xantippe*, Prinsengracht 290 (☎23 58 54) a women's bookshop with a wide selection of feminist titles in English.

travel details

Trains

From Amsterdam to Haarlem (6 an hour; 15min); Schipol/Leiden/The Hague/Rotterdam/Dordrecht/Rosendaal (2 an hour; 16min/33min/47min/1hr/1hr30min/1hr45min); Alkmaar/Den Helder (2 an hour; 30min/1hr 10min); Hoorn/Enkhuizen (2 an hour; 35min/55min); Utrecht/Den Bosch/Eindhoven (2 an hour; 30min/1hr/1hr 25min); Maastricht (hourly; 2hr 30min); Arnhem/Nijmegen (2 an hour; 1hr 10min/1hr 30min); Amersfoort/Apeldoorn/Enschede (hourly; 40min/1hr 5min/2hr); Zwolle (hourly; 1hr 20min); Leeuwarden (hourly; 2hr 25min); Groningen (hourly; 2hr 25min); Middelburg/Vlissingen (hourly; 2hr 35min/2hr 45min).

CHAPTER TWO

NORTH HOLLAND

T he province of **North Holland** is one of the country's most explored regions. Though not as densely populated as its sister province to the south, it's still a populous area, and holds some of Holland's prime tourist attractions. The landscape is typically Dutch, the countryside north of Amsterdam for the most part a familiar polder scene of flat fields, cut by trenches and canals, stretching far into the distance, the vast horizons broken occasionally by the odd farmhouse or windmill. Lining most of the western coast are rugged areas of dune and long and broad sandy beaches, while on the other side the coast of the Ijsselmeer, formerly the Zuider Zee, is home to old ports turned yachting communities, which sport the vestiges of a glorious past in picturesquely preserved town centres.

As with much of South Holland, and indeed parts of provinces further afield, the majority of North Holland is easily visited by means of day trips from Amsterdam. But this would be to only skim the surface of the region. The urban highlight is undoubtedly **Haarlem**, a very easy day trip from Amsterdam but definitely worth treating as an overnight stop. It also gives access to some wild stretches of dune and beach, and one of the country's largest seaside resorts in **Zaandvoort**. **Alkmaar**, too, to the north, is usually visited by day-excursionists from Amsterdam to see its rather bogus ceremonial Friday cheese market, but is worth taking in for longer if you're keen to experience small-town provincial Holland. In the eastern part of the province, the villages nearest Amsterdam – **Marken**, **Volendam** and **Edam** – are twee places full of tourists in search of clogs and windmills during summer, and probably worth avoiding at any time of year. Further north, towns like **Hoorn** and **Enkhuizen** are of more interest, formerly major Zuider Zee ports, now pretty towns with yacht-filled harbours that again make either a good day trip from Amsterdam, or pleasant stopoffs if you're travelling up to Friesland by car and are in no hurry. In the far north of the province, the island of **Texel** is the most accessible and busiest of the Wadden Sea islands. It's very crowded during summer, but don't be put off by the numbers: with a bit of walking you can find places well off the beaten tourist track – and far away from the hustle of Amsterdam.

Transport in North Holland is, as ever, by a mixture of train to the main centres and then bus. For moving on, there's a fast road link along the top of the 20km-long dike between Enkhuizen and Lelystad, on the reclaimed Flevoland polders. It was completed in 1976, the first stage of a plan to reclaim the enclosed area in the so-called **Markerwaard** scheme. This met considerable opposition when proposed and has now been indefinitely postponed (you'll still see posters and graffiti against the plan in places like Hoorn and Enkhuizen), but the road it spawned is still a useful way of getting to the east of the country without passing through Amsterdam.

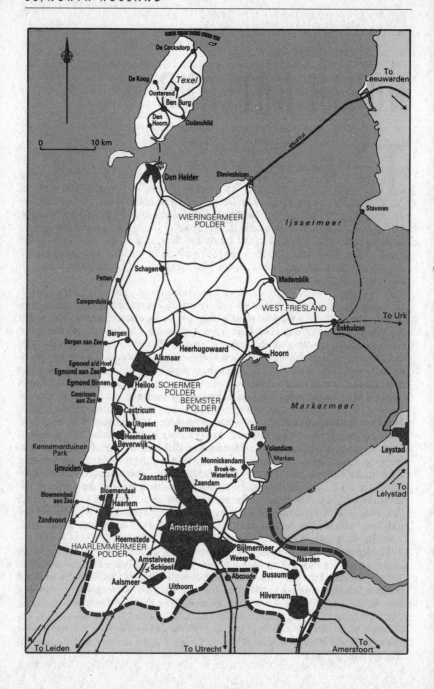

Muiden, Naarden and Hilversum

Most of the province of North Holland is located, logically enough, north of Amsterdam. But the borders of the province also dip down beneath the capital, taking in Schipol and parts of the bulb-growing areas (covered in the following chapter) and a suburban agglomeration which sprawls east towards Amersfoort. The area is hardly essential viewing: you're really more likely to pass through on your way to somewhere else than make a special trip. However, if you have time on your hands in Amsterdam and have seen all the more obvious attractions, a couple of low-key towns might draw your attention – not to mention some modern architecture highlights further east.

Muiden and Naarden

The first town you reach, **MUIDEN** is squashed around the Vecht, a river usually crammed with pleasure boats and dinghies sailing out to the Ijsselmeer. Most of the sightseeing is done by weekend sailors eyeing up each other's boats, although the **Muiderslot** (April–Sept Mon–Fri 10am–4pm, Sun 1–5pm; Oct–March Mon–Fri 10am–4pm, Sun 1–4pm; f3.50) provides an extra spark of interest. In the thirteenth century this was the home of Count Floris V, a sort of aristocratic Robin Hood who favoured the common people at the nobles' expense. They replied by kidnapping the Count, imprisoning him in his own castle and stabbing him to death. Destroyed and rebuilt in the fourteenth century, Muiderslot's interior is these days a recreation of the period of a more recent occupant, the poet Pieter Hooft. He was chatelain here from 1609 to 1647, a sinecure that allowed him to entertain a group of artistic and literary friends who became known as the Muiden Circle, and included Grotius, Vondel, Huygens and other Amsterdam intellectuals. The obligatory guided tours centre on this clique, in a restoration that is both believable and likeable – two things period rooms generally aren't.

Look at a postcard of **NAARDEN**, about 5km east, and it seems as if the town was formed by a giant pastry cutter: the double rings of ramparts and moats, unique in Europe, were engineered between 1675 and 1685 to defend Naarden and the eastern approach to Amsterdam. They were still used in the 1920s, and one of the fortified spurs is now the wonderfully explorable **Fortification Museum** at Westwalstraat 6 (end March–Oct Mon–Fri 10am–4.30pm, Sat & Sun noon–5pm; f2.50), whose claustrophobic underground passages show how the garrison defended the town for 250 years.

The rest of Naarden's tiny centre is peaceful rather than dull. The small, low houses mostly date from after 1572 when the Spanish sacked the town and massacred the inhabitants, an act designed to warn other settlements in the area against insurrection. Fortunately they spared the late Gothic **Grote Kerk** (May–Sept daily except Fri 2–4pm) and its superb vault paintings. Based on drawings by Durer, these twenty wooden panels were painted between 1510 and 1518 and show an Old Testament on the south side, paralleled by a New Testament story on the north. To study the paintings without breaking your neck, borrow a mirror at the museum's entrance. A haul up the Grote Kerk's **tower** (hourly tours 1–4pm; f2) gives the best view of the fortress island and, less attractively, of Hilversum's TV tower.

If you've never heard of Jan Amos Komenski or Comenius, a seventeenth-century polymath and educational theorist, it's unlikely that the **Comenius**

Museum at Turfpoortstraat 27 (Tues–Sun 2–5pm; free) will fire your enthusiasm for the man. A religious exile from Moravia (now in Czechoslovakia), Comenius lived in Amsterdam and is buried in Naarden. He's a national hero to the Czechs, and they donated most of the exhibits in the museum and also constructed his **Mausoleum** in the **Waalse Kapel** on Kloosterstraat – a building permanently on loan to the Czech people.

Practical details

CN buses #136, #137 and #138 leave Amsterdam every half-hour from the Amstel railway station, stopping first at Muiden (travel time 40min) then Naarden (55 min). The Naarden **VVV** is at Adriaan Dortmansplein 1b (Mon–Fri 9.15am–5pm, Sat 10am–4pm, Sun noon–4pm; mornings only in winter; ☎021/594 2836).

Hilversum

The main town of this corner of North Holland is **HILVERSUM**, a nineteenth-century dormitory suburb for wealthy Amsterdammers, who created a well-heeled smugness that survives to this day. Their villas have been flashily converted into studios for Dutch broadcasting companies, and behind the neatly trimmed hedges and net curtains live some of the country's more comfortably-off.

In the middle of all this tidy bourgeois greenery is the town's **Raadhuis** of 1931, the work of the Frank Lloyd Wright-influenced architect W.M. Dudok. If you've any interest at all in modern architecture, it's a trip well worth making. A deceptively simple progression of straw-coloured blocks rising to a clock tower, the eye drawn across the buildings by long slender bricks, it is open to the public during office hours (ask at the reception for information). Inside is a series of lines and boxes, marble walls margined with black like an uncoloured Mondrian painting, all coolly and immaculately proportioned. Dudok also designed the interior decorations, and though some have been altered, his style confidently continues, even down to the ashtrays and light-fittings.

Dudok was Hilversum's principal architect, and the **Information Centre** on Kerbrink publishes a walking tour that takes in the many other buildings he designed in the town; the centre's free town map is also worth picking up. The **VVV**, near the station at Emmastraat 2, can help with rooms, though with Amsterdam so close, and connections on to more interesting towns so easy, there's little reason to stay.

Haarlem and around

Just over ten minutes from Amsterdam by train, **HAARLEM** has quite a different pace and feel from the capital, an easily absorbed city of around 150,000 people that sees itself as a cut above its neighbours. If you've any time at all to spare you'd be mad to miss it. The Frans Hals Museum, in the almshouse where the artist spent his last – and for some his most brilliant – years, is worth an afternoon in itself; there are numerous beaches within easy reach, as well as some of the best of the bulbfields (see Chapter Three). In short, if you're tired of the crowds and grime of Amsterdam, Haarlem makes a good alternative base for exploring North Holland, or even the capital itself.

Arrival, information and accommodation

The **railway station** is located on the north side of the city, about ten minutes' walk from the centre; **buses** stop right outside. The **VVV**, attached to the station (Mon–Fri 9am–5pm, Sat 10am–4pm; ☎31 90 59), have maps (50c) and copies of the monthly events guide, "Swinging Haarlem". They can also book **private rooms** for around f24 a head, though you'll find more choice in Zandvoort, about fifteen minutes away by hourly bus #81. The same goes for **hotels**, though Haarlem has a few reasonably priced alternatives. The *Carillon*, at Grote Markt 27 (☎31 05 91), has doubles from about f70 and is centrally placed; the *Piccolo*, a few doors along at Riviersvismarkt 1 (☎32 68 49), is a little cheaper at around f60; or try the *Waldor*, close to the station at Jansweg 40 (☎31 26 22), which has doubles for f75. There's also a **youth hostel** at Jan Gijzenpad 3 (open April–Oct; ☎37 37 93); take bus #2 or #6 from the station. **Campers** should either try the campsites among the dunes along Zeeweg out at Bloemendaal-aan-zee (bus #81), though these tend to be open during spring and summer only, or Haarlem's own site at Liewegie 17, which is open all year.

> The Haarlem area telephone code is ☎023

The Town

For a long time the residence of the counts of Holland, Haarlem was sacked by the Spanish under Frederick of Toledo in 1572. There are reminders of this all over the town, since, after a seven-month siege, the revenge exacted by the inconvenienced Frederick was terrible: very nearly the whole population was massacred, including the entire Protestant clergy. Recaptured in 1577 by William the Silent, Haarlem went on to enjoy its greatest prosperity in the seventeenth century, becoming a centre for the arts and home to a flourishing school of painters.

Nowadays, the place retains an air of quiet affluence, with all the picturesque qualities of Amsterdam but little of the sleaze. The core of the city is **Grote Markt**, an open space flanked by a concentration of Gothic and Renaissance architecture, most notably the gabled and balconied **Stadhuis**, at one end. This dates from the fourteenth century, though it has been much rebuilt over the years, the last time in 1630 – a date recorded on the facade. Inside, the main hall is normally left open for visitors during office hours; it's decorated with a few fifteenth-century paintings. At the other end of Grote Markt there's a statue of one **Laurens Coster**, who, Haarlemmers insist, is the true inventor of printing. Legend tells of him cutting a letter "A" from the bark of a tree and dropping it into the sand by accident. Plausible enough, but most authorities seem to agree that Gutenburg was the more likely source of the printed word.

Coster stands in the shadow of the **Grote Kerk of St Bavo** (Mon–Sat 10am–4pm; f1.50), where he is believed to be buried. If you've been to the Rijksmuseum, the church may seem familiar, at least from the outside, since it was the principal focus of the seventeenth-century painter Berckheyde's many views of this square – only the black-coated burghers are missing. Finished in the early sixteenth century, it dwarfs the surrounding clutter of streets and houses, and serves as a landmark from almost anywhere in the city. Inside, it is breathtakingly high, its beauty enhanced by the bare, white-painted power of the Gothic vaulting. The mighty Christian Muller organ of 1738 is said to have been played by Handel and Mozart and is one of the biggest in the world, with 5000 pipes and razzamatazz baroque embellishment. Beneath the organ, Xaverij's lovely group of draped marble figures represents Poetry and Music, offering thanks to the town patron for her generosity, while in the choir there's a late fifteenth-century painting that the church traditionally (though dubiously) attributes to Geertgen tot Sint Jans, along with memorials to painters Pieter Saenredam and Frans Hals – both of whom are buried here. Outside, at the western end of the church, the **Vishal** and, opposite that, Lieven de Key's profusely decorated **Vleeshal** (the former fish and meat markets), hold regular art exhibitions, to which admittance is normally free.

The Frans Hals Museum

Haarlem's chief attraction, the **FRANS HALS MUSEUM** (Groot Heiligland 62; Mon–Sat 10am–5pm, Sun 1–5pm; f4), is just a five-minute stroll from Grote Markt, housed in the Oudemannhuis almshouse where the aged Hals is supposed to have lived out his last destitute years on public funds. Little is known about Frans Hals. Born in Antwerp, the son of Flemish refugees who settled in Haarlem in the late 1580s, his extant oeuvre is relatively small: some 200 paintings and nothing like the number of sketches and studies left behind by Rembrandt – partly because Hals wasn't fashionable until the nineteenth century, and a lot of his work was lost before it became collectable. His outstanding gift was as a portraitist, showing a sympathy with his subjects and an ability to capture fleeting expression that some say even Rembrandt lacked. Seemingly quick and careless flashes of colour form a coherent whole, leaving us a set of seventeenth-century figures that are curiously alive.

The museum begins with the work of other artists: first a small group of **sixteenth-century works**, the most prominent a triptych by Gerard David, and an early anti-imperialist painting – *West Indian Scene* by Jan Mostaert, in which the naked natives try fruitlessly to defend themselves against the cannon and sword of their invaders. Van Scorel's *Baptism of Christ* and *Knights of Jerusalem* follow, along with works by van Goyen, Brouwer and van Ostade, and a good group of paintings by the **Haarlem mannerists**, including works by Carel van Mander, leading light of the Haarlem School and mentor of many of the other painters represented here. Cornelis Cornelisz van Haarlem best follows van Mander's guidelines: *The Marriage of Peleus and Thetis* was a popular subject at the time, probably because it was interpreted as a warning against discord, appropriate during the long war with Spain – though Cornelisz gives as much attention to the arrangement of elegant nudes as to his subject. The same is true of his *Massacre of the Innocents*, which could refer to the siege of Haarlem just twenty years earlier.

Frans Hals was a pupil of van Mander too, though he seems to have learned little more than the barest rudiments from him. His paintings in the west wing – a set of "Civic Guard" portraits of the companies initially formed to defend the country from the Spanish, later on just local social clubs – established his reputation as a portraitist, and earned him a regular income. There was a special skill involved in painting these: for the first time Hals made the group portrait a

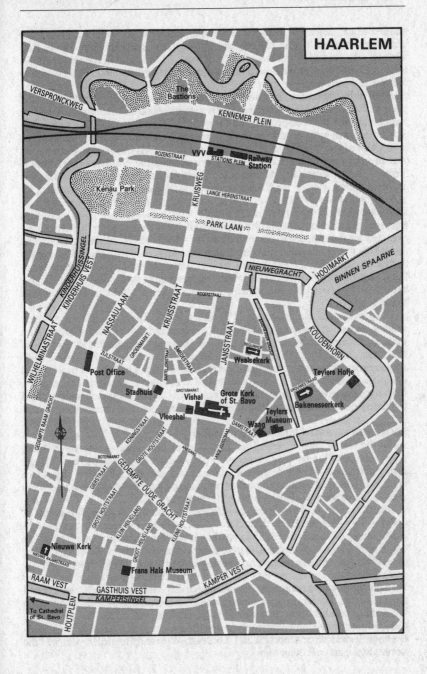

HAARLEM

VERSPRONCKWEG

The Bastions

KENNEMER PLEIN

ROZENSTRAAT

VVV

STATIONS PLEIN

Railway Station

KRUISWEG

Kenau Park

LANGE HERENSTRAAT

PARK LAAN

HOOIMARKT

BINNEN SPAARNE

NIEUWEGRACHT

KINDERHUISSINGEL

KINDERHUIS VEST

NASSAULAAN

KRUISSTRAAT

RIDDERSTRAAT

JANSSTRAAT

ZOUTKEET GRACHT

KOUDENHORN

WILHELMINASTRAAT

ZIJLSTRAAT

GROENMARKT

BARTELJORISSTRAAT

SMEDESTRAAT

BEGIJNHOF

Wealsekerk

NIEUWE GRACHT

Post Office

Teylers Hofje

GEDEMPTE RAAM GRACHT

Stadhuis

GROTEMARKT

Vishal

Grote Kerk of St. Bavo

Bakenesserkerk

Vleeshal

Teylers Museum

Waag

DAMSTRAAT

LANGE VEERSTRAAT

KONINGSTRAAT

GROTE HOUTSTRAAT

ANEGANG

BOTERMARKT

GEESTRAAT

GEDEMPTE OUDE GRACHT

GROTE HOUTSTRAAT

KLEIN HEILIGLAND

GROOT HEILIGLAND

KLEINE HOUTSTRAAT

Nieuwe Kerk

NIEUWE RAAMSTRAAT

Frans Hals Museum

KAMPER VEST

RAAM VEST

GASTHUIS VEST

KAMPERSINGEL

HOUTPLEIN

To Cathedral of St. Bavo

unified whole instead of a static collection of individual portraits; his figures are carefully arranged, but so cleverly as not to appear contrived. For a time, Hals himself was a member of the Company of Saint George, and in the *Officers of the Militia Company of Saint George* he appears in the top left-hand corner – one of his few self-portraits.

After this, there are numberless scenes of Haarlem by Berckheyde and Saenredam, among others; landscapes by the Ruisdaels and Berchem; and some group portraits by Veerspronck and the elderly Frans Hals. Hals' later paintings are darker, more contemplative works, closer to Rembrandt in their lighting. The *Governors of the Saint Elizabeth Gasthuis*, painted in 1641, is a good example, as are the portraits of the *Regents* and *Regentesses of the Oudemannhuis* itself – perhaps the museum's finest treasures. These were commissioned when Hals was in his eighties, a poor man despite a successful painting career, hounded for money by the town's tradesmen and by the mothers of his illegitimate children, and dependent on the charity of the people depicted here. Their cold, hard faces stare out of the gloom, the women reproachful, the men only slightly more affable – except for the character just right of centre who has been labelled (and indeed looks) completely drunk. There are those who claim Hals had lost his firm touch by the time he painted these, yet the sinister, almost ghostly power of these paintings, facing each other across the room, suggests quite the opposite. Van Gogh's remark that "Frans Hals had no less than twenty-seven blacks" suddenly makes perfect sense.

Other galleries hold lesser works by lesser artists. There's a new wing, which houses temporary exhibitions, usually of modern and contemporary artists, and permanent paintings by Israëls, Appel & Jan Sluyters – though lamentably few of the latter. More interesting is the Oudemannhuis itself, a fairly typical *hofje* whose style of low buildings and peaceful courtyards you'll see repeated with slight variations all over town – and indeed the country. Classical concerts are held here regularly throughout the year, usually in the afternoon on the third Sunday of each month; prices are around f3, phone ☎31 91 80 for details.

The Hofjes ... and Haarlem's other sights

As for the rest of town, Haarlem has a greater number of **hofjes** than most Dutch cities – proof of the town's prosperity in the seventeenth century. The VVV can give information on where to find them; most are still inhabited, so you're confined to looking around the courtyard, but the women who sit outside seem used to the occasional visitor and won't throw you out.

Second in the pecking order of Haarlem sights, the **Teylers Museum**, at Spaarne 16 (Tues–Sat 10am–5pm, Sun 1–5pm, winter until 4pm; f4), is Holland's oldest museum, founded in 1778 by wealthy local philanthropist Pieter Teyler van der Hulst. This should appeal to scientific and artistic tastes alike, containing everything from fossils, bones and crystals, to weird, H.G. Wells-type technology (including an enormous eighteenth-century electrostatic generator), and sketches and line drawings by Michelangelo, Raphael, Rembrandt and Claude, among others. The drawings are covered for protection from the light, but don't be afraid to pull back the curtains and peek. Look in, too, on the rooms beyond, filled with work by eighteenth- and nineteenth-century Dutch painters, principally Breitner, Israëls, Weissenbruch and, not least, Wijbrand Hendriks, who was the keeper of the art collection here.

Teyler also lent his charity to the **Teyler's Hofje**, a little way east around the bend of the Spaarne, a solid late eighteenth-century building that is more monumental in style than the town's other *hofjes*. Nearby, the elegant tower of the **Bakenesser Kerk** forms the other main protrusion on the Haarlem skyline, a late-fifteenth-century church which is usually kept closed. Two other sights which may help structure your wanderings are on the opposite side of town. Van Campen's **Nieuwe Kerk** was built – rather unsuccessfully – on to Lieven de Key's bulbed, typically Dutch tower in 1649, though the interior is symmetrical with a soberness that is quite chilling after the soaring heights of the Grote Kerk. Just beyond, and much less self-effacing, the Roman Catholic **Cathedral of St Bavo** (March–Oct daily 9.30am–noon & 2–4pm) is one of the largest ecclesiastical structures in Holland, designed by Joseph Cuijpers and built between 1895 and 1906. It's broad and spacious inside, cupolas and turrets crowding around an apse reminiscent of Byzantine churches or mosques, the whole surmounted by a distinctive copper dome.

Eating and drinking

For **lunches and snacks**, try *Café Mephisto*, Grote Markt 29, which is open all day and serves Dutch food for f12–20, snacks for much less. *Café 1900*, Barteljorisstraat 10, is also a good place for lunch, a trendy locals' hangout serving drinks and light meals in an impressive turn-of-the-century interior (it also has live music on Sundays); *H. Ferd. Kuipers* is an excellent patisserie and tearoom at Barteljorisstraat 22. In the evening, there's *Alfonso's* Mexican restaurant just behind the Grote Kerk, which does Tex-Mex meals for around f19; the *Piccolo* restaurant serves pasta and decent pizzas from f12; or try the Indonesian food at *De Lachende Javaen*, on Frankestraat, which serves *rijstaffels* from f32 per person.

Once you've eaten, the *Crack*, at the junction of Lange Veerstraat and Kleine Houtstraat, is a dim, smoky **bar** with good music and – unsurprisingly perhaps – lots of English people and beer by the pint if you want it. On the same street, closer to Grote Markt at Lange Veerstraat 7, *'t Ouwe Proef* is more typically Dutch, a *proeflokaal* that also sells beer – lively early evening. Later on, *Stalker*, at Elleboogsteeg 20, is one of the city's more renowned **clubs**, open Thursday until Sunday and with a variety of music depending on the night you visit – from funk to hip-hop to jazz. Entry is free on Thursday and Sunday; Fridays and Saturdays it costs f5.

Around Haarlem

You'll find most of interest **west** of Haarlem. Take bus #80 from the railway station, and the monied Haarlem suburbs quickly give way to the thick woodland and rugged dune landscape of the **Kennemerduinen National Park**, which stretches down to the sea. **BLOEMENDAAL-AAN-ZEE** is the rather grandiose name for a group of shacks that house a thriving ice-cream trade, while a little further south, **ZANDVOORT**, an agglomeration of modern and faceless apartment complexes that rise out of the dunes, is a major Dutch seaside resort. As resorts go it's pretty standard – packed and oppressive in summer, depressingly dead in winter. The best reason to visit is the championship motor racing circuit, which provides background noise to everyone's sunbathing. If you come for the beach, and manage to fight your way through the crush to the water, watch out – the sea here is murky and ominously close to the smoky chimneys of **IJMUIDEN** to the north. This is a sprawling, depressing town, with a modern centre spread along the wide North Sea Canal. The part around the enormous sea locks and fishing harbour is of most interest, but the detour isn't really worth making.

A few miles **north** of Haarlem, **SPAARNDAM** is well known for its statue commemorating the boy who saved the country from disaster by sticking his finger in a hole in the dike. This tale has no basis at all in reality and few Dutch people even know it, but it had a sufficient ring of truth for a little-known American writer to weave a story around it, and so create a legend. The monument to the heroic little chap was unveiled in 1950 – more, it seems, as a tribute to the opportunistic Dutch tourist industry than anything else.

Continuing north, the train line cuts up through unrelenting suburbia to **BEVERWIJK**, not much of a place in itself but very much worth a visit if you're staying in either Haarlem or Alkmaar (or even Amsterdam) for its weekend **market** – a Turkish bazaar basically, rather incongruously situated on the outskirts of town in a number of large warehouses on an industrial estate. People come from all over the surrounding area at weekends to buy cheap hi-fi and clothes, leatherwear, Turkish clothes and *rai* cassettes from a huge number of stalls. There are places, too, selling spices, olives, turkish delight and dried fruits, as well as some excellent – and authentic – places to eat, serving up shoarma and thin crispy Turkish pizzas, spread with minced meat, at tables on which huge pots of chilli and yoghurt are arranged. The market is a fifteen-minute walk from the railway station – right out of the station, first right under the motorway and first left onto Parallelweg; follow this for 500m or so and turn right onto Buitenlanden.

North of Amsterdam

The polders immediately north of Amsterdam and the small towns and villages that line the Ijsselmeer are Holland at its most enforcedly quaint and touristed. The area is a favourite for day-trippers from Amsterdam, who arrive here by way of numerous bus excursions from the capital, and it can be packed to the gills during the summer. Don't expect anything too pristine.

Zaandam, Zaanse Schans and Purmerend

Most of the trains heading north from Amsterdam pass through the build-up of settlements that spreads north from the banks of the Ij and is known as **ZAANSTAD**. Looking out of the train window, it's arguable that there's no real reason to get off, and you really wouldn't be missing all that much if you didn't. But some people take an hour or so out to visit the central core of Zaanstad, known as **ZAANDAM**, a small, largely modern town that was a popular tourist hangout in the nineteenth century, when it was known as "La Chine d'Hollande" for the faintly oriental appearance of its windmills, canals, masts, and row upon row of brightly painted houses. Claude Monet spent some time here in the 1870s, and, despite being suspected of spying and under constant police surveillance, immortalised the place in a series of paintings.

Follow the main street of Gedempte Gracht from the railway station for five minutes, turn right down Damstraat, right again and left down Krimp, and you can see something of this former look, the harbour spiked with masts beyond a little grouping of wooden houses. On Krimp itself is Zaandam's main claim to fame, the **Czaar Petershuisje** (Tues–Fri 10am–1pm & 2–5pm, Sat & Sun 1–7pm; f1.50), a house in which the Russian Tsar Peter the Great stayed when he came to study shipbuilding here. In those days Zaandam was an important centre for ship-building and the Tsar made four visits to the town, the first in 1697 when he arrived incognito and stayed in the simple home of one Gerrit Kist, who had formerly served with him. A tottering wooden structure enclosed within a brick shelter, the house is no more than two rooms really, decorated with a handful of portraits of the benign-looking emperor and the graffiti of tourists that goes back to the mid-nineteenth century. Among the few things to see is the cupboard bed in which Peter is supposed to have slept, together with the calling cards and pennants of various visiting Russian delegations; around the outside of the house is a display on the shipbuilding industry in Zaandam. As Napoleon is supposed to have remarked on visiting the house, "Nothing is too small for great men".

Most visitors to Zaanstad are, however, here to visit **ZAANSE SCHANS** (April–Nov daily 10am–5pm; f8), a re-created Dutch village made up of houses, windmills and workshops assembled from all over the country. An energetic, but ultimately rather fake attempt to reproduce a Dutch village as it would have looked at the end of the seventeenth century, it's a pretty enough place, but it gets crammed in summer, and is not frankly worth the bother for its clogmaking displays and pseudo artisans' premises. However, it does represent the closest chance to Amsterdam to see windmills if that's what you're after, some of them working mills producing mustard and oil. Among other specific attractions are a clock museum and period room, and you can also take boat trips on the river. To get to Zaanse Schans from Zaandam catch bus #97; direct from Amsterdam take bus #94 – a thirty-minute journey.

Further up the rail line from Zaandam, **PURMEREND** has a once-weekly summer cheese market on Thursday at 11am – a slightly less crowded affair than its counterpart at Alkmaar. That apart, though, there's not much reason to stop. Purmerend is a rather dull suburb of Amsterdam these days, and aside from a local museum, it has little of much interest.

Marken, Volendam and Edam

The majority of visitors heading out of Amsterdam head further east from here, to the settlements on the banks of the Ijsselmeer. **MARKEN** is the first of these settlements, accessible direct from Amsterdam by way of bus #11 from opposite the St Nicolaaskerk. It's a popular place, a former island in the Zuider Zee that was, until its road connection to the mainland in 1957, largely a closed community, supported by a small fishing industry. At one time its biggest problem was the genetic defects caused by close and constant intermarrying; now it's how to contain the tourists, whose numbers increase yearly. Marken's distinctness has in many ways been its downfall; its character – that which remains – has been artificially preserved: the harbour is still brightly painted in the local colours, and local costumes and clogs are worn. Although visitors now supply the income lost when the Zuider Zee was closed off, it turns out to have been a desperate remedy.

The road follows the dike as far as **VOLENDAM**, accessible on bus #110, a larger village which retains some semblance of its fishing industry in conjunction with the more lucrative business of tourism – into which it too has thrown itself wholeheartedly. This is everyone's picture-book view of Holland: fishermen in baggy trousers sit strategically along the harbour wall, women scurry about picturesquely to piped music, clad in the winged lace caps that form the most significant part of the well-publicised village costume. Stop off if it's lunchtime, when you can snack your way along the waterfront fish stalls; otherwise give the place a wide berth.

Further on down the #110 bus route, almost connected to Volendam, you might expect **EDAM** to be just as bad, especially considering its reputation for the small red balls of cheese that the Dutch produce for export. In fact, it's a relief after the mob rule of Volendam, a pretty little town that is these days more a suburb of the capital than a major cheese-producer. It has only a fraction of the souvenir shops of its neighbours, and a charm that they have long since lost. The main draw is the **Grote Kerk**, an enormous building almost totally rebuilt after a fire in 1602, with some remarkable stained glass dating from that time. Damplein, Edam's nominal centre, is home to the eighteenth-century **Raadhuis**, which, although rather plain from the outside, has a superabundance of luxuriant stucco work within. In a distinctive step-gabled building across the bridge there's a small **museum** (Easter–Sept Mon–Sat 10am–4.30pm, Sun 2–4.30pm). The **VVV** is housed in the leaning Speeltoren on Kleine Kerkstraat (April–Oct Mon–Fri 10am–12.30am/1.30–5pm, Sat noon–5pm; Oct–March Mon–Sat 10.30am–noon; ☎02993/71727), but there's no great reason to bother them unless you're staying.

West Friesland: Hoorn, Enkhuizen and Medemblik

A little way north of Edam, the Ijsselmeer shore curves east to form the jutting claw of land that makes up an area known as **West Friesland**, whose two main towns – Hoorn and Enkhuizen – can be visited either as day trips from Amsterdam (both are connected by twice-hourly train), or, more interestingly, as overnight stops on the way across the Afsluitdijk into Friesland proper. West Friesland is these days not actually a part of Friesland at all, but was one of the three Frisian districts recognised by Charlemagne and at one time boasted its own regional council, whose authority extended as far away as Alkmaar and Purmerend. The area clings jealously to its supposedly separate identity from the rest of North Holland, though it's hardly very different – the same flat polder landscapes, punctured by farmhouses and the odd windmill, that you see throughout the rest of the province. However, as long as the Markerwaard is never reclaimed, Hoorn and Enkhuizen are the best, and most appealing, examples of old Zuider Zee ports you'll find.

Hoorn

HOORN, the ancient capital of West Friesland, "rises from the sea like an enchanted city of the east, with its spires and its harbour tower beautifully unreal". So wrote the English travel writer E.V. Lucas in 1905, and the town is still very much a place you should either arrive at or leave by sea – though you probably won't get the chance to do either. During the seventeenth century this was one of the richest of the Dutch ports, referred to by the poet Vondel as the trumpet and capital of the Zuider Zee, handling the important Baltic trade and that of the Dutch colonies. The Dutch East India Company was run from here, Tasman went off to "discover" Tasmania and New Zealand, and in 1616 William Schouten sailed out to navigate a passage around South America, calling its tip "Cape Hoorn" after his native town. The harbour silted up in the eighteenth century, however, stemming trade and gradually turning Hoorn into one of the so-called "dead cities" of the Zuider Zee – a process completed with the creation of the Ijsselmeer.

The Town

Not surprisingly, Hoorn's former glories are hard to detect in what is today a quiet provincial backwater: the harbour is a yacht marina and the elegant streets and houses, almost entirely surrounded by water, give only the faintest of echoes of the town's balmy seventeenth-century prosperity. The centre is **Rode Steen**, literally "red stone", an unassuming square that used to hold the town scaffold and now focuses on the swashbuckling statue of **J.P. Coen**, founder of the Dutch East Indies Empire and one of the bright lights of the seventeenth century. Coen was a headstrong and determined leader of the Dutch imperial effort, under whom the Far East colonies were consolidated, and rivals, like the English, were fought off. His settling of places like Moluccas and Batavia was something of a personal crusade, and his austere, almost puritanical way of life was in sharp contrast to the wild and unprincipled behaviour of many of his compatriots on the islands.

On one side of Rode Steen stands the early-seventeenth-century **Waag**, designed by Hendrik de Keyser and now a posh restaurant. On the other side, and dominating the square, the **Westfries Museum** (Mon–Fri 11am–5pm, Sat & Sun 2–5pm; f3.50) is Hoorn's most tangible sight, housed in the elaborately gabled former West Friesland government building, and decorated with the coats of arms of the house of Orange-Nassau, West Friesland and the seven major towns of the region. Inside, the museum re-creates – convincingly – the interiors of the time, when Hoorn's power was at its height. Along with any number of unascribed portraits, furniture and ceramics, the walls of the council chamber (room 7) are covered with militia portraits by Jan Rotius, who portrays himself in the painting by the window – he's the figure by the flag on the left – and employs some crafty effects in the other canvases. Walk past the figure in the far right of the central painting and watch his foot change position from left to right as you pass. On the first floor, in room 16, there's a 1632 painting by Jan van Goyen (*Landscape with a Peasant Cart*), and a wooden fireplace carved with tiny scenes showing a whaling expedition – Hoorn was once a whaling port of some importance. Other items of interest include a view of Hoorn painted in 1622, a room containing portraits of various East India Company dignitaries, including one of the severe Coen, while on the top floor are mock-ups of trades and shops of the time, even a prison cell.

There's not all that much of special interest in the rest of Hoorn, but it's a good place to drift around aimlessly, and the old **harbour**, and the canals which lead down to it (follow G. Havensteeg from Rode Steen), is very pretty, the waterfront lined with gabled houses looking out to the stolid **Hoofdtoren**, a defensive gateway from 1532. On the other side of Rode Steen, on Kerkstraat, the **St Jans**

Gasthuis puts on temporary exhibitions for the Westfries Museum, a delightful building with a so-called trap-gable, tapering to a single window and built at an angle to the main body. Opposite, the Grote Kerk is a nineteenth-century church since converted into apartments. Back towards the station, the **Noorderkerk** on Kleine Noord is a fifteenth-century church that wouldn't be of much interest but for its small model showing Hoorn in 1650, together with an audiovisual display on the history of the city (May 14–Sept 30 daily 11am–5pm).

Practical details

Hoorn's **railway station** is on the northern edge of town, about ten minutes' walk from the centre and the **VVV**, which occupies the leaning former town hall at Nieuwstraat 23 (Sept–June Mon 1.30–5pm, Tues–Fri 10am–12.30pm & 1.30–5pm, Sat 10am–2pm; July & Aug Mon 1–6pm, Tues–Sat 10am–6pm; ☎02290/18342). They have maps of the town and can help out with **rooms** for f22.50–30 a head. Of Hoorn's **hotels**, the cheapest are *De Magneet*, close to the harbour at Kleine Oost 5–7 (☎02290/15021), and *De Posthoorn*, Breed 25–27 (☎02290/14057), both of which have doubles from about f80. As for **eating**, *Sweet Dreams* on Rode Steen is a good place for lunch, and couldn't be more central, with omelettes for about f9 and Mexican dishes for f15 – though it closes at 9pm. Later on there's *Isola Bella*, Grote Oost 65, five minutes from Rode Steen, which has pizza and pasta for f10–15, or *Het Witte Paard*, by the Grote Kerk at Lange Kerkstraat 27, which has Dutch food and vegetarian dishes for f15–25, or lighter meals for around f8. There are also a number of bars and restaurants grouped around the harbour.

Between May and September, Hoorn is the starting-point of **steam train services** to Medemblik. These run regularly from the railway station between 10am and 6pm, and can be a nice way of getting to the town if you have kids – journey time is one hour. Outside summer, if you want to get from Hoorn to Medemblik, catch express bus #139, which takes about 25 minutes. For the full picture see "Travel Details".

Enkhuizen

Another "dead city", though much smaller than Hoorn, **ENKHUIZEN**, twenty minutes by train further east, was also an important port during the seventeenth century, with the largest herring fleet in the country. However, it too declined at the end of the seventeenth century and the town now offers much the same sort of attractions as Hoorn, retaining its broad mast-spattered harbours and peaceful canals. It also has a genuinely major attraction in the Zuider Zee Museum, which brings coachloads of tourists up here during the summer to experience what is a very deliberate attempt to capture the lifestyle that existed here when the town was still a flourishing port – and which was destroyed once and for all with the building of the Afsluitdijk. Enkhuizen is also a good place to visit for its summer ferry connections to Stavoren and Urk across the Ijsselmeer.

The Town ... and the Zuider Zee Museum

A few hundred metres from the two main harbours, **Westerstraat** is Enkhuizen's main spine, a busy pedestrianised street that is home to most of the town's shops and restaurants. At one end, the **Westerkerk** is an early fifteenth-century Gothic church with an odd wooden belfry, added in 1519. A right turn from here leads into a residential part of town, very pretty, with its canals crossed by white-painted footbridges. The other end of Westerstraat is marginally more monumental, zeroing in on the mid-sixteenth-century **Waag** on Kaasmarkt, which houses a small local **museum** (Tues–Sat 10am–noon & 2–5pm, Sun 2–5pm; f1.30), and, nearby, the solid classically styled mid-seventeenth-century **Stadhuis** – behind which the dangerously leaning **Gevangenis** was once the town prison. This is closed to the public, but a peek through its barred windows gives some idea of the bleakness of conditions for the average prisoner in those days, most of the main fittings still being in place.

Close by here, along the waterfront at Wierdijk 18, the indoor section of the Zuider Zee Museum, the **Binnenmuseum**, is closed for restoration until the middle of 1991, by which time its collection of fishing vessels and equipment, and Zuizer Zee arts and crafts, will have been spruced up and will hopefully be displayed in bright new surroundings. Exhibits include regional costumes and painted furniture from Hindeloopen (see Chapter Four), an ice-cutting boat from Urk, once charged with the responsibility of keeping the shipping lanes open between the island and the port of Kampen, displays of sail- and rope-making implements – and much else besides.

Even when it was open, most people gave the Binnenmuseum a miss and made straight for the **Buitenmuseum** on the far side of the harbour (early April–end Oct daily 10am–5pm; f9, children f7), where buildings have actually been transported from 39 different locations to form a period portrayal of the vanished way of life around the Zuider Zee in a mock-up of numerous towns and villages. The only way to get there is by boat, either from the railway station, or, if you're driving, from the museum parking area by the end of the Lelystad road. Once there, you can either tour the museum by way of the free hourly guided tours, or – rather nicer – simply wander around taking it all in at your own pace.

Close by the ferry jetty there's a series of lime kilns, conspicuous by their tall chimneys, from which a path takes you through the best of the museum's many intriguing corners. A little way beyond the kilns is a line of cottages from Monnickendam, nearby which there's an information centre. Further on, a cottage from Hindeloopen doubles up as a restaurant. Inevitably, fishing is a dominant theme in the museum: there is an exhibition in one house describing the trauma of three fishermen who survived three weeks floating on a small block of ice, and there are any number of buildings that were formerly devoted to the fishing industry – the fish auction house from Volendam, curing and salting sheds, and several modest, precisely furnished fishermen's houses. Other trades are represented by way of a baker's shop from Hoorn, a grocer's from Harderwijk, a cheese warehouse (also a restaurant), and a tannery consisting of two huge masts between which sheets of leather were hung to dry. It all sounds rather kitsch, and in a way it is: there are regular demonstrations of the old ways and crafts, and the exhibition is mounted in such an earnest way as to almost beg criticism. But the attention to detail is very impressive, and the whole thing is never overdone, with the result that many parts of the museum are genuinely picturesque. If you see nothing else in Enkhuizen (and many people don't), you really shouldn't miss it.

Practical details

Trains to Enkhuizen – the end of the line – stop right on the corner of the harbour, close by the main **bus stops** and **ferry jetties**. There's a VVV office in the railway station (Tues–Sat 10am–5pm; ☎02280/13164) which has free maps but can't help with much else. From here it's a five- to ten-minute walk to Westerstraat and the centre of the small town. If you're staying, the cheapest **hotel** is *Het Wapen van Enkhuizen*, conveniently located close to the Zuider Zee museums and the harbours at Breedstraat 59 (☎02280/13434), which has double rooms for around f80 – though apart from camping that's about it on the budget accommodation front. For **campers**, there are two sites handily located on the northern side of town: closest is the *Enkhuizer Zand* on the far side of the Zuider Zee Museum at Kooizandweg 4; there's also *De Vest* – follow Vijzelstraat north off Westerstraat, continue on down Noorderweg and take a left by the old town ramparts.

Restaurants in Enkhuizen tend to be expensive. *'t Shoutwje*, Westerstraat 98, is less pricey than most and has daily specials, but the food is only average; *Holle Bolle Gijs*, on the waterfront of the outer harbour, has main meals for f17 and up, and cheaper lunch dishes; and there's also a good **bar** which serves food in the stout Dromedaris tower, also in the outer harbour.

During summer you can travel on from Enkhuizen **by ferry** to Stavoren, Urk or Medemblik. These leave from behind the railway station and go roughly four times daily in high season to Stavoren, three times daily during the same period to Urk; to Medemblik, boats run regularly between 11am and 3pm. To Stavoren and Urk, reckon on paying around f9 one-way, plus f5 or so for a bike. For more, see "Travel Details".

Medemblik, the Wieringermeer polder . . . and into Friesland

Just a few miles up the coast from Enkhuizen, **MEDEMBLIK** is one of the most ancient towns in Holland, a seat of pagan kings until the seventh century, though there's not much to entice you there nowadays. The only sign of Medemblik's ancient beginnings is the **Kasteel Radboud**, named after the most famous of the town's kings, a much-restored thirteenth-century fortress that sits by the harbour – though you can't actually go in. The old railway station, where the summer steam train draws in, houses a **steam train museum** (May–June & Sept–Oct Wed–Sat 10am–5pm, Sun noon–5pm; July & Aug Tues–Sun 10am–5pm, Sun noon–5pm; f4), with an assembly of ancient steam engines in a former pumping station. Otherwise most people come to Medemblik for its sailing interest, the harbour busy throughout summer with the masts of visiting and resident yachtspeople.

North of Medemblik, the **Wieringermeer Polder** was the first of the Zuider Zee polders, created in the 1920s when the former island of Wieringen was connected to the mainland and the area behind it reclaimed. During their occupation, and only three weeks before their surrender, the Germans flooded the area, boasting they could return Holland to the sea if they wished. After the war it was drained again, leaving a barren, treeless terrain that had to be totally replanted. Almost forty years later, it's virtually back to normal, a familiar polder landscape of flat, geometric fields, highlighted by farmhouses and church spires, that most people only pass through on their way to Friesland by way of the Afsluitdijk motorway.

The sluices on this side of the **Afsluitdijk** are known as the **Stevinsluizen**, after Henry Stevin, the seventeenth-century engineer who first had the idea of reclaiming the Zuider Zee. He was, of course, constrained by the lack of technology, but his vision lived on, to be realised by Cornelis Lely in 1932. Close to the North Holland end, there's a statue of Lely by the modern Dutch sculptor Mari Andriessen, though the engineer died before the dike was completed. Further along, at the point where the barrier was finally closed, there's an observation point on which an inscription reads: "A nation that lives is building for its future".

Alkmaar and around

An hour from Amsterdam by train, **ALKMAAR** is typical of small-town Holland, its pretty, partially canalised centre surrounded by water and offering a low-key, undemanding provincialism which makes a pleasant change after the rigours of the big city. It's also a good base for exploring the nearby dunes and beaches, or even the towns of West Friesland.

Alkmaar is probably best known for its **cheese market**, an ancient affair which these days ranks as one of the most extravagant tourist spectacles in Holland. Cheese has been sold on the main square here since the 1300s, and although no serious buying goes on here now, it's an institution that continues to draw crowds – though nowadays they're primarily tourists. If you do want to see it (it's held every Friday morning, mid-April to Sept), be sure to get there early, as by the 10am opening the crowds are already thick. The ceremony starts with the buyers sniffing, crumbling and finally tasting each cheese, followed by heated bartering. Once a deal has been concluded, the cheeses – golden discs of Gouda mainly, laid out in rows and piles on the square – are borne away on ornamental carriers by four groups of porters, for weighing. Payment, tradition has it, takes place in the cafés around the square.

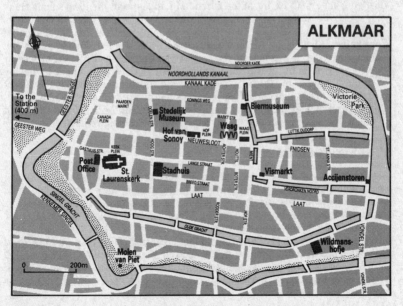

The Town

Even if you've only come for the cheese market, it's a good idea to see something of the rest of the town before you leave. On the main square, the **Waag** was origi-nally a chapel dedicated to the Holy Ghost, but was converted, and given its magnificent east gable, shortly after the town's famous victory against the Spanish in 1573, when its citizens withstood a long siege by Frederick of Toledo – a victory which marked the beginning of the end for the Spaniards. Nowadays the Waag houses the **VVV** (see below) and the **Kaasmuseum** (April–Oct Mon–Sat 10am–4pm, Fri 9am–4pm; f2), which has displays on the history of cheese and cheese-making equipment and suchlike. Across the other side of the square, the **Biermuseum de Boom**, Houttil 1 (Tues–Sat 10am–4pm, Sun 1–5pm, reduced times between Nov and April; f2), is housed in the building of the old De Boom brewery, and has displays tracing the brewing process from the malting to bottling stage, aided by authentic props from this and other breweries the world over. There's lots of technical equipment, enlivened by mannikins and empty bottles from once innumerable Dutch brewers – though few, curiously, from De Boom itself. It's an engaging little museum, lovingly put together by enthusiasts; it also has a top floor shop in which you can buy a huge range of beers and asso-ciated merchandise, as well as a downstairs bar serving some eighty varieties of Dutch beer.

The **Stedelijk Museum**, (March–Dec Tues–Sat 10am–5pm, Sun 1–5pm; f2), on the other side of the town centre in Doelenstraat displays pictures and plans of the siege of 1573, along with a *Holy Family* by Honthorst and portraits by Maerten van Heemskerk and Caesar van Everdingen, the latter a local and very minor seventeenth-century figure who worked in the Mannerist style of the Haarlem painters. Close by, at the far end of **Langestraat**, the town's main shop-ping street, the **St Laurenskerk**, a Gothic church of the later fifteenth century, is worth looking into for its huge organ, commissioned at the suggestion of Constantijn Huygens by Maria Tesselschade, local resident and friend of the Golden Age elite. It was designed by Jacob van Campen and painted by Caesar van Everdingen. In the apse is the tomb of Count Floris V, penultimate in the line of medieval counts of North Holland, who did much to establish the indepen-dence of the towns hereabouts but who was murdered by nobles in 1296 (p.89). On Langestraat itself the only notable building is the **Stadhuis**, a florid affair, half of which (the eastern side and tower) dates from the early sixteenth century.

Practical details

Alkmaar's **railway station** is about ten minutes' walk west of the centre of town on Stationsstraat; to get to the centre from the station, turn right outside, then left, and follow the road for five minutes to the St Laurenskerk. The **VVV** is five minutes on from here, housed in the Waag on Waagplein (Mon–Wed 9am–5.30pm, Thurs & Fri 9am–6pm, Sat 9am–5pm; ☎072/11 42 84). They have **private rooms** for f25 per person, including breakfast; failing that, *De Nachtegaal* is the cheapest and most central **hotel**, opposite the town hall at Langestraat 100 (☎072/40 14 14), with reasonable double rooms, without bath, from about f85. If you're **camping**, there's a site northwest of the town centre; take bus #168 or #169 from the railway station.

There are quite a few decent places to eat. *Jelle's Eethuisje*, between Laat and Oude Gracht at Ridderstraat 26, is good for light lunches and cheap evening meals; full menus go for around f14. *Ikan Mas*, one of several restaurants in the old part of town at Fnidsen 101–103, is an OK Indonesian that does a reasonable *rijstaffel* for under f30 a head, while *Rose's Cantina*, next door but one, serves Tex-Mex dishes for about f18. For splurges, try *Bistro Wladimir* at Waagplein 36, which offers French-Dutch food in an intimate atmosphere for f25–30. **Drinking**, too, is well catered for. There are two main groupings of bars: one on Waagplein itself, the other on the nearby canal of Verdronken Noord, by the old Vismarkt. Of the former, *De Kaasbeurs* is a lively place during the day but closes in the early evening; *Café Corridor*, virtually next door, is a lively hangout that plays loud music late into the night and has a small dancefloor at the back. On Verdronken Noord, *De Pilaren* is also noisy, though catering to a slightly older crowd; *Café Stapper*, next door, is a good refuge if the music gets too much. Across the water by the Vismarkt, *The String* is a loud, amicable bar which has weekly live bands and the rest of the time plays records from its own, vast collection.

If you just want to have a quick look around Alkmaar after the cheese market, *Voltheus Cruises*, Kanaalkade 62, close to the Waag, offer **boat trips** around the town during summer, lasting forty minutes and costing f5 per person.

Around Alkmaar – and points north

The seaside close to Alkmaar is the area's best feature and, if the weather is warm, it's a good place to cool off after the crush of the cheese market. Bus #168 runs out to **BERGEN**, a cheerful village that has been something of a retreat for artists since the Expressionist Bergen School of the early twentieth century worked here. There are a number of galleries around the village, including the **KCB** gallery next door to the VVV. Bergen also has a small collection in the **Sterkenhuis Museum** on Oude Prinsweg, which contains documentation on the defeat of the Duke of York here in 1799, along with period rooms and old costumes. There's a permanent exhibition of Bergen School paintings on display at the **Smithuizen Museum**, Van Renesselaan 42 in CASTRICUM, to the south of Alkmaar (phone first for an appointment).

Alkmaar is also centre of one of North Holland's more major bulb-growing areas, and there's a **museum** devoted to bulb cultivation south of the town in **LIMMEN**, with exhibits on two centuries of bulb-growing in Holland (Dusseldorpweg 64; mid-April to mid-Sept Mon–Tues 9am–noon & 2–4pm, Fri 9am–noon; free). Closer to Alkmaar, **HEILOO** is also important for bulbs, and has a summer exhibition of flowers and plants in its **Hortus Bulborum** – fair compensation if you missed the Keukenhof.

Bus #168 runs on from Bergen to **BERGEN-AAN-ZEE**, a bleak place in itself but with access to some strikingly untouched dunes and beach. About 3km south, **EGMOND-AAN-ZEE** (also directly accessible from Alkmaar) is a little larger but not much more attractive, though it also has huge expanses of sand. A short way inland across the dunes, in **EGMOND-AAN-DE-HOEF**, you can see the remains of the castle of the counts of North Holland, destroyed in 1574. Egmond is also an entry point of the **Noordhollands Duinreservaart**, an area of woods and dunes that stretches south beyond Castricum and holds a couple of campsites and any number of cycle paths, not to mention the superb beach.

The coast north of Bergen, from CAMPERDUIN to PETTEN, has no dunes, and the sea is kept at bay by means of a 4.5km-long **dike** – something you can learn more about at the **"de dijk te kijk"** (the dike on show) exhibition near Hondsbossche Zeewering, which has old maps, photos and drawings illustrating the building of the defence.

SCHAGEN, inland from Petten, draws visitors for its summer market, held every Thursday morning between June and August, when the small town centre is entirely taken over by stalls. Twenty minutes further north by train, **DEN HELDER** is a town of around 60,000, though it was little more than a fishing village until 1811, when Napoleon, capitalising on its strategic position at the very tip of North Holland, fortified it as a naval base. It's still the principal home of the Dutch navy, though otherwise not a place of very much interest, its centre an uninspiring muddle of modern architecture prefacing a seedier old quarter down near the harbour. The only reason to come here at all is to take one of the plentiful ferries across the water to the island of Texel. If this is what you are doing, take bus #3 direct from the railway station to the harbour and miss out the town altogether.

Texel

The largest of the islands of the Wadden Sea – and the easiest to get to – **TEXEL** is a lush, green thumb of land, speckled with small towns and lined on its western side by large areas of dune and vast beaches. Much of it has actually been reclaimed from the sea, and, until the draining of its main polder on the northeastern side of the island during the nineteenth century, it was shaped quite differently, the dunes providing a backbone to a much less even expanse of farmland. It's an incredibly pretty island, and very diverse – something borne out by the crowds that congregate here during the summer months. When the weather's hot, Texel is far from empty.

Ferries leave for Texel from Den Helder roughly every hour all year round. The journey takes twenty minutes and costs f9.50 per person, plus f42 for a car, f4.75 if you're taking a bicycle across. For further information call ☎02220/19441.

Around the island

Ferries from the mainland drop you in the middle of nowhere, though there are generally onward buses to **DEN BURG**, the main town – no more than a large village really, but home to the island's principal **VVV** office, located on the shady central square of Groenplaats (Mon–Fri 9am–6pm, Sat 9am–5pm; ☎02220/14741). Here you can book **private accommodation** throughout the island for between f22.50 and f30 per person. The cheapest **hotel** in Den Burg is *'t Koogerend*, Kogerstraat 94 (☎02220/13301), which has doubles starting at about f60. There are also two **youth hostels** on either side of Den Burg on the roads to De Koog and Oudeschild – one called *Panorama* at Schansweg 7 (☎02220/2197), the other, *De Eyercoogh*, at Pontweg 106 (☎02220/2907). As for sights, there's not much to see in Den Burg beyond a small **museum** of local history, but it is a good place to hire **bikes** – much the best way to get around the island; try *Zegel*, Parkstraat 16. And it makes a decent base for seeing the rest of Texel. The VVV has booklets detailing good cycling routes, as well as the best places to view the

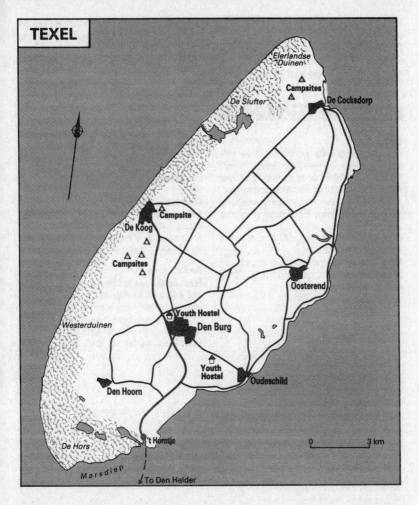

island's many **bird colonies**, protected in sanctuaries right across Texel (the island is one of the most important breeding grounds in Europe). Though you can see them well enough from a distance, you may want to get closer – in which case you need permission from the VVV.

As regards other villages, a little way southeast of Den Burg, **OUDESCHILD** is worth a quick look for its **Beachcombers Museum** (Tues–Sat 10am–5pm; f2.50), a fascinating collection of marine junk recovered from offshore wrecks – everything from aeroplane engines to messages in bottles. Otherwise, in the opposite direction, **DE KOOG**, halfway up the western coast of Texel, is the island's main resort. It's a very crowded place throughout the summer, with campsites galore dotted all over the surrounding area, many restaurants and hotels, as well as a nature centre, **Ecomare**, with a small natural history museum.

In the southern part of the island, **DEN HOORN** is a tiny village surrounded by bulbfields that's handy for some very remote spots, including a nudist beach to the southwest. North of De Koog, the **De Slufter** nature reserve feels similarly distanced from the modern world, the scrubby dunes meeting massive stretches of sand in an almost frighteningly windswept environment.

travel details

Trains

From Amsterdam CS to Haarlem (4 an hour; 15min); Hilversum (every 2 hours; 30min); Zaandam (4 an hour; 10min); Alkmaar (2 an hour; 30min); Castricum (2 an hour; 30min); Schagen (2 an hour; 55min); Purmerend/Hoorn/Enkhuizen (2 an hour; 23/35/55min); Den Helder (2 an hour; 1hr).

From Haarlem to Zaandvoort (2 an hour; 10min); Alkmaar (2 an hour; 25min).

From Alkmaar to Hoorn (2 an hour; 25min).

From Hilversum to Utrecht (3 an hour; 20min); Amersfoort (2 an hour; 15min).

Buses

From Amsterdam to Muiden/Naarden (*CN* bus #136, #137 or #138, half-hourly; 40min/55min).

From Muiden to Naarden (*CN* bus #136 or #138; 30min).

From Edam to Hoorn (*NZH* bus #114; 25min).

From Hoorn to Medemblik (*NZH* bus #139, #140, #141; 25–45min).

From Alkmaar to Harlingen/Leeuwarden (hourly; 1hr 50min/2hr 30min).

Ferries

From Enkhuizen to Stavoren (May–July & end Aug–mid Sept 3 daily, July & Aug 4 daily; 1hr 20min); Urk (May–July & end Aug to mid-Sept 2 daily, July & Aug 3 daily; 1hr 30min); Medemblik (hourly during summer; 1hr 15min).

From Den Helder to Texel (hourly; 20min).

CHAPTER THREE

SOUTH HOLLAND AND UTRECHT

S outh Holland is the most densely populated province of The Netherlands, with a string of towns and cities that make up most of the **Randstad** or rim-town. Careful urban planning has stopped this from becoming an amorphous conurbation, however, and each has a pronounced identity – from the refined tranquillity of **The Hague** to the seedy low-life of **Rotterdam**'s docklands. All the towns have good museums and galleries; some, like The Hague's **Mauritshuis**, Leiden's **Van Oudheden museum** and Rotterdam's **Boymans-van Beuningen**, outstanding. Since it too now forms part of the Randstad, **Utrecht** is included here, again a city rich in galleries.

Historically, South Holland is part of what was simply **Holland**, the richest and most influential province in the country. Throughout the Golden Age Holland was far and away dominant in the political, social and cultural life of the Republic, overshadowing its neighbours, whose economies suffered as a result of Holland's success. There are constant reminders of this pre-eminence in the buildings of this region: elaborate town halls proclaim civic importance and even the usually sombre Calvinist churches allow themselves little excesses – the later windows of Gouda's Janskerk a case in point. Many of the great painters either came from or worked here, too – Rembrandt, Vermeer, Jan Steen – a tradition that continued into the nineteenth century with the paintings of the Hague School. Outside of the coastal strip of cities, the countryside around the ancient port of **Dordrecht** is of most interest, featuring the windmills of the Kinderdijk, the Biesbosch reed forest and, around **Gouda**, the rural charms of the tidy town of **Oudewater**.

Uniformly flat, the countryside is brightened only by rainbow flashes of bulb-fields. Travelling around is never a problem: none of South Holland's towns are more than 20km apart, and they're linked by a fast and efficient rail network with buses as a cheap alternative.

Leiden and around

The home of Holland's most prestigious university, **LEIDEN** has an academic air. Like Haarlem to the north, you get the feeling it regards itself as separate from, and independent of, Amsterdam – which is fair enough. There's enough here to justify at least a day trip, and the town's energy, derived largely from its students, strongly counters the myth that there's nothing worth experiencing outside the capital. Leiden's museums, too, are varied and comprehensive enough to merit a visit in themselves – though be selective. The town's real charm lies in the peace and prettiness of its gabled streets and canals.

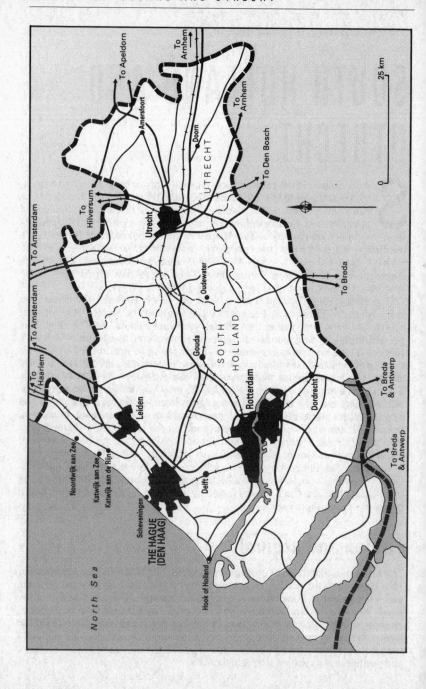

The university was a present from William the Silent, a reward for Leiden's enduring (like Haarlem and Alkmaar) a year-long siege by the Spanish. The town emerged victorious on October 3, 1574, when William cut through the dykes around the city and sailed in with his fleet for a dramatic eleventh-hour rescue. This event is still commemorated with an annual fair, fireworks and the consumption of two traditional dishes: herring and white bread, which the fleet was supposed to have brought with them, and *hutspot*, or stew – a cauldron of which was apparently found simmering in the abandoned Spanish camp.

> The Leiden area telephone code is ☎071

Arrival, information and accommodation

Leiden's **railway and bus stations** are situated on the northwest edge of town, about ten minutes' walk from the centre. The VVV is opposite at Stationsplein 210 (Mon–Fri 9am–5.30pm, Sat 9am–4pm; ☎14 68 46); they have maps and various leaflets and can advise on **accommodation** or make **room** bookings in private homes for f30–35 a person. Other than that, Leiden is fairly short on **hotel** space for a town of its size, and there are no special bargains. The *De Ceder*, out beyond the station at Rijnsburgerweg 80 (☎17 59 03), is about the least expensive option at f75 up for a double; turn left outside the station and left again under the rail tracks. On the whole, though, accommodation is cheaper in the seaside resorts of Katwijk and Noordwijk (p.114). Of the two, Katwijk is the more pleasant place to stay, with several hotels and pensions along its seafront Boulevard; try *Het Anker*, at Boulevard 129 (☎18/13890), or the *Seahorse*, Boulevard 14 (☎01718/15921), both of which have rooms starting at about f30 per person. The nearest **youth hostel** is in Noordwijk, at Langevelderlaan 45 (☎02523/72920) – take bus #40 or #42 from opposite the station. If you're **camping**, the closest large site is the *Koningshof* in Rinjsburg, north of Leiden; again take bus #40: otherwise, Noordwijk has several campsites, Katwijk one.

The Town

Leiden's most appealing quarter is that bordered by Witte Singel and Breestraat, focusing on Rapenburg, a peaceful area of narrow pedestrian streets and canals. Here, at Rapenburg 28, is perhaps the city's best-known attraction, the **Rijksmuseum Van Oudheden** (Tues–Sat 10am–5pm, Sun 1–5pm; f3.50, children f2) – Holland's principal archaeological museum, with a huge collection. You can see one of its major exhibits, the *Temple of Taffeh*, for free. Situated in a courtyard in front of the museum entrance, this was a gift from the Egyptian government in gratitude for the Dutch part in the 1960s UNESCO excavations in Abyssinia (Ethiopia), which succeeded in uncovering submerged Nubian monuments. Dating back to the first century AD, the temple was adapted in the fourth century to the worship of Isis, eventually being sanctified as a Christian church 400 years later. The Egyptians placed very firm conditions on their legacy: no one should have to pay to see it, and the temperature and humidity must be carefully regulated, with the lights overhead simulating the passage – and shadow – of the sun.

Inside the museum proper, the first exhibit is the remains of a temple to Nehellania – a goddess of seamen – which was uncovered in Zeeland. Next come classical Greek and Roman sculpture, leading chronologically through Hellenistic works to busts, statues and friezes of Imperial Rome. The best collection, though, is the Egyptian, beginning with wall reliefs, statues and sarcophagi from tombs and temples and continuing in the rooms immediately above with a set of mummies and sarcophagi as complete as you're likely to see outside Egypt. The *Three Figures of Maya*, to name just one exhibit, are exceptionally well preserved. The second floor is specifically Dutch: an archaeological history of the country, from prehistoric, Roman and medieval times, that is, perhaps inevitably, less interesting than the rest of the museum.

Further along Rapenburg, at no. 73, the original home of the **university** still stands, part of which is open as a **museum** (Wed–Fri 1–5pm; free) that details its history. Through the courtyard, the **Hortus Botanicus** gardens are a lovely spot, lushly planted and subtly landscaped across to the Witte Singel canal. Planted in 1587, they are supposedly among the oldest botanical gardens in Europe, a mixture of carefully tended beds of shrubs and hothouses full of tropical foliage. Leave by the exit off to the left, across the canal, where a red door hides a reconstruction of the original garden, the **Clusiustuin**, named after the botanist who first brought tulips to Holland.

Cross Rapenburg from the university museum, and you're in the network of narrow streets that constituted the medieval town, converging on a central square and the **Pieterskerk** (daily 1.30–4pm; free), the town's principal church. This is deconsecrated now, used for exhibitions, concerts and a Saturday antique market, and it has an empty warehouse-like feel. But among the fixtures that remain are a simple and beautiful Renaissance rood screen in the choir, and a host of memorials to the sundry notables buried here – among them **John Robinson**, leader of the Pilgrim Fathers.

Robinson lived in a house on the site of what is now the **Jan Pesijn Hofje** at Pieterskerkhof 21. A curate in England at the turn of the seventeenth century, he was suspended from preaching in 1604, later fleeing with his congregation to pursue his Puritan form of worship in the more tolerant atmosphere of Holland. Settling in Leiden, Robinson acted as pastor to growing numbers but still found himself at odds with the establishment. In 1620, a hundred of his followers ("The Pilgrim Fathers") sailed via Plymouth for the freedom and abundance of America, though Robinson died before he could join them; he's buried in the church.

If you want to find out more, stroll down to the **Leiden Pilgrim Collection** at Vliet 45 (Mon–Fri 9.30am–4.30pm; free), part of the city archives and a mine of information on Robinson's group during their stay in Leiden. Otherwise, continue east onto **Breestraat**, which marks the edge of Leiden's commercial centre, flanked by the long, ornate Renaissance front of the late sixteenth-century **Stadhuis**, the only part of the building to survive a fire in 1929. Behind, the rivers which cut Leiden into islands converge at the busiest point in town, the site of a vigorous Wednesday and Saturday general **market** which sprawls right over the sequence of bridges into the blandly pedestrian **Haarlemmerstraat** – the town's major shopping street.

The junction of the Oude and Nieuwe Rijn is marked by the mid-seventeenth-century **Waag**, a replacement for a previous Gothic structure, built to a design by Pieter Post and fronted with a naturalistic frieze by Rombout Verhulst. Across the water from here, on the island formed by the split in the two sections of river, the

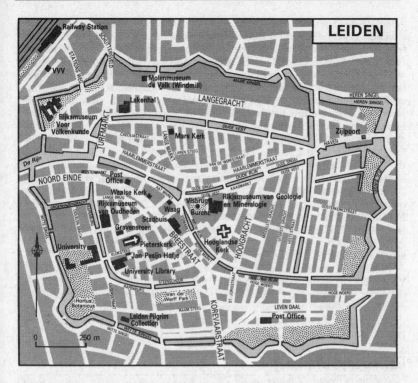

Burcht is the rather ordinary, graffiti-daubed shell of a fort perched on a mound, the battlements of which you can clamber up for a view of Leiden's roofs and towers. The **Hooglandsekerk** (May–Sept Mon 1–3.30pm, Tues–Sat 11am–3.30pm), nearby, is a light, lofty church with a central pillar that features an epitaph to the burgomaster at the time of the 1574 siege, Pieter van der Werff, who became a hero during its final days. When the situation became so desperate that most people were all for giving up, the burgomaster, no doubt remembering the massacre of Haarlem, offered his own body to them as food. His invitation was rejected, but – the story goes – it succeeded in instilling new determination in the flagging citizens.

A short walk away, on Hooglandsekerkgracht, the **Rijksmuseum van Geologie en Mineralogie** (Mon–Fri 10am–5pm, Sun 2–5pm; f3) is one of Leiden's three national museums, though its predictable display of minerals, fossils, bones and skeletons can be missed with a clear conscience. More interesting, across Oude Rijn from here towards the railway station, is the **Museum Boerhaave** (Tues–Sat 10am–5pm; Sun 1–5pm; f3.50), named after a seventeenth-century Leiden surgeon, and a brief but absorbing guide to scientific and medical developments over the last three centuries, with particular reference to Dutch achievements, including some gruesome surgical implements, pickled brains and suchlike. It's due to reopen in 1991 after refurbishment. Five minutes' walk away, Leiden's municipal museum, housed in the old **Lakenhal** (cloth-hall) at Oude

Singel 28–32 (Tues–Sat 10am–5pm, Sun 1–5pm; f2.50), is similarly engaging, with a picture gallery devoted to natives of the town as well as mixed rooms of furniture, tiles, glass and ceramics. Upstairs, the rooms are grouped around the *Grote Pers* (Grand Press), and look much as they would have when Leiden's cloth trade was at its height – though most have since been decorated with paintings or now house temporary exhibitions. Downstairs are sixteenth-century paintings centring around Lucas van Leyden's *Last Judgement* triptych, plus canvases by Jacob van Swanenburgh, the first teacher of the young Rembrandt, by Rembrandt himself and associated Leiden painters – among them Jan Lievens (with whom he shared a studio), Gerrit Dou (who initiated the Leiden tradition of small, minutely finished pictures), and the van Mieris brothers. There's also a painting depicting the sixteenth-century siege that shows the heroic van der Werff in full flow.

Around the corner on Molenwerf, the **Molenmuseum de Valk**, 2e Binnenvestgracht 1 (Tues–Sat 10am–5pm, Sun 1–5pm; f3), is a restored grain mill, one of twenty that used to surround Leiden. The downstairs rooms are furnished in simple, period style; upstairs a slide show recounts the history of windmills in Holland, while displays detail their development and showcase their tools and grinding apparatus, all immaculately preserved. An absorbing way to spend an hour, and only five minutes' stroll from the station.

There's one other museum between here and the station, the **Rijksmuseum Voor Volkenkunde** at Steenstraat 1 (Tues–Sat 10am–5pm, Sun 1–5pm; f3.50), the national ethnological museum, which has complete sections on Indonesia and the Dutch colonies, along with reasonable ones on the South Pacific and Far East. However, it gives most other parts of the world a less than thorough showing and is not an essential stop by any means.

Eating and drinking

It's easy to **eat and drink** cheaply in Leiden. The streets around the Pieterskerkhof and the Hoogslandskerk both hold concentrations of bars and restaurants. For lunch, *Noroc*, just off Breestraat on Pieterskerk Choorsteeg, is a pleasant café with a light menu; *Barrera*, opposite the old university building on Rapenburg, is a cosy bar that serves sandwiches. In the evening, the *Eethuisje de Engelenbak*, Lange Mare 38, has Dutch food for f12 upwards; *Eethuis de Trommelaar* is a pleasant and reasonably priced vegetarian restaurant at Apothekersdijk 22; *Eethuis de Stoep*, Oude Rijn 1a, has à la carte dishes from f15 and cheap three-course menus ranging in price from f22.50 to f45 for a very varied selection of food. With more money, you might try *Bistro Malle Jan*, just off Pieterskerkhof at Nieuwesteeg 9, which serves evening meals from around f17.50, and includes a vegetarian dish on its menu. If you want something non-Dutch, *Radja Mas*, on Maarsmansteeg, next door to *Vroom & Dreesman* off Breestraat, is a reasonably priced Indonesian restaurant serving main courses starting at under f10; *Cojico*, at Breestraat 33, is an amiable Mexican restaurant with main dishes for f12–25.

Because of the university Leiden is a good place to buy **books**. *Kooyker*, Breestraat 93, has a marvellous selection of books in English; there's also a decent branch of *De Slegte* at Breestraat 73. Consider also taking a **canal trip** around the city centre. These run from Beestenmarkt during summer and cost f7 per person for an hour-long tour.

Around Leiden: the bulbfields and the coast

Along with Haarlem to the north, Leiden is the best base for seeing something of the Dutch **bulbfields**, which have flourished here since the late sixteenth century when one Carolus Clusius, a Dutch botanist, brought the first tulip bulb over from Asia Minor and watched it prosper on Holland's sandy soil. Although bulbs are grown in North Holland too, the centre of the Dutch bulb-growing industry is the area around Leiden and up towards Haarlem. The flowers are inevitably a major tourist pull, and one of Holland's most lucrative businesses, supporting some 10,000 growers in what is these days a billion-guilder industry. Obviously spring is the best time to see something of the blooms, when the view from the train – which cuts directly through the main growing areas – can be sufficient in itself, the fields divided into stark geometric blocks of pure colour. With your own transport you can take in the full beauty of the bulbfields by way of special routes marked by hexagonal signposts – local VVVs sell pamphlets listing the best vantage points.

THE BRITISH BULBERS: EXPLOITATION AND EXCESS

Behind the dazzling surface of the bulbfields lies the misery of exploitation. Each summer the bulbs need to be packed and labelled, and the core of the workforce for this is around 500 young British men, many of whom come back year after year to work sixteen-hour shifts for wages no Dutch person would look at. Many of the workers are migrant labourers who follow the various harvests throughout Europe, moving on south afterwards for oranges and, later, work in the vineyards. Others simply come for a good time: beer is cheap in Holland, as are soft drugs, which are plentifully – and legally – available. The "bulbers", as they refer to themselves, line up for work at 7.30am and work until the late evening packing and labelling tulip and hyacinth bulbs. The rest of the time they spend drinking in the English bars of Hillegom, Haarlem or Leiden, sleeping in makeshift camps outside the bulb warehouses. Not only are the terms and conditions of the job dire, it is also painful work. The dust from tulip bulbs rots the fingers of the packers, leading to a condition known as "bulb finger" – sometimes fingers become infected and swell up. Hyacinth bulbs are even worse: the dust from them lodges in the skin, causing itching and – again – infection. Bulbers are provided with coats and gloves to protect themselves, but the heat in the warehouses is intense, and most simply don't bother with them. There is a bulb-workers union, the Voedingsbind FNV, but the British aren't members, and employers break every rule in the book each year when they take them on. Apart from the bulb barons, the Dutch see the British as a bizarre subculture during their time here, amazed at their capacities for excessive intake of booze and dope; the Brits, for their part, are unconcerned, playing up to the role of "the crazy English".

Lisse and the Keukenhof Gardens

Should you want to get closer to the flowers, **LISSE**, halfway between Leiden and Haarlem, is the place to look at the best of the Dutch flower industry, home to the **Keukenhof Gardens** (late March–end of May daily 8am–6.30pm; f12.50), the largest flower gardens in the world. The Keukenhof was set up in 1949, designed by a group of prominent bulb growers to convert people to the joys of growing flowers from bulbs in their own gardens. Literally the "kitchen garden", its site is the former estate of a fifteenth-century countess, who used to grow herbs and vegetables for her dining table here – hence the name. Some seven million flowers are on show for their full flowering period, complemented, in case of especially harsh winters, by 5000 square metres of greenhouses holding indoor displays. You could easily spend a whole day here, swooning among the sheer abundance of it all. There are three restaurants in the seventy acres of grounds, and well-marked paths take you right the way through the gardens, which hold daffodils, narcissi and hyacinths in April, and tulips from mid-April until the end of May. Special express buses – #54 – run to the Keukenhof from Leiden bus station twice an hour at ten and forty minutes past each hour, every day including Sunday.

If you can't visit in the spring, the **Bulbdistrict Museum**, also in Lisse at Heereweg 219 (June–March Tues–Sun 1–5pm, Sun 11.30am–5pm; f2.50), offers the history of the bulb business, dating from the time the first tulip was brought over from Turkey – but it's a poor substitute for the real thing.

Aalsmeer and more bulbs

You can see the industry in action in **AALSMEER**, 23km north of Leiden towards Amsterdam, whose flower auction, again the largest in the world, is held daily in a building approximately the size of 75 football pitches (Mon–Fri 7.30–11.30am). The dealing is fast and furious, and the turnover staggering. In an average year around f1.5 billion (about £500 million) worth of plants and flowers are traded here, many of which arrive in high-street florists in Britain the same day.

There are other places, too, with bulbs and flowers, though none as spectacular as the Keukenhof, nor as vibrant as the Aalsmeer auction. The **Frans Roozen nurseries** at Vogelenzangseweg 49 in **VOGELENZANG**, a little way south of Haarlem (April–May Mon–Sun 8am–6pm July–Sept Mon–Fri 9am–5pm; f2), have a show greenhouse displaying blooms. **RIJNSBURG**, just north of Leiden, has a flower parade in early August each year, from Rijnsburg to Leiden and Noordwijk. And there's a similar parade from Haarlem to Noordwijk (see below) at the end of April, culminating with a display of the floats in the town.

The coast: Katwijk and Noordwijk

Like all of the towns in this part of Holland, Leiden has easy access to some fine beaches, though the coastal resorts themselves aren't much to write home about, and unless you're keen to swim the only reason for visiting is for their larger – and cheaper – supply of accommodation and campsites. **KATWIJK-AAN-ZEE**, accessible by bus #31, #32 or #41 from the stop opposite the bus station, is the stock Dutch seaside town, less crowded than Zandvoort and without the pretensions of Scheveningen, but pretty dreary nonetheless – although it does preserve some of the features of an old seaside village in the lines of terraced housing that spread out around the seventeenth-century lighthouse. Its expanse of undeveloped sand dune, though, which stretches along the shore south towards The Hague, is an ideal area for secluded sunbathing. Otherwise its main attraction is the **Katwijk Sluices**, just north of the resort area, beside the main bus route. Completed in 1807, these are a series of gates that regulate the flow of the Oude Rijn as it approaches the sea: around high tide, the gates are closed; when they are opened, the pressure of the accumulated water brushes aside the sand deposited at the mouth of the river by the sea – a simple system that finally determined the course of the Oude Rijn, which for centuries had been continually diverted by the sand deposits, turning the surrounding fields into a giant quagmire.

NOORDWIJK-AAN-ZEE, some 3km up the coast and reachable on bus #40 or #42 from the same stop, is of even less appeal, not much more than a string of grandiose hotel developments built across the undulating sand dunes behind the coast. However, it again offers some excellent stretches of beach – and a flower festival in April (see above).

The Hague and Scheveningen

With its urbane atmosphere, **THE HAGUE** is different from any other Dutch city. Since the sixteenth century it's been Holland's political capital and the focus of national institutions, in a country built on civic independence and munificence. Frequently disregarded until the development of central government in the nineteenth century, The Hague's older buildings are a rather subdued and modest collection with little of Amsterdam's flamboyance. Most of the city's canal houses are demurely classical with an overpowering sense of sedate prosperity. In 1859 Matthew Arnold wrote: "I never saw a city where the well-to-do classes seemed to have given the whole place so much of their own air of wealth, finished cleanliness, and comfort; but I never saw one, either, in which my heart would so have sunk at the thought of living." Things haven't changed much: today's "well-to-do classes", the diplomats in dark Mercedes and multi-national businessmen, ensure that many of the city's hotels and restaurants are firmly in the expense account category, and the nightlife is similarly packaged. But, away from the mediocrity of wealth, The Hague does have cheaper and livelier bars and restaurants – and even its share of restless adolescents hanging around the pizza joints.

The town may be rather drab, but it does have some excellent museums, principally the famed collection of old Dutch masters at the **Mauritshuis**, and more modern works of art at the **Gemeente Museum**.

> The Hague area telephone code, including Scheveningen, is ☎070.

Arriving and staying

The Hague has two **railway stations** – *Den Haag H.S.* (*Hollands Spoor*) and *Den Haag C.S.* (*Centraal Spoor*). Of the two, Den Haag C.S. is the more convenient, sited in the same complex as the **VVV** (Mon–Sat 9am–8pm, Sun 10am–5pm; ☎354 6200) and the bus and tram stations, five minutes' walk east of the town centre. Den Haag H.S. is 1km to the south, and frequent rail services connect the two. The Hague may be the country's third largest city, but almost everything worth seeing is within easy walking distance of Den Haag C.S.; if you intend to use the city's buses and trams, the VVV sells the standard *strippenkaart* and a *dagkaart* – the best bet if you're only here for the day.

Accommodation in The Hague proper is hard to find and/or expensive – you might be better off basing yourself in Scheveningen, twenty minutes' ride away by tram (see below), where rooms are more plentiful and slightly cheaper. If you do want to stay in town, the best bet is to pay the odd guilder and let the VVV arrange somewhere for you to stay – especially as the cheaper pensions are spread out all over the city. Otherwise, there's a cluster of seedy, but reasonably

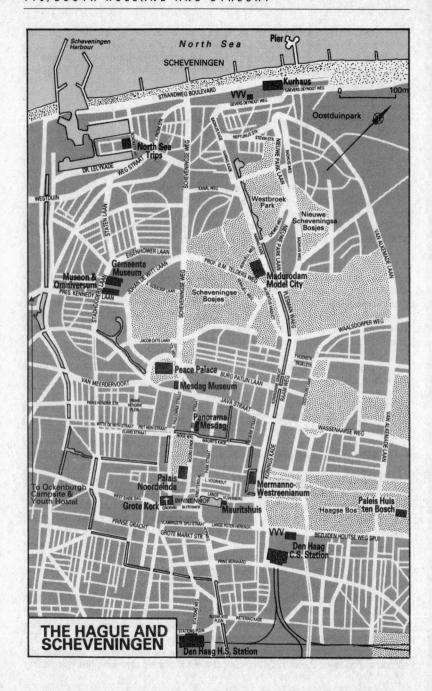

THE HAGUE AND SCHEVENINGEN

priced **hotels** just outside Den Haag H.S. station, with singles at f40–50, doubles from f70 per night: the *Aristo*, Stationsweg 164-6 (☎389 0847); the *Astoria*, Stationsweg 139 (☎384 0401); the *Limburg*, Stationsplein 49 (☎384 0102); and the *Du Commerce*, Stationsplein 64 (☎380 8511). There are also two relatively central **pensions** with doubles at f80 per night, the *Huize Bellevue*, northwest of the centre along Laan Van Meerdervoort, right at Groot Hertoginne, first left on the northern part of Beeklaan at no. 417 (☎360 5552); and the *Minnema*, a short journey north of the centre just east of Koningskade/Raamweg at Dedelstraat 25.

The **youth hostel** *Ockenburgh* (☎397 0011) is at Monsterseweg 4, some 8km to the west of the town centre just behind the beach at Kijkduin (bus #122, #123, #124 from Centraal Station). It's attached to a small budget hotel and adjoins the best and largest **campsite** in the area, *Camping Ockenburgh*, Wijndaelerweg 25 (☎325 2364), bus #4 from the station. Both the youth hostel and the campsite are about ten minutes' walk from the nearest bus stop – ask the driver to put you off. Another solution, if you're visiting between mid-June and the end of August, is to use the student flats in **Delft** as a base; they're only a quarter of an hour away by train (see below).

The City Centre

Right in the centre, and the oldest part of the city, the **Binnenhof** ("inner court") is the home of Holland's two-chamber parliament. Count William II built a castle here in the thirteenth century, and the settlement that grew up around it became known as the "Count's Domain" – *'s Gravenhage*, literally "Count's Hedge" – which is still the city's official name. As the embodiment of central rather than municipal power, the Binnenhof had a chequered history – empty or occupied, feted or ignored – until the nineteenth century when The Hague shared political capital status with Brussels during the uneasy times of the United Kingdom of the Netherlands. Thereafter it became the seat of government, home to an effective legislator. The present rectangular complex is a rather mundane affair, a confusing mixture of shape and style that irritated nineteenth-century Dutch parliamentarians with its obvious lack of prestige.

The best view is from the front, where a small lake – the **Hof Vijver** (Court Pond) – mirrors the attractive symmetry of the front facade. Behind the lake, the Binnenhof is a major tourist attraction, but there's precious little to see except the **Ridderzaal** (Hall of the Knights), a slender-turreted structure used for state occasions. It's been a courtroom, market, and stable, and so repeatedly replaced and renovated that little of the thirteenth-century original remains. An undramatic guided tour of the Ridderzaal and the chambers of parliament (often closed on Mon & Tues) starts regularly from the information office at Binnenhof 8a (Mon–Sat 10am–4pm & July–Aug Sun noon–4pm; f4).

The Mauritshuis collection

To the immediate east of the Binnenhof, the **Royal Picture Gallery Mauritshuis** (Tues–Sat 10am–5pm, Sun 11am–5pm; f6.5) is located in a magnificent seventeenth-century mansion. Generally regarded as one of the best galleries in Europe, it's famous for its extensive range of Flemish and Dutch paintings from the fifteenth to the eighteenth centuries, based on the collection accumulated by Prince William V of Orange (1748–1806). All the major Dutch artists are represented and it's well laid out, with multi-lingual cards in each room providing background notes on all the major canvases. At present the rooms are not numbered and the policy of the museum is (rather awkwardly) to spread the works of many of the key artists through several rooms, rather than place them together. For further detailed information, the museum shop sells an excellent guidebook for f25, or you can join one of the irregular and expensive conducted tours – prices depend on length; ask at reception for times.

The entrance and museum shop are in the **basement** on the east side of the building, together with **Andy Warhol**'s *Queen Beatrix*, a twentieth-century aperitif to the collection above. Heading up the stairs to the **ground floor**, walk back towards the old front doors and enter the room on the left, where **Hans Memling**'s *Portrait of a Man* is a typically observant work, right down to the scar on the nose. Close by, **Rogier van der Weyden**'s *The Lamentation of Christ* is a harrowing picture of death and sorrow, the Christ's head hanging down towards the earth, surrounded by the faces of the mourners, each with a particular expression of anguish and pain. **Quinten Metsys** was the first major artist to work in Antwerp, where he was made a master of the Guild in 1519. An influential figure, the focus of his work was the attempt to imbue his religious pictures with spiritual sensitivity, and his *Descent from the Cross* is a fine example – Christ's suffering face under the weight of the Cross contrasted with the grinning, taunting onlookers behind.

Proceeding in an anticlockwise direction, through a series of rooms on either side of the Italianate dining room, exhibits include two giant allegorical canvases by **Jan Sanders van Hemessen**; **Lucas Cranach the Younger**'s spirited *Man with a Red Beard*; and two works by **Hans Holbein the Younger**, a striking *Portrait of Robert Cheeseman*, where all the materials – the fur collar, the falcon's feathers and the cape – seem to take on the appropriate texture, and his *Portrait of Jane Seymour*, one of several pictures commissioned by Henry VIII, who sent him abroad to paint possible wives. Holbein's vibrant realism was later to land him in hot water: an over-flattering portrait of Anne of Cleves swayed Henry into an unhappy marriage with his "Flanders' Mare" that was to last only six months.

Of a number of paintings by **Adriaen Brouwer**, *Quarrel at a Card Table* and *Inn with Drunken Peasants* are two of the better known, with thick, rough brushstrokes recording contemporary Flemish low-life. Brouwer could approach this subject with some authority, as he spent most of his brief life in either tavern or prison. **Peter Paul Rubens**, the acclaimed painter, draughtsman and diplomat, was a contemporary of Brouwer, though the two could hardly be more dissimilar: Rubens' *Portrait of Isabella Brant*, his first wife, is a typically grand, rather statuesque work, not perhaps as intriguing as *Adam and Eve in Paradise*, a collaboration between Rubens, who painted the figures, and **Jan Brueghel the Elder**, who filled in the dreamlike animals and landscape behind. In the same room are two examples of the work of Rubens' chief assistant, **Anthony van Dyck**, a portrait specialist who found fame at the court of Charles I. His *Pieter Stevens of Antwerp* and *Quinton Simons of Antwerp* are good early examples of his tendency to flatter and ennoble that no doubt helped him into the job. Nearby, and again showing the influence of Rubens, is the robust *Adoration of the Shepherds* by Jacob Jordaens.

On the **first-floor** landing, the broad brush-strokes of **Frans Hals'** *Laughing Boy* are far removed from the restrained style he was forced to adopt in his more familiar paintings of the burghers of Haarlem. **Carel Fabritius**, pupil of Rembrandt and (possibly) the teacher of Vermeer, was killed in a gunpowder

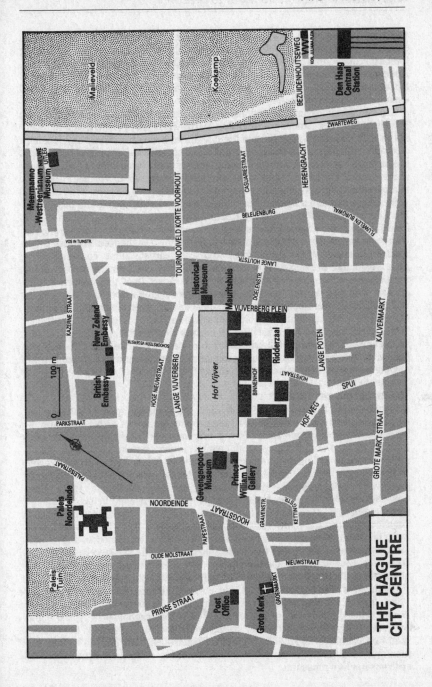

THE HAGUE
CITY CENTRE

Malieveld

Koekamp

BEZUIDENHOUTSEWEG

VVV

KON. JULIANA PLEIN

Den Haag
Centraal
Station

ZWARTEWEG

Meermanno
-Westreenianum
Museum

NIEUWE UITLEG

TOURNOOIVELD KORTE VOORHOUT

CASUARIESTRAAT

BELEIJENBURG

HERENGRACHT

FLUWELEN BURGWAL

VOS IN TUINSTR.

LANGE HOUTSTR.

Historical
Museum

Mauritshuis

VIJVERBERG PLEIN

DOELENSTR.

KAZERNE STRAAT

New Zeland
Embassy

SCHOOLSTEN VOORSTRA.

HOGE NIEUWSTRAAT

LANGE VIJVERBERG

Hof Vijver

Ridderzaal

Binnenhof

HOFSTRAAT

LANGE POTEN

KALVERMARKT

British
Embassy

100 m

0

PARKSTRAAT

HOF WEG

SPUI

PALEISSTRAAT

Paleis
Noordeinde

NOORDEINDE

Gevangenpoort
Museum

Prince
William V
Gallery

HOOGSTRAAT

PAPESTRAAT

GRAVENSTR.

KETTINGSTR.

GROTE MARKT STRAAT

Paleis
Tuin

OUDE MOLSTRAAT

NIEUWSTRAAT

PRINSE STRAAT

Post
Office

Grote Kerk

GROENMARKT

explosion at Delft when he was only 22. Few of his canvases have survived, but an exquisite exception is *The Goldfinch*, a curious, almost impressionistic work, with the bird reduced to a blur of colour. One of his Delft contemporaries was Gerard Houckgeest, who specialised in church interiors, like *The Tomb of William of Orange*, a minutely observed study of exact architectural lines lightened by expanses of white marble.

Off the first-floor landing, on the left at the front of the museum, is the Mauritshuis's most famous painting, **Jan Vermeer's** *View of Delft*, a superb townscape of 1658, with the fine lines of the city drawn beneath a cloudy sky, a patchwork of varying light and shade – though the dispassionate, photographic quality the painting has in reproduction is oddly lacking in the large canvas. In the same room, Gerard Ter Borch's *Lice Hunt* is in striking contrast to Vermeer's detachment, a vignette of seventeenth-century domestic life.

Heading in an anticlockwise direction, other highlights include the busy sticklike figures of the *Winter Scene* by Hendrik Avercamp, the deaf and dumb artist from Kampen, and Paulus Potter's lifelike *Young Bull*, a massive canvas complete with dung and rather frightening testicles. Best known of the **Rembrandts** is the *Anatomy Lesson of Dr Tulp*, from 1632, the artist's first commission in Amsterdam. The peering pose of the "students" who lean over the corpse solved the problem of emphasis falling on the body rather than the subjects of the portrait, who were in fact members of the surgeons' guild. Hopefully Tulp's skills as an anatomist were better than his medical advice, which included the recommendation that his patients drink fifty cups of tea a day.

Dotted throughout the museum are no less than thirteen paintings by **Jan Steen**, including a wonderfully riotous picture carrying the legend *"The way you hear it, is the way you sing it"* – a parable on the young learning bad habits from the old – and a typically salacious *Girl eating Oysters*.

The rest of the city centre

A few metres to the west of the Binnenhof, the **Gevangenpoort**, Buitenhof 33 (Prisoner's Gate Museum; Mon–Fri 10am–5pm, April–Sept also Sat & Sun 1–5pm; tours only; last tour 4pm; f4), was originally part of the city fortifications. Used as a prison until the nineteenth century, it now contains an array of instruments of torture and punishment centred around its Chamber of Horrors. As well as the guillotine blades, racks and gibbets, the old cells are in a good state of preservation – including the *ridderkamer* for the more privileged captive. Here Cornelius de Witt, Burgomaster of Dordrecht, was imprisoned before he and his brother Johan, another staunch Republican and leader of the States of Holland, were dragged out and murdered by an Orangist mob in 1672. The brothers were shot, beheaded and cut into pieces which were then auctioned to the crowd; Johan's tongue is preserved for a macabre posterity in the storerooms of the Gemeente Museum. The Gevangenpoort is understandably popular; join the queue about fifteen minutes before each half-hourly tour to guarantee a place.

Down the street at Buitenhof 35, the **Prince William V Gallery** (Tues–Sun 11am–4pm; f2.50) has paintings by Rembrandt, Jordaens and Paulus Potter among others, but it's more interesting as a reconstruction of a typical eighteenth-century gallery – or "cabinet" as they were known. The fashion then was to sandwich paintings together in a cramped patchwork from floor to ceiling: but though it's faithful to the period, this makes viewing difficult for eyes trained by spacious modern museums.

A five-minute walk away to the west, and easily the best of The Hague's old churches, St Jacobskerk or the **Grote Kerk** (May–Sept Mon–Sat 11am–4pm; f2) is a hall church with an exhilarating sense of breadth and warmly decorated vaulting. The one thing you can't miss, as it's placed where the high altar should be, is the memorial to the unmemorable Admiral Opdam, who was blown up with his ship during the little-remembered naval battle of Lowestoft in 1665. Keep an eye open for the Renaissance pulpit: similar to the one in Delft's Oude Kerk, it has carved panels framing the apostles in false perspective. For the energetic, the **church tower** is occasionally open and provides blustery views over the town.

Back in the centre, **Lange Voorhout** is fringed by an impressive spread of diplomatic mansions and the *Hotel des Indes*, where the ballerina Anna Pavlova died in 1931 and where today you stand the best chance of being flattened by a chauffeur-driven limousine. Just to the east, the **Meermanno-Westreenianum Museum**, Prinsessegracht 30 (Mon–Sat 1–5pm; free), has a small collection of remarkably well-preserved medieval illuminated manuscripts and Bibles; and nearby, the **Hague Historical Museum**, Korte Vijverberg 7 (Tues–Sun noon–4pm; f3), mixes local history with temporary exhibitions on topical issues.

To the immediate west of Lange Voorhout, the sixteenth-century **Palais Noordeinde** (no admission) is one of several royal buildings that lure tourists to this part of town. In 1980, Queen Juliana abdicated in favour of her daughter Beatrix, who proceeded to return the royal residence from the province of Utrecht to The Hague. Despite the queen's attempts to demystify the monarchy, there's no deterring the enthusiasts who fill the expensive "Royal Tours" around the peripheries of the palace and Beatrix's other residence just outside town, the seventeenth-century **Huis ten Bosch** (House in the woods; no entrance).

Much of the rest of the centre is drab and dreary, an apparently unformulated mixture of the stately old and the brashly new (the giant "Babylon" shopping complex by the Centraal Station wins the ugliness award). During the war years the occupying German forces built a V2 launching site just outside the city: as a result it was almost as thoroughly bombed by the RAF as its neighbour Rotterdam had been by the Luftwaffe.

> In July and August, a **museum bus** (daily 10am–4.30pm; every 30min; f2 each trip) plies between all The Hague's main museums. Up-to-date timetables from the VVV.

North of the city centre

Ten minutes' walk north of the centre along Noordeinde, the **Panorama Mesdag**, Zeestraat 65b (Mon–Sat 10am–5pm, Sun noon–5pm; f4), was designed in the late nineteenth century by Hendrik Mesdag, banker turned painter and local citizen become Hague School luminary. His unremarkable seascapes are tinged with an unlikeable bourgeois sentimentality, but there's no denying the achievement of his panorama, a depiction of Scheveningen as it would have appeared in 1881. Completed in four months with help from his wife and the young G.H. Breitner, the painting is so naturalistic that it takes a few moments for the skills of lighting and perspective to become apparent. Five minutes' walk from the Panorama at Laan van Meerdervoort 7f is the house Mesdag bought as a home and gallery. At the time it overlooked one of his favourite subjects, the dunes, the inspiration for much of his work, and today contains the **Mesdag Museum** (Tues–Sat 10am–

5pm, Sun 1–5pm; f3.5). His collection includes a number of Hague School paintings which, like his own work, take the seascapes of the nearby coast as their subject. There are also paintings by Corot, Rousseau, Delacroix and Millet, though none of them represent the artists' best achievements. Perhaps the most interesting exhibits are the florid and distinctive paintings of Antonio Mancini, whose oddly disquieting subjects are reminiscent of Klimt.

The Peace Palace

Round the corner from the Mesdag Museum, framing the Carnegieplein, the **Peace Palace** (Mon–Fri guided tours 10am–noon & 2–4pm; check with the VVV for times of English-speaking tours) is home to the Court of International Justice and, for all the wrong reasons, a monument to the futility of war. Towards the end of the nineteenth century, Tsar Nicholas II called an international conference for the peaceful reconciliation of national problems. The result was the First Hague Peace Conference of 1899 whose purpose was to "help find a lasting peace and, above all, a way of limiting the progressive development of existing arms". This in turn led to the formation of a Permanent Court of Arbitration housed obscurely in The Hague until Andrew Carnegie donated $1.5 million dollars for a new building – the Peace Palace. These honourable aims came to nothing with the mass slaughter of World War I: just as the donations of tapestries, urns, marble and stained glass were arriving from all over the world, so Europe's military commanders were preparing their offensives. Backed by a massive law library, fifteen judges are still in action today, conducting trade matters in English and diplomatic affairs in French. Widely respected and generally considered neutral, their judgements are nevertheless not binding.

The Gemeentemuseum, Museon and Omniversum

North of the Peace Palace, the **Gemeentemuseum**, Stadhouderslaan 41 (Tues–Sun 11am–5pm; f5; bus #4 from Centraal Station), is arguably the best and certainly the most diverse of The Hague's many museums. Designed by H.P. Berlage in the 1930s, its confused and awkward layout doesn't help you find your way around the large and varied collection. To make matters worse, there appears to be no consistent policy about each display's language cards – some rooms are Dutch only, others multi-lingual. However, the musical instruments are outstanding – especially the harpsichords and early pianos – and the selection of Islamic ceramics is extraordinary. The museum's collection of modern art is frustrating, but it does attempt to outline the development of Dutch painting through the Romantic, Hague and Expressionist schools to the De Stijl movement. **Mondrian**, most famous member of the De Stijl group, dominates this part of the gallery: the museum has the world's largest collection of his paintings, though much of it consists of (deservedly) unfamiliar early works painted before he evolved the abstraction of form into geometry and pure colour for which he's best known.

Adjoining the Gemeentemuseum is a modern building that houses the **Museon** (Tues–Fri 10am–5pm, Sat & Sun noon–5pm; f3), a sequence of non-specialist exhibitions of human activities related to the history of the earth. Self-consciously internationalist, it's aimed at school parties, as is the adjoining **Omniversum** or "Space Theatre" (shows on the hour, Tues–Thurs 11am–4pm, Fri–Sun 11am–8pm; f13). A planetarium in all but name, it possesses all the technical gadgetry you'd expect.

The Madurodam Miniature Town

Halfway between The Hague and Scheveningen, the **Madurodam Miniature Town** (daily March–Dec 9am–6pm; June–Aug 9am–11pm; f9.50) is heavily plugged by the tourist authorities, though its origins are more interesting than the trite and expensive present, a copy of a Dutch town on a 1:25 scale. The original money was put up by a J.M.L. Maduro, who wished to establish a memorial to his son who had distinguished himself during the German invasion of 1940, and died in Dachau concentration camp five years later. There's a memorial to him just by the entrance and profits from the Miniature Town are used for general Dutch social and cultural activities.

Eating and drinking

For cheap **food**, there's a cluster of places along Herenstraat, off Plein near the Binnenhof, the best of which is the *De Apendans* at no 13, a no-frills, popular restaurant serving a simple Dutch menu. Other reasonably priced, centrally sited alternatives include good fishy snacks at *Noordzee*, Spuistraat 44; pizzas at *Pinelli*, on the way to the Grote Kerk at Dag. Groenmarkt 31; good quality shoppers' lunches at *Brasserie Renoir* (Mon–Sat 9.30am–6.30pm), at the bottom of Noordeinde, no. 2a; vegetarian meals at *De Dageraad*, just east of Lange Voorhout at Hooikade 4; and more expensive snacks at the *Bodega De Posthoorn*, Lange Voorhout 39a.

The Hague has literally dozens of prestige **restaurants** serving gourmet dishes from all over the world. Try the seafood delights of the *Oesterbar Saur*, or the *Saur* on the first floor up above, at Lange Voorhout 47–53; Italian specialities at *La Liguria*, Noordeinde 97; or fish and French cooking at *Le Gobelet*, Noordeinde 143.

For **bars**, head for the streets to the immediate east of Lange Voorhout, including the quiet canals around Smidswater and Hooikade, where the *De Landeman* and the *Pompernickel* are at Denneweg 48 and 27.

Listings

Bikes Can be hired from either of The Hague's railway stations for f7 a day, plus a f200 deposit.

Bookshop *Boekhandel Plantijn*, Noordeinde 62. Good for art books.

Car hire *Avis*, Theresiastraat 210 (☎385 0698); *Budget*, Juliana van Stolberglaan 214 (☎382 0609); *Europcar* (at the *Hotel Sofitel*), Koningin Julianaplein 35 (☎385 1708).

Dentist 24hr service ☎397 4491.

Embassies Australia, Koninginnegracht 23 (☎64 79 08); Britain, Lange Voorhout 10 (☎64 58 00); Canada, Sophialaan 7 (☎61 41 11); Eire, Dr Kuyperstraat 9 (☎63 09 93); USA, Lange Voorhout 102 (☎62 49 11).

Gay scene There are several gay bars: try *Aquarius*, Herengracht 7a, or *Stairs*, Nieuwe Schoolstraat 11.

Hospital Ambulances ☎322 2111; general medical care ☎345 5300.

Information A free monthly magazine with details of concerts, theatre performances, special events and entertainments in The Hague and environs is available from the VVV.

Jazz records *Jazz Inn*, Groenmarkt 32. A superb jazz record shop.

Markets General: Herman Costerstraat (Mon, Fri & Sat from 8am). Food: Markthof, Gedempte Gracht/Spui (Mon 11am–6pm, Tues–Sat 9am–6pm). Antiques, books and curios: Lange Voorhout (mid-May to Sept Thurs & Sun 9am–9pm); Plein (Oct to mid-May Thurs 9am–9pm).

Pharmacies Evening and weekend opening details ☎345 1000.
Post office Nobelstraat; Prinsenstraat; Kerkplein (Mon–Fri 8.30am–7pm, Sat 9am–noon).

> The **North Sea Jazz Festival**, held every year in mid-July, is The Hague's most
> prestigious event, attracting international media coverage and many of the world's
> most famous musicians. Details of performances are available from the VVV, who
> will also reserve accommodation, which is virtually impossible to find after the festi-
> val has begun.

Scheveningen

Situated on the coast about 4km from the centre of The Hague, the old fishing
port of **SCHEVENINGEN*** has none of its neighbour's businesslike air, enjoying instead its status as Holland's top seaside town, attracting more than nine
million visitors a year to its beach, pier and casino. It's not a particularly attractive
place, but it can make a good alternative base if you're keen to see something of
The Hague, since, not surprisingly, hotels are cheaper and more plentiful. At
certain times of year, too, it's worth a special visit – in mid-June for example,
when the town hosts a massive international **kite festival** that takes over the
beach and much of the town.

Scheveningen was a fashionable resort in the nineteenth century, but faded
after the 1920s; it's currently being redeveloped as an all-year resort. The centre
of town is called **Scheveningen Bad**, grouped around the massive **Kurhaus**
hotel that's the most potent symbol of the town's bygone era. Sadly, it's the only
reminder, the rest of the town centre a rather tacky mix of shopping precinct,
guesthouses and amusement arcades, both around the hotel and along the busy
seafront. Inside, the *Kurhaus* has recently been refurbished and is worth a peek
into its main central hall, which looks much as it would have done in the town's
heyday, richly frescoed, with mermaids and semi-clad maidens cavorting high
above the gathered diners. You can enjoy the atmosphere for the price of a
coffee, or attend one of the classical concerts occasionally held here.

The town **museum** at Neptunusstraat 92 (Tues–Sat 10am–4.30pm; f3) recap-
tures some of the atmosphere of old Scheveningen, with a collection of figures in
nineteenth-century costume, dioramas showing the cramped conditions on board
the primitive fishing boats, and items such as nets and compasses from the boats
themselves. But most people come here for the **beach** – a marvellous strand,
though very crowded in summer, and it's hard to be sure about the condition of
the water. The **pier** isn't especially impressive either, its appendages packed with
the rods of fishermen and various amusements, and you'd do better to either
indulge yourself in the **Wave Pool** recreation centre, complete with a sub-
tropical climate, whirlpools and waterslides, or stroll a little way north to emptier
stretches of beach and dune in the **Oostduinpark**. Otherwise, a kilometre or so
in the opposite direction, Scheveningen's harbour and fishing port still flourish in

---

* One of the difficulties involved in getting to Scheveningen is pronouncing the name.
During World War II, resistance groups tested suspected Nazi infiltrators by getting
them to say "Scheveningen" – an impossible feat for a German-speaker apparently, and
not much easier if you happen to be British.

the more workaday environs of **Scheveningen Haven**: the site of a large container depot and an early morning **fish auction**, by the more northerly of the two docks, at Visafslagweg 1 (Mon–Sat 7–10am) – though this is very much a technical, computerised affair. Boat trips on the **North Sea** (June–Sept daily at 4pm) start from Dr. Lelykade, beside the southern dock.

Practical details: rooms, food and drink

Trams #1, #7 and #9 run from The Hague C.S. to Scheveningen, stopping by the *Kurhaus*; from The Hague H.S., take tram #8. Tram #1 also connects with Delft. If you decide to stay in Scheveningen, the **VVV** at Gevers Deyjnootweg 126 (Mon–Sat 9am–6pm, summer also Sun 10am–5pm) can book **rooms** in private homes for about f30 a head. Failing that there are plenty of **hotels**. Try the *Martin*, Gevers Deyjnootweg 23 (☎355 6047), which has double rooms starting at f90, or, more cheaply, the *Albion* across the road (☎355 7987). Or there's a grouping of hotels on the other side of the *Kurhaus* on the seafront Zeekant, including the "youth hotel" *'t Zeehuys* (☎55 95 85), which charges f16–21 for a bed with breakfast, and the more expensive, and comfortable, *Aquarius*, which charges upwards of f95 for a double. There's another, smaller youth hotel, the *Marion*, at Havenkade 3a (☎354 3501), with rooms for f25 a head. Other cheap options include the *Meyer*, near the town museum at Stevinstraat 64 (☎355 8138), the *Hage*, closer to the sea at Seinpostduin 23 (☎351 4696), and the *El Cid*, Badhuisweg 51 (☎354 6667) – each of which has double rooms for f60–75.

As for **eating**, the *Big Bell*, on the seafront next to the *Kurhaus*, is about the cheapest place to eat in the town centre, serving huge portions of Dutch food for under f20; the *Olympiada*, underneath the *Martin* hotel, is a cosy Greek eatery. In Scheveningen Haven there are a couple of decent waterside fish restaurants, both by the outer harbour: the *Havens* restaurant is simple and inexpensive, the *Mero*, further down towards the sea, is posher and pricier. For evening **drinking**, try the *Kings Arms*, a friendly mock-pub outside the *Kurhaus* on Gevers Deyjnootplein.

Delft

DELFT has considerable charm: gabled red-roofed houses stand beside tree-lined canals, and the pastel colours of the pavements, brickwork and bridges give the town a faded, placid tranquillity – a tranquillity that from spring onwards is systematically destroyed by tourists. They arrive by air-conditioned coachloads and descend to congest the narrow streets, buy an overpriced piece of gift pottery, and photograph the spire of the Nieuwe Kerk. And beneath all the tourists, the gift shops and the tearooms, old Delft itself gets increasingly difficult to find.

Why is Delft so popular? Apart from its prettiness, the obvious answer is **Delftware**, the clunky and monotonous blue-and-white ceramics to which the town gave its name in the seventeenth century. If you've already slogged through the vast collection in Amsterdam's Rijksmuseum it needs no introduction; and though production of the "real" Delftware is down to a trickle, cheap mass-produced copies have found a profitable niche in today's shops. For those sufficiently interested, *De Pocelyn Fles* at Rotterdamsweg 119 runs **tours** of its Delftware factory throughout the day, and the **Huis Lambert van Meerten Museum** at Oude Delft 119 (Tues–Sat 10am–5pm, Sun 1–5pm; f3.50) has a large collection of Delft (and other) tiles.

The other reason for Delft's popularity is the **Vermeer** connection. The artist was born in the town and died here too – leaving a wife, eleven children, and a huge debt to the local baker. He had given the man two pictures as security, and his wife bankrupted herself trying to retrieve them. Only traces remain of the town as depicted in Vermeer's famous *View of Delft*, now in the Mauritshuis in The Hague. To find them, you'll do best on foot – it's not a difficult place to explore. The **Markt** is the best place to start, a central point of reference with the Renaissance Stadhuis at one end and the Nieuwe Kerk at the other. Lined with cafés, restaurants and teenagers blaring disco music on ghetto-blasters, it really gets going with the Thursday general market – not, therefore, the ideal day to visit.

The **Nieuwe Kerk** (April–Oct Mon–Sat 9am–5pm; Nov–May Mon–Fri 10am–noon & 1.30–4pm; f2; tower f3.25 extra) is new only in comparison with the Oude Kerk, as there's been a church on this site since 1381. Most of the original structure, however, was destroyed in the great fire that swept over Delft in 1536, and the remainder in a powder magazine explosion a century later – a disaster, incidentally, which claimed the life of the artist Carel Fabritius, Rembrandt's greatest pupil and (debatably) the teacher of Vermeer. The most striking part of the restoration is in fact the most recent – the 100m spire, replaced in 1872 and from whose summit there's a wonderful view of the town. Unless you're a Dutch monarchist, the church's interior is rather uninspiring: it contains the burial vaults of the Dutch royal family, the most recent addition being Queen Wilhelmina in 1962. Only the Mausoleum of William the Silent grabs your attention, an odd hotchpotch of styles concocted by Hendrik de Keyser, architect also of the Stadhuis opposite.

South of the Stadhuis, signs direct you to the **Koornmarkt**, one of the town's most characteristic seventeenth-century streets. At number 67 is the **Museum Tétar van Elven** (May–Oct Tues–Sat 1–5pm; f2.50, children f1.50), slightly drab in appearance but an authentic restoration of the eighteenth-century patrician house that was the studio and home of Paul Tétar van Elven, a provincial and somewhat forgettable artist/collector. **Wynhaven**, another old canal, leads to Hippolytusburt and the Gothic **Oude Kerk** (April–Oct Mon–Sat noon–4pm; f2), arguably the town's finest building. Simple and unbuttressed, with an unhealthily leaning tower, it's the result of a succession of churches here from the thirteenth to the seventeenth century; the strong and unornamented vaulting proves interiors don't have to be elaborate to avoid being sombre. The pride of the church is its pulpit of 1548, intricately carved with figures emphasised in false perspective, but also notable is the modern stained glass, depicting and symbolising the history of The Netherlands – particularly the 1945 liberation – in the north transept. If you're curious about the tombs – including that of Admiral Maarten van Tromp, famed for hoisting a broom at his masthead to "sweep the seas clear of the English" as he sailed up the Medway – take a look at the *Striking Points* pamphlet available at the entrance.

Opposite the Oude Kerk is the former Convent of Saint Agatha or **Prinsenhof** as it came to be known (Tues–Sat 10am–5pm, Sun 1–5pm; f3.50). Housing Delft's municipal art collection (a good group of works including paintings by Aertsen and Honthorst), it has been restored in the style of the late sixteenth century – an era when the building served as the base of **William the Silent** in his Protestant revolt against the Spanish invaders. From here William planned sorties against the Imperial Catholic troops of Phillip II, achieving considerable success with his *Watergeuzen* or sea-beggars, a kind of commando-guerilla unit that initially operated from England. Here, too, he met his death at the hands of a French assassin: the bullets that passed through him, made by three pellets welded into one, left their mark on the Prinsenhof walls and can still be seen. Tickets for the Prinsenhof also include admission to the unremarkable **Nusantra** ethnographical museum and the Huis van Meerten tile collection.

Finally, if you have the time, the **Royal Army and Weapon Museum** (Tues–Sat 10am–5pm, Sun 1–5pm; f2), near the station, is worth a visit. It has a good display of weaponry, uniforms and military accoutrements – which may sound supremely dull, but isn't, even if you're not an enthusiast. The museum attempts to trace the military history of The Netherlands from the Spanish wars up to the imperialist adventures of the 1950s – which are shown in surprisingly candid detail.

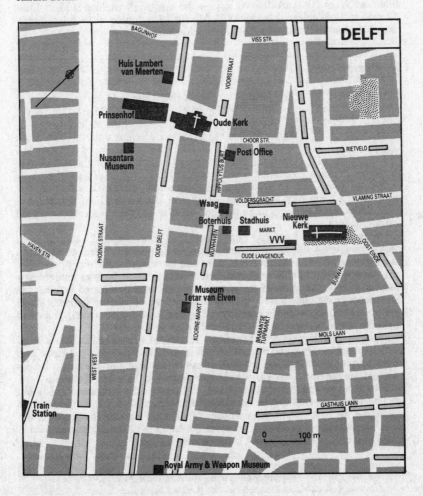

Practical details

From the train station it's a short walk into town and the **VVV** at Markt 85 (Mon–Sat 9am–7pm, Sun 11am–3pm; ☎015/12 61 00). For **eating**, the *Hotel Monopole*, centrally located on the Markt, is pretty tourist-oriented but has pancakes, *uitsmijters* and other light meals for under f10. *Locus Publicus*, Brabantse Turfmarkt 67, is a popular local hangout, serving a staggering array of beers as well as sandwiches. Try, also, *Café de Wynhaven* on Wynhaven and *Café der Oude Jan* opposite the Oude Kerk. *Exprezzo*, at Oude Delft 135, is a trendy art gallery-cum-Italian restaurant-café. Cheapest **accommodation** is in the pensions around the station: expect to pay f55–60 for a double; details from the VVV. Cheapest hotel is *De Kok*, Houttuinen 15 (☎015/12 21 25), with doubles from f75. Between June and August it's possible to stay in the spartan Krakelhof Student Flats, Jacoba van Beierenlaan 9 (☎015/13 59 53), for f28 a double; or there's a **campsite** at Hoflaan (bus #60 from the station to Korftlaan).

Rotterdam

ROTTERDAM lies at the heart of a maze of rivers and artificial waterways that form the seaward outlet of the rivers Rijn (Rhine) and Maas (Meuse). An important port as early as the fourteenth century, it was one of the major cities of the Dutch Republic, sharing its periods of fortune and decline, until the nineteenth century when it was caught on the hop, for the city was ill-prepared for the industrial expansion of the Ruhr, the development of larger ships and the silting up of the Maas. Prosperity returned in a big way with the digging of an entirely new ship canal (the "Nieuwe Waterweg") between 1866 and 1872, and was only brought to a temporary halt during World War II when, without warning, the Germans bombed the city centre to pieces in 1940 and systematically destroyed the port in 1944.

The postwar period saw the rapid reconstruction of the docks and the town centre, and great efforts were made to keep Rotterdam ahead of its rivals. Consequently, when huge container ships and oil tankers made many port facilities obsolete, the Dutch were equal to the challenge and built an entirely new deep-sea port some 25km to the west of the old town. Completed in 1968, the **Europoort** juts out into the North Sea and can accommodate the largest of ships, contributing to Rotterdam's handling of 300 million tonnes of fuel, grain and materials needed or sold by western Europe each year.

Rapid postwar rebuilding transformed Rotterdam's town centre into a giant covered shopping area, a sterile and formless assembly of concrete and glass. This prospect of docks and shops probably sounds unalluring, but Rotterdam has its moments: in the **Boymans-Van Beuningen Museum** it has one of the best – and most overlooked – galleries in the country, and between the central modernity and dockland sleaze is **Delfshaven**, an old area that survived the bombs. There's not much else, but redevelopment hasn't obliterated Rotterdam's earthy character: the prostitution and dope peddling are for real, not for tourists, and if you want to avoid the high spots of the low life, stick to the centre.

The telephone code for Rotterdam is ☎010

Arriving and staying

Rotterdam has a large and confusing centre edged by its main rail terminal, **Centraal Station**, that serves as the hub of a useful tram and metro system for the city and its suburbs – though it's a seamy, hostile place late at night. In the station concourse, a sub-office of the **VVV** (Mon–Sat 9am–10pm, Sun 10am–10pm) provides all the usual tourist information, plus a useful city brochure incorporating a street map for f1, and free maps of the tram, bus and underground system, divided into zones for the calculation of fares (one section of a *strippenkaart* or f1.85 for a single trip in the central zone). There's also a separate leaflet on the metro. The main VVV office, ten minutes' walk away at Coolsingel 67 (Mon–Thurs 9am–6pm, Fri 9am–9pm, Sat 9am–5pm & April–Sept Sun 10am–4pm; ☎413 6000), offers similar information, concentrating on theatre and concert reservations and more general details on Holland as a whole. Both VVVs operate an **accommodation** booking service, the best bet for finding somewhere to stay, as Rotterdam's cheaper hotels and pensions are dotted all over the city and are often full in summer. However, the VVV's listings tend to be cautious, excluding many of the places to the immediate west of the station that they consider undesirable.

Otherwise, there are a clutch of central, reasonably priced **hotels** and **pensions** a kilometre or so to the southwest of the station, charging between f65 and f75 per double per night. These include the *Rox-Inn*, 's-Gravendijkwal 14 (☎436 6109; tram #1, #7 or #9); the *Heemraad*, Heemraadssingel 90 (☎477 5461; tram #1, #7 or #9); and the *Metropole* (☎436 0319). To the immediate north of Centraal Station, the *Bagatelle*, Provenierssingel 26 (☎467 6348), has doubles at f55, and the *Holland* (☎465 3100), along the street at no. 7, has doubles from f90. For the stouthearted, the **youth hostel** is 3km from the station at Rochussenstraat 107 (☎436 5763; tram #4 or metro stop Dijkzigt), and the nearest **campsite** is north of the station at Kanaalweg 84 (☎415 9772; bus #33). The summer **Sleep In**, Mauritsweg 29b, a five-minute walk south of the station, has dormitory accommodation for f10 per person, and there's a handy unlisted hotel, the *Statendam*, close by on Diergaardesingel with doubles from f40.

The City

From Centraal Station, Kruisplein leads south onto Westersingel/Mauritsweg, cutting this part of the city into two sections – to the west is the down-at-heel housing of many of the city's migrant workers, and to the east is the **Lijnbaan**, Europe's first pedestrianised shopping precinct, completed in 1953. The Lijnbaan connects into a baffling series of apparently endless shopping areas hemmed in by Weena, Coolsingel, Westblaak and Mauritsweg. To the east of Coolsingel, just off Beursplein, the fifteenth-century **St Laurenskerk** (Grote Kerk; June–Sept Tues–Sat 10am–4pm; Oct–May Thurs noon–2pm; free) has been the object of a clumsy renovation which has left it cold and soulless. Nearby, and marginally more exciting, is the redevelopment of the **Blaak** area with a New Central Library adjoining a remarkable series of cubist houses, replacing a part of the old city centre destroyed by the bombing. If you're curious, **Kijk-Kubus** (Cube House; Jan–March Sat & Sun 11am–5pm; April–May & Oct–Dec Tues–Sun 11am–5pm; June–Sept daily 10am–5pm; f2.50), at Overblaak 70, near Blaak railway station, is furnished and open to visitors, though there's not much to look at and you're likely to bang your head on a beam or go giddy if you peer out of the windows.

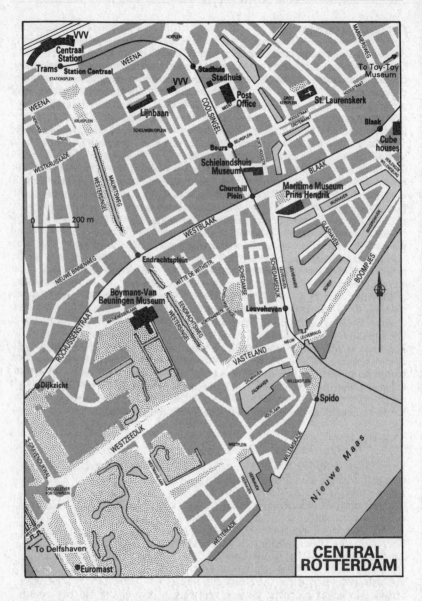

CENTRAL
ROTTERDAM

Heading west, the **Maritime Museum Prins Hendrik** (Tues–Sat 10am–5pm, Sun 11am–5pm; f3.50) is situated in the old harbour area beside the Leuvehaven. Apart from an enterprising programme of temporary nautical exhibitions, the outside area has been spruced up for the museum's prime exhibit – an immaculately restored mid-nineteenth-century ironclad, the *Buffel*, complete with communal washbasins shaped to match the angle of the bows, a couple of ships' figureheads and a string of luxurious officers' cabins.

Across the boulevard to the north, surrounded by tower blocks, the **Schielandshuis Museum** (same times) is housed in a seventeenth-century mansion at Korte Hoogstraat 31, and has a variety of displays on the history of Rotterdam, incorporating the *Atlas van Stolk* collection of drawings and prints, which includes fascinating sketches of pre-colonial "Indonesia". A couple of minutes to the south, the old city docks are enclosed by the Boompjes, a former sea dyke that's now a major freeway, which leads southwest to the **Euromast**, on a rather lonely park corner beside the Nieuwe Maas. This was originally just a drab grey observation platform thrown up in 1960: the **Spacetower** (March–Sept daily 10am–9pm; Oct–Dec daily 11am–4pm; Jan & Feb Sat & Sun 11am–4pm) was added later, its revolving lift rising on the outside of the 185-metre tower. The view is spectacular, but at f12.50 no less than you'd expect.

If nothing in the city centre can be called exactly picturesque, **DELFSHAVEN** goes part of the way to make up for it. It's a good 45-minute walk southwest of Centraal Station – fifteen minutes by tram #4 (direction Schiedam, tram stop Spanjaardstraat), or a couple of minutes on foot from Delfshaven metro. Once the harbour that served Delft, it was from here that the Pilgrim Fathers set sail in 1620, changing to the more reliable Mayflower in Plymouth before continuing onwards to the Americas. Delfshaven was only incorporated into Rotterdam in 1886 and managed to survive World War II virtually intact. Long a neglected area, the town council has recently recognised its tourist potential and has set about conserving and restoring the whole locality as rapidly as possible. Most of the buildings lining the canals are eighteenth- and nineteenth-century warehouses, seen today as "desirable residences" by the upwardly mobile, who are set to turn Delfshaven into a chichi suburb. The **Dubbelde Palmboom Museum**, Voorhaven 12 (Tues–Sat 10am–5pm, Sun 1–5pm; f3.50, but free on Wed), once a jenever distillery, is now an historical museum with a wide-ranging, if unexceptional, collection of objects representing work and leisure in the Maas delta. Nearby, the **Zakkendragershuisje**, Voorstraat 13 (Tues–Sat 10am–5pm, Sun 1–5pm; free), was originally the guild room of the Grain Sack Carriers, who decided the allocation of duties by dice. Today, it's a privately owned, fully operational tin foundry, selling a variety of items made in the old moulds.

The Boymans-Van Beuningen Museum

To the northeast of Delfshaven, back towards the centre, the **Boymans-Van Beuningen Museum**, Mathenesserlaan 18–20 (Tues–Sat 10am–5pm, Sun 11am–5pm; f3.50, but free on Wed), is Rotterdam's one great attraction, accessible from Centraal Station by tram #5 or from Eendrachtsplein metro. Amid the enormous collection of paintings, from Flemish Masters to Pop Art, it's impossible not to find something to your liking, though the sheer size of the displays can be overpowering, while the constant rotation of exhibits can make guidebooks confusing. The information desk provides an updated and simplified diagrammatic outline of the museum, but in general terms pre-nineteenth-century paintings are in the old wing, modern paintings in the new wing, and both wings are divided into two interconnecting floors.

The entrance to the new wing leads to the modern paintings, best known of which are the **Surrealists**. De rigueur for student bedrooms in the 1970s, it's difficult to appreciate Salvador Dalí's *Spain* as anything more than the painting of the poster – not that Dalí would have been bothered. Other works by René Magritte, Max Ernst and Giorgio de Chirico provide a representative sample of a movement whose images seem to have lost much of their power. Surrealism was never adopted by Dutch artists, though the Magic Realism of **Carel Willink** has its similarities in the precise, hallucinatory technique he uses to distance and perturb the viewer in *Self Portrait with a Pen*. **Charley Toorop**'s *Three Generations* is also realism with an aim to disconcert – the huge bust of her father, Jan, looms in the background and dominates the painting. Most of the rest of the ground floor is given over to various displays of applied art and design, including a comprehensive range of tiles.

The **Van der Vorm collection**, housed on the first floor, has paintings from many of Europe's most famous artists, including Monet, Van Gogh, Picasso, Gauguin, Cézanne and Munch, alongside a series of small galleries containing most of the significant artists of the Barbizon and Hague schools, notably **J.H. Weissenbruch**'s *Strandgezicht*, a beautiful gradation of radiant tones.

Adjoining the Vorm collection, and arranged in roughly chronological order (from Room 1), are the museum's earlier paintings, beginning with an excellent **Flemish and Nederlandish religious art section**, whose sumptuous *Christ in the House of Martha and Mary* by Pieter Aertsen is outstanding. **Hieronymus Bosch**, famed for his nightmarish visions, is represented by four of his more mainstream works. Usually considered a macabre fantasist, Bosch was actually working to the limits of oral and religious tradition, where Biblical themes were depicted as iconographical representations, laden with explicit symbols. In his *St Christopher*, the dragon, the hanged bear and the broken pitcher lurk in the background, representations of danger and uncertainty, whereas the Prodigal Son's attitude to the brothel behind him in *The Wanderer* is deliberately ambivalent. Bosch's technique never absorbed the influences of Renaissance Italy, and his figures in the *Marriage Feast at Cana* are static and unbelievable, uncomfortably arranged around a distorted table. Other works in this section include paintings by **Jan van Scorel**, who was more willing to absorb Italianate styles as in his *Scholar in a Red Cap*; the Bruges artist **Hans Memling**, whose capacity for detail can be seen in his *Two houses in a Landscape*; **Pieter Brueghel the Elder**'s mysterious, hazy *Tower of Babel*; and **Geertgen tot Sint Jans**' beautiful, delicate *Glorification of the Virgin*.

Further on, a small selection of **Dutch Genre** paintings reflects the tastes of the emergent seventeenth-century middle class. The idea was to depict real life situations overlaid with a symbolic moral content. Jan Steen's *Extracting the Stone* or *The Physician's Visit* are good humorous examples, while Gerrit Dou's *The Quack*, ostensibly just a passing scene, is full of small cameos of deception – a boy catching a bird, the trapped hare – that refer back to the quack's sham cures.

Dotted across the museum are a number of **Rembrandts**, including two contrasting canvases: an analytic *Portrait of Alotta Adriaensdr*, her ageing illuminated but softened by her white ruff, and a gloomy, indistinct *Blind Tobias and his Wife* painted twenty years later. His intimate *Titus at his Desk* is also in marked contrast to the more formal portrait commissions common to his day. Most of the work of Rembrandt's pupil **Carel Fabritius** was destroyed when he was killed in a Delft gunpowder explosion in 1654; an exception is his *Self-Portrait*, reversing his master's usual technique by lighting the background and placing the subject in shadow.

Waterway excursions

One way of exploring the waterways you can see from the Euromast is on the
Spido cruises that leave from beside the Willemsplein, to the south of Centraal
Station (tram #5 or Leuvehaven metro). Itineraries, times of departure and duration vary, but harbour tours run several times a day and on summer evenings,
starting at f11.50 per person. They head off past the wharfs, quays, docks and
silos of this, the largest port in the world, though it's most impressive at night,
when the illuminated ships and refineries gleam like Spielberg spaceships. In
season, there are also longer, less frequent trips to Dordrecht, the windmills of
Kinderdijk, the Europoort and the Delta Project (see below), starting at around
f40 per person. Further details are available from the VVV, or the boat operators
at Willemsplein (☎413 5400).

The Spido excursion to the series of colossal dams that make up the **Delta
Project**, along the seaboard southwest of Rotterdam, only provides the briefest of
glances, and it's best to visit by bus: take the underground to Spijkenisse (30min)
and catch bus #104 for Vlissingen (Mon–Sat hourly, Sun every 2hr), which travels along the road that crosses the top of the three dams that restrain the
Haringvliet, Grevelingen and Oosterschelde estuaries. For more on the Delta
Project and Delta Expo, see Chapter Six.

SPECIAL INTEREST MUSEUMS

Accessible by bus and tram from Centraal Station, Rotterdam has a number of
special interest **museums**, including a collection of rare dolls and mechanical toys
dating from 1700 to 1940 at the *Toy-Toy Museum*, east of the city centre at Groene
Wetering 41 (Sun–Thurs 11am–4pm, closed July & Aug; f5; tram #3, #7). The
National Museum of Schools, south of the station at Nieuwe Markt 1a (Tues–Sat
10am–5pm, Sun 11am–5pm; f3.50, free on Wed; metro Blaak), has six fully furnished
classrooms of various periods. The Marine Corps museum, *Mariniersmuseum*,
southeast of the centre at Maaskade 119 (Tues–Sat 10am–5pm, Sun 11am–5pm;
f2.50; bus #32 from Churchillplein), outlines the history of the brigade from its establishment in 1665. There's African art in the *African Culture Centre*, Eendrachtsweg
41 (Wed & Fri–Sun noon–6pm; f1; tram #5); the *Trammuseum*, Nieuwe Binnenweg
362 (April–Nov Sat 11am–4pm; free; tram #4), has several interesting old trams; and
there are shiny steam trains and engines at *Steam Depot Museum*, Giessenweg 82
(Sat 10am–5pm; free; bus #38).

Eating and drinking

The cheapest sit-down **meal** in town is served just near the Centraal Station, next
door to the Sleep In, at *De Eend*, Mauritsweg 28 (5.30–8.30pm). Opposite, the *De
Consul*, Westersingel 28, serves a variety of dishes at reasonable prices, as does
the *Statenhof*, whose vegetarian specialities are to be found just northwest of the
station at Bentinckplein 1–4 (tram #3, #9). Alternatives include excellent
Hungarian fare at the *Boris Grill*, Diergaardesingel 93b; extravagant Italian dishes
at *La Gondola*, Kruiskade 6; cheaper Italian food at *Leonardo da Vinci*, Coolsingel
207; and standard Dutch meals at *De Hazzebaz*, Coolsingel 63a.

If you want to dig out a traditional brown café, try the streets west of Centraal Station, though many have been knocked down and many more are scheduled for modernisation. The *Double Diamond*, at the corner of West Kruiskade and Westersingel, dubiously proclaims itself an English pub, whilst *Jazzcafe Dizzy*, 's-Gravendijkwal 127, and the *Harbour Jazzclub*, Delftsestraat 15, offer some good **live music**.

Listings

Airport enquiries Rotterdam airport, Heathrowbaan 4 (☎415 7633; bus #33).

Car hire *Avis*, Rotterdam airport (☎415 8842); *Hertz*, Heervrankestraat 64–68 (☎465 1144).

Dental care ☎455 2155.

Exchange At most banks (Mon–Fri 9am–4pm & Fri 6.30–8pm). Exchange agency at Centraal Station (Mon–Sat 7.30am–10pm, Sun 9am–10pm).

Football At *Feyenoord* stadium – bus #49 or Stadion train from Centraal Station. Fixture details from the VVV; most games are on Sundays.

Left luggage Coin-operated lockers at the railway station.

Markets General, including antiques, on Mariniersweg (Tues & Sat 9am–5pm). Stamps, coins and books on Grotekerkplein (Tues & Sat 9.30am–4pm).

Medical assistance ☎411 5504.

Pharmacies 24hr service details ☎411 0370.

Police Police Station, Haagseveer 23 (☎424 2911).

Post office Coolsingel 42 (Mon–Fri 8.30am–7pm); Delftseplein 31 (Mon–Fri 8.30am–9pm, Sat 8.30am–noon).

Taxis *Rotterdam taxi* ☎462 6060; *St Job* ☎425 7000.

Train enquiries Domestic ☎06/899 1121; international ☎411 7100.

What's on *Deze Maand* is a monthly magazine on events and entertainments in Rotterdam. Free and useful, it's available from the VVV.

Gouda and Oudewater

A pretty little place some 25km northeast of Rotterdam, **GOUDA** is almost everything you'd expect of a Dutch country town: a ring of quiet canals that encircle ancient buildings and old quays. More surprisingly, its **Markt**, a ten-minute walk from the railway station, is the largest in Holland – a reminder of the town's prominence as a centre of the medieval cloth trade, and later of its success in the manufacture of cheeses and clay pipes.

Gouda's main claim to fame is its **cheese market**, held in the Markt every Thursday morning in July and August. Traditionally, some 1000 local farmers brought their home-produced cheeses here to be weighed, tested and graded for moisture, smell and taste. These details were marked on the cheeses and formed the basis for negotiation between buyer and seller, the exact price set by an elaborate hand clapping system, which itself was based on trust and memory, for deals were never written down. Today, the cheese market is a shadow of its former self, a couple of locals in traditional dress standing outside the Waag, surrounded by modern open-air stalls. The promised mixture of food and tradition is mercilessly milked by the tour operators, who herd their victims into this rather dreary scene every week – but don't let this put you off a visit, since Gouda's charms are elsewhere.

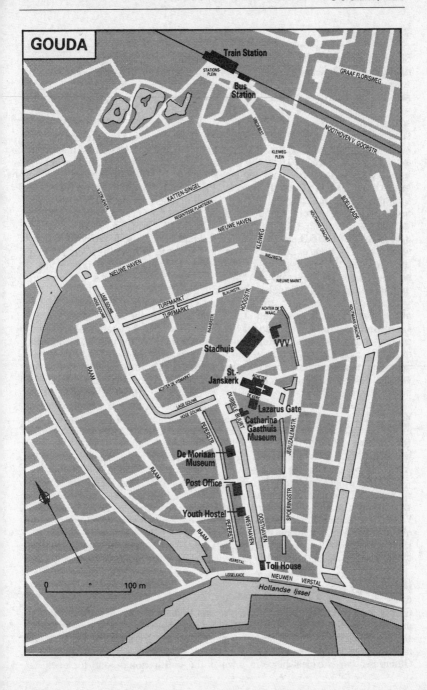

GOUDA

Train Station

STATIONS-
PLEIN

Bus
Station

GRAAF FLORISWEG

NOOTHOVEN V. GOORSTR

DREBEST

KLEIWEG
PLEIN

KATTEN-SINGEL

REGENTESSE PLANTSOEN

NIEUWE HAVEN

KLEIWEG

NIEUWSTR.

HOUTMANS GRACHT

BOELEKADE

NIEUWE HAVEN

NIEUWE MARKT

LAGE GOUWE

HOGE GOUWE

TURFMARKT

TURFMARKT

BLAUWSTR.

HOOGSTR.

ACHTER DE
WAAG

NAAIERSTR.

RAAM

Stadhuis

VVV

ACHTER DE VISMARKT

LAGE GOUWE

HOGE GOUWE

St.
Janskerk

ACHTER
DE KERK

Lazarus Gate

DUBBELE BUURT

Catharina
Gasthuis
Museum

JERUZALEMSTR.

HOUTMANS GRACHT

PEPERSTR.

De Moriaan
Museum

RAAM

Post Office

SPIDERINGSTR.

Youth Hostel

PEPERSTR.

WESTHAVEN

OOSTHAVEN

RAAM

VERSTAL

Toll House

IJSSELKADE

NIEUWEN

VERSTAL

0   100 m

Hollandse Ijssel

The Town

Slap-bang in the middle of the Markt, the **Stadhuis** is an elegant Gothic building dating from 1450, whose facade is fringed by statues of counts and countesses of Burgundy above a twee carillon that plays every half-hour. Nearby, on the north side of the square, the **Waag** is a tidy seventeenth-century building, decorated with a detailed relief of cheese weighing, with the remains of the old wooden scales inside. To the south, just off the Markt, **St Janskerk** (April–Oct Mon–Sat 9am–5pm; Nov–March Mon–Sat 10am–4pm; f2) was built in the sixteenth century and is famous for its magnificent **stained-glass windows**. As well as their intrinsic beauty, the windows show the way religious art changed as Holland moved from a Catholic to a Protestant dominated society. The Biblical themes executed by Dirk and Wouter Crabeth between 1555 and 1571, when Holland was still Catholic, have an amazing clarity of detail and richness of colour. Their last work, *Judith Slaying Holofernes* (window no. 6) is perhaps the finest, the story unfolding in intricate perspective. By comparison, the post-Reformation windows, which date from 1572 to 1603, adopt an allegorical and heraldic style typical of a more secular art. *The Relief of Leiden* (window no. 25) shows William the Silent retaking the town from the Spanish, though Delft and its burgomasters take prominence – no doubt because they paid the bill for its construction. All the windows are numbered and a detailed guide is available at the entrance for f3.

By the side of the church, the flamboyant **Lazarus Gate** of 1609 was once part of the town's leper hospital, until it was moved to form the back entrance to the **Catharina Gasthuis**, a hospice till 1910. A likeable conglomeration of sixteenth-century rooms and halls, including an old isolation cell for the insane, the interior of the Gasthuis has been turned into the municipal **Museum** (Mon–Sat 10am–5pm, Sun noon–5pm; f3). The collection incorporates a fine sample of early religious art, notably a large triptych, *Life of Mary*, by Dirk Barendsz and a characteristically austere *Annunciation* by the Bruges artist Pieter Pourbus. Other highlights include a spacious hall, *Het Ruim*, that was once a sort of medieval hostel, but is now dominated by paintings of the civic guard, principally two group portraits by Ferdinand Bol; the intricate silver-gilt *Chalice and Eucharist Dish* was presented to the guard in the early fifteenth century. Two later rooms have a modest selection of Hague and Barbizon School canvases, notably work by Anton Mauve and Charles Daubigny.

Gouda's other museum, **De Moriaan** (Mon–Fri 10am–5pm, Sat 10am–12.30pm & 1.30–5pm, Sun noon–5pm; f3), is in a cosy old merchant's house at Westhaven 29, with a mixed bag of exhibits from clay pipes to ceramics and tiles. Westhaven itself is a charming jumble of old buildings that head off towards the old toll house and a dilapidated mill beside the Hollandse Ijssel river, on the southern edge of the town centre. There's a restored, fully operational **corn mill** (Mon–Sat 9am–5pm; f1.50) to the immediate west of the Markt, at Vest 65.

Practical details

Gouda's **rail** and **bus stations** are to the immediate north of the town centre, ten minutes from the VVV, Markt 27 (Mon–Fri 9am–5pm, Sat 10am–4pm; ☎01820/13666), which has a limited supply of private **rooms**, from f60 for a double per night; they will ring ahead to make a booking, and there's a cover charge of f3.5. Otherwise, the cheapest place in town is the **youth hostel**, and for once it's conveniently sited at Westhaven 46 (☎01820/12879). The most reasonably priced **hotel** is the *Het Blauwe Kruis*, Westhaven 4 (☎01820/12677), where grim and grimy doubles start at f65. There are two other, more agreeable hotels in the centre, the *De Keizerskroon*, to the west of Westhaven at Keizerstraat 11 (☎01820/28096), with doubles from f80; and the *De Utrechtse Dom*, a couple of minutes' walk to the east of St Janskerk at Geuzenstraat 6 (☎01820/27984), with doubles from f60.

For **food**, Gouda has literally dozens of cafés and snack bars catering for the hundreds of tourists who day-trip here throughout the season. There are vegetarian delights at the *Borsalino*, Naalerstraat 4; Yugoslav specialities at the *Balkan*, Markt 10; pretty pancakes at *'t Goudse Winkeltje*, Achter de Kerk 9a; and cheap pizzas at the *Rimini*, Markt 29.

Oudewater

Eleven kilometres east of Gouda and easily accessible by bus, **OUDEWATER** is a compact and delightful little town that holds a unique place in the history of Dutch witchcraft.

It's estimated that over a million people were burned or otherwise murdered in the widespread **witch-hunts** of the sixteenth century, and not only from fear and superstition: anonymous accusation to the authorities was an easy way of removing an enemy – or even a wife, at a time when there was no divorce. Underlying it all was a virulent misogyny and an accompanying desire to terrorise women into submission.

There were three main methods for investigating accusations of witchcraft: in the first, **trial by fire**, the suspect had to walk barefoot over hot cinders or have a hot iron pressed into the back or hands. If burn blisters appeared, the accused was innocent as witches were supposed to burn less easily than others; naturally, the (variable) temperature of the iron was crucial. **Trial by water** was still more hazardous: dropped into water, if you stayed afloat you were a witch, if you sank you were innocent – and probably dead from drowning. The third method, **trial by weight**, presupposed that a witch would have to be unduly light to fly on a broomstick, so many towns – including Oudewater – used the Waag (town weighhouse) to weigh the accused. If the weight didn't accord with a notional figure derived from the height, the woman was burnt.

The last Dutch woman to be burnt as a witch was a certain Marrigje Ariens, a herbalist from Schoonhaven, whose medical efforts, not untypically, inspired mistrust and subsequent persecution. She died in 1597.

Oudewater's Waag gained its fame from the actions of Charles V (1516–52), who saw a woman accused of witchcraft in a nearby village. The weighmaster, who'd been bribed, stated that the woman weighed only a few pounds, but Charles was dubious and ordered the woman to be weighed again in Oudewater, where the officials proved unbribable, pronouncing a normal weight and acquitting her. The probity of Oudewater's weighmaster impressed Charles and he granted the town the privilege of issuing certificates, valid throughout the empire, stating that "The accused's weight is in accordance with the natural proportions of the body". Once in possession of the certificate, one could never be brought to trial for witchcraft again. Not surprisingly, thousands of people came from all over Europe for this life-saving piece of paper, and to Oudewater's credit no one was ever condemned.

Oudewater's sixteenth-century Waag has survived, converted into the **Heksenwaag** (witches' weigh house; April–Oct Tues–Sat 10am–5pm, Sun noon–5pm; f2), a family-run affair, where you can be weighed on the original rope and wood balance. The owners dress up in national costume and issue a certificate in olde-worlde English that states nothing, but does so very prettily. There's not much else to see here, but it's a pleasant little place, whose traditional stepped gables spread out along the river Hollandse Ijssel as it twists its way through town.

If you decide to **stay**, the VVV, Ijsselveere 17 (Mon–Fri 9am–6pm; ☎03486/1871), a couple of minutes' walk from the bus stop towards town, has details of several private **rooms** and **pensions** from f65 for a double; there are no hotels.

Dordrecht

Some 15km southeast of Rotterdam, the ancient port of **DORDRECHT**, or "Dordt" as it's often called, is a likeable town beside one of the busiest waterway junctions in the world, where tankers and containers from the north pass the waterborne traffic of the Meuse and Rhine. Eclipsed by the expansion of Rotterdam and left relatively intact by World War II, Dordrecht has been spared the worst excesses of postwar development and preserves a confusion of ancient and dilapidated buildings that stop it from being just another tidy Dutch showpiece. Within easy reach is some of the province's prettiest countryside, including the windmills of the **Kinderdijk** and the **Biesbosch** nature reserve.

Granted a town charter in 1220, Dordrecht was the most important and powerful town in Holland until well into the sixteenth century. One of the first cities to declare against the Habsburgs in 1572, it was the obvious site for the first meeting of the Free Assembly of the Seven Provinces, and for a series of doctrinal conferences that tried to solve a whole range of theological differences amongst the various Protestant sects. After all, the Protestants may have hated the Catholics, but they also inherited the medieval church's desire for arcane debate. In 1618, at the Synod of Dordt, the Remonstrants or Arminians had prolonged arguments with the Calvinists over the definition of predestination, though this must have seemed pretty important stuff compared to the Synod of 1574, when one of the main rulings had required the dismantling of church organs.

From the seventeenth century, Dordrecht lost ground to its great rivals to the north, slipping into comparative insignificance, its economy sustained by trade and shipbuilding.

> The telephone code for Dordrecht is ☎078

Arriving and staying

Well connected by train to all the Randstad's major cities, Dordrecht's adjoining **rail** and **bus** stations are a ten-minute walk from the town centre, straight down Stationsweg/Johan de Wittstraat and left at the end along Bagijnhof/Visstraat. A couple of minutes from the station, the VVV, Stationsweg 1 (Oct–April Mon–Fri 9am–5.30pm, Sat 9.30am–1pm; May–Sept daily 9.15am–5pm; ☎132800), has a list of **pensions** and **private rooms**, which they will reserve for a cover charge of f1.25; doubles start at f60, but most of their addresses are far from the centre.

There are three central **hotels**: the *Klarenbeek*, near the VVV at Johan de Wittstraat 35 (☎144 133), with doubles from f90 and some of the smallest single rooms imaginable from f45; the *Dordrecht*, by the river near the west end of Spuiboulevard at Achterhakkers 12 (☎136011), doubles from f120; and the excellent *Bellevue*, overlooking the Maas from the northern tip of the old town by the Groothoofdspoort, doubles from f125. There are three cheaper alternatives approximately 4km east of town along Baanhoekweg, the road that forms the northern perimeter of the Biesbosch (bus #4 from the station). These are the *Budget Hotel* at no. 25 (☎211 311), doubles at f85; a campsite, *De Hollandse Biesbosch* (April–Oct), in the same complex; and a **youth hostel**, at no. 52 (May–Dec; ☎133310). The most agreeable **campsite**, *De Kleine Rug* (☎163555; advance bookings essential in July & Aug), is about 1km south of Baanhoekweg on a sandspit at Loswalweg 1: take bus #5 to Stadspolder, walk fifteen minutes down to the end of Loswalweg and, at the jetty, yell and wave furiously until the boat appears; if there's no sign of life, *Camping 't Vissertje*, Loswalweg 3 (☎162751), is a reasonable second choice.

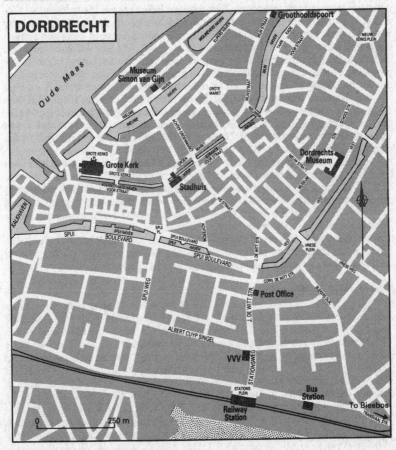

The Town

The old part of Dordrecht juts out into the Maas, divided by three concentric waterways that once protected it from attack. From the railway station, the second canal is the heart of the town, flowing beside the **Voorstraat**, today's main shopping street. At the junction of Voorstraat and Visstraat, the Groenmarkt spans the canal with a heavy-handed **monument** to the De Witt brothers, Jan and Cornelius, prominent Dutch Republicans who paid for their principles when they were ripped to pieces by an Orangist mob in The Hague in 1672. To the right, Voorstraat bends its way northeast, a chaotic mixture of the old, the new, the restored and the decayed, intersected by a series of tiny alleys that once served as the town's quays. Cutting off Voorstraat at Nieuwebrug, the **Wijnhaven** was used by the city's merchants to control the import and export of wine when they held the state monopoly from the fourteenth to the seventeenth centuries.

Straight ahead, the **Groothoofdspoort** was once the main city gate and has a grand facade of 1618, pushed up against the *Hotel Bellevue*, with its fine views over the surrounding waterways. For a better look at the harbour front, a renovated **steamship**, the *Pieter Boele*, leaves from beside the *Bellevue* for hour-long excursions on some Saturday and Sunday afternoons between June and August (schedules from the VVV; tickets on the boat, f4.50). The town's innermost canal is just along the waterfront from here, divided into two harbours, home to the cruisers, barges and sailing boats that slip up and down the Maas. Fringed by stately buildings and criss-crossed by rickety footbridges, it's an attractive setting for the **Museum Simon van Gijn**, Nieuwe Haven 29 (Tues–Sat 10am–5pm, Sun 1–5pm; f2.5), whose collection of local memorabilia and period rooms is of some moderate interest, best the eighteenth-century Brussels tapestries and a fine Renaissance chimneypiece of 1550, transferred from the old guild house of the arquebusiers.

Near the southwest end of Nieuwe Haven, the **Grote Kerk** (April–Oct Tues–Sat 10.30am–4.30pm, Sun noon–4pm; Nov & Dec 1st & 3rd Sat of the month 2–4pm; free) is visible from all over town, its fourteenth-century **tower** (same times; f2) topped with incongruous seventeenth-century clocks. One of the largest churches in Holland, it was built to emphasise Dordrecht's wealth and importance, but it's heavy and dull, despite its attractive environs, and there's only an elaborately carved choir inside to hold your interest. Climb the tower for a great view over the town and its surrounding waters. From beside the church, Grotekerksbuurt leads to the stolid classicism of the **Stadhuis**, back on the Voorstraat.

The Dordrechts Museum

To the southeast of the town centre, the **Dordrechts Museum**, Museumstraat 40 (Tues–Sat 10am–5pm, Sun 1–5pm; f5), is a ten-minute walk from the train station, turn right off Johan de Wittstraat on the far side of the first canal as you head into town, and follow the signs. Well presented and clearly labelled, the museum concentrates on the work of local artists both in its permanent and temporary displays. Highlights of the permanent collection include a couple of finely drawn portraits by Jacob Cuyp, and a whole room devoted to the work of his son, Aelbert. Born in Dordrecht in 1620, **Aelbert Cuyp** was influenced by those of his contemporaries who had visited Italy, modulating his work with the soft, yellowish tones of the Mediterranean. Noted for his Italianate landscapes, seascapes and town scenes, his *Resting Riders in a Landscape* is representative of

In March 1989, several of the museum's principal paintings, including two works by Aelbert Cuyp and one by Nicolaes Maes, were attacked by a madman with a knife. Under repair, they are scheduled to be re-exhibited in 1991.

his work, in contrast to the muted tones of traditional Dutch landscape painting, as illustrated by Jan van Goyen's *View of Dordrecht*, the city's bustle restricted to the bottom section of the canvas, beneath a wide sky and flattened horizon.

A student of Rembrandt, Nicolaes Maes first specialised in informal domestic scenes, as in *The Eavesdropper*, turning his skills to portrait painting after his visit to Antwerp in 1670. A good example of his later work is his flattering picture of *Jacob de Witt the Elder*. More curiously, *De Dordtse Vierling* (the Dordt quadruplets) is an odd, unattributed seventeenth-century painting of a dead child and her three trussed siblings, a simple, moving tribute to a lost daughter; and on the staircase nearby, the massive *Gezicht op Dordt* (View of Dordt) is a masterpiece of minutely observed naturalist detail by Adam Willaertz (1577–1644).

On the first floor, there's a selection of work by the later and lesser Ary Scheffer, who was born in Dordrecht in 1795, but lived in Paris from 1811. His much reproduced *Mignon Pining for her Native Land* struck a chord in the sentimental hearts of the nineteenth century. Jozef Israels' *Midday Meal at the Inn* and G.H. Breitner's *Lauriergracht 1891* are among a small collection of Amsterdam and Hague School paintings, though the collage style of their Italian associate, Antonio Mancini, is of more immediate appeal.

Eating and drinking

Dordrecht has two excellent **restaurants**, the *Costa d'Oro*, Voorstraat 444, which serves a wide range of tasty Italian dishes, and the *Crimpert Salm*, Visstraat 5, which has an imaginative seafood menu and exquisite daily specials. Alternatives include *De Troubadour*, Vriesplein 8; fish at the *De Stroper*, Wijnbrug 1; and snacks at *In de Klandermuelen*, Statenplein 86. For **bars**, try *'t Avontuur*, at Voorstraat 193, or the more staid *De Pul*, on the Spuiplein. There's **live music** at the *Jazz and Folk Club* on the Grote Kerksplein, with a list of future attractions pinned to the door.

Around Dordrecht: the Biesbosch and the Kinderdijk

On November 18, 1421, South Holland's sea defences gave way and the "St Elizabeth Day flood" formed what is now the Hollands Diep sea channel and the **Biesbosch** (reed forest) – an expanse of river, creek, marsh and reed covering some forty square miles to the south and east of Dordrecht. It was a disaster of major proportions, destroying some seventy towns and villages, and early accounts put the death toll at over 100,000. The catastrophe disrupted the whole of the region's economy, breaking up the links between South Holland and Flanders and accelerating the shift in commercial power to the north. Even those hamlets and villages that did survive took generations to recover, subject, as they were, to raids by the wretched refugees of the flood.

Indundated twice daily by the rising tide, the Biesbosch produced a particular **reed culture**, its inhabitants using the plant for every item of daily life, from houses to baskets and boats, selling excess cuttings at the local markets. It was a harsh and gruelling existence that lasted well into the nineteenth century, when the reeds were no longer of much use, replaced by machine-manufactured goods.

Today, the Biesbosch is a nature reserve and national park whose delicate eco-system is threatened by the very scheme that aims to protect the province from further flooding. The Delta Project (see *Chapter Six*) dams have controlled the rivers' flow and restricted the tides' strength, forcing the reeds to give ground to other forms of vegetation, incompatible with the area's special mixture of bird and plant life. Large areas of reed have disappeared, and no one seems to know how to reconcile the nature reserve's needs with those of the seaboard cities.

The park divides into two main sections, north and south of the Nieuwe Merwede channel, which marks the provincial boundary between South Holland and North Brabant. The undeveloped heart of the nature reserve is the **Brabantse Biesbosch**, the chunk of land to the south, whereas tourist facilities have been carefully confined to the north, on a strip of territory to the immediate east of Dordrecht, along the park's perimeter. Here, the **Bezoekerscentrum Merwelanden**, Baanhoekweg 53 (Visitors' Centre; Tues–Sun 10am–5pm; ☎01840/18047), accessible by bus #4 from Dordrecht train station, has displays on the flora and fauna of the region. **Boat trips** for the Brabantse Biesbosch leave from the jetty beside the Bezoekerscentrum once or twice daily six days a week in July and August, and once on Sundays only in May, June, September and early October. Prices vary according to the itinerary, but start at f22.50 for the day ("Dagtocht") and at f8.50 for a two-hour excursion ("Panoramatocht"). There are similar trips at similar prices from the **Bezoekerscentrum Drimmelen**, Dorpsstraat 14, Drimmelen (Wed–Fri 10am–5pm, Sun 11am–5pm, March–Oct also Sat 1–5pm, June–Aug also Tues 10am–5pm; ☎01626/2991), on the southern bank of the Amer, about 20km north of Breda – though this cannot readily be reached by public transport from Dordrecht. From Drimmelen, boats leave for the Brabantse Biesbosch twice on Sundays only from mid-April to mid-June and in September, and twice daily in July and August.

Some of the longer excursions visit the **Biesboschmuseum**, on the southern shore of the Nieuwe Merwede at Spieringsluis 4 (Mon 1–5pm, Tues–Sun 10am–5pm; f2), where there are further details on the ecology of the Biesbosch and the origins of its distinctive reed culture. Further details of boat trips are available at the Dordrecht VVV and direct from both of the Visitors' Centres.

The other way of visiting the nature reserve is by **bike**, on hire at standard rates from Dordrecht railway station and the VVV, who also sell detailed maps of the district and brochures on suggested cycle routes. The ride from town to the Brabantse Biesbosch takes about half an hour, via the shuttle passenger boat service that runs from the quay by Kop van 't Land, 5km southeast of the town centre, to a point about 1km northeast of the Biesboschmuseum.

The Kinderdijk

Some 12km north of Dordrecht, the **Kinderdijk** (child's dyke) sits at the end of a long drainage channel which feeds into the river Lek, whose turbulent waters it keeps from flooding the polders around Alblasserdam. Sixteenth-century legend suggests it takes its name from the time when a cradle, complete with cat and kicking baby, was found at the precise spot where the dyke had just held during a particularly bad storm. A mixture of symbols – rebirth, innocence and survival – the story encapsulates the determination and optimism with which the Dutch fought the floods for hundreds of years, and is repeated in many different forms across the whole province.

Today, the Kinderdijk is famous for its picturesque, quintessentially Dutch **windmills**, all eighteen stringing alongside the main channel and its tributary beside the Molenkade for some 3km. Built around 1740 to drive water from the Alblasserwaard polders, the windmills are put into operation every Saturday afternoon in July and August and one of them is open to visitors from April to September (Mon–Sat 9.30am–5.30pm; f2). Without a car, the easiest way to explore the district from Dordrecht is by **bike**, and if you decide to **stay**, the tiny village of Kinderdijk is to the immediate west of the dyke, on the banks of the Lek. There's one **hotel**, *Kinderdijk*, West Kinderdijk 361 (☎01859/12425), with doubles from f95, and one **pension**, *De Waaier*, Molenstraat 6 (☎01859/12694), with doubles at f50. Advance booking is essential from June to August.

Utrecht

"I groaned with the idea of living all winter in so shocking a place", wrote Boswell in 1763, and **UTRECHT** still promises little as you approach: surrounded by shopping centres and industrial developments, the town only begins to reveal itself in the old area around the Dom Kerk, roughly enclosed by the Oude and Nieuwe Grachts. These distinctive sunken canals date from the fourteenth century and their brick cellars, used as warehouses when Utrecht was a river port, have been converted to chic cafés and restaurants. Though the liveliest places in town, they don't disguise Utrecht's provincialism: just half an hour from Amsterdam, all the brashness and vitality of the capital is absent, and it's for museums and churches rather than nightlife that the town is enjoyable.

Founded by the Romans in the first century AD, the city of Utrecht became the site of a wealthy and powerful medieval bishopric, which controlled the surrounding region under the auspices of the German emperors. In 1527 the bishop sold off his secular rights and shortly afterwards the town council enthusiastically joined the revolt against Spain. Indeed, the **Union of Utrecht**, the agreement that formalised the opposition to the Habsburgs, was signed here in 1579. Some two hundred years later the **Treaty of Utrecht** brought to an end some of Louis IV of France's grand imperial ambitions.

The focal point of the centre is the **Dom Tower**, at around 120m the highest church tower in the country. It's one of the most beautiful too, soaring, unbuttressed lines rising to a delicate octagonal lantern added in 1380. A guided tour (April–Oct Mon–Fri 10am–5pm, Sat & Sun noon–5pm; f1.50, no museumcards) takes you unnervingly near to the top, from where the gap between the tower and Gothic **Dom Kerk** is most apparent. Only the eastern part of the great cathedral remains, the nave having collapsed (with what must have been an apocalyptic crash) during a storm in 1674. It's worth peering inside (May–Sept daily 10am–5pm; Oct–April Mon–Sat 11am–4pm, Sun 2–4pm; free) to get a sense of the hangar-like space the building once had, and to wander through the **Kloostergang**, the fourteenth-century cloisters that link the cathedral to the chapterhouse, now part of the university.

Except for the Dom, Utrecht's churches aren't all that interesting: the oldest is the **St Pieterskerk** (Fri & Sat 9am–noon & 2–4pm), a shabbily maintained building that's a mixture of Romanesque and Gothic styles with twelfth-century paintings and reliefs. The **Buurkerk** was the home of one sister Bertken until her death in 1514; she was so ashamed of being the illegitimate daughter of a cathedral priest that she hid away in a small cell here – for 57 years. Now the church is a peculiar home to the **Speelklok tot Pierement Museum** (Tues–Sat 10am–4pm, Sun 1–4pm; f6, children f3), a collection of burping fairground organs and ingenious musical boxes worth an hour of anyone's time.

The city's other museums are a little way from the centre. The national collection of ecclesiastical art, the **Catherine Convent Museum** (Tues–Fri 10am–5pm, Sat & Sun 11am–5pm; f3.50, children f2), at Nieuwe Gracht 63, has a mass of paintings, manuscripts and church ornaments from the ninth century on, brilliantly exhibited in a complex built around the old convent. This excellent collection of paintings includes work by **Geertgen tot Sint Jans**, **Rembrandt**, **Hals** and, best of all, a luminously beautiful *Virgin and Child* by **van Cleve**. Part of the convent is the late Gothic St Catherine's church, its radiant white interior enhanced by floral decoration.

Keep walking down along Nieuwe Gracht and you reach Utrecht's other important museum, the **Centraal**, at Agnietenstraat 1 (Tues–Sat 10am–5pm, Sun 2–5pm; f2.50). Its claim to hold "25,000 curiosities" seems a bit exaggerated, but it does have a good collection of paintings by Utrecht artists of the sixteenth and seventeenth centuries. **Van Scorel** lived in Utrecht before and after he visited Rome, and he brought the influence of Italian humanism north. His paintings, like the vividly individual portraits of the *Jerusalem Brotherhood*, combine High-Renaissance style with native Dutch observation. The central figure in white is van Scorel himself: he made a trip to Jerusalem around 1520, which accounts for his unusually accurate drawing of the city in *Christ's Entry into Jerusalem*. A group of painters influenced by another Italian, Caravaggio, became known as the Utrecht School. Such paintings as Honthorst's *The Procuress* adapt his chiaroscuro technique to genre subjects, and develop an erotic content that would itself influence later genre painters like Jan Steen and Gerrit Dou. Even more skilled and realistic is Terbrugghen's *The Calling of St Matthew*, a beautiful balance of gestures dramatising the tax collector's summoning by Christ to become one of the apostles.

Gerrit Rietveld, the de Stijl designer, was most famous for both his zig-zag and his brightly coloured geometrical chairs, displayed in the applied art section. Part of the de Stijl philosophy (see *Contexts*) was that the approach could be used in any area of design, though Rietveld's angular furniture is probably better to look at than to sit on. Out of town, his **Schröder House**, at Prins Hendriklaan 50, is one of the most influential pieces of modern architecture in Europe, demonstrating the organic union of lines and rectangles characteristic of the movement. To join a conducted tour (Tues–Sun; f7.50, children f3.75), phone first: (☎030 51 79 26).

Two final museums that might detain you: the **Phonographic Museum** (Tues–Sat 10am–4.30pm; f3.75, children f2.50) in the Hoog Catharijne centre has a collection of sound-oriented devices from the earliest Edison up to the compact disc; and east of the centre, at Johan van Oldenbarneveldtlaan 6, the **National Railway Museum** (Tues–Sat 10am–5pm, Sun 1–5pm; f7.50, children f4.50) has trains, buses and trams sitting in Utrecht's out-of-use railway station – not much information, but enthusiastic attendants.

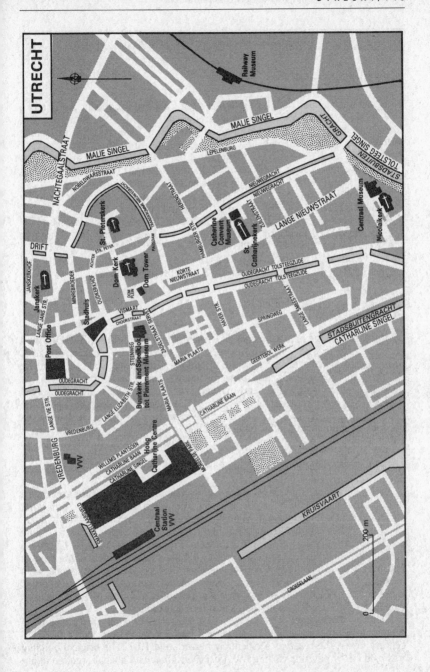

> The telephone code for Utrecht is ☎030

Practical details

Train and bus stations both lead into the Hoog Catharijne shopping centre and a VVV kiosk: the **main VVV office** is at Vredenburg 90 (Mon–Sat 9am–8pm, Sun 10am–3pm; ☎030 31 41 32), a seven-minute walk away. They offer the usual help with accommmdation – the cheapest pensions, such as *Van Ooijen*, Dantelaan 117 (☎93 81 90), or *Hensen* A.H.G. Fokkerstraat 59 (☎44 41 85), cost around f60 a double, basic hotels such as the *Domstad*, Parkstraat 5 (☎31 01 31), a few guilders more. The **youth hostel** at Rhijnauwenselaan 14, Bunnnik, linked to town by bus #40, is a little far out, but the well-equipped **campsite** at Arienslaan 5 can be conveniently reached by a #57 bus from the Central Station.

Restaurants are mainly along the Oude Gracht; the best are *Oudaen* at no. 99 and the mostly vegetarian *De Werfkring* at no. 123. The junction of Oudegracht and Wed has the town's best collection of **bars**: *Café Graf Floris*, opposite the central Vismarkt, is a good place to hear the Dom Tower's carillon concerts, and the nearby *De Witte Ballons* at Vismarkt 12 has a lively atmosphere.

Amersfoort

On the eastern edge of the province of Utrecht, the town of **AMERSFOORT** was first fortified in the eleventh century and received its charter in 1259. Surprisingly, it managed to avoid the attentions of the rival armies during the Revolt of the Netherlands, and some of today's centre has survived from the fifteenth century, lying at the heart of a series of twisting canals that once served to protect the town from assault and to speed the import and export of goods. The main square, the Hofplein, is edged by the giant hulk of the **St Joriskerk**, an unusual, predominantly Gothic edifice finished in 1534. The nave and aisles are of equal height, and only the south porch stops the exterior from resembling an aircraft hangar. Like most churches of the period, it was an enlargement of an earlier building, but here the original Romanesque tower was left inside the later fifteenth-century construction.

A few minutes' walk northeast along Langestraat, the **Kamperbinnenpoort** is a turreted thirteenth-century gate, extensively renovated in the 1930s. From here, north and south of Langestraat, Muurhuizen follows the line of the old city moat, its houses either built into the original city walls or draped beside the canal. At the northern end of Muurhuizen, the **Museum Fléhite**, Westsingel 50 (Tues–Fri 10am–5pm, Sat & Sun 2–5pm), sits prettily behind another section of the moat, a fancifully gabled building of neo-Renaissance design. This is the town's main museum, but it's packed with a dreary assortment of items of strictly local interest. Close by, the ridiculously picturesque **Koppelpoort** is a fifteenth-century town gate that once defended Amersfoort's northern approaches.

Back on Westsingel, 500 metres past the museum, all that remains of Amersfoort's other main church, the **Onze Lieve Vrouwekerk**, is the fifteenth-century tower, the rest was accidentally blown up in 1797. The original building was paid for by pilgrims visiting the *Amersfoort Madonna*, a small wooden figure that had been thrown into the town canal by a young girl in 1444. Legend has it that the girl was on her way to enter one of Amersfoort's convents when she became ashamed of her simple figurine, so she decided to throw it away. In the manner of such things, a dream commanded her to retrieve the statuette, which subsequently demonstrated miraculous powers. Part morality play, part miracle, the story fulfilled all the necessary clichés to turn the figure into a revered object, and the town into a major centre of medieval pilgrimage.

Practical details

Amersfoort **train station** is opposite the **VVV**, Stationsplein 22 (Mon–Fri 9am–6pm & Oct–April Sat 10am–1pm, May–Sept Sat 10am–3pm; ☎033/635 151), which is a good ten-minute walk west of the centre of town, the Hofplein: turn left out of the station building along Stationsstraat and keep going. The VVV has a good supply of private **rooms** and **pensions** from f60 for a double per night and they'll ring ahead to make a booking, though most of their addresses are way out of the town centre. There's only one convenient, reasonably priced **hotel** in Amersfoort, the *De Witte*, just to the southwest of the Onze Lieve Vrouwetoren at Utrechtseweg 2 (☎033/614 142), with doubles from f80. **Camping** *De Bokkeduinen* is about 2km west of the station at Barchman Wuytierslaan 81 (☎033/619 902; April–Sept), take bus #70 or #72, direction Soest, from the bus stop outside the train station. For **food**, there are a number of snack bars and restaurants on the main shopping street, Langestraat: try the pleasant *Den Grooten Slock*, beside St Joriskerk.

travel details

Trains
From Amersfoort to Amsterdam CS (4 hourly; 35min); Utrecht (4 hourly; 20min); Zwolle (2 hourly; 35min).
From Leiden to The Hague CS (2 hourly; 35min); Amsterdam CS (2 hourly; 35min).
From The Hague to Delft/Rotterdam (4 hourly; 12/25min); Dordrecht (2 hourly; 40min); Gouda/Utrecht/Amersfoort (3 hourly; 20min/40min/1 hour).
From Rotterdam to Gouda/Utrecht (3 hourly 20/45min); Dordrecht (6 hourly; 20min).

International trains
From Leiden/The Hague HS/Rotterdam/Dordrecht to Antwerp (1 hourly; 1hr 50min/1hr 35min/1hr 15min/1hr). Trains continue to Brussels a further 40min away.
From The Hague HS/Rotterdam CS to Antwerp Berchem (1 hourly; 1hr35min/1hr10min); Brussels Midi (1 hourly; 2hr 10min/1hr 50min); Paris Nord (1hourly; 5hr 10min/4hr50min).

Buses
Buses from Leiden station make the 3km journey west to the coast at **Katwijk-aan-Zee** every 10min, taking 25min to complete the trip.
From Gouda to Oudewater (bus #180, Mon–Sat every 30min, Sun hourly; 30min).
From Leiden to Katwijk-aan-Zee (every 30min; 30min).

CHAPTER FOUR

THE NORTH AND THE FRISIAN ISLANDS

U ntil the opening of the Afsluitdijk in 1932, which bridged the mouth of the Zuider Zee, the **north** of Holland was a relatively remote area, a distinct region of small provincial towns that was far from the mainstream life of the Randstad. Since the completion of the dyke, the gap between north and west Holland has narrowed, and fashion and custom seem almost identical. The main exception is linguistic: Friesland has its own language, more akin to Lower German than Dutch, and its citizens are keen to use it.

Three provinces make up the north of the country – **Drenthe**, **Groningen** and **Friesland** – though for a long time the Frisians occupied the entire area that is now northern Holland. Charlemagne recognised three parts of Friesland: West Frisia, equivalent to today's West Friesland, across the Ijsselmeer; Central Frisia (today's Friesland); and East Frisia – now Groningen province. At this time much of the region was prey to inundation by the sea, and houses and sometimes entire settlements would be built on artificial mounds or *terpen* (*wierden* in Groningen), which brought them high above the water level. It was a miserable sort of existence, and not surprisingly the Frisians soon got around to building dykes to keep the water out permanently. You can still see what's left of some of the mounds in Friesland, though in large settlements they're usually obscured.

During the Middle Ages the area that is now Friesland proper remained independent of the rest of Holland, asserting its separateness regularly until it was absorbed into the Hapsburg empire by Charles V in 1523. It's still something of a maverick among Dutch provinces, although the landscape is familiar enough – dead flat and very green, dotted with black-and-white cattle and long thatched farmhouses crowned with white gable finials or *uleburden*, in the form of a double-swan motif, that were originally meant to deter evil spirits. Of the towns, **Leeuwarden**, the provincial capital of Friesland, is a pleasant, if sedate town with two outstanding museums, one of which has the largest collection of tiles in the world. However, many visitors prefer the west coast of the province, where a chain of small towns prospered during the sixteenth-century trading heyday of the Zuider Zee. Each coastal town has its own distinct charm and character, from the splendid merchant houses of **Harlingen**, to the painted furniture and antique neatness of **Hindeloopen** and the tile manufacturers of **Makkum**. Inland, southwest Friesland is a chaos of lake and canal that's been transformed into one of the busiest water sports areas in the country, centring on the town of **Sneek**.

East of Friesland, the province of Groningen, equivalent to Charlemagne's East Frisia, has comparatively few attractions. Its villages tend to be dull and suburban and most tourists stick to the university town of **Groningen**, a lively cosmopolitan place that makes up for its shortage of historic sights with its busy bars and

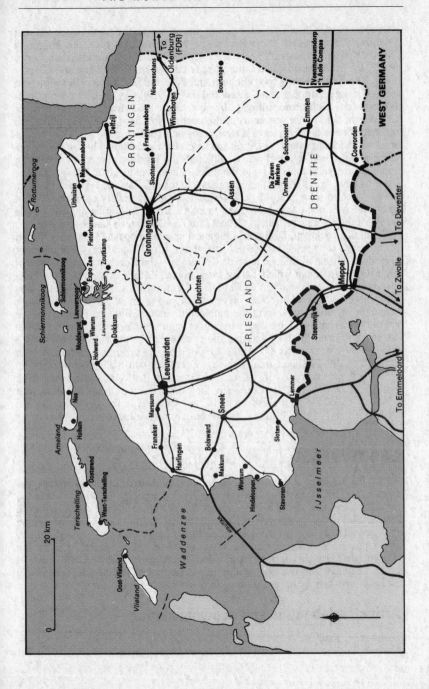

restaurants and a thriving contemporary arts scene. To the north lie the **Frisian Islands**, a fragmented extension of the sandbank that runs the length of Holland's western coastline. There are five populated Dutch islands in all, four of which are in Friesland (Texel, the fifth, is part of North Holland; see Chapter Two). The most westerly two, **Vlieland** and **Terschelling**, are accessible by boat from Harlingen; further east, **Ameland** is reachable by bus and ferry from Leeuwarden, **Schiermonnikoog** by bus and boat from Leeuwarden or Groningen. One of the few areas of the country you have to put any effort into reaching, the islands preserve a rare peace and constitute an important nature area, with thriving colonies of birds and a rich flora and fauna. They're also, inevitably, popular holiday destinations, although the tourists who arrive here each summer are easily absorbed into the miles of beach and wide expanses of dune. Plans to build dykes connecting the islands to the mainland and reclaim the shallows all around were met with such resistance from naturalists and islanders that they have now been abandoned, and there's a strong feeling among the people here that they should remain as distinct from the Dutch mainland as possible.

South of Groningen, **Drenthe** is the most sparsely populated and least visited of the Dutch provinces, and it's not hard to see why. The range of low hills that spreads northeast of Emmen towards Groningen – the Hondsrug – as a centre of prehistoric settlement which, dating from around 2500 BC, constitutes the earliest sign of any civilisation in Holland. But for most of its history, Drenthe was little more than peat bog and barren moor, a region of no real military or economic significance. During the nineteenth century, the face of much of the province was changed by the founding of innumerable peat colonies, whose labourers drained the land and dug the peat to expose the subsoil below. As a result of their work, parts of Drenthe are given over to prosperous farmland, with agriculture the dominant local industry. Drenthe's two main towns are of no special interest and have only a couple of attractions that could conceivably bring you this far off the beaten track: **Assen**, the capital, has the Drents Museum, with a superb collection of prehistoric finds, and **Emmen** is the best place to see Drenthe's most original feature – its *hunebeds*, or megalithic tombs.

Leeuwarden

An old market town at the heart of an agricultural district, **LEEUWARDEN** was formed from the amalgamation of three *terpen* that originally stood on an expanse of water known as the Middelzee. Later it was the residence of the powerful Frisian Stadholders, who vied with those of Holland for control of the United Provinces. These days it's the neat and distinctly cosy capital of Friesland, with an air of provincial prosperity and a smug sense of independence. It lacks the concentrated historic charm of many other Dutch towns, but it has a number of grand buildings and two outstanding museums, not to mention an appealingly compact town centre that is almost entirely surrounded and dissected by water.

Arrival, information and accommodation

Leeuwarden's **rail** and **bus** stations virtually adjoin each other, five minutes' walk south of the town centre. The VVV at the train station (Mon–Fri 9am–5.30pm, Sat

9am–2pm; ☎13 22 24) has a short list of private **rooms** that covers the whole of Friesland, including the town itself; last-minute vacancies are rare, but if there is one you should reckon on paying about f25 per person per night. There are only two reasonably priced **hotels** in town: the *De Pauw*, near the train station at Stationsweg 10 (☎12 36 51), is the best bet for getting a room late at night – doubles rooms from f80; the *Hotel 't Anker*, on the north side of the centre in Eewal (☎12 52 16), with double rooms from f70, is a reasonable alternative, though it's used as visiting workers' lodgings and so is often full during the week. **Camping Kleine Wielen** is about 6km out towards Dokkum (take bus #51 from the station).

> The Leeuwarden area telephone code is ☎058.

The Town

If you've swallowed all the tourist office myths about Friesland being a land of historic beauty, rural charm and the like, Leeuwarden is initially a bit of a disappointment, with the southern part of the town centre near the station an indeterminate, rather careless mixture of the old and new. Here, at Zuiderplein 9, is the revamped **Frisian Resistance Museum** (Tues–Sat 10am–5pm, Sun 1–5pm; f2), a chronological exhibition tracing the early days of the Nazi invasion, through collaboration and resistance on to the Allied liberation. A variety of photographs and bits and pieces from the war years illustrate the text, but the emphasis is very much on the local struggle rather than the general war effort.

Heading north, high-rise blocks and shopping centres line Wirdumerdijk into the centre of town at **Waagplein**, a long narrowing open space cut by a canal and flanked by cafés and large department stores. The **Waag** itself dates from 1598, but it's been converted into a restaurant and bank. Walking west, **Nieuwestad** is Leeuwarden's main shopping street, from where Kleine Kerkstraat, a turning on the right, leads to the **Oldehoofster Kerkhof** – a large square-cum-car park near the old city walls. At the end of the square stands the precariously leaning **Oldehove**. Something of a symbol for the city, this is part of a cathedral started in 1529 but never finished because of subsidence, a lugubrious mass of disproportion that defies all laws of gravity and geometry. To the right stands a statue of the Frisian politician and Trade Unionist P.J. Troelstra, who looks impassively on, no doubt admonishing the city on their choice of architects. Those brave enough can climb the tower for a guilder (Tues–Sat 10am–4pm).

Along Grote Kerkstraat

Grote Kerkstraat leads east from the square, following the line of the track that connected two of Leeuwarden's original *terpen*, Oldehove and Nijehove. Close by, at Grote Kerkstraat 11, is **Het Princessehof** (Mon–Sat 10am–5pm, Sun 2–5pm; f3), a house from 1650 that was once the residence of the Stadholder William Friso. It's now a ceramics museum, with the largest collection of tiles in the world, though sadly the layout is confusing and there are no English guidebooks available; one is promised for 1991. If you're really interested in ceramics you could spend days here; if not, be selective, as the sheer quantity of material is overwhelming.

Of the many displays, two are outstanding. The first, through the ornamental arch at reception and up the stairs to the second floor, is the collection of **Chinese, Japanese and Vietnamese ceramics**, which outlines the rise and fall of Far Eastern "china" production. In the sixteenth century Portuguese traders first began to bring back Chinese porcelain for sale in Europe. It proved tremendously popular, and by the seventeenth century the Dutch, among others, had begun to muscle in. Ships crammed with plates and dishes shuttled backwards and forwards to the China coast, where European merchants bargained with local warlords for trade and territorial concessions or "hongs" – hence Hong Kong. The benefits of the trade were inevitably weighted in favour of western interests, and the Chinese could only watch with dismay as the bottom fell out of the market when European factories began to reproduce their goods. The Dutch soon modified the original, highly stylised designs to more naturalistic patterns with a lighter, plainer effect, with the result that Chinese producers were forced to make desperate attempts to change their designs to fit western tastes.

The earliest pieces on display in this section date from the sixteenth century, notably several large blue and white plates of naive delicacy, decorated with swirling borders and surrealistic dragons. Although Chinese producers began to work to European designs in the early eighteenth century, it was many years before the general deterioration in manufacture became apparent, and some of the most exquisite examples of Chinaware date from as late as the middle of the eighteenth century – not least those from the Dutch merchantman *Geldermalsen*, which sank in the waters of the South China Sea in 1752 and was salvaged in 1983. Some 150,000 items of cargo were retrieved, and there's a small sample here, including a magnificent dish of bright blue twisting fish bordered by a design of flowers and stems – in stark contrast to the crude, sad-looking Chinese imitations of western landscapes and coats of arms across the room.

On the first floor, to the left of the stairs, you'll find another room devoted to the development of **Chinese porcelain** from prehistory onwards, with representative examples illustrating major trends. The finest work dates from the Ming Dynasty (1368–1644), with powerful open-mouthed dragons, billowing clouds and sharply drawn plant tendrils. This room leads to the other section you shouldn't miss, a magnificent array of **Dutch tiles**, with good examples of all the classic designs – soldiers, flowers, ships, etc – framed by uncomplicated borders. Well documented and clearly laid out, the earliest tiles date from the late fifteenth century, the work of Italians based in Antwerp, who used a colourful and expensive tin-glazing process. By the seventeenth century, tiles were no longer an exclusive product, and the demands of a mass market transformed the industry. Popular as a wall covering – the precursor of wallpaper – thousands of identical tiles were churned out by dozens of Dutch factories (there were seven in Friesland alone). The emphasis was on very simple designs, characteristically blue on white, the top end of the market distinguished by extra colours or the size of the design: the more tiles it took to make the "picture", the more expensive the tile.

Heading east from the museum along Grote Kerkstraat is the house where **Mata Hari** spent her early years – a native of Leeuwarden whose name has become synonymous with the idea of the "femme fatale". A renowned dancer, she was arrested in 1917 by the French on charges of espionage and subsequently shot, though what she actually did remains a matter of some debate. In retrospect it seems likely that she acted as a double agent, gathering information for the Allies while giving snippets to the Germans. Something of a local heroine, her old home has become the **Frisian Literary Museum** (Mon–Fri 9am–12.30pm & 1.30–5pm), a repository for a whole range of Frisian documents, together with a few derisory exhibits on Mata Hari herself. Better is the permanent display on P.J. Troelstra, the Frisian socialist politician and poet, who set up the Dutch Social Democratic party in 1890 and was at the head of the Dutch labour movement until 1924.

At the far end of Grote Kerkstraat, the **Grote** or **Jacobijner Kerk** (July–Aug Tues–Fri 10–11am & 2–4pm) has recently undergone a very extensive restoration, though it's still an unremarkable Gothic construction. Another victim of subsidence, the whole place tilts slightly towards the newer south aisle, where some tattered remnants of sixteenth-century frescoes are exhibited. In front of the church is a modernistic **memorial** to Leeuwarden's wartime Jewish community, based on the class registers of 1942; it's an imaginative and harsh reminder of suffering and persecution.

The Fries Museum and around

South of here, on Turfmarkt, the **Fries Museum** (Tues–Sat 10am–5pm, Sun 1–5pm; f3) is one of the best regional museums in the country, founded by a society that was established in the nineteenth century to develop interest in the language and history of Friesland, and with displays that trace the development of Frisian culture from prehistoric times up until the present day. On the ground floor, among a chain of period rooms, is an extensive collection of silverware. A flourishing Frisian industry throughout the seventeenth and eighteenth centuries, most of the work was commissioned by the local gentry, who were in their turn influenced by the fashions of the Frisian Stadholder and his court. The earliest piece is an elegant drinking horn of 1397 and there are some particularly fine examples of chased silver in Baroque style, where each representation is framed by a fanciful border or transition. This distinctive "Kwabornament" design flourished in Friesland long after it had declined in the rest of Holland. Some of the more curious exhibits here date from the middle of the seventeenth century when it was fashionable to frame exotic objects in silver: a certain Lenert Danckert turned a coconut into a cup and Minne Sikkes fitted silver handles to a porcelain bowl to create a brandy cup. Most of the later exhibits are ornate, French-style tableware.

On the first floor there's a selection of early majolica, many examples of different sorts of porcelain, and a mundane collection of seventeenth-century Frisian painting enlivened by a painting of his wife, Saskia, by Rembrandt. Other highlights include rooms given over to the island of Ameland and, notably, the painted furniture of Hindeloopen – rich, gaudy and intense, with tendrils and flowers on a red, green or white background. Most peculiar of all are examples of the bizarre headgear of eighteenth-century Hindeloopen women – large cartwheel-shaped hats known as *Deutsche muts* and (the less specifically Frisian) *oorijzers*, gold or silver helmets that were an elaborate development of the hat clip or brooch. As well as an indication of social standing, a young girl's first *oorijzer* symbolised the transition to womanhood.

Opposite the Fries Museum stands one of the most striking buildings in Leeuwarden – the **Kanselarij**, a superb gabled Renaissance structure of 1571. The original plan placed the gable and the corresponding double stairway in the centre of the facade, but they are in fact slightly to the right because the money ran out before the work was finished – making the Kanselarij an early example of public expenditure cuts. A little way north, the Catholic church of **St Boniface** is a neo-Gothic building of 1894 designed by P.J.H. Cuypers, its ornamented spire imposing itself on what is otherwise a rather flat skyline. The spire was almost totally destroyed in a storm of 1976 and there were many people who wanted to take the opportunity to pull the place down altogether – even to replace it with a supermarket. Fortunately the steeple was replaced at great expense and with such enormous ingenuity that its future seems secure, making it one of the few Cuypers churches left in Holland.

Eating and drinking

One of the best places to **eat** in Leeuwarden is *Eetcafé Spinoza* on Eewal, an elegant, reasonably priced restaurant with a good range of vegetarian dishes; for lunch, try the excellent *De Brasserie* on Wirdumerdijk. Alternatively, *Pizzeria Sardegna*, Grote Hoogstraat 28 (closed Mon), serves an extravagant variety of pizzas from f7 – as does *Pizzeria Antonio*, Uniabuurt 6. You can eat Mexican food at the *Yucatan* on St Jacobsstraat; or, for an arm and a leg, enjoy haute cuisine at the *Restaurant Maestral* by the junction of Zaailand and Prins Hendrikstraat. For **drinking**, the bar of the *Hotel De Pauw*, Stationsweg 10, is quiet and has some delightful old furniture; the *Herberg De Stee*, next door, is busy and boisterous. The *Spoekepolle*, on St Jacobsstraat, is a students' favourite; and the town's adolescents gather in the series of bars on the Doelesteeg.

Listings

Boat tours For information on guided boat trips to the Frisian lakes (੮nr; f15 per person) contact the VVV.
Books *Van der Velde*, Nieuwestad 90, has a good stock of English-language titles.
Car hire *Interrent*, Marshallweg 12–14 (☎12 55 55).
Emergencies ☎0011
Left luggage At the station (daily 6am–12pm).
Markets General market on Friday, Wilhelminaplein.
Pharmacy Details of nearest (emergency) pharmacy from ☎13 52 95
Police Holstmeerweg 1 (☎13 24 23)
Post office Opposite the station (Mon–Fri 8.30am–6pm, Sat 9am–2pm).

Around Leeuwarden: Popta Slot

On the western outskirts of Leeuwarden, the tiny village of **MARSSUM** incorporates **Popta Slot** (April–Sept Mon–Fri guided tours at 11am, 2pm & 3pm; f3) – a trim onion-domed eighteenth-century manor house, which sits prettily behind its ancient moat. Inside is a series of period rooms, furnished in the style of the local gentry. Doctor Popta was an affluent lawyer and farmer who spent some of his excess wealth on the neighbouring **Popta Gasthuis**, neat almshouses cloistered behind an elaborate portal of 1712. Bus #91 leaves Leeuwarden bus station for the ten-minute trip to Marssum once every hour during the week, every two hours on Sundays.

West of Leeuwarden: Franeker, Harlingen and the islands

Seventeen kilometres west of Leeuwarden, **FRANEKER** was the cultural hub of northern Holland until Napoleon closed the university in 1810. Nowadays it's a quiet country town with a spruce old centre of somewhat over-restored old buildings. The train station is five minutes' walk to the southeast of town – follow Stationsweg round to the left and over the bridge, first left over the second bridge onto Zuiderkade and second right along Dijkstraat. Buses from Leeuwarden (#97, hourly; 25min) drop passengers on Kleijenburg, at the northwest corner of the old town centre.

All the town's key sights are beside or near the main street, **Voorstraat**, a continuation of Dijkstraat, which runs from east to west to end in a park, **Sternse Slotland** – the site of the medieval castle. Near the park at Voorstraat 49, the

VVV is housed in the **Waag** of 1657, which also serves as the entrance to the **Museum 't Coopmanshus** (Tues–Sat 10am–5pm, April–Sept also Sun, 1–5pm; f2.75), next door, whose ground floor has bits and pieces relating to the university and its obscure alumni. In the old senate room, a pile of slim boxes carved to resemble books contain dried samples of local flora and fauna, the gift of Louis Bonaparte. Upstairs, a couple of rooms are devoted to trophies and pictures of the Frisian game of *kaatsen* – apparently a cross between fives and baseball.

Heading east along Voorstraat, past the stolid **Martenahuis** of 1498, the Raadhuisplein branches off to the left, edged by the **Stadhuis**, with its twin gables and octagonal tower – a magnificent mixture of Gothic and Renaissance styles built in 1591. Opposite, there's a curious, primitive eighteenth-century **Planetarium** (Tues–Sat 10am–12.30pm & 1.30–5pm; May–Aug Mon same times & Sun 1–5pm; f3.50) built by a local woolcomber, Eise Eisinga, in the living room of his house. Born in 1744, Eisinga was something of a prodigy: he taught himself mathematics and astronomy, publishing a weighty arithmetic book at the age of only 17. In 1774, the unusual conjunction of Mercury, Venus, Mars and Jupiter under the sign of Aries prompted a local paper to predict the end of the world. There was panic in the countryside, and an appalled Eisinga decided on his life's work, the construction of a planetarium that would dispel superstition by explaining the workings of the cosmos. It took him seven years, almost as long as he had to enjoy it before his distaste for the autocratic Frisian Stadholder caused his imprisonment and exile. His return signalled a change of fortunes. In 1816 he was presented with the order of the Lion of the Netherlands and, two years later, a royal visit persuaded King Willem I to buy the planetarium for the state, granting Eisinga a free tenancy and a generous annual stipend until his death in 1828.

The planetarium isn't of the familiar domed variety, but was built as a false ceiling in the family's living room, a series of rotating dials and clocks indicating the movement of the planets and associated phenomena, from tides to star signs. The whole apparatus is regulated by a clock which is driven by a series of weights hung in a tiny alcove beside the cupboard-bed. Above the face of the main dials, the mechanisms are open for inspection, hundreds of hand-made nails driven into moving slats. A detailed guidebook explains every aspect and every dial.

Of other buildings, the quaint **Korendragerhuisje** (no admission), just east along the canal from the planetarium, was built for the Corn Porters' Guild in 1634. There's also an extraordinarily dull provincial **coin collection** (Munt en Penningkabinet; May–Sept Mon–Fri 1–5pm; f1.50), stored above a bank on Dijkstraat.

Practical details

Franeker's **VVV** is at Voorstraat 51 (Mon–Fri 9am–5pm; ☎05170/4613), five minutes' walk northwest of the train station. There are four **hotels** in town, with doubles for f30–40 per person per night: *De Bleek*, near the station at Stationsweg 1 (☎05170/2124); *De Stadsherberg*, on the continuation of Stationsweg at Oude Kaatsveld 8 (☎05170/2686); *De Doelen*, where Dijkstraat joins Voorstraat at Breedeplaats 6 (☎05170/2261); and *De Bogt Fen Gune*, on the left turn at the west end of Voorstraat, Vijverstraat 1 (☎05170/2416). The town **campsite** (April–Sept) is a couple of minutes' walk east of the train station down Schurmansingel and across Tzummerweg on J. Stapertlaan. For **food**, try *La Terraz*, near the Korendragerhuisje at Zilverstraat 7, or the hotel *De Bogt Fen Gune*.

Harlingen

Just north of the Afsluitdijk, 30km west of Leeuwarden, **HARLINGEN** is more compelling than Franeker, an ancient and historic port that serves as the ferry terminal for the islands of Terschelling and Vlieland. A naval base from the seventeenth century onwards, the town sits astride the **Vliestroom** channel, once the easiest way for shipping to pass from the North Sea through the shallows that surround the Frisian islands and on into the Zuider Zee. Before trade moved west, this was Holland's lifeline, where corn, fish and other foodstuffs were brought in from the Baltic to feed the expanding Dutch cities.

Harlingen has two railway stations, one on the southern edge of town for trains from Leeuwarden, the other, Harlingen Haven, right next to the docks, handling trains connecting with boats to the islands. From Harlingen Haven the old town spreads east, sandwiched between the Noorderhaven and Zuiderhaven canals, a mass of sixteenth- to eighteenth-century houses that reflect the prosperity and importance of earlier times. However, Harlingen is too busy to be just another cosy tourist town: there's a fishing fleet, a small container depot, a shipbuilding yard and a resurgent ceramics industry. The heart of town is the **Voorstraat**, a long tree-lined avenue that's home to an elegant eighteenth-century **Stadhuis**, the VVV and the town **museum** (no. 56; July & Aug Tues–Sat 10am–5pm; May, June & Sept Mon–Fri 2–5pm). Sited in an eighteenth-century merchant's house, the museum concentrates on the history of the town and includes some interesting displays on shipping and some lovely, locally produced tiles – for once in manageable quantities. All the information is in Dutch, but an English guide is promised to coincide with the museum's expansion.

Harlingen was once a tile-making centre, and the industry flourished here until it was undermined by the rise of cheap wallpaper. The last of the old factories closed in 1933, but the demand for traditional crafts has led to something of a recovery, with the opening of new workshops in 1974. If you like the look of Dutch tiles, this is a good place to buy. The **Harlinger Aardewerk en Tegelfabriek** at Voorstraat 84 sells an outstanding range of contemporary and traditional styles – if you've got the money. Dutch handicrafts don't come cheap.

Practical details

Another of Harlingen's specialities is fresh **fish**: dotted all over the centre of town are fish stalls, fish restaurants and snack bars. Best is *Veltman's* on the edge of the Noorderhaven at Rommelhaven 2, a combined snack bar and restaurant with a wide range of North Sea delicacies. More expensive alternatives are the *'t Noordeke* at Noorderhaven 17 and the hotel restaurants. If you're planning to stay, there are three reasonably priced **hotels** in Harlingen. The *Heerenlogement*, on the eastern continuation of Voorstraat at Franekereind 23 (☎05178/15846), and the *Zeezicht*, near the harbour at Zuiderhaven 1 (☎05178/12536), both charge around f100 per person per night for doubles with private bath – though the former has some rooms without. The *Anna Casparii* (☎05178/12065) only costs a little more and is superbly sited, overlooking the canal at Noorderhaven 67. For about half the price, the VVV at Voorstraat 34 (Mon–Fri 9am–5pm, Sat 9am–1pm & 2–5pm; ☎05178/17222) have a small stock of **rooms** and **pensions**, though they go fast in the summer. The nearest **campsite**, *De Zeehoeve* (April–Sept), is a fifteen-minute walk along the sea dyke to the south of town at Westerzeedijk 45 – follow the signs from Voorstraat.

Terschelling and Vlieland

Boats leave Harlingen for the ninety-minute crossings to the islands of Terschelling and Vlieland at least three times daily throughout the summer and twice daily during the winter. The return fare for both trips is f30, bikes a further f11, and the ferries dock at West Terschelling and Oost-Vlieland, the islands' main settlements. An additional service joins Terschelling and Vlieland but only runs two days a week between June and August, once a week at other times (f15 return). Visitors' cars are not allowed on either island.

Terschelling

A major tourist resort in its own right, the town of **WEST TERSCHELLING** is a rather unappealing sprawl of chalets, bungalows and holiday complexes that spreads out from what remains of the old village – a mediocre modernity that belies West Terschelling's past importance as a port and safe anchorage on the edge of the Vliestroom channel, the main shipping lane from the Zuider Zee. Strategically positioned, West Terschelling boomed throughout the seventeenth century as a ship supply and repair centre, with its own fishing and whaling fleets, paying the price for its prominence when the British razed the town in 1666. The islanders were renowned sailors, much sought after by ships' captains who also needed them as pilots to guide ships through the treacherous shallows and shifting sandbanks that lay off the Vliestroom. Despite the pilots, shipwrecks were common all along the island's northern and western shores – the VVV sells a sketch of the island marked with all the known disasters. The most famous victim was the *Lutine*, which sank carrying gold and silver to British troops stationed here during the Napoleonic wars. The remains are still at the bottom of the sea, and only the ship's bell was recovered – now in Lloyd's of London, where it's still rung if ever a big ship goes down.

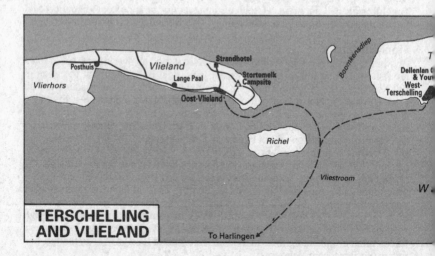

TERSCHELLING AND VLIELAND

The best place to bone up on Terschelling's past is the excellent town **Museum** (April–Oct Mon–Fri 9am–5pm & in Aug Sat 9am–5pm; f3), near the ferry terminal at Commandeurstraat 30. The prime exhibits here include maps of the old coastline illustrating Terschelling's crucial position, various items from the whaling fleet, lots of sepia photos of bearded islanders, and a shipwreck diving room. There's also a rather desultory tribute to the local explorer Willem Barents, who came unstuck when ice trapped his ship in the Arctic in 1595. Undaunted, he and his crew managed to survive the whole winter on the ice and sailed back in the spring. Barents mounted other, more successful expeditions into the Arctic regions, discovering Spitzbergen and naming the Barents Sea – all in the fruitless search for the northern route to China. He died in the Arctic in 1597.

Throughout the summer West Terschelling is packed with tourists sampling the restaurants and bars that line the main streets, while others trudge off across the island to the beach at **WEST-AAN-ZEE**. If you want to stay, **accommodation** is hard to come by in July and August when all the cheaper places tend to be booked up months in advance. At other times you have a wide choice, including **pensions** for about f30 – try *De Boekanier*, Commandeurstraat 19 (☎05620/2524), or the *De Holland*, Molenstraat 5 (☎05620/2302); both are near the ferry terminal. There's a **youth hostel** at Burgmeester Van Heusdenweg 39 (April–Sept; ☎05620/2338), with an adjoining **campsite**, the *Dellewal* (☎05620/2305), the nearest of several sites, some 25 minutes' east of town along the southern shore.

The **VVV** (Mon–Fri 9am–noon & 2–5pm, Fri also 7.30–9pm, Sat 11am–noon & 4–5pm; ☎05620/3000), also near the ferry port, provides a full list of pensions and **rooms** and operates a reservation service (f5). They also take bookings for the rest of the island; if you're after a bit of peace and quiet, aim for **pensions** between the villages of FORMERUM and OOSTEREND – far enough east to escape most of the crowds.

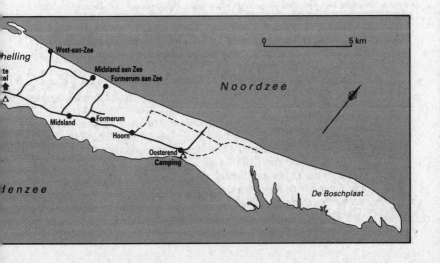

From West Terschelling, the other villages stretch out along the southern part of the island, sheltered from winter storms by the sand dunes and occasional forest that lie to the immediate north. The island **bus** service leaves from beside the ferry terminal and is excellent, connecting all the villages in a matter of minutes; alternatively **bikes** can be hired at about f6 a day from a number of shops near the harbour and from the VVV. Quite simply, the further east you go the more attractive the island becomes: the last two settlements, **HOORN** and **OOSTEREND** are particularly pleasant places within easy reach of empty tracts of beach and the nature reserve **De Boschplaat**, where thousands of birds congregate in the marshy shallows of the southeastern shore. To protect the birds, De Boschplaat is closed during the breeding season (March 15–Aug 15), though the VVV run guided tours for bird enthusiasts. Oosterend also has a **café**, *De Boschplaat*, one of the best places to eat on the island, and three **campsites** – including the cosy *'t Wantij*.

Vlieland

The complex pattern of sandbank shallows that lie to the south of **VLIELAND**, just west of Terschelling, helped to make the island one of the most isolated and neglected parts of nineteenth-century Holland. Of minor importance during the great days of the Zuider Zee trade, Vlieland lost one of its two villages to the sea in the eighteenth century and there was never enough money to have it rebuilt. Tourism has brought wealth to the 1000 or so islanders, but it's all very low-key: development has been restrained and the island is popular for family holidays – cycling, windsurfing, beaches and country walks. The quietest of the Frisian islands, no cars are allowed; and the only settlement, **OOST-VLIELAND**, is little more than a restaurant-lined main street surrounded by second homes, chalets and bungalows. There's little to see in the village as such, though the plastic globe in the small square is a surprising tribute to Esperanto, and the Armenhuis behind it a particularly attractive seventeenth-century country dwelling. The town's **Museum**, Dorpsstraat 99 (Mon–Sat 10am–noon & 2–5pm), has a mundane collection of antiques and Vlieland bygones.

Accommodation is limited and virtually impossible to find throughout the summer, though the **VVV** (Mon–Fri 9am–5pm; Oct–April also Sat 11am–noon; May–Sept also Sat & Sun 11am–noon & 4-5pm; ☎05621/1357) do their best with the few private **rooms**, from f30 per person per night, and will help groups rent out apartments and "dune houses". Vlieland has nine **hotels**, cheapest of which is the *De Herbergh van Flielant* on the main street at Dorpsstraat 105, with doubles for about f80 (☎05621/1400); the only **pensions** are down the road at nos. 163 and 173 – f35–40 for bed and breakfast per person. The most convenient **campsite**, *De Stortemelk* (☎05621/1225), is sited on the sand dunes behind the beach, about half an hour's walk northeast of Oost-Vlieland at Kampweg 1.

The best way of seeing the island is by **bike**, available from several village shops and the VVV for f8 per day, though there's also a limited **bus** service that travels along the southern shore from near the ferry terminal. For **excursions**, the VVV run birdwatching expeditions, and private operators organise day-long trips to the northern tip of Texel (f10 return) by way of a tractor-like lorry, which crosses the great expanse of sand ("Vliehors") that forms Vlieland's western extremity, to connect with a boat.

South of Leeuwarden: Sneek, the lakes and the Ijsselmeer ports

The Leeuwarden–Stavoren rail line passes through a series of small Frisian towns with a speed that gainsays their earlier isolation. Until well into the nineteenth century, the lakes, canals and peat diggings south and east of Sneek made land communications difficult and the only significant settlements were close to the sea or on major waterways. Dependent on water-borne trade, these communities declined with the collapse of the Zuider Zee trade, but, because of their insularity, some maintained particular artistic and cultural traditions – from the painted furniture and distinctive dialect of Hindeloopen to the style and design of many of Makkum's tiles. Nowadays, all the tiny old towns are popular holiday destinations, of which Sneek, the centre of a booming pleasure-boat industry, is by far the busiest.

Sneek

Twenty minutes by train from Leeuwarden, **SNEEK** (pronounced "snake") was an important shipbuilding centre as early as the fifteenth century, a prosperous maritime town protected by an extensive system of walls and moats. Clumsy post-war development has robbed the place of most of its charm, but there are still some buildings of mild interest.

Sneek's **rail** and **bus** stations are five minutes' walk from the old centre, directly east down Stationsstraat. This leads to the main square, **Martiniplein**, whose ponderous sixteenth-century **Martinikerk** is edged by an old wooden belfry. Around the corner at the end of Grote Kerkstraat, the **Stadhuis**, Marktstraat 15, is all extravagance, from the Rococo facade to the fanciful outside staircase; inside (Mon–Fri 2–4pm) there's a mediocre display of ancient weapons in the former guardroom. Heading east along Marktstraat, veer right after the VVV and follow the signs to the nearby **Scheepvart Museum en Oudheidkamer**, Kleinzand 14 (Mon–Sat 10am–noon & 1.30–5pm; f2), a well displayed collection of maritime models, paintings and related miscellany. There's also a room devoted to the Visser family, who made a fortune in the eighteenth century, transporting eels to hungry Londoners. Lastly, directly south of the Martiniplein, the grandiose Renaissance **Waterpoort** is all that remains of the town walls.

Practical details

If you want to stay in Sneek, the **VVV**, right in the centre of town near the Stadhuis at Marktstraat 18 (May–Aug Mon–Sat 9.30am–5pm; Sept–April Mon 1–5pm, Tues–Fri 9.30am–5pm, Sat 10am–2pm; ☎05150/14096), will arrange private **rooms**, from f25 per person per night, for a small booking fee. The town's cheaper **hotels** include the *Ozinga,* immediately to the south of the Waterpoort at Lemmerweg 8 (☎05150/12216), with doubles for around f60 per night; the *Bonnema*, by the station at Stationsstraat 64 (☎05150/13175), has doubles for f100 a night, the *De Wijnberg*, Marktstraat 23 (☎05150/12421), for f90. The Sneek **youth hostel** (☎05150/12132; mid-June to mid-Sept) is some 3km southeast of the town centre at Oude Oppenhuizerweg 20 – head east to the end of Kleinzand, turn right down Oppenhuizerweg and it's the first major turning on the left. The nearest **campsite** is *De Domp*, Domp 4 (☎05150/12559; no buses), a couple of kilometres northeast of the centre on Sytsingawiersterleane, a right turn off the main road to Leeuwarden. *Camping De Potten*, Paviljoenweg (☎05150/15205; April–Sept), lies some 5km east of town beside the **Sneekemeer**, the nearest of the Frisian lakes, but again there are no buses; taxis can be arranged at the VVV. *De Potten* hires out a good range of water sports equipment at reasonable prices.

If you want to see more of the lakes, **boat trips** leave from the Oosterkade, over the bridge by the east end of Kleinzand, throughout the summer. Itineraries and prices vary and there's no fixed schedule of sailings; contact the VVV or the boat owners at the quay for up-to-date details.

One word of warning: expect Sneek to be exceptionally busy and accommodation impossible to find during **Sneek Week**, the annual regatta held at the beginning of August, when the flat green expanses around town are thick with the white of slowly moving sails.

Bolsward

Some 10km west of Sneek, **BOLSWARD** is the archetypal Frisian country town, with tractors on the roads and geese in the streets. Founded in the seventh century, there are only two sights to speak of – the scant ruins of the **Broerekerk**, opposite the VVV, and the **Stadhuis**, a magnificent red-brick, stone-trimmed Renaissance edifice of 1613. The facade is topped by a lion holding a coat of arms over the head of a terrified – or surprised – Turk, and below a mass of twisting, curling carved stone frames a series of finely cut cameos, all balanced by an extravagant external staircase.

Bus #99 connects Sneek railway station with Bolsward (Mon–Sat 3 hourly, Sun 1 hourly; 15min), and should you decide to **stay**, the VVV, Broereplein 1 (Mon–Fri 9am–noon & 1.30–5pm; ☎05157/2727), has a handful of private **rooms** from f30 per person per night. There are two cheap and convenient **hotels**, *The Centraal*, Nieuwmarkt 10 (☎05157/2589), with doubles for f60, and *De Wijnberg*, Marktplein 5 (☎05157/2220), which charges f75 plus.

Workum and Makkum

Ten minutes' southwest of Sneek by train, **WORKUM**, with its neat grid-iron rows of houses, has the appearance of a comfortable city suburb, protected by several kilometres of sea defences. In fact, until the early eighteenth century it was a seaport, and nowadays indications of a more adventurous past are confined to the central square, 3km from the railway station, with its seventeenth-century **Waag** and flamboyant **Stadhuis**. The VVV (Mon–Fri 9am–5pm; ☎05151/1300) is on the ground floor of the Waag and can sometimes sort out a private **room**.

From Workum train station a minibus service (#102, Mon–Sat every 2–3 hours, no Sun service) heads south to Hindeloopen (see below) or north to the agreeable town of **MAKKUM** – in fact more easily accessible from Bolsward, by bus #98 (Mon–Sat hourly, Sun afternoon every 2hr; 20min). The minibus follows part of Friesland's "Heritage Trail", passing ancient red and black tiled farmhouses among green and flattened fields. Though saved from postcard prettiness by a working harbour, Makkum's popularity as a centre of traditional Dutch ceramics manufacture means it can be overwhelmed by summer tourists. The local product rivals the more famous Delftware in quality, varying from the bright and colourful to more delicate pieces. The VVV (April–Oct Mon–Fri 10am–5pm; summer also Sat 10am–5pm & Sun 1.30–5pm; ☎05158/1422) is sited beneath a **museum** which features, predictably enough, representative samples of local work. If you haven't seen enough tiles here to satisfy your curiosity, there's plenty more, notably in the Tichelaar family **workshops** at Turfmarkt 61, open to the public for f3 – or you can visit their two shops for free. There are no bargains, though, and most of the modern tiles have either staid traditional motifs or ooze an unappealing domestic cosiness; the vases and larger plates are more exciting but also more expensive. If you decide to **stay**, the *De Prins* at Kerkstraat 1 (☎05158/1510), with doubles from f70 per night, is the cheapest hotel in town with good views over the harbour; the *De Waag*, at Markt 13 (☎05158/1447), is a reasonable second choice with rooms for about f80. Details of a few private **rooms** are available from the VVV.

Hindeloopen

The next stop down the railway line, the village of **HINDELOOPEN** juts into the Ijsselmeer twenty minutes' walk west of the railway station, its primness extreme even by Dutch standards. Until the seventeenth century Hindeloopen prospered as a Zuider Zee port, concentrating on trade with the Baltic and Amsterdam. A tightly-knit community, the combination of rural isolation and trade created a specific culture, with a distinctive dialect – *Hylper*, Frisian with Scandinavian influences – a sumptuous costume, and, most famous of all, an elaborate style of painted furniture. Adopting materials imported into Amsterdam by the East India Company, the women of Hindeloopen dressed in a florid combination of colours where dress was a means of personal identification: caps, casques and trinkets indicated marital status and age, and the quality of the print indicated social standing. Other Dutch villages adopted similar practices, but nowhere were the details of social position so precisely drawn. The development of dress turned out to be a corollary of prosperity, for the decline of Hindeloopen quite simply finished it off.

Similarly, the furniture was an ornate mixture of Scandinavian and oriental styles superimposed on traditional Dutch joinery. Each item was covered from top to tail with painted tendrils and flowers on a red, green or white background, though again the town's decline led to the lapsing of the craft. Tourism has revived local furniture making, and countless shops line the main street selling modern versions, though even the smallest items aren't cheap, and the style is something of an acquired taste. You can see original examples in the small village **museum** (March–Oct Mon–Sat 10am–5pm, Sun 1.30–5pm; f3), but there's a wider display at the Fries Museum in Leeuwarden.

Tradition apart, Hindeloopen is a delightful little village pressed against the sea in a tidy jigsaw of old streets and canals. There are no particular sights, but the church has some Royal Air Force graves in memory of airmen who came down in the Zuider Zee, while the small **Schaats Museum** is really a furniture shop with some skating mementoes – Hindeloopen is one of the towns included in the route of the great Frisian ice-skating race, De Friese Elfstedentocht (see below). Hindeloopen is also popular with windsurfers, who benefit from the shallow, sloping beach to the south of the town, where a brand new marina and leisure centre have just been completed.

Hindeloopen's popularity makes **accommodation** a problem in summer, and the only cheap hotel, *Skipshotel*, Oosterstrand 3 (☎05142/2452), with doubles for f60 or so, is nearly always full. The VVV (summer Mon–Fri 9am–noon & 1–5pm; ☎05142/2550) have the odd private **room**, and the only other alternative is the **campsite** a kilometre or so south of town near the coast at Westerdijk 11. For **eating**, try *De Gasterie*, Kalverstraat 13, or *De Kastanjehof*, Nieuwe Weide 1.

Sloten

Close to the southern coast of Friesland, the main problem with **SLOTEN** is getting there. Of the possible permutations, the easiest option is to take bus #42 (Mon–Fri every half-hour, Sat & Sun hourly; 35min) from Sneek train station to the bus change-over point on the motorway at Spannenburg, where connecting services #44 or #41 (same frequency; 5min) continue west to Sloten and Bolsward or Balk. Double-check your destination with the driver as there are connecting buses with the same numbers on them heading east.

THE ELFSTEDENTOCHT

The **Elfstedentocht** is Friesland's biggest spectacle, a gruelling ice-skating marathon around Friesland that dates back to 1890, when one Pim Muller, a local sports journalist, skated his way around the eleven official towns of the province – simply to see whether it was possible. It was, and twenty years later the first official Elfstedentocht or "Eleven Towns Race" was born, contested by 22 skaters. Weather – and ice – permitting, it has taken place regularly ever since, nowadays a major ice-skating event, attracting skaters from all over the world.

The race is organised by the Eleven Towns Association, and you have to be a member of this association to take part. Perhaps not surprisingly, the current interest in the race means membership is restricted and very difficult to obtain, over-subscribed by around 17 times at the last count. The route of the race, which measures about 200km in total, takes in all the main centres of Friesland, starting in the capital, Leeuwarden, at about 5am in the town's Friesland Hall, when the racers sprint, skates in hand, 1500m to the point where they start skating. The first stop after this is Sneek, taking in Hindeloopen and the other old Zuider Zee towns before finishing in Dokkum in the north of the province. The contestants must stop briefly at each town to have their card stamped. These days the event is broadcast live on TV across the country, and the route lined with spectactors. Of the 17,000 or so who take part in the race, only around 300 are serious skaters; the rest are there just to see if they can complete the course. In 1986 the winning time was just under 7 hours – managed by one Evert van Benthem, a Frisian dairy farmer who has won the Elfstedentocht two years in a row and is something of a national celebrity as a result.

All the skaters need to have all-round fitness. They attempt to skate the whole route, but it's not always possible, and at times – crossing from one canal to another, for example, or avoiding a stretch of thin ice – they have to try something called *kluning*, a Frisian word which basically means walking on dry land in skates: not easy. Casualties are inevitably numerous. Of the 10,000 who took part in 1963, only 70 or so finished, the rest beaten by the fierce winds, extreme cold and snowdrifts along the way. On the last few occasions things have been a little gentler, around three-quarters of those who started out crossing the finishing line. But competitors still go down with frostbite, and many have to drop out because their sweat turns to ice and clogs up their eyes – a condition only a trip to hospital will put right.

The smallest of Friesland's eleven towns, Sloten was ruined by the demise of the Zuider Zee trade, and, robbed of its importance, became something of a museum-piece. Little more than a main street on either side of a central canal, it's undeniably charming, even if there are a lot of other people sharing its delights. With its cobbled streets, windmill, old locks and decorated gables, Sloten's homely prettiness is only disturbed by a large concrete tower that's part of a milk processing factory – surely a prime target for demolition. **Accommodation** is limited to a few **campsites** at opposite ends of town, and the **pension** *'T Brechje* at Voorstreek 110 (☎05143/298) with doubles from f60 per night – ring ahead to make sure of a vacancy. The **VVV** at Heerenwal 57 (☎05143/583) rarely have **rooms** to rent.

Stavoren

At the end of the railway line, **STAVOREN** was also once a prosperous port, but is now an ungainly combination of modern housing and old harbour, from where **ferries** make the crossing to Enkhuizen for connecting trains to Amsterdam (see Chapter Two for rough frequencies and prices). Named after the Frisian god Stavo, Stavoren is a popular boating centre and has a large marina adjoining a **campsite** that in turn is just behind a pleasant sandy beach, some ten minutes' walk south of the railway station. The campsite is surrounded by a swampy strip of water, so come equipped with mosquito repellent. The best place to **stay** is the hotel *De Vrouwe van Stavoren* (☎05149/1202), attractively sited by the harbour and surprisingly cheap at around f40 per person per night. The **VVV** (June–Aug Mon–Sat 10am–noon & 1.30–5pm; ☎05149/1616) has details of **pensions** and private **rooms**, but you'll probably want to move straight on.

North of Leeuwarden: Dokkum and the islands

Edged by the Lauwersmeer to the east and protected by interlocking sea-dykes to the north, the strip of Friesland between Leeuwarden and the Waddenzee is dotted with tiny agricultural villages that were once separated from each other by swamp and marsh. Sparsely inhabited, the area's first settlers were forced to confine themselves to whatever higher ground was available, the *terpen* which kept the treacherous waters at bay.

DOKKUM, the only significant settlement and one of Friesland's oldest towns, is half an hour by bus from Leeuwarden (#51; Mon–Fri 2 hourly; Sat & Sun hourly). The English missionary Saint Boniface was murdered here in 754 while trying to convert the pagan Frisians to Christianity. In part walled and moated, Dokkum has kept its shape as a fortified town, but it's best by the side of the **Het Grootdiep** canal, which cuts the town into two distinct sections. This was the commercial centre of the old town, and is marked by a series of ancient gables, including the **Admiralty Building** which serves as the town's mediocre museum. There's not much else: a couple of windmills, quiet walks along the old ramparts, and all sorts of things named after Saint Boniface. Give it a couple of hours and move on. If you decide to stay, the **VVV** (Mon–Fri 9am–5pm; ☎05190/3800) has a supply of private **rooms** from f25 per person per night. The cheapest **hotel** is the *Van der Meer*, Woudweg 1 (☎05190/2380); reckon on f35 per person per night.

Wierum and Moddergat

Of all the tiny hamlets in northern Friesland, two of the most interesting are Wierum and neighbouring Moddergat. **MODDERGAT**, the more easterly of the two, spreads out along the road behind the sea-wall some 10km north of Dokkum, merging with the village of PAESENS. At the western edge of the village, a memorial commemorates the tragedy of 1893 when 17 ships were sunk by a sudden storm with the loss of 83 lives. Opposite, the **'t Fiskerhuske Museum** (March–Oct Mon–Sat 10am–5pm) consists of three restored fishermens' cottages with displays on the history and culture of the village and details of the disaster. Huddled behind the sea-dyke 5km to the west, **WIERUM** has one main claim to fame, its twelfth-century church with a saddle-roof tower. The **Wadloopcentrum** here organises guided walks across the mud flats: times vary with conditions and tides; further details from Dokkum VVV.

Readily accessible from Dokkum, Moddergat and Wierum are on the same bus route (#52; Mon–Sat 7 times daily, Sun 2 daily). There's only one place to **stay**, the pension *Meinsma* (☎05199/396), Meinsmaweg 5 in Moddergat, where beds run at about f25 per person per night.

Ameland and Schiermonnikoog

It only takes 35 minutes by bus #66 from Leeuwarden to Holwerd, where you can catch the connecting ferry to **Ameland**. Boats leave five or six times daily throughout the year, but on summer weekends the service increases to nine. The trip takes 45 minutes and costs f12 return. For **Schiermonnikoog** island, bus #51 runs from Dokkum (30min) and Leeuwarden (1hr 30min), and bus #63 from Groningen (1hr), for the port of Lauwersoog, where connecting boats make the crossing two to six times daily (f15 return; 50min). Cars aren't allowed on either island.

Ameland

Ameland is one of the major tourist resorts of the northern Dutch coast, with a population that swells from a mere 3000 to a staggering 35,000 during summer

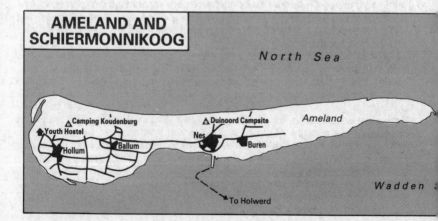

weekends. Boats dock near the principal village, **NES**, a tiny place that snuggles amongst the green fields behind the enclosing dyke. Once an important centre of the Dutch whaling industry, Nes has its share of cafés, hotels and tourist shops, though quite a bit of the old village has survived and high-rise development has been expressly forbidden. Perhaps surprisingly, the crowds rarely seem to overwhelm the village, but rather to breathe life into the place. Nes has a wide range of **accommodation**, but prices do rise dramatically in summer, when many places are full; off-season rooms cost about f30 per person per night, rising to f50 at peak weekends. It's advisable to ring ahead if you are visiting in July and August. For a few guilders, the **VVV** (July & Aug Mon–Sat 9am–5pm & 7–8pm; otherwise Mon–Fri 9am–noon & 2–5pm; ☎05191/2020) will fix you up with a **pension** or private **room** anywhere on the island, or you could try the centrally sited *Hotel De Jong* (☎05191/2016) at Reeweg 29, where you'll pay between f35 and f55 per person per night. The best appointed **campsite** is *Duinoord* (☎05191/2070), by the beach about half a mile north of Nes at Jan van Eijckweg 4.

If you fancy some peace and quiet, it's fairly easy to escape the crowds on all but the busiest of days, and **bikes** are for hire at a number of shops in Nes for about f5 a day (f25 per week). Ameland is only 2km wide, but it's 25km long, and its entire northern shore is made up of a fine expanse of sand and dune laced by foot and cycle paths. The east end of the island is the most deserted, and you can cycle by the side of the marshy shallows that once made up the whole southern shore before the construction of the sea-dyke. Of the smaller villages that dot the island, the prettiest place to stay is **HOLLUM**, a sedate settlement of old houses and farm buildings west of Nes. Here, the **hotel** *De Zwaan* (no phone) is cheap, friendly and convenient; **camping** *Koudenburg* (☎05191/4367) is by the heath to the north; and to the west, near the lighthouse and the tip of Ameland, is a better-than-average **youth hostel** (☎05191/4133; April–Sept), surrounded by sand dune and forest.

If you're heavily laden, a summer island **bus** service connects the principal villages between three and nine times daily. There are a variety of **boat** excursions from Nes, including trips to Terschelling, Schiermonnikoog and the sandbanks to see the sea-lions – though these have been decimated following a recent pollution-based viral epidemic. Details from the VVV or tour operators in Nes.

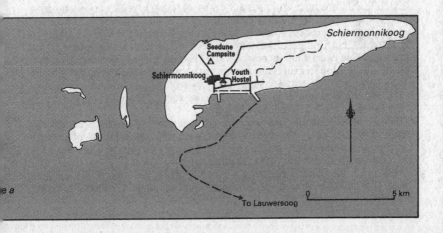

Schiermonnikoog

Until the Reformation, **SCHIERMONNIKOOG** was the property of the monastery of Klaarkamp, back on the mainland; its name means literally "island of the
grey monks". Nothing remains of the monks, however, and these days
Schiermonnikoog's only settlement is a prim and busy village bordering on long
stretches of muddy beach and sand dune to the north, mud flat and farmland to
the south. Once you're clear of the weekend homes that fringe the village, the
island's a wild, uncultivated place, criss-crossed by cycle paths, and not surprisingly it's a popular spot for day-trippers.

Boats from Lauwersoog dock at the island quay, some 3km from the village,
and there's a connecting bus service which drops you outside the VVV in the
centre. It's even possible to walk to the island across the mud flats from
Kloosterburen, a distance of about 8km, but this is not feasible without a guide;
see the box opposite for details.

Accommodation is hard to find in season, when prices rise sharply, and it's
advisable to ring ahead. The **VVV** (Mon–Sat 9.30–11.30am & 2.30–6.30pm; July &
Aug also Sun 10am–noon; ☎05195/1233) will help by booking private **rooms** and
pensions. The cheapest **hotel** on the island is the *Zonneweelde* (☎05195/1304),
situated in the heart of the village at Langestreek 94; a double room costs f80. A
good second bet is the *Duinzicht* (☎05195/1218), to the north of town on the way
to the beach at Badweg 17, where they have rooms for about the same price.
Schiermonnikoog's **campsite**, *Seedune* (☎05195/1398), is also to the north, in the
woods just east of Badweg at Seeduneweg 1. The **youth hostel** at Knuppeldam 2
(☎05195/1257; July–Aug) is on the east side of the village, fifteen minutes' walk
from the VVV.

The *Strandhotel*, twenty minutes from the VVV, overlooks the beach at the end
of Badweg and hires out **windsurfing** equipment; **bikes** (f5 per day) are available
from several small shops in the village, and the VVV sells good **maps**.

Groningen and around

Nominally a fiefdom of the Bishops of Utrecht from 1040 until 1536, the city of
GRONINGEN was once an important centre of trade, in reality an autonomous
merchant state ruled by a tightly defined oligarchy, whose power was exercised
through the city council or *Raad*. In 1536 Charles V forced the town to submit to
his authority, but Groningen was nevertheless still hesitant in its support of the
Dutch rebellion against his successors. The dilemma for the city fathers was that
although they stood to gain economically from independence, the majority of the
town's citizens were Catholic, deeply suspicious of their Protestant neighbours.
In the end, the economic argument won the day and the town became the capital
of the Dutch province of Groningen in 1594.

Heavily bombed in the last war, the city has few sights and is an eclectic
jumble of architectures. However, it does benefit from the presence of its large
and prestigious university, which gives the place a cosmopolitan and vigorous
feel quite unexpected in this part of the country.

Very much the cultural centre of northern Holland, Groningen offers a wide
range of contemporary arts performances and exhibitions, especially during
term-time.

WADLOPEN

Wadlopen, or mud-flat walking, is a popular and strenuous Dutch pastime, and the stretch of coast on the northern edge of the provinces of Friesland and Groningen is one of the best places to do it; twice daily, the receding tide uncovers vast expanses of mud-flat beneath the Waddenzee. It is, however, a sport to be taken seriously, and far too dangerous to do without an experienced guide – the depth of the mud is too variable (you have to walk up to thigh-deep in places) and the tides inconsistent. In any case, channels of deep water are left even when the tide has receded and you need to be aware of the whereabouts of these; the currents, too, can be perilous. The VVVs in **Dokkum, Leeuwarden** and **Groningen** will provide details of organised excursions, whose timing depends on weather and tidal conditions. It's important to be properly equipped, not least with adequate clothing. The weather can change rapidly up here, and group leaders request you take or wear walking shorts or swimming trunks, a sweater, a wind jacket, knee-high wool socks, high-top gym shoes and a complete change of clothes stored in a watertight packet.

Arrival, information and accommodation

Groningen's **bus** and **railway** stations are side by side on the south side of town, ten minutes' walk from the VVV, on the east side of the Grote Markt at Naberpassage 3 (Mon–Fri 9am–5pm, Sat 10am–4pm; ☎13 97 00). The VVV provide a wide range of services, from tourist information on the town and province through to tickets for visiting bands, theatre groups and orchestras, as listed in their free booklet *Uit in Groningen*. They also have a short list of **private rooms** in both Groningen and the surrounding area, averaging out at about f25 per person per night, though hardly any are near the city centre. Otherwise, Groningen has only three reasonably priced **hotels**, all situated just south of the Grote Markt: the rather seedy *Tivoli* (☎12 57 28), and the *Weeva* (☎12 99 19), at Gedempte Zuiderdiep 67 and 8, which have double rooms for about f60 and f80 respectively, and the *Garni Friesland* at Kleine Pelsterstraat 4 (☎121307), which has doubles ffor f80 upwards. If you're camping, catch bus #2 from the main square for the ten-minute journey to **Camping Stadspark** (March–Oct).

The Groningen area telephone code is ☎050.

The Town

The centre of town is **Grote Markt**, a wide open space that was badly damaged by wartime bombing and has been reconstructed with little imagination. At its northeast corner is the tiered tower of the **Martinikerk** (April–Sept Tues–Sat noon–4pm; f1), a beacon of architectural sanity in the surrounding shambles. Though the oldest parts of the church go back to 1180, most of it dates from the mid-fifteenth century, the nave being a Gothicised rebuilding undertaken to match the added choir. The vault paintings in the nave are beautifully restored, and in the lofty choir there are two series of frescoes on the walled-up niches of the clerestory. On the right, a series of eight depicts the story of Christmas,

beginning with an *Annunciation* and ending with a portrayal of the young Christ in the temple. On the left, six frescoes complete the cycle with the story of Easter. Adjoining the church is the essentially seventeenth-century **Martinitoren** (April to mid-Oct daily noon–4.30pm; f1.50). If you've got the energy, it offers a view that is breathtaking in every sense of the word – fainthearts be warned. Behind the church is the lawn of the **Kerkhof**, an ancient piece of common land that's partly enclosed by the **Provinciehuis**, a rather grand neo-Renaissance building of 1915, seat of the provincial government.

On the opposite side of the Grote Markt, the classical **Stadhuis** dates from 1810, tucked in front of the mid-seventeenth-century **Goudkantoor** (Gold Office): look out for the shell motif above the windows, a characteristic Groningen decoration. From the southwest corner of the Grote Markt, the far side of Vismarkt is framed by the **Korenbeurs** (Corn Exchange) of 1865. The statues on the facade represent, from left to right, Neptune, Mercurius (god of commerce) and Ceres (goddess of agriculture). Just behind, the **A-kerk** is a fifteenth-century church with a Baroque steeple, attractively restored in tones of yellow, orange and red. Immediately to the west along A-Kerkhof NZ, the **Noordelijk Scheepvaart Museum**, Brugstraat 24 (Tues–Sat 10am–5pm, Sun 1–5pm; f3.50), is one of the best-equipped and most comprehensive maritime museums in the country, tracing the history of north Holland shipping from the sixth to the twentieth centuries. Housed in a warren of steep stairs and timber-beamed rooms, each of the museum's twenty displays deals with a different aspect of shipping, including trade with the Indies, the development of peat canals and a series of reconstructed nautical workshops. The museum's particular appeal is its imaginative combination of models and original artefacts, which are themselves a mixture of the personal (seamen's chests; quadrants) and the public (ship figureheads; tile designs of ships). Next door, the much smaller **Niemeyer Tabacologisch Museum** is devoted to tobacco smoking from 1600 to the present day. Exhibits include a multitude of pipes and an outstanding collection of snuff paraphernalia in all sorts of material, from crystal and ivory to porcelain and silver. The Niemeyer family built their fortune on the tobacco trade and here you can see the origins of those familiar blue tobacco packets.

A short walk south (left out of the museum and left at the canal, along Klein der A), the **Groninger Museum**, at Praediniussingel 59 (Tues–Sat 10am–5pm, Sun 1–5pm; f2), is divided into three main sections. On the ground floor, a melange of arts and applied arts outlines Groningen's history from early *terp* culture to the twentieth century, according to periods rather than different media. In the basement, there are displays of local silverware and Far Eastern ceramics, notably a 200-piece sample of porcelain rescued from the *Geldermalsen*, which sank in the South China Sea in 1572 (see "Leeuwarden"). Of the examples on display, several are still encrusted with accumulated detritus, but others have been cleaned and polished to reveal designs of delicate precision, fine drawings of flowers and stems, and bamboo huts where every stick is distinct. On the first floor, the museum's collection of paintings is sometimes displaced by exhibitions, but when on view it includes Rubens' energetic *Adoration of the Magi* among a small selection of seventeenth-century works, Isaac Israels' inviting *Hoedenwinkel* from a modest sample of Hague School paintings, and a number of later works by the Expressionists of the Groningen *De Ploeg* association, principally Jan Wiegers, whose *Portrait of Ludwig Kirchner* is typically earnest. An adventurous acquisition policy has also led the museum to dabble in some of the more unusual trends of modern art, like Carel Visser's 1983 collage *Voor Dali* and the bizarre *Can the bumpsteers while I park the chariot* by Henk Tas.

Groningen's final sight is its **railway station**: built in 1896 at enormous cost, it was one of the grandest of its day, decorated with the strong colours and symbolic designs of Art Nouveau tiles from the Rozenburg factory in The Hague. The grandeur of much of the building has disappeared under a welter of concrete, glass and plastic suspended ceilings, but the old First and Second Class waiting rooms have survived pretty much intact and were recently refurbished as restaurants. The epitome of high Gothic style, the oak-panelled walls are edged by extravagantly tiled chimney pieces, while a central pillar in each room supports a papier-maché fluted ceiling. The Third Class waiting room is now a travel agency, but a yellow, blue and white tiled diagram of the Dutch railway system still covers one wall.

Eating, drinking and nightlife

The cheapest **food** in town is served at the student *Mensa*, Oosterstraat 44 (Mon–Fri noon–1.30pm & 5–7pm), where reliable, filling canteen meals cost about f12. Other more appetising places include exquisite daily specials from f15 in the elegant surroundings of the *Schimmelpenninck Huys*, Oosterstraat 53; Mexican-

American food at the *Four Roses*, at the junction of Oosterstraat and Gedempte Zuiderdiep; excellent vegetarian meals at the *Brussels Lof*, A-Kerkstraat 24; pizzas from f11 at *Isolabella*, above the Naberpassage, and Dutch snacks at *Het Pakhuis*, Peperstraat 82.

For **drinking**, there are several good **bars** on the south side of the Grote Markt, notably the cosy *Der Witz* at no. 48, and the boisterous *De Drie Gezusters* at no. 39 – near the rather more polished *Café Montparnasse*. There are further lively bars down neighbouring Poelestraat, for instance the vaguely alternative *De Opera*, at no. 17, and the slick *Brasserie* at no. 32.

For **live music**, try the "rock pub" *De Vestibule*, Oosterstraat 24; *Vera*, in the basement below the *Mensa*, at Oosterstraat 44, also has live bands – as does *Troubadour*, Peperstraat 19. Most major visiting **bands** play in the municipal concert hall, the *Stadsschouwburg*, Turfsingel 86 – details from the VVV; others sometimes perform on July and August Sundays in the **Stadspark**, about 3km southwest of the town centre (bus #2 from the Grote Markt to Peizerweg on the northern edge of the park, but confirm with the driver as routes vary). The **cinema** with the most varied programme is the *Filmhuis*, Poelestraat 30. **Listings** of all events are contained in *Groninger Zomer Manifestatie* and *Uit in Groningen*, both available free from the VVV.

Listings

Boat trips Summer trips along the old town moat around the town centre, f6 for 75min. Times of sailings and reservations at the VVV.

Books A good range of English titles at *Scholtens*, Grote Markt 42.

Car hire From *Interleasing*, Vechtstraat 72 (☎261659).

Emergencies ☎0611

Left luggage At the railway station (daily 8am–noon & 1–5.30pm); also coin-operated storage units in the ticket hall.

Markets General market, including fruit and vegetables, on the Grote Markt (Tues–Sat from 8am), with curios and miscellaneous antiques best on Tuesdays, Fridays and Saturdays.

Police Schweitzerlaan 1 (☎131313)

Post office Stationsweg 10 (Mon–Fri 9am–5pm, Sat 9am–noon).

Travel agent *NBBS*, Oude Kijk in 't Jatsraat 52.

Around Groningen

A patchwork of industrial complexes and nondescript villages, the **province of Groningen** has little going for it, and there's nowhere that really warrants an overnight stay. Of possible day trips from Groningen city, the most agreeable is to the village of UITHUIZEN, 25km to the north (hourly trains; 35min), where the moated manor house of **Menkemaborg** (April–Sept daily 10am–noon & 1–5pm; Oct–Mar Tues–Sun 10am–noon & 1–4pm; closed Jan) is a signposted ten-minute walk from the station. Dating from the fifteenth century and surrounded by formal gardens in the English style, the house has a sturdy compact elegance and is one of the very few mansions, or *borgs*, of the old landowning families to have survived. The interior consists of a sequence of period rooms furnished in the style of the seventeenth century.

The trip to Uithuizen can be combined with a guided walk across the coastal **mud flats** (*wadlopen* – see above) to the uninhabited sand spit island of

Rottumeroog. Guided excursions leave from outside Menkemaborg, by bus to the coast, between three and four times monthly from June to September. The cost is f20 per person and prior booking is essential; further details and reservations at Groningen VVV. Without a guide, it's too dangerous to go on the mud flats, but it is easy enough to walk along the enclosing dyke that runs behind the shoreline for the whole length of the province. There's precious little to see as such, but when the weather's clear, the browns, blues and greens of the surrounding land and sea are unusually beautiful. From Uithuizen, it's a good hour's stroll north to the nearest point on the dyke, and you'll need a large-scale map for directions – available from Groningen VVV.

The Lauwersmeer

Some 35km northwest of Groningen, the **Lauwersmeer** is a broken and irregular lake that spreads across the provincial boundary into neighbouring Friesland. Once an arm of the sea, it was turned into a freshwater lake by the construction of the Lauwersoog dam, a controversial Sixties project that was vigorously opposed by local fishermen, who ended up having to move all their tackle to ports on the coast. Spared intensive industrial and agricultural development because of the efforts of conservationists, it's a quiet and peaceful region, popular with anglers, windsurfers, sailors and cyclists. The local villages are uniformly dull, however; the most convenient base is **ZOUTKAMP**, near the southeast corner of the lake on the river Reitdiep, accessible by bus from Groningen (#65; hourly; 1hr). Zoutkamp has one **hotel**, the *De Zeearend*, Dorpsplein 1 (☎05956/1647), where bed and breakfast costs f40 per person, and a **VVV**, Dorpsplein 1 (June–Aug Mon–Fri 10am–noon & 1.30–4.30pm, Sat 1.30–4.30pm; Sept–May Mon–Fri 10am–noon & 1.30–4pm; ☎05956/1957), with a limited supply of private **rooms**. These can also be reserved at the Groningen VVV office.

Situated at the mouth of the lake, some 10km north of Zoutkamp, the desultory port of **LAUWERSOOG** is where **ferries** leave for the fifty-minute trip to the island of Schiermonnikoog (see above). It's also the home of **Expo Zee** (April–Sept Tues–Fri 10am–5pm, Sat–Sun 2–5pm; f2), 500m south of the harbour, which gives background information on the Lauwersmeer, the Waddenzee and Dutch land reclamation in general. Bus #63 connects Groningen with Lauwersoog and the ferries (5 daily; 1hr).

Fraeylemaborg and Bourtagne

There are two other minor attractions in the province. The first, 21km east of Groningen on the northern edge of the small town of SLOCHTEREN (no buses), is **Fraeylemaborg** (March–Dec Tues–Sun 10am–noon & 1–4pm), a well-preserved, seventeenth-century moated mansion set within extensive parkland. The second, some 60km southeast of Groningen, is **BOURTAGNE**, a restored fortified village close to the German frontier. Founded by William of Orange in 1580 to protect the eastern approaches to Groningen, Bourtagne fell into disrepair in the nineteenth century, only to be entirely refurbished as a tourist attraction in 1964. Today it's possible to walk round the old bastions of the star-shaped fortress. There's a **campsite**, *'t Plathuis*, Vlagtwedderstraat 88; one **hotel**, *De Staakenborgh*, up the road at no. 33, with doubles from f40 a head (☎05993-54216; closed Sept–May); and a **VVV** at Marktplein 4 (April–Oct Mon–Fri 9am–noon & 1–5pm, Sat & Sun 1–5pm; Nov–March Mon–Fri 9am–noon; ☎05993/54600).

Drenthe

The sparsely populated province of **DRENTHE** was little more than a flat expanse of empty peat bog, marsh and moor until well into the eighteenth century. Its only conspicuous geographical feature is a ridge of low hills that runs northeast for some 50km from Emmen towards Groningen. This ridge, the **Hondsrug**, was high enough to attract prehistoric settlers whose **hunebeds** (megalithic tombs) have become Drenthe's main tourist attraction. There are few others. **Assen**, the provincial capital, is a dull place with a good museum, and **Emmen**, the other major town, can only be recommended as a convenient base for visiting some of the *hunebeds* and three neighbouring open-air folk-culture museums.

Governed by the Bishops of Utrecht from the eleventh century, Drenthe was incorporated into the Hapsburg empire in 1538. The region sided with the Protestants in the rebellion against Spain, but it had little economic or military muscle and its claim to provincial status was ignored until the days of the Batavian Republic. In the nineteenth century, work began in earnest to convert the province's peat bogs and moors into good farmland. *Veenkulunies* (peat colonies) were established over much of the south and east of Drenthe, where the initial purpose of the labourers was to dig drainage canals (*wiels*) and cut the peat for sale as fuel to the cities. Once cleared of the peat, the land could be used to grow crops, and today the region's farms are some of the most profitable in the country.

Assen

Some 16km south of Groningen, **ASSEN** is a possible first stopoff, though not at all a place to get stuck in. Its rail and bus station are five minutes' walk from the centre of town, straight ahead across the main road down Stationsstraat. On the east side of the central square, Brink is home to both parts of the **Drents Museum** (Tue–Fri 9.30am–5pm, Sat & Sun 1–5pm; f1), the only thing that makes a stop worthwhile. Of the two buildings, the *Ontvangershuis*, Brink 1, is no more than a predictable plod of period rooms, but on the first floor of Brink 5 there's an extraordinary assortment of prehistoric bodies, clothes and other artefacts that have been preserved for thousands of years in the surrounding peat bogs. The bodies are the material remains of those early settlers who built the *hunebeds*, and the museum has a modest display dealing with what is known of their customs and culture. There's also the much vaunted *Pesse Canoe*, the oldest water vessel ever found, dating from about 6800 BC and looking its age.

Five kilometres west of the centre of Assen, straight down Torenlaan, is an **Automuseum**, Rode Heklaan 3 (May–Oct Mon–Fri 9am–5pm, Sat & Sun 11am–5pm; f9) which has a wide selection of antique and vintage cars. To get there take a bus marked *Verkeerspark* from the railway station.

The Assen VVV is in the town centre at Brink 42 (Mon–Fri 8.30am–5pm, Sat 10am–1pm, July & Aug until 4pm; ☎05920/14324). The cheapest place to **stay** is the *Christerus* (☎05920/13517), on the way in from the station at Stationsstraat 17, which has doubles for f70. The *De Nieuwe Brink Hotel*, Brink 13, is a reasonable place to **eat**.

Emmen and around

To all intents and purposes **EMMEN** is a new town, a twentieth-century amalgamation of strip villages that were originally peat colonies. The centre is a modernistic affair, mixing the remnants of the old with boulders, trees and shrubs and a selection of municipal statues that vary enormously in quality. Emmen **rail** and **bus** stations adjoin each other five minutes' walk north of the town centre: head straight down Stationsstraat into Boslaan and turn left down Hoofdstraat, the main drag. The **VVV** (Mon–Fri 9am–5pm, Sat 10am–1pm; ☎05910/13000), in the centre on the Raadhuisplein, will arrange **accommodation** if required. Their list includes **pensions** and **private rooms** from f25 per person per night and **hotels** from f35. The cheapest pension is the *Centrum* at Sterrenkamp 9 (☎05910/14158), first left after the zoo, heading south; the cheapest hotel is the *Bos en Zon* at Burg. Tijmesstraat 1 (☎05910/11369), which is immediately behind the railway station. For **food**, try the ground-floor café of the *Hotel Boerland*, Hoofdstraat 57.

Emmen is well known for two things: its *hunebeds* and its zoo. The **Zoo** (daily 9am–5pm; f12) is right in the middle of town at Hoofdstraat 18 and claims to be one of the most modern zoos in the world. It boasts an imitation of an African savanna, where the animals roam "free", a massive sea lion pool, the biggest in Europe, and a giant, brand-new hippo house. Emmen is also the most convenient place to see *hunebeds*, of which the best is the clearly sign-posted **Emmerdennen Hunebed**, in the woods a kilometre or so east of the station along Boslaan. This is a so-called passage-grave, with a relatively sophisticated entrance surrounded by a ring of standing stones. The other interesting *hunebed* within easy walking distance is the **Schimmer-Es**, a large enclosure containing two burial chambers and a standing stone; to get there follow Hoofdstraat north from the VVV, take a left down Noorderstraat, right along Noordeinde, left along Broekpad and first right at Langgrafweg – a distance of about 2km. If you want to see more, the VVV sell detailed maps of a circular car route along the minor roads to the north of town that covers all the principal remains. A particular highlight is the largest *hunebed* of the lot, 25m long, on the northeast edge of the village of BORGER, some 20km from Emmen.

Around Emmen

Approximately 11km east of Emmen, towards the German border, the **Veenmuseumdorp 't Aole Compas** (daily 9am–5pm; f10; bus #43 hourly from Emmen station; 30min) is a massive open-air museum-village which traces the history and development of the peat colonies of the moors of southern Groningen and eastern Drenthe. The colonies were established in the nineteenth century, when labour was imported to cut the thick layers of peat that lay all over the moors. Isolated in small communities, and under the thumb of the traders who sold their product and provided their foodstuffs, the colonists were harshly exploited and lived in abject poverty until well into the 1930s. Built around some old interlocking canals, the museum consists of a series of reconstructed villages that span the history of the colonies. It's inevitably a bit folksy, but very popular, with its own small-gauge railway, a canal barge, and working period bakeries, bars and shops. A thorough exploration takes the whole day.

Thirteen kilometres northwest of Emmen, **De Zeven Marken** (April–Oct daily 9am–5pm; f3; bus #21), on the northern edge of the village of SCHOONOORD, is another open-air museum concerned with life in Drenthe. The exhibits here concentrate on the end of the nineteenth century and cover a wide range of traditional community activities – from sheep farming to education and carpentry. Seven kilometres to the west, tiny **Orvelte** (Mon–Fri 9.30am–5pm, Sat & Sun 11am–5pm; f7) is another village-museum, fully operational and inhabited this time. Owned by a trust who exercise strict control over construction and repair, Orvelte's buildings date from the seventeenth to the nineteenth centuries and include examples of a toll house, a dairy, a farmhouse and a number of craft workshops. Most are open to the public, but you'll need a car to get here.

travel details

Trains
From Emmen to Zwolle (2 hourly; 70min).
From Groningen to Amsterdam (2 hourly; 2hr 25min); Assen (2 hourly; 20min); Leeuwarden (2 hourly; 50min); Zwolle (2 hourly; 70min).
From Leeuwarden to Amsterdam (2 hourly; 2hr 25min); Franeker/Harlingen (2 hourly; 15/30min); Groningen (2 hourly; 50min); Sneek/Hindeloopen/Stavoren (hourly; 20/35/50min); Zwolle (2 hourly; 70min).

Buses
From Groningen to Emmen (hourly; 1hr 10min); Zoutkamp (hourly; 1hr).
From Leeuwarden to Franeker (hourly; 25min); Alkmaar (hourly; 2hr 20min); Dokkum (1–2 hourly; 30min).
From Sneek to Bolsward (3 hourly; 15min).
From Bolsward to Makkum (hourly; 20min).

Buses and connecting ferries
From Groningen to Lauwersoog (*GADO* Bus #63: 5 daily; 1hr) for boats to Schiermonnikoog (2–6 daily; 50min).
From Leeuwarden to Holwerd (*FRAM* bus #66: 5–7 daily; 50min) for boats to Ameland (4–8 daily; 45min); Lauwersoog (*FRAM* bus #51: 4–7 daily; 90min) for boats to Schiermonnikoog (2–6 daily; 50min).

Ferries
From Harlingen to Vlieland (2–3 daily; 1 hr 30min); Terschelling (2–3 boats daily; 1hr 30min).
From Terschelling to Vlieland (2–3 boats weekly; 65min).
From Vlieland to Terschelling (2–3 boats weekly; 65min).
From Stavoren to Enkhuizen (May–Sept, 3 boats daily; 1hr 20min).

International trains
From Groningen to Oldenburg, West Germany (2 or 3 daily; 2hr 10 min).

CHAPTER FIVE

OVERIJSSEL, FLEVOLAND AND GELDERLAND

With the eastern provinces of Holland, the flat polder landscapes of the north and west of the country begin to disappear, the countryside growing steadily more undulating as you head towards Germany. Coming from the north, **Overijssel** is the first province you reach, "the land beyond the Ijssel", which forms the border with Gelderland to the south. Its more appealing western reaches are a typically Dutch area, in part cut by lakes and waterways around the picturesque water-village of **Giethoorn**, the rest home to a series of towns – **Kampen**, **Deventer**, **Zutphen** and the provincial capital of **Zwolle** – which enjoyed a period of immense prosperity during the heyday of the Zuider Zee trade, from the fourteenth to the sixteenth centuries. At the junction of trade routes from Germany in the east, Scandinavia to the north and South Holland in the west, their future seemed secure and all of them were keen to impress their rivals with the splendour of their public buildings. The bubble burst in the seventeenth century, when trade moved west and the great merchant cities of South Holland undercut their prices, but today all are well worth a visit for their ancient centres, splendid churches and extravagant defensive portals. Southeast of here, **Twente** is an industrial region of old textile towns that forms the eastern district of the province, near the German frontier. It's one of the least visited parts of the country, and rightly so, only **Enschede**, the main town, providing a spark of interest with an excellent local museum.

The boundary separating Overijssel from the reclaimed lands of Holland's twelfth and newest province, **Flevoland**, runs along the old shoreline of the Zuider Zee. Divided into two halves, the drab **Northeast Polder** in the east and the later **Flevoland Polder** to the west, there's not really much to attract the visitor here, except for the fishing village of **Urk**, which was an island until the land reclamation scheme got under way. The provincial capital is **Lelystad**, a pretty dire modern town with one point of interest, the **Nieuw Land** centre, providing background information on the draining of the Ijsselmeer.

Gelderland, spreading east from Utrecht to the German frontier, takes its name from the German town of Geldern, its capital until the late fourteenth century. As a province it's a bit of a mixture, varying from the fertile (but dull) agricultural land of the **Betuwe** ("Good Land"), which stretches west from Nijmegen as far as Gorinchem, to the more distinctive – and appealing – **Veluwe** (literally "Bad Land"), an expanse of heath, woodland and dune that sprawls down from the old Zuider Zee coastline to Arnhem. Infertile and sparsely populated, the Veluwe separated two of medieval Holland's most prosperous regions, the ports of the river Ijssel and the cities of the Randstad, and today it constitutes one of the most popular holiday destinations in the country, strewn with camp-

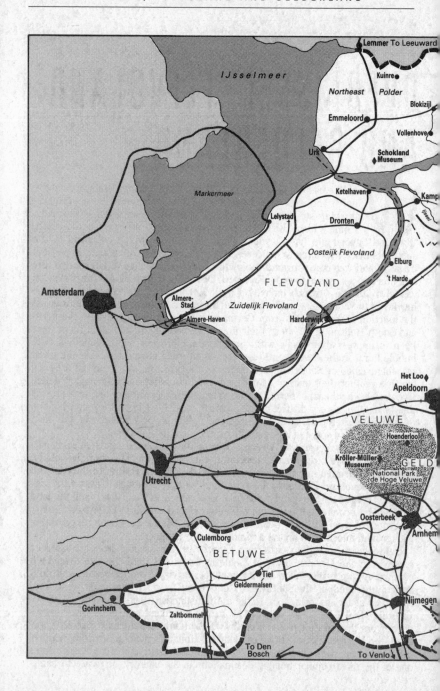

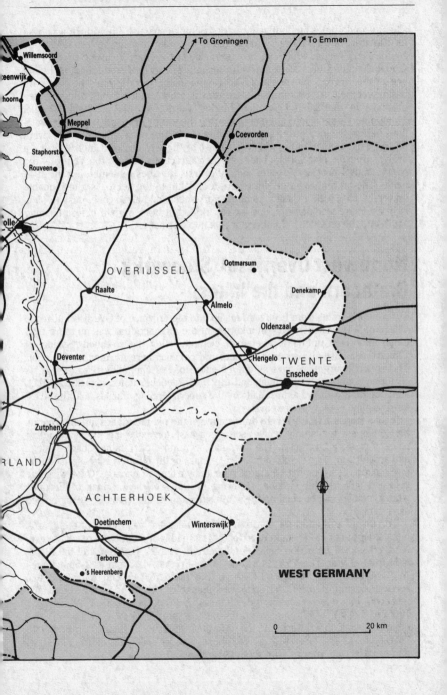

To Groningen

To Emmen

Willemsoord

eenwijk

hoorn

Meppel

Coevorden

Staphorst

Rouveen

olle

OVERIJSSEL

Ootmarsum

Raalte

Denekamp

Almelo

Oldenzaal

Deventer

Hengelo

TWENTE

Enschede

Zutphen

RLAND

ACHTERHOEK

Doetinchem

Winterswijk

Terborg

's Heerenberg

WEST GERMANY

0   20 km

sites, second homes and bungalow parks. Some people use **Apeldoorn** as a base for the area, but it's a dreary town, and if you want to visit the less developed southeastern sector, which has been set aside as the Hoge Veluwe National Park (and its Kroller-Muller Museum with a magnificent array of modern art, including one of the largest collections of Van Goghs in the world), you'd be better off basing yourself in Arnhem itself. **Arnhem** is most famous for its bridge, a key objective in the failed Operation Market Garden of 1944 – Field Marshal Montgomery's audacious attempt to shorten the war by dropping parachute battalions behind enemy lines to secure a string of advance positions across the rivers of southeast Gelderland – which left most of the city centre ruined. But it's a lively, agreeable place, and a base for other attractions besides the Veluwe – the Netherlands Open-Air Museum, and, of course, the sites remembering the 1944 battle. The ancient town of **Nijmegen**, too, 21km to the south, is a fashionable university city, with a quality contemporary music and arts scene, despite similarly extensive war damage, and makes a good, if brief, stopoff before heading south into the province of Limburg or east into Germany.

Northwest Overijssel: Steenwijk, Giethoorn and the lakes

Twice-hourly trains from Leeuwarden slip into the province of Overijssel near the village of **WILLEMSOORD**, in a corner of the province that was no more than empty moorland until the nineteenth century, when the so-called "Society of Charity" established a series of agricultural colonies here to cater for the poor. The Dutch bourgeoisie was as apprehensive of the unemployed pauper as its Victorian counterpart in Britain, and the 1900 Baedeker noted approvingly that, "the houses are visited almost daily by the superintending officials, and the strictest discipline is everywhere observed".

Trains stop at **STEENWIJK**, on the edge of the old moorlands, an unremarkable settlement that's only really useful as a base for exploring the surrounding lakes of western Overijssel. The town has seen more than its fair share of siege and assault, and, as a result, the towering mass of the Grote Kerk is an inconclusive mixture of styles that's suffered repeatedly from war damage. Otherwise, the centre is still roughly circular, following the lines of the original fortifications whose remains can be seen on the south side of town in a chain of steep, moated earth ramparts.

The town's **rail** and **bus stations** are five minutes' walk north of the centre; head straight out of the station and follow the road round until you reach the ring road, cross over onto Doelenstraat, take a right at the T-junction, and the Markt is in front of you. The **VVV**, Markt 60 (Mon–Fri 9am–12.30pm & 2–5pm; June–Aug Sat 9am–noon; ☎05210/12010), is the place to can find out about bus services around the lakes; for up-to-date timetables, ask for the **NWH** bus book. Steenwijk has one reasonably priced **hotel**, *De Gouden Engel*, at Tukseweg 1 (☎05210/12436), with rooms from f50 per person per night. The hotel is five minutes' walk northwest of the Markt – follow Kerkstraat round into Paardenmarkt and Tukseweg is dead ahead. The VVV also has details of a small number of private **rooms** from about f30 per person.

Meppel and Staphorst

South of Steenwijk, the railway lines from Leeuwarden and Groningen join at **MEPPEL**, a second possible base for travelling on to the lakes, though frankly it's a dull town and its **bus** and **rail stations** are a good ten minutes' walk south-east of the centre. The town's **VVV**, at Kleine Oever 11 (Mon–Fri 9am–5pm, Sat 10am–noon; ✆05220/52888), has a limited supply of private **rooms** from f30 and will help with local bus schedules. The **youth hostel**, at Leonard Springerlaan 14 (✆05220/51706; May–Sept), is signposted from outside the railway station and takes about ten minutes to reach.

Beyond Meppel lie the elongated villages of **STAPHORST** and **ROUVEEN**, tiny squares of brightly shuttered and neatly thatched farmhouses that line some ten kilometres of road in the shadow of the motorway. Despite significant industrial development in the last decade, both these communities still have strong and strict Calvinist traditions: the majority still observe the Sabbath and many continue to wear traditional costume as a matter of course – and do not wish to be photographed. That said, apart from the custom of painting their houses in vicious shades of green and sky blue, Staphorst and Rouveen are fairly undistinguished.

BUSES AROUND THE LAKES

From Steenwijk railway station #72 to Giethoorn/Zwartsluis (Mon–Fri hourly; Sun 3 daily; 15/30min); change at Zwartsluis for connecting #71 to Vollenhove (Mon–Fri 2 hourly; Sun 3 daily; 20min). To Blokzijl #75 (Mon–Fri hourly; Sun 3 daily; 20min).

From Meppel railway station #73 to Zwartsluis (Mon–Fri 2 hourly; Sun 3 daily; 35min); change at Zwartsluis for Vollenhove, as above.

From Zwolle railway station #71 to Zwartsluis & Vollenhove (Mon–Fri 2 hourly; Sun every 2 hours; 30/50min); change at Zwartsluis for connecting #72 to Giethoorn and Steenwijk (Mon–Fri hourly; Sun 3 daily; 15/30min).

Giethoorn and the lakes

Meppel and Steenwijk in the east, and the old seaports of Vollenhove and Blokzijl in the west, rim an expanse of lake, pond, canal and river that's been formed by centuries of haphazard peat digging. Although it's a favourite holiday spot for water sport enthusiasts, public transport is limited, and in any case you really miss the quiet charm of the region if you aren't travelling by **boat**. Fortunately these are available for hire at all the major villages, in a variety of shapes and sizes, from canoes to motorboats and dinghies. Prices vary, but reckon on f80 per day for a motorboat down to f20 for a canoe. The other alternative is to come on a **boat trip** from Kampen (see p.186). Itineraries vary, but once or twice weekly, from mid-July to mid-August, boats sail from Kampen to Vollenhove, Blokzijl and Giethoorn. Further details from Kampen VVV.

Giethoorn

The best known and most picturesque lakeland village is **GIETHOORN**, which flanks a series of interlocking canals that lie some 200m east of the road from

Steenwijk to Zwolle – not to be confused with the modern village of the same name on the main road itself. Bus #72 from Steenwijk station travels right through modern Giethoorn before reaching the VVV at its southern end. Make sure the driver puts you off here – ask either for the VVV or the adjoining *Hotel Giethoorn*.

Giethoorn's origins are rather odd. The marshy, infertile land here was given to an obscure sect of flagellants in the thirteenth century by the lord of Vollenhove. Isolated and poor, the colonists were dependent on local peat deposits for their livelihood, though their first digs only unearthed the horns of hundreds of goats who had probably been the victims of prehistoric flooding, leading to the settlement being named "Geytenhoren" (goats' horns). Nowadays Giethoorn's postcard-prettiness of thatched houses and narrow canals crisscrossed by arching footbridges draws tourists in their hundreds, Dutch and German weekenders swarming into the village throughout summer to jam the busy footpaths and clog the waterways in search of some sort of northern Venice. The high prices and water-borne hubbub are certainly similar, although sadly Giethoorn has little else to offer besides.

If you decide to stay, Giethoorn **VVV**, Beulakerweg 130 (June–Aug daily 9am–noon & 1–6pm; April, May & Sept Mon–Sat 10am–noon and 1–5pm; Oct–March Mon–Fri 10am–noon & 1–4pm; ☎05216/1248), has a list of private **rooms** and **pensions** from about f25 per person per night, and they'll telephone ahead to make a reservation; clarify the exact location before you make a booking, though, or you could end up walking for miles. Two of the more convenient **hotels** are the *'t Centrum* (☎05216/1225) and the *'t Pannekoekenhuis* (☎05216/1321), approximately 2km north of the VVV by Giethoorn's central canal, at Ds. Hylkemaweg 39 and 7, with rooms from f45 per person per night. Another alternative, *Hotel Giethoorn* (☎05216/1216), next door to the VVV, charges from f70 per person per night. Accommodation is very tight between June and August.

A couple of minutes' east of old Giethoorn, **Lake Bovenwijde** has no less than seven **campsites** on its western shore. The two nearest ones, towards the southern end of the lake, are the *De Punter*, Langesteeg 12, and the *Scholten*, Binnenpad 139 (both April–Sept), about twenty minutes' walk from the VVV – head straight down the footpath opposite and turn left at the end. Both campsites and all three hotels hire out **boats**. **Water taxis** leave from the canal opposite the VVV and cost about f15 per hour for a trip round the village.

Zwartsluis, Vollenhove and Blokzijl

South of Giethoorn, bus #72 travels the length of the dyke across Lake Belterwijde before cutting down into **ZWARTSLUIS**, once the site of an important fortress at the junction of waterways from Zwolle and Meppel. The **Natural History Museum**, on the north side of the village at Zomerdijk 13 (May–Sept Mon–Sat 9am–noon & 2–5pm), is devoted to displays of local fauna and flora.

At the bus station on the edge of Zwartsluis passengers change for the journey west to **VOLLENHOVE**, one of the most agreeable little towns in northwest Overijssel. Once a maritime fortification guarding the approach to Zwolle, Vollenhove spreads out east from the Vollenhover Kanaal that marks the path of the old Zuider Zee coastline. Buses stop on Clarenberglaan, a five-minute walk away from the main square (straight up Doelenstraat), where the **Onze lieve Vrouwekerk** is a confusion of towers, spires and gables. The elegant, arcaded **Stadhuis** is attached to the church, and, across Kerkplein, the weathered stone gateposts outside the bank were originally part of the entrance to the **Latin**

School. Around the corner from the church is the town's charming ancient harbour, a cramped, circular affair encased in steep grass banks.

Vollenhove **VVV**, Bisschopstraat 24 (June–Aug Mon–Sat 10am–noon & 2–4pm; ☎05274/1700), is a couple of minutes east of the Kerkplein; when it's closed there's usually a town map and a short list of pensions pinned up on the notice board outside the church. There's one **hotel**, the *Saantje*, Kerkplein 14 (☎05274/3234), where bed and breakfast starts at f60 per person. **Restaurant** *De Vollenhof* is a couple of doors away and serves good fish dishes.

Some 6km to the north, **BLOKZIJL** is of less immediate appeal, and can only be easily reached by bus from Steenwijk. Formerly a seaport, the settlement has a large marina and a number of restored seventeenth-century terraces. The **VVV** is in the centre at Kerkstraat 12 (June–Aug Mon–Sat 9am–6pm, Sun 1–4pm; ☎05272/414) and has details of a handful of **pensions** from f30 per person per night – though they're usually booked months in advance.

Zwolle

The first major railway junction as you come from the north, **ZWOLLE** is the small and compact capital of Overijssel. An ancient town, it achieved passing international fame when Thomas à Kempis settled here in 1399, and throughout the fifteenth century Zwolle prospered as one of the principal towns of the Hanseatic League, its burghers commissioning an extensive programme of public works designed to protect its citizens and impress their rivals. Within the city walls, German textiles were traded for Baltic fish and grain, or more exotic products from Amsterdam, like coffee, tea and tobacco. The boom lasted for some two hundred years, but by the middle of the seventeenth century the success of Amsterdam and the general movement of trade to the west had undermined its economy – a decline reflected in Zwolle's present-day status as a small market town of no particular significance.

Re-fortified in successive centuries, today's centre is still in the shape of a star fortress, nine roughly triangular earthen bulwarks encircling both the old town and its harbour, whose waters separate a northern sector off from the rest. Prettily moated and still partly walled, Zwolle is engaging, though the surrounding suburbs, by comparison, are an unattractive modern sprawl.

Arriving and staying

Well connected by train to many of Holland's major cities, and by bus to most of Overijssel's tourist attractions, Zwolle's **rail** and **bus** stations are some ten minutes' walk south of the centre, a little way from the moat down Stationsweg. The **VVV** is at Grote Kerkplein 14 (Mon–Fri 9am–5.30pm, Sat 10am–4pm; ☎038/213900), and has details of a small number of **pensions** for a rather pricey f40 per person per night, though you can expect all their addresses to be way out of the centre. There are several more convenient alternatives: the *Hotel Beniers*, Oosterlaan 6 (☎038/219141), is opposite the bus station and charges from f70 a double; the hostile *Hotel Fiddler*, Wilhelminastraat 6 (☎038/218395), ten minutes' walk southwest of the centre on a turning off Willemskade/Veerallee, has rooms from f80. There's also the *Hotel Weenik*, Rode Torenplein 10 (☎038/218182), just northwest of the Grote Markt at the end of Melkmarkt, with doubles from f150.

The best bargain is the no-frills *Sleep Inn* at Rode Torenplein 4 (☎038/217828; June–Aug), where you can get your head down for a mere f10.

The town's nearest **campsite**, *Het Vechterstrand*, Haersterveerweg 23 (April–Sept), is by the river Vecht on the northeastern outskirts of town and difficult to reach without a car; take the Meppel bus, #40, from Zwolle station and ask for the campsite. You'll be let off on the east side of the bridge across the Vecht on the A28. Immediately east of the bus stop, Ordelseweg goes under the A28 and leads north to the turning for the campsite, a distance of about 2km.

The Town

In the centre of the Grote Markt stands the **Grote Kerk** (July–Aug Fri 10am–1pm, Sat 2–4pm; July Wed 10am–4pm), dedicated to Saint Michael, patron saint of the town. If the exterior seems a little plain it's because it's been dogged by ill

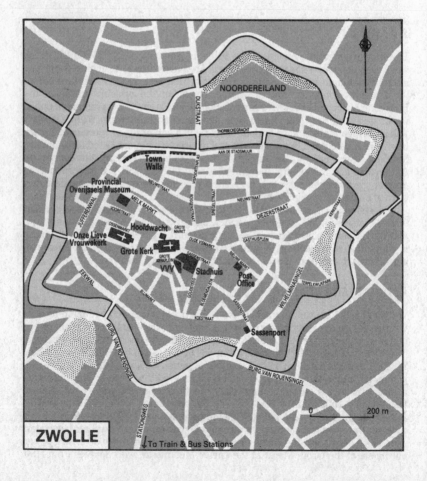

luck. Its bell tower used to be one of the highest in the country and was struck by lightning three times in 1548, 1606 and 1669. After the third time it was never rebuilt and eventually the bells were sold. Inside, the church has the familiar austerity of Dutch Protestantism, with the choir a bare and dusty forgotten corner and the seats arranged on a central pulpit plan. The pulpit itself is an intricate piece of Renaissance carving by the German Adam Straes, where the grace of Christ is emphasised by the brutal ugliness of the faces of the sinners.

Attached to the church is the **Hoofdwacht** of 1614, an ornately gabled building which once served as a guardhouse. In front was the place of public execution, the remaining inscription "Vigilate et Orate" (Watch and Pray) a stern piece of advice to the crowds who gathered to witness these bloody spectacles. Appropriately, the building later housed the town's main police station.

A little way west, down an alley off the Grote Markt, the **Onze Lieve Vrouwekerk** (July–Aug Fri 10am–1pm, Sat 10am–4pm) is a discordant mixture of styles dating from the fifteenth century. Once again, the church has been plagued with difficulties – the original building contractor ran off with an advance payment, and the tower was rebuilt after a fire in 1815 with an odd-looking turret on top, giving rise to its nickname "Peperbus" (pepperpot).

From beside the Grote Kerk, Sassenstraat twists and turns its way southeast towards the old city walls. Number 33, the **Karel V Huis**, is all that's left of the mansion built for the Emperor Charles V in case he decided to pay the town a visit. He never did, but then all the major cities of his empire were obliged to construct similarly grand buildings for his possible convenience. Strangely, the bas-relief medallion of Charles on the gable is dated 1571, thirteen years after his death in 1558. At the end of the Sassenstraat, the massive **Sassenpoort** is a fine example of a fifteenth-century defensive portal, complete with boiling oil and water holes; it gives some idea of just how grand the medieval town must have been.

West of the Grote Markt, at Melkmarkt 41, is the main entrance to the **Provinciaal Overijssels Museum** (Tues–Sat 10am–5pm, Sun 2–5pm; f2), which is divided between two houses: the **Drostenhuis** (Bailiff's house) on Melkmarkt, a grand sixteenth-century mansion topped with an uncomfortable Rococo pediment, and the **Gouden Kroon**, through the garden at the side on Voorstraat. Pride of place in the Drostenhuis goes to the Blokzijl room, a meticulous reconstruction of a wealthy local family's seventeenth-century living quarters. The walnut, leather-upholstered chairs are a good illustration of Dutch furniture making, and the mantelpiece holds some examples of Chinese ceramics. There's not much else of note, but of the items displayed on the first floor, there's a bizarre Vollenhove drinking cup in the shape of a bearded man in a doublet, and a group of distinctive Art Nouveau Rozenburg vases – all deep strong colours with insects and flowers at the heart of the design – made by the same Hague company that tiled Groningen railway station. The Gouden Kroon, around the back, is used for modest temporary exhibitions and houses a tiny natural history museum.

North of the Grote Markt, Roggenstraat and subsequently Vispoortenplas lead to a bridge over what was once the city harbour. On its south side much of the old town wall has been restored, including sections with a covered defensive parapet and a couple of fortified towers – principally the **Wijndragerstoren** (wineporters' tower), which dates from the fourteenth century.

Eating and drinking

Zwolle isn't a marvellous place to **eat**. The most imaginative menu in town is offered at the *Poppe* at Luttekestraat 66, on the way from the station to the Grote Kerkplein, where they serve dishes with names like "Perestroika" and "Berlin Wall". Otherwise, there's *De Sassenpoort*, at Sassenstraat 54, which offers reasonably-priced meals, a branch of *Nordzee*, Diezerstraat 25, serving takeaway seafood, or the *Bella Napoli*, Grote Kerkplein 11 – the most appetising of a number of pizzerias. If money's no object, *Le Clochard*, Sassenstraat 34, and *De Palm*, Melkmarkt 38, cater for the upper income bracket. Zwolle is deadly dull at night; the best of the **bars** is the *De Konijn* beside the Grote Kerk.

West of Zwolle: Kampen and Elburg

Just ten minutes from Zwolle by train, the small town of **KAMPEN** strings along the dull flat flood plain of the Ijssel, a bold succession of towers and spires that, together with the other towns along the river, enjoyed a period of real prosperity in the fifteenth century as members of the Hanseatic League. Their success was short-lived, however, and by the late sixteenth century they were in decline as trade moved west and Amsterdam mopped up what was left by undercutting their merchants. Indeed, the Ijssel towns slipped into obscurity just as Amsterdam rose to the full height of its glory.

The Town

Sidelined by history, Kampen nowadays is little more than four roughly parallel streets edging the river, dotted with the remnants of the town's heyday. A bridge from beside the station spans the Ijssel, leading directly into the centre. Clearly visible to the right of the bridge is a leaning tower with a bizarre top that resembles a hollowed-out onion. This is part of the Stadhuis, and is Kampen's main tourist attraction every summer on five consecutive Thursdays, beginning in early July, when the **Kampen cow** is pulled up to its top. Insult turned to civic celebration, the cow is a symbol of the stupidity of the inhabitants of Kampen, who are unlucky enough to be the butt of the Dutch equivalent of "Irish jokes". The legend is that when grass began to grow at the top of the tower, local farmers asked if they could graze their cattle up there, without considering how the animals could get up and down. To commemorate this daft request, an animal has been hoisted up the tower every year ever since, though thankfully it's recently been replaced by a stuffed model.

The **Stadhuis** itself (Mon–Thurs 11am–noon & 2–4pm, plus May–Sept Sat 2–5pm; f1) is divided into two parts, the **Oude** and **Nieuwe Raadhuis**: the former was built in 1543, the latter added during the eighteenth century. Of the two, it's the old building which has most of interest, namely the *Schepenzaal* or Magistrates' Hall, a claustrophobic medieval affair with dark-stained walls capped by a superbly preserved barrel-vault roof and a magnificent stone chimneypiece – a grandiloquent, self-assured work carved by Colijn de Nole in tribute to Charles V in 1545, though the chimney's typically Renaissance representations of Justice, Prudence and Strength speak more of municipal pride than royal glory. To the right, the Magistrate's bench is the work of a more obscure local carpenter, a Master Frederik, who didn't get on with de Nole at all. Angry at not getting the more important job of the chimneypiece, his revenge can still be seen on the left-hand pillar, where a minute malevolent satyr laughs maniacally at the chimney. For further details, pick up the glossy booklet on your way in – entry through the Nieuwe Raadhuis.

From outside the Stadhuis, Oudestraat leads directly south to the **Bovenkerk** (April to mid-May Mon–Fri 1–5pm; mid-May to early Sept Mon & Tues 1–5pm, Wed–Fri 10am–5pm; mid-Sept to mid-Oct Tues 1–5pm), a lovely Gothic church with a light, spacious sandstone interior. Generally regarded as one of the most important Dutch medieval churches, its choir – with thirteen radiating chapels – was the work of Rotger of Cologne, a member of the Parler family of masons who worked on Cologne Cathedral. In the south transept an urn contains the heart of Admiral de Winter, a native of Kampen who fought to rid his country of what he considered to be the yoke of the House of Orange. A staunch republican, he took part in the successful French invasion of 1795 that created the Batavian Republic; the rest of him lies in the Pantheon in Paris. Beside the church is the earliest of Kampen's three surviving gates, the fourteenth-century **Koornmarktspoort**. The others, the **Cellespoort** and the **Broederpoort**, are of a later, more ornamental design and lie on the west side of town along Burgwal, reached from the Bovenkerk via Schoolstraat.

Practical details

It takes ten minutes for the twice-hourly train from Zwolle to reach Kampen **station**, five minutes' walk from the town centre. Unfortunately, finding somewhere to **stay** is difficult in the high season. Of the town's three **hotels**, the cheapest is the *De Steur*, Oudestraat 8 (☎05202/13094; closed Sun), where rooms cost f35 per person per night. The alternatives are far more expensive, though they are more likely to have vacancies: the *Van Dijk*, Ijsselkade 30 (☎05202/14925), and the *D'Olde Brugge*, Ijsselkade 48 (☎05202/24927), both charge f60 for a single and f95 for a double, although you do get a river-view. The nearest **camp-site** is the *Seveningen*, some 2km northeast of town at Frieseweg 7 (April–Sept): heading out of Kampen, cross the bridge and turn left; follow the main road round until it crosses the Ganzendiep canal, and the campsite is on the minor road to the immediate right. If you're in difficulties, the Kampen **VVV** is on the main street at Oudestraat 85 (Mon–Fri 9am–5pm, Sat 10am–12noon; ☎05202/13500); they may be able to suggest alternatives.

If you do manage to get fixed up, Kampen makes a good base for **day trips** into Flevoland and the Northeast Polder. Throughout July and August **boat trips** leave Kampen to explore the surrounding waterways; there are once- or twice-weekly excursions to Urk, Giethoorn and Enkhuisen. Prices vary according to the itinerary, but the longest trips will only set you back about f25; up-to-date schedules and reservations are available at the VVV. Alternatively, **bikes** can be hired, as ever, from the railway station or from *Potkamp*, Oudestraat 152 (☎05202/13495), for f7.50 a day.

For **food**, there's rather stolid Dutch fare at all three hotels, or you can try either the fish and Dutch specialities of *D'Olde Vismark*, Ijsselkade 45, or one of Kampen's four Chinese restaurants: the most popular are the *Peking* and the *Happy Garden* at Oudestraat 28 and 184.

Elburg

Half an hour from Zwolle by bus, just across the provincial boundary in Gelderland, the tiny coastal town of **ELBURG** once looked out across the Zuider Zee, whose perimeter is now marked by the path of the Veluwemeer as it snakes its way between the mainland and the polders of Flevoland. These days it's one of the most popular day-trip destinations in this part of Holland, awash with visitors throughout the season, here to enjoy the town's seaside flavour and to tour the homeopathic gardens on the outskirts.

Elburg was a successful port with its own fishing fleet from as early as the thirteenth century. However, in 1392 the governor, a certain Arent thoe Boecop, moved the whole town a little inland as a precaution against flooding. Familiar with the latest developments in town planning, Boecop and his overlord, the Count of Zutphen, laid out the new town in the shape of a grid-iron, encircled by a protective wall and moat. Not all of Elburg's citizens were overly impressed – indeed the street by the museum is still called Ledigestede, literally "Empty Way" – but the basic design, with the notable addition of sixteenth-century ramparts and gun emplacements, survived the decline that set in when the harbour silted up, and can still be observed today. Elburg's two main streets are Beekstraat, which forms the north–south axis, and Jufferenstraat/Vischpoortstraat, which runs east–west; they intersect at right angles to form the main square, the Vischmarkt, and all of Elburg's streets radiate from one or the other.

Buses from Zwolle drop visitors at the VVV, opposite the **Gemeentemuseum**, Jufferenstraat 6 (Mon 2–5pm, Tues–Fri 9.30am–noon & 2–5pm; f2.75), with its predictable period rooms and objects of local interest. The entry fee covers all three town museums. Heading south across Jufferenstraat, the tower of the **St Nicolaaskerk** (July & Aug Mon–Fri 10am–noon & 2–4.30pm) dominates the landscape, even without its spire, which was destroyed by lightning in 1693. West of the church, down Van Kinsbergenstraat, are the attractive stepped gables and tidy shutters of the old **Stadhuis**, which once served as Boecop's home. At the end of Van Kinsbergenstraat, turn left into Beekstraat for the town's main square, the Vischmarkt, from where Vischpoortstraat leads straight to the best preserved of the medieval town gates, the **Vispoort**, a much restored brick rampart tower dating from 1594. Inside there's a modest exhibition on the local fishing industry (mid-June to Aug Mon 2–4.30pm, Tues–Fri 9.30am–noon & 2–4.30pm).

Outside the gate, the pattern of the sixteenth-century defensive works is clear to see – from interior town wall, to dry ditch, to earthen mound and moat. The interior of one of the subterranean artillery **Kazematten** (casemates) is open during July and August (Mon 2–4.30pm, Tues–Fri 9.30am–noon & 2–4.30pm). Cramped and poorly ventilated, it's easy to see why the Dutch called such emplacements *Moortkuijl*, literally "Pits of Murder". From the Kazematten it's about an hour's stroll right round the ramparts.

Ten minutes' walk northwest from the Vispoort – turn right along Havenkade and take the second left – lie the **De Vier Jaargetijden** homeopathic gardens (guided tours only; April–Oct Mon–Fri 9.30am–4pm plus June–Aug Sat 10am–3.30pm; ☎05250/7373), six hectares of land that hold a comprehensive collection of homeopathic plants, the life's work of one Alfred Vogel. They form part of a successful business and are Elburg's main tourist attraction. In the summer, free guided tours of two hours' duration begin at the Visitors' Centre every hour, on the hour, subject to demand and within opening times. It's easy to tag on to any of the groups visiting the gardens, but if you're keen to have the tour in English, ring ahead to make arrangements. It's also possible to negotiate a tour in English on the spot, but you may have to wait a couple of hours. There's also a Visitors' Centre, or **Bezoekerscentrum**, at Industriestraat 15 (Mon–Fri 9.30am–4pm), which has a variety of illustrative displays and a mock-up of an old pharmacy. However, it's all in Dutch and the gardens are of far more interest.

Practical details

Elburg is easily reached from **Zwolle bus station** by service #101 (Mon–Sat 2 hourly, Sun hourly; 35min). The nearest **railway station** is 8km from town at 'T HARDE, on the Zwolle–Amersfoort line, with trains in both directions every half hour; however, buses from 't Harde station to Elburg are irregular (Mon–Fri 5 daily; Sat 3 daily; none on Sun; 15min).

Elburg **VVV**, Jufferenstraat 9 (Mon–Sat 9am–12.30pm & 1.30–5pm; ☎05250/ 1520), is by the bus stop on the way in from Zwolle and they have a list of private **rooms** starting at f25 per person per night. The VVV will ring round to make a booking, but try to get a room in the old centre, and come early in high season when accommodation often runs short. There's one **hotel**, *Het Smeede*, Smedestraat 5 (☎05250/3877), off Beekstraat on the southwest side of the centre, with double rooms for f95 per night. The nearest **campsite** is the *Old Putten*, Zuiderzeestraatweg 65 (Easter–Sept), some 500m east of the VVV; head out of the old town along Zwolseweg and Zuiderzeestraatweg is the first on the right.

Of Elburg's many **restaurants** it's difficult to find any of real note. However, *'t Olde Regthuys*, Beekstraat 33, serves an excellent range of fish dishes underneath fishing nets and ship models; the *'t Scheepje*, Vischpoortstraat 16, is lively and cheap; and the *Beekzicht*, Beekstraat 39, is fine for snacks.

For **boat trips**, there are hour-long excursions from Elburg around the Veluwemeer throughout the summer (f5 per person). There are also three times weekly day trips to Urk in July and August (f20), and occasional sailings to Ketelmeer and Harderwijk, among other destinations, in a nineteenth-century clipper (prices by negotiation). The VVV have the latest schedules and will make reservations on your behalf.

The **strip of coast** on both sides of the Veluwemeer around Elburg is popular with Dutch holidaymakers for its water sports, nature reserves and forests. The whole region is dotted with campsites and the best way to explore it all is by **bike**. Cycles are available for hire in Elburg at *Koops*, Beekstraat 1 (☎05250/4461), for about f7 a day. The VVV have a comprehensive range of suggested cycle routes.

Flevoland

With the damming of the Zuider Zee and the creation of the Ijsselmeer, the coast-line north and west of Kampen and Elburg has been transformed, creating two new polder areas, the **Oostelijk and Zuidelijk Flevoland polders**, which form an island of reclaimed land in front of the old shoreline and make up the greater part of Holland's twelfth and newest province – **Flevoland**. To the north, the reclaimed land mass of the **Northeast Polder** forms the rest of the new province, the small towns that mark the line of the old coast – Vollenhove, Blokzijl and Kuinre – cut off from open water and now marking the provincial boundary between Flevoland and Overijssel.

The Northeast Polder

The **Northeast Polder** was the first major piece of land to be reclaimed as part of the Zuider Zee reclamation scheme, which began in earnest with the Zuider Zee Reclamation Act of 1918. The key to the project was the completion of the Afsluitdijk between Den Oever in North Holland and Zurich in Friesland in 1932, which separated the open sea from the Zuider Zee and thereby created the fresh-water Ijsselmeer lake. The draining of the polder was completed in 1936: drained and dried, it provided 119,000 acres of new agricultural pasture, which the government handed out under an incentive scheme to prospective settlers. The original aims of the project were predominantly agricultural, and (unlike later polders) little consideration was given to the needs of the settlers, with the result that most of the Northeast Polder is unimaginably boring (the only town of any size, Emmeloord, is like a vast housing estate), and it's no surprise that, even with the incentives, there were difficulties in attracting settlers. Also, a number of design faults soon became apparent. Without trees the land was subject to soil erosion, and the lack of an encircling waterway meant the surrounding mainland dried out and began to sink – problems that have persisted until the present day.

The Schokland Museum

The Northeast Polder incorporates the former Zuider Zee islands of Urk and Schokland, which in Roman times were actually connected as one island. Schokland, however, was abandoned in the last century because of the threat of flooding and only the church of 1834 has survived, converted into the **Schokland Museum** (April–Sept daily 10am–5pm; Oct–March Tues–Sun 11am–5pm), with displays of all sorts of bits and pieces found during the draining of the polders. From beside the museum, a circular foot and cycle path follows the old shoreline of the island, a distance of about 10km.

The Schokland Museum is a 400-metre walk south of the minor road between Ens and Nagele/Urk – some 4km west of Ens. Buses drop you on the stretch of road nearest the museum, but it's an awkward journey without a car: take bus #141 from Zwolle or Kampen station to Ens bus station (Mon–Fri every half-hour, Sun hourly), from where you can either walk or take the connecting #142, which passes Schokland on its way to Urk (Mon–Fri 4 daily; none at weekends; 5min).

Urk

The only place really worth a visit in the Northeast Polder is **URK**, a trim harbour and fishing port that was a reluctant addition to the mainland. Centuries of hard-ship and isolation bred a tight-knit island fishing community here, with its own distinctive dialect and version of the national costume – aspects that have inevita-bly become diluted by connection to the mainland. However, the island's earlier independence does to some extent live on, rooted in a fishing industry which marks it out from the surrounding agricultural communities.

The damming of the Zuider Zee posed special problems for the islanders, and it's hardly surprising that they opposed the Ijsselmeer scheme from the begin-ning. Some feared that when the Northeast Polder was drained they would simply be overwhelmed by a flood of new settlers, but their biggest concern was that their fishing fleet would lose direct access to the North Sea. After futile nego-tiations at national level, the islanders decided to take matters into their own hands: the larger ships of the fleet were sent north to fish from ports above the line of the Afsluitdijk, particularly Delfzijl, and transport was organised to transfer the catch straight back for sale at the Urk fish auctions. In the meantime, other fishermen decided to continue to fish locally and adapt to the freshwater species of the Ijsselmeer. These were not comfortable changes for the islanders, and the whole situation deteriorated when the Dutch government passed new legislation banning trawling in the Ijsselmeer in 1970. When the inspectors arrived in Urk to enforce the ban, years of resentment exploded in ugly scenes of quayside violence and the government moved fast to sweeten the pill by offering substantial subsidies to compensate those fishermen affected. This arrangement continues today, and the focus of conflict has moved to the attempt to impose EC quotas on the catch of the deep-sea fleet.

There's nothing spectacular about Urk – it's neither especially pretty nor particularly picturesque, but its setting is attractive, its quayside a pleasant mixture of the functional and the ornamental, and an appealing series of narrow lanes of tiny terrace houses indicate the extent of the old village. A surprising number of the islanders still wear traditional costume and further examples are on display by the harbour in the **Visserijmuseum**, Wijk 2, no. 2, (Mon–Fri 10am–1pm & 2–5pm, Sat 10am–1pm; f2.50).

The only convenient way of reaching Urk by **bus** is to take #141 from Kampen and Zwolle (Mon–Sat 2 hourly, Sun 4 daily after 2pm; 60–80min); ask the driver to drop you off at the stop nearest the centre. From early May to mid-September, Monday to Saturday, **ferries** cross the Ijsselmeer between Enkhuizen and Urk two or three times daily; a day return costs f15, a single f9, and the trip takes ninety minutes; check with any VVV for times.

Adjoining the museum, Urk **VVV**, Wijk 2, no. 2, (Mon–Fri 10am–1pm & 2–5pm, Sat 10am–1pm; ☎05277/4040), will help arrange **accommodation** in both private **rooms** from f25 and **pensions** from f30 per person per night. There are two cheap pensions near the harbour: *De Kroon*, Wijk 7, no. 54, (☎05277/1216), with prices from f35 per person, and the unnamed pension of Mw. J. Bakker at Wijk 3, no. 76 (☎05277/2363), where the rate is f30 per person per night. The nearest **campsite** is *De Vormt*, Vormtweg 9 (April–Sept), in the woods some 4km north of Urk along the coastal road. Finally, Urk is a great place to eat **fresh fish** – try the *De Kaap* near the lighthouse at Wijk 1, no. 5, or the *De Zeebodem*, further down at no. 67.

The Flevoland Polders

The Dutch learned from their mistakes on the Northeast Polder when, in the 1950s and 1960s, they drained the two polders that make up the western portion of the province of Flevoland, ringing the new land with a water channel to stop the surrounding mainland drying out and sinking. The Dutch government have tried hard to make these polders attractive: they're fringed by trees and water sports facilities. But it remains an uphill struggle, and people have moved here slowly and reluctantly, only persuaded by large financial carrots and very cheap housing. **LELYSTAD**, accessible direct from Kampen on bus #143 (Mon–Sat half-hourly, Sun hourly; 55min) or by train from Amsterdam CS (half-hourly; 40min), is where most of them end up, a characterless expanse of glass and concrete surrounded by leafy suburbs. The epitome of 1960s and early 1970s urban design, Lelystad is something of a disaster, and things may get worse if plans to expand the city to accommodate some 100,000 by the year 2000 proceed.

The new railway link to Amsterdam was completed early in 1990, and should go the whole way to making both Lelystad and the other new town of ALMERE, 25km to the west, a dormitory suburb of the capital, and home to some of its most poorly paid workers.

Lelystad takes its name from the pioneer engineer who had the original idea for the Zuider Zee Scheme, and for those with a passing interest in land reclamation there is at least one reason to stop – the **Informatiecentrum Nieuw Land**, at Oostvaardersdijk 1–13 (April–Oct Tues–Sun 10am–5pm; Nov–March Tues–Fri 10am–5pm; f2.50). This gives the background on the Zuider Zee plan, with photos, models, films and slides. Most of the information has been translated into English, and you get a good idea of what's happened, and what's scheduled to happen. The main problem is getting there: from the rail and neighbouring bus stations, walk north beside the busy road that runs along the east side of the railway tracks and turn left at the first main intersection – a 1500-metre walk; the information centre is straight ahead across the island at the end of the road, a further 1500m on. If you're travelling by car from Enkhuizen, take the first major right as you come off the dyke, and it's right again at the first island.

The area's other attraction, the **Scheepsarcheologisch Museum** (daily 11am–5pm; f1.50), is on the northeastern edge of the polder at tiny **KETELHAVEN**. It's a collection of all sorts of material retrieved as the land was drained. Most of the exhibits come from the extraordinary number of ships that foundered in the treacherous shallows of the Zuider Zee, notably much of the hull of a seventeenth-century merchant ship. Once again, though, you really need a car to get here: the nearest bus stop is some 6km away on the main Dronten–Kampen road. For the determined, take bus #143 from Kampen station and tell the driver where you're going. The bus stop is a couple of hundred metres east of Colijnweg, a turning to the right that takes you from the main road right into Ketelhaven .

Eastern Overijssel: Twente

Southeast of Zwolle, the flat landscape of western Holland is replaced by the lightly undulating, wooded countryside of **Twente**, an industrial region whose principal towns – **Almelo**, **Hengelo** and **Enschede** – were once dependent on the textile industry. Hit hard by cheap Far Eastern imports, they were forced to diversify their industrial base with mixed success: the largest town, Enschede, still has around ten percent unemployment.

Enschede

If you visit anywhere in Twente it should really be **ENSCHEDE**, the region's main town. Laid waste by fire in 1862, it has a desultory modern centre that's been refashioned as a large shopping precinct, but it's a lively place, with regular festivals, exhibitions and the like, and it has a museum with an excellent collection of Dutch art, and some interesting 1930s architecture. All in all it's a worthwhile detour if you're heading east into Germany.

The Town

Five minutes' walk south of the train station, **Langestraat** is Enschede's main street. At its northern end, **Markt** is the town's main square, home to the nineteenth-century **Grote Kerk** (Wed & Sun 2–4pm) in the middle, with its Romanesque tower, and the **St Jacobuskerk** just across the Markt, completed in 1933 on the site of a previous church that burnt down in 1862. The severe rectangular shape of the building is punctured by angular copper-green roofs, huge circular windows and a series of Gothic arches. It's normally kept closed, but if you call at the presbytery next door someone should open up the place for you. It's worth the trouble, as the church is built in a beautiful domed and cloistered neo-Byzantine style, with some good modern sculpture and stained glass. The **Stadhuis**, a couple of minutes away down Langestraat, was finished in the same year and is also something of an architectural landmark, its brown brick tower topped by four eye-catching blue and gold clocks. No expense was spared in its construction, and the interior is richly decorated with mosaics, and, again, stained glass.

Fifteen minutes' walk north of the centre at Lasondersingel 129 – over the railway line at the crossing beside the station, first right, second left and follow the road to the end – the **Rijksmuseum Twente** (Tues–Fri 10am–5pm, Sat & Sun 1–5pm; f3) is housed in a building of the same era, an Art Deco mansion of 1929, the gift to the nation of a family of mill owners, the Van Heeks, who used the profits they made from their workers to build up one of eastern Holland's finest art collections. Clearly laid out and labelled, the museum has three main sections: fifteenth- to nineteenth-century art to the right of the entrance in rooms 1 to 11a; modern art, primarily Dutch with the emphasis on Expressionism, to the left of the entrance in rooms 12 to 21 and 23 to 32 (though many of these rooms are used for temporary exhibitions); and applied art, based on exhibits from the region of Twente, in the rooms at the back of the museum – prehistoric and medieval artefacts, tiles and porcelain, tapestries and a reconstructed farm.

It's the paintings, inevitably, that provide the most interest, especially the Dutch and Flemish sections. Among a fine sample of early religious art are seven brilliant blue and gold fragments from a French hand-illuminated missal; a primitive twelfth-century wood carving of *Christ on Palm Sunday*; a delightful cartoon strip of contemporary life entitled *De Zeven Werken van Barmhartigheid* (The Seven Acts of Charity); and an extraordinary pair of fifteenth century altar doors by one Tilman van der Burch, where a deep carved relief of a pastoral scene resembles a modern pop-up book. Of later canvases, Hans Holbein's *Portrait of Richard Mabott* is typical of his work, the stark black of the subject's gown offset by the white cross on his chest, and the face so finely observed it's possible to make out the line of his stubble. Pieter Bruegel the Younger's *Winter Landscape* is also fastidiously drawn, down to the last twig, and contrasts with the more loosely contoured bent figures and threatening clouds of his brother Jan's *Landscape*. Lucas Cranach's studies of a bloated *Frederick Grootmoedige* and the spectacularly ugly *Barbara van Saksen* must have done little for the self-confidence of their subjects. Jan Steen's *The Alchemist* is all scurrilous satire, from the skull on the chimneypiece, to the lizard suspended from the ceiling and the ogre's whispered advice, and compares with the bulging breasts and flushed countenance of the woman in his *Flute Player*, where the promise of forthcoming sex is emphasised by the vague outline of tussling lovers on the wall in the background. The modern section, too, has a few highlights – Claude Monet's volatile *Falaises pres de Pourville*; a characteristically unsettling canvas by Carel Willink, *The Actress Ank van der Moer*; and examples of the work of less well-known Dutch modernists like Theo Kuypers, Jan Roeland and Emo Verkerk.

From beside the Stadhuis, it's a twenty-minute walk southwest to Enschede's **Textielindustrie Museum** (Tues–Fri 10am–5pm, Sat–Sun 1–5pm; f1.50), at the junction of Haaksbergerstaat and Industriestraat: head straight down Van Loenshof, turn right at Boulevard 1945 and take the first left. Housed in a former mill and devoted to portraying everyday life in Twente from the nineteenth century onwards, the most intriguing displays are a series of representative living rooms and a bewildering variety of looms reflecting the development of the textile business from its origins as a cottage industry to large-scale factory production.

A third museum, the **Natuurmuseum**, De Ruyterlaan 2 (Tues–Sat 10am–5pm, Sun 2–5pm; f2.50), is also worth a peek: there's a vivarium on the first floor, some well presented fossils at ground level, and a mineralogy section in the basement. To get there, turn right out of the train station along Stationsplein and it's down the first major road on the left – a five-minute walk.

Practical details

The best place to **stay** in Enschede is the unpretentious *Hotel Atlanta*, right in the centre at Oude Markt 12 (☎053/31 67 66), where rooms cost f90 per night. The **VVV**, in the centre of town at Oude Markt 31 (Mon–Fri 10am–5.30pm, Sat 9am–1pm, June–Aug to 5pm; ☎053/32 32 00), has details of a limited number of private **rooms** from f30 per person per night. For **food**, the *Atlanta* serves reasonable snacks; the *Atrium*, behind the *Atlanta Hotel* on Stadsgravenstraat, is cheap and popular; and the *Poort van Kleef*, Oude Markt 13, is a good place for lunch.

Around Enschede: Hengelo, Almelo, Oldenzaal, Ootmarsum and Denekamp

Some 10km northwest of Enschede, **HENGELO** has about 80,000 inhabitants and is Twente's second town, a grim place whose old centre was destroyed during World War II. **ALMELO**, a further 17km northwest, is the region's third largest town, but this too has few attractions: the only buildings of any real interest are the centrally sited **Waag**, whose stepped gables date, surprisingly enough, from 1914, and, in a park east of the Marktplein, a stately seventeenth-century mansion, the **Huize Almelo** (no entry).

Things pick up a little northeast of Enschede with **OLDENZAAL**, the most agreeable of Twente's other settlements. Founded by the Franks, it was a medieval city of some importance, and it was from here, too, that Overijssel's textile industry began its rapid nineteenth-century expansion, spurred by the introduction of the power loom by Thomas Ainsworth of Bolton. The town's principal sight, the **St Plechelmusbasiliek**, is right in the centre, an impressive essentially Romanesque edifice dating from the thirteenth century. Named after Saint Plechelm, the Irish missionary who brought Christianity here, the interior (visits organised by the VVV) is an exercise in simplicity – strong, sturdy pillars supporting a succession of low semicircular arches. Above, the bell tower is the largest in Europe with a carillon of no less than 46 bells.

Bus #60 leaves Enschede for the twenty-minute trip to Oldenzaal train station twice-hourly from Monday to Saturday and once hourly on Sunday. The approach by **rail** is less convenient as passengers have to change at Hengelo, where it's a half-hour wait for the right connection. Oldenzaal's **train station** is ten minutes' walk south of the centre – head down Stationsplein, turn right at the end onto

Haerstraat, first left along Wilhelminastraat and it's dead ahead – where the **VVV**, Ganzenmarkt 3 (Mon–Fri 9am–noon & 2–5pm, June–Aug also Sat noon–4pm; ☎05410/14023), has information on private **rooms**. There are several **hotels**: the *Muller* at Markt 14 (☎05410/12093), with doubles from f60, is the cheapest. For **eating**, Markt is lined with **bars** and **restaurants**, try the *'t Geveltje* at no. 19 or the *Los Carretas* at no. 21.

Oldenzaal is a good base for visiting the wooded countryside that stretches northeast from near the town to the German border. This is a popular holiday area, littered with campsites, summer cottages and bungalow parks. The village of **OOTMARSUM** (bus #64 from the station hourly; 15min) is noted for its half-timbered houses and quaint Markt. By comparison, **DENEKAMP** (bus #52 from the station; Mon–Sat every 15min, Sun hourly; 15min) is rather drab, though the elegant classicism of the **Kasteel Singraven**, some 2km west of the centre, partly makes up for it. Details of guided tours around the castle (mid-April to Oct Tues–Fri only) are available from the Denekamp VVV, Kerkplein 2 (Mon–Fri 9am–12.30pm & 2–5pm, June–Aug also Sat 1–4pm; ☎05413/1205), but entry to the extensive grounds with their working watermill is free.

Deventer and Zutphen

South of Zwolle, the river Ijssel twists its way through flat, fertile farmland as it marks out the boundary between Overijssel and Gelderland. For 200 years the towns of the lower Ijssel, **Deventer** and **Zutphen**, shared with Zwolle and Kampen a period of tremendous prosperity as the junction of trade routes from Germany, the Baltic and Amsterdam. Although both towns suffered grievously during the wars with Spain, the underlying reasons for their subsequent decline were economic – they could do little to stop the movement of trade to the west and could not compete with the great cities of South Holland. By the eighteenth century, they had slipped into provincial insignificance.

Deventer

Twenty minutes by twice-hourly train from Zwolle, **DEVENTER** sits calmly on the banks of the Ijssel, an intriguing and – in tourist terms – rather neglected place, whose origins can be traced to the missionary work of the eighth-century Saxon monk, Lebuinus. An influential centre of medieval learning, it was here in the late fourteenth century that Gerrit Groot founded the Brotherhood of Common Life, a semi-monastic collective that espoused tolerance and humanism within a philosophy known as *Moderne Devotie* (Modern Devotion). This progressive creed attracted some of the great minds of the time, and Thomas à Kempis and Erasmus both studied here.

The Town

Five minutes from the train station, the centre of town is **Brink**, an elongated marketplace that runs roughly north to south, dividing the old town in two. The **Waag** edges the southern end of the square, a late Gothic edifice that retains an ancient dignity despite something of a rickety appearance. Inside, the **Town Museum** (Tues–Sat 10am–5pm, Sun 2–5pm) has a thin collection of portrait paintings and a few antique bicycles. More intriguing is the large pan that's nailed to the outside of the Waag's western wall. Apparently, the mintmaster's assistant was found making a tidy profit by debasing the town's coins, so he was put in the pan and boiled alive. The bullet holes weren't an attempt to prolong the agony, but the work of idle French soldiers taking, quite literally, "pot shots".

Behind the Waag, the VVV is housed in a sixteenth-century merchant's mansion, *De Drie Haringen* (The Three Herrings), close by which is the **Speelgoed en Blikmuseum** (Toy and Tin Museum; Tues–Sat 10am–5pm, Sun 2–5pm), which specialises in mechanical dolls. Walking west from here, Assenstraat's **window cuts** were completed in the early 1980s by a local artist, J. Limburg. Precise and entertaining, each illustrates a particular proverb or belief: at no. 119 the hedgehog's inscription translates as "Thrift yields big revenues" and at no. 81, on a house called *Gevaarlijke Stoffen* (Dangerous Materials), the totem pole is surrounded by slogans including *E pericolose sporcare* (To pollute is harmful). Continuing west along Assenstraat, and veering left down Grote Poot (Big Leg), the **Lebuinuskerk** (Mon–Fri 10am–5pm, Sat 1.30–5pm; free) is one of the most impressive Gothic buildings in eastern Holland, an expression of Deventer's fifteenth-century wealth and self-confidence. Carefully symmetrical, the massive nave is supported by seven flying buttresses, trimmed by an ornate stone parapet. The interior has recently been restored and today the expanse of white stone is almost startling, high arched windows and slender pillars reaching up towards a distant timber roof. Below, the church has two magnificent Baroque organs, the delicate remnants of some medieval murals, and an eleventh-century crypt with a simple vaulted roof supported by Romanesque, spiral columns.

Back outside, the rear of the Lebuinuskek is joined to the fourteenth-century **Mariakerk** (no entry). Services haven't been held here since 1591 and the town council considered demolishing it as early as 1600, but in the event it survived as the town's arsenal. Back at Brink, east of the Waag, Rijkmanstraat heads into the **Bergkwartier**, an area of ancient housing that was tastefully refurbished in the 1960s, one of Holland's first urban renewal projects. Turning left onto Kerksteeg, there's a small piece of iron, the remnants of a ring, embedded in a hole on the right-hand wall. Fearful of marauding Spanish armies, the 1570s were desperate times for the inhabitants of Deventer, and, in their efforts to reinforce the town's defences, iron rings were cut into the walls of many of the streets so that chains could be hung across them. At the end of Kerksteeg, the **Bergkerk** is fronted by two tall towers dating from the thirteenth century, the differences in the colouring of the brick indicating the stages of construction. From the church, Roggestraat leads downhill to the east side of Brink; opposite is a tiny triangle edged by the **Penninckshuis**, whose florid Renaissance frontage is decorated with statuettes of six virtues. The inscription *Alst Godt behaget beter benyt als beclaget* is smug indeed – "If it pleases God it is better to be envied than to be pitied".

Practical details

Deventer's **bus** and **rail** stations are a five-minute walk north of the town centre – straight down Keizerstraat and onto the Brink. For a place of this size, **accommodation** is thin on the ground: there are no pensions or private rooms, and there's only one central **hotel**, the *Royal*, Brink 94 (☎05700/11880), where doubes start at f90 a night. The only alternative is the **campsite**, *De Worp*, west of the centre in the fields across the Ijssel. A shuttle boat service crosses the river from the landing stage at the bottom of Vispoort, and on the other side it's a five-minute walk down the first turning on the right, Langelaan.

Bars and **restaurants** line both sides of Brink: *De Waagschaal*, no. 77, is a pleasant brown café; good snacks are available at *Marts*, no. 82, and the *Hans en Grietje*, no. 76; there's excellent Italian food at *Ti Amo*, no. 7, and a varied French and Dutch menu at *La Balance*, no. 72. The local speciality is a sort of honey gingerbread, *Deventer koek*, and the best place to try it is the antique cake shop *Bussink* at no. 84.

The **VVV**, Brink 55 (Mon–Fri 10am–5pm, Sat 10am–4pm; ☎05700/16200), sells a detailed town guide (f2) and has details of **boat trips** up the Ijssel. A weekly programme throughout July and August includes excursions to Enkhuizen, Urk, Kampen, Zwolle and Zutphen; prices vary according to the itinerary, but for the longer trips reckon on f25 per person.

Zutphen

A sleepy little town some 15km south of Deventer, **ZUTPHEN** was founded in the eleventh century as a fortified settlement at the junction of the Berkel and Ijssel rivers. It took just one hundred years to become an important port, and today's tranquillity belies an illustrious and sometimes torrid past. Attacked and sacked on numerous occasions, the massacre of its citizens by Spanish forces in 1572 became part of Protestant folklore, strengthening their resolve against Catholic cruelty and absolutism. It was also here that Sir Philip Sidney, the English poet, soldier and courtier, met his death while fighting with Leicester's forces against the Spanish in 1586. Sir Philip personified the ideal of the Renaissance man and died as he had lived – in style: wounded in the thigh as a consequence of loaning his leg-armour to a friend, he had every reason to feel outraged by his poor luck. Instead, realising he was about to die, he offered his cup of water to another wounded soldier, uttering the now commonplace phrase "thy need is greater than mine".

The Town

A five-minute walk from the rail station, the effective centre of Zutphen is the **Wijnhuis**, a confused building of pillars, urns and platforms that was begun in the seventeenth century and now houses the VVV. All the old town's main streets radiate from here, and although there aren't many specific sights, the place does have charm, a jangle of architectural styles within much of the medieval street plan.

Around the corner from the Wijnhuis, Lange Hofstraat cuts down to the **Grote Kerk** of St Walburga (early May to mid-Sept, Mon 2–4pm, Tues–Sat 11am–4pm; guided tours on the hour; f2.50), an indifferent Gothic church in need of external restoration. Inside, the most impressive features are an extravagant brass baptismal font and the remarkable medieval **Library**, sited in the sixteenth-century chapterhouse. Established in 1560, the library has a beautiful low vaulted ceiling that twists round in a confusion of sharp-edged arches rising above the original wooden reading desks. It has all the feel of a medieval monastery, but it was in fact one of the first Dutch libraries to be built for the general public, a conscious effort by the Protestant authorities to dispel ignorance and superstition. Stored here are some 700 books and manuscripts, from early incunabula to later sixteenth-century works, a selection of which are still chained to the lecterns on which they were once read. The collection also includes two handwritten volumes – one a beautiful sixteenth-century illuminated missal, the other an origi-

nal manuscript attributed to Thomas à Kempis. Curiously, the tiles on one side of
the floor are dotted with paw marks, which some contemporaries attributed to
the work of the Devil.

Down the alleys east of the church entrance is the fifteenth-century
Drogenapstoren, one of the old city gates. This is a fine example of a brick
rampart tower, taking its name from the time when the town trumpeteer, Thomas
Drogenap, lived here.

Heading back towards the Wijnhuis along the Zaadmarkt, you'll come to the
Museum Henriette Polak at no. 88 (Tues–Fri 11am–5pm, Sat & Sun 1.30–5pm)
which has a modest collection of twentieth-century Dutch paintings, notably
Landschap by Wim Oepts, a profusion of strong colours, roughly brushed, that
manages a clear impression of a Dutch landscape.

Finally, the **Stedelijk Museum** (same times), on the other side of town
towards the station at Rozengracht 3, is housed in the shell of a thirteenth-
century Dominican monastery and has a fairly predictable selection of shards,
armour and silverware. In the old refectory on the first floor there's an altarpiece
from around 1400, originally from the Grote Kerk.

Practical details

Zutphen's **VVV**, in the Wijnhuis (Mon–Fri 9am–5.30pm, Sat 10am–12.30pm;
☎05750/19355), has details of a couple of centrally situated **rooms**, from f35 per
person per night, though in July and August it's advisable to arrive early as they
disappear fast. There's only one **hotel**, the pleasant *Berkhotel*, straight down the
Groenmarkt from the VVV at Marschpoortstraat 19 (☎05750/11135), with
doubles from f75.

As far as **eating** is concerned, there are two good and reasonably priced
restaurants in Zutphen: *Pizzeria da Enzo*, near the Drogenapstoren at
Pelikaanstraat 1a, and the *Berkhotel*'s vegetarian café *De Kloostertuin*,
Marschpoortstraat 19 (closed Mon). For **bars**, try *'t Winkeltje*, Groenmarkt 34, or
the quieter *De Korenbeurs*, Zaadmarkt 84.

Boats trips run north up the Ijssel in July and August with occasional excursions to Deventer, Zwolle and Kampen. Prices vary according to the route, but a
day trip will cost about f25. Times of sailing from the VVV.

Around Zutphen: the Achterhoek

Extending some 40km southeast from Zutphen to the German border, the
Achterhoek (Back Corner) is a quiet rural region of small towns and villages
criss-crossed by cycle tracks. Small enough to tour from Zutphen, there are no
really noteworthy monuments, with the possible exception of the old frontier
settlement of **'S-HEERENBERG**, where the restored castle, **Huis Bergh**, dates
from the early fifteenth century and sits prettily within the surrounding woods.
Inside (May, June, Sept & Oct tours daily at 2pm; July & Aug noon–4pm), there's
a mixed bag of antiques, but it's the setting which really pleases. The old
Stadhuis, the original castle chapel – now the village church – and what remains
of the ramparts are nearby. 'S-Heerenberg is accessible by bus from the railway
station at DOETINCHEM, about 9km to the north, once every two hours. Once
there, the **VVV** (Mon–Fri 2–5pm, Sat 10am–2pm; ☎08346/63131) has good
suggestions for walking and cycling, and **bicycles** can be hired from *G. Nijland*,
Klinkerstraat 36.

Through the Veluwe: Apeldoorn

Extending west of the river Ijssel, the **Veluwe** (literally Bad Land) of the province of Gelderland is an expanse of heath, woodland and dune edged by Apeldoorn and Amersfoort to the east and west, and the Veluwemeer and Arnhem to the north and south. For centuries these infertile lands lay almost deserted, but today they make up the busiest holiday area in Holland, a profusion of campsites, bungalow parks and second homes that extends down to the Hoge Veluwe National Park, a protected zone in the southeast corner that is much the prettiest part, and the best place to experience the area – though it's more sensibly seen from Arnhem.

Apeldoorn

The administrative capital of the Veluwe, **APELDOORN** was no more than a village at the turn of the century, but it's grown rapidly to become an extensive garden city, a rather characterless modern place that spreads languidly into the surrounding countryside. However, as one-time home of the Dutch royal family, Apeldoorn is a major tourist centre in its own right, popular with those Dutch pensioners who like an atmosphere of comfortable, rather snobbish privilege. The one annual show of life is the **Jazz in the Woods** festival held over a weekend in either late May or early June, which attracts artists of international standing who perform in the pubs and bars around town, culminating in a Saturday night show at the *Orpheus* concert hall. Further details from the **VVV**, Postbus 1142, 7301 BJ Apeldoorn (☎055/78 84 21), who will also reserve accommodation.

The Paleis Het Loo

Apeldoorn is most famous for the **Paleis Het Loo** (Tues–Sun 10am–5pm; f7), situated on the northern edge of town and reachable by buses #102 and #104 (about once hourly) from the bus stop around the back of the *Hotel Suisse*, opposite the train station. Designed in 1685 by Daniel Marot for William III and his queen Mary, shortly before he acceded to the throne of England and Scotland, the palace was later the favourite residence of Queen Wilhelmina, who lived here until her death in 1962. No longer used by the Dutch royals – they moved out in 1975 – it was opened as a national museum in the early 1980s, illustrating 300 years of the history of the House of Orange-Nassau. Inside, seven years of repair work have restored an apparently endless sequence of bedrooms, ballrooms, living rooms and reception halls to their former glory, supplemented by displays of all things royal – from costumes and decorations in the West Wing, to documents, medals and gifts in the East Wing, and dozens of royal portraits and miscellaneous memorabilia spread across the main body of the palace. You can view the rooms of William and Mary, including their colourful individual bedchambers, as well as the much later study of Queen Wilhelmina. It's an undeniably complete display but, unless you've a special interest in the House of Orange, not especially diverting. Better are the formal **gardens** (both William and Mary were apparently keen gardeners), a series of precise and neatly bordered flowerbeds of geometric design that are accessible by long walkways ornamented in the Dutch Baroque style, with fountains, urns, statuettes and portals. The other part of the palace, the **Royal Stables** of 1906 (April–Oct only; same times), next to the entrance on Amersfoortweg, has displays of some of the old cars and carriages of past monarchs, including a pram that's rigged up against gas attack.

Practical details

The Apeldoorn **VVV** (Mon–Fri 9am–5pm, Sat 10am–1pm; ☎055-78 84 21) adjoins the railway station, and has maps of the town and the surrounding area and (if you need to stay) lists of **rooms** from about f30 per person per night; in season it's advisable to ask them to ring ahead to confirm vacancies. The most reasonably priced **hotel** in or near the town centre is the *De Poort van Kleef*, dead in the centre at Martplein 11 (☎055/21 39 90), which has double rooms from f70 a night. There's also an unofficial **youth hostel**, 4km to the west of town at Asselsestraat 330 (☎055/55 31 18; April–Sept; bus #2 or #4 from beside the railway station), with beds for f17.50. The nearest **campsite**, *De Veldekster*, is some 5km southwest of the centre, off Europaweg at Veldekster 25 (bus #110 from the train station).

Apeldoorn's popularity means that cheap **eating** is difficult, and you have to fall back on either pizza houses or fast food joints. For something a little more nutritious, try the centrally sited *Café de Paris*, Raadhuisplein 5, or the Greek restaurant, *Parthenon*, at no. 2.

An easy way to see the countryside around town is by **bike**. Details of suggested routes are available from the VVV, and cycles can be hired at *Janssen*, Koninginnelaan 54 – head down Hoofdstraat and onto its continuation, Loolaan; take the second turning right, Kerklaan, and then the first turning left.

Arnhem and around

Around 20km south of Apeldoorn, on the far side of the heathy Hoge Veluwe National Park, **ARNHEM** was once a wealthy resort, a watering-hole to which the merchants of Amsterdam and Rotterdam would flock to idle away their fortunes. This century it's become better known as the place where thousands of British and Polish troops died in the failed Allied airborne operation of September 1944, codenamed "Operation Market Garden". The operation gutted the greater part of the city and most of what you see today is a postwar reconstruction – inevitably not particularly enticing. However, Arnhem is a lively town that makes a good centre for seeing the numerous attractions scattered around its forested outskirts – the war museums and memorials, the Dutch open-air museum, and the Hoge Veluwe park itself, incorporating the Kröller-Müller Museum and its superb collection of modern art.

The Town

Since the war, Arnhem has been something of a place of pilgrimage for English visitors, who flock here every summer to pay their respects to the soldiers who died, or to view the spots immortalised by the battle; only recently have the graves begun to seem distant reminders of an ancient conflict, as World War II veterans age and memories fade. Predictably, the postwar rebuilding has left Arnhem a patchy place with the usual agglomerations of concrete and glass, surrounded by formless empty spaces. Five minutes' walk southeast from the rail station, the best part of what's left is the area northwest of the centre, around the **Korenmarkt**, a small square which escaped much of the destruction and has one or two good facades. The streets which lead off the Korenmarkt are pleasantly lively, full of restaurants and bars, while the **Filmhuis**, at Korenmarkt 42, has an excellent programme of international films and late-night showings.

Arnhem deteriorates as you walk southeast from the Korenmarkt and into the area most badly damaged by the fighting. Here you can find "The Bridge too Far", the **John Frostbrug**, named after the commander of the battalion that

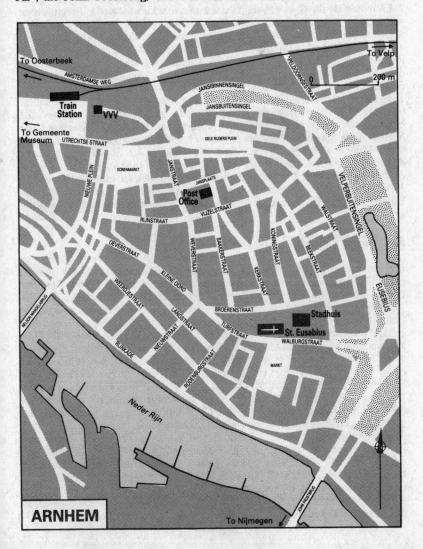

defended it for four days. It's just an ordinary bridge, but it remains the symbol and centre of people's remembrance of the battle, Dutch and British alike. Around its north end you can see the results of the devastation – wide boulevards intersect broad open spaces edged by haphazardly placed high-rise blocks and car parks. Overlooking this rather desolate spot, at the end of the characterless **Markt**, is the church of **St Eusabius**, with the fifteenth-century **Stadhuis** tucked in behind. The church is a fifteenth- to sixteenth-century structure surmounted by a valiantly attempted but rather obvious replacement tower. Fenced off for repair works of indefinite duration, it really does look rather forlorn.

From outside the train station, it's a ten-minute walk west along Utrechtsetraat to the **Gemeentemuseum** at no. 87 (Tues–Sat 10am–5pm, Sun 11am–5pm; free), whose speciality is temporary exhibitions of modern Dutch art. The permanent collection, displayed in the main part of the museum and the annexe opposite at no. 74, includes numerous archaeological finds from the surrounding area; a display of Chinese, Japanese and Delft ceramics from the seventeenth and eighteenth centuries; Dutch silverware, notably several *guild beakers*, whose size and degree of decoration indicated the status of the owner; and a modest selection of paintings from the sixteenth to the nineteenth centuries, with the emphasis on views of the landscape, villages and towns of Gelderland. The nucleus of the modern art section is the work of the **magic realists**, particularly Carel Willink and Pyke Koch, whose *Vrouwen in de Straat* is a typically disconcerting canvas, the womens' eyes looking out of the picture in a medley of contrasting emotions. The paintings of Renier Lucassen, for example *The Kiss* of 1976, establish the stylistic link between the magic realism of the 1930s and Dutch contemporary art, the familiar once again given a disturbing and alienating slant.

Practical details

Arnhem is a major rail junction, well connected with both Dutch and German cities. The town's **rail** and **bus stations**, a couple of minutes' walk from the centre, are next door to the **VVV**, Stationsplein 45 (Mon–Fri 9am–5.30pm, Sat 10am–5pm, until 8pm July & Aug; ☎085/42 03 30), who have a good selection of Dutch maps, books on "Operation Market Garden", brochures, and up-to-date cultural information, including rock and film listings, in *Uit in Arnhem* (f1). They also operate an **accommodation** booking service – useful in July and August when Arnhem's handful of reasonably priced **pensions** and **hotels** can fill up early. The cheapest double rooms in town – f65 – are at *Pension Warnsborn*, Schelmseweg 1 (☎085/42 59 94), but it's a fair way out (bus #11 or #2, direction Hoogkamp). Of the cheaper places to stay in or near the centre, *Hotel Pension Parkzicht*, Apeldoornsestraat 16 (☎085/42 06 98), ten minutes' walk from the station, has doubles from f70 per night; *Hotel Rembrandt*, Paterstraat 1 (☎085/42 01 53), on the second right off Apeldoornsestraat, costs f70 a night. There's also the *Hotel Rijnoever*, by the river at Rijnkade 86 (☎085/45 31 94), which has doubles at f80. There's a **youth hostel** some 5km north of town at Diepenbrocklaan 27 (bus #3, direction Cranvelt; ☎085/42 01 14). The nearest **campsite** is *Camping Warnsborn*, northwest of the centre at Bakenbergseweg 257 (☎085/42 34 69; bus #11 direction Schaarsbergen), though there are many others around the edge of the Hoge Veluwe park, 5km further north.

If you have problems finding something, there's a good alternative, the *Pension Little Tower*, Vijverlaan 29 (☎085/63 51 76), in the leafy suburb of VELP (trains twice hourly, 10min), bookable at Arnhem VVV. Untouched by the war, parts of Velp are still much as they were at the turn of the century – comfortable country mansions and landscaped streets and gardens. The *Little Tower* is right in the middle of Velp, ten minutes' walk from the railway station, a snip at f30 per person per night. To get there, turn right along Stationsstraat, left at the main road, first right down Overbeeklaan and first left.

Walking is the best way to **get around** Arnhem town centre, although to see any of the outlying attractions, and for some of the accommodation, you'll need at some point to use a **bus**. Arnhem has a rather odd system of trolley buses which describe a figure-of-eight pattern over town. This means there'll often be two buses at the station with the same number and different destinations, so it's important to get the direction as well as the number right.

Cheap **eating** isn't too much of a hassle, and the streets around Korenmarkt are best for restaurants, including *Pizzeria Da Leone*, Nieuwe Plein 24; the excellent *Nola Rae*, Marienburgstraat 2, with its vegetarian specialities (closed Mon); and, around the corner, Turkish food at the *Mozaik*, Ruiterstraat 43. For more traditional Dutch fare try the *Old Inn*, Stationsplein 40.

World War II memorials: Oosterbeek

The area around Arnhem is scattered with the graveyards of thousands of soldiers who died during **Operation Market Garden**. If you're a devotee of battle grounds and battle plans, Arnhem VVV sells specialist books on the campaign and provides details of organised tours. Otherwise, the easiest way to get some idea of the conflict and its effect on this part of Holland is to visit **OOSTERBEEK**, once a small village and now a prosperous suburb of Arnhem (4 trains hourly; 4min).

Following the signs from beside Oosterbeek railway station, it's a five-minute walk east to the **Airborne Cemetery**, a neat, symmetrical tribute to several hundred paratroopers whose bodies were brought here from the surrounding fields. It's a quiet secluded spot; the personal inscriptions on the gravestones are especially poignant. Ten minutes south of the station down Stationsweg, the village proper has spruce lawns and walls dotted with details of the battle – who held out where and for how long – as the Allied forces were pinned back within a tighter and tighter perimeter.

The **Airborne Museum** (Mon–Sat 11am–5pm, Sun noon–5pm; f3, no museumcards) is just to the west of the village centre along Utrechtseweg, housed in the former *Hotel Hartenstein*, where the British forces were besieged by the Germans for a week before retreating across the river, their numbers depleted from 10,005 to 2163. With the use of an English commentary, photographs, dioramas and original military artefacts – from rifles and light artillery to uniforms and personal memorabilia – the museum gives an excellent outline of the battle, and to a lesser extent aspects of World War II as it affected Holland as a whole. The Army Film and Photographic Unit landed with the British forces, and, perhaps more than anything else, it's their photographs that stick in the memory – grimly cheerful soldiers hauling in their parachutes, tense tired faces during the fighting, shattered Dutch villages.

OPERATION MARKET GARDEN

By September 1944 most of France and much of Belgium had been liberated from Nazi occupation. Fearing that an orthodox campaign would take many months and cost many lives, Field Marshal Montgomery decided that a pencil thrust north through Holland and subsequently east into the Ruhr, around the back of the Siegfried line, offered a good chance of ending the war early. To speed the advance of his land armies, Montgomery needed to cross several major rivers and canals in a corridor of territory stretching from Eindhoven, a few kilometres north of the front, to Arnhem. The plan, **Operation Market Garden**, was to parachute three Airborne armies behind enemy lines, each responsible for taking and holding particular bridgeheads until the main army could force their way north to join them. On Sunday September 17, the 1st British Airborne Division parachuted into the fields around Oosterbeek, their prime objective to seize the bridges over the Rhine at Arnhem. Meanwhile, the 101st American Airborne Division was dropped in the area of Veghel to secure the Wilhelmina and Zuid-Willemsvaart canals, and the 82nd were dropped around Grave and Nijmegen, for the crossings over the Maas and the Waal.

All went fairly well with the American landings and, by the night of September 20, sections of the main British army, 30 Corps, had reached the American bridgehead across the river Waal at Nijmegen. However, despite Polish reinforcements, the landings around Arnhem had run into problems. Allied Command had estimated that immediate opposition was unlikely to exceed a force of some 3000 men, but as luck would have it, the entire 2nd S.S. Panzer Corps was refitting near Arnhem just when the 1st Division landed. Taking the enemy by surprise, 2nd Parachute Battalion, under Lieutenant-Colonel John Frost, did manage to capture the north end of the road bridge across the Rhine, but it proved impossible to either reinforce them or capture the southern end. Surrounded, out-gunned and outmanned, the 2nd Battalion held their position from the 17th to the morning of the 21st, far longer than anybody could have anticipated, a story of extraordinary heroism. There were more heroics elsewhere, for the Polish and British battalions of the rest of the Division had concentrated around the bridgehead at Oosterbeek, which they held at tremendous cost under the command of General Urquhart. Elements of 30 Corps made desperate efforts to join up with them, but by the morning of the 25th it was clear that it was not going to be possible to provide reinforcements in sufficient numbers. Under cover of darkness, a dramatic withdrawal saved 2163 soldiers from an original force of 10,005.

The Nederlands Openluchtmuseum

Immediately north of Arnhem, the **Nederlands Openluchtmuseum** (April–Oct Mon–Fri 9am–5pm, Sat & Sun 10am–5pm; f8), reachable by bus #3, direction Alteveer (every 20min), or direct by special bus #12 (July–Aug only; every 30min), is a huge collection of Dutch buildings open to public view. One of the first of its type, the museum was founded in 1912 to try to "present a picture of the daily life of ordinary people in this country as it was in the past and has developed in the course of time". Over the years, original and representative buildings have been taken from all over the country and assembled here in a large chunk of the Veluwe forest. Where possible, buildings have been placed in groups that resemble the traditional villages of the different regions of Holland – from the farmsteads of Friesland to the farming communities of South Holland and the peat colonies of Drenthe. There are about 120 buildings in all, including examples of every type of Dutch windmill, most sorts of farmhouse, a variety of bridges, and several working craft shops, demonstrating the traditional skills of papermaking, milling, baking, brewing and bleaching. Other parts of the museum incorporate one of the most extensive regional costume exhibitions in the country and a comparatively modest herb garden.

All in all, it's an imaginative attempt to recreate the rural Dutch way of life over the past two centuries, and the museum's own guidebook explains everything with academic attention to detail – at f8 certainly worth every cent. It recommends three signposted routes – red (1hr), green (2hr) and blue (4hr); the green route, with certain selected forays into other sections, is perhaps a reasonable compromise.

The Hoge Veluwe National Park and Rijksmuseum Kröller-Müller

Spreading north from the Open Air Museum is the **Hoge Veluwe National Park**, an area of sandy heath and thick woodland that was once the private estate of Anton and Helene Kröller-Müller. Born near Essen in 1869, Helene Müller came from a wealthy and influential family whose money was made in the blast-furnace business. She married Anton Kröller of Rotterdam, whose brother ran the Dutch side of their trading interests, and the couple's fortunes were secured when the death of her father and his brother's poor health placed Anton at the head of the company at the age of 27. Apart from extending their business empire and supporting the Boers, they had a passionate desire to leave a grand bequest to the nation, a mixture of nature and culture which would, she felt, "be an important lesson when showing the inherent refinement of a merchant's family living at the beginning of the century". She collected the art, he the land, and in the 1930s ownership of both was transferred to the nation on the condition that a museum was built in the park. The museum opened in 1938 and Helene acted as manager until her death in 1939. Today, the park is one of Gelderland's most popular day-trip destinations, although it's large enough to absorb the crowds quite comfortably on all but the sunniest of summer weekends.

Around the park

The Hoge Veluwe park has three entrances – one near the village of Otterlo on the northwest perimeter, another near Hoenderloo on the northeast edge, and a third to the south at Rijzenburg, near the village of Schaarsbergen, only 10km from Arnhem. The park is open daily (8am–sunset; f6.25), though in September and early October certain areas are off-limits during the rutting season. The entry fee includes the museum, but cars are charged f6 extra.

There are a number of ways to get to the park by **bus**; easiest is to take the museum special from outside Arnhem railway station (May–Sept, bus #12 direction Hoge Veluwe; hourly; f8.40 for a day return plus f6.25 entry ticket: pay the driver) direct to the **Bezoekers Centrum** (Visitors' Centre; April–Oct daily 10am–5pm; Nov–March Sun 11am–4pm only), in the middle of the park not far from the museum. The centre has information on the park and is a good place to pick up one of the white bicycles that are left out for everyone's use at no extra charge – much the best way of getting around once you're here. When the bus isn't running, you can either hire a bike at Arnhem railway station or take bus #107 (direction Lelystad; hourly; 25min) to the entrance at Otterlo. From here it's a four-kilometre walk east to the Visitors' Centre, unless you're lucky enough to find a museum bike by the entrance.

Once mobile you can cycle around as you wish, along clearly signposted tracks and through stretches of dune and woodland where it's possible to catch sight of some of the park's big game – principally red deer, roe and moufflon (Corsican sheep). By comparison, the park's wild boar keep to themselves. Apart from the Kröller-Müller Museum (see below), the only thing to see is the **Jachtslot St Hubertus** (May–Oct Mon–Fri 10am–noon & 2–5pm), some 3km north of the Visitors' Centre, a hunting lodge and country home built for the Kröller-Müllers by the modernist Dutch architect, H. P. Berlage, in 1920. Dedicated to the patron saint of hunters, it's an impressive Art Deco monument, with lots of plays on the hunting theme. The floor plan – in the shape of branching antlers – is representative of the stag bearing a crucifix that appeared to Saint Hubert, the adopted patron of hunters, while he was hunting, and each room of the sumptuous interior symbolises an episode in the saint's life – all in all a somewhat unusual commission for a committed socialist who wrote so caustically about the *haute bourgeoisie*.

The Rijksmuseum Kröller-Müller

Most people who visit the Hoge Veluwe park come for the **Rijksmuseum Kröller-Müller** (All year round Tues–Sat 10am–5pm; April–Oct Sun 11am–5pm; Nov–March 1–5pm), made up of the private art collection of the Kröller-Müllers. It's one of the country's finest museums, a wide cross-section of modern European art from Impressionism to Cubism and beyond, housed in a low-slung building that was purpose-built in 1938 by the Belgian architect Van de Velde. Entry is included in the price of admission to the park (see above).

The bulk of the collection is in one long wing, starting with the most recent Dutch painters and working backwards. There's a good set of paintings, in particular some revealing *Self-portraits*, by Charley Toorop, one of the most skilled and sensitive of twentieth-century Dutch artists. Her father Jan also gets a good showing throughout the museum, from his pointillist studies to later, turn-of-the-century works more reminiscent of Aubrey Beardsley and the Art Nouveau movement. Piet Mondrian is well represented too, his 1909 *Beach near Domburg* a good example of his more stylised approach to landscape painting, a development from his earlier sombre-coloured scenes in the Dutch tradition. In 1909 he moved to Paris and his contact with Cubism transformed his work, as illustrated by his *Composition* of 1917 – simple flat rectangles of colour with the elimination of the object complete, the epitome of the De Stijl approach. Much admired by Mondriaan and one of the most influential of the Cubists, Fernand Léger's *Soldiers Playing Cards* is typical of his bold, clear lines and tendency towards the monumental. One surprise is an early Picasso, *Portrait of a Woman*, from 1901, a classic Post-impressionist canvas very dissimilar from his more famous works.

The building as a whole gravitates towards the works of **Vincent Van Gogh**, with one of the most complete collections of his work in the world, housed in a large room around a central courtyard and placed in context by accompanying, contemporary pictures. The museum owns no less than 278 examples of his work and doesn't have the space to show them all at any one time; consequently exhibits are rotated, with the exception of his most important paintings. Of earlier canvases, *The Potato Eaters* and *Head of a Peasant with a Pipe* are outstanding, rough unsentimental paintings of labourers from around his parents' home in Brabant. From February 1886 till early 1888 Van Gogh lived in Paris, where he came into contact with the Impressionists whose work – and arguments – convinced him of the importance of colour. His penetrating *Self-portrait* is a superb example of his work of this period, the eyes fixed on the observer, the head and background a swirl of grainy colour and streaky brush-strokes. One of his most famous paintings, *Sunflowers*, dates from this period also, an extraordinary work of alternately thick and thin paintwork of dazzling, sharp detail and careful colour.

The move to Arles in 1888 spurred Van Gogh to a frenzy of activity, inspired by the colours and light of the Mediterranean. The joyful *Haystacks in Provence* and *Bridge at Arles*, with its rickety bridge and disturbed circles of water spreading from the washerwomen on the river bank, are from these months, one of the high points of his troubled life. It was short-lived. The novelty of the south wore off, Gauguin's visit was a disaster, and Van Gogh's desperate sense of loneliness intensified. At the end of the year he had his first attack of madness – and committed his famous act of self-mutilation. In and out of mental hospital till his suicide in July of the following year, his *Prisoners Exercising* of 1890 is a powerful, sombre painting full of sadness and despair: heads bent, the prisoners walk round in a pointless circle as the walls around them seem to close in.*

Finally, outside the museum, behind the main building, there's a **Sculpture Park** (same times), spaciously laid out with works by Auguste Rodin, Alberto Giacometti, Jacob Epstein and Barbara Hepworth, all appearing at manageable intervals. Noteable is Jean Debuffet's *Jardin d'email*, one of his larger and more elaborate jokes.

Nijmegen

One of the oldest towns in Holland, **NIJMEGEN**, some 20km south of Arnhem, was built on the site of the Roman frontier fortress of *Novio Magus*, from which it derives its name. Situated on the southern bank of the Waal, just to the west of its junction with the Rhine, the town's location has long been strategically important. The Romans used Nijmegen as a buffer against the unruly tribes to the east; Charlemagne, Holy Roman Emperor from 800 to 814, made the town one of the principal seats of his administration, building the Valkhof Palace, an enormous complex of chapels and secular buildings completed in the eighth century. Rebuilt in 1155 by another emperor, Frederick Barbarossa, the complex dominated Nijmegen right up until 1769, when the palace was demolished and the stonework sold; what was left suffered further demolition when the French occupied the town in 1796. More recently, in September 1944, the town's bridges were a key objective of "Operation Market Garden" (see "Arnhem" above), and although they were captured by the Americans, the disaster at Arnhem put the town on the front-line for the rest of the war. The results are clear to see: the old town was largely destroyed and has been replaced by a centre reconstructed to a new plan.

The Town

The town centre is **Grote Markt**, a good fifteen-minute walk from the railway station, or five minutes by bus #6 from the stop immediately outside. Much of the Grote Markt survived the shelling and is surprisingly well preserved, in stark contrast to the modern shopping streets across the road. The **Waag**, with its traditional stepped gables and shuttered windows, stands beside a vaulted passage, the **Kerkboog**, which leads through to the peaceful precincts of the

---

* On the night of December 12, 1988, thieves broke into the Rijksmuseum Kröller-Müller and took several key paintings, principally Van Gogh's *Sunflowers* and *The Potato Eaters*. After a long police search, the canvases were recovered under somewhat mysterious circumstances – there are reports of them being "found" in a tree. All sustained some minor damage and are at present under repair in preparation for display in 1991.

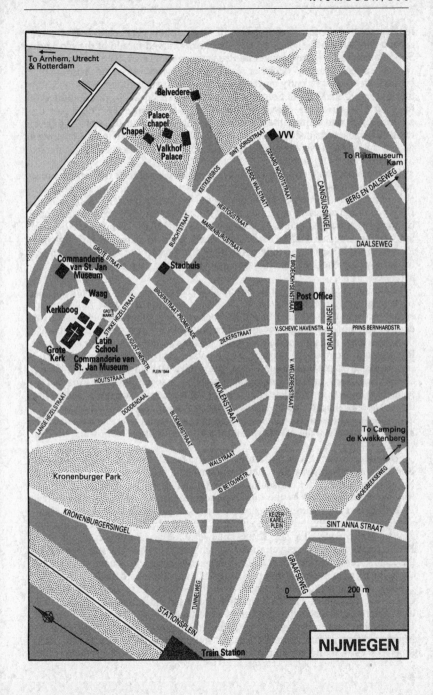

To Arnhem, Utrecht & Rotterdam

Belvedere

Palace chapel

Chapel

Valkhof Palace

VVV

To Rijksmuseum Kam

SINT JORISSTRAAT

GERARD NOODTSTRAAT

REGE WALSTRAAT

KETKENSBOS

CANISIUSSINGEL

BERG EN DALSEWEG

BURCHTSTRAAT

HERTOGSTRAAT

MARIENBURGSTRAAT

DAALSEWEG

GROTE STRAAT

Commanderie van St. Jan Museum

Stadhuis

V. BROECKH SENSTRAAT

Post Office

ORANJESINGEL

Waag

BROERSTRAAT PROMENADE

PRINS BERNHARDSTR.

Kerkboog

STIKKE HEZELSTRAAT

GROTE MARKT

ZIEKERSTRAAT

V.SCHEVIC HAVENSTR.

Grote Kerk

Latin School

Commanderie van St. Jan Museum

AUGUSTIJNENSTR.

PLEIN 1944

V. WELDERENSTRAAT

LANGE HEZELSTRAAT

HOUTSTRAAT

DODDENDAAL

To Camping de Kwakkenberg

MOLENSTRAAT

BLOEMERSTRAAT

WALSTRAAT

GROESBEEKSEWEG

Kronenburger Park

ID BETOUWSTR.

KRONENBURGERSINGEL

KEIZER KAREL PLEIN

SINT ANNA STRAAT

GRAAFSEWEG

0   200 m

TUNNELWEG

STATIONSPLEIN

Train Station

NIJMEGEN

much-renovated Gothic **Grote Kerk of St Stephen**. The church is entered around the back to the left, past the attractively carved facade of the old **Latin School**, and inside there's some fine Renaissance woodwork. The **tower**, with its vaguely oriental spire, offers a commanding vista over the surrounding countryside for just f1; entry into the church will cost you another f1.50 (mid-May to mid-June & mid-Aug to Sept Mon–Fri 10am–12.30pm & 1–5pm; mid-June to mid-Aug Mon–Fri 10am–5pm, Sat 10am–1pm, Sun 2–5pm). The view over the streets beside and behind the church isn't what it used to be – the huddle of medieval houses that sloped down to the Waal was almost totally destroyed during the war and has been replaced by a hopeful but rather sterile residential imitation.

A few metres away, down towards the river, the **Commanderie van St Jan** is more authentic-looking, a reconstruction of a seventeenth-century building that now houses the **Municipal Museum** (Mon–Sat 10am–5pm, Sun 1–5pm; free). Here you'll find a variety of exhibits with a local flavour, including innumerable paintings of Nijmegen and its environs – none particularly distinguished except for Jan van Goyen's *Valkhof Nijmegen*, which used to hang in the town hall. Painted in 1641, it's a large, sombre-toned picture – pastel variations on green and brown – where the Valkhof shimmers above the Waal, almost engulfed by sky and river.

Returning to the Grote Markt, Burchtstraat heads east roughly parallel to the river, past the dull reddish-brown brick of the **Stadhuis**, a square, rather severe edifice with an onion-domed tower, another reconstruction after extensive war damage. A couple of minutes away, in a park beside the east end of Burchtstraat, lie the scanty remains of the **Valkhof Palace** – a ruined fragment of the Romanesque choir of the twelfth-century palace chapel and, just to the west, a sixteen-sided chapel built around 1045, in a similar style to the palatinate church at Charlemagne's capital, Aachen. The smaller chapel (May–Oct Mon–Sat 1–5pm, Sun 2–5pm) is complete, though the atmosphere is somewhat marred by the crowds and piped choral music. These bits and pieces are connected by a footbridge to a **belvedere**, which was originally a seventeenth-century tower built into the city walls; today it's a restaurant and a look-out platform with excellent views over the river.

Some fifteen minutes' walk southeast of the town centre, the **Rijksmuseum Kam**, Museum Kamstraat 45 (Tues–Sat 10am–5pm, Sun 1–5pm; f3), is the best of Nijmegen's many other museums. Devoted mainly to the history of Roman Nijmegen and founded by the eminent archaeologist G. M. Kam, who died in 1922, the museum features his collection alongside other artefacts that have been added more recently; together they form a comprehensive picture of the first Roman settlements. To get there walk east along Burchtstraat and onto Kelfkensbos, which brings you to the island beside the VVV. Heading south off the island, down Mr. Franckenstraat, you reach Mariaplein, where you turn left down Berg en Dalseweg; Museum Kamstraat is the third on the left.

More bizarre, southeast of Nijmegen on the road to Groesbeek, the **Biblical Open Air Museum**, Profetenlaan 2 (Heilig Land Stichting; Easter–Oct daily 9am–5pm; f7.5), is accessible by bus #84 (destination Groesbeek; twice hourly), from beside the rail station. Ask the driver to indicate your stop on Nijmeegsebaan, from where it's a five-minute walk northeast along Meerwijkselaan to the museum. Here you'll find a series of reconstructions of the ancient Holy Land including a Galilean fishing village, a complete Palestinian hamlet, a town street lined with Egyptian, Greek, Roman and Jewish houses and, strangely enough, "Bedouin tents of goats' hair as inhabited by the patriarchs". An experience not on any account to be missed . . .

There's another unusual museum 2km east of here, along Meerwijkselaan – the **Afrika Museum** at Postweg 6 (April–Oct Mon–Fri 10am–5pm, Sat & Sun 11am–5pm; Nov–Mar Tues–Fri 10am–5pm, Sat & Sun 1–5pm; f5; no buses), where there's a purpose-built West African village, a small animal park and a museum full of totems, carved figurines and musical instruments.

Practical details

Nijmegen's **rail** and **bus stations** are a good fifteen-minute trudge west of the town centre and the **VVV** at St Jorisstraat 72 (Mon–Fri 9am–6pm, Sat 10am–4pm, June–Aug also Sun 10am–2pm). If you don't fancy the walk, bus #6 leaves the bus station for Grote Markt and the VVV three times hourly.

Cheap **accommodation** is pretty thin on the ground in Nijmegen; it's easiest to let the VVV ring round to make a reservation. Alternatively, there are two **pensions** not far southeast of the railway station with doubles at f80 a night – the *Catharina*, St Annastraat 64 (☎080/23 12 51), and *Mrs Fortuin's*, Groesbeekseweg 9 (☎080/22 42 98). To reach them head east along one of the southern pair of roads from the station to the Keizer Karelplein; from here St Annastraat is the road heading southeast, with Groesbeekseweg the first turning on the left. The cheaper **hotels** are no more expensive and tend to be more convenient: the *Apollo* is on the turning running east off Keizer Karelplein, at Bisschop Hamerstraat 14 (☎080/22 35 94), and has rooms for about f100; the rather seedy *Europa Hotel* (☎080/22 66 45) is between the station and Grote Markt at Bloemerstraat 65, and has doubles for f80. If you're stuck, the *Atlanta*, right in the centre at Grote Markt 38, isn't as pricey as you'd imagine, with single rooms for f60 per night. The nearest **campsite** is *De Kwakkenberg*, Luciaweg 10 (April–Sept), a few kilometres south of town, reachable from the station by bus #5, direction Berg en Dal. Ask the driver to put you off at your stop, which will be on the main road, Kwakkenbergweg; Luciaweg runs roughly parallel, a block to the south.

Nijmegen is a university city so there are plenty of cheap places to **eat**. A good area to try is beside the Valkhof Palace, along Kelfkensbos, where you can find the *So What*, at no. 49 (closed Tues), the more upmarket *Les Entrees*, no. 30, and *Het Poortwachtershuys*, at no. 57. Otherwise, there are several pleasant cafés and bars around the Grote Markt, including *In de Boterwaag*, no. 26, and *De Druivenkelder*, no. 38.

Every inch a fashionable town, Nijmegen attracts some top-name rock **bands**, especially during term-time. Most perform at the municipal concert hall, the *Stadsschouwburg*, at Van Schaeck Mathonsingel 2, close by the railway station; for latest details see the VVV. For **films**, the *Filmcafé*, Hertogstraat 71 (☎080/22 19 05), and the *Filmcentrum*, Marienburg 59 (☎080/22 16 12), have good international programmes and some late-night showings. Between June and August, there are a variety of **boat trips** on the Waal. Prices vary according to the itinerary, but excursions range from an hour's river tour to sailings to Rotterdam (once weekly; f47).

travel details

Trains
From Apeldoorn to Amersfoort (2 hourly; 25min); Deventer (2 hourly; 12min); Zutphen (2 hourly; 15min).

From Arnhem to Amsterdam (3 hourly; 1hr 10min); Cologne (15 daily; 2hr 15min); Nijmegen (3 hourly; 15min); Roosendaal (2 hourly; 1hr 45min).

From Zutphen to Arnhem (4 hourly; 20min).

From Zwolle to Amersfoort (3 hourly; 35min); Amsterdam CS/Schiphol (1 or 2 hourly; 1hr 15min/1hr 40min); Arnhem/Nijmegen (2 hourly; 65/75min); Deventer/Zutphen (2 hourly; 25/35min); Emmen (2 hourly; 50min); Enschede (1 hourly; 1hr 10min); Groningen (2 hourly; 1hr 5min); Kampen (2 hourly; 10 min); Steenwijk (2 hourly; 15min); Leeuwarden (2 hourly; 55min); Meppel (4 hourly; 15min).

Buses
From Steenwijk to Giethoorn (*NWH* bus #72; Mon–Sat hourly, Sun 4 daily; 20min).

From Zwolle to Elburg (2 an hour; 35min); Urk (2 an hour; 1hr 20min).

From Kampen to Lelystad (2 hourly; 55min); Urk (2 hourly; 60min).

From Enschede to Oldenzaal (2 an hour; 20min).

Ferries
From Urk to Enkhuizen (May, June & Sept 2 daily, July & Aug 3 daily; 1hr 30min).

CHAPTER SIX

THE SOUTH

Three widely disparate provinces make up Holland's south: Zeeland, North Brabant and Limburg. **Zeeland** is a scattering of villages and towns whose wealth, survival, and sometimes destruction has long depended on the vagaries of the sea. Secured only when the dykes and sea walls of the Delta Project once and for all stopped the chance of flooding, at their best (for example in the small wool town of **Veere** or the regional market centre of **Middelburg**) they seem in suspended animation from a richer past.

As you head across the arc of towns of **North Brabant** the landscape slowly fills out, rolling into a rougher countryside of farmland and forests, unlike the precise rectangles of neighbouring provinces. Though the change is subtle, there's a difference in the people here, too – less formal, less Dutch, and for the most part Catholic, a fact manifest in the magnificent churches of **Breda** and **'s Hertogenbosch**. But it's in solidly Catholic Limburg that a difference in character is really felt.

European rather than Dutch, **Limburg** has only been part of Holland since the 1830s, but way before then the presence of Charlemagne's court at Aachen deeply influenced the identity of the region. As Holy Roman Emperor, Charlemagne had a profound effect on early medieval Europe, revitalising Roman traditions and looking to the south for inspiration in art and architecture. Some of these great buildings remain, like **Maastricht's** St Servaas, and most have a wealth of devotional art that comes as a welcome change after the north. What's more, the landscape has steepened sharply, and you're within sight of Holland's first and only hills.

ZEELAND

Formed by the delta of three great rivers, the Rhine, the Schelde and the Maas, Zeeland comprises three main "islands": Walcheren and North and South Beveland, Schouwen-Duiveland, and Goree–Overflakkee. These claw-like prongs jut out into the North Sea, protected from flooding by the Delta dyke-barriers which also give them their main lines of communication. Before the Delta Project secured the area, silting up and fear of the sea had prevented any large towns developing, and Zeeland remains a condensed area of low dunes and nature reserves, popular with holidaymakers escaping the cooped-up conurbations nearby. Getting around isn't a problem, with bus services making up for the lack of north–south rail connections, though undoubtedly the best way to see these islands is to cycle, using Middelburg as a base and radiating out to the surrounding smaller towns.

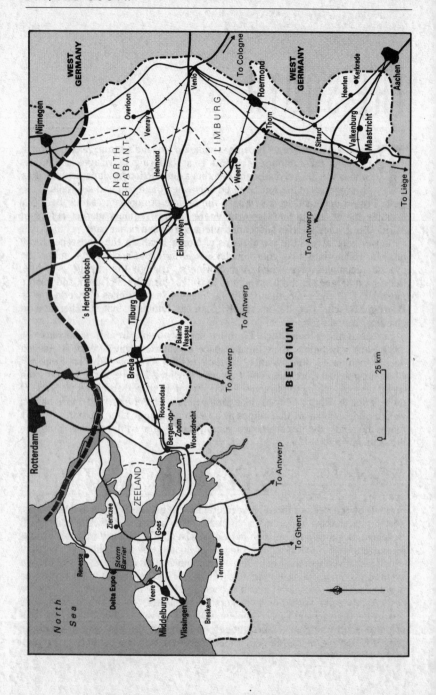

Vlissingen

VLISSINGEN is an important ferry terminal, linked to Sheerness in England by twice-daily ferries. The best thing to do on arrival at the bleak ferry terminal is leave; a bus takes you to the train station, from where there are hourly departures to Amsterdam and intermediate stations. There's also a ferry service, leaving from outside the train station, to BRESKENS on the southern side of the Westerschelde estuary (Mon–Fri 4.50am–11.35pm every 30min; Sat & Sun 9.25am–6.55pm hourly), from where buses go on to Bruges.

If you do want to go into town, take a bus from the ferry terminal to the centre. Here you'll find the unremarkable **St Jacobskerk** on Kleine Markt, and a **Stedelijk Museum** at Bellamyplein 19 (Tues–Fri 10am–5pm, Sat–Sun 1–5pm; f1), whose collection includes a room devoted to local naval hero Michiel de Ruyter. Should you need to stay, the **VVV** at Nieuwendijk 15 (☎01184/12345; Sept–June Mon–Fri 9am–5pm, Sat 9am–1pm; July and Aug Mon–Sat 9am–6pm, Sun 1–6pm) have a list of **pensions** for around f30 per person, including the *Pension El Porto*, nearby at Nieuwendijk 5 (☎01184/12807).

Middelburg

MIDDELBURG is the largest town in Zeeland, and by any reckoning the most likeable. While not crammed with things to see, its streets preserve some snap-shots of medieval Holland, and a few museums and churches provide targets for your wanderings. Rimmed with the standard shopping precinct, its centre holds a large Thursday market, and, if you can only make it for one day, this is the best time to visit, as the local women still wear traditional costume – to picturesque effect. But really Middelburg is best used as a base for exploring the surrounding area: it forms the hub for regional bus connections, and accommodation is plentiful and inexpensive.

The telephone code for Middelburg is ☎01180

Arriving and practical details

The train station is a short walk from town: head straight out across the bridge, onto Seghersstraat and Lange Delft and you're on the Markt, where the **VVV** office at Markt 65a (Sept–June Mon–Fri 9am–5pm, Sat 9am–1pm; July & Aug Mon–Sat 9am–6pm; ☎16851) offers the usual booking service. Most of Middelburg's **hotels and pensions** are within spitting distance of the Markt: the friendly *Wapen van Middelburg* hotel, Pottenmarkt 16–20 (☎14706), is most central of all, across the street from the VVV, with doubles at f62. Other pension options include *De Geere*, Langeviele 51 (☎13083; doubles f55–f60); *Huize Orliëns*, Nieuwstraat 23 (☎27529; f60–65); and *Bij de Abdij*, Bogardstraat 14–16 (☎27135; f60–f80). The nearest **campsite**, *De IJsbaan*, Koninginnelaan 55 (April 1–Oct 31), is about 2km out of town. Head down Zaandstraat and Langeviele Weg, south and east of the Koveniersdoelen (see map), or check with the VVV for bus connections.

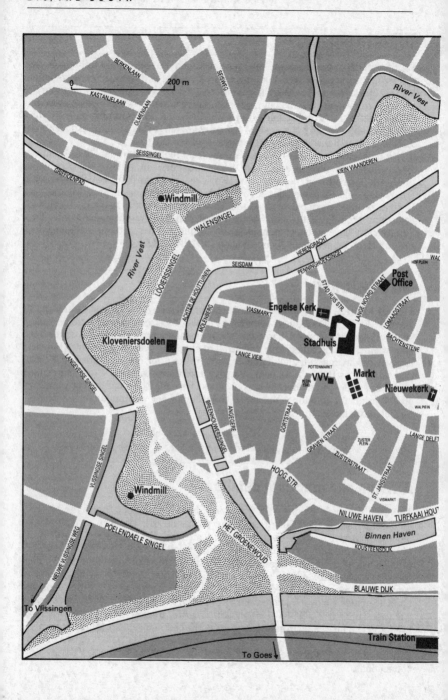

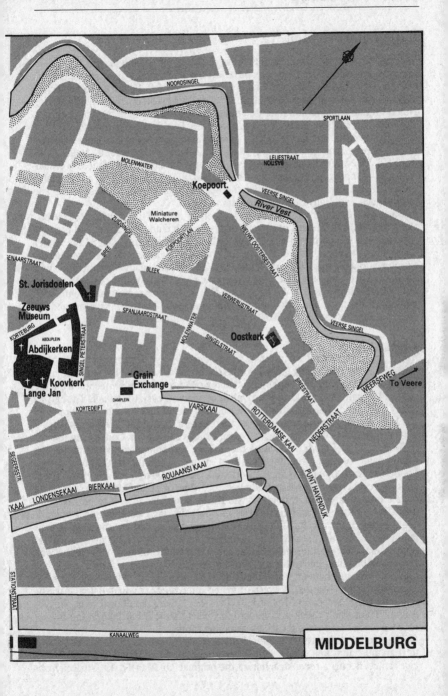

MIDDELBURG

Eating and drinking

Vlasmarkt, the street running northwest of Markt, has Middelburg's best selection of **restaurants**. *La Piccola Italia* at no. 19 offers cheap pizzas from f10; the café-bar *De Lachende Vis* at no. 20 has a *dagschotels* at f10–15 and a good selection of beers – it closes at 9pm. Best of all, *De Mug*, Vlasmarkt 56, has mouthwatering Dutch-French cooking at moderate prices: between f20 and f35 for main courses. To tempt you further, there's live jazz here every last Tuesday of the month. Most other restaurants are on or around Markt, and most seem tourist-geared and pricey for what you get: *De Ploeg*, Markt 55, offers best value with main dishes from f16. Elsewhere in town, *Surabaya*, Stationstraat 20, is an Indonesian restaurant with *rijsttafels* for f19, and *De Kabouterhut*, Oostkerkplein 7–8, a reasonable crêperie. On Thursday and Saturday the market stalls supply limitless cheap and tasty snacks, especially fresh fishy things.

Bars and cafés are also concentrated on or around the Markt. *De Herberg*, Pottenmarkt 2a, is the best of a group of places with outdoor seating, and the *Café American* on the corner of Plein 1940 is the chosen drinking spot of the town's long-haired stonewashed set. Damplein is another good stretch for drinking: the *Rhythm en Blues Kroeg "Bloesbak"* at no. 20 is a rough and ready bar with loud tapes by day and live blues by night; *Café Meccano* at no. 27 has a young clientele spilling out from the large disco at the back; *Café Solo* at no. 48 is more mainstream, with outdoor drinking on its garden terrace in summer; and *Meneer Jansen*, around the corner at Reigerstraat 5 is a small, relaxed bar that attracts older custom.

About town

Middelburg owed its early growth to the comparative safety of its situation in the centre of Walcheren. The slight elevation gave the settlement protection from the sea, and its site on a bend in the river Arne made it easy to defend. Though its abbey was founded in 1120, the town's isolation meant that it did not develop until the late Middle Ages, when, being at the western end of the Scheldt estuary, it began to get rich off the back of Antwerp, Bruges and Ghent. Conducting its own trade in wool and cloth, it became the market and administrative centre of the region, and some of the town's street names – Houtkaai (Timber Quay), Londense Kaai (London Quay), Korendijk (Corn Dyke) and Bierkaai (Beer Quay) – reveal how various its trade became. Most of Middelburg's best building comes from this period, though its **Stadhuis**, generally agreed to be Zeeland's finest, is a junkshop of architectural styles. The towering Gothic facade is magnificent, dating from the mid-fifteenth century and designed by the Keldermans family from Mechelen. Ranged in niches across the front are twenty-five statues of the counts and countesses of Holland, starting with Charles V and ending with queens Wilhelmina and Juliana placed above the **Vleeshal**, a former meat hall that now houses changing exhibitions of contemporary art (May–Sept Tues–Sat 11am–5pm, Sun 1–5pm). If you're further interested, conducted tours of the Stadhuis (April 9–Oct 19 Mon–Fri 10.30am & 11.15am; additional tours July 9–Aug 17 11am–4pm; check noticeboard for exact times; f2.55) take in the mayor' office, council chamber and various reception rooms.

The Stadhuis's impressive pinnacled tower was added in 1520, but it's as well to remember that this, along with the Stadhuis itself and much of Middelburg's city centre, is only a reconstruction of the original. On May 17, 1940 the city was practically flattened by German bombing in the same series of raids that destroyed Rotterdam. In 1944, in an attempt to isolate German artillery in Vlissingen, Walcheren's sea defences were breached, which resulted in severe flood damage to Middelburg's already treacherous streets.

Restoration was a long and difficult procedure, but so successful has it been that only occasionally can you tell that the city's buildings have been patched up. Middelburg's most distinctive tower, that of the **Abdijkerken (Abbey Churches)** on Onderdentoren, collapsed under German bombing, destroying the churches below. Today the abbey complex – really three churches in one – seems pretty bare inside, considering that it's been around since the twelfth century. Middelburg was an early convert to Protestantism following the uprising against the Spanish: in 1574 William the Silent's troops slung out the Premonstratensian monks and converted the abbey to secular use. The abbey's three churches were adapted to Protestant worship, and most of what can be seen inside dates from the seventeenth century. The **Nieuwe Kerk** has an organ case of 1692, and the **Wandel Kerk** the triumphantly over-the-top tomb of admirals Jan and Cornelis Evertsen, brothers killed fighting in a naval battle with the English in 1666. The **Koor Kerk**, on the eastern side of the tower, retains the oldest fittings, including a Nicolai organ of 1478. To see all this you'll need to join a conducted tour (May 1–Nov 1 Mon–Sat 1.30pm & 3.30pm; additionally July & Aug Tues–Fri 11am; f5, f3.50 with museumcards, includes entrance to Zeeuws museum), but best fun of all is to climb the tower (April 2–Oct 1 Mon–Sat 10am–5pm; f1.95). Known locally as *Lange Jan* (Long John), from its 91-metre summit there's a tremendous view across Middelburg and over Walcheren as far as the Zeelandbrug and the eastern Scheldt, giving a good idea of how vulnerable Zeeland is to the sea and estuaries.

At the rear of the abbey, housed in what were once its dormitories, the **Zeeuws Museum** (Zeeland Museum; Tues–Fri 10am–5pm, Sat–Mon 1.30–5pm; f3.50) holds a mixed bag of collections and finds from the Zeeland area. The museum kicks off with a tiny but choice collection of twentieth-century painting by Mesdag, Jan and Charlie Toorop and other (local) artists. Downstairs, there's a well-documented assembly of Roman and medieval artefacts, including Nehallenia altar stones. Like those in Leiden's Van Oudheden museum, these seem to have been votive offerings, given by sailors in Roman times in thanks for safe passage across the English channel. Little more is known about the goddess Nehallenia, though it's possible she was also a goddess of flowers, akin to Flora. Elsewhere in the museum are lively tapestries, a cabinet of curiosities and a comprehensive display of local costumes.

East of the abbey, **Damplein** was recently restored to its original breadth by the demolition of a couple of rows of houses. It forms a quieter focus for bars than the Markt and is the site of the **Graanbeurs**, a grain exchange rebuilt in the nineteenth century and today containing some intriguing (and humorous) stone plaques by international artists. To the western side of the square, the **Blauwpoort** (also known as the **Gistpoort** or Yeast Gate) forms a decorative entrance to the abbey complex. Built at the beginning of the sixteenth century from blue limestone, it was all but destroyed in the last war, and what you see today is a rather scruffy renovation.

Directly north of Damplein on Molenwater, **Miniature Walcheren** (April 12–Oct 21, daily 9.30am–5pm; July & Aug until 6pm; f5, kids f3) has scaled-down models of Walcheren island's best buildings. It's about as enjoyable as you'd imagine, but might entertain kids for an hour or so. Further east, the distinctive profile of the domed, octagonal **Oostkerk** (mid-July to mid-Aug Thurs 10am–4pm; also Sun 10am for services only) stands high above the surrounding suburbs, near the main road to Veere: built in 1647 to designs by Pieter Post and others, it was one of the first churches in Holland to be built expressly for Protestant use.

While the streets around the Abdijkerken and Stadhuis are the most atmospheric, it's worth walking to the western edge of town, to reach the landmark of the **Kloveniersdoelen** at the end of Langeviele. Built in 1607 in exuberant Flemish Renaissance style, until the end of the eighteenth century this was the home of the city's civic guard, the Arquebusiers, later becoming the local headquarters of the East India Company, later still a military hospital. Restored in 1969 (as you might have guessed if you've spotted the weather vane), it's now a venue for concerts and is particularly renowned for presenting new and experimental music. A short walk north or south of the Kloveniersdoelen, by the edge of Middelburg's old encircling defensive canal, are a couple of eighteenth-century **windmills**: *De Hoop* mill to the south was once a barley peeling mill; *De Seismolen* to the north a corn mill. Though it's not possible to enter either mill today, should you fancy a paddle around the canal it's possible to **hire boats** from alongside *De Seismolen*.

Middelburg's other museums

François Ryckhals Museum, Dam 71 (April 1–Oct 1 Thurs–Sat 1–5pm; f2). The life story of the unmemorable local artist, as revealed through an exhibit of his paintings in the house in which he was born.

Holografie Museum, Gortstraat 36 (Tues–Fri 10.30am–5.30pm, Sat & Sun 10am–5pm; f3.50). Gallery for the gimmicky art form.

Military Administration Corp Collection, Zuidsingel 24 (Tues & Thurs 2–4pm). Uniforms, photos and other dull exhibits relating to the Dutch army's pen-pushers.

Ramschipde Schorpioen, moored off Loskade, opposite the train station (usually spring–Oct Tues–Sat 10am–5pm; check with VVV). One of only three remaining iron ramming ships left in the world, the *Schorpioen* is a floating maritime museum. The ship itself, built in France in 1867, is worth a scramble around for its ornate, if cramped, interior.

Roosevelt Study Centre, Abdij 9 (Wed & Thurs 9.30am–12.30pm & 1.30–4.30pm). Centre for the study of twentieth-century American history (one of the largest in Europe) and an exhibition on presidents Theodore and Franklin Delano Roosevelt, and the latter's remarkable wife Eleanor. Often has talks by visiting big-league politicians.

Listings

Boat trips The *Madeleine* sails from Loskade to the Veerse Meer daily at 1.30pm, from Ascension Day to mid-Sept. Trips last three hours and cost f9.50. Tickets from the VVV.

Car hire *Autoservice Leo van Liere*, Kanaalweg (10am–noon; ☎27680); *Louisse Auto Bv*, Kalverstraat 1 (☎25851).

Carillon concerts At Lange Jan May–Sept Sun noon–1pm; July & Aug also Sat 11am–noon, Wed 7–7.30pm .

Cycling If you intend to bike around, get hold of a copy of the yellow *Zuid-Holland Fietskaart*, from the VVV or any bookshop/newsagent: cycle routes in the South aren't as well signposted as in the rest of the country.

Launderette *Wassalon Wolders*, Maasstraat 52 (Mon–Fri 8am–5pm).

Markets General market on the Markt Thurs 8.30am–4pm; flower, fruit and veg market Sat 8.30am–4pm. Vismarkt has a flea market on the first Sat of the month, 8am–2pm; and an antique and curio market from June 14 to Aug 30, Sun 9am–4pm.

Police station Achter de Houttuinen (☎88000).

Post office Lange Noordstraat 48.

Ring tilting *Ringrijderij*, a horseback competition where riders try to pick off rings with lances, takes place at the Koepoort city gate near Molenwater each July and Aug.

Taxis *Taxicentral*, ☎12600 or ☎13200; *Blanker*, ☎13900.

East of Middelburg: a note on Goes

GOES, 22km east of Middelburg and the centre of South Beveland, is an undistinguished town only worth stopping off at if you're heading this way into North Brabant. Its late Gothic basilica, the **Grote Kerk** (July & Aug Mon–Fri 10am–noon & 2–4pm), has a seventeenth-century organ and there's a **Museum van Noord en Zuid Beveland** (Tues–Fri 10am–4pm, Sat 11am–4pm) – very much inferior to the Zeeuws museum. Basically, if you're travelling via Goes to Bergen-op-Zoom, there's no need to stop en route.

Veere

Eight kilometres northeast of Middelburg, **VEERE** is a resolutely picturesque little town by the banks of the Veerse Meer. Today it's a centre for all things aquatic, its small harbour jammed with yachts and its cafés packed with yachting types: but a handful of buildings and a large church point to a time when Veere was rich and quite independent of other, similar towns in Zeeland.

Veere earned its money from an odd Scottish connection: in 1444 Wolfert VI van Borssele, the lord of Veere, married Mary, daughter of James I of Scotland. As part of the dowry, van Borssele was granted a monopoly on trade with Scottish wool merchants; in return, Scottish merchants living in Veere were granted special privileges. A number of their houses still stand, best of which are those on the quay facing the yacht harbour: *Het Lammetje* (The Lamb) and *De Struys* (The Ostrich), dating from the mid-sixteenth century, were combined offices, homes and warehouses for the merchants; they now house the **Museum Schotze Huizen** (April–Oct Mon 1–5pm, Tues–Sat 10am–5pm; f2), a rather lifeless collection of local costumes, old books, atlases and furniture, along with an exhibit devoted to fishing. Elsewhere there's plenty of Gothic building, whose rich decoration leaves you in no doubt that the Scottish wool trade earned a tidy packet for the sixteenth- and seventeenth-century burgers of Veere: many of the buildings (which are usually step-gabled with distinctive green and white shutters) are embellished with whimsical details that play on the owners' names or their particular line of business. The **Stadhuis** at Markt 5 (June–Aug Mon–Sat 11am–5pm, Sept noon–5pm; f2) is similarly opulent, dating from 1477 with an out-of-scale, boastful Renaissance tower added a century later. Its facade is decorated with statues of the lords of Veere and their wives (Wolfert VI is third from the left), and, inside, a small museum occupies what was once the courtroom, pride of place going to a goblet that once belonged to Maximilian of Burgundy.

Of all Veere's buildings the **Grote Kerk** (May–Oct Mon–Sat 10am–5pm, Sun 2–5pm; f2.25) seems to have fared worst: finished in 1560, it was badly damaged by fire a century later, and restoration removed much of its decoration. In 1808 invading British troops used the church as a hospital, and three years later Napoleon's army converted it into barracks and stables, destroying the stained glass, bricking up the windows and adding five floors in the nave; later, in the nineteenth century, it became a workhouse. Despite all this damage, the church's blunt 42-metre tower adds a glowering presence to the landscape, especially when seen across the misty polder fields. According to the original design, the tower was to have been three times higher, but even as it stands there's a great view from the top, back to the pinnacled skyline of Middelburg and out across the breezy Veerse Meer.

Veere fell from importance with the decline of the wool trade. The opening of the Walcheren Canal in the nineteenth century, linking the town to Middelburg and Vlissingen, gave it a stay of execution, but the construction of the Veersegatdam and Zandkreekdam in the 1950s finally sealed the port to seagoing vessels, and simultaneously created a freshwater lake ideal for watersports. The VVV office, Oudestraat 28 (Sat 11am–3pm; ☎01181/1365), can advise on hire of all manner of watercraft and help with **accommodation**: the cheaper of Veere's two hotels, *'t Waepen van Veere* at Markt 23–27 (☎01181/1231), has rooms starting at f33 per person; any of the town's B&Bs, such as that run by M.A. de Rijk, Kapellestraat 14 (☎01181/1414), costs f25 per person, with an additional f2.50 payable for stays of one night only. To reach Veere from Middelburg, catch a frequent #33 bus, or hire a bike from Middelburg train station and take either the main road or the circuitous but picturesque routes leaving from the north of the town.

The Delta Project – and the Delta Expo

On February 1, 1953, a combination of an exceptionally high spring tide and powerful northwesterly winds drove the North Sea over the dykes to flood much of Zeeland. The results were catastrophic: 1855 people drowned, 47,000 homes and 500km of dykes were destroyed, and some of the country's most fertile agricultural land was ruined by salt water. Towns as far west as Bergen-op-Zoom and Dordrecht were flooded, and Zeeland's road and rail network wrecked. The government's response was immediate and on a massive scale. After patching up the breached dykes, work was begun on the **Delta Project**, one of the largest engineering schemes the world has ever seen, and one of phenomenal complexity and expense.

The plan was to ensure the safety of Zeeland by radically shortening and strengthening its coastline. The major estuaries and inlets would be dammed, thus preventing unusually high tides surging inland to breach the thousands of kilometres of small dykes. Where it was impractical to build a dam – such as across the Westerschelde or Nieuwe Waterweg, which would have closed the seaports of Antwerp and Rotterdam respectively – secondary dykes were to be greatly reinforced. New roads across the top of the dams would improve communications to Zeeland and south Holland, and the freshwater lakes that formed behind the dams would enable precise control of the water table of the Zeeland islands .

It took thirty years for the full Delta Project to be completed. The smaller, secondary dams – the Veersegat, Haringvliet and Brouwershaven – were completed first, a plan designed to provide protection from high tides as quickly as possible, and a process that enabled engineers to learn as they went along. In 1968, work began on the largest dam, intended to close the **Oosterschelde** estuary that forms the outlet of the Maas, Waal and Rhine rivers. It soon ran into intense opposition from environmental groups, who realised the importance of the flora and fauna in and around the Oosterschelde: at low tides, the mud flats and sandbanks were an important breeding ground for birds, and the estuary itself formed a nursery for plaice, sole and other North Sea fish. Local fishermen saw their livelihoods in danger: if the Oosterschelde were closed the oyster, mussel and lobster beds would be destroyed, and even without taking into account the social problems caused by the loss of jobs in an area dependent on fishing and related industries, the loss to the economy was estimated (then) at f200 million.

The environmental and fishing lobby argued that strengthening the estuary dykes would provide sufficient protection; the water board and agricultural groups raised the emotive spectre of the 1953 flood. In the end a compromise was reached, with the design of a supremely elegant and intelligent piece of engineering: in 1976 work began on the **Storm Surge Barrier**, a device that would stay open under normal tidal conditions, allowing water to flow in and out of the estuary, but close ahead of unusually high tides.

It's on this barrier, completed in 1986, that the fascinating **Delta Expo** (April–Oct daily 10am–5pm regular conducted tours start with a boat trip around the barrier f10; Nov–April Wed–Sun 10am–5pm, tours without boat trip. Last tours 4pm; f8, no museumcards) is housed. The conducted tours point out the huge computer-controlled sluice gates, but it's only once you're inside the Expo itself that you get an idea of the scale of the whole project. It's best to start with the film history of the barrier before taking in the exhibition, which is divided into three areas: the historical background of Holland's response to its water problems; the mechanical and scientific developments that enabled it to protect itself; the environmental problems caused by the project, and the solutions that have minimised the damage. The Surge Barrier (and the Delta Project as a whole) have been completely successful. Computer simulations are used to predict high tides, though if an unpredicted rise occurs the sluice gates are programmed to close automatically in a matter of minutes. On average, a dangerously high tide occurs once every eighteen months.

Reaching the Delta Expo is easily managed: from Middelburg take a #104 bus or allow an hour and a half to cycle; from Rotterdam, ask the VVV for details of daily coach trips.

Brouwershaven and Zierikzee

Continuing north from the Storm Surge Barrier, the "island" of **Schouwen-Duiveland** makes up the middle finger of Zeeland's claw. Most of the Dutch tourists who come here head directly west for the two thousand acres of beach and dune between HAAMSTEDE and RENESSE, themselves pretty villages but with only the **Slot Moermond** (mid-June to mid-Aug; contact Renesse VVV for times of tours; ☎01116/2120), a castle built for the local lords just north of Renesse, worth breaking your journey for. Ideally, you need your own transport to see the villages, and it's a necessity should you want to carry on to **BROUWERSHAVEN**, in the middle of Schouwen-Duiveland's northern coast. Until the building of the Nieuwe Waterweg linked Rotterdam to the coast, Brouwershaven was a busy seaport, with boats able to sail right into the centre of town. Other than a few narrow streets around the Markt, the **Stadhuis** is the single thing to see, an attractive Flemish Renaissance building of 1599.

Schouwen-Duiveland's most interesting town, though, lies to the south. **ZIERIKZEE**'s position at the crossroads of shipping routes between England, Flanders and Holland led to it becoming an important port in the late Middle Ages. It was also famed for its salt and madder – a root that when dried and ground produces a brilliant red dye.

Encircled by a defensive canal and best entered by one of two sixteenth-century watergates, Zierikzee's centre is small and easily explored, easier still if you arm yourself with a map from the **VVV** at Havenpark 29 (Mon–Sat 10am–5pm; ☎01110/12450). A few minutes' walk from the office, the Gothic **'s Gravensteen** building at Mol 25 (May–Sept Mon–Sat 10am–5pm, Sun noon–5pm; f1.50) was once the town's gaol and is today home to a maritime museum. But the building is far more interesting than the exhibits: the old cells from the prison are much as they were when built, and the removal of plaster walls in 1969 uncovered graffiti and drawings by the prisoners. The basements contain torture chambers, and iron cage cells built to contain two prisoners.

Zierikzee's **Stadhuis** (May–Sept Mon–Fri 10am–5pm) is easy enough to find – just head for the tall, fussy spire on Meelstraat 6. Inside, the **Gemeentemuseum** (May–Sept Mon–Fri 10am–noon & 1.30–4.30pm; f1.50) has collections of silver, costumes and a regional history exhibition. Also worth seeing is the **Munstertoren** (June–Aug daily 10am–5pm), a tower designed by the Keldermans family on which work was stopped when it reached 97 of its planned 167 metres .

If you need to **stay over**, Zierikzee has one pension, *Beddegoed* at Meelstraat 53 (☎01110/15935), which has rooms from f27.50. Least expensive hotel is the *Van Oppen*, Verrenieuwstraat 11 (☎01110/12288), with rooms at f35. Heading to or from GOES from Zierikzee you'll pass over the **Zeelandbrug**, a graceful bridge across the Oosterschelde that at 5022 metres is the longest in Europe.

NORTH BRABANT

North Brabant, Holland's largest province, stretches from the North Sea to the German border. Originally, it was part of the independent Duchy of Brabant, which was taken over by the Spanish, and, eventually, split in two when its northern towns joined the revolt against Spain. This northern part was ceded to the United Provinces under the terms of the 1648 Treaty of Munster; the southern part formed what today are the Belgian provinces of Brabant and Antwerp.

The **Catholic influence** is still strong in North Brabant: it takes its religious festivals seriously, and if you're here in March the boozy **carnivals** (especially in the province's capital, 's Hertogenbosch) are well worth catching – indeed, it's difficult to miss them. Geographically, woodland and heath form most of the natural scenery, and the gently undulating arable land is distinctive in a country whose landscape is ruthlessly featureless.

Bergen-op-Zoom

BERGEN-OP-ZOOM is an untidy hotchpotch of a town, a jumble of buildings old and new that are the consequence of its being kicked around by the various powers from the sixteenth century onwards. In 1576 Bergen-op-Zoom sided with the United Provinces against the Spanish, and as a result was under near continuous siege until 1622. The French bombarded the city in 1747 and took it again in 1795, though it managed to withstand a British attack in 1814.

Walk straight out of the train station and pretty soon you'll find yourself on the Markt, a rough and tumble square-cum-car park that holds the **VVV** office at Hoogstraat 2 off the south side (Mon–Fri 9am–6pm, Sat & Sun 9am–5pm; ☎01640/66000), and the **Stadhuis** (Mon–Fri 8.30am–12.30pm & 1.30–5.30pm), Bergen's most attractive building, on the the north. Much spruced up following a recent renovation, the Stadhuis comprises three separate houses: to the left of the gateway an alderman's house of 1397, to the right a merchant's house of 1480, and on the far right a building known as "De Olifant" whose facade dates from 1611. Ask politely inside the Stadhuis and someone will show you the council chamber and the *Trouwzaal*, the room where marriages take place. All of this is a lot more appealing than the blunt ugliness of the **Grote Kerk**, a singularly unlucky building that's been destroyed by siege, fire and neglect innumerable times over the last 400 years – most recently in 1972, when it was undergoing a restoration .

Fortuinstraat, to the left of the Stadhuis, leads to the **Markiezenhof Museum**, Steenbergsestraat 8 (Sept–May Tues–Sun 2–5pm; June–Aug Tues–Fri 11am–5pm, Sat & Sun 2–5pm; f5), a first-rate presentation of an above average collection that has a little of everything: domestic equipment and samplers from the sixteenth century onwards, sumptuous period rooms, architectural drawings, pottery and galleries of modern art. All this is housed in a palace built by Anthonis Keldermans between 1485 and 1522 to a late Gothic style that gives it the feel of an Oxford college. Before you reach the main entrance to the Markiezenhof on Steenbergsestraat, you pass the **Galerie Etcetera** (Tues–Sun 2–5pm), an exhibition space for twentieth-century artists, worth popping in to if what's on show takes your fancy.

Of the rest of old Bergen-op-Zoom little remains: at the end of Lievevrouwestraat, near the entrance to the Markiezenhof, the **Gevangenpoort** is practically all that's left of the old city defences, a solid-looking fourteenth-century gatehouse that was later converted to a prison.

Practical details

It's hard to imagine a reason why you'd want to stay over in Bergen, and there are only two **pensions** in town: *De Lantaarn*, Bredastraat 8 (☎01640/36488; f35 per person), is conveniently between the train station and the town centre; *De Valk*, Antwerpsestraatweg 25 (☎01640/52299; f30 per person), is some way out to the south. The **youth hostel**, *Klaarvelden*, is 4km out of town at Boslustweg 1; take bus #1 or #2 from the station. Cheapest hotel is the *Old Dutch*, Stationstraat 31 (☎01640/35780), with rooms at f40 per person. The VVV offers the usual services, including a walking tour of the town on Wednesdays between June and August, and a free map of the centre.

Woensdrecht

WOENSDRECHT, 8km south of Bergen, merits a mention on the dubious basis of its being the site of Holland's contribution to the European nuclear arms build-up. Despite some of the largest demonstrations of recent times (including a petition signed by over 4 million people, some 28 percent of the country's population), the small town was selected as the site for deployment of American **cruise**

missiles in 1985. Like Greenham Common, Woensdrecht quickly became the focus for anti-missile protest; but the fact that the missiles were never deployed owed more to shifts in superpower bargaining than the Dutch government taking heed of the wishes of its people.

Breda

BREDA is the prettiest town of North Brabant, and the most immediately likeable place in all of the south: its centre is compact and eminently strollable, with a magnificent church and a couple of good museums; there's a range of well-priced accommodation, inexpensive restaurants and lively bars; and it's an excellent springboard for exploring central North Brabant. In short, it's an ideal target, whether you're visiting for the day or looking for a base from which to branch out to Zeeland, Dordrecht, 's Hertogenbosch, or even Antwerp.

Some history

Though there's little evidence of it today, Breda developed as a strategic fortress town, and was badly knocked about following its capture by the Spanish in 1581. The local counts were scions of the House of Nassau, which in the early sixteenth century married into the House of Orange. The first prince of the Orange-Nassau line was **William the Silent**, who spent much of his life in the town and would probably have been buried here – had Breda not been in the hands of the Spanish at the time of his assassination in Delft. In 1566 William was amongst the group of Netherlands nobles who issued the **Compromise of Breda** – an early declaration against Spanish domination of the Low Countries. The town later fell to the Spanish, was retaken by Maurice, William's son, captured once more by the Spanish, but finally ceded to the United Provinces in 1648.

King Charles II of England lived in the town for a while (it was here that he issued his **Declaration of Breda** in 1660, the terms by which he was prepared to accept the throne), as did (though less reliable historically) Oliver Cromwell and Daniel Defoe. Breda was last fought over in 1793, when it was captured by the French, who hung on to it until 1813.

Finding somewhere to stay

The VVV office, Willemstraat 17 (Mon–Fri 9am–6pm, Sat 9am–5pm; ☎076/22 24 44) is straight out from the train station, about six minutes' walk from the Grote Markt and the town centre. It offers guided tours between mid-July and mid-August (f5), a detailed guide, *Strolling through Breda* (f2), and help with accommodation. Since some of the pensions are on the southern side of town, it's worth using their booking service in high season – or at least phoning ahead to check on room availability.

Pensions include *Graumans* (☎076/21 62 71), which should be your first choice as it's near the station at Delpratsingel 14. The others are all too far to reach on foot – take a yellow #130 bus from the station and ask to be dropped at Duivelsbruglaan. *De Jonge*, Duivelsbruglaan 78 (☎076/65 44 09), *Leenders* Duivelsbruglaan 92 (☎076/65 16 66), and *Donkers*, Duivelsbruglaan 72 (☎076/65 43 32), each cost f30 per person. *Vissers*, Prins Hendrikstraat 171 (☎076/65 55 19),

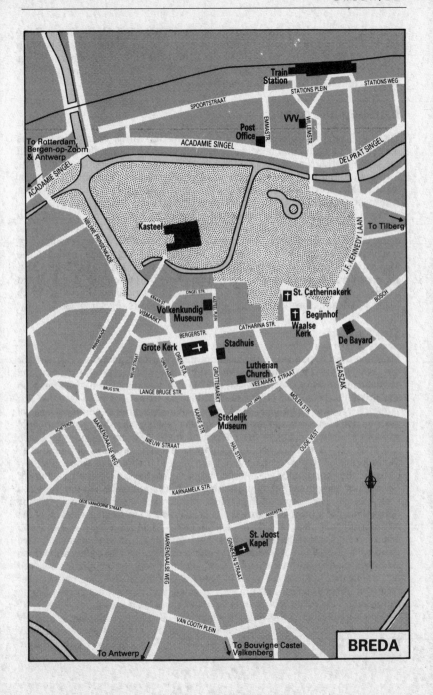

BREDA

is also to the south and charges f25 per person. Of the **hotels**, *De Klok* at Grote Markt 26–28 (☎076/21 40 82) is about as central as you could wish to be, with doubles at f90; the *Lion d'Or*, Stationsweg 4 (☎076/21 11 83), has rooms at f40 per person and *Van Ham*, Van Coothplein 23 (☎076/21 52 29), has doubles at f80. The nearest **campsite**, *Liesbos*, is 8km out of town on the #111 bus route.

Drinking and eating

For down-to-earth **drinking**, try *De Groene Sael*, Havermarkt 8, an unpretentious bar serving draught *Palm* beer, and with a small dance floor at the back. Just off the Grote Markt, *Hemeltjelief*, Veemarktstraat 5, also has a good range of beers. *Nickelodeon*, Halstraat 2, is a more upmarket affair, with a swish interior popular with an older crowd; *Bommel*, across the road at Halstraat 3, is *the* place to drink in town, a large and lively café-bar with a good mix of customers.

Breda has decent range of places to **eat**. For cheap central food, *Da Attilio* is a pizzeria at Grote Markt 35, and *Willy's Pizza* on Halstraat is handy for snacks, doing takeaway slices for f3. *De Graanbeurs*, Reigerstraat 20, is a late-closing Thai restaurant with meals from f10 to f30, including vegetarian options; the *Maharajah of India*, Havermarkt 25, has curries from f16; *Het Voske*, Grote Markt 15, is a smart French place with prices from f20; *Pols*, Halstraat 15, is a small and excellent *eetcafé* with meals starting at f16; and *De Korenbloom*, Ginnekenweg 2b (daily 5–7.30pm), is worth the walk out to the south for its vegetarian food.

The Centre

From the train station and VVV, head down Willemstraat and cross the park for the town centre. The **Grote Markt** is the focus of life, site of a general and second-hand **market** every Tuesday and Friday morning, when stalls push up against the pocket-Gothic **Grote Kerk** (Mon–Sat 10am–5pm; May–Oct also Sun 1–5pm; f1.75, tower open June–Aug), whose intimate interior generates a sense of awe you don't usually associate with so small a building, the short nave and high, spacious crossing adding to the illusion of space. Like the majority of Dutch churches, the Grote Kerk had its decorations either removed or obscured after the Reformation, but a few paintings have been uncovered and reveal just how colourful the church once was. At the end of the southern aisle there's a huge *St Christopher*, and other decorations in the south transept embellish the walls and roof bosses. The Grote Kerk's most remarkable feature, though, is the **Mausoleum of Count Engelbrecht II**, a Stadholder and Captain-General of the Netherlands who died in 1504 of consumption – vividly apparent in the drawn features of his intensely realistic face. Four kneeling figures (Caesar, Regulus, Hannibal and Philip of Macedonia) support a canopy that carries his armour, so skilfully sculpted that their shoulders sag slightly under the weight. It's believed that the mausoleum was the work of Tomaso Vincidor of Bologna, but whoever created it imbued the mausoleum with grandeur and power without resorting to flamboyance: the result is both creepily realistic and oddly moving.

During the French occupation the choir was used as a stable, but fortunately the sixteenth-century misericords, showing rustic and everyday scenes, survived. A couple of the carvings are modern replacements – as you'll have guessed from their subject matter.

Breda's two museums are close to the church. The **Stedelijk en Bisschoppelijk Museum** (City and Episcopal Museum; Wed–Sat 10.30am–5pm, Tues & Sun 1–5pm; f3) at Grote Markt 19 holds a forgettable collection of ecclesiastical art and oddments, along with exhibits concerning Breda's history. The **Volkenkundig Museum**, Kasteelplein 25 (Tues–Sat 10am–5pm, Sun 1–5pm; f3), has a large ethnological collection that, for once, hasn't only been gathered from former Dutch colonies. Exhibits include particularly good Japanese and Native American rooms.

At the top of Kasteelplein sits the **Kasteel**: too formal to be forbidding, and much rebuilt since the Compromise of Breda was signed here in 1566. Twenty-five years later the Spanish captured Breda, but it was regained in 1590 thanks to a nifty trick by Maurice of Nassau's troops: the Spanish garrison was regularly supplied by barge with peat, so, using the Trojan Horse technique, 70 troops under Maurice's command hid beneath the peat of the barge and were towed into the castle, jumping out to surprise the Spanish and regain the town. The Spanjaardsgat, an early sixteenth-century watergate with twin defensive bastions that's just west of the Kasteel, is usually (but inaccurately) identified as the spot where this happened. Today the Kasteel is a military academy, and there's no admission to its grounds.

To the east of Kasteelplein on Catherinastraat, the **Begijnhof**, built in 1531, was until quite recently the only *hofje* in Holland still occupied by Begijns (see *Contexts* "Glossaries"). Today it has been given over to elderly women, some of whom look after the dainty nineteenth-century chapel at the rear, the St Catherinakerk, and tend the herb garden that was laid out several hundred years ago. They also run a fitfully opening little museum of Begijn life. To the right of the Begijnhof entrance, incidentally, is the **Walloon Church**, where Pieter Stuyvesant, governor of New York, was married.

Catherinastraat, which is lined with stately houses from the seventeenth century, twists round to **De Beyaard**, Boschstraat 22 (Tues–Fri 10am–5pm; f2), a cultural centre with changing exhibitions of contemporary art housed in what was once a lunatic asylum.

Tilburg

TILBURG is a faceless and unwelcoming industrial town, its streets a maze of nineteenth-century housing and anonymous modern shopping precinct. Three of its four museums are a stone's throw from the train station, and if that's as far as you get into town, you haven't missed much.

Tilburg developed as a textile town, though today most of its mills have closed in the face of cheap competition from India and southeast Asia. The **Netherlands Textielmuseum**, housed in an old mill at Goirkestraat 96 (out of the station, walk west along Spoorlaan, turn right along Gasthuisring, and Goirkestraat is the fourth turning on the right; Tues–Fri 10am–5pm, Sat & Sun noon–5pm; f5), displays all aspects of the industry, from simple domestic looms to the elaborate industrial machines of the nineteenth century. There's a collection of textile designs from around the world, and demonstrations of weaving and spinning. If you've any interest in the subject, you'll find it fascinating. The shiny new **Scryption**, Spoorlaan 434a (Tues–Fri 10am–5pm, Sat & Sun 1–5pm; f3.50), is a fancy name for a collection of writing implements – everything from lumps of chalk to word processors. Particularly good are the old, intricate typewriters, some of which you can operate yourself. Next door, the **Noordbrabants Natuurmuseum** (Tues–Fri 10am–5pm, Sat & Sun 1–5pm; f3.50) is basically a load of dead animals and (live) creepy crawlies.

If you do go into town you'll need a map from the **VVV** office at Stadhuisplein 128 (ask for directions) to stand any chance of finding the **Poppenmuseum** at Telefoonstraat 13–15 (Sun & Wed 2–4pm; f2.50), a small private collection of dolls. Unless you're mad or desperate there's no earthly reason why you'd want **to stay** in Tilburg, but, for the record, the least expensive room in town is at the *Het Wapen van Tilburg* hotel, Spoorlaan 362 (☎013/42 26 92).

's Hertogenbosch (Den Bosch)

Capital of North Brabant, **'s HERTOGENBOSCH** is officially known as Den Bosch and universally referred to as **'s Bosch**, the name deriving from the words "the Count's Woods" after the hunting lodge established here by Henry I, Duke of Brabant, in the twelfth century. The great draw is its cathedral, but a number of lesser museums and an enjoyable nightlife make it worth a couple of days stopover at least.

> The telephone code for 's Bosch is ☎073

Arriving and finding somewhere to stay

's Bosch's centre is a quarter of an hour's walk from the train station. The **VVV** office in "De Moorian", Markt 77 (Mon–Fri 9am–5.30pm, Sat 9am–4pm; June–Aug Sat until 5pm; ☎12 30 71) claims to know of no pensions in town and only two budget range **hotels**, the *Terminus* at Stationsplein 19 (☎13 06 66), where rooms go for f40 per person, and the *Bosch*, Boschdijkstraat 39a (☎13 82 05), which has singles for f50, doubles for f80. It's worth knowing, then, that there's a scruffy but friendly central hotel, *All In* (☎13 40 57), just down the road at Gasselstraat 1, on the corner of Hinhamerpromenade: rooms without breakfast are f35 per person.

Eating and drinking

's Bosch's **restaurants** can be pricey: many of those in the centre are geared to expense accounts and are poor value for money. *Da Peppone*, Kerkstraat 77, *Taormina*, Verwerssstraat 46, and *Il Brigantino*, Hinthamerstraat 122, are all inexpensive (f14 and up) pizzerias. *Bagatelle*, Hinthamerpromenade 29, has well-priced Dutch food; *De Twee Blaauwe Lelien*, Hinthamerstaat 78, is a chic café-restaurant with good views of the cathedral and meals from f10. *De Opera*, Hinthamerstraat 115–117, has wonderful Dutch-French cooking in a relaxed setting: worth every penny of the f18–30 for main courses. *Dry Hamerkens*, Hinthamerstraat 57 (closed Tues), is pricey, with main courses costing f25–32: what you pay for is the ambience of the building, a tidily elegant seventeenth-century house that looks as if it's fallen out of a Vermeer. For lunch, *In den Brouw Ketel*, Hinthamerstraat 76, is a reasonably inexpensive alternative to the other places around the cathedral, with soups, salads and sandwiches as well as full meals. A little way from the centre, *Van Puffelen* at Van Molenstraat 4 is an attractive *eetcafé* above a canal.

For **drinking**, it's easy enough to wander up and down Hinthamerstraat or the streets that radiate from the Markt and find somewhere convivial. *Keulse Kar*, Hinthamerstraat 101, is as good a starting point as any, a fairly conservative bar near the cathedral. At Hinthamerstaat 97, *'t Bon Palet* is a tiny, popular, and hence often crowded bar that's good for a swift one as you're working your way along the street. Up a few notches on the trendiness scale, *Café Cordes*, A. de Backer Parade 4 (just southwest of the cathedral), is a stylish, aluminium-clad café-bar that brings in 's Bosch's bright young things. *Café Pavlov*, Kerkstraat 38, is also a popular meeting place for the city's youth. *De Blauwe Druif*, at the corner of Markt and Kolperstraat, is a big, boozy pub that takes off on market days, and the bar at 13 Kolperstraat is a friendly place to drink and smoke dope. *Duvelke*, Verwersstraat 59, is a deftly decorated drinking den near the Noordbrabants Museum.

About town

If you were to draw a mental picture of the archetypal Dutch Markt it would probably look like the one in 's Bosch: broad and cobbled, the market that takes place here on Wednesday and Saturday is the largest in the province, and the houses that rim the square are typically seventeenth-century. The sixteenth-century **Stadhuis** (Mon–Fri 10am–5pm) has a carillon that's played every Wednesday between 10 and 11am, and that chimes the half-hour to the accompaniment of a group of mechanical horsemen.

From just about anywhere in the centre of town it's impossible to miss **St Jan's Cathedral** (daily 10am–5pm; restricted entrance during services). Generally regarded as the finest Gothic church in the country, it was built between 1330 and 1530 and has recently undergone a massive restoration. But if Breda's Grote Kerk is Gothic at its most intimate and exhilarating, then St Jan's is Gothic at its most gloomy, the garish stained glass – nineteenth-century or modern – only adding to the sense of dreariness that hangs over the nave. You enter beneath the oldest and least well-preserved part of the cathedral, the western tower: blunt and brick-clad, it's oddly prominent amidst the wild decoration of the rest of the exterior, which includes some nasty-looking creatures scaling the roof – symbols of the forces of evil that attack the church. Inside, there's much of interest. The **Lady Chapel** near the entrance contains a thirteenth-century figure of the Madonna known as *Zoete Lieve Vrouw* (Sweet Dear Lady), famed for its miraculous powers in the Middle Ages and still much venerated today. The brass **font** in the southwest corner was the work of Alard Duhamel, a master mason who worked on the cathedral in the late fifteenth century. It's thought that the stone pinnacle, a weird twisted piece of Gothicism at the eastern end of the nave, was the sample piece that earned him the title of master mason.

Almost filling the west wall of the cathedral is an extravagant **organ case**, assembled in 1602. It was described by a Victorian authority as "certainly the finest in Holland and probably the finest in Europe . . . it would be difficult to conceive a more stately or magnificent design". Equally elaborate, though on a much smaller scale, the south transept holds the **Altar of the Passion**, a retable (a piece placed behind and above the altar to act as a kind of screen) made in Antwerp in around 1500. In the centre is a carved Crucifixion scene, flanked by

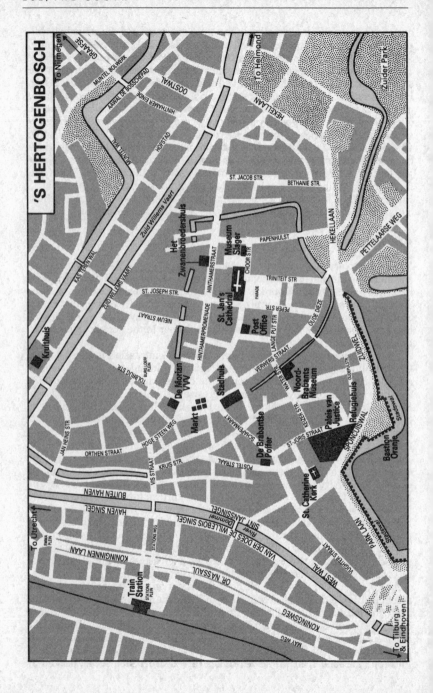

'S HERTOGENBOSCH

Christ bearing the Cross on one side and a Lamentation on the other. Though rather difficult to make out, a series of carved scenes of the life of Christ run across the retable, made all the more charming by their attention to period (medieval) costume detail.

Though a few painted sections of the cathedral remain to show it would have been decorated before the Reformation, most works of art that it possessed were destroyed in the Iconoclastic Fury of 1566. These included several paintings by **Hieronymus Bosch**, who lived in the town all his life: only two works by Bosch remain (in the north transept) and even their authenticity is doubtful. What is more certain is that Bosch belonged to the town's Brotherhood of Our Lady, a society devoted to the veneration of the Virgin, and that as a working artist he would have been expected to help adorn the cathedral. Though none of his major works remain in 's Bosch today, there's a collection of his prints in the Noordbrabants Museum (see below).

Opposite the cathedral at Hinthamerstraat 94, the **Zwanenbroedershuis** (Fri 11am–3pm) has a collection of artefacts, liturgical songbooks and music scores that belonged to the Brotherhood of which Bosch was a member. Founded in 1318, there's nothing sinister about the Brotherhood: membership is open to all, and its aim is to promote and popularise religious art and music.

South and east of the cathedral, the **Museum Slager**, Choorstraat 16 (Tues–Fri & Sun 2–5pm), contains the works of three generations of the Slager family who lived in 's Bosch. The paintings of the family's doyen, P.M. Slager, such as *Veterans of Waterloo*, have the most authority, but some of the other works are competent, taking in the major trends in European art as they came and went. Over the hundred and thirty years they have been active (the remaining Slager, Tom, lives in France) the Slager family seem to have spent most of their time painting 's Bosch – or each other.

A few minutes' walk southwest of the cathedral, the **Noordbrabants Museum**, Verwersstraat 41 (Tues–Fri 10am–5pm, Sat 11am–5pm), is housed in an eighteenth-century building that was once the seat of the provincial commissioner. The good-looking collection of local art and artefacts here is uniformly excellent and interesting – unlike many regional museums. It includes drawings and prints by Hieronymus Bosch, work by other medieval painters, and assorted early torture equipment. There's also a rare *Schandhuik* or "Cloak of Infamy", a wooden cloak carved with adders and toads, symbols of unchastity. In it, women who had been unfaithful to their husbands were paraded on a cart through the city streets in the seventeenth century.

's Bosch's other museum of local interest, **De Brabantse Poffer**, Postelstraat 3a, was firmly closed last time I visited, and looked set to be so for some time. If, by the time you come, it has opened, take a look at its reputedly wacky assembly of North Brabant odds and sods that ranges much wider than the poffers, a type of bonnet, after which it is named. Just down the road, the **Refugiehuis** at the end of St Jorisstraat (Mon–Sat 9am–5pm), originally a sixteenth-century safe house for those persecuted for their religious beliefs, is today a commercial crafts centre.

St Jorisstraat leads down to the site of the old city walls, which still marks the southern limit of 's Bosch. The **Bastion Oranje** once defended the southern section of the city walls, but, like the walls themselves, it has long gone. Still remaining is a large cannon, **De Boze Griet** (The Devil's Woman), cast in 1511 in Cologne and bearing the German inscription "BRUTE FORCE I AM CALLED, DEN BOSCH I WATCH OVER".

For more information on the town's back streets and lesser sights, it's worth picking up the VVV leaflet *Wandering around Old Den Bosch*, which lists most of the better facades and buildings. To name just one, the **Kruithuis** (Tues–Sat 11am–5pm, Sun 1–5pm) at Citadellelaan 6, northwest of the centre, is an old gunpowder magazine that's been converted into an arts centre, with changing exhibitions of (mostly) contemporary art.

Eindhoven

You might wonder why a town the size of **EINDHOVEN** only merits a page in a guidebook; half an hour there, and a few statistics, will tell you why.

In 1890 Eindhoven's population was 4500. In 1990 it was around 197,000. What happened in between was **Philips**, the electrical firm, and the name of Eindhoven's benevolent dictator is everywhere – on bus stops, parks, even the stadium of the famous local football team. The town is basically an extended industrial and research plant for the company, and, save for one impressive art gallery, there's no need to come here unless business (or a football match) forces you.

The city centre: bars and other important attractions

On a more positive note, Eindhoven's modern streets contain some stylish **bars** that have sprung up over the last few years to assuage the thirst of the town's affluent youth. **Kleine Berg** is the best street to drink your way down, starting at *Artys* at no. 10, whose outdoor seating allows you to people-watch those heading this way. The *Grand Café Berlage* at no. 16, as slick as anything you'll find in Amsterdam, has a good menu, but for a full sit-down meal *Eetcafé Bert* at no. 38 has bargain food for f15 to f25. *Eetcafé Jez* at no. 34b is trendier and pricier. At no. 26 *Café Troost*'s marble-covered interior attracts local poseurs, but *Café Bommel*, a little further down, is a more old-fashioned traditional bar – and quite a relief if you've bar-hopped your way down the street.

Eindhoven's other strip for drinking is **Stratumseind**, which starts just south of Cuypers' gloomy neo-Gothic **St Catherinakerk**. The *Miller* bar at Stratumseind 51 is usually packed with teenagers; *De Krabbedans* at no. 32 is an arts complex with a pricey bar; *De Bakkerij* at no. 95 is popular with locals and stoners; *La Squale* at no. 35 is an distinctively different bar with changing wall paintings.

Since the Evoluon, a science museum, was closed down because of poor attendances, Eindhoven's only real pull has been the **Van Abbe Museum**, Bilderdijklaan 10 (Tues–Sun 11am–5pm; f5), with its collection of modern paintings that includes works by Picasso Klein, Chagall, Kandinsky and Bacon. To see this, you need to come between June and September: at other times the Van Abbe has changing exhibitions, and nothing of the main collection can be seen.

Some practicalities – and top soccer action

Eindhoven's **VVV** is outside the train station (Mon–Fri 9am–6pm, Sat 10am–4pm; ☎040/44 92 31). It can provide a handy brochure on the city and a list of pensions, of which only *De Swaan*, Wilhelminaplein 5 (☎040/44 89 92), is anywhere near the centre: rooms go for f35 per person, phone through or ask at the VVV for directions. The only truly central, affordable accommodation is the

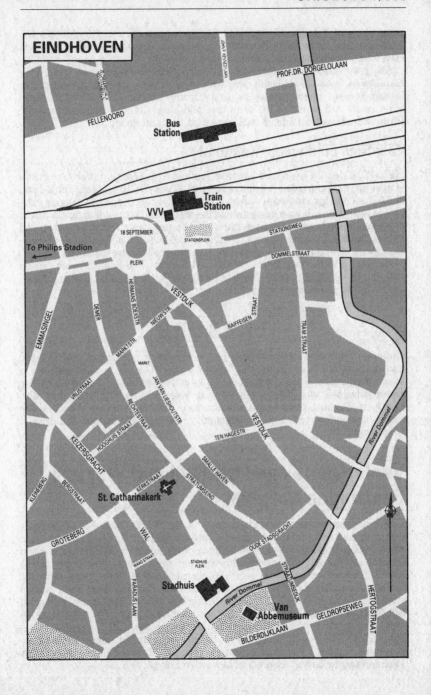

Hotel Corso at Vestdijk 17 (☎040/44 91 31), with singles at f40, doubles f70. There's a good campsite at Landsard 15, but it's a long way out and a fair walk even from the nearest #149/150 bus stop.

Along with Ajax Amsterdam and Rotterdam, Eindhoven's football team, **PSV Eindhoven**, is one of Holland's best, with some valuable home-grown talent like Ronald Koeman among its players. Unfortunately it's renowned for the violence of its fans – and famed as the team that sold Ruud Gullitt. Catch games at the **Philips Stadion**, ten minutes' walk west from the train station.

East from Eindhoven: Helmond

HELMOND, on the main train line from Eindhoven to Venray, just about merits a stopoff for its moated late medieval **Kasteel** (Tues–Fri 10am–5pm, Sat 2–5pm; f2.50) that contains a museum with a small historical collection and changing exhibitions of art (though wandering around the castle itself is most fun); and a collection of futuristic houses, the **Speelhuis** (Playhouse), designed by Piet Blom and opened in 1977. Designed to look like Cubist tree-huts, the buildings most resemble a group of tumbling dice – try and get into the small theatre to have a look.

Helmond's VVV at Markt 211 (☎04920/43 155) has free English brochures on both the Kasteel and the Speelhuis: but once you've spent an hour seeing these, there's nothing to stop you moving on.

LIMBURG

Limburg is Holland's most southerly province, a finger of land that pushes down into Belgium and runs against the Belgian border. The north, around **Venlo**, is mostly farmland and woods; the centre, around **Roermond**, dominated by the rivers and canals; and in the south, down to Maastricht, rise Holland's only hills. Like North Brabant it's a deeply Catholic area (if anything even more so), and one that's been influenced both architecturally and socially by the countries it neighbours.

Venlo, Venray and the National War and Resistance Museum

Only a few miles from the Dutch–German border, **VENLO** has been repeatedly destroyed and recaptured throughout its history, particularly during the last war, when a good number of its ancient buildings were knocked out during the Allied invasion of Europe. Wandering through the town today, you come across random, broad spaces where wartime destruction has never been replaced, though this isn't the case for the area around the Stadhuis. Here the cramped streets wind medievally, eventually delivering you to the fancy, pinnacled **Stadhuis**, a free-standing building of the sixteenth century. From the Stadhuis signs direct you to the **Goltziusmuseum**, Goltziusstraat 21 (Tues–Fri 10am–4pm, Sat & Sun 2–5pm; f2.50, ticket includes entry to Van Bommel-Van Dam museum), the city's historical collection. Best exhibit is the nineteenth-century kitchenware, the largest assortment in western Europe.

Venlo's other museum, the **Van Bommel-Van Dam**, Deken van Oppensingel 8 (Tues–Fri 10am–4pm, Sat & Sun 2–5pm; f2.50), has changing exhibitions of the work of contemporary, mostly local artists. From the train station, take the second exit off the roundabout and then turn first right.

Venlo's **VVV**, Koninginneplein 2 (Mon–Fri 9am–5.30pm, Sat 9am–4pm; ☎077/ 54 38 00), outside the train station, hands out glossy leaflets and can help with accommodation. The only **pension** is the *Knapen*, Puteanussstraat 6 (☎077/51 57 63), with rooms for f27.50 per person; **hotels** include the *Grolsche Quelle*, Eindhovenseweg 3–5 (☎077/51 365 60), and the *Stationshotel*, Keulsepoort 16 (☎077/51 82 30), both of which have rooms for f40 per person. For **eating and drinking**, try the street named Parade.

Venray and the National War and Resistance Museum

A few minutes by train from Venlo, VENRAY is a cosy residential town and a stepping stone to OVERLOON, site of the **National War and Resistance Museum**. To reach the museum from Venray you'll need to hire a bike, either from the station or from *Jacob's Bike Shop* at the end of Radhuisstraat (f9 plus f50 deposit or passport). A fifteen-minute ride through fields of wheat and you're in Overloon (which is actually over the provincial border and back in North Brabant), an affluent little town that was rebuilt following destruction in the last war, when it was the site of a fierce battle in October 1944 in which 2400 men died. The final stages took place in the woods to the east, where hand-to-hand fighting was needed to secure the area, and it's on this site that the museum (Sept–May daily 10am–5pm; June– Aug daily 9.30am–6pm; f6 plus f2 for essential guidebook) now stands, founded with the military hardware that was left behind after the battle. Its purpose is openly didactic: "Not merely a monument for remembrance, it is intended as an admonition and warning, a denouncement of war and violence". This the museum powerfully achieves, with the macabre machinery of war (which includes tanks, rocket launchers, armoured cars, a Bailey bridge and a V1 flying bomb) forming a poignant prelude to the excellent collection of documents and posters. To tour the whole museum takes a couple of hours, and it's a moving experience.

Roermond

ROERMOND, the chief town of central Limburg, is an oddity. Save for a few churches and a museum of fairly specialised interest, there's precious little to see here: its nightlife can't hold a candle to that of Maastricht to the south, cultural happenings are few, and, to be honest, it's not one of Holland's prettier towns either. Yet the town has great personality, caused in part by its long adherence to **Catholicism**. In 1579, seven years after William the Silent had captured Roermond from the Spanish, it fell back into their hands without a struggle and remained under the control of the Spanish (or Austrian) Hapsburgs, who actively encouraged Catholic worship, until the town was finally incorporated into the Netherlands in 1839. Reminders of the pre-eminence of the faith are everywhere, most visibly in the innumerable **shrines** to the Virgin built into the sides of houses. Usually high enough off the street to prevent damage, they contain small figures of the Virgin, sometimes decorated with flowers. And it was in Roermond that P.J.H. Cuypers, the architect who crowded the country with Gothic revival

Catholic churches in the nineteenth century, lived and had his workshops. Roermond is also a handy stopover on the way to Maastricht and the south, Aachen, or Düsseldorf and Cologne in Germany, and useful as a base for visiting nearby THORN.

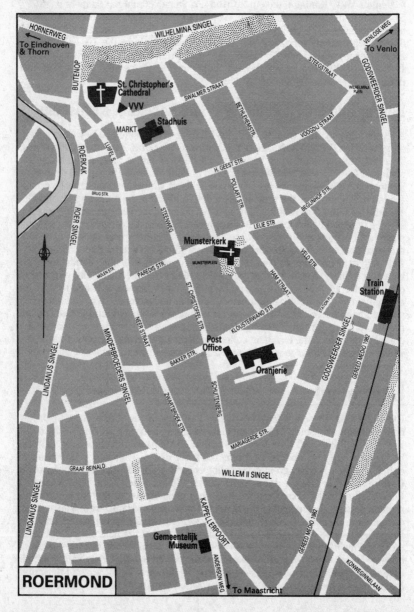

ROERMOND

> The telephone code for Roermond is ☎04750

Arrival and practicalities

Though it looks straightforward enough on the map, Roermond is a confusing place to walk around, its series of wide streets and broad squares aggravatingly similar to the unacquainted. Use the Munsterkerk and river as landmarks, consult our map, and you shouldn't get lost for too long.

The VVV office, Markt 24 (April–Sept Mon–Fri 9am–5.45pm, Sat 10am–6pm; Oct–March closes 2pm Sat; ☎33 205), is a fair walk from the train station, which makes it worth deciding on accommodation before you arrive. A good range of inexpensive **hotels** includes *De Toerist*, Mariagardestraat 3 (☎18 831); *Fuserhof*, Raadhuisstraat 1(☎29 298); *De Herberg*, Borgeind 48 (☎51 5474); and *De Roodververij*, Hertenerweg 2 (☎15 661); all have rooms for f35–40 single, f55–75 double. *De Pauw*, Roerkade 1–2 (☎16 597), charges f50/f80, and *Cox*, Maalbroak 104 (☎28 946), f55/f85. *Willems*, Godsweerdersingel 58 (☎33 021), comes in cheapest of the lot at f35 per person, or there's a single **pension**, *Van Eyden*, Burg. Moorenhof 22 (☎20 771), which charges f25.

The Centre

Walk into town from the train station and you'll come to the **Munsterkerk** (Fri 10am–noon & 2–6pm, Sat 10am–4.30pm) on Munsterplein, built in Romanesque style in the thirteenth century, but much cut about and gothicised by Cuypers in the nineteenth century. Inside, the chief thing to see is the polychrome thirteenth-century **tomb** of Gerhard III and his wife Margaret of Brabant.

From here it's a short walk to the **Markt**, a large sloping square that hit the headlines in May 1990, when two Australian tourists were gunned down by members of the **provisional IRA**, who were under the mistaken belief that they were British soldiers. Its proximity to the German border made Roermond a particularly attractive site for such an action: soldiers often pass through the town en route to their Rhine bases; and fleeing into Germany lessened the likelihood of capture for the assassins, since the Dutch police are not allowed to chase over the border, and the minutes taken to alert the German force allowed additional time for a getaway. The town's early eighteenth-century **Stadhuis** stands on the Markt's eastern side, a dull building that's easily overlooked. More noticeable (though no more interesting), **St Christopher's Cathedral** (April–Sept Sat 2–5pm) was rebuilt following damage in World War II.

Making you way down the larger streets leading south from the Markt – Marktstraat, Neerstraat and Minderbroeders Singel – you'll come across some later, and much more attractive, architecture. Wherever you are in town, it's worth keeping an eye open for Roermond's alluring twentieth-century **facades**: the majority are Art Nouveau, often strongly coloured with heavily moulded vegetal patterns and designs, sometimes with stylised animal heads and grotesque characters.

Roermond's principal architectural claim-to-fame is celebrated at the **Gemeentelijk Museum**, Andersonweg 2–8 (Tues–Fri 11am–5pm, Sat & Sun 2–5pm; f1). **P.J.H. Cuypers** (1827–1921) was Holland's foremost ecclesiastical architect in the nineteenth century, his work paralleling that of the British Gothic revivalist, Augustus Pugin. Almost every large city in the country has a Catholic church by him – those in Eindhoven, Leeuwarden and Hilversum are notable – though his two most famous buildings aren't churches, but the Rijksmuseum and the Centraal Station in Amsterdam. The museum is the building in which Cuypers lived and worked for much of his life, and preserves a small private chapel as well as a large extension in which masses of decorative panels, mouldings and fixtures were produced. Other exhibits show his plans and paintings, along with a collection of works by other local artists, chiefly Hendrik Luyten.

Drinking and eating

The three main areas to **eat and drink** are those around the Markt, the Munsterkerk, and the train station, though *Il Corso*, an excellent value and smartly decorated Italian restaurant, is away from all these places at Willem II Singel 16a, the continuation of Godweerder Singel: pizzas cost from f10 to f20. On Stationsplein, *Le Journal* and *De Tramhalte*, both at no. 17, are café-bars with inexpensive eats; while pricey for dinner, the restaurant of the *De La Station* hotel, Stationsplein 9, is worth checking out for its fixed-price lunches; *Le Châpeau* is a croissanterie ideal for breakfast and snacks, just down from Stationsplein at Hamstraat 4; *Jugoslavija*, Munsterstraat 16, is a better-than-average Yugoslav restaurant with dishes starting at f12; *Tin San* is the best of several Chinese places, just south of the Markt at Varkensmarkt 1; while a little further south, *Marni* at Schoenmakersstraat 16a (the continuation west of H. Geeststraat) has inexpensive Dutch–French food.

None of the bars in these areas are outstanding, and Roermond seems to lack any first-rate boozeries. Try *Herman's Beer Boetiek*, Schuitenberg 32, for a good range of beers, or *De Boag*, Veldtstraat 11, which can get lively. For a more artistic night out, check out the *Orangerie*, a multicultural centre on Kloosterwplein.

Thorn

If you do end up staying in Roermond, the village of **THORN** makes for an enjoyable half-day's outing. Regular buses link it to the town, but it's more fun to hire a bike from the train station and cycle the 14km through the almost rolling Limburg farmland. If you do cycle, take a map that shows cycle routes – the signposting off the main road is none too good.

Once you get here, it's easy to see why Thorn is a favourite for travel agents' posters. Its houses and farms are all painted white, a tradition for which no-one seems to have a creditable explanation, but one that distinguishes what would, in any case, be a resolutely picturesque place. The farms intrude right into the village itself, giving Thorn a barnyard friendliness that's increased by its cobbled streets, the closed-shuttered propriety of its houses, and, at the centre, the **Abdijkerk** (March–Oct daily 10am–5pm; Nov–Feb by request from the VVV; f2).

The abbey was founded at the end of the tenth century by a powerful count, Ansfried, and his wife Hilsondis, as a sort of religious retirement home after Ansfried had finished his days as bishop of Utrecht. Under his control the abbey and the land around it was granted the status of an independent principality under the auspices of the Holy Roman Empire, and it was in the environs of the abbey that the village developed. The abbey was unusual in having a double clois-ter that housed both men and women (usually from local noble families), a situa-tion that carried on right up until the French invasion of 1797, after which the principality of Thorn was dissolved, the monks and nuns dispersed, and all the abbey buildings save the church destroyed. Most of what can be seen of the church today dates from the fifteenth century, with some tidying up by P.J.H. Cuypers in the nineteenth. The interior decoration, though, is congenially restrained Baroque of the seventeenth century, with some good memorials and side chapels. If you're into the macabre, the crypt under the chancel has a couple of glass coffins containing conclusively dead members of the abbey from the eighteenth century: this, and other highlights are described in the notes (in English) for a self-guided walking tour, that you can pick up on entry.

Thorn has several small museums worth catching: the good-natured **Radio en Gramofoon Museum** at Hofstraat 10 (mid-April to mid-Oct daily 10.30am–4.30pm; f2), a collection of ancient radios, record players, telephones and televi-sions; a **Poppenmuseum**, Akkerwal 27 (April to mid-Oct daily 10am–6pm; f2), packed with dolls, glove puppets, marionettes and old porcelain dolls; and the **Carnivalsmuseum**, Kloosterberg 4a, which records the history of the celebra-tion of the Shrovetide carnival in South Holland along with oddments from carni-vals the world over.

The **VVV**, Wijngaard 8 (Mon–Fri 10am–5pm; ☎04756/25 55), can do little more than sell you postcards. Thorn makes a great place to stay if you want to get away from it all: the cheaper of two **hotels** is the *Crasborn*, whose rooms go for f55 per person, though the atmospheric *Golden Tulip* offers surprisingly affordable luxury, with rooms starting at f70 per person. There's also a private **campsite**, reached by turning right halfway down Hofstraat.

Maastricht

Situated in the corner of the thin finger of land that reaches down between Belgium and Germany, **MAASTRICHT**, the capital of the province of Limburg, is one of the most delightful cities in Holland, quite different in feel to the twee waterland centres of the north, with its feet firmly planted in the heart of Europe – vibrant, youthful, and, in a sense, markedly un-Dutch. A cosmopolitan place, where three languages and currencies happily co-exist, it's also one of the oldest towns in the country. The first settlers here were Roman, when Maastricht became an important stop on the trade route between Cologne and the coast – the town's name derives from the words *Mosae Trajectum* or "Maas Crossing". The Romans left relatively few obvious traces, but the later legacy of Charlemagne – whose capital was at nearby Aachen – is manifest in two churches that are among the best surviving examples of the Romanesque in the Low Countries.

Nowadays Maastricht is a key industrial centre, with long-established industries like Mosa (who produce domestic ceramic products from their plant on the east bank of the river), and Sphinx just north of the city centre, whose name graces toilets nationwide, spearheading Maastricht's prosperity. The town's "heart of Europe" position is also being traded on by the local authorities, in the hope of drawing new money into the region – exemplified in projects like the newly-completed MECC conference centre to the south of the city.

> The Maastricht area telephone code is ☎043

Arrival, information and accommodation

The centre of Maastricht is on the west bank of the river, and most of the town spreads out from here towards the Belgian border. You're likely to arrive, however, on the east bank, in the district known as **Wijk**, a sort of extension to the centre that's home to the railway and bus stations and many of the city's hotels. The railway station is about ten minutes' walk from the St Servaas bridge, which crosses the river into the centre. All local (ie non-yellow) buses connect with Markt from here, but really, if you have no luggage, it's easy enough to walk. If you're flying direct to Maastricht, the **airport** is north of the city at BEEK, a twenty-minute journey away by bus; take bus #61, which runs every thirty minutes to Markt and the railway station, or a taxi – a f25 ride.

For information, the **VVV** (Mon–Sat 9am–6pm; ☎25 21 21) is housed just across the river in the Dinghuis, a tall late fifteenth-century building at the end of Grote Straat, the main shopping street. They have bumph on the city, decent maps for f1.50, and copies of *Uit in Maastricht*, a weekly rundown on film, theatre and music events around town. **Getting around**, you only really need to use buses to get from the station to the town centre at Markt, or out to St Pietersburg; otherwise you may as well walk everywhere.

For **accommodation**, there's nothing super-cheap. The VVV have **private rooms** for about f25 per person upwards; they'll either book them for you at the usual fee or sell you their list for f1. Otherwise, of the city's **hotels**, the *De la Guide*, at Stationsstraat 17a (☎21 61 76), and – more comfortably – *De Poshoorn*, Stationsstraat 47 (☎21 73 34), both have doubles from about f85; more upmarket is the *Le Roi*, almost opposite the station on the corner of St Martenslaan (☎25 38 38), which has doubles with private bath for just over f100. If you want to stay across the river (though Wijk is quite pleasant and not at all far out), the *La Colombe*, at Markt 30 (☎21 57 74), is reasonably priced at f95 or so for a double room. There's also a *Hotelboot* (☎21 90 23), moored on the river on Maasboulevard, not far from the Helpoort – cheap at upwards of f65 for a double. If you're **camping**, the *De Dousberg* site, almost in Belgium on the far western side of town, is large and well-equipped; take bus #7 from the railway station and walk for about a kilometre. There's also a **youth hostel** nearby at Dousbergweg 4 (☎43 44 04) – again, bus #7.

The Town

The busiest of Maastricht's many squares is **Markt**, at its most crowded on Wednesday and Friday mornings, when people nip over the nearby borders for the town's cheap general market. At the centre of the square, which is a car park the rest of the time, the **Stadhuis** of 1664 was designed by Pieter Post, a square, grey limestone building that is a fairly typical slice of mid-seventeenth-century Dutch civic grandeur. Its double staircase was designed so that the rival rulers of Brabant and nearby Liège didn't have to argue about who should go first on the way in. Inside, the building has an imposing main hall, which gives way to a rear octagonal dome supported by heavy arches. Wander in for a poke around during office hours – the doors are normally open and nobody's likely to bother you.

The second of the town's main central squares, **Vrijthof**, is just west of the Markt, a larger, rather grander open space flanked by a couple of churches on one side, and a line of cafés on the other, with tables smothering the wide pavement in summer. During the Middle Ages, Vrijthof was the scene of the so-called "Fair of the Holy Relics", a seven-yearly showing of the bones of Saint Servaas, the first bishop of Maastricht, which brought plenty of pilgrims and funds into the town but resulted in such civil disorder that it was eventually banned. The church which holds the relics now, the **St Servaaskerk** (daily 10am–5pm; f3.50), dominates the far side of the square. Dating originally from 950, it's the elaborate outcome of an earlier shrine dedicated to Saint Servaas, and the site of his burial in 384. Only the crypt remains of the tenth-century church, containing the tomb of the saint himself, and the rest is mostly of medieval or later construction. The building looks better than it has done for some time following a recent thorough restoration. Entry is through the mid-thirteenth-century Bergportaal on the south side of the church, into a rich and imposing interior, the round-arched nave supporting freshly painted Gothic vaulting. On the northern side of the church, the fifteenth-century Gothic cloister leads into the treasury, which holds a large collection of reliquaries, goblets and liturgical accessories, including a bust reliquary of Saint Servaas, decorated with reliefs telling the saint's story, which is carried through the town in Easter processions. There's also a coffin-reliquary of

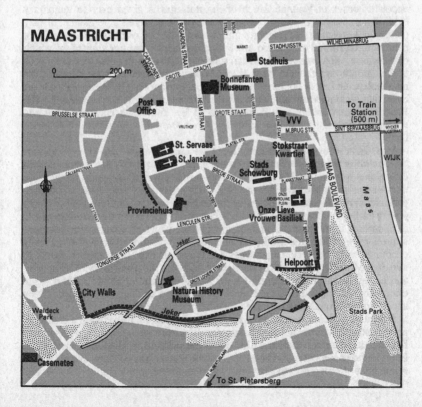

the saint, the so-called "Noodkist", dating from 1160, and bristling with saints, stones and ornate copperwork, as well as a jewelled crucifix from 890 and a twelfth-century Crucifixion in ivory.

The second most prominent building on the square, next door, is Maastricht's main Protestant church, the fourteenth-century **St Janskerk** (June 15–Sept 15 Tues–Fri 11am–4pm, July & Aug also Sat; free), the baptistery of the church of St Servaas when it was a cathedral and nowadays competing for attention with its high and faded red fifteenth-century delicate Gothic tower. Inside are some medieval murals but otherwise a climb up the tower is the church's main point of appeal. On the south side of the square, the sixteenth-century **Spanish Government House** (Wed 2–5pm, Thurs 10am–1pm, April 1–Oct 31 also Sat 10am–1pm; free) has an attractive Renaissance arcade and a number of period rooms furnished in Dutch, French and the more local Liège-Maastricht style. Among various exhibits are statues and figurines, porcelain and applied arts, and a handful of seventeenth-century paintings, though none is exactly essential viewing.

The **Bonnefanten Museum** (Mon–Fri 10am–5pm, Sat & Sun 11am–5pm; f5) is more engaging – Maastricht's main city museum, so-called because of its former home in the eighteenth-century convent of the same name, southwest of the city centre, and since rehoused in a functional modern structure just off the opposite corner of Vrijthof. Much of the museum is given over to temporary exhibitions of varying quality, but on the second floor there's a permanent display of artefacts relating to Limburg and Maastricht, as well as a collection of paintings. Of the former, there are lots of archaeological finds, many of which date from the Roman era hereabouts, religious statuary and other bits and pieces of limited interest; if you're lucky there'll also be ceramics from the Mosa works on display, and a scale model of Maastricht in 1748. Of the museum's art collection, among many indifferent sixteenth-century works are paintings by the Bruegels, van Mander and Bernard van Orley, and some canvases from the Italian Renaissance, notably a coolly executed *Mary adoring Christ* by Filippino Lippi.

Maastricht's other main church, the **Onze Lieve Vrouwe Basiliek**, is a short walk south of Vrijthof, down Bredestraat, in a small shady square crammed with café tables in summer. It's unusual for its fortified west front, with barely more than one or two slits for windows. First built around the year 1000, it's a solid, dark and eerily devotional place after the bright Protestant churches of the North – or even the relative sterility of the St Servaaskerk. The Gothic vaulting of the nave springs from a Romanesque base, while the galleried choir is a masterpiece of proportion, raised under a high half-dome, with a series of capitals exquisitely decorated with Old Testament scenes. Off the north aisle, the treasury (Easter to mid-Sept Mon–Sat 11am–5pm, Sun 1–5pm; f2) holds the usual array of reliquaries and ecclesiastical garments, most notably the dalmatic of Saint Lambert – the evangelical bishop of Maastricht who was murdered at Liège in 705, allegedly by a local noble whom he had rebuked for adultery.

Around the corner from the square, on Plankstraat, on the edge of a district of narrow streets known as the **Stokstraat Kwartier** after its main gallery- and boutique-lined spine, Stokstraat, is the **Museumkelder Derlon** (Sun 1–5pm; free), in the basement of the hotel of the same name. This contains one of the few remnants of Roman Maastricht – the remains of a temple to Jupiter, a well, and several layers of pavement, discovered before the building of the present hotel in the mid-1980s. On the other side of Onze Lieve Vrouweplein lies another of Maastricht's most appealing quarters, narrow streets winding out to the remains of the town battlements alongside the fast-flowing river Jeker, which weaves in and out of the various houses and ancient mills. The best surviving part of the walls is the **Helpoort** of 1229, close to a stretch overlooking the river at the end of St Bernadusstraat; and from here you can walk along the top of the walls almost as far as the **Natural History Museum** at De Bosquetplein 6 (Mon–Fri 10am–12.30pm & 1.30–5pm, Sun 2–5pm; F2.50), where there's a small collection on the geology, flora and fauna of the surrounding area, along with a small lush garden display. A little way south of here, the **Casemates** in the Waldeck Park (mid-April to early Sept tours daily at 2pm; f4) are further evidence of Maastricht's once impressive fortifications, a system of galleries created through mining between 1575 and 1825 that were used in times of siege for surprise attacks on the enemy. There used to be many more casemates around the town, but only these survive, making for a fairly draughty way to spend an hour, tours taking you through a small selection of the 10km or so of damp passages. Probably the most interesting thing about them is the fact that the fourth "musketeer" d'Artagnan was killed here, struck down while involved in an attack on the town as part of forces allied to Louis XIV in 1673.

Outside the centre: St Pietersberg

There are more dank passageways to explore fifteen minutes' walk from the case-mates on the southern outskirts of Maastricht, where the flat-topped hill of **St Pietersberg** rises up to a height of about 110m – a popular picnic spot on warm summer weekends. Again these aren't so much caves as galleries created by quarrying, hollowed out of the soft sandstone, or marl, which makes up the hill – an activity which has been going on here since Roman times. The marl hardens in exposure to the air, so is a much more useful material than might at first be imagined. Of the two cave systems, the **Zonneberg** is probably the better, situated on the far side of the St Pietersberg hill at Casino Slavante (Oct to mid-May hourly tours on Sun only; mid-May to Sept daily tours hourly; f4). The caves were intended to be used as air-raid shelters during the last war and were kitted out accordingly, though they were only in fact utilised during the last few days before Maastricht's liberation. There is some evidence of wartime occupation, plus what everyone claims is Napoleon's signature on a graffiti-ridden wall. Also on the walls are recent charcoal drawings, usually illustrating a local story and acting as visual aids for the guides, not to mention the ten varieties of bat that inhabit the dark (and cold) corridors.

The other, more northerly system of caves, the **Grotten Noord** (Oct to mid-April once daily tours; mid-April to Sept tours several times daily; f4), is easier to get to (fifteen minutes' walk from the centre of town) but it has less of interest. The entrance is at Chalet Bergrust, on the near side of St Pietersberg close by **Fort St Pieter**, a low brick structure, pentagonal in shape and built in 1702, which nowadays houses a pricey restaurant. You can visit – there are guided tours that leave from the restaurant – but (especially if you've had your fill of forti-fications) you'd probably do just as well nursing a drink on the restaurant's terrace, which gives wide-ranging views over the town and surrounding countryside.

Eating, drinking and nightlife

Eating is never a problem in Maastricht. The city has a huge number of restaurants, covering the spectrum in quality; indeed, in Holland Maastricht is renowned for its good food. At the bottom end of the price scale, on Graanmarkt, just off Onze Lieve Vrouweplein towards the river, *Le Chevalier* is an *eetcafé* with most main dishes for around f15–20 and plenty for much less, including omelettes, *uitsmijters* and the like. Nearby, *D'n Blind Genger*, on Koestraat, has a varied menu and a nice atmosphere – main courses around f15–25. *Da Giovanni*, just off Vrijthof on Platielstraat, does a creditable plate of pasta and reasonable pizzas from f7 – though, oddly, it doesn't sell beer. *Jansen*, on A.H. Vleeshius, near St Amorsplein, is an *eetcafé* with lots of cheap things to eat, including good salads and vegetarian dishes, although it tends to close up early. With a little more money, *Galerie*, Onze Lieve Vrouweplein 28, is rather self-consciously trendy but has good French-Dutch food for f25–30 a dish. You might also try *L'Escale*, Havenstraat 19, the cheaper arm of the fancy *t'Klaoske*, which does excellent three-course menus from f25 and *dagschotels* (with a glass of wine) for just under f20.

Drinking, too, you're spoilt for choice – there are, apparently, around 400 bars in Maastricht. Those that line the east side of Vrijthof are packed throughout the day and evening in summer, with outside spaces at a premium. *In den Ouden Vogelstruys*, on the corner of Platielstraat, is one of the nicest, though really any of them make good places to while away the end of the day sipping a drink – and prices are barely more expensive than anywhere else. Away from Vrijthof, *De Bobbel*, on Wolfstraat just off Onze Lieve Vrouweplein, is a bare-boards bar, lively early evening and serving some well-priced bar snacks. *Falstaff*, on St Amorsplein, just down Platielstraat from Vrijthof, is younger and noisier, playing good music and serving a wide range of beers; it also has outside seating. *Touchdown*, further up Platielstraat, is a good bar with pool and regular live bands, usually playing for free. There are also a few good bars on the Wijk side of the river: *Casjet*, on Corversplein, is one of several close to the St Servaasbrug overlooking the river; *De Gijsbrecht*, towards the station on Wycker Brugstraat, is a very busy bar, packed of an evening and serving cheap meals and snacks during the day.

If you don't want to drink, bear in mind that the *Lumière Flimhuis*, Bogaardenstraat 40b (☎21 40 80), regularly shows interesting **movies**, often English or American and always with Dutch subtitles: details in *Uit in Maastricht*.

Listings

Airport Situated north of Maastricht at Beek and connected to the railway station and Markt by bus #61, which runs twice hourly until about 8pm, then hourly until 10pm – a twenty-minute ride; otherwise taxis cost about f25. Flight enquiries on ☎66 64 44.

Boat trips Between mid-April and the end of September, *Stiphout Cruises* run hourly cruises down the Maas daily between 10am and 5pm, price f6 per person. *Stiphout* also offer (less frequent) trips taking in the St Pietersberg caves (f9.75) – or even as far as Liège. Phone ☎25 41 51 for details.

Books There's a branch of *De Slegte* at Wolfstraat 8, good for second-hand English paperbacks and much else besides. Try also *Bergmans* on Nieuwestraat, off Markt, which has a good selection of new English books.

Car hire *Avis*, Spoorweglaan 18 (☎25 23 77); *Hertz*, St Martenslaan 36 (☎25 19 71); *Europcar*, St Martenslaan 21 (☎21 21 21). The major companies also have desks at the airport.

City tours The VVV organise guided tours, leaving from their office, of the city and its fortifications, usually daily at 2pm between Easter and early October. They last around 1hr 30min and cost f4 per person.

Exchange There's a GWK office at the railway station, open every day.

Post office The main city post office is on Keizer Karelplein, just off the northwest corner of Vrijthof.

Around South Limburg

South Limburg boasts Holland's only true hills, and as such is a popular vacation area for the Dutch, many of the villages crammed in summer with walkers from the north taking in the scenery. And this is certainly worth doing, the countryside green and rolling, studded with castles (many of which have been converted to hotels), seamed with river valleys and dotted with the timber-framed houses that are unique to the area. Everywhere is within easy reach of Maastricht, and perfectly feasible on day trips, though without a car you shouldn't try and cover too much in one day as public transport connections are patchy. **Valkenburg**, the main resort, is perhaps the easiest place to visit, on the main rail line from Maastricht to Aachen, though it is packed throughout the summer. Further east down the train line, **Heerlen** and **Kerkade** are also easily reached, though neither is any great shakes. To the south of the rail line, towards the Belgian border, the countryside is wilder and more impressive, the roads switchbacking over hills and giving long, expansive views all around. It's not at all a Dutch scene, and perhaps not what you came to Holland for. But after the grindingly flat landscapes of the northern provinces, it can be excellent therapy – as numerous hotels, one for every tiny village, testify.

Cadier-en-Keer, Margraten and Gulpen

Five kilometres east of Maastricht, the first stop on the #54 bus route – which eventually goes to Vaals on the German border – **CADIER-EN-KEER** is a small suburb of the city best known for its **Africa Centre** (Mon–Fri 1.30–5pm, Sun 2–5pm; f2.50), ten minutes' walk off to the left of the main road (follow the signs). Housed in the headquarters of the African Missionaries Society, this contains a small museum of (mainly West) African artefacts, masks, jewellery and statuary arranged by tribe and dating back as far as the thirteenth century – as well as giving details on the contemporary way of life of African peoples.

Bus #54 continues on to **MARGRATEN**, where just before the town proper there's an **American War Cemetery** (mid-April to end Sept daily 8am–6pm; rest of the year 8am–5pm), a peaceful and in some ways moving memorial to over 8000 American servicemen who died in the Dutch and Belgian campaigns of late 1944 and 1945. Buses stop right outside. The centrepiece is a stone quadrangle recording the names of the soldiers, together with a small visitors' room and a pictorial representation and narrative describing the events in this area leading up to the German surrender – while beyond the quadrangle, the white marble crosses that mark the burial places of the soldiers cover a depressingly huge area.

There's not much else to Margraten, nor is there to **GULPEN**, a few kilometres beyond, a nondescript place though with good bus connections all over South Limburg. The town is known for its *Gulpener* beer, the name of which you see all over the province, and indeed the rest of Holland, though that aside the only thing that sets Gulpen apart is the 161-metre-high **Gulpenberg**, which rises roundly behind the town and is home to a **campsite**. South of Gulpen, the countryside rises higher, and makes for a pretty route back to Maastricht, either driving yourself or by way of the # 57 bus route from Gulpen's bus station, taking in the scenically sited villages of MECHELEN, EPEN and SLENAKEN.

Valkenburg, Heerlen and Kerkrade

Set in the gently wooded valley of the Geul river, **VALKENBURG**, ten minutes' east of Maastricht by train, is southern Limburg's major tourist resort, the unloading point for coaches full of tourists throughout the summer, with innumerable hotels, restaurants, and even a casino. While you wouldn't want to stay here, it's a nice enough place to visit, about as far away from the clogs and canals of the rest of the country as it's possible to get, with a feel more of a Swiss or Austrian alpine resort, its small restaurant-ridden centre sloping up from its fake castle railway station to the surrounding green hills, full of grottoes, castles and thermal centres.

Theo Dorrenplein, five minutes' walk from the railway station, is the centre of town, fringed with cafés and home to the VVV, from where the main Grote Straat leads up through the pedestrianised old centre through the old **Grendelpoort** arch to **Grendelplein**, which provides a second focus, the streets which lead off going to Valkenburg's main attractions. A great many of these are directed at children – things like bobsleigh runs, a fairytale wood, a hopeful reconstruction of Rome's catacombs – and even those that aren't are the kind of things kids enjoy.

It's worth a walk up to the **Castle** (April 1–Nov 1 daily 10am–6pm; f1.50; entrance off Grendelplein), a ruined edifice which overlooks the town from a neatly placed peak above Grote Straat. It was blown up in 1672 on the orders of William III, after he had retrieved it from its French occupiers. Repair and restoration on the castle began in 1921 and continue still, uncovering a series of underground passages that served as an escape route in times of siege. These form part of the **Fluwelengrot** (April–Nov daily 9am–5pm; f4.50), further up the road on the left, a series of caves formed – like those of St Pietersberg in Maastricht – by the quarrying of marl, which has been used for much of the building in this area over the years. Tours leave every ten minutes or so in high summer (much less frequently outside this period) but on the whole they're a damp, cold way to spend an hour, the most interesting features the signatures and silhouettes of American soldiers who wintered here in 1944–45, and a clandestine chapel that was used during the late eighteenth-century French occupation.

If you particularly like caves, or can't be bothered to walk around the Fluwelengrot, the **Gemeentegrot** (same times and prices), just off Grendelplein on Cauberg, is similar, but has a train which whips you around its charcoal drawings, memorials to local dignitaries, giant sculptures of dinosaurs and fish hewn out of the rock, and, most engagingly, a weirdly, brightly-lit underground lake. The whole tour takes about half an hour and costs a guilder extra. Further up the same road as the Fluwelengrot, on the left, the **Steenkolemijn** (April–Nov Mon–Fri 9am–5pm) is a mocked-up coal mine whose hour-and-a-quarter-long tours take in a short film on coal-mining, some fake mine-workings and a small fossil museum. Again, good for the kids but not exactly riveting viewing. If the idea of trudging around dank underground passages doesn't appeal, you can ascend to the top of the hill above the castle by way of a **cable car** (daily noon–5pm; f4.50 return), five minutes' walk down Berkelstraat from the top of Grote Straat – or you can cut through the passage between the castle and the Fluwelengrot. This, a fairly primitive structure of the kind used for ski-lifts, with two-person open carriages, takes you up to the **Wilhemina Toren**, where you can either enjoy the view from the terrace of the inevitable bar-restaurant or, for another f2, ascend further to the top of the tower.

The **VVV** at Theo Dorrenplein 5 (Mon–Fri 9am–5pm, Sat 11am–3pm; ☎04406/ 13364) has maps and information on all Valkenburg's attractions, as well as lists of **hotels** and **private rooms** should you want to stay. Bear in mind, though, that despite the enormous number of rooms here, availability can be a problem in high season. **Camping**, the nearest site is a short walk up Dahlemerweg from Grendelplein on the left. As virtually every other building in Valkenburg is a restaurant, there's little point in listing specific places to **eat**. Suffice to say you can dine cheaply and fairly reasonably at most of the places in the centre – though don't expect haute cuisine.

Heerlen and Kerkrade

HEERLEN, ten minutes on from Valkenburg by train, is quite different, an ugly modern town that sprawls gracelessly over the rolling countryside. But it has one definite attraction in the excellent **Thermen Museum** (Tues–Sat 10am–5pm, Sat & Sun 2–5pm), which incorporates the excavations of a bath complex from the Roman city of Coriovallum here – a key settlement on the Cologne–Boulogne trade route. These have been enclosed in a gleaming hi-tech purpose-built structure, with walkways leading across the ruins, and tapes (in English) explaining what's what. An adjacent room displays finds and artefacts from the site, including glasswork from Cologne, shards of pottery, tombstones and coins, all neatly labelled. To get to the museum, follow Saroleastraat from the station as far as Raadhuisplein and turn right.

Fifteen minutes on from Heerlen lies **KERKRADE**, again an unappealing place, but worthy of a visit for its **Abdij van Rolduc** complex, situated on the far side of town, twenty minutes or so's walk from the station. Originally founded by one Ailbert, a young priest who came here in 1104, this is now almost entirely sixteenth-century, used as a seminary and conference centre, but it does preserve a fine twelfth-century church, a model of simplicity and elegance, with contemporary frescoes and a marvellous mosaic floor. The clover-leaf-shaped crypt, dark and mysterious after the church and with pillar capitals carved by Italian craftsmen, contains the relics of Ailbert, brought here from Germany where he died; while next door to the church, a **Mine Museum** describes mining through the ages in the area – appropriate enough in the shadow of the giant slagheaps nearby.

travel details

Trains
From Vlissingen to Middelburg (2 hourly; 7min).
From Middelburg to Goes (2 hourly; 12min); Bergen-op-Zoom (2 hourly; 37min); Roosendaal (2 hourly; 47min).

From Roosendaal to Dordrecht (2 hourly; 22min); Breda (2 hourly; 18min); Antwerp (2 hourly; 29min).
From Breda to 's Hertogenbosch (2 hourly; 35min); Dordrecht (2 hourly; 20min).

From Tilburg to Eindhoven (2 hourly; 23min); 's Hertogenbosch (2 hourly; 15 min).
From 's Hertogenbosch to Eindhoven (2 hourly; 22min).
From Eindhoven to Roermond (2 hourly; 32min); Venlo (2 hourly; 48min).
From Roermond to Maastricht (2 hourly; 33min); Venlo (2 hourly; 26min).
From Maastrict to Liège (hourly; 30min).

Buses

From Middelburg to Veere (7 daily; 20min); Delta Expo (8 daily; 30min); Haamstede (8 daily; 45min).
From Goes to Zierikzee (8 daily; 15min).

PART THREE

BELGIUM AND LUXEMBOURG

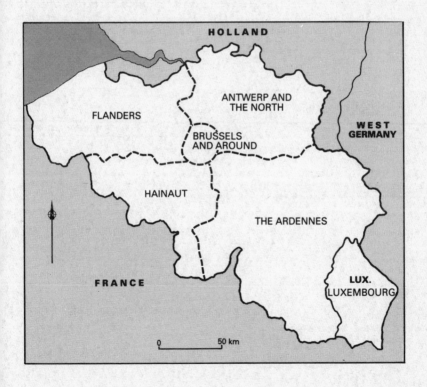

Introduction

A federal country, with three official languages and an intense regional rivalry, Belgium has a cultural mix and diversity which belies its rather dull reputation amongst travellers. Luxembourg, too, though known as a tiny refuge of bankers and diplomats, has surprises in store, scenically one of the most beautiful countries in northern Europe, its green, wooded hills rolling down to its strikingly situated capital.

■ The Belgian language divide

Belgium is the land where the French- and German-speaking nations meet, the tensions between the two a consistent historical threat to the prosperity and welfare of its people. Today, the country's population of around ten million is fairly evenly divided between Flemish-speakers (about sixty percent) and Walloons (about forty percent), who speak French as their first language; there are even, in the far east of the country, a few pockets of German-speakers around the city of Eupen. Certainly, Belgium's language problems are not to be taken lightly, reflecting, as they do, deep class and economic divisions. Prosperity has shifted back and forth between the two communities over the centuries: in medieval times Flanders grew rich on its textile trade; later Wallonia developed mining and steel industries. But through the ages the Francophones have always represented the aristocracy, the Flemings the bourgeoisie. The setting-up of the Belgian state in 1830 crystallised the antagonism, with the final arrangements favouring the French-speakers. French became the official language, Flemish was banned in schools (the Belgian Civil Code was only translated into Flemish in 1961), and the industries of Wallonia were dominant. Nowadays, however, Flanders is the industrial powerhouse of Belgium – a fact championed by Flemish nationalist parties like the *Volksunie*, who would also like to see Brussels become a totally Flemish city.

The line between the two cultures – officially called the "language divide" and effectively cutting the country in half, west to east – was drawn in 1962, but in response to increasing acrimony between the two communities the constitution has since been redrawn (in 1982) on a federal basis, with three separate entities – the Flemish North, the Walloon South, and Brussels, which is officially bilingual (although its population is eighty percent French-speaking). However, the division between Flemish Flanders and French Wallonia still influences every aspect of working and social life. Schools, political parties, literature, culture – all break down along linguistic lines. Neighbours refuse to speak to one another because of the conflict, and stereotypes are deeply ingrained, leading to a set of complex, face-saving rules and regulations which can verge on the absurd. Press conferences, for example, must have questions and answers repeated in both languages, one after the other. Bitterness about the economy, unemployment and the government smoulders within the framework of this linguistic division, and individual neighbourhoods can be paralysed by language disputes. The communities of Fourons (Voeren), for example, a largely French-speaking collection of villages in Flemish Limburg, known as the *voerstreek*, almost brought down the government in the mid-Eighties when the Francophone mayor, Jose Happart, refused to take the Flemish language exam required of all Flanders officials. He was divested of office several times, and each time stood for mayor again and was re-elected, prompting the prime minister at the time, Wilfred Martens, to offer his own resignation. The Fourons affair was symptomatic of the obstinacy that besets the country to this day. Jose Happart could probably pass that Flemish exam easily, indeed rumour has it that he is fluent in the language. He simply chooses not to submit.

All this said, it would be wrong to assume that Belgium's language differences have yet gone beyond the level of personal animosity and institutionalised mutual suspicion. Belgian language extremists have been imprisoned over the years, but very few, if any, have died in the fight for supremacy. Indeed, some might see a bilingual nation as a positive thing in a Europe where trading – and national – barriers are being increasingly broken down. Suggesting this to a Belgian, however, is useless. He or she will only turn away in disgust.

■ Where to go

There's more to the Flemish–Walloon divide than just language: the North and South of **Belgium** are visually very different places. The **North**, made up of the provinces of West and East

Flanders, Antwerp, Limburg and the top half of Brabant, is mainly flat, with a landscape and architecture not unlike Holland. **Antwerp** is the largest city, a big, sprawling, bustling old port with doses of sleaze and high art in roughly equal measure. Further south, in the Flemish heartland of Flanders, are the great Belgian historic cities, **Bruges** and **Ghent** – tourist attractions in themselves, with a stunning concentration of Flemish art and architecture. Bruges especially is the country's biggest tourist pull, and although this inevitably means it gets very crowded, you shouldn't miss it on any account. Beyond lies the Belgian **coast**, which makes valiant attempts to compete with the rest of Europe but is ultimately let down by the crassness of its development and the coldness of the North Sea. Far better to spend time in some of the other inland Flanders towns, not least **Ieper**, formerly and better known as Ypres to the British, many of whom come to visit the stark sights of the nearby World War I **battlefields**.

Marking the meeting of the Flemish and Walloon parts of Belgium, **Brussels**, the capital, is central enough to be pretty much unavoidable, a culturally varied city, more exciting and varied than its reputation as bland Euro-capital would suggest. Because Belgium is not a large country, you can also use it as a base for day trips out: Bruges and Ghent are easily feasible, as is the old university city of **Leuven** to the north, or even the cathedral city of **Mechelen**, halfway to Antwerp.

The southern part of Brussels' province, **Brabant**, is French-speaking, and merges into the solely Walloon province of **Hainaut** – rich agricultural country, dotted with ancient cities like **Tournai**, and industrial centres like **Charleroi** and **Mons**. East of here lies Belgium's most scenically rewarding region, the **Ardennes**, spread across the three provinces of **Namur**, **Liège** and **Luxembourg**: an area of deep, wooded valleys, high elevations and heathy plateaux and caverns that, beyond the main tourist resorts, is very wild indeed – by any standards, let alone those of normally tame Belgium. Use either Liège or Luxembourg as a jumping-off point, before heading into the heart of the region at **St-Hubert**, **Han-sur-Lesse** or **La Roche**.

Luxembourg

The Ardennes reach across the Belgian border into the northern part of the **Grand Duchy of Luxembourg,** a high, green, almost Alpine landscape of high hills topped with crumbling castles overlooking rushing rivers. **Vianden**, **Echternach** and **Clervaux** are perhaps the three best of very few centres for touring the countryside – quiet small towns with little life outside the tourist industry. However, the country's status as European nonentity is quite unjust; in fact it packs more scenic highlights into its tight borders than many other, more renowned holiday spots. And while its southern reaches are much more ordinary, **Luxembourg city** at least is worth a stop. Dramatically sited, it's about the closest the country gets to a proper urban environment, although its population of 75,000 people (around a fifth of the Grand Duchy's total) is still tiny by capital city standards.

Getting Around

As with Holland, travelling around Belgium is rarely a problem. Once again, the fact that it's a small country means distances are short, and there's a well-organised – and reasonably-priced – train service linking them, supplemented by plentiful buses. Luxembourg, on the other hand, can be problematic for such a tiny country: the train network is not extensive, and bus timetables often demand careful study if you're doing much independent travelling.

■ Trains

Like Holland, too, the best way of getting around Belgium is by **train**. Run by the *Societé National Chemin de Fer de Belgique/Belgische Spoorwegen* (*Belgian Railways*), denoted by a simple "B" in an oval, the system is comprehensive and efficient, and fares – at least compared to much else in the country – are affordably low, around F300 for a journey of

100km. Reckon on paying around F400 to travel from, say, Bruges to Namur, one of the longer journeys you're likely to make; you can travel the length of the country for another F300 or so on top of this.

You can, of course, cut costs further by investing in a **rail pass** – though this is only really worth it if you're going to be doing a lot of travelling. The Belgian Tourrail pass gives entitlement to five days' unlimited rail travel within a seventeen-day period for F1700 (F1300 if you're under 26). There is also the so-called Half-Fare Card, which for F500 allows you to purchase first- and second-class tickets at half-price during the period of a month, or the recently introduced TTB Pass, giving validity for a month on all the country's trains, trams and buses – price F2200 (under-26s F1700). Consider also the **Benelux Tourrail Card**, valid for any five days within a seventeen-day period on the Belgian, Dutch and Luxembourg national networks, as well as Luxembourg buses, for F2490 – under-26s F1790. If you're travelling to a town for a specific attraction, you might also consider taking one of *Belgian Railways*' organised **excursions**, whereby you pay a price – usually upwards of F200 – that includes return travel plus entry prices and sometimes a meal.

Belgian Railways publish lots of **information** on their various offers and services, available in advance from their office in London at Premier House, 10 Greycoat Place, London SW1P 1SB (☎071/233 0360). They'll sell you national (F150) and international (F50) timetables, though these are of course also available from railway stations inside the country.

In **Luxembourg** the railways are run by *Chemins de Fer de Luxembourg – CFL* – and are not at all as wide-reaching as those in Belgium. There's one main north–south route down the middle of the country to Luxembourg city, but apart from that only a few lines branching out from the capital, and the system is mainly supplemented by buses. There are a number of passes available if you're going to be doing a lot of travelling, giving unlimited train (and bus) travel for periods lasting from one day to a month. The price for a one-day pass is F217; a five-day pass allows unlimited travel for any five days within a month-long period and costs F658; the monthly pass, valid for a full calendar month, costs F1748. Obviously the Benelux Tourrail Card is also valid on both trains and *CFL* buses.

■ Buses

As so much of the country is covered by the rail network, **buses** in Belgium (run by *SNCV*, the national bus company) are only really used for travelling short distances, and whenever there are alternatives, the train is generally quicker and not greatly more expensive. Where you will use buses is to travel around and into the environs of major towns and cities, or in the Botte de Hainaut and some parts of the Ardennes, where the train network is less comprehensive. In most towns the main bus terminal is next door to the rail station.

In Luxembourg the reverse is true: because of the sparsity of the rail system, buses are a much more usual way of getting around, many of them run by *Luxembourg Railways* and indeed replacements in many cases for former branch rail lines. In all cases, the bus services are fully integrated with the rail lines. Fares are comparable, and it's worth knowing that at weekends and on holidays the price of a single and return ticket are the same. There are also a number of passes available if you're doing a lot of travelling; see "Trains" for details.

■ Driving and hitching

In either Belgium or Luxembourg, **driving** is not something that will cause many problems. Both countries are well covered by networks of main roads and (toll-free) motorways, and congestion is normally tolerable outside the major cities.

Rules of the road are much the same as in Holland: you drive on the right, and the speed-limit in built-up areas is 60kph, on main roads 90kph and on motorways 120kph. You need a full driver's licence in order to drive, as well as a green card of insurance. In general, petrol costs are slightly below those of Britain. The national motoring organisation in Belgium is the *Tourist Club Belgique* (*TCB*), whose headquarters are at rue de la Loi 44 (☎02/233 22 11); in Luxembourg it's the Automobile Club ACL, route deLonguly 54 (☎45 00 45) Both organisations have reciprocal arrangements with AA/RAC members and can be called upon in case of **breakdown**. Most major roads in Belgium have roadside phones. Seat belts in both countries are compulsory, and penalties for drunken driving stiff. Spot fines are common for some offences, and in Luxembourg it's obligatory to always carry at least F600 on you for payment of fines.

Car hire in both countries is quite pricey, and works out cheaper if you book it before you leave

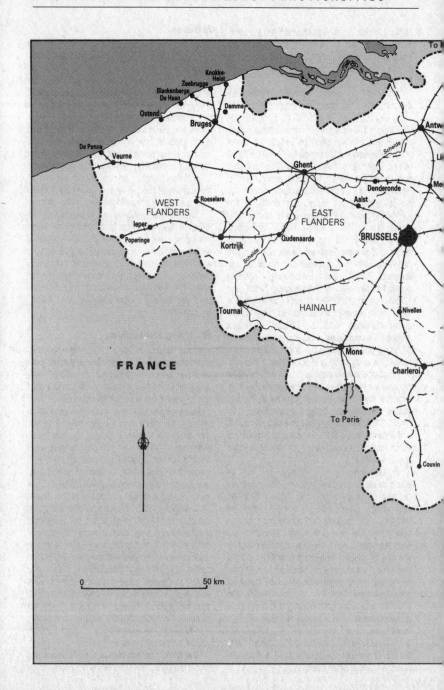

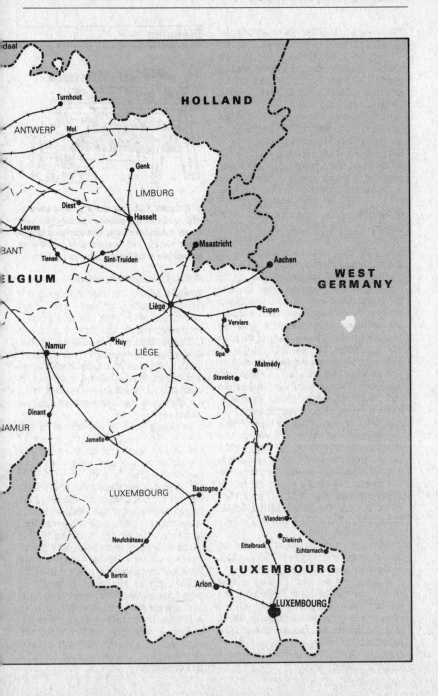

home – about F10,500 a week with unlimited mileage as opposed to F15,000 once in Belgium or Luxembourg, though as usual there are cheaper weekend rates, bringing it down to around F2000 a day. However, as in Holland it is possible to cut costs greatly by means of special weekends deals and the like.

As for **hitching**, this is easy: the Belgians give lifts to hitchhikers frequently, and the size of the country makes it a perfectly feasible way of getting around. Hitching on motorways is illegal, but the major towns of both countries are well connected by a good network of main roads, so this isn't usually a problem.

■ Cycling

Cycling is something of a national sport in Belgium, and it is also a viable way of getting around, the short distances largely flat terrain making it a fairly effortless business for the non-enthusiast – and keen cyclists have, in the Ardennes, some ideal and very scenic terrain to indulge their pleasure. Most roads have bicycle lanes (use the outer one where there's a choice), and the *Geocart* maps, detailed on p.12, are adequate for route planning; many of the country's tourist offices also have details, and sometimes maps, of recommended cycling routes.

If you haven't brought your own machine (for details on which see *Basics*), you can **hire** one from around sixty railway stations nationwide, returning it to the station of your choice (normally open daily 7am–9pm). Rates are cheap: F100 a day with a valid train ticket, F150 without; for a period of three days or more, the price is F90 a day, and during summer at least, it's advisable to book. No deposits are required. For a list of railway stations offering this service, get hold of *Belgian Railways' Train & Vélo (Trein & Fiets)* leaflet, available in advance from the Belgian Tourist Office, *British Rail* in London or railway stations in Belgium itself.

Whether you have your own, or have hired one from elsewhere, it is possible to take your **bike on the train**; rates are F160 per journey.

In Luxembourg you can hire bikes at local offices throughout the country for around F250 a day; local tourist offices have details of locations where they're not mentioned in the guide. Bear in mind also that you can take your bike on trains anywhere in Luxembourg for F18 a machine. The Luxembourg Tourist Office issues a booklet showing possible cycling routes.

Sleeping

In Belgium and Luxembourg, accommodation is one of the major expenses you will incur: hotels, even the grottiest places, are never cheap, and hostels only provide an alternative in the larger cities and resorts.

■ Hotels and private rooms

Hotels in Belgium and Luxembourg are roughly classified according to cost: prices range upwards from around F1000 for a double room in the cheapest one-star establishment to between F5000 and F8000 in the big city luxury hotels, though prices vary according the tourist interest-rating of the town. In cheaper establishments breakfast isn't always included in the price, in which case you should add on F200 or so to the cost of the room – or, cheaper and better, use the nearest café.

In summer you'd be well advised to book rooms in advance, especially in the larger cities and Ardennes resorts. You can either do this by phoning the hotel direct – we've given phone numbers throughout the guide – or by using the free *Belgium Tourist Reservations* service (*BTR*), Post Box 41, 1000 Brussels 23 (☎02/230 50 29), through which you can book rooms nationwide. Reservations can also be made through most tourist offices, again for free, though they'll often charge you a deposit which will be deducted from your final bill. For a full list of approved hotels throughout the country, with details of prices and facilities, pick up the Belgian Tourist Office's guide before you leave Britain, especially as it can be surprisingly difficult to get hold of a copy once in Belgium. The Luxembourg Tourist Office also produces a booklet of approved hotels, with prices, which is again well worth getting hold of before you leave – though it is possible to pick it up once there.

Private accommodation is sometimes a possible, slightly cheaper alternative. Many towns have a limited supply of rooms in private homes which local tourist offices will book for you at no charge. On average, reckon on spending about F900 a night on a double room – and expect them to sometimes be inconveniently situated.

■ Hostels, sleep-ins, student rooms

Belgium has 28 official IYHF **youth hostels**, rather oddly run by two separate organisations, one for Flanders, another for Wallonia. Each operates a similar number of hostels, though they are rather different in many ways, the Flanders hostels large, ruthlessly organised affairs often used by large parties, while those in Wallonia are smaller and more informal. Flanders hostels charge a flat rate per person throughout the country of F240–280 for a bed in a dormitory, F330–550 in Ostend and Brussels; in Wallonia the rate is F195–210, F330–550 in Brussels. Breakfast is usually included at hostels in Flanders, and not in Wallonia, where it costs about F75; charges are levied for sleeping bag hire in both regions – normally around F90. Many hostels in both Flanders and Wallonia also offer lunch and dinner, at prices of around F100–150 for lunch, F200 or so for dinner.

It's a good idea to join the YHA before you leave Britain, since the prices above will be considerably higher if you're not a member. Their head office is at 14 Southampton St, London WC2 (☎01/836 8542), and membership costs £4 a year for those under 21, £7 otherwise.

During the summer at least, you should book in advance wherever possible, since in high season, many hostels can be completely booked up. We've detailed many of the hostels, with phone numbers, in the guide, but for a complete list contact either the YHA in Britain or one of the Belgian youth hostels organisations direct: the *Vlaamse Jeugdherbergcentrale*, Van Stralenstraat 40, B-2008 Antwerp (☎03/232 72 18); or the *Centrale Wallone des Auberges de la Jeunesse*, rue Van Oost 52, B-1030 Brussels (☎02/215 31 00). The Belgian Tourist Office's *Budget Holidays* leaflet also has details of official youth hostels.

Some of the larger cities – Antwerp and Brussels, for example – have a number of **unofficial youth hostels** in addition to the IYHF establishments. These normally cost F250–300 for a dormitory bed and are often just as comfortable; they also have the advantage of being open to

non-YHA members. You'll also come across places known as **Sleep-ins**, which, as in Holland, offer dormitory accommodation for rock-bottom prices – sometimes as low as F180 per person. Where they exist, we've given details in the guide. Finally, you might also find some cities offering **student accommodation** during the summer holidays – in Ghent, for example, where the university opens up its dorms to travellers at very cheap rates. Again we've given details, where relevant, in the guide.

Luxembourg has about a dozen youth hostels, all members of the *Auberges de la Jeunesse de Luxembourg (AJL)*, place d'Armes 18, Luxembourg (☎25588). Rates for YHA members are F170 per person for a dorm bed, F210 if you're over 26, in all but the Luxembourg city hostel, where you'll pay F210 and F250 respectively. Breakfast is usually about F80 extra, evening meals F200. There are no other, unofficial youth hostels in Luxembourg.

■ Campsites, farms, gîtes, apartments

Considering the cost of other forms of accommodation, **camping** is an option well worth considering in both Belgium and Luxembourg. There are around 400 sites in **Belgium**, most of them well-equipped and listed, with details of facilities, in the Belgian Tourist Office's *Camping* leaflet. Many are situated close to main roads for the convenience of motorists, and are broadly classified on a one- to four-star coding. The vast majority of sites are one-star establishments, for which you should expect to pay F30–70 per person per night, plus about F40 for a tent, F40 or so for a car or motorcycle. **Luxembourg** has a little over 100 campsites, all detailed in the free booklet available from the national tourist board. Price again vary, but are usually between F50 and F100 per person, plus F30–60 for a tent, sometimes including hot showers. During peak season it can, in both countries, be a good idea to book ahead if you have a car and large tent or caravan; phone numbers are listed in the free directories, and in Luxembourg there's also a special telephone number you can ring if you're having difficulty finding somewhere – ☎48 11 99, between 11am and 7.30pm daily.

As for other alternatives, in Luxembourg there's the option of taking an **apartment**. These are also listed in a booklet available from the national tourist board and it's unusual to rent them for less than a week. In Belgium there are also so-called **farm holidays**, whereby you stay on a farm for a small amount and help out with work that needs doing. Prices vary from province to province and depend partly on the amount of work you are expected to undertake. Advance arrangements are essential. Both countries also offer **gîte d'etapes** – hostels really, situated in relatively remote parts of the country and accommodating between 30 and 100 people in each establishment. Reckon on about F100 per person per night. Again, the Belgian Tourist Office's *Budget Holidays* leaflet has details of these and of farm holidays. The Luxembourg Tourist Office publishes a leaflet showing gîte locations and prices, or you can contact the *Gîtes d'Etapes Luxembourgeois*, boulevard Prince Henri 23, 1724 Luxembourg (☎23 698).

Costs, Money and Banks

Belgium and Luxembourg are, by a whisker, the most expensive of the Low Countries. Of the two, Belgium is the cheaper, but in both places prices for just about everything are above what you will be used to paying at home. A notable exception is beer, which is dirt cheap, especially in Luxembourg. Travel, also, if only because both countries are so small, isn't a major expense.

Those camping or staying in hostel accommodation and self-catering should be able to manage on around £15 a day. Staying in hotels, and eating out in restaurants most nights, you'll get through at least £30 a day – in Luxembourg it might be more.

■ Money and Banks

The **currency** in both Belgium and Luxembourg is the franc, normally written as "F" or "BF" and "FLux". The Belgian and Luxembourg franc are actually separate currencies, but they are virtually interchangeable: they have the same rate of exchange against all other currencies, but although Belgian francs are legal tender in Luxembourg, the reverse isn't true in Belgium. Also, it is advisable to change all spare Luxembourg francs into Belgian notes before you leave for home, since this is the more acceptable currency in foreign banks. Both currencies divide into 100 centimes, and come in **coins** worth 1, 5, 20 and 50 francs, and **notes** worth 50, 100, 500, 1000 and 5000 francs. At the time of writing the exchange rate was F55–60 to the pound sterling.

Banks are the best places to change money. In Belgium they are open Monday–Friday 9am–noon and 2–4pm, in Luxembourg 9am–noon and 12.30–4.30pm; some banks also open on Saturday mornings. You can also change money in larger cities at railway stations, some hotels, and bureaux de change, though the rates are less favourable, and if you have a Eurocheque card with a PIN number you can use the *MISTERCASH* dispensers in Brussels and elsewhere. The major **credit cards** – *Access, Visa, American Express, Diner's Club* – are accepted widely in shops, hotels and restaurants. You can also get cash advances on these from some high street banks, though there is usually a F5800 minimum.

Communications

Post and phones in Belgium and Luxembourg are very efficient. Unlike Holland, however, English newspapers are seldom available on the day of publication.

■ Post

Post offices in Belgium and Luxembourg are plentiful: in Belgium they are open Monday–Friday 9am–noon and 2–5pm and in Luxembourg Monday–Friday 8am–noon and 1.30–5pm. Some post offices open Saturday mornings too, and in larger centres like Brussels and Luxembourg city the main offices do not shut at lunchtime. **Postage** costs F14 for a postcard, the same for a letter under 20g inside Europe, and F25 to countries outside. Mail to the UK takes 3–5 days. **Post boxes**, painted red in Belgium and yellow in Luxembourg, are, as in Holland, attached to walls.

INTERNATIONAL DIALLING CODES

Great Britain ☎0044	
Ireland ☎00353	
Australia ☎0061	
New Zealand ☎0064	
USA and Canada ☎001	

USEFUL NUMBERS	Belg	Lux
Operator calls	☎997	☎0010
Directory enquiries	☎1307	☎017
International enquiries	☎1304	☎016
Emergencies	☎100/101	☎012
International Collect calls	☎1324	☎0010

■ Phones

Both countries have reliable **phone systems**. Public call boxes are the usual continental kind, where you deposit the money before you make your call. In both countries phone boxes take F20 and F50 coins, though in Belgium there are also public phones that take cards – available from newsagents, post offices and railway stations for F100 or F500. Area **phone codes** for Belgium are given in the guide; you'll notice, however, that Luxembourg is small enough to not need any kind of area coding system – everywhere in the country simply has a five-digit number.

If **calling abroad**, remember that some post offices have booths where you can make your call and settle up afterwards. You can also, of course, make calls from your hotel, though as usual this is much more expensive than any other method.

■ Media

British newspapers are widely available in both Belgium and Luxembourg, though normally a day later than they appear in Britain. Railway station bookstalls in the large cities are a good bet; expect to pay about F50.

As for the **domestic Belgian press**, the major newspapers in Wallonia are the influential, independent *Le Soir*, the left-of-centre *Journal et Independance*, the liberal *Dernière Heure* and the right-wing *Libre Belgique*. In Flanders you'll see the leftish *De Morgen*, *Het Volk*, which is the paper of the Christian Democrats, and the right-leaning *De Standaard* and *Het Laatste Nieuws*. There's also an **English-language weekly magazine**, the Brussels-based *Bulletin* (F70),

catering to the sizeable ex-pat community here. Though inevitably orientated towards the capital, it's worth buying wherever you are in Belgium, for its entertainments and TV listings, and slices of Belgian news in English. It also carries a fair-sized classified section – useful if you've just arrived for an extended stay and are looking for an apartment or even work. In **Luxembourg**, the highest circulation newspaper is the *Luxemburger Wort*. There's also an English-language weekly, the *News Digest*, though this is very dry and not really worth the bother.

British TV and radio stations can, as in Holland, be picked up in Belgium and Luxembourg, on the same frequencies. You'll find BBC Radio 4 on 1500m long wave, the World Service on 463m medium wave and shortwave frequencies between 24m and 75m at various times throughout the day. BBC1 and BBC2 can also be found, though more so in Belgium than in Luxembourg, as well as the usual pan-European cable and satellite channels – Sky, Superchannel, Eurosport and the rest (see p.26 for details of these). You can also, in most parts of both countries, pick up all the Dutch and German stations, and sometimes those from France and Italy too.

Food and Drink

The attitude to food in Belgium and Luxembourg is quite different from that in Holland. Belgian cuisine is held in high regard worldwide, and in Europe at least is regarded as second only to French in quality. The food of Luxembourg isn't as appealing or as varied, but you can still eat out well in much of the country, albeit at high prices. As for drink, beer is one of the real delights of Belgium, and Luxembourg produces some very drinkable white wines along its side of the Moselle.

■ Food

Southern Belgian cuisine is not unlike French, retaining the fondness for rich sauces and ingredients that the latter has to some extent lost of late. In Flanders the food is more akin to that of Holland, plainer and simpler on the whole, though here too there are many interesting traditional dishes. For such a small country there's a surprising amount of regional variation, but in general it's true to say that pork, beef and game, and fish and seafood, especially mussels, are staple items, often cooked with butter, cream and herbs, or sometimes beer – which is, after all, the Belgian national drink. Soups, too, are common: hearty affairs, especially in the south and Ardennes, where it's usual to be served a huge tureen of the stuff from which you can help yourself – a meal in itself. The Ardennes is also well-known for its smoked ham (similar to Italian proscuitto) and, of course, its pâté, made from pork, beef, liver and kidney – though it often takes a particular name from an additional ingredient, for example *pâté de faisan* (pheasant) or *pâté de lièvre* (hare).

Among common **Belgian dishes** you'll come across are *waterzooi*, a Flanders stew consisting of chicken or fish boiled up with fresh vegetables; *truite à l'Ardennaise* – trout cooked in a wine sauce; *carbonnades de porc Bruxelloise* – pork with a tarragon and tomato sauce; *carbonnades à la boeuf* – cubes of beef marinated in beer and cooked with herbs and onions; *fricassée Liègeois* – basically, fried eggs, bacon and sausage or black pudding; and *konijn met pruimen* – rabbit with prunes. An Antwerp speciality is *paling in 't groen*, eel braised in a white sauce with herbs; *fricadelles à la bière*, or meatballs in beer, is a Brabant delicacy. Among many salads you'll find are *salade de Liège*, made from beans and potatoes, and *salade wallonie*, a warm salad of lettuce, fried potatoes and bacon bits.

Luxembourg cuisine is similar to that of Belgium, but, as you might expect, it has more Germanic influences, with sausages and sauerkraut featuring on menus, as well as pork, game and river fish. Favourite dishes include smoked pork with beans, liver dumplings with sauerkraut and potatoes, and *tripe à la Luxembourgoise*.

Breakfast, snacks and sweets

In most parts of Belgium and Luxembourg you'll **start the day** in routine continental fashion with a cup of coffee and a roll or croissant, the sumptuous affairs served in Holland never having caught on this far south. Coffee, however, is often served Dutch-fashion, with a small tub of evaporated rather than fresh milk.

Later in the day, the most obvious **snack** is *frites* – served everywhere in Belgium from *friture* stalls or parked vans, with just salt or mayonnaise, or, as in Holland, with more exotic dressings. Mussels, cooked in a variety of ways,

with chips, is virtually the Belgian national dish, and makes a good fast lunch in cafeterias. On the coast you'll see stalls selling all kinds of fish delicacies, much the same as in Holland. Other street stalls, especially in the north, sell various sorts of sausage (*worst*), especially black pudding (*bloedworst*); and everywhere there are stands selling waffles (*gaufres*), served up piping hot with jam and honey. There are also, of course, the usual multinational burger joints, of which the indigenous *Quick* chain is a reasonable approximation.

As for cakes and sweets, Belgium is known best for its **chocolate**. Each Belgian, apparently, eats 12.5kg of chocolate annually, and chocolates are the favoured gift when visiting friends. The big Belgian chocolatiers, *Godiva* and *Leonidas*, have shops in the main towns and cities, and though by no means cheap, their *pralines* (filled chocolates) are marvellous. Regular chocolate by the bar (*Cote d'Or* is one of the major manufacturers) is also delicious. Apart from chocolate, look out for *speculaas*, a speciality of the northen part of the country (and also found in Holland) – a rich spiced cake that was originally baked in the form of saints and religious figures but now comes in all shapes and sizes.

Sit-down food

At the cheaper end of the **sit-down meal** scale, many **bars** serve food, at least at lunchtimes, and there are normally a host of **cafeterias** around serving up basic dishes, omelettes, fricassées, soups, chicken or steak with chips and suchlike. Nothing comes cheap, but the quality will regularly be excellent, even with the most humble dishes, and portions are usually enormous. In bars, basic restaurants and cafeterias, you can expect to pay about F200 on average for an omelette or something similar; a more substantial meat-and-chips affair might cost F300–400. Most bars and cafeterias that serve food normally have a *plat du jour* on offer, too, usually for around F300, which often includes a starter and a sweet.

Though there's often a thin dividing line between the two as regards the food, **restaurants** are not surprisingly more expensive than bars; they will also probably only be open during the evening. Even in the cheapest restaurant, a main course will rarely cost under F400, and it's more likely that prices for most things will be more like F500–700, especially in Luxembourg, where things are that much more expensive.

As for **other cuisines**, in the larger cities there is a huge variety, especially in Brussels, where the authenticity of the ethnic restaurants is one of the city's strengths. However, in country areas of both Belgium and Luxembourg choice is much more limited. Traditional Belgian (and Luxembourgois) food is fairly meat-based, which means **vegetarians** are in for a difficult time, especially if they want to sample the local specialities – though this is considerably easier if you eat fish. Vegetarian restaurants exist, but are much rarer than in Holland. In the cities, **Italian** and **French** are the most widespread available cuisines aside from Belgian and Luxembourgois, and restaurants are invariably of good quality. Among less often found alternatives are **Turkish** and **Greek** restaurants (good in Brussels particularly); **Yugoslav** restaurants pop up here and there but are generally overpriced. Of far eastern options, **Vietnamese** restaurants are more common in Belgium than in Britain; **Chinese** restaurants are also fairly widespread; while Luxembourg's sizeable Portuguese minority has spawned a higher than average quota of **Portuguese** eateries. There are also a fair few **African** and **North African** restaurants, in Belgium at least – worth sampling, if not cheap.

■ Drinking

The price of food in both Belgium and Luxembourg is more than compensated for by the cost of **drinking**, especially if you like beer, which is always good and comes in numerous varieties. There's a bar on almost every corner in both countries: most serve at least twenty types of beer, and in some beer lists run into the hundreds. Usually they're cosy, unpretentious places, the walls, as in Holland, stained brown by tobacco smoke; they're normally frequented by locals and sometimes serve simple food.

Beer

Beer has been a passion in Belgium since the Middle Ages, when monks did much of the brewing; later the brewers' guilds were founded, and became among the most influential institutions in the region. Today there are up to 500 different kinds of beer in Belgium, many brewed by small family breweries, some still produced by monasteries. Most of these are of the lager – or pilsener – type, but it would be wrong to assume this is all that's on offer.

In both Belgium and Luxembourg, ask for a *bière* in a **bar** and you'll be served a roughly half-pint glass, larger than in Holland, of whatever the bar has on tap. The most common beers you'll see in Belgium are the Leuven-based *Stella Artois*, *Jupiter* from Liège (the country's biggest-selling beer), *Maes* and *Lamot*. In Luxembourg the most widespread brands are *Diekirch* (the largest domestic brewer), the Luxembourg-based *Mousel* and *Bofferding*. **Bar prices** don't vary greatly: in Belgium you'll pay F30–40 for a glass of beer in all but the swankiest places; in Luxembourg count on F25–30 – about the only thing that is cheaper in Luxembourg than Belgium. For speciality bottled beers like *Duvel* and *Chimay* (see below) you'll pay around F90. As for buying **beer in a supermarket**, you can buy large, 75cl bottles of pilsener beer for about F25; six-packs of 25cl bottles go for about F90. Speciality beers cost about F30 for a 33cl bottle.

In addition to the ordinary draught pilsener beers, there are any number of **speciality beers**, usually served by the bottle but occasionally on draught. These are often regionally based but many are available everywhere. They are usually strong and should be drunk (and sometimes poured) with care – those in the bottle sometimes carry sediment at the bottom. The most famous speciality beer in perhaps the whole of Belgium is *lambic* – the generic title for beer brewed in the Brussels area (mainly Payottenland) which is fermented by contact with the yeast naturally available in the air and matured in oak casks. *Lindemans* are one of the best-known producers, but there's also the *Cantillon* museum-brewery in Anderlecht, which brews genuine *lambic* beers. A blend of old and young lambic beers is known as *gueuze*. Of other pilsener brands, *Duvel* stands out: the name means "devil", which is an appropriate tag for a brew that's not far short of the strength of wine – though you wouldn't know it from the taste. Belgium also has plenty of dark beers or ales. *De Koninck*, brewed in Antwerp, is like an English bitter but smoother, with a yeasty taste; *Mort Subite* (literally "sudden death") is, despite the name, not especially strong, actually named after a bar in Brussels. Try also some of the beers traditionally (and still) brewed by Belgium's five Trappist monasteries, strong, top-fermented ales that are usually over six percent alcohol by volume. The best-known – and most widely available – is *Chimay*, brewed at the

FRENCH FOOD AND DRINK TERMS

Basics

Beurre	Butter	*Oeufs*	Eggs
Chaud	Hot	*Pain (complet)*	Bread
Dessert	Dessert	*Poisson*	Fish
Fromage	Cheese	*Poivre*	Pepper
Froid	Cold	*Salade*	Salad
Fruit	Fruit	*Sel*	Salt
Hors d'Oeuvre	Starters	*Sucre*	Sugar
Legumes	Vegetables	*Viande*	Meat

Typical Snacks

Un sandwich/une baguette . . .	A sandwich . . .	*brouillés*	scrambled eggs
		Omelette . . .	Omelette . . .
jambon	with ham	*nature*	plain
fromage	with cheese	*au fromage*	with cheese
saucisson	with sausage	*Salade de . . .*	Salad of
à l'ail	with garlic	*tomates*	tomatoes
au poivre	with pepper	*concombres*	cucumbers
Croque-monsieur	Grilled cheese and ham sandwich	*Crêpes*	Pancakes
		au sucre	with sugar
Oeufs . . .	Eggs . . .	*au citron*	with lemon
au plat	fried eggs	*au miel*	with honey
à la coque	boiled eggs	*à la confiture*	with jam
durs	hard-boiled eggs		

Soups and Starters

Bisque	Shellfish soup	*Potage*	Thick soup, usually vegetable
Bouillabaisse	Fish soup from Marseilles	*Assiette anglaise*	Plate of cold meats
Bouillon	Broth or stock		
Consommé	Clear soup	*Crudités*	Raw vegetables with dressing

Meat and Poultry

Agneau	Lamb	*Hamburger*	Hamburger
Bifteck	Steak	*Jambon*	Ham
Boeuf	Beef	*Lard*	Bacon
Canard	Duck	*Porc*	Pork
Cheva	Horsemeat	*Poulet*	Chicken
Dindon	Turkey	*Saucisse*	Sausage
Foie	Liver	*Veau*	Veal

Fish

Anchois	Anchovies	*Maquereau*	Mackerel
Anguilles	Eels	*Morue*	Cod
Carrelet	Plaice	*Moules*	Mussels
Cervettes roses	Prawns	*Saumon*	Salmon
Escargots	Snails	*Sole*	Sole
Hareng	Herring	*Truite*	Trout
Lotte de mer	Monkfish		

Terms

A point	Medium	*Mijoté*	Stewed
Au four	Baked	*Pané*	Breaded
Bien cuit	Well-done	*Rocircumflexti*	Roast
Bouillir	Boiled	*Saignant*	Rare
Frit/friture	Fried/deep fried	*Sauté*	Lightly cooked in butter
Fumé	Smoked	*Tourte*	Tart or pie
Grillé	Grilled		
Hollandaise	Egg yolk, butter and vinegar sauce, often served with fish		

Vegetables

Pommes (de terre)	Potatoes	*Genièvre*	Juniper
Choufleur	Cauliflower	*Poireau*	Leek
Asperges	Asparagus	*Riz*	Rice
Champignon	Mushrooms	*Laitue*	Lettuce
Petits pois	Peas	*Oignon*	Onions
Ail	Garlic	*Carotte*	Carrots
Concombre	Cucumber		

Sweets and Desserts

Crème fraiche	Sour cream	*Madeleine*	Small, shell-shaped sponge cake
Crêpes	Pancakes		
Crêpes suzettes	Thin pancakes with orange juice and liqueur	*Parfait*	Frozen mousse, sometimes ice cream
Frappé	Iced	*Petits fours*	Bite-sized cakes or pastries
Glace	Ice cream		

Fruit and Nuts

Amandes	Almonds	*Noisette*	Hazelnut
Ananas	Pineapple	*Pamplemousse*	Grapefruit
Cacahouète	Peanut	*Poire*	Pear
Cérises	Cherries	*Pomme*	Apple
Citron	Lemon	*Prune*	Plum
Fraises	Strawberries	*Pruneau*	Prune
Framboises	Raspberries	*Raisins*	Grapes
Marrons	Chestnuts		

Drinks

Bière	Beer	*Tea*	Thé
Café	Coffee	*Vin*	Wine
Eaux de vie	Spirits distilled from various fruits	*Rouge*	Red
		Blanc	White
Jenever	Dutch/Flemish gin	*Brut*	Very dry
Milk	Lait	*Sec*	Dry
Orange/citron pressé	Fresh orange/lemon juice	*Demi-sec*	Sweet
		Doux	Very Sweet

For a list of Dutch food and drink terms – detailing the words and phrases you need when travelling in the Flemish-speaking north of Belgium – see p.28.

biggest of the country's monastery breweries in Hainaut. Other examples are *Orval*, from the southern province of Luxembourg, *Westmalle*, from north of Antwerp, and there are smaller breweries at Rochefort in Namur and at the monastery of St Sixtus in Westvleteren near Ieper, the last of which produces a beer that is said to be the strongest in the country – over ten percent alcohol by volume.

Besides these there are some other, rather odd brews. *Hoegaarden*, for example, is a so-called "white beer" (*witbier* or *bière blanche*) – actually cloudy rather than white, and drunk in summer, sometimes with lemon. There's also the more commonly drunk *kriek*, which is a pilsener beer with cherries added during the final fermentation, producing a refreshing, not-too-sweet brew that comes in champagne-style bottles or on draught. *Lindemans*, the well-known *lambic* producer, make *kriek*, but with cherry juice these days rather than the real thing; only *Cantillon* of Anderlecht and the *Liefmans* brewery in Oudenaarde use actual cherries. You'll also come across beers flavoured with other fruits – strawberries (*framboise*) or even peaches.

Wine and spirits

The presence of **wine** in Belgium is obviously much overshadowed by the beer, but it is widely available, at about F120 a bottle from the supermarket, F250 or so for a half-litre in a restaurant. French wines are the most commonly drunk, although **Luxembourg** is, in a small way, a wine producer, and its white wines, produced from vines grown along the north bank of the Moselle – which forms the border between Luxembourg and Germany – are very drinkable, not unlike those of Germany, but drier and fruitier than those of France. They also produce some very palatable sparkling wines. As with beer, Luxembourg wines are relatively cheap to buy in shops: the sparkling, *methode champenoise* varieties go for under F200 a bottle (try the *St Martin* brand, which is excellent and dry); ordinary white wine costs about F100.

Unlike Holland, there's no one national Belgian **spirit**, but all the usual kinds are available, at about F60 a glass in a bar. You will also find jenever in most bars, especially in Limburg where it is made. In Luxembourg spirits are cheaper than elsewhere in Europe – a fact reflected by a thriving cross-border trade from France and Germany. You'll also come across home-produced bottles of *eau de vie* – distilled from various fruits and around fifty percent alcohol by volume.

Museums, Churches and Castles

Like Holland, Belgium, and to a lesser extent Luxembourg, are strong on museums and galleries. The legacy of Flemish art is apparent in a good many decent galleries, and the strong Belgian sense of regionalism has spawned a number of museums devoted to specific provinces.

■ Museums

Most **museums** in Belgium are open, with variations, Tuesday until Saturday from 9am to 4pm, and sometimes on Sunday; Monday is a common closing day. However, travelling outside the April–September period, you can expect a lot of places to be closed unless they're of really prime touristic importance; a number of museums don't actually open until Easter or May 1, closing up again in the middle or end of September. Displays vary, and are normally of better quality in the historic north Belgian towns, where there are usually at least a handful of Flemish paintings on show, and other trinkets from the era of medieval prosperity. In both countries, most towns of any size at all have some kind of local display, which you can normally miss with a clear conscience – exceptions again being the major Flemish towns, and places like Liège with its important Walloon museums.

■ Churches and castles

Churches in Belgium and Luxembourg are normally quite different places from those in Holland: Catholicism is the main religion, with the result that places of worship are not the cold, unadorned buildings you find to the north – though most of the great churches of Flanders have little decoration, dating from the ransackings of Flemish Protestants. Churches which are interesting touristically are normally open all day, at least during the summer, only closing up for a couple of hours at lunchtime (often noon–2pm). Otherwise you'll only be able to enter during a Mass.

Southern Belgium and Luxembourg are also blessed with a wealth of **castles and chateaux**, usually perched in isolated – and nowadays picturesque – locations, that can be difficult to reach without a car. Luxembourg, especially, has a dense concentration – some almost entirely ruined now but worth visiting for the views, others sumptuously restored in period fashion. During the summer, opening times are generally all day every day for the most interesting sites, though again outside the April–September period you can expect many places to be closed.

Festival and annual events

Both Belgium and Luxembourg are big on festivals and annual events – everything from religious processions to carnivals to more contemporary-based jazz binges and the like. Apart from the obvious exception of carnival, most events, as in Holland, take

place in summer. As always, the national tourists offices at home, and offices within Belgium and Luxembourg, can supply details of exact dates, which tend to change from year to year. For more on the events themselves, see the appropriate entry in the guide.

The best annual fun is probably to be had at the many (mainly Belgian) annual **carnivals**, held in February and early March. One of the most renowned of these is held at Binche, in Hainaut, when there's a procession involving some 1500 dancers – or *Gilles* – alone. There are also carnivals in Ostend and Aalst, in Eupen, with events lasting over the weekend before Shrove Tuesday and culminating with *Rosenmontag* on the Monday – a pageant of costumed groups and floats through the town centre – and, most uniquely, in Stavelot, where the so-called "Blancs Mousis" (featured on the cover of this book) take to the streets.

FESTIVALS DIARY

January
Jan–May Luxembourg international festival of opera and ballet.

February
Early Feb Binche Carnival.
Weekend before Shrove Tuesday Eupen Carnival, climaxing with the *Rosenmontag* procession and festivities on the Monday.
Last weekend Carnivals in Aalst, Vianden.
End Feb–end March Luxembourg City Carnival.

March
Early March Ostend Carnival.
Early March *Buergsonndeg* or "Bonfire Day" all over Luxembourg.
Mid-Lent Stavelot Carnival Parade with the famous "Blancs Mousis".
Last Sun *Bretzelsonndeg* ("Pretzel Day"), markets, processions and displays of folk art in the Luxembourg Moselle towns.
Last Sun Petange Carnival (Luxembourg).

April
Easter weekend Leuven International Folklore Festival.
End April Ghent Flower Show.

May
Early May Bruges: Procession of the Holy Blood.
Second Sun Ieper Cat Festival.
Mid-May *Octave*, Luxembourg City, an annual pilgrimage culminating in front of the cathedral.
End May Mechelen Handswijk Procession.
Whit Tuesday Echternach Dancing Procession to commemorate St Willibord.

June
Second Sun Tournai Day of the Four Processions, notably a carnival parade and the traditional procession of the Knight of the Tower.
June 23 Luxembourg National Day
Last weekend Ieper 24-hour car rally.
June–Sept Knokke-Heist Cartoon Festival.
June–Sept Mechelen Carillon concerts at St Rombout's tower, every Mon, Sat and Sun.

July
July weekends and first week of Aug Middlekerke Folklore Festival.
July and Aug Wiltz International Music Festival.
Early July Brussels Ommegang.
Early July Schoten Folklore Festival.
Early July Torhout-Wecher Rock Festival.
Third weekend Diekirch beer festival.
End July Veurne Penitents Procession.
End July Eeklo hot air balloon festival.

August
Aug 9 Brussels *Meiboom*.
Mid-Aug Leuven *Marktrock* rock festival.
Mid-Aug Liège Outremeuse Folklore Festival.
End Aug Lochristi Begonia Festival.
End Aug Blankenberge Flower Procession.
End Aug to early Sept Luxembourg: *Schueberfouer*, a former shepherds' market that's now the capital's largest funfair.
Aug–Sept Ghent Festival of Flanders – concerts, etc, held in the ancient buildings of the medieval town centre.
Aug–Oct Wine festivals in the Moselle Valley.

September
Early Sept Dendermonde International Jazz Festival.
First weekend Kortirjk Golden River City Jazz Festival.
Second weekend Grevenmacher wine and grape festival, with processions, wine-tasting and fireworks.

Second Sun Mechelen horticultural and floral pageant.
Second Sun Tournai Procession of the Plague, to remember an epidemic of 1090.
End Sept Nivelles Sixteen-kilometre procession from St Gertrude's tower out through the countryside and back again.

October
Early Oct Vianden Walnut Market.

November
Nov 1 Diest Pilgrimage to All Saints Hill, accompanied by the offering of ex-votos, etc.
Nov 10 Vianden: *Miertchen* or "St Martin's Fire" celebrating the end of the harvest.
Nov 11 Eupen St Martin's Procession through the town, with children bearing candles and Roman legionaries, finishing with a bonfire.

December .
Dec 6 Arrival of St Nicholas, celebrated by processions and the giving of sweets to children.

Both countries' **religious-inspired festivals** are among the most intriguing events you're likely to come across. The Brussels *Ommegang* is the best-known, a largely secular event these days, held on the first Thursday in July, that nominally commemorates the arrival by boat of a miraculous statue of the Virgin Mary from Antwerp in the fourteenth century. If you want see anything on the Grand Place, however, where most of the action is, you have to book months in advance, and you might be better off visiting the town of Veurne in Flanders for its annual Processions of the Penitents, on the last Sunday in July, where cross-bearers dressed in sacking process through the town – a slightly macabre sight. Other religious events include the Procession of the Holy Blood in Bruges, when a shrine brought back from the Holy Land during the crusades that supposedly contains the blood of Christ is carried solemnly through the streets; and the procession of dancers in memory of St Willibord that winds its way through the streets of Echternach in Luxembourg.

More secular events include the *Meiboom*, held in Brussels on August 9, Ieper's Cat Festival in May, with floats and costumes on a cat theme, and any number of folklore events and fairs. There are also a number of annual sporting occasions, not least the Ieper 24-hour car rally and the Grand Prix at the circuit near Spa.

Directory

AIRPORT TAX Not charged when leaving either Belgium or Luxembourg.

BIKE HIRE See p.258.

CAR PROBLEMS See p.255.

CONTRACEPTIVES Condoms are available from chemists (*pharmacie* in French, *apotheek* in Flemish), though for the pill you need a presciption.

DISABLED VISITORS Unlike Holland, access for the physically disabled is rarely considered in either Belgium or Luxembourg – lifts and ramps are few, and steep steps and rough pavements are common. The trains, too, unlike Dutch railways, make few concessions.

ELECTRIC CURRENT 220v AC – the same as in Britain.

EMERGENCIES Belgium: Ambulance/fire brigade ☎100; police ☎101. In Luxembourg the emergency number is ☎012, which can also get you details of late-opening chemists, doctors, dentists, etc.

LEFT LUGGAGE Major railway stations have luggage offices (normally open daily 6am–midnight); smaller stations have coin-operated lockers, taking F20 and F50 pieces.

SHOPPING Both countries have a number of things worth buying to take home. In Belgium, chocolates are obviously a major enticement, though you won't find them a lot cheaper than in Britain. Beer, on the other hand, providing you're up to carrying it, is worth a raid on a supermarket on the way to the airport. The same goes for Luxembourg, where beer is equally affordable; it's also worth buying wine in shops rather than duty-free, since the home-produced stuff is cheap and good – particularly the sparkling variety.

TIME One hour ahead of Britain.

TIPPING As in Holland, there's no necessity to tip, although it's common to round up the bill to the nearest ten francs or so in restaurants and cabs. In public toilets, such as they exist, it's usual to leave F5–10.

TRAVEL AGENTS *Wasteels*, *Acotra* and *JEST* are three organisations with branches in both countries that are good places for discount flights, *BIJ* tickets, student cards, etc. Where relevant, we've given addresses in the guide.

WAR CEMETERIES There are a number of war cemeteries in Belgium and Luxembourg, from both world wars. Most, of course, are centred on the World War I battlefields around Ieper. There are others, from World War II, in the Ardennes region, from the heavy fighting there in late 1944. Again, full details are available from the Commonwealth War Graves Commission, 2 Marlow Road, Berks.

CHAPTER SEVEN

BRUSSELS AND AROUND

Wherever else you go in Belgium, it's likely that at some point you'll wind up in **Brussels**. The city is the major air gateway for the country; it's on the main routes heading inland from the channel ports via the Flemish art towns; and it's also a convenient stopover on the railway between France and Holland. As such Brussels is somewhat hard to avoid. But despite the city's reputation as a dull, faceless centre of commerce and diplomacy, full of dark-suited diplomats and sleazy businessmen, you could do worse than stop over for a while. It has architecture and museums to rank with the best of Europe's capitals, a well-preserved medieval centre, and a vibrant, energetic streetlife and nightscene, especially in its immigrant quarters. It's also small enough to be easily absorbed over a few long days.

It's true to say that since Brussels became home of the European Commission in 1959, parts of it have been sacrificed to a grey district of business and government. And it's also true that at times the medieval centre can feel like a purpose-built playground for tourists and ex-pats. But the most striking aspect of the city is the sharp contrast between the contrived internationalism of the centre and EC zone, and the vital, authentic foreignness of the non-indigenous quarters. This is something that the city's compact nature only heightens: in five minutes you can walk from a designer shopping mall into an African ghetto, or from a depressed slum quarter to a snooty square of antique shops and exclusive cafés.

Brussels is, and always has been, a fragmented place. Indeed, the city's historic class divisions are embodied in its very layout. Since the eleventh century, monarchs, aristocrats and the wealthy have lived in the **Upper Town**, tradespeople and workers in the **Lower Town** – a distinction which is still in part true. In addition to this, the French-Flemish language disputes which have plagued the region for so long continue here in full and concentrated force – so much so that the capital has been officially bilingual since 1962, and by law all road signs, street names and virtually all published information must be in both languages. Nowadays the city is even more diverse, with communities of European bureaucrats, diplomats and business people, and immigrants from North Africa, Turkey, the Mediterranean and Zaire, constituting a quarter of the population.

Each of these communities leads a very separate, distinct existence, something which only increases the allure of the city – not least in the number and variety of affordable ethnic **restaurants**. Without these, Brussels would still be a good place to eat: its gastronomic reputation rivals that of Paris, and though traditional meals in homegrown restaurants are rarely cheap, there is great-value food to be had in many of the **bars**. The bars themselves are sumptuous, basic, traditional or trendy, and one of the capital's real pleasures.

As the capital of a country where the cost of living is high, prices in Brussels are no joke. But although it's no place to get gripped by a consumer frenzy,

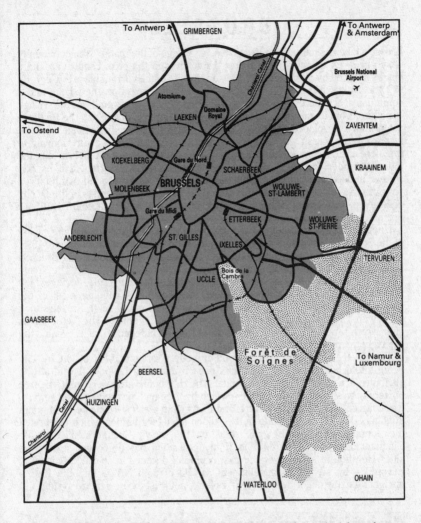

numerous antique and contemporary art galleries, some wonderful markets, a host of chocolatiers and shops devoted solely to comic books, make **window-shopping** a joy.

The capital is also a feasible base for a number of attractions in **the countryside around**, and – not least because Belgium is such a small country – even further afield. Close by, and accessible on public transport from central Brussels, are the battlefield of **Waterloo** and the intriguing **Museum of Central Africa at Tervuren**. You might also consider trips further afield, to **Leuven**, or even Ghent or Mechelen – all of which can be easily seen in a day out from the capital.

BRUSSELS

Brussels takes its name from Broekzele, or "village of the marsh", the community which grew up on the wide, shallow Senne river in the sixth century around a chapel founded by Saint Géry, roughly on the site of the current place St Géry. By 979 the Dukes of Lower Lotharingia had built a fortress on the island, and a community of soldiers and merchants soon grew up around it, the village benefiting from its position on the trade route between Cologne and the (in those days) more developed towns of Bruges and Ghent. As the village's wealth increased, the marsh was drained and houses were built, the centre moving to the more easily defended hill where the Upper Town now stands. Before long the town fell under the control of the Dukes of Brabant, who granted it its first charter in 1229 and controlled things here, on and off, for around two hundred years. In the early fifteenth century, marriage merged the interests of the Duchy of Brabant with that of Burgundy, which in turn fell under Hapsburg and later Spanish rule.

Under the Spanish, the town flourished and grew, eventually becoming capital of the Spanish Netherlands and enjoying a period of comparative calm until 1695, when Louis XIV, keen to incorporate the area into France, bombarded Brussels for 36 hours, leaving it decimated, especially around the Grand Place. The Treaty of Utrecht in 1713 left what is now Belgium under Hapsburg rule, during which time the city once again enjoyed peace, the Hapsburgs building most of the monumental buildings of the Upper Town. From 1815 until 1830, Brussels took turns with The Hague as capital of the new United Kingdom of The Netherlands, after which time, with the establishment of Belgian independence, it became the capital of the new Belgian state.

The nineteenth century was a period of modernisation and expansion, the city being kitted out under Burgomaster Anspach and King Leopold II with all the attributes of a modern European capital. The ring boulevards were built; the free university was founded; the Senne – which by then had become an open sewer – was covered over in the city centre; and many slum areas were cleared and grand buildings erected, culminating in the golden jubilee exhibition which celebrated the founding of the Belgian state in the newly inaugurated Parc de Cinquantanaire. Since World War II modernisation has proceeded apace, the city's elevation in status over the past couple of decades to so-called "capital of Europe" – by way of its appointment as HQ of both NATO and the EEC – instigating many major development projects, not least the new metro system.

Arrival, information and getting around

Brussels has three main **railway stations** – Gare Centrale, Gare du Nord and Gare du Midi, each a few minutes apart – and most national and international trains stop at all three. A notable exception is the train from Milan via Switzerland, which stops only at Midi and Nord. **Gare Centrale** is, as its name suggests, the most central of the three, a five- to ten-minute walk from the Grand Place; **Gare du Nord** lies in a sleazy red-light district just north of the main ring road, and **Gare du Midi** in a depressed immigrant area to the south of the city centre. The stations are linked across the city centre by underground tram and railway. Line #3 (green) connects Gare du Nord and Gare du Midi; to reach Gare Centrale from either station take Line 3 and change to Line 1 (red) at de Brouckère (direction Stokkel or Veeweyde). If you're heading straight to the Grand Place from Nord or Midi, take Line #3 to Bourse – a couple of minutes' walk from the Grand Place. Solo women arriving late at night at either Nord or Midi would be wise to take a taxi to their hotel or hostel.

Arriving by **coach** from the UK, *Hoverspeed* coaches drop you at place de la Bourse,. *Eurolines* at place de Brouckère. Belgium's comprehensive rail network means that it's unlikely that you'll arrive in the city by long-distance domestic bus, but if you do, Gare du Nord is the main terminal.

Coming by air, you'll land at **National Airport** in Zaventem, 12km northeast of the city centre. There's a tourist information desk in the arrivals hall, open throughout the year (Mon–Fri 8am–9pm; Sat & Sun 8am–8pm; ☎722 30 00) which has information on accommodation and transport, sells tickets for the metro/bus/tram network and can make hotel reservations in Brussels (or indeed anywhere else in Belgium). The service is free – you just pay a percentage of the room rate upfront. There is also a branch of *Acotra* (open daily 7am–11pm; ☎720 35 47), which will book you a bed or room in a hostel. There are exchange bureaux open from 7am to 9pm and from 7am to 10pm daily.

From the airport, trains run every 20 to 30 minutes to the Gare du Nord and the Gare Centrale, with one train an hour going on to Midi. The journey time to Gare Centrale is about 17 minutes; the cost is F70 one-way and tickets can be bought from the train information kiosk (daily 6.40am–10pm) before you go through customs, or from the ticket office in the station. The trains run until around 11.45pm; after that you'll need to take a taxi into the city centre – reckon on paying upwards of F1000 for the trip.

Information

Aside from the office at the airport, there are two **tourist information offices** in Brussels, both located in the centre of town.

The main one, the **TIB** (Tourist Information Brussels) in the Hôtel de Ville on the Grand Place (June–Sept daily 9am–6pm; Oct–April Mon–Sat 9am–6pm; ☎513 89 40), handles information on the city only. It has various bumph, free public transport maps, can sell you a city guide with a map and make hotel reservations. The map is adequate for the city centre, but if you want to explore areas outside the ring, it's advisable to get the *Falkplan* map of the city, which includes a street directory, before leaving Britain. The TIB also has a theatre and concert booking office, open daily between 11am and 5pm, which charges a F25 booking fee.

The **National Tourist Office**, nearby at rue Marche aux Herbes 61 (June–Sept Mon–Fri 9am–8pm, Sat & Sun 9am–7pm; rest of the year Mon–Fri 9am–6pm, Sun 1pm–5pm, closed Sat; ☎513 30 30), has information on the whole of Belgium and will also make hotel reservations. The *Acotra* office at 51 Rue de la Madeleine 9 (Mon–Fri 10am–6pm, Sat 10am–1pm; ☎512 85 07/512 55 40) will book accommodation in youth hostels. The best English-language source of **what's on listings** is the weekly magazine *The Bulletin* (F70); the weekly pull-out in the newspaper *Le Soir* is also useful – it comes out every Thursday, but is available throughout the week at TIB.

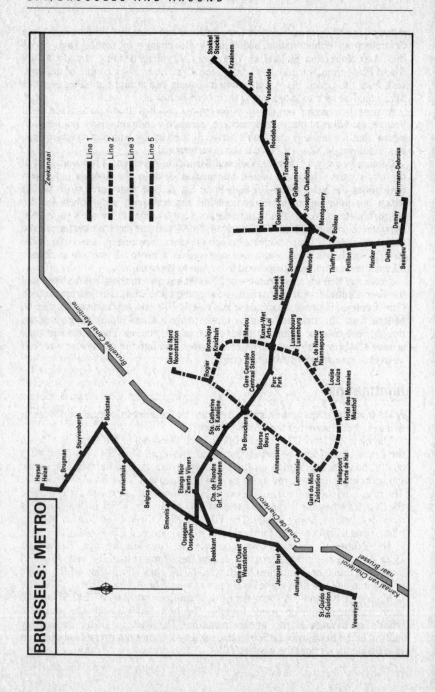

BRUSSELS: METRO

Line 1
Line 2
Line 3
Line 5

Zeekanaal

Bruxelles Canal Maritime

Stokkel
Stockel
Kraainem
Alma
Vandervelde
Roodebeek
Tomberg
Gribaumont
Joseph-Charlotte
Montgomery
Boileau
Hermann-Debroux
Demey
Beaulieu
Delta
Hankar
Pétillon
Thieffry
Merode
Schuman
Maalbeek
Maalbeek
Georges-Henri
Diamant

Medou
Kunst-Wet
Arts-Loi
Luxembourg
Luxemburg
Pte. de Namur
Naamsepoort
Louise
Louiza
Hotel des Monnaies
Munthof
Hallepoort
Porte de Hal
Gare du Midi
Zuidstation
Lemonnier
Anneessens
Bourse
Beurs
De Brouckere
Ste. Catherine
St. Katelijne
Rogier
Botanique
Kruidtuin
Gare du Nord
Noordstation
Gare Centrale
Centraal Station
Parc
Park

Etangs Noir
Zwarte Vijvers
Cte. de Flandre
Grf. V. Vlaanderen

Bockstael
Stuyvenbergh
Brugman
Heysel
Heizel
Pannenhuis
Belgica
Simonis
Ossegem
Osseghem
Beekkant
Gare de l'Ouest
Weststation
Jacques Brel
Aumale
St-Guido
St-Guidon
Veeweyde

Canal de Charleroi
Kanaal van Charleroi
naar Brussel

Getting around the city

To get around the city centre, within the ring of boulevards, the easiest thing to do is **walk**: you'll end up seeing more and appreciating the transition between the different neighbourhoods. To get from one side of the centre to the other, or to reach some of the more widely dispersed attractions, you'll need to use **public transport**. Operated by *STIB* (☎515 30 64), the urban system runs on a mixture of bus, tram and metro lines and covers the city comprehensively. It's a user-friendly network, with the times of arrival and all stopping-points displayed on metro platforms and at bus and tram stops. The metro system consists of two underground train lines: Line 1 (red) running west–east through the centre, and splitting into two branches at either end, and Line 2 (orange) circling the centre. There are also two underground tram, or "pre-metro" lines, of which Line 3 (green) is the most useful, running from the Gare du Nord, through de Brouckère and Bourse, to the Gare du Midi.

Tickets are cheap by any standards. A single ticket costs F35, a strip of five F155, and a strip of ten F220, available either from tram or bus drivers or from metro kiosks; you can also buy the multi-journey strips from the tourist office, metro kiosks and selected newsstands. Single tickets can also be obtained from automatic machines at most stations. A go-as-you-please *carte*, for F140, allows for 24 hours of travel on public transport. You're relied upon to stamp tickets yourself in the machines provided, after which it is valid for an hour, during which you can get on and off as many trams, metros and buses as you wish. The system is wide open to abuse, as once your ticket has been validated you are free to pass through barriers at metro stations and to get on buses and trams without showing the ticket. Spot fines, however, are heavy – F1000, or double that if you don't have it on you. Finally, remember that doors on metros and some trams and buses have to be opened manually. **Route maps** are available free from the tourist office and from information kiosks at Porte de Namur, Rogier and Midi metro stations. Services run from 6am until midnight, after which there's a very sporadic **night bus** service – often just one between midnight and around 3am. Women on their own should avoid the metro late at night, especially around Midi and Nord.

Taxis don't cruise the city but can be picked up from the ranks spread around the city – notably on Bourse, Brouckère, Grand Sablon and Porte de Namur, at the railway stations and outside swanky hotels. Prices are on a par with London. When you can't find one, phone ☎511 22 44 or ☎513 62 00.

In addition to the STIB network are **local trains**, run by Belgian railways, which connect different parts of the inner city and the outskirts, though unless you're living and working in the city, you're unlikely to need to use them. Supplementing these are the **SNCV buses** (☎526 28 28) which run (mainly) from the Gare du Nord and Place Rouppe (just off boulevard Lemonnier) to the suburbs of greater Brussels. A few run to other Belgian cities but they can take up to four times longer than the train. They are all listed on the back of the route map.

Guided tours

If you're only around for a short while or just want to get your bearings, it might be a good idea to take an **organised tour**. There are, of course, the regular 2–3 hour **coach tours** in a variety of languages which take in all the sights but give little opportunity to see anything. These cost around F600 per person and are run by *De Boeck*, rue de la Colline 8 (☎513 77 44) and *Panorama Tours*, rue Marché aux Herbes 105 (☎513 61 54). TIB also run a *Sightseeing Line*, where you are driven around the city by minibus, listening on headphones to a commentary in your own language.

Less conventionally, a company known as *Chatterbus* (☎673 18 35) offer options of **walking tours** of central Brussels and **bus tours of the less obvious sights**, together with **beer-tasting evenings**. Another organisation, *ARAU* (Atelier de recherches et d'Actions Urbaines), rue Henri Maus 37, next to the Bourse (☎513 47 61), an architectural action group, also runs good introductions to the city, taking in its **architectural specialities** (such as Art Nouveau) or the more undiscovered architectural attractions. Sadly, the commentary is usually only in French. Most of these tours are scheduled from March through November, although *Chatterbus* conducts its beer-tasting nights sporadically throughout the winter; booking in advance is normally essential. As an example, tours of the city's Art Nouveau houses, including the interiors of five of the best ones, currently run between March and November on the second Saturday of the month, and also on Mondays in July and August. Saturday tours leave at 9.45am, and Monday tours at 5.45pm from the Bourse post office, and cost F500. They also run a tour of the city's Art Deco buildings between March and November at 9.45am on the third Saturday of the month.

> The Brussels area telephone code is ☎02

Finding a place to stay

Brussels has no shortage of **places to stay,** but given the number of people passing through the city, finding a room can be hard, particularly in spring and summer – to be sure of a bed, it's best to book at least your first night. The tourist offices in the Grand Place and on rue Marché aux Herbes can provide a list of hotels and book hotel rooms, taking a percentage of the room rate as a (refundable) deposit. The *Acotra* office rue de la Madeleine 51 (☎512 85 07/512 55 40) will book rooms in youth hostels for free, though again you'd be better off doing it yourself well in advance.

Hostels

Jacques Brel, rue de la Sablonnière 30 (☎ 218 01 87). An official IYHF hostel – modern, comfortable and with a hotel-like atmosphere. Facilities include showers in every room, bar, restaurant and meeting room. Beds in 6–12 bed dorms F340, triples or quads F385, doubles F460, singles F560. No access to rooms between 10am and 3pm; 1am curfew. Prices include breakfast, sheets can be hired for F100; temporary membership of the IYHF costs F80. Metro stops Madou, Botanique.

Bruegel, just behind Notre Dame de la Chapelle at rue de St Esprit 2 (☎511 04 36). The other official IYHF hostel, also in a new building, and with identical prices to the Brel, though with the disadvantage of shared showers. It is, however, more central – close to the Sablon, the Musée des Beaux Arts and the Upper Town. Bus #20 from Midi or bus #48 from Porte de Halle.

CHAB (Centre de'Hébergement de l'Agglomeration de Bruxelles), rue Traversiere 8 (☎217 01 58). A rambling, spacious hostel with a good reputation and slightly lower prices than the official youth hostels, though it can seem chaotic. Bike-hire F150 a day (F1000 deposit), left luggage lockers and laundry facilities. Sinks in all rooms, but shared showers and toilets.

Meals are basic, but there's a reasonably priced restaurant across the road. Sleep-in beds (own sleeping bag obligatory) cost F240, dorm beds F290, triples or quads F370, doubles F440, singles F540. All prices include breakfast. Sheet hire F70. Open until 2am, rooms closed 10am–3pm. Metro Botanique.

Maison Internationale, chaussèe de Wavre 205 (☎648 97 87). An unofficial hostel, and for cleanliness, privacy and conscientious management, the best value-for-money in Brussels. Singles F340 per person, doubles F290 (sheets F60 extra). There are no dormitories; showers and toilets are shared, but there are sinks in every room. Handy for the chaussèe d'Ixelles shopping district.

Sleep Well, rue de la Blanchisserie 27 (☎218 50 50). Cheap and conveniently located off rue Neuve, with summer prices ranging from F280 in a dorm to F430 for a single. Be warned, however – it tends to be crowded and sometimes dirty during the height of the summer season. Metro Rogier.

Hotels

Albert Premier place Rogier 20 (☎217 21 25). Fairly recently renovated hotel, which has doubles with bath for F3000.

Bosquet, rue Bosquet 70 (☎538 52 30). Spick and span hotel with doubles for upwards of about F1000, including breakfast. Metro Hotel des Monnaies.

De Boeck's, rue Veydt 40 (☎537 40 33). In a pretty neighbourhood close to Avenue Louise. Pleasant rooms for between F1900 and F2500 for a double with toilet, sink and shower. Breakfast included. Metro Louise.

De L'Yser, 9–13 rue d'Edimbourg (☎511 74 59). Large hotel with clean, if basic rooms, in the Zairean quarter just off chausée de Wavre. Doubles without shower F1000, with shower F1250. Triples without shower F1315, with shower F1475. Breakfast not included.

Derby, avenue de Tervuren 24 (☎733 08 19). On the edge of the Parc du Cinquantenaire, with large, somewhat run-down rooms (all have shower or bath). Doubles with bath F1650–1800. Metro stop Merode.

George V, rue 't Kint 23 (☎513 50 93). A ramshackle period hotel in a quiet neighbourhood a five-minute walk to the west of Bourse. Prices are set to rise after August 1990, but until then doubles without bath cost around F1000, with bath for F1200–1750. Breakfast included. Metro Bourse.

Hotel du Congrès rue du Congrès 42/44 (☎217 18 90) Shabby, but within walking distance of the main business and tourist areas, and used by the European Commission for their visiting guests. Doubles without bath F1275, with bath F1450–F1580. Breakfast included. Metro Madou.

Madou and 't **Zilveren Tasje**, rue du Congrès 45 and 48 (☎218 83 75/217 32 74). Two fin-de-siècle hotels under the same management. Rooms vary from the simple to the scruffily splendid, and all have shower and toilet. Doubles cost F1250–1350. Breakfast F120. Book well ahead. Metro Madou.

Osborne Residence, 67 rue Bosquet (☎537 92 51). A hotch-potch of rooms in an 1860s town house just off avenue Toison d'Or, a short walk from Avenue Louise. Doubles without shower for around F1000, with shower F1400. Breakfast included. Two minutes' walk from metro Munthof.

Pension des Eperonniers, rue des Eperonniers 1 and 28–30 (☎513 53 66). A simple, clean hotel conveniently located between Gare Centrale and the Grand Place. The main hotel is above a bakery, but there is an annexe further up the street, in a converted hospital. Doubles without bath F1300–1500, with bath F1400–1700. Breakfast, which is included, is provided by the bakery. Metro or train to Gare Centrale.

Sabina, rue du Nord 78 (☎218 26 37). Spruce, pretty rooms, in a wonderful turn-of-the-century house with a beamed and panelled breakfast room. Prices are surprisingly low: doubles without bath F1030, with bath F1150–1400. A two-minute walk from metro Madou, in a relatively safe, commercial district of town.

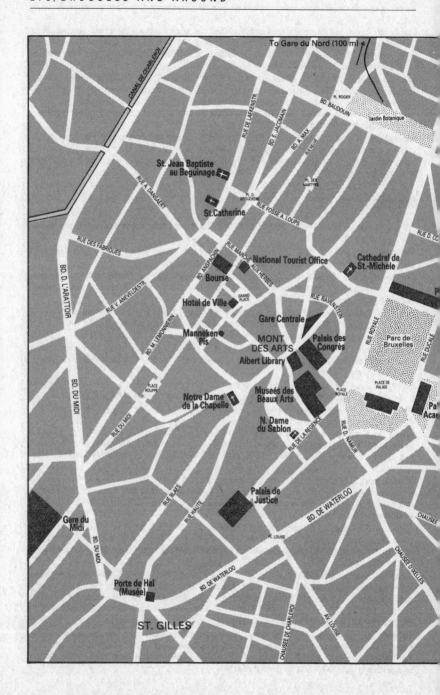

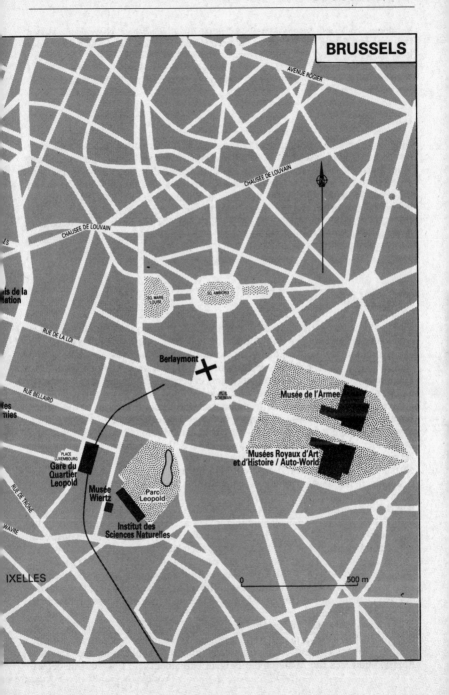

BRUSSELS

AVENUE ROGIER

CHAUSEE DE LOUVAIN

CHAUSEE DE LOUVAIN

ES

is de la
ation

RUE DE LA LOI

SQ. MARIE
LOUISE

SQ. AMBIORIX

Berlaymont

RUE
SCHUMAN

RUE BELLIARD

Musée de l'Armee

les
nies

PLACE
LUXEMBOURG

Gare du
Quartier
Leopold

Musées Royaux d'Art
et d'Histoire / Auto-World

RUE DE TRONE

Musée
Wiertz

Parc
Leopold

WAVRE

Institut des
Sciences Naturelles

IXELLES

0   500 m

Vendôme, boulevard Adophe Max 98 (☎218 00 70). A smart hotel conveniently located between place Rogier and Brouckère, with comfortable rooms, some of which have fridge bars. Good place to stay if you want to pamper yourself. Doubles F2575–3175.

Windsor, place Rouppe 13 (☎511 20 14). Strikingly clean and cheerful rooms for as low as F1220 for a single without bath, up to F2450 for a double with bath. Breakfast included. Metro Anneessens.

Camping

Although there are a number of **campsites** in the Greater Brussels area, only two make feasible bases for the city. One, the *Grimbergen*, is near the Atomium at Veldkantstraat 46 in Grimbergen (☎269 25 97/269 79 28). Take bus G from Gare du Nord to the terminus, after which it's roughly a ten-minute walk. The other, the *Paul Rosmant*, is east of the city, at Warandenberg 52 (☎782 10 09) in Wezembeek–Oppem. To get there, take the metro to Kraainem (Line 1B) and from there bus #30 to place St Pierre. Failing that, it's not much more difficult, or time-consuming, to escape the sway of the big city, and to go further afield, to Leuven, Villers-la-Ville or one of the smaller towns in Flanders or Antwerp province. See the appropriate chapters for details.

The City

The centre of Brussels sits neatly within the rough pentagon of boulevards that enclose it, a "petit ring" which follows the course of the fourteenth-century city walls, running from place Rogier in the north round to porte de Halle in the south. The city centre divides in turn into the **Upper and Lower Towns**, the neighbourhoods generally becoming more expensive the higher you go. By far the greater part of the city centre is occupied by the **Lower Town**, which is slung between rue Royale in the east (running from the Jardin Botanique to the Palace Royale), and the north–south central boulevard – slicing though the city from Place Rogier to the Gare du Midi – variously named Adolphe Max, Anspach and Lemonnier. Just east of this main thoroughfare, the medieval core of Brussels zeroes in on the Grand Place – the unquestionable centre of Brussels and perhaps the finest preserved city square in Europe, a focus for both tourists and residents. In the Lower Town, keep your position in relation to the Grand Place in mind and you won't go far wrong. South of the Grand Place the busy centre fades into the old working-class streets of the Marolles district and Gare du Midi – now a depressed, and predominantly immigrant, area. To the north is the rather tacky rue Neuve, a pedestrianised highstreet that's home to Brussels' mainstream shops and department stores, leading up to the place Rogier and the tawdry area around the Gare du Nord. It's here that a rather sad Red Light district lurks, spilling into the side streets off Adolphe Max, where neon signs advertise peep shows and "sexy girls". West of these streets, however, is an appealingly workaday district, centring on the church of St Catherine, with many fish restaurants along the (now dry) docks.

The *haute de la ville*, or **Upper Town**, is quite different in feel from the rest of the city centre, a self-consciously planned, more monumental quarter, with statuesque buildings lining wide, classically imposed boulevards and squares. Appropriately, it's the home of the Belgian parliament and government departments, some of the major museums, the swishest shops (around place Louise), and the massive Palais de Justice, which lords it over the rest of the city, commanding views that on clear days reach as far as the Atomium and the park at Laeken, way north of the city centre.

There's much of interest, too, in the **outer boroughs** that radiate from the **petit ring**. From the Palais de Justice, avenue Louise stretches southeast, a fashionable strand that leads into the **St Gilles** neighbourhood, and the concentration of houses of the Art Nouveau architect, Victor Horta. There is more Art Nouveau, a good art gallery, and some excellent bars and shops in the adjacent quarter, **Ixelles**, leading down to the city's most popular park, the Bois de la Cambre, and the bucolic expanses of the Forêt de Soignes. North of Ixelles, **Etterbeek** is home to the EC and European Parliament buildings, and the rather dull Parc de Cinquantenaire. **St Josse**, beyond, is home to the city's Turkish community, and somewhere you're most likely to go at night to eat. North of the centre, there's **Laeken**, city residence of the Belgian royal family but visited more for the Atomium, a rather monstrous leftover from the 1958 World's Fair; west lies the suburb of **Anderlecht** – with its famous football team, the fascinating Gueuze brewery, and the Erasmus house.

The Lower Town

The **LOWER TOWN** is the commercial heart of Brussels, a bustling quarter that's home to the major shops, hotels and restaurants. The Grand Place is the centre, though its modern-day rival, place de Brouckère, a little way north, also serves as a major focus, as do the nearby place de la Monnaie and the seedy place Rogier on the edge of the ring road.

The Grand Place

The obvious place to begin any tour of Brussels is the **Grand Place**, where the magnificently gilded facades of Baroque guildhouses and the elaborate Gothic Hôtel de Ville create a splendid arena for gawping tourists and gin and tonic slugging businessmen. In the pavement cafés, and in the maze of narrow cobbled streets to the north of the square, you'll hear more British, American and German spoken than French or Flemish, and the whole area is almost overwhelmingly geared to tourists and expats. That said, the square is stunning, and there's no better place to get a taste of Brussels' past – and its Eurocapital present.

For centuries the Grand Place was the town's main market place. Now there's just a small daily flower market and a rather mournful caged bird market on Sunday mornings. Originally an area of marsh, it was drained in the twelfth century, and in the thirteenth century covered markets for bread, meat and cloth were erected. Evidence that the market developed beyond the boundaries of the square is obvious from the names of the narrow streets that tangle around it, rues du Beurre, des Bouchers, Marché aux Herbes, Poulets, and Fromages all combining to evoke an image of medieval bustle. On the square itself, the city's merchant guilds built themselves headquarters, cementing the Grand Place's role as commercial hub of the city.

In the fifteenth century, with the building of the splendid Gothic town hall, the square took on a civic and political function as well, with the ruling Dukes descending from their Upper Town residences to meet the people or show off in tournaments. Official decrees and pronouncements were read here, and public executions took place. The majority of those executed were Protestants, rebelling at the oppressive Catholic regime of Philip II, who in 1567 sent the Duke of Alva and an army of 12,000 to quash the dissenters. Thousands fled from the town, and a period of severe famine ensued, during which a contemporary source described "the poor wrestling with the dogs for the blood and entrails of slaughtered cows and sheep".

Of the square's medieval buildings only the Hôtel de Ville and one guildhouse survive, due to a 36-hour bombardment of the city by the French in 1695, which destroyed 4000 houses and virtually the whole of the Grand Place. Unperturbed, the city's guildsmen swiftly had their headquarters rebuilt, adopting a distinctive and flamboyant Baroque style, making the square fancier and more imposing than ever. The **Hôtel de Ville** still dominates the proceedings, its splendour little diminished by the scaffolding that currently encases the elegant 330-foot spire. You'll probably be content to take in the intricacies of its pinnacle-and-statue encrusted facade from a pavement café, but if you're interested to see inside there are guided tours (Tues–Fri 9.30am–5pm; Sun & hols 10am–4pm; closed Sat and election days; F50). These take in various official rooms, most dazzling of which is the sixteenth-century council chamber, decorated with gilt moulding, faded tapestries and an oak floor inlaid with ebony. On a more contemporary note, take a look at the electronic interpreting system, installed to facilitate discussion between French and Flemish speaking councillors. You'll also see the Gallery of the Spanish Kings, with its amazingly sharp and clear full-length portraits, painted between 1715 and 1718 after the monarchs were all dead.

But the the real glory of the Grand Place lies in the **guildhouses**, their slender, gilded facades swirling with exuberant, self-publicising carving and sculpture, pompously promoting the aims and practices of the guildsmen. Each house has a name, usually derived from one of the statues, symbols or architectural quirks decorating its facade. Some of the most spectacular line the western side of the square. At no. 7, the **Maison du Renard** was the house of the haberdashers' guild: on the ground floor cute cherubs in bas relief play at haberdashery, while a gilded fox, after which the house is named, squats above the door; up on the second storey a statue of Justice flanked by statues symbolising the four continents suggests the guild's designs on world markets – an aim to which Saint Nicholas, patron saint of merchants, glinting above, clearly gives his blessing. Next door, at no.6, is the **Maison du Cornet**, headquarters of the boatsman's guild, a fanciful creation of 1697 whose top storey resembles the stern of a ship. Adjoining it, the **Maison de la Louve** is one of the few guildhouses to have survived the French bombardment, its elegant pilastered facade fronting the former home of the Archers' guild, studded with pious representations of concepts like Peace and Discord, together with a pediment relief of Apollo firing at a python. The three lower storeys of the **Maison de Sac**, next door, also escaped; the headquarters of the joiners and coopers, the upper storeys were appropriately designed by a cabinet-maker, and feature pilasters and caryatids which resemble the ornate legs of Baroque furniture. At the end of the row is the **Roi d'Espagne**, headquarters of the guild of bakers and now housing the most famous of the square's bars. The house is named after the bust of Charles V on the facade, flanked by a Moorish and Indian prisoner, symbolising his mastery of a vast empire. Balanced on the balustrade are allegorical statues of Energy, Fire, Water, Wind, Wheat and Prudence, presumably meant to represent the qualities necessary for baking the ideal loaf.

Most of the northern side of the Place is taken up by the sturdy neo-Gothic **Maison du Roi**, a reconstruction of a sixteenth-century Gothic building commissioned by Charles V. It now houses the **Musée de la Ville de Bruxelles** (Mon, Tues, Wed, Fri 10am–12.30pm & 1.30–4pm; Thurs 10am–4pm; Sat & Sun 10am–1pm; F80) which painlessly summarises the history of Brussels. On the ground floor are sculptural fragments from the Hôtel de Ville, and Pieter Bruegel's *Wedding Procession*, but it's the first floor which is most interesting, with maps and 3D models of the city at various points in its development. The second floor houses the Manneken Pis's vast wardrobe, 400 sickeningly saccharine costumes ranging from Mickey Mouse to a maharaja, all of them gifts from various visiting dignitaries.

Just beyond the Maison du Roi is **Le Pigeon** (no.26), where Victor Hugo lived during his exile from France; he was expelled for his support of the French insurrection of 1848. On the opposite side of the square, **Le Cygne** (no.9), once housed a bar where an equally famous exile, Karl Marx, would meet up with Engels. It was in Brussels in February 1848 that they wrote the Communist Manifesto, only to be deported as political undesirables the following month. Appropriately enough, the Belgian Labour Party was founded here in 1885, though ironically the building now shelters one of the city's most exclusive restaurants. Next door, the **Maison des Brasseurs** (no.10) is the only house still to be owned by its original guild – the Brewers' – and it houses a small **Brewery Museum** (Mon–Fri 10am–noon & 2–5pm; Sat 10am–noon, April–Oct; F50) in the cellar. Here you can sit over a free beer, look at various ancient bits of brewing paraphernalia, and listen to a self-congratulatory commentary in which beer figures as a health-giving, friendship-promoting panacea for the world's problems. On the other side of Le Cygne is the **Maison d'Etoile**, a nineteenth-century rebuilding of the medieval home of the city magistrate. In rue Charles Buls, around the corner, the exploits of one Everard 't Serclaes are commemorated: in 1356 the francophile Count of Flandre attempted to seize power from the Duke of Brabant, occupied the magistrate's house and flew his standard from the roof. 't Serclaes scaled the building, replaced Flandre's standard with that of the Duke of Brabant, and went on to lead the recapturing of the city, events represented in bas relief above a reclining statue of 't Serclaes. His arm is polished smooth from the long-standing superstition that good luck will come to those who stroke it.

Around the Grand Place

Rue Charles Buls takes you to rue des Brasseurs, scene of a bizarre incident in 1873 when the French Symbolist poet Paul Verlaine shot his fellow poet and lover Arthur Rimbaud, earning himself a six-month prison sentence. There's still a slightly offbeat feel to the quarter, totally at odds with the respectable tourism of the Grand Place, with gutsy bars and cheap Greek eateries running up to rue des Eperonniers and the Galerie Agora, both of which are good hunting-grounds for second-hand and alternative clothes.

Rue de la Violette, in contrast, leads down to two of the city's most hyped tourist attractions. The **Musée de Costume et de la Dentelle**, at rue de la Violette 6, is undergoing restoration at present, and only opens for occasional exhibitions. It's due to close completely for a period at the end of 1990. When it does reopen it should be worth a visit, for it holds fine examples of antique and contemporary lace. Lace became an important local product in the seventeenth century, and by

CENTRAL BRUSSELS

Gare du Nord
Jardin Botanique
PORTE DE SCHAERBEEK
RUE DE L'ENSEIGNEMENT
RUE D. CONGRÈS
Palais de la Nation
RUE DE LA LOI
BD. DU JARDIN BOTANIQUE
BD. PACHECO
City Council Buildings
Colonne du Congrès
RUE DES COLONIES
Cathedral St. Michele
PL. CH. ROGER
City 2
Rogier ★
RUE DE LA BLANCHISSERIE
RUE DU MARAIS
BD. DE BERLAIMONT
RUE DES COMEDIENS
Gare Centrale
IMPERATRICE
Notre Dame de Finistere
RUE NEUVE
BD. ADOLPHE MAX
BLD. EMILE JACQMAIN
PL. DES MARTYRS
RUE DES HERBES POTAGÈRES
RUE MONT AUX HERBES POTAGÈRES
RUE D'ARGENT
RUE DE L'ÉCUYER
Théâtre de la Monnaie
RUE DE LA MONTAGNE
Agora
Musée Communal
RUE DE LAKEN
RUE DU FOSSÉ-AUX-LOUPS
PL. DE BROUCKÈRE
RUE DU FOSSÉ AUX LOUPS
PL. DE LA MONNAIE
RUE DE L'ÉVÊQUE
Centre Monnaie
RUE DE LA FOURCHE
RUE DES BOUCHERS
RUE DU MARCHÉ AUX HERBES
AU BEURRE
Tourist Office
GRAND PLACE
Hôtel de
Musée Communal
St.-Jean Baptiste au Beguinage
BOULEVARD BAUDOUIN
BOULEVARD D'ANVERS
RUE DU CANAL
RUE DU GRAND-HOSPICE
De Broeckère ★
BOULEVARD ANSPACHLAAN
RUE DES FRIPIERS
RUE DES PIERRES
RUE AUX POULETS
St. Nikolas
Bourse ★
Bourse ★
RUE DU MIDI
QUAI AU BOIS À BRÛLER ★
QUAI AUX BRIQUES
Ste. Catherine ★
St.-Catherine
R. ST.-CATHERINE RUE DU MARCHÉ AUX PORCS
RUE DES RICHES CLAIRES
BOULEVARD D'YPRES
RUE DE FLANDRE
RUE ANTOINE DANSAERT
RUE DES CHARTREUX
RUE VAN ARTEVELDE
CANAL DE CHARLEROY
BD. BARTHELEMY
Graaf V. Vilanderen ★
CANAL DE CHARLEROI
BD. BARTHELEMY
RUE DES FABRIQUES
BD. DE L'ABATTOIR

250 m

0

RUE ROYALE

DU RÉGENT

Palais des
Acadamies

Luxembourg ★

Parc de
Bruxelles

BOULEVARD

★ Pte. de Namur

CHAUSEE D'IXELLES

Palais des
Beaux Arts

RAVENSTEIN

Palais des
Congrès

P. ROYALE

Palais Royal

RUE DU PEPIN

Palais
d'Egmont

RUE DE STASSART

MONT
DES ARTS

RUE LEBEAU

Gare Centrale

BD. DE L'EMPEREUR

RUE
ALBERT

P. DE
L'ALBERTINE

Musée des
Beaux Mrts

RUE DE LA REGENCE

RUE DU
GRAND SABLON

P. DU
GRAND SABLON

Notre Dame
du Sablon

Musée
Instrumental

BOULEVARD DE WATERLOO

R. LOUISE

★ Pl. Louise

AVENUE LOUISE

P. STEPHANIE

Albert Library

RUE POLLAERT

Palais de
Justice

LA VIOLETTE

Notre Dame
de la Chapelle

RUE DE LÉTOILE

RUE DU CHÊNE

Manneken
Pis

R. LOMBARD

Bruegel
Youth Hostel

RUE HAUTE

RUE BLAES

RUE DES BRIGITTINES

RUE DES URSULINES

RUE ST-GHISLAIN

RUE DU POINÇON

QUARTIER

RUE DES RENARDS

MAROLLES

RUE DES BOGARDS

RUE DU MIDI

PL. FONTAINAS

PL. ROUPPE

RUE TERRE NEUVE

AVENUE DE STALINGRAD

PAS.
DU JEU DE
BALLE

RUE DE LA RASIERE

PORTE DE HAL

Anneessens ★

BOULEVARD M. LEMONNIER

RUE DES FOULONS

BD. Lemonnier

BD. DU MIDI ZUIDLAAN

Gare du Midi

the eighteenth century, when the industry reached its peak, the city had reputedly 10,000 lacemakers, all of them women. The lace made here was renowned for the intricacy of the designs, and was in demand worldwide, bought by the rich to embellish their clothes. Nowadays lace is still made in Brussels, though on a much smaller scale, and it's still very expensive – especially from any of the shops around the Grand Place.

At the foot of rue de la Violette, rue de l'Etuve runs along to the **Manneken Pis**, a diminutive statue of a little boy pissing – normally concealed behind hoards of camera-clicking tourists – that's supposed to embody the "irreverent spirit" of the city (or so visitors are told). Jerome Duquesnoy cast the original statue in the 1600s, but it was stolen several times, notably by a French convict in 1817, who broke it into pieces. The thief and the smashed Mannekin were apprehended, the former publicly branded on the Grand Place and sentenced to a life of forced labour, while the fragments were used to create the mould in which the present-day Manneken was cast. It is kitsch culture at its most extreme, and you wouldn't be missing much if you bypassed it altogether.

North of the Grand Place, the quarter hinging on **rue des Bouchers** is the city centre's restaurant ghetto, the narrow cobbled streets transformed at night into fairy-lit tunnels where restaurants vie for custom with elaborate displays of dull-eyed fish and glistening seafood. There's a feverish atmosphere here, of hard-selling and high-spending, as buskers and street vendors attempt to distract Amex-armed tourists and expense-account businesspeople from the serious task of selecting an eatery. Although it's worth seeing what Brussels' role as Euro-capital has done for the city centre, you're unlikely to want to hang around for long.

Things are slightly more subdued in the nearby **Galeries St Hubert**, bisected by rue des Bouchers – one of Europe's first shopping arcades. It consists of three glass-vaulted galleries – du Roi, de la Reine and des Princes – which, with their refined shops, exclusive restaurants and cafés, a theatre and cinema, still retain an aura of sophistication.

The Bourse and Around

Walking out of the Grand Place along rue du Beurre, the tiny Gothic church of **St Nicholas** stands incongruously hemmed in by touristy shops. The outer shell is in fact a 1950s reconstruction, but the rarely open interior retains a fourteenth-century choir and a painting attributed to Rubens. Beyond rises the **Bourse**, the grandiose home of the city's stock exchange, a neoclassical structure of 1873 caked with fruit, fronds, languishing nudes and frolicking putti – details most effortlessly absorbed from a pavement table at the Art Nouveau *Falstaff* café alongside. **Place de la Bourse** itself is little more than an unsightly, heavily trafficked pause along Boulevard Anspach, over-endowed with familiar fast-food outlets.

The streets on the other side of the boulevard have more appeal, where **place St Géry** stands at the core of a tangle of semi-gentrified streets. The nineteenth-century covered market on the square has been recently renovated and looks set to become a mini-Covent Garden, prompting a face-lift for the rest of the area: tall terraces of decayed houses are being returned to their former glory, and the occasional designer boutique or bar is already open in anticipation of the new tenants.

For a taste of what place St Géry was like in its heyday, head north to the neighbourly bustle of **place St Catherine's** daily market. It's held outside the church of **St Catherine**, a blackened, eroded nineteenth-century replacement for a Baroque church, of which only the creamy, curvy tower remains. Pop inside if it's open, ignoring the piped muzak and digital display flashing Christ's message, to see a fourteenth-century Black Madonna, chucked into the Senne by Protestants, but fished out while floating on a fortuitous clod of peat.

The **river**, however, is no longer viewable here. By the nineteenth century it had become intolerably polluted – in the words of the Brussels' writer, Lemonnier, "the dumping ground, not only of industry, but also of the houses lining the river: it was not unusual to see the ballooned stomach of a dog mixed pêle mêle with its own litter..." After an outbreak of cholera in 1866, which killed nearly 3500 people, the river was piped underground and paved over. Some of the quays were also filled in (notably Quai aux Briques and parallel Quai aux Bois à Brûler), but, lined with small nineteenth-century buildings, they still have a bank-side feel – an impression heightened in the early morning when the streets are choked with lorries bearing loads of fish for the fish restaurants and fishmongers. It's a refreshingly workaday scene after the razz of the streets around the Grand Place. Set back from the quays is another peaceful spot, the triangular **place de Béguinage**, dominated by the supple, billowing Baroque facade of **St Jean de la Béguinage**, a church so decayed that it has a falling rocks sign pasted to its front door. The interior echoes with the flapping and cooing of pigeons, providing an eerie soundtrack as you wander along a nave studded with the chubby faces of curly headed angels to a mock-rustic pulpit resembling a grotesque tree-house.

North of the Grand Place

Further north from the Grand Place, beyond the rue des Bouchers quarter, **place de la Monnaie** is home to the **Theatre de la Monnaie**, Brussels' opera house, a neoclassical structure built in 1819 and with an interior added in 1856 to a design by Poelaert, the architect of the Palais de Justice. The square itself is otherwise uninteresting (though in summer it's a venue for live bands), its fringe of modern buildings, notably the huge sprouting **Centre Monnaie**, housing offices, shops and the main city post office. On the far side, the central boulevard Anspach opens out at **place de Brouckère**, Brussels modern centre, a busy traffic-choked junction surrounded by advertising hoardings.

From place de la Monnaie, **rue Neuve** forges north, a gaudy pedestrianised shopping street meeting the inner ring at the junction of **place Rogier**, beyond which lies the Gare du Nord and the seedy Red Light area. Stop instead, about a third of the way up rue Neuve, at **place des Martyrs**, a cool, rational square imposed on the city by the Hapsburgs that is nowadays one of its most haunting sights, a forlorn, abandoned open space, and magnet for the lonely and down-and-out – the cracks between the cobbles are encrusted with glass shards, the fountain no longer flows, and many of the windows are smashed and boarded up. The square's position over an underground shrine to the 445 rebels against Dutch rule, who died in the Belgian revolution of 1830, only adds to the desolate mood.

Beyond the square, narrow lanes trace their medieval route past soulless modernistic monoliths up to rue des Sables, where, at no.20, the city's only surviving Horta-designed department store, the **Magasins Waucquez**, has just been restored to house the **Centre Belge de la Bande Desinée** (Tues–Sun 10am–6pm; F80), devoted to the history of the Belgian comic strip. It's worth visiting for the building alone, a wonderfully airy, summery construction, with light flooding through the stained glass that surrounds the central courtyard;

even if you're not interested in comics, the *Horta Brasserie* especially, with its exposed girders and slender, silvered Corinthian columns, is attraction enough. At present the museum, which opened only in March 1990 has displays tracing the techiques and development of the comic strip until 1960. For the moment it's labelled in French and Flemish only so means little if you speak neither language, but from 1991 there will be explanations in English, and the history brought right up-to-date.

The South: the Marolles and Midi

There's little of interest along the series of dead straight boulevards that run down to the **Gare du Midi**, which is best reached direct by metro from Bourse. The area around the station is home to the city's many North African and Greek immigrants, a severely depressed and at times seedy quarter with an uneasy undertow by day and a sometimes overtly threatening one at night. There's a closed, ghettoised feel to the streets and in many of the cheap cafés and bars: the exceptions are listed under "Eating". The best time to go is on a Sunday morning, when a vibrant souk-like **market** is held under the rail arches of the station (see "Shops").

If you'd rather avoid Midi, you could instead take bus #48 from Bourse to **Notre Dame de la Chapelle**, a clumsy sprawling Gothic structure, grimed by weather and pollution and currently undergoing a much-needed restoration. The city's oldest church, built between 1210 and 1300, its main claim to fame is the tomb of Pieter Bruegel the Elder in the third chapel of the south aisle (he's supposed to have lived and died round the corner at rue Haute 132). For the time being, however, there's little to see inside, as everything save one of the transepts is boarded up.

Rue Haute and parallel rue Blaes form the double spine of the **Quartier Marolles**, stacked on the slopes below the Palais de Justice. An earthy neighbourhood of run-down housing, and cheap, basic restaurants, shops and bars, it's one of the few places in the city where you can still hear older people using the traditional dialect, "Brusselse Sproek", or "Marollien". A brand of Flemish which has, over the centuries, been influenced by the languages of the city's overlords, it is now in danger of dying out, and local people have set up an academy to preserve it, supported by such powerful figures as Jacques Delors. They propose that all newcomers to Brussels should learn 100 words of the dialect. It's a colourful, earthy language; you could make a start with *dikenek*, "big mouth", *schieve lavabo*, "idiot" (literally a twisted toilet) or *fieu* – "son of a bitch".

The Marolles neighbourhood grew up in the seventeenth century as a centre for artisans working on the nearby mansions of Sablon, and remained a thriving working-class district until the 1870s, when the paving over of the Senne led to the riverside factories closing down and moving out to the suburbs. The workers and their families followed, abandoning Marolles to the old and poor. Today, a tide of gentrification is sweeping through the district, and along rues Haute and Blaes there are dilapidated houses in the process of restoration and the occasional swanky restaurant or antique shop sprouting up alongside a basic bar or cheap clothes shop. Even at **place Jeu de Balle**, the heart of Marolles and scene of the city's best flea market (see "Shops") there's a swish enclave of arty shops and smart eateries tucked away on rue des Renards – although the market itself has so far made few concessions to fashion. Piles of rusty junk lie alongside a muddle of eccentric bric-a-brac that might range from a chipped buddha, rococo angel, or African idol, to horn-rimmed spectacles, a top hat, or a pair of antlers.

The Upper Town

The division between lower and upper town is in part a blurred one, the slopes to the **UPPER TOWN** rising only minutes from the Grand Place itself. The gentle slope is home to the city's cathedral and the so-called Mont des Arts, whose rigorous layout is little preparation for the exuberant neoclassicism along the rue Royale and rue de la Regence, which make up the Upper Town's formal spine. Though heavily trafficked, the wide avenues and grand architecture of what was once the aristocratic quarter, lend a dignified feel that's markedly different from the bustle of the lower town. It is, however, very much a part of town you visit and then leave, not very neighbourly or residential. Climb up and admire the views and the museum collections, and then descend back into the maelstrom below – or push on into the outer boroughs.

The Cathedral and lower slopes

Climbing the steep slope above rue Marché aux Herbes, rue de Montagne leads up to the city's **Cathedral** (Mon–Sat 7.30am–7pm, Sun 2–7pm), a Brabant-Gothic building which occupies a commanding position just below the topmost ridge, though sadly it's becoming jostled by modern blocks. Begun in 1220, the cathedral is dedicated jointly to Saint Michel and Saint Gudule, the patron and patroness of Brussels – though it's more often known as the church of St Gudule. It was severely damaged during the Restoration and – like so much else in the city – by the French shelling a century later. Napoleon later tentatively restored the building, and another major restoration is in progress now. Flooded with light from the clerestory windows, it's a fine church, though the present restoration means that the choir, the earliest example of the style in the Low Countries, is boarded off. There is, however, some superb sixteenth-century stained glass in the transepts – panegyrics to the Hapsburgs designed by Bernard van Orley.

South of the cathedral is the **Gare Centrale**, a bleak Art Deco creation of Victor Horta, who was also responsible for the drab **Palais des Beaux Arts** just above. A complete contrast with his flamboyant earlier works, it has only one storey to avoid blocking the monarch's view from his palace. It holds a theatre, concert hall, numerous exhibitions, and the **Musée du Cinema**, which shows old and silent movies every night from 6.15pm, and has displays on the history of film to browse around between screenings. (Full listings in *The Bulletin*.)

Beyond is the so-called **Mont des Arts**, a collection of severe geometric buildings given over to a variety of arts-related activities, instituted in 1934 as a memorial to King Albert and built in the late Fifties and early Sixties. They flank a broad flight of steps which link the upper and lower towns, emerging at the foot of rue Coudenberg, which climbs up to place Royale.

Place Royale, the Palais du Roi and the Parc de Bruxelles

Imperiously neoclassical, **place Royale** forms a fitting climax to rue Royale, the dead straight backbone of the upper town which runs all the way up to the Turkish suburb of St Josse. Ostentatious mansions built for the city's aristocrats flank the equally ostentatious church of **St Jacques Coudenberg**, a fanciful version of a Roman temple with a colourfully frescoed pediment. In the centre of the square, posing above a sea of jammed traffic, is a dashing equestrian statue of Saint Godfrey, a Belgian-born Crusader who became Jerusalem's first Christian king.

Around the corner, the **Palais du Roi** is something of an anticlimax, a sombre downbeat 1904 conversion of some eighteenth-century town houses, fronted by bored guards, unkempt hedges, and trams rattling across the cobbled place de Palais. The Belgian dynasty is relatively young, founded in 1831. The second of its five kings, Leopold II, was responsible for gracing Brussels with such pompous monuments as the Palais de Justice, the Cinquantenaire arcades, and the mock-medieval prison of Saint Gilles, partially financed by his private income from the Congo, which was his personal property. His successor, Leopold III, was one of Europe's least popular monarchs. His first wife died in a suspicious car crash, and he nearly lost his kingdom by remarrying (anathema in a Catholic country); later on, during the German occupation, he remained in the country rather than go into exile, fuelling rumours that he was a Nazi collaborator. His supporters maintained that he prevented thousands of Belgians from being deported, and in 1950, in a referendum which showed a clear French/Flemish split, the country (or rather, the French-speaking majority) voted to retain the monarchy and Leopold returned. Perhaps fortunately for Belgium, he abdicated in 1951 in favour of his son, the present King Baudouin, who hit the news in April 1990 by standing down for a day so that an abortion bill (which he as a Catholic had refused to sign) could be passed.

Although this is their official residence, the current Belgian Royals have, not surprisingly, elected to live elsewhere (in Laeken) and the palace is open to the public during August. Sumptuous rooms, and tapestries designed by Goya, make a visit worthwhile – which is more than can be said for the fancy collection of furniture, porcelain and glass of the **Hôtel Bellevue** (Sat–Thurs 10am–5pm; free) housed in the dull palace annexe. A third royal exhibition, the **Musée de la Dynastie** (Wed & Sat 2–5pm; and in Aug, Tues–Sat 11am–5pm; free), behind the palace in rue Brederode, charts the brief history of the Belgian royal family, and will thrill only ardent monarchists.

Opposite the Palais, the **Parc de Bruxelles** is the most central of the city's parks, along whose dusty, tree-shaded avenues businesspeople, civil servants and office workers stroll at lunchtime, or race to catch the metro in the evenings. Surrounded by trees with branches tortured to form continuous parallel lines, and dotted with classical statues, it's a dreary, vacuous place, and somewhere you're only likely to want to pause briefly.

Musées Royaux des Beaux Arts

Facing onto place Royale, the **MUSÉES ROYAUX DES BEAUX ARTS** comprise two museums, one displaying modern art, the other older works – the two linked by a passageway. Together they make up Belgium's most satisfying, all-round collection of fine art, with marvellous collections of work by Bruegel, Rubens and the Belgian surrealist painters.

Both galleries are large, and to do them justice you should see them in separate visits. Finding your way around the larger of the two collections, **Musée d'Art Ancien**, is made easy by following the colour-coded routes: the **blue route** takes in paintings of the fifteenth and sixteenth centuries, including Bruegel; the **brown route** concentrates primarily on paintings of the seventeenth and eighteenth centuries, with the collection of Rubens (for which the museum is internationally famous) as the highlight; the **yellow route** is devoted to nineteeth-century works, notably the paintings and sculptures of workers by the social realist Constantin Meunier. The second collection, the **Musée d'Art Moderne** is laid out on eight subterranean levels, a stimulating collection of works by twentieth-century artists, most of them Belgian, though a handful of French Impressionists, a couple of Chagalls and a Francis Bacon, provide more familiar moments.

Musée d'Art Ancien

Tues–Sun 10am–noon & 1–5pm; free (route plan F10)

It's best to start a visit to the **Musée d'Art Ancien** with the **blue route**, which begins with the **Flemish primitives**. Room 12 holds a couple of delicately realistic paintings by Rogier van der Weyden, city painter to Brussels in the fifteenth century, and room 13 *Justice of Otto* by his contemporary Deric Bouts, a powerful work of deep characterisation and almost photographic realism. Room 14 has some plain, no-nonsense portraits by Hans Memling, and room 17 a *Temptation of St Anthony* by Hieronymous Bosch, painted in the nightmarishly fantastic style that would later so influence Pieter Bruegel the Elder.

Works by the **Bruegel** family, notably Pieter the Elder, are in rooms 31, 32 and 41. The influence of Bosch is clearest in the *Fall of the Rebel Angels* in room 31, which was actually attributed to Bosch until Bruegel's signature was discovered under the frame. However, it's for his distinctive use of contemporary life in the treatment of religious and mythical scenes that Bruegel is rightly famed, and there are some wonderful examples here. *The Census at Bethlehem* and *Massacre of the Innocents* are particularly absorbing, with the traditionally momentous events happening, almost incidentally, among the bustle of everyday life. There are almost identical versions by both Pieter the Elder and Pieter the Younger. The gallery also holds what is possibly Bruegel the Elder's most haunting work, *The Fall of Icarus*, whose mood is perfectly captured by Auden in his poem *Musée des Beaux Arts*:

> *...In Bruegel's* Icarus, *for instance: how everything turns away*
> *Quite leisurely from the disaster; the ploughman may*
> *Have heard the splash, the forsaken cry,*
> *But for him it was not an important failure; the sun shone*
> *As it had to on the white legs disappearing into the green*
> *Water; and the expensive delicate ship that must have seen*
> *Something amazing, a boy falling out of the sky,*
> *Had somewhere to get and sailed calmly on.*

The **brown route** concentrates on work of the seventeenth and eighteenth centuries, notably some glorious canvases by Rubens, stunning refutations of the popular misconception that he painted nothing but flabby nude women. *Landscape with the Chase of Atlanta* in room 52 is a case in point, a brilliant evocation of the depth, light and shade of a forest; *Studies of a Negro's Head* is likewise wonderfully observed, a preparation for the black magus in the *Adoration of the Magi* next door in room 62. This is a luminous work, with the light sheening textures of skin and fabric. In the same room *The Climb to Cavalry* is an intensely physical painting, capturing the confusion, agony and strain as Christ struggles on all fours under the weight of the cross up the hill.

The **yellow route** of nineteeth-century works is the gallery's dullest, largely devoted to derivative city- and landscapes, portraits, forgettable canvasses by Belgian impressionists and some rather disagreeable symbolist paintings. Most worth seeing are the paintings and sculptures of workers by the Belgian social realist Constantin Meunier in room 79.

Musée d'Art Moderne

Tues–Sun 10am–1pm & 2–5pm; free

Revamped in the Eighties, the **Musée d'Art Moderne**, accessible by escalator from the Ancient collection, is the city's most innovative museum, a startlingly varied collection of modern art and sculpture, laid out on eight semicircular subterranean floors. As a gallery it's both enjoyable and challenging. Level 1 is devoted to temporary exhibitions of contemporary art, and levels 2 and 3 are largely reception areas; of the rest, levels 4, 6 and 8 are the most interesting.

The fourth level is as good a place to start as any, with a handful of works by Bonnard, Gauguin and Matisse, a Dufy *View of Marseille*, and two fanciful paintings by Chagall – including the endearingly eccentric *The Frog that wanted to make itself as big as a bull*. Undoubted highlights, however, are the series of solitary women by James Ensor, and Leon Spillaert's evocations of intense loneliness, from virtually monochromatic beaches to empty rooms and railway carriages.

Level 6 is devoted to Expressionists, Cubists and Surrealists, of which the last are by far the most gripping. There's a fine Dali, *The Temptation of St Anthony*, a hallucinatory work in which spindly legged elephants tempt the saint with fleshy women; and a couple of de Chirico's paintings of dressmakers' dummies. Of the Belgian Surrealists, Paul Delvaux, one of whose less provocative works graces the Bourse metro station, is represented by such diverse paintings as the oddly erotic *Pygmalion*, a *Crucifixion* in which all the figures are skeletons, and *La voix publique*, in which a tram approaches a reclining nude. Even more elusive is the gallery's small collection of paintings by Magritte – perplexing works, whose weird, almost photographically realised images and bizarre juxtapositions aim firmly to disconcert.

There are some equally unsettling works down on level 8, most of them by living artists. Undoubted highlight is Francis Bacon's *Pope with Owls*, but the rest of the collection is always a surprise, ranging from the wacky psychodelic sculpture of a fluorescent flower by Bailleux, to the swirling abstracts of Pierre Alechinsky.

Rue de la Regence and the Sablon neighbourhood

From the Beaux Arts it's a short walk along rue de la Regence to the **place du Petit Sablon**, a rectangular area off to the left which was formerly a horse market. It was laid out as a park in 1890, surrounded by a wrought iron fence decorated with 48 statues representing the medieval guilds. At one end a fountain decorated with larger statues recounts the story of Counts Egmont and Hoorn, beheaded on the Grand Place for their opposition to Spanish tyranny in the 1500s. Count Egmont is further remembered by the **Palais d'Egmont** on the other side of the square. This was originally built in 1548 for Francoise of Luxembourg, mother of the executed Count; it was rebuilt in 1750 and again in the 1890s, and it was the palace where in 1972 Britain signed the treaty that admitted them to the EC. On the other corner of the park, back on rue de la Regence, is the **Musée Instrumental du Conservatoire Royal de Musique** (Tues, Thurs, Sat 2.30–4.30pm, Wed 4–6pm, Sun 10.30am–12.30pm; free). Although at present there is room to show only a fraction of its 5000 exhibits, the long process of preparing a new home in a mansion on place Royale has begun, though this is not likely to be ready for another five years. What you can see of the collection today bodes well for the new museum – exquisitely inlaid and painted keyboard instruments, strings ranging from the unwieldy viola da gambas to mini-violins designed to be slipped into the pockets of street musicians. There's also a display devoted to Adolphe Sax, the Belgian-born inventor of the saxophone, which includes some of his wilder contraptions, like the oddly contorted saxhorn.

On the other side of the street, the fifteenth-century church of **Notre Dame du Sablon** began life as a chapel for the medieval guild of archers. But after a statue of Mary with powers of healing was brought by boat from Antwerp to the chapel, it became a centre of pilgrimage and a proper church was built to accommodate its visitors. The statue of Mary no longer exists, but a wooden carving of a boat over the entrance, and a stained-glass boat in the west window, commemorate its legendary means of transport, and the occasion of its arrival is still celebrated annually in July by the Ommegang procession (see "Listings").

If you can find the sacristan (he's available most weekday mornings and weekend afternoons) he will take you round the church (for the price of a donation) and into the black and white marble chapel containing the tomb of the Tour et Taxis family (who founded the Belgian postal system), dominated by a Baroque set-piece showing Life and Time fighting a tug-of-war. Considerably more interesting are the spandrels along the aisles, carved with different figures and animals, and the grotesque tomb of one Claude Bouton, chamberlain of Charles V, at the back of the church, which features a graphically realistic skeleton.

Behind the church, the **place du Grand Sablon**, a sloping wedge of cobbles surrounded by artisans' houses, is centre of one of the city's wealthiest districts, and is busiest at weekends, when a high-priced antique market clusters below the church. Most of the shops on Sablon and the surrounding streets are devoted to antiques and art, and you could easily spend an hour or so window-browsing from one to another – a cheaper pursuit, at any rate, than eating or drinking in one of Sablon's pavement cafés.

From the square follow rue de la Regence up the hill to **place Poelaert**, named after the architect who designed the immense **Palais de Justice** behind, a great Greco-Roman wedding cake of a building, dwarfing everything around, not least the poor Marolles quarter below. Built in 1883, it's actually larger than St Peter's in Rome; you may recognise it from the TV pictures of the Heysel stadium trial, which took place here. It's possible to wander into the main hall of the building, though really it's the size alone that is impressive.

A stone's throw from the Palais de Justice, **place Louise**, a chaotic traffic junction on the inner ringroad, dominated by fast-food restaurants and flashing ad hoardings, provides an unlikely setting for the discreet shops of *Hermés, Gucci, Chanel* and the like. They herald the start of the city's most exclusive shopping district – an area of designer boutiques, jewellers and glossy shopping malls where the air is spiked with the scents of expensive French perfumes.

Rue Royale, the Jardin Botanique and St Josse

It's a long, dreary walk up rue Royale to the Jardin Botanique and the St Josse district. The only landmark is the 154-foot high **Colonne de Congrès**, erected in 1850 to commemorate the country's first national parliament, with a blue flame at its base eternally burning to honour Belgian's dead of the two world wars. It dominates a vast, bleak belvedere, flanked by the blank glass and concrete city administration buildings, and offering a singularly unflattering view of the city.

The main reason for heading this way is to eat cheaply, or to visit the cultural centre housed in the impressive greenhouses of the **Jardin Botanique**, something you're most likely to do in the evening for a concert or play, as the gardens themselves are exposed to the noise and fumes of traffic whipping along the petit ring. **ST JOSSE**, too, is somewhere you'll probably want to go only at night, the main draw being its numerous (and cheap) Turkish restaurants. It's a compelling, uncompromisingly foreign neighbourhood, where men while away their days and nights over glasses of tea in cafés and head-scarved women emerge only during the day to shop. The vast, domed and severely dilapidated **Eglise de St Marie**, standing at the head of rue Royale, is the quarter's landmark, but life centres on **chausée de Haecht**, joining rue Royale just beyond the Botanique metro station, packed with restaurants, snack bars and the odd shop selling fruit and veg, Turkish videos and gimcrackery.

Outside the petit ring: the parks and outer boroughs

Brussels by no means ends with the petit ring. The city burst beyond its ancient boundaries back in the last century, and there's much worth seeing in the districts which lie outside the centre. Admittedly you won't miss much if you don't visit the self-glorifying monuments and stodgy museums of the Parc de Cinquantenaire, or the concrete jungle around the EC buildings. But the boroughs of Ixelles and St Gilles are a different matter – animated neighbourhoods holding the best of the city's Art Nouveau architecture and some of its most congenial nightspots.

East of the ring: Parc Leopold, the EEC and Parc Cinquantenaire

East of the inner ringroad, the **QUARTIER LEOPOLD** is possibly the most visited part of Brussels outside the centre. Taking its name from the late nineteenth-century king of Belgium, who laid out much of the area, with large boulevards and monuments and statues, it's home to two of the capital's largest parks, museums, and, of course, the European Community – in the form of the huge, winged **Berlaymont** building. It's this institution which inevitably colours much of the neighbourhood, not least in its relentless growth – at present the offices of Berlaymont overlook a vast building site. Along rue Archimède, past sundry Euro-bars, you reach a peaceful little island of nineteenth-century town-planning – interlinking garden squares and a tiny lake overlooked by some fine Art Nouveau houses. **Square Ambiorix** is the least alluring, now overshadowed by modern blocks on two sides, but don't miss the superb wrought iron and windows of no.11, one of the city's most ornate examples of the Art Nouveau style. Below, at the foot of avenue Palmerston, are three wonderfully subtle **houses** by Brussels' most innovative Art Nouveau architect, Victor Horta, overlooking the artificial lake of **place Marie Louise**. From here, rue de Taciturne will take you to rue de la Loi, from where you can cut across the building site to **Parc Leopold**.

Parc Leopold (metro Luxembourg or Maalbeek) is the pleasanter of the quarter's two parks, a hilly enclave landscaped around a lake, holding within its borders the **Institut des Sciences Naturelles** (daily 9.30am–4.45pm; F50) the city's rather old-fashioned natural history collection. It's a good place for kids on a rainy day, with a great army of dinosaurs on the ground floor, a vivarium with some vicious-looking scorpions and a Mexican orange-kneed tarantula, and scores of stuffed animals. Upstairs are some striking displays of tropical shells, and in the midnight-blue room, the immense white skeleton of a *Balaenoptera Musculus*.

Just outside the park gates, at rue Vautier 62, the **Musée Wiertz** (Tues–Sun 10am–noon & 1–5pm; closes at 4pm Nov–March; free) is devoted to the works of the city's most disagreeable nineteenth-century artist. Once immensely voguish – so much so that Thomas Hardy in *Tess of the d'Urbervilles* could write of "the staring and ghastly attitudes of a Wiertz museum" – Antoine Wiertz painted vast religious and mythological canvasses, featuring gory hells and coy nudes, and displayed a penchant for such nasty subjects as *The Burnt Child, The Thoughts and Visions of a Severed Head*, and *Premature burial*.

Further east, just beyond the Berlaymont complex and accessible by metro to Merode, lies the much larger **Parc du Cinquantenaire**, laid out for an exhibition to mark the golden anniversary of the Belgian state in 1880. It's a far-from-peaceful place these days, traffic surging up its middle, and its grounds home to trade fairs, yearly car shows, and occasional military exercises. But you might want to come out here to visit some of Brussels' largest museums, housing collections of art and applied art, not to mention weapons and motor cars.

The museums are in the Palais de Cinquantenaire, a vast edifice at the eastern end, with an entrance guarded by the mammoth **Cinquantenaire Arch**, topped by a bronze four-horse chariot, built by Charles Girault in 1905. The **Musée Royal d'Art et Histoire**, in the south wing of the palace (Tues–Sun 9.30am–12.30pm & 1.30–4.45pm; free), is made up of a maddening (and badly labelled) maze of pottery, carving, furniture, tapestries, glassware and lacework from all over the world – at its best in the opulent homegrown Belgian sections, less engaging in the Ancient civilisations sections. There is, in any case, almost too much to take in in its entirety. There are enormous galleries of – mostly run-of-the-mill – Greek, Egyptian and Roman artefacts, enough to soon become monotonous. If you do go, it's mildly diverting to spot the wobbles on the slap-dash Corinthian pottery (room 3) or to see mummies of a jackal, crocodile and falcon (room 5), and there's also a pretty impressive partially reconstructed Syrian synagogue, with some well-preserved mosaics.

The European applied arts sections have more immediacy, much of them devoted to Belgian clocks, silver and brasswork. There are reliefs of fourteenth-century knights, in chain mail, exhibits of Brussels tapestries, woven between 1427 and 1521, and some fabulously animated wooden relief altarpieces – one notable object displays the saga of Saint George's tortures from the chapel of Notre Dame in Leuven. An adjacent display, complete with wax dummy workmen, explains the process of carving a small altarpiece.

The museum is currently being rearranged, and for the moment the main sections close on alternate days; it's a good idea to know what's accessible before you actually come out here. Supposedly, the Ancient Civilisations sections, and those devoted to Islamic and Christian Art from the East, are open on even days, Sculpture and Decorative Arts on odd dates. Special exhibits such as Glasswork, the Far East and American pre-Colombian art are accessible by telephoning ☎733 96 10 (ext. 331) and making an appointment.

Also in the south wing of the palace is **Autoworld** (daily 10am–5pm; F150) – a good, if expensive, place to take the kids, although its extensive displays of vintage cars, motorcycles, fire engines, even an ice-cream truck from Glasgow, should appeal to anyone, tracing the history of the car as a stylesetter, military machine and economic indicator. In the north wing of the palace, the **Musée Royal de l'Armee et d'Histoire Militaire** (9am–noon & 1–4.45pm; closed Mon & hols; free) has collections detailing the history of the Belgian army from the eighteenth century to the present-day by means of weapons, uniforms and paintings. Most spectacular are the galleries devoted to armoured cars and artillery and military aircraft, though it's far from the required viewing unless you're a war buff.

The Horta Houses

Victor Horta, who died in 1947, is perhaps Belgium's most famous architect, a well-known champion of the Art Nouveau movement who spent much of his life in Brussels, dotting the city with some marvellous small-scale examples of his work, some of the best of which lie on the fringes of Ixelles and St Gilles.

The **Musée Victor Horta** at rue Americain 25 (Tues–Sun 2–5.30pm; F50), accessible by tram #92 from place Louise, was built, along with the studio next door, between 1898 and 1901, and served as his home until 1919. From the outside, the house is quite modest, a dark, narrow terraced house with a fluid facade and almost casually knotted and twisted ironwork. But it is for his interiors that Horta is noted, and the inside is a sunny sensuous dwelling, with all the architect's familiar trademarks – wide, bright rooms spiralling around a superbly worked staircase, wrought iron, stained glass, sculpture, and ornate furniture and panelling made from several different types of wood. He designed everything for his houses from the floor plans to the wallpaper, and he never used a straight line or a sharp angle where he could use a curve instead. His use of light was also revolutionary, often filtering through from above, atrium-like, using skylights and as many windows as possible.

The delight Horta took in his work is clear, especially when employed on private houses, but sadly there's not much of this early period left in Brussels, and much of his work has been neglected or destroyed; indeed he actually destroyed many of the drawings he had made for his earlier works himself. That said, there are a couple of other Horta creations nearby, though access is possible only through *ARAU*. (See "Guided tours".)

Somewhere you *can* go inside is the Horta-designed patisserie, *Bardat*, rue Bailli 75, a five-minute walk from the museum, a pretty pastel confection of stained glass and gilt-framed mirrors, and a fitting stage for the elaborate cakes and pastries. From here a left turn up rue Faider takes you past another fine Art Nouveau house (no. 83) with ironwork foliage tracing the windows, and faint frescoes of languishing pre-Raphaelite women. Around the corner, the **Tassel House** at rue Paul Emile Jansen 6, is the building that first placed Horta at the forefront of the Art Nouveau movement. The sinuous facade is appealing enough, with clawed columns, stained glass and curvaceous ironwork, but it was again with the interior that Horta really made his mark, an uncompromising fantasy featuring a flamboyant wrought-iron staircase and walls covered with linear decoration. It's also a striking example of the way in which Horta tailor-made his houses to suit the particular needs of clients. In this case it was built for an amateur photographer and includes a studio and projection room. Continuing along rue Paul Emile Jansen you hit avenue Louise, with, at no. 224, the **Hotel Solvay** – reckoned to be Horta's masterpiece, and like the museum, containing most of the original furniture and fittings. The 33-year-old Horta was given complete freedom and unlimited funds by the Solvay family (they made a fortune in soft drinks) to design this opulent town house. He commissioned an artist to paint a scene from the Solvay's summer cottage at the first staircase landing, choosing the dominant colours himself.

St Gilles

ST GILLES is the most intriguing of the inner boroughs, stretching from the refinement of avenue Louise in the east, to the solidly immigrant quarters towards the Gare du Midi. Here, a tense multi-racialism, brought about by generations of political and economic refugees from the Mediterranean and North Africa, contrasts sharply with the bland internationalism of the centre, and you begin to absorb something of the city's grim undertow.

The district's most distinctive landmark is a fake medieval castle on. avenue Ducpetiaux (bus #54 from Porte de Namur), which houses a **prison**. By night it's floodlit; by day sad clusters of women huddle outside the gates waiting to visit relatives, a disturbing proportion of them veiled, giving some notion of the problems facing Brussels's non-European communities. Ironically, the prison building only increases the picturesqueness of the surrounding streets, whose turn-of-the-century and Art Nouveau houses are numbered among the city's trendiest residences.

Facing the prison at the foot of avenue Jef Lambeaux is the **Hôtel Communal de St Gilles**, the showy, mock-Renaissance seat of local government, which dominates the **Barrière de St Gilles**, a seven-road junction that until the middle of the last century was the site of a toll gate at which taxes were levied on all merchandise passing into the city. It is here that St Gilles begins to slip down the social scale, the cafés getting cheaper, the shops tackier, and the general feel of the streets more depressed. If you want to halt here, and have F700 to spare, you could do worse than blow it on a sauna and Turkish bath at the turn-of-the-century **St Gilles' Baths** (8am–6pm; Tues & Fri for women, Mon, Wed, Thurs & Sat for men) just off avenue du Parc, at rue de la Perche 38 (☎538 28 57); if the price seems high, you can swim for around F50.

Pressing on down the chausée de Waterloo, past the daily morning market of the **Parvis de St Gilles**, you reach **rue Vanderschrick**, a tall terrace of elaborate, if slightly run-down Art Nouveau houses, the furthest of which now houses the chic café *Porteuse d'Eau*; see "Bars and cafés". This, however, is the only sign of gentrification in the neighbourhood, and continuing along the street, you penetrate further into the poor, immigrant heartland of the city. As an outsider, you are bound to feel intrusive, even more so if you decide to eat in one of the cheap Spanish, Portuguese, and Greek restaurants around the soulless **place de Bethlehem**. Rather than hanging around, walk on along the chausée de Forest, named for the rather dismal **Parc de Forest** at its head. Far nicer is the **Parc Duden**, just beyond, whose elegant towering trees make it perhaps the loveliest of the city's open spaces – an ideal escape or picnicking spot. Bus #48 will take you back to Bourse and the city centre.

Ixelles

IXELLES lies southwest of the petit ring, with the chausée d'Ixelles as its axis. Traditionally an immigrant quarter, and the favoured hang-out of arty and Bohemian types, there are now the inevitable pockets of yuppification, a handful of designer shops and a growing number of chic bars and restaurants joining the more congenial student and ethnic haunts. Less intimidating than either St Josse or the Marolles, Ixelles' greatest appeal remains its nightlife, but its shops, a couple of museums, and the sprinkling of Art Nouveau houses around the pretty Ixelles lakes, make for an interesting, and tourist-free, daytime wander.

At first sight, the beginning of the chausée d'Ixelles looks like any other of the city's shopping streets, and things don't get really interesting until you step into the Galerie d'Ixelles. In sharp contrast to the designer boutiques in the Galerie Toison d'Or across the road, this is the shopping and social centre of Ixelles' Zairean community, packed with tiny shops selling batik cloths, and cheap, cramped snack bars playing African music. Though the neighbouring side streets are a great source of night action, there's little to detain you by day until you reach rue J. van Volsem, with Ixelles' **Musée des Beaux Arts** (Tues–Fri 1-7.30pm, Sat & Sun 10am-5pm, closed Mon & hols; free.) at no. 71. This holds a modest but palatable collection of mostly French and Belgian modern artists – a couple of Magrittes, including the disturbing *Face of a Genius*, a luminescent *Cannes 1923* by Dufy, an Ixelles street scene by Delvaux and some dark, lonely canvases by Spillaert. There's also a room containing a series of signed posters by Toulouse-Lautrec, and a powerful *Head of an Italian Woman* by Constantin Meunier, with the years of wisdom and resignation written in the lines of her face.

If you liked Meunier, and have already seen his sculptures and paintings in the Musée d'Art Ancien, it's worth visiting the **Musée Constantin Meunier**, rue de L'Abbaye 59, housed in the artist's old studio on the other side of avenue Louise from the Ixelles lakes, the **Etangs d'Ixelles**, at the foot of the chausée (Tues–Sun 10am–noon & 1–5pm, closed Mon & hols; free). Whether the artist appeals or not, the benches by the two lakes, are a restful place to picnics, after which you could wander along avenue General de Gaulle, to see more of Brussels' Art Nouveau houses. Further south, you could also head for the **Bois de la Cambre**, unpleasantly criss-crossed by the main commuter access roads in its upper reaches, but opening out around a lake in the centre. It's Brussels most popular park, bustling with joggers, dog-walkers, families and lovers at weekends, and is part of the vast **Forêt de Soignes** – through which, if you've the stamina, you could walk the 13km to Tervuren (see p.310).

North of the Ring: Laeken

To the north of the ringroad, **LAEKEN** (tram #92 from rue Royale or pre-metro #52 from anywhere along Line #3) is the royal suburb of Brussels, home to the Belgian royal family – who occupy a large off-limits estate not far from the railway station – and a large public **park** close by, laid out in the nineteenth century by Leopold II. Leopold brought a **Chinese Pavilion** here from the Paris World's Fair of 1900, with the intention of transforming it into a fancy restaurant. The restaurant never materialised, and the pavilion now houses a collection of Chinese porcelain (Tues–Sun 9.30am–12.30pm & 1.30–4.30pm; free) – though this is currently under restoration and is in case less interesting than the building itself, decorated on the outside with bas reliefs of comic faces. There are also other monuments dotted around, including a fountain that's a replica of Giambologna's on Piazza Nettuno in Bologna, and a **planetarium**. But the park is perhaps best-known for the **Atomium** (metro Heysel), an imposing model of a molecule built for the 1958 World's Fair, which has since become something of a symbol of the city. It contains a museum – an unremarkable display on the peaceful uses of atomic energy – and a restaurant within its metallic spheres, but the main sensation is the disorientating feeling of travelling from sphere to sphere by escalator. Unfortunately, grey weather often obscures the view from the top sphere, around 110m above the ground, and if you're short of money you may want to save the rather high entrance fee by simply viewing the structure from the outside – at its base there's a scaled-down version of Europe, complete with Channel Tunnel and TGV.

West of the ring: Anderlecht, Koekelberg and around

It's little surprise that the suburb of **ANDERLECHT**, famous only for its football team, is little-visited by foreigners. It's a dull, grimy quarter, starting at Midi station and bisected by the city's bleak canal, and were it not for a couple of museums, there'd be little point in going. Make an effort, at least, however, to see the **Musée Gueuze**, rue Gheude 56 (Oct 20–May 30; Mon–Fri 8am–4.30pm, Sat 10am–12.30pm;F50), a short walk from Midi. It's a mustily evocative working brewery, still brewing Gueuze according to the traditional methods. Though there are guided tours on Saturdays at 11am, 2pm and 3.30pm, it's probably more fun to go around alone, using the excellent English language leaflet. The beer is made only of wheat, malted barley and hops, is allowed to ferment naturally, reacting with natural yeasts peculiar to the Brussels air, and is bottled for two years before it is ready to drink. The result is unique, as you can find out at the tasting at the end of the tour.

Rather than trekking on through Anderlecht, head back towards Midi, and catch tram #103 to place de la Vaillance, dominated by the lacily carved spire of the late-fifteenth century church of **St Pierre**. Across from the church, is the mellow red-brick **Maison d'Erasme,** rue du Chapitre 31 (daily 10am–noon & 2–5pm, except Tues & Fri; F20), the house where the humanist philosopher died. Though it contains none of Erasmus's actual belongings, it does have a display of portraits of the man by Holbein, Dürer and others, together with a collection of ancient editions of his writings, some of which include censors' marks. There's also a mould of the philosopher's skull, and seals made with two of his signet rings ("concedo nulli"). Get hold of the guidebook (which you can borrow for F20) giving the full lowdown, and try and time your visit to coincide with one of the occasional Renaissance music concerts that are held here.

North of here, in the adjoining borough of **KOEKELBERG**, the **Basilique Nationale Sacre Coeur** (metro Simonis) is another of Brussels' Art Nouveau attractions, a huge church (462 feet long with a 295-foot-tall dome), decorated sumptuously inside with marble and stained glass. Begun in 1905 and still unfinished, it was originally supposed to have six towers but has since been modified; it's dedicated to all those who have died in wars on behalf of their country (March 1–Nov 30 Mon–Fri 9am–5pm, Sun 2–5.45pm; visits to the gallery, F30, and terrace, F50, are possible at 11am and 3pm).

Eating and drinking

Whichever way you look at it, Brussels isn't a cheap city in which to **eat**, with the *cheapest* main courses going for about F350. The lowest-priced of the mainstream, centrally located restaurants are Italian, with pizza and pasta dishes starting at around F200. Fortunately, however, there is a good range of takeaway food, and meals in the Turkish restaurants of St Josse, and the Greek restaurants around the Gare du Midi, are very good value; the city's Spanish, Vietnamese, Japanese and Buddhist vegetarian restaurants are also worth investigating –

though they don't come as cheap. As for Belgian food, many bars serve food, often just spaghetti, sandwiches and croque monsieurs, but some have wider ranging menus, taking in traditional Brussels' fare. You can also eat excellent fish and seafood, especially in the old fish market district on quais aux Briques and aux Bois à Brûler.

For fast food, aside from the multinational burger and pizza chains, there are plenty of *frites* stalls around the Grand Place, notably on rue Marché aux Fromages and at the beginning of rue des Boucheurs. Rather more unusual are the carts around place St Catherine selling hot mussels, and *caricoles*, a poorman's version of the escargot. Pitta is also popular, stuffed with a wide range of fillings – though vegetarian ones are rare. The pitta snack bars along rue Marché aux Fromages are cheap, convenient and open late. Even better value, and far more substantial, are the enormous long, thin Turkish pizzas, or *pide*, topped with combinations of cheese, minced meat or even a fried egg, sold at any number of restaurants along the chausée de Haecht and rue Meridien. For picnic lunches, try the city's street markets or the Italian delis around place St Catherine.

Fast food, breakfast and snacks

L'Abricot Gourmand, rue Finistère, between rue Neuve and boulevard Adolphe Max. Unassuming snack bar with omelettes from F80 and spaghetti from F180.

Au Suisse, 73–75 boulevard Anspach. Long-established, and extremely popular New York-style deli, serving a vast range of sandwiches, milkshakes, ice creams and pastries. Eat at the bar or takeaway.

Bardat, rue Bailli 75. Elaborate cakes, croissants and pastries in a luscious Horta-designed patisserie en route to the Horta museum. The pastel stained glass is currently being restored and the café at the back is closed, though the bakery remains open.

Bistro 48, chausée d'Ixelles 48. Substantial, healthy breakfasts from F195, freshly squeezed juices, and a wide range of vegetable quiches.

Le Croissantin, rue Marché aux Herbes 81. Snack bar which serves sandwiches, croissants and pastries – a good place for a cheap breakfast. Also serves soup, spaghetti and sandwiches.

Crousty, rue des Fripiers, corner rue Marché aux Herbes. Popular place for a swift breakfast, with croissants, pastries and cakes baked on the premises.

Efe's, chausée de Haecht 129. Turkish restaurant with takeaway *pide* from F100.

Horta Brasserie, rue des Sables 20. The café of the recently opened *Centre Belge de la Bande Dessinée* (see p.287). Classy food, including smoked salmon, good salads, and a generally inventive menu in a summery Art Nouveau setting.

Jaffa, rue Fourche. Kebabs and falafel to eat in or takeaway.

Nasreddin, chaussée de Haecht 100. Turkish snack bar in St Josse serving great *pide* with a small side salad thrown in for F120. Closed Mon.

Nolido, corner rue des Renards and place Jeu de Balle. Sandwich and salad bar where the young and trendy retreat after scouring the Jeu de Balle flea market.

Pizza Uno, corner rue Fripiers and place de la Monnaie. Takeaway pizza slices for F60.

Resto Snack, corner rue Eperonniers and Brasseurs. Falafel and salad for F150.

Vlady, rue Marché au Fromage 15. One of many cheap pitta snack bars on this street. Also serves sandwiches, grills and salads. Eat in or takeaway.

Wittamer, place du Grand Sablon 12–13. Brussels' most famous patisserie, established in 1910 and still run by the Wittamer family. Gorgeous, if pricey, pastries and cakes.

Restaurants

L'Auberge des Chapeliers, rue des Chapeliers 1–3. Specialises in mussels prepared in a variety of ways, and soups. Mussels as a starter cost F295, as a main course F450. Open daily noon–3pm and 6pm–1am.

Le Canard à Trois Pattes, rue des Bouchers 5. Excellent omelettes or *gratins* (vegetable-meat-cheese casseroles) for around F300. The atmosphere and service are gourmet level.

Casa Rafael, rue des Tanneurs 144. Simple but comfortable neighbourhood restaurant in the Marolles quarter, with steaks for F260, brochettes for F100 and deep-fried anchovies for F150. Open daily except Tues from 11am until late.

Au Caveau des Comtes d'Egmont et Hoorn, Grand Place 14. Cheap fixed meals right on the Grand Place – ground beef or pork, frites and a vegetable for around F300. Mussels and chips F350. Closed Mon.

Carrefour St Gilles, 1 avenue de Parc. Unassuming but comfortable restaurant/café on the Barrière de St Gilles. Convenient place to stop for lunch while exploring the area. Sandwiches, spaghetti, and steak, salad and chips for F275.

Chez Léon, rue des Bouchers 18–22. Touristy restaurant near the Grand Place serving traditional Belgian fare like *carbonnades à la Flamande*, though it's most famous for its mussel dishes. Open daily noon–midnight.

Chez Mille et Alice, rue de Flandre 101. Unpretentious neighbourhood restaurant where you can get a mountain of mussels and a large plate of chips for F360.

Le Forestière, bottom of rue de Rollebeek. The most reasonable place to eat lunch in the Sablon area, with seats outside on an exclusive pedestrianised street of designer shops. Spaghetti from F160, omelettes, quiche and salad F100–200.

La Grande Porte, rue Notre–Seigneur 9. Long, narrow, cosy and crowded seventeenth-century *estaminet*, whose walls are plastered with old posters and photos. Rather too popular with ex-pats for comfort, but the food is good, hearty and traditional, and you're quite free to just go for a drink. Main meals cost F350–400, and include *waterzooi* and *carbonnades à la Flamande*. Open daily 6pm–2am, later at weekends.

De Hoef, rue Edith Cavell 218. One of the best-value restaurants in town for committed carnivores. Belgian grilled meat dishes a speciality.

Jacques, quai aux Briques 44. Fish restaurant serving a sedate, middle-aged clientele at lunchtime but attracting a raucous international crowd in the evenings. It's not cheap, with some dishes costing well over F500, but if you feel like splashing out, the *cabillaud de poche* is highly recommended. Reservations always necessary.

Le Perroquet, 58 rue de Minimes. Chic café-bar on a street of private art galleries and antique shops. Imaginative range of stuffed pitta and salads, and a superb selection of tarts. Open daily 11.45am–2.30pm and 7pm–1am. Closed Sat & Sun lunchtimes.

Ethnic and vegetarian restaurants

Atanas, rue de l'Argonne 20, and **Athenes,** rue de l'Argonne 22. Cheap, popular Greek restaurant in the dodgy quarter around Gare du Midi, serving large portions of standard, usually lukewarm, taverna fare. Plats du jour F170–200.

Restaurant Beograd, rue de Flandre (opposite *Au Portugal*). Goulash for F290, stuffed fish for F270.

Chez Emir, rue de la Meridien 62. A small Turkish restaurant with almost obtrusively amiable service.

Hoa Binh, rue Marché aux Fromages 18. Abundant, spicy Vietnamese dishes in a casual atmosphere perfect for children.

Iberia, rue de Flandre 8. Spanish restaurant at the place St Catherine end of rue de Flandre that does paella for F350.

Le Paradoxe, chaussée d'Ixelles 329. Buddhist-run wholefood restaurant and tearoom, with a preciously ascetic feel, and an eclectic programme of live music on most Fri & Sat evenings. Main courses go for F290–350, and it's a peaceful place to retreat during the day for a herbal tea and savoury toast. Open Mon–Sat, noon–2pm, 7pm–10pm.

Au Portugal, rue de Flandre 118. Fixed Portuguese meals for F230.

Quartier Latin, boulevard General Jacques 212. Relaxed, studenty hang-out serving excellent Vietnamese food. Dim sum a speciality.

Sahbaz, chaussée de Haecht 102. Reckoned to be the city's best Turkish restaurant. Amazingly, the prices remain low – grilled meats served with rice and crudités for F175–F225. Open daily 11.30am–1am.

La Strada de Spoleto, rue de la Colline 15, and **Pizzeria Napoli,** rue de la Colline 17. Good value pizza and pasta just off the Grand Place from around F200.

Den Teepot, rue de Chartreux 29. Simple and peaceful vegetarian and fish restaurant, where you eat to a soundtrack of classical music and jazz. The plat du jour is usually a selection of pulses, grains, vegetable salads and maybe a sushi roll, and costs around F200. Open Mon–Sat noon–2pm only.

Tsampa, rue de Livourne 109. Congenial Buddhist vegetarian restaurant, with full meals for around F350, salads and pasta for much less. Open noon–2pm & 7–10pm, closed Sat & Sun evenings.

Un Violin sur le Toit, place du Nouvelle Marché aux Grains 35. Jewish deli that serves lunch until 3pm every day except Saturday. A good stopoff in the middle of the day.

Yamato, corner rue Francart and rue St Boniface. Japanese restaurant where you eat sitting at the central, circular bar. Dishes from F230. Closed Sun & Mon.

Bars and cafés

Boozing in Brussels, as in the rest of the country, is a joy. The city has an enormous variety of **bars and cafés** – sumptuous Art Nouveau cafés, traditional bars with ceilings stained brown by a century's smoke, bars whose walls are plastered with sepia photographs and ancient beer ads, speciality beer bars with literally hundreds of different varieties of ale, and, of course, more modern hang-outs. Many of the centrally located places, especially those considered particularly typical, are much-frequented by tourist and ex-pats, but outside the centre, and even tucked away off the Grand Place, there are places which remain refreshingly local. A number serve meals as well as snacks, often far better value than eating in a restaurant. Bars also stay open late – most until 2 or 3am, some until dawn.

L'Aiglon, place Houwert 2. Small African bar in St Josse playing loud reggae and African music. Open daily until dawn.

African Wangata, rue St Alphonse 60–62. A good place to move on to after visiting L'Aiglon, from which it is a five-minute walk.

Amadeus, rue Veydt 13. Trendy wine bar in the one-time studio of Auguste Rodin. Open noon–1am, closed Mon.

L'Amor Fou place Fernand Cocq. Ixelles bar to which the studiously alternative come to pose. Tequila, mezcal, and pepper vodka feature among the accessorising drinks; there's also good, reasonably priced food (spinach flan, spaghetti with basil) and occasional live music.

Au Brasseur, rue des Brasseurs, just off Grand Place. Unpretentious place ideal for late-night drinks – it often stays open until first light. The beer is cheap, and you can usually find a table.

Le Cercueil, rue des Harengs 10–12. Funereal concept bar, where the tables are coffins, the only light UV, and the music alternates between Gregorian chants and Chopin's Funeral March. Expensive. Open daily 11am–3am, until dawn on Fri & Sat.

DNA, rue Plattesteen 18. Young, lively hang-out for the studenty and street-credible. Don't expect to find a seat after 10pm, and expect to have your conversation drowned out by Madonna and The Cure. Open weekdays noon–3am, weekends 3pm–3am.

't Dolle Mol, rue des Eperonniers 52. Predominantly Flemish-speaking bar, with a cliquey clientèle. Music ranges from manic punk to kitschy music-hall, and everyone sits looking thoroughly miserable. Open daily 11am–1am, 3am at weekends.

L'Estaminet de Toone, petite rue des Bouchers 21. Largely undiscovered bar belonging to the Toone puppet theatre, just off the Grand Place. Two small, beamy rooms with old posters on rough plaster walls, a reasonably priced beer list, a modest selection of snacks, and a soundtrack of classical and jazz, make it the centre's most congenial bar. Open noon–1am, although this can be slightly erratic.

Falstaff, rue Henri Maus 17–23. Art Nouveau café next to the Bourse, attracting a mixed bag of tourists, fashionable young things, Eurocrats and the bourgeois Bruxellois. Full of atmosphere, and so crowded in the evenings that you're unlikely to find a seat. Inexpensive beer and sandwiches. Open daily 9am–3am.

Greenwich, rue des Chartreux 7. Brussels' traditional chess café, and with a peace that makes it an ideal place to retreat from the pace of the city.

Interférences, rue de la Tête d'Or 1. Video bar which gets lively later in the evening with a mainly young crowd. Many different kinds of videos, and handily situated just off the Grand Place.

Café Metropolitan, place de Brouckère 31. Sumptuously ritzy fin-de-siècle café, belonging to an equally opulent hotel. Astonishingly many people prefer to sit outside, for a view of flashing ads and zipping traffic. Expect to pay F80 for a *kriek*, and F20 for the privilege of using the palatial lavatories. If you've got cash to spare, splurge on a brunch of smoked salmon or caviare. Open daily 9am–1am.

Moeder Lambic, rue de Savoie 68, St Gilles. Over a thousand beers on offer, including 500 Belgian varieties, and not at all expensive. Open weekdays 11am–4am, weekends 4pm–4am.

La Mort Subite, rue Montagne-aux-Herbes-Potagères. 1920s bar that lent its name to a widely available bottled beer. A long, narrow room with nicotine-stained walls and mirrors, a thirtysomethingish clientèle, and an animated atmosphere. Open daily 9am–1am.

Le Pantin, chaussée d'Ixelles 355. Relaxed, vaguely arty bar just above place Eugene Flagey, playing a wide range of music.

Pitt's Bar, rue des Minimes 53. Business-drinkers at lunchtime, rather yuppie at night. They serve tapas and pasta. Open weekdays 11am–2pm, evenings only Sat & Sun.

La Portuese d'Eau, avenue Jean Volders 48a, on the corner with rue Vanderschrick, St Gilles. The last in a terrace of ornate Art Nouveau houses near the Parvis de St Gilles, and one of the few signs of gentrification in this run-down quarter of the barrière. The food is not cheap, but it's worth the price of a beer to see the swanky interior. Open daily 10am–1am. Food from noon–2pm & 7pm–10pm.

Roi d'Espagne Grand Place 1. Supremely touristy bar in a seventeenth-century guildhouse, worth wandering inside for a look, if only to view the collection of inflated animal bladders suspended from the ceiling, but don't bother staying for a drink. Open daily until 1am.

SiSiSi, chaussée de Charleroi 174A, St Gilles. Youthful bar worth the journey for its splendid range of salads and stuffed pittas. Open daily 9am–midnight.

Stella au Grand Place rue de la Colline, corner Grand Place. Unassuming bar, with prices to match, tucked into a corner of the Grand Place and, amazingly, totally ignored by tourists. Open daily 7am–1am.

Stoemelings, place de Londres 7, Ixelles. Small, modern and congenial bar with a good range of Belgian beers and excellent food, including gargantuan portions of inexpensive spaghetti and lasagne, as well as sandwiches.

Vossegat Nord, boulevard Adolphe Max 54. Strange old café with a predominantly aged clientele who sit surrounded by stuffed foxes while drinking dark, syrupy *Vossegat* beer, served with cubes of cheese. Open daily 9am–midnight.

De Ultieme Hallucinatie, rue Royale 316. Fanciful Art Nouveau bar featuring a grotto, helicopter fans and pretty stained-glass, and a nonchalantly-dressed crowd. Reasonably priced drinks and food – omelettes, lasagne, etc – and an extremely sumptuous restaurant in front. Sun–Mon 11am–3am, Sat 4pm–4am. Live music on Fri from 10.30pm.

L'Ultime Atome, rue Saint-Boniface 14, Ixelles. Congenial café. Good range of beers, superb food and youngish clientele. Food – at lunchtime and 7pm–12.30am – ranges from pasta and elaborate salads to more exotic fare, such as ravioli with artichokes and *osso bucco* .

English, Irish and American bars

Chez Richard, rue de Minimes 4. Irish bar that's a favoured hang-out of the younger EC crowd. Sometimes intimate in feel, other times crazy.

Conways, Porte de Namur. American bar full of men on the make, especially on Thurs nights when drinks are half-price for women – though if you're in a mixed group this can, of course, be turned to your advantage.

Henry J. Beans, rue Mont aux-Herbes-Potagères 40 (in the *SAS Royal Viking Hotel*). Youthful bar with a contrived Fifties decor that is renowned for its heavy pick-up scene. More of a singles bar than anything else. Cheap cocktails, though.

James Joyce, rue Archimède 34. Cliquey and sometimes boisterous hang-out for the ex-pat Irish, within staggering distance of the EC building. Worth braving on Tues at 8.30pm if you like Irish folk music.

Rick's Café Americain, avenue Louise 344. Situated in a ritzy part of Brussels, this bar-restaurant has been a gathering-place of resident English-speakers for close on thirty years. The bar can get lively, and there's a full menu available, though it's most famous for its ribs.

Twickers, rue Archimède 55. The most authentic of the so-called British pubs, popular with Berlaymont *stagières*.

Nightlife: music, clubbing, film and theatre

As far as **nightlife** goes, you may be perfectly happy to while away the evenings in one of the city's bars or restaurants – there are plenty in which you can drink until sunrise. However, although it's not as lively at night as some European cities, Brussels is also a good place to catch **live bands**: the city is – with Antwerp – a regular stop on the European tours of major and up-and-coming artists. On a more local level, the music bars clustered around place Fernand Cocq and the lower end of the chausée d'Ixelles are great for Friday/Saturday night bar-hopping. **Clubs and discos** are rather less impressive, but they are sometimes free – although at least one, overpriced, drink is usually obligatory.

There is also a thriving **classical concert scene** – notably the recently established *Ars Musica* festival of contemporary music held annually in March, and the prestigious four-yearly *Concours Musical Reine Elisabeth*, competition for piano, violin and composition, which numbers among its prize-winners Vladimir Ashkenazy, David Oistrach and Gidon Kremer.

For **listings** of concerts and events, check *The Bulletin* or the Thursday pull-out section of *Le Soir*. **Tickets** for most things are available from *FNAC* in City 2, or from the booking office at *TIB* on the Grand Place.

Concert halls and performance venues

Forest National, avenue du Globe 36 (☎347 03 55). Brussels' main venue for big-name international concerts, holding around 6000 people. Recent gigs included Adeva, Tears for Fears and Bowie.

Palais des Beaux Arts, rue Ravenstein 23 (☎512 50 45). With a concert hall holding around 2000, as well as some smaller theatres, the Palais is used for anything from contemporary dance to Tom Jones.

Ancienne Belgique, boulevard Anspach 114 (☎512 59 86). The main venue for home-grown and international indie bands. Also showcases jazz and folk.

Le Botanique, rue Royale 236 (☎217 63 86) Housed in the 150-year old conservatory of the Jardin Botanique – includes an art gallery, two theatres and a small cinema. Occasional concerts, and some good, mostly contemporary theatre.

RTBF/BRT, place Flagey 18 (☎737 28 45) Home of the French (RTBF) and Flemish (BRT) radio and TV symphony orchestras, with concerts almost every Fri & Sat.

Live music bars and clubs

Le Bierodrome, place Ferdinand Cocq 21. Smoky jazz bar whose live gigs (mostly Fri, Sat & Sun from 10.30pm) attract a mixed, comfortably unpretentious crowd. On other evenings, it's just a nice place to drink.

Blues Corner, rue des Chapeliers 12. No-frills bar with local bands playing most nights – you'll be able to hear from outside whether it's worth going in. Occasional touring British and American bands.

Do Brasil, rue de la Caserne 88 (☎513 50 88) Brazilian music and food from Tues–Sat.

Machado, rue des Chapeliers 14 (☎513 36 91). Jazz and Latin concerts till dawn, just off the Grand Place. Closed Mon.

Le Paradoxe, chaussée d'Ixelles 329. Buddhist vegetarian restaurant with an esoteric range of live jazz, folk, classical and world music every Fri & Sat night. See also "Ethnic and vegetarian restaurants".

Sounds rue de la Tulipe 28. Scruffy, smoky American-orientated bar, serving up a noisy blend of R & B.

Travers, rue Traversière 11. (☎218 15 09). Informal jazz club with an impressive reputation for showcasing up-and-coming Belgian musicians.

Clubs and discos

Le Garage, rue Duquesnoy 16. The best of the capital's large clubs, playing a frenetic mix of House, Techno and New Beat.

Le Mirano Continental, chaussée de Louvain 38. The club of the posturing media crowd, with a door policy that favours anyone who looks like a model.

The New Memphis, rue de Dublin 40. Ixelles club with mixed black and white crowd, playing disco and funk.

The Rainbow, rue Leopold 7. A bar during the week, disco on Sat, and supposed to resemble a saloon set from a Western. Normally patronised by a very young crowd of US high school kids and UK au pairs. The music can be good, however, and it's fairly cheap to get in.

Film and theatre

About half the films shown in Brussels' cinemas are in English with French and Flemish subtitles (coded VO, *version originale*). *The Bulletin* has comprehensive listings of the week's films – the best night to go is Monday, when entry is half-price. Though most screens are devoted to the big US box-office hits, programmes at the **Actor's Studio**, petit rue des Bouchers 16, and the **Arenberg/Galeries**, Galerie de la Reine 26, are more adventurous, often showing foreign films. Failing that, the **Musée du Cinema**, rue Baron Horta 9, shows a nightly selection of silent films and old talkies for just F35. There's also an annual **Film Festival** in January at the Palais du Congrès on the Mont des Arts, highlight of which is the "Tremplin" or Springboard section, which features international films favoured by critics but not yet taken on by Belgian distributors.

Obviously most of Brussels' **theatre** is staged in French or Flemish, although the various amateur British, American and Irish theatre groups frequently put on high-quality productions. More famously, there's the **Toone Puppet Theatre**, at rue des Bouchers 21 (☎511 71 37/513 54 86), which has been around for over twenty years in this location putting on puppet plays in the Bruxellois dialect. It's run by one Jose Gael, the seventh of a long line of puppet masters dating back to the 1830s. He revived the theatre in the Sixties and now stages performances at 8.30pm from Wednesday to Saturday.

Shops and markets

Brussels compares pretty well with most European capitals for **shops**. But while the range and variety will suit most tastes, prices for some things are virtually twice those charged in Britain. This includes the goods in British stand-bys like *Marks & Spencer*, the *Body Shop* and *WH Smith*, so beware of running out of underwear, hair gel, or reading matter.

High-street shopping, books , clothes and the Galeries

The main central shopping street is **rue Neuve**, which runs from place de la Monnaie to place Rogier and is home to most of the mainstream chains, including *Marks and Spencer* – indistinguishable from its branches back home. At the top end, **City 2** is the ultimate in glossy, sanitised shopping malls, with cinemas, restaurants, department stores and boutiques, and, most usefully, a large supermarket.

WH Smith at boulevard Adolphe Max 71–75 is not surprisingly one of the best places in town to buy **English books**. Other English-language bookshops include *House of Paperbacks*, chaussée de Waterloo 813, in the suburb of Uccle, and the *Strathmore Bookshop* rue St Lambert 131 in Woluwe St Lambert.

For **clothes and accessories**, **chaussée d'Ixelles** is another mid-market shopping street, but merits a visit for the African shops in the **Galerie d'Ixelles**, and for the cluster of design shops in its lower reaches, beyond place Fernand Cocq. *Sous Sol*, chaussée d'Ixelles 196, has an unusual range of designer jewellery, *Z'Art*, across the road at no.223, trendy accessories; *Luxiol*, at no.221, sells wooden toys and contemporary and Art Deco-style jewellery. Aiming at the same market is the city's latest shopping gallery: the trendily refurbished **Saint-Géry market**, not yet open, but likely to become a small-scale Covent Garden.

Apart from the conservative boutiques of the **Galeries St Hubert**, **upmarket shops** are mostly confined to the upper town: classic French and Italian designers at place Louise, Porte de Namur, and on avenue Louise. Lesser-known but nonetheless pricey outlets shelter in the snooty **Galerie Louise**; for wackier creations by Gaultier, Moschino and the like try *Ottime* or *Blue* in the **Galeries Toison d'Or**.

Alternative and second-hand clothes

Alternative and second-hand clothes shops are concentrated on rue des Eperonniers, while clothes in the adjacent Galerie Agora are by turns trashy, eccentric, hippy and punk. Second-hand prices are mostly on a par with those in London, alternative stuff more expensive, and, in the main, rather tame – exceptions being a cluster of young designers in the Galerie Agora and the young Belgian names on rue Dansaert. You'll also be able to pick up period clothes (and some amazing accessories) at the Jeu de Balle flea market (see below).

For **second-hand**, try *Killiwatch*, at rue des Eperonniers 20, *Ark* (no. 54) and *Fever* (no. 63). *Anik*, rue des Eperroniers 1A has hippy jewellery and punk T-shirts, *L'Astrolabe* (no. 2) jewellery, and *Virgin* (no. 13) Junior Gaultier and vastly overpriced DMs. Further out from the centre, close to the Jeu de Balle flea market *Leo Ellébas Boutique*, corner rue Tanneurs and rue Ghislaine, sells mostly 50s and 60s clothes; while off Avenue Louise, *La Boutique*, rue de Stassaert 114 has second-hand designer clothes for women (the men's branch is a few doors further up).

Art, antiques, bric-a-brac and markets

Though prices are predictably prohibitive, the window displays, and – if you've the nerve – the interiors of the numerous **private galleries** selling contemporary art, antiques, archaeological, oriental and African artefacts, can be as fascinating as any museum. Most lie on and around **place du Grand Sablon** – where there's an expensive **antiques market** every weekend – in the swanky shopping mall, **Jardin de Sablon**, and on rues Ernest Allard, Minimes, Watteau and Jansens; there are also a few places on rue de la Madeleine and rue St Jean. Less exclusive, and more affordable, is the **Jeu de Balle flea market** in the Marolles quarter, held every morning, but at its best at weekends, where the eccentric muddle of colonial spoils, quirky jumble and domestic and eccelesiastical bric-a-brac give an impression of a century's bourgeois fads and fashions. Perhaps more useful, if you've just moved to Brussels and have an apartment to furnish is the junk **Marché aux Jeunes**, held on the first Sunday of the month (7am–1pm) at place St Lambert in the suburb of Woluwe St Lambert, or the similar **Marché Dailly** on place Dailly in Schaarbeek held on Tuesdays from 8am until 1pm.

As for the city's many **other markets**, the largest and most colourful is the one held every Sunday morning at the **Gare du Midi**, a bazaar-like affair, with traders crammed under the railway bridge and spilling out into the surrounding streets. Stalls sell pitta, olives, *Rai* tapes, spices, herbs and pulses, among the more familiar fruit, veg and cheap clothes.

Specialities: lace, chocolate, comics

If you like **lace**, you'll pick up far nicer pieces at Jeu de Balle than in any of the much-hyped hand-made lace shops on and around the Grand Place, where you could pay F650 for a souvenir handkerchief. The other Bruxellois speciality, **chocolate**, is another matter: *pralines* come filled with cream, liqueurs, or *ganache* (a fine dark chocolate); truffles, made of chocolate, butter, cream and sugar, can be rather more sickly. Though only die-hard chocaholics will feel like blowing more than the price of a meal on a 100g of chocolates at *Godiva* on the Grand Place, *Neuhaus* in the Galerie de la Reine or *Corné* in the Galerie du Roi have lower prices, and the quality is way above that of any British chocolates. *Leonidas* has a

number of branches around the city, most centrally at Boulevard Anspach 46.
Don't omit either, to try the *speculaas* made by *Dandoy* at rue au Beurre 31.

Hergé, creator of Tin Tin, was a Belgian, and the cult of the **comic strip** or
bande dessinée continues to flourish in the capital. As well as the latest publications, there are a number of shops selling second-hand comic books, notably a
good selection at *Slumberland*, rue des Sables 20, the bookshop in the newly
opened *Centre Belge de la Bande Dessinée* . *Multi BD*, boulevard Anspach 126, on
the corner with rue Plattesteen, sells second-hand as well as new comics, as does
Jonas Comics Exchange, place Fernand Cocq 4. *Espace BD*, place Fernand Cocq 2
is also worth a browse. Just off the Grand Place there's a whole shop dedicated to
Hergé's quiffed hero: *La Boutique de Tin Tin*, rue de la Colline 13, which has
Tin Tin books, postcards, figurines, T- shirts and jumpers.

Listings

Airlines *British Airways*, Centre Rogier, 9th floor (☎217 74 00); *Aer Lingus*, 91–91 avenue
Louise (☎537 24 10); *Sabena*, rue Cardinal Mercier 35 (☎511 90 30 or ☎723 60 10); *KLM*, rue
des Princes 8 (☎217 63 00); *Luxair*, avenue Louise 104 (☎646 03 70); *London City Airways*
(contact *Sabena*); *Air Europe,* avenue Louise 66 (☎511 39 39).

American Express place Louise 2 (☎512 17 40); open Mon–Fri 9am–5pm, Sat 9am–noon.

Baby-sitters Phone ☎647 23 85.

Car hire *Hertz*, boulevard Lemonnier 8 (☎513 28 86, airport arrivals ☎720 60 44); *Avis*, rue
Americaine 145, Ixelles (☎537 12 80, airport arrivals ☎720 09 44); *Europcar*, avenue Louise
235 (☎640 94 00), rue St Denis 117 (☎344 91 47), and airport arrivals (☎721 05 92).

Dental problems If you need a dentist, call ☎426 10 26 or ☎428 58 88, weekends and evenings after 9pm.

Embassies *UK*, rue Joseph II 28, Etterbeek (☎217 90 00)); *Ireland*, rue du Luxembourg 19
(☎513 66 33); *Australia*, avenue des Arts 52 (☎213 05 00); *New Zealand*, boulevard de Regent
47–48 (☎512 10 40); *USA*, boulevard de Regent 27 (☎513 38 30); *Canada*, avenue de Telvurel
2 (☎735 60 40).

Emergencies Police ☎101; ambulance/fire brigade ☎100. For young people, there's also
SOS-Jeunes, rue Mercelis 27 (☎512 90 20), open 24 hours a day to deal with emotional and
other problems.

English-speaking Brussels If you've recently come to Brussels to live, there are a number
of social groups all advertising in *The Bulletin*: Of them, *Fringe* is the least stiff and formal.
Amateur dramatics is also a big part of the ex-pat scene: if you're at all into acting or doing
backstage work, check out the amateur dramatic groups listed in *The Bulletin*, most of whom
put on a wide range of plays. See also our listings of English and American bars, and visit the
British Council office and library at rue Joseph II, Etterbeek (☎219 36 00).

Exchange Outside bank hours you can change money and travellers' cheques at offices at
the Gare du Nord and Gare du Midi (daily 7am–11pm), Gare Centrale (daily 8am–9pm), *Paul
Laloy*, rue de la Montagne 6 (Mon–Fri 9am–6pm, Sat 10am–6pm; June–Sept also Sun 11am–
1pm), and *Thomas Cook*, Grand Place 4 (Mon–Sat 9am–5pm). There are also bureaux de
change at the airport. Remember too that a few central banks also open on Sat morning, and
if you have a Eurocheque card with a PIN number, you can use the numerous
MISTERCASH dispensers scattered throughout the city.

Festivals Brussels has a number of festivals and annual events worth timing a visit around.
Best-known is the *Ommegang*. A medieval procession from Grand Sablon to the Grand Place
that began in the fourteenth century as a religious event, celebrating the arrival by boat of a
statue of the Virgin from Antwerp (see p.293). The celebration became increasingly secular –
an excuse for the nobility, guilds and civic big-wigs to parade their finery, reaching a peak in
1549, when it was witnessed by Charles V. Today's Ommegang, which finishes up with a

dance on the Grand Place, is so popular that it is now held twice annually on the first Tuesday and Thursday of July; if you want a ticket for the finale, you'll need to book (at the TIB on the Grand Place) at least six months ahead. Another fun annual event, is the more modest *Planting of the Meiboom*, which takes place every August 9 – a procession from rue des Sables to the Grand Place, which involves much boozing, food and general partying. The story goes that in 1213 a wedding party was celebrating outside the city gates when they were attacked by a street gang from Louvain. They were beaten off (with the help of a group of archers, who just happened to be passing by) and in thanks, the local Duke gave them permission to plant a maypole (Meiboom) on the eve of their Patron Saints' feastday. Other events include the *Foire du Midi*, which takes place every year from mid-July to the end of August around the Porte de Hal – good for sampling local food and beer – and the biannual *flower carpet*, in mid-August, when the entire Grand Place is covered with an intricate design made entirely of begonias.

Football Brussels has several teams, of which *Anderlecht* are by far the best-known and most consistent, ranging among the contenders for the Belgian league championship. Their stadium is the Vanden Stock, at avenue Theo Verbeeck 2 (☎522 94 00), reachable by taking tram #103 or bus #46, #74 or #76. The more infamous Heysel stadium, out on avenue de Marathon in Laeken (☎478 93 00), is the home of the rather less impressive *Racing Jet de Bruxelles* – a second division side since their relegation a couple of years back. To see them, take tram #81, or the metro to Heysel.

Gay and lesbian life For the most up-to-date information on the Brussels gay scene, phone the Gay/Lesbian Line on ☎233 25 02 (daily 9am–9pm). Brussels' gay men meet up in a number of city centre bars, among which the following are well-known: *Chewing-Gum*, place de las Vieille Halle aux Blés 25; *Le Forum*, rue des Bouchers 71; *Duquesnoy*, rue Duquesnoy 12; and the disco, *Le Why Not?*, rue des Riches Claires 7. For more information, contact *Tels Quels Meeting Point*, rue Marché au Charbon 81 (☎512 45 87). There is less of a lesbian scene, but the *Capricorne*, rue d'Anderlecht 8 (off place Fontainas) is a long-established lesbian disco, which attracts a crowd spanning the ages (men admitted too). It's open at weekends only. You could also try the bar *Madam*, Galerie du Roi 25, which is about the only truly lesbian bar in town.

Hospital For medical assistance call ☎479 18 18 or ☎648 80 00, day or night.

Infor-Jeunes rue du Marché aux Herbes 27 (☎512 32 74). An information centre for young people new to the city, giving advice on accommodation, the law and other matters; it's open Mon–Fri 10am–6pm, Sat 10am–1pm.

Launderette *Salon Lavoir*, rue Haute 5, around the corner from the Bruegel youth hostel.

Lost property For articles lost on public transport, call ☎515 23 94; on a train ☎219 28 80; on a plane ☎720 91 13.

Pharmacies Outside normal working hours, all pharmacies display a list of open alternatives outside. Weekend rotas are also listed in the Saturday newspapers.

Post office The main central post office is upstairs in the Centre Monnaie building at the bottom end of place de Brouckère; it's open Mon–Sat 9am–5pm. There's also a 24-hour post office at the Gare du Midi.

Swimming pools There's a reasonably central swimming pool at rue du Chevreuil 28 (☎511 24 68).

Telephones rue de Lombard 30a (daily 10am–10pm).

Train enquiries ☎219 26 40; *Netherlands Railways*, boulevard de l'Empereur 66 (☎512 83 45); *British Rail*, rue de la Montagne (☎511 69 25).

Travel agents *Acotra*, rue de la Montagne 38 (☎513 44 80); *Nouvelles Frontières*, rue de la Violette 21 (☎511 80 13); *Europabus*, place de Brouckère 50 (☎217 00 25).

Women's contacts The English-speaking *Women's Organisation for Equality* (WOE), rue Blanche 29, off avenue Louise (☎538 47 73), holds public meetings on the third Wednesday of the month, at 8pm. There's a cafeteria on the premises, *Les Dames Blanches* (Mon, Tues & Fri 11am–6pm, Wed & Thurs 11am–10pm), which does cheap *plats du jour*. *Artemys*, Galerie Bortier, rue St Jean 8–10, is Brussels' only feminist bookstore, and stocks a large number of books in English; it has a women's tearoom upstairs.

AROUND BRUSSELS: TERVUREN, WATERLOO AND LEUVEN

The bilingual city of Brussels constitutes one third of the federation which these days makes up Belgium, and lies at the centre of the province of **Brabant**, which is divided more or less equally between French-speakers and Flemings. Much of the province is covered in other chapters, but there are one or two high spots close to the city which are worth getting out to see if you're here for a few days. The battlefield at **Waterloo** is the most popular attraction, though perhaps more interesting is the Central African museum in the quiet suburb of **Tervuren**. Further afield, the old university city of **Leuven** is worth a day trip too, though it can also be seen on the way to places further out.

Tervuren

Avenue de Tervuren leads out of Brussels towards the suburb of **TERVUREN**, lined with embassies and mansions in its upper reaches, and then delving through the wooded areas of the northern Forêt de Soignes, a route most easily covered by tram #44 from place Montgomery. The main attraction of Tervuren, aside from the mere pleasure of escaping the city for a couple of hours, is the **Musée Royal de L'Afrique Centrale** (mid-March–mid-Oct daily 9am–5.30pm; rest of the year 10am–4.30pm; free), a short walk along the main road from the tram terminus – housed in a grandiose purpose-built pile constructed on the orders of King Leopold II early this century. Leopold owned the Belgian Congo himself, its income making him one of the country's richest men, and it was he who sent the explorer Stanley there (of Livingstone fame) on a five-year fact-finding mission. In 1908, one year before the museum opened, the Belgian government took over the colony, replacing Leopold's chaotic, extraordinarily cruel, regime with a marginally more liberal state bureaucracy. The country gained independence as Zaire only in 1960. The museum was Leopold's own idea, a blatantly colonialist and racist enterprise which treats the Africans as a naive and primitive people, and the Belgians as their paternalistic benefactors. However, the collection is undeniably rich, and should not be missed. Displays are devoted to many aspects of Congo society, from export crops like coffee, cocoa and seed oils, to masks, idols, musical instruments, weapons and an impressive array of dope pipes. The museum's grounds are also worth a stroll, the formal gardens, set around a series of geometric lakes, flanked by wanderable woods. Afterwards, if you've not brought a picnic, head for *Il Paradiso* behind the museum car park, which serves reasonably priced and authentic Italian pizza – so popular you're unlikely to find a table on Sunday.

Waterloo

About 18km south of Brussels, accessible by orange bus #W from place Rouppe, **WATERLOO** has a resonance far beyond its size. Today, a bland small town with a large American community and a glut of fast-food outlets, it was here on June

18, 1815 that Wellington masterminded the battle which put an end to the imperial ambitions of Napoleon, and so changed the course of European history. The battlefield not surprisingly gets lots of visitors, although frankly it doesn't really live up to expectations, and unless you're especially interested in the battle, there's little reason to go – unless it's to see an annual re-enactment by a local historical society in June.

Actually, the battle is still something of a bone of contention between the French-speakers and Flemings hereabouts. Broadly speaking, French-speakers fought for Napoleon, while the Flemings fought on the side of Wellington, and the souvenir shops and monuments that have gone up in years since have divided along linguistic lines – the shops that sell Napoleonic souvenirs are unlikely to be run by Flemish-speakers; the sights that honour the British will not have been erected by Walloons.

The best starting-point if you do visit is the *Name* inn in the centre of town. It was here that Wellington slept the night before the battle and Gordon, Wellington's aide-de-camp, was brought to die. It now houses the **Musée Wellington**, chaussée de Bruxelles 147 (April–mid-Nov 9.30am–6.30pm; mid-Nov–end March 10.30am–5pm; F60), detailing the events of the battle with plans and models, the assorted personal effects of Wellington, Gordon and Napoleon, and a display of amputating instruments – the need for which becomes clearer in the small **chapel** across the street, where a plaque reads "Here is buried the leg of the illustrious, brave and valiant Count Uxbridge". "I say, I've lost my leg", Uxbridge is reported to have said, to which Wellington replied "By God sir, so you have!" In fact, although Uxbridge's leg was initially buried here it was returned to London when he died to join the rest of his body; as a consolation his artificial leg was donated to the museum.

The Waterloo **tourist office** (daily 9.30am–6.30pm; ☎02/354 99 10), next door to the Musée Wellington, has a pamphlet suggesting walking tours in and around the town, though you'd be better off picking up orange bus #W again and heading down to the **battlefield** itself – a deadly flat landscape of fields spiked by the odd clump of trees. The best vantage point is from the 100m high **Butte de Lion**, built by local women with soil from the battlefield to mark the spot where Holland's Prince William of Orange – later King William II of the Netherlands – was wounded. It's a commanding monument, a regal 28-ton lion atop a stout column, up which it's possible to climb – some 226 steps (May–Aug 8.30am–12.30pm & 1.30pm–7pm; Sept, Oct, March & April 9.30am–12.30pm & 1.30pm–5pm; Nov–Feb 10am–12.30pm & 1.30pm–3pm; free). Close by, a rotunda-like building holds an enormous panoramic circular **painting** of the battle, 110m in circumference, the work of the French artist Louis Demoulin, naturalistically depicting the French cavalry charge on the opposing forces (Mon–Sat 9.30am–6pm, Sun 9.30am–6.30pm; F70). Afterwards, you could take a look at the **Musée de Cires** (Easter–Oct daily 9am–6.30pm; winter daily 10.15am–4.45pm) – which has wax figures of the leading characters, and shows a 1936 film of the proceedings.

Napoleon spent the eve of the battle at **Le Caillou**, a white brick farmhouse about 3km down the road from the Butte de Lion, and you can visit this too (the curator lives on the premises; F40). The mementoes here, including Napoleon's camp bed, death mask and the skeleton of a dead soldier (just one of the 39,000 who died) are something of a memorial to the emperor, as well as doing something to bring home the chill reality of battle.

Leuven

Less than half an hour away by train, **LEUVEN** makes for an equally easy day trip from Brussels. It's home to Belgium's oldest university, and has a fine Gothic square and studenty atmosphere that combine to give an impression of a relaxed, low-key provincial town. Apart from an extraordinary Gothic town hall and a handful of churches, there's not a great deal to see, as the city centre is, for the most part, an undistinguished tangle of streets lined with modern shops and snack bars. But it's something of a miracle that any of Leuven's ancient buildings have survived at all: in World War I some 1500 houses were destroyed, and the university library and main church gutted, only to suffer further damage in the last war too. The atmosphere of the town, also, can appear an odd one, with an acute disjunction between town and gown that only begins to reveal itself the longer you stay.

The history of the **university**, founded in 1425, isn't a particularly happy one. By the early sixteenth century it rated among Europe's most prestigious educational establishments: the cartographer Mercator was a student at Leuven, and Erasmus worked here, founding the *Collegium Trilingue* for the study of Hebrew, Latin and Greek, as the basis of a liberal (rather than Catholic) education. However, in response to the rise of Lutheranism, the authorities insisted on strict Catholic orthodoxy, and drove Erasmus into exile. In 1797 the French completely suppressed the university, and, after the defeat of Napoleon, when Belgium fell under Dutch rule, William I replaced it with a Philosphical College – one of many blatantly anti-Catholic measures which fuelled the Belgian revolution. Re-established after the revolution, as a bilingual Catholic institution, it became a hotbed of Flemish Catholicism, and for much of this century French and Flemish speakers here were locked into a sometimes violent nationalist dispute. In 1970 it was decided to found a separate, French-speaking university at Louvain-la-Neuve, just south of Brussels, and today Leuven has been re-established as a power-base of Flemish thinking, wielding considerable influence over the country's political and economic thought.

The City

The centre of town is marked by two adjacent squares – **Fochplein** (buses from the station drop off here), a road junction whose one remarkable feature is the **Font Sapienza**, a wittily cynical fountain of a student literally being brainwashed by the book he is reading, and the wedge-shaped **Grote Markt**. The latter is Leuven's architectural high spot, dominated by two magnificent fifteenth-century Gothic buidings – the Sint Pieterskerk and the Stadhuis. The **Stadhuis**, or town hall, is the more flamboyant of the two buildings, an extraordinarily light, lacy structure, studded with statues and tracery and crowned by soaring pinnacles. The statues, representing everything from important citizens, artists and nobles, to virtues, vices and municipal institutions, actually date from the nineteenth century: until then, the lavishly carved niches stood empty for lack of money. More appealing than these are the exuberant, sometimes grotesque, medieval figures protruding from the niche bases.

After the lavishness of the exterior, the inside of the Stadhuis is something of an anticlimax, with guided tours (Mon–Fri 11am & 3pm; Sat, Sun, hols 3pm; F50) taking you through a succession of heavily elaborate rooms, some of which are incongruously decked out in the fancy French styles of Louis XIV and XV. Even the Gothic hall upstairs is a disappointment, featuring a neo-Gothic chimneypiece and nineteenth-century portraits of people involved in the building of the Stadhuis, including the Leuven artist, Dieric Bouts. The basement – accessible by a separate entrance on Naamsestraat – holds a **Brasserie Museum** (Tues–Sat 10am–noon & 2–5pm; Easter–end Sept; also open Sun & hols 2–5pm), which holds a singularly unremarkable collection of brewing equipment.

There are few surviving works by Bouts, who worked for most of his life in Leuven, and had considerable influence on fifteenth-century German painting. His figures tend to be rather stiff and bony, but his use of colour is masterful, as you can see in two tryptychs housed in the late Gothic **Sint Pieterskerk** across the road, whose ambulatory – the only part of the church that is open right now, due to restoration – holds a **Museum of Religious Art**. Of the paintings, the *Last Supper* is of most interest, showing Christ and his disciples in a Flemish

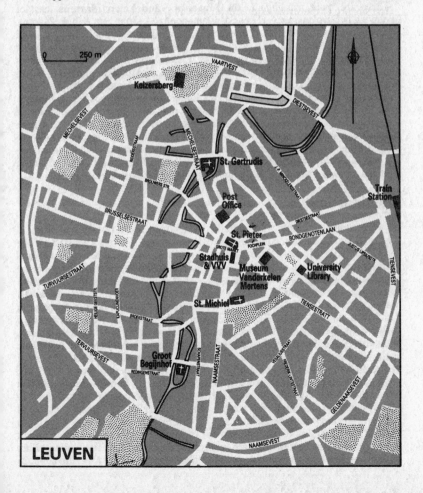

dining room, with the (half-built) Stadhuis just visible through the left-hand window. Look also for a copy of Rogier van der Weyden's marvellous *Descent from the Cross*, now in Madrid, which is said to have influenced Bouts' work, and the shrine and paintings in chapels 8 and 9, dedicated to one Saint (Proud) Margareth, Patron of Serving Girls. A thirteenth-century servant, she witnessed the murder of her employers, was abducted by the murderers, and then killed for refusing to marry one of them. The paintings in the second chapel, by Pieter Vrhagen, retell her story.

From the ambulatory there is access to the **crypt**, uncovered by World War II bomb damage, and still retaining some faint eleventh-century graffiti scratchings on the pillars. Have a peek, too, at the immense eighteenth-century **pulpit**, a weighty wooden confection carved with foliage and animals and showing Saint Norbert being thrown off his horse by lightning – a brush with death that prompted his conversion.

There are more paintings in the **Museum Vandekelen Martens**, east of Fochplein at Savoyestraat 6 (Tues-Sat 10am–noon & 2–5pm; Sun & hols 2–5pm), an eclectic collection that takes in everything from Japanese porcelain to stained glass. It's rather badly labelled, where at all, but its array of art exhibits includes work by Quentin Matsys, Cornelis de Vos, Pieter Aertsen and others, as well as polychromatic medieval and Renaissance sculpture. South of the museum, **Oude Markt** is the lively core of Leuven's student scene, a large cobbled rectangle surrounded by bars in gabled houses. It's home to a bustling market on Fridays. Above Oude Markt, Naamsestraat leads south past the supple Baroque facade of the Jesuit **Sint Michielskerk**, restored after wartime damage, to the **Groot Begijnhof**, a sixteenth-century enclave of mellow red-brick houses, once home to around three hundred *begijns:*. In 1962 the Begijnhof was bought by the university and painstakingly restored as student residences. Even now by day, when the students are out, a wonderfully tranquil, timeless atmosphere pervades.

Practical details

It's a ten- to fifteen-minute walk from the train station, down Bondgenotenlaan, to the Grote Markt, but you could also take bus #5 or #10. There's a **Tourist Office** just off the Grote Markt at Naamesestraat 1a (Mon–Fri 8am–5pm, Sat, Sun & hols 10am–5pm) which has maps, what's-on information and a useful booklet on the town listing all hotels and restaurants as well as sights and museums. There are some reasonable **hotels** directly opposite the station: *Hotel Industrie*, Martelarenplein 7 (☎016/22 13 49) with plain, clean and basic doubles for around F1000 without bathroom, F1200 with, and *Mille Colonnes*, Martelarenplein 5 (☎016/22 86 21), which has neat, simple doubles for F950 without bathroom, otherwise F1400. Alternatively, unless you're an unmarried couple, you could stay at the *Majestic*, Bondgenotenlaan 20 (☎016/22 43 65), which has doubles with bathroom from F1000, including breakfast in a wonderful period dining room.

To **drink**, the best place to head for is Oude Markt. *Bagatelle*, at no. 38 is a trendy hi-tech bar, *Café Allee* at no. 41 a cavernous student hang-out, and the self-service bar at no. 30, cheap and scruffy with beer for F30. The cheapest places to **eat** here are *Pizzeria il Fornello* at no. 37 with pizza from F150 and pasta from F160, or the bakery at no. 43. The densest concentration of **sandwich** and **snack bars** is on Tienenstraat which runs southeast from Fochplein. Try *Aquino*, at no. 93 or *Pistoleke*, at no. 84 which do massive filled baguettes, or *'t Overitje* at no. 25

which has takeaway pizza and hot savoury croissants. Below the Groot Bejinhof *Dijlemolens*, at the foot of Zwarte-Zusterstraat, is a student bar with filled baguettes, pasta dishes and omelettes; the *Cambridge*, at the corner of Parkstraat and Naamsestraat, is similar.

For more substantial fare you can get a meal for F285 with a student card at the university canteen *Alma*, Bondgenotenlaan 69 (11.30am–2pm & 5.30–8pm). Otherwise prices at *Ascoli*, Muntstraat 17, are lower than its smart decor might suggest, with pizza and pasta courses for under F200. There is good **vegetarian** food at *Lukemieke*, Vlamingenstraat 55 (noon–2pm & 6–8.30pm), behind the St Donatuspark, with main courses starting at F210.

travel details

Trains

All trains stop at Midi, Centrale and Nord unless otherwise indicated.

From Brussels to Ghent/Bruges/Ostende (hourly 40min/1hr/1hr 23min); Charleroi (hourly; 50min); Leuven (half-hourly; 30min); Liège/Maastricht (hourly; 1hr 20min/2hr); Mons (hourly; 55min); Antwerp (half-hourly; 40min); Antwerp/ Rotterdam/Amsterdam (hourly; 40min/2hr/3hr); Brussels Midi and Nord to Paris (10 daily; 3hr); Brussels Midi and Nord to Luxembourg/Metz/ Strasbourg/Basle (5 daily; 2hr 30min/3hr 45min/ 5hr/7hr 30min).

CHAPTER EIGHT

FLANDERS

The Flemish-speaking provinces of **East** and **West Flanders** spread out from the North Sea coast as far as Antwerp in the east and Kortrijk in the south. As early as the thirteenth century, Flanders was one of the most prosperous areas of Europe, with an advanced, integrated economy dependent on the cloth trade. By the sixteenth century, the region was in decline as trade slipped north towards Holland, and England's cloth manufacturers began to undermine Flanders' economic base. The speed of the collapse was accelerated by religious conflict, for the great Flemish towns were by inclination Protestant, their kings and queens Catholic, and, once Hapsburg domination was assured, thousands of weavers, merchants and skilled artisans poured north to escape religious persecution. The ultimate economic price was the closure of the Scheldt at the insistence of the Dutch in 1648. Thereafter, Flanders sank into poverty and decay, a static and traditional society where nearly every aspect of life was controlled by decree, and only three percent of the population could read or write. As Voltaire quipped:

In this sad place wherein I stay,
Ignorance, torpidity,
And boredom hold their lasting sway,
With unconcerned stupidity;
A land where old obedience sits,
Well filled with faith, devoid of wits.

The Flemish peasantry of the seventeenth and eighteenth centuries saw their lands crossed and re-crossed by the armies of the great powers, a region where the relative fortunes of dynasties and nations were decided. Only with Belgian independence did the situation begin to change: the towns started to industrialise, tariffs protected the cloth industry, Zeebrugge was built and Ostend was modernised, all in a flurry of activity that shook the land from its centuries-old torpor. Today, despite the devastating dislocation of World War I and the occupation of World War II, Flanders has emerged prosperous, its citizens maintaining a distinctive cultural and linguistic identity that's become a powerful political force in opposition to their Walloon neighbours.

With the exception of the range of low hills around Ronse and the sea dunes along the coast, Flanders is unrelentingly flat, and, frankly, rather dreary. However, there are many reminders of its medieval greatness, readily accessible by means of a comprehensive public transport network. The ancient cloth cities of **Bruges** and less well-known **Ghent** both hold marvellous collections of early Flemish art; and, of the smaller towns, **Oudenaarde** has a delightful Stadhuis and is famed for its tapestries, and **Kortrijk** and **Veurne** are pleasant old places worth stopping off at on the way south into France. There is also, of course, the legacy of World War I. The trenches extended from the North Sea coast, just near Westende, as far as Switzerland, cutting across West Flanders via Dijksmuide and

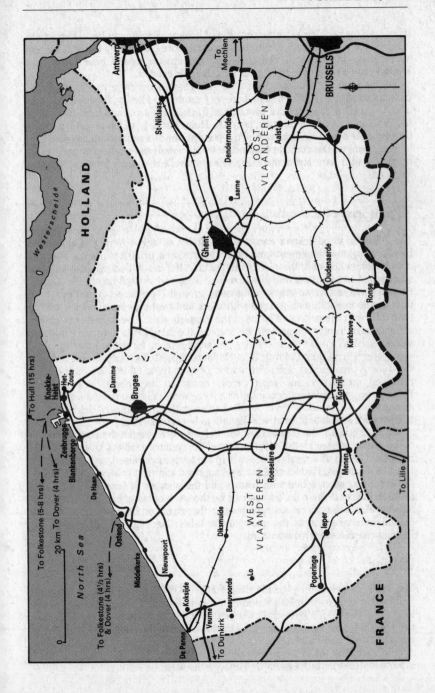

Ieper, and many of the key engagements of the war were fought here. Every year hundreds of visitors head for **Nieuwpoort** and more particularly **Ieper** (formerly Ypres) to see the numerous cemeteries and monuments around these towns – sad reminders of what proved to be a desperately futile conflict.

Not far from the battlefields, the Belgian coast is beach territory, an almost continuous stretch of golden sand that every summer is filled by thousands of tourists. An excellent **tram** service connects all the major resorts, and although a lot of the development has been crass, cosy **De Haan** has kept much of its turn-of-the-century charm, and **Knokke** has all the pretensions of a sophisticated resort. The largest town on the coast is **Ostend**, a lively, rough-and-ready port and resort crammed with bars and restaurants full of travellers waiting for the ferries to England.

The Coast

The 70km or so of Belgian **coast** groans under an ugly covering of apartment blocks, bungalow settlements and caravan parks, obscuring a landscape that was largely untouched until the nineteenth century, the beach backing onto a line of sand dunes on which nothing grew except rushes and stunted Lombardy poplars. Behind them, a narrow strip of undulating ground ("Ter Streep"), seldom more than a mile in width and covered with moss and bushes, connected the barren sand-hills with the cultivated farms of the Flemish plain. The dunes were always an inadequate protection against the sea, and the inhabitants here were building dykes as early as the tenth century, an arrangement formalised two hundred years later when Count Baldwin IX of Flanders appointed guardians charged with the duty of constructing defensive works. Despite these efforts, life on the coast remained precarious, and most people chose to live inland; indeed, when Belgium achieved independence in 1830, there were only two coastal settlements of any size – Ostend, a small fortified town with an antiquated harbour, and Nieuwpoort, in a state of what was thought to be terminal decay.

It was Leopold I, the first king of the Belgians, who began the transformation of the coast, assisted by the development of the country's railway system. In 1834 he chose Ostend as a royal residence, had the town modernised, and connected it by rail to Brussels. Fashionable by royal approval and readily accessible by train, the coast was soon dotted with resorts and the number of seaside visitors shot through the roof. The next king carried on the work of his father, building a light railway along the shore and completing the chain of massive sea-walls that extend from one end of the coast to the other. Barring the remarkable, the Belgian coastline seemed safe at last.

Ostend

The 1900 Baedeker travel guide distinguished **OSTEND** as "One of the most fashionable and cosmopolitan watering places in Europe". The gloss is, however, long gone, the town's aristocratic visitors have moved on to more exotic climes, and Ostend is now among Belgium's largest ports and the main ferry terminal for boats to Dover and Folkestone. It's also the pivot of the region's public transport system, including the fast, frequent and efficient trams that run behind the beach to Knokke-Heist in the east and De Panne in the west.

The old fishing village of Ostend was given a town charter in the thirteenth century, in recognition of its growing importance as a port for trade across the Channel. Flanked by an empty expanse of sand dune, it remained the only important harbour along this stretch of the coast until the construction of Zeebrugge in the nineteenth century. Like so many other towns in the Spanish Netherlands, it was attacked and besieged time and again, winning the admiration of Protestant Europe in resisting the Spaniards during a desperate siege that lasted from 1601 to 1604. Later, convinced of the wholesome qualities of sea air and determined to impress other European rulers with their sophistication, Belgium's first kings, Leopold I and II, turned Ostend into a chi-chi resort, demolishing the town walls and dotting the outskirts with prestigious buildings and parks – some of which were destroyed during World War II, when the town was a prime bombing target.

Arriving, sleeping and eating

The **ferry terminal** at Montgomerydok is next to the **railway station**, a couple of minutes' walk from the centre of town – you couldn't wish for a more convenient setup if you're heading straight through. The station's **information office** (Mon–Fri 7am–7pm, Sat & Sun 8.30am–7pm) has comprehensive details of international train times. For destinations along the coast, **trams** leave from beside the railway station and head off east to Knokke-Heist and west to De Panne, putting all the Belgian resorts within easy striking distance. Winter services in both directions depart every half-hour, in summer every ten minutes. Fares are relatively inexpensive – Ostend to De Panne, for instance, costs F135; you can also buy tickets for unlimited tram travel, valid either one day (F260) or five days (F750). If you are pushing on immediately, **car hire** is available from *Budget*, Groentemarkt 22 (☎059/50 35 08), *Hertz* Leopold III Laan 17 (☎059/70 28 20), and *Inter-rent*, Verenigde Natieslaan 43 (☎059/70 65 89).

If you decide to stay, Ostend has a small **tourist kiosk** just outside the station (July–Aug 10am–12.30pm & 2–6pm) and a main **tourist office** a few minutes' away on the Wapenplein (July–Aug daily 9am–1pm & 2–8pm; Sept–June Mon–Fri 8.30am–noon & 1.45–5.45pm, Sat 9am–noon & 2–5pm; ☎059/508 988). They will help you find **accommodation** in one of many hotels and guesthouses. One of the more pleasant and convenient areas to stay is in the series of side streets sandwiched between Albert 1 Promenade, the Casino and Van Iseghemlaan: there are a number of hotels on Louisastraat, including the *Coventry*, no. 8a (☎059/70 58 55), which has doubles from F850; other include the *Marion*, no. 19 (☎059/50 28 56), *Mayfair*, no. 18 (☎059/70 96 50), and the *Empire*, no. 31 (☎059/ 70 42 59), all of which charge F500 per person. The more upmarket *Louisa*, no. 8b (☎059/50 96 77), has doubles for F2000, while nearby the pleasant *Royal Astor*, Hertstraat 15 (☎059/50 49 70), is a good deal with doubles from F1600. The **youth hostel** is spick, span and handily placed at Langestraat 82 (☎059/80 52 97), though it's often full in summer. The nearest **campsite** is *Ostend Camping-Coppin* at Nieuwpoortsesteenweg 514 (☎059/70 55 73), just behind the beach several kilometres to the west of town (take bus #6 from the railway station).

The sheer variety of places to **eat** is almost daunting. Along Visserskaai and through the central city streets are innumerable snack bars, coffee houses and restaurants. Many of them serve some pretty mediocre stuff, alhough all offer good plates of mussels and chips. Two of the better restaurants are on the seafront near the station – the pricey *Lusitania*, Visserskaai 35, and the *Marina*, Albert I Promenade 2.

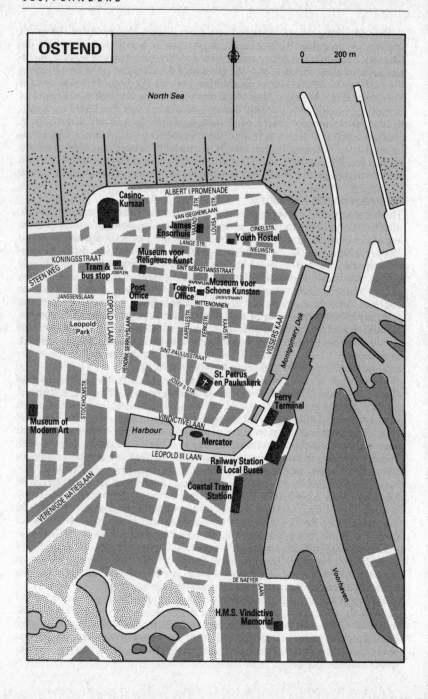

OSTEND

North Sea

0   200 m

ALBERT I PROMENADE

Casino-
Kursaal

VAN ISEGHEMLAAN

James
Ensorhuis

CIRKELSTR.

Youth Hostel

LANGE STR.

NIEUWSTR.

Museum voor
Religieuze Kunst

KONINGSSTRAAT

SINT SEBASTIANSSTRAAT

Tram &
bus stop

MARIE
JOSEPLEIN

STEEN WEG

WAPENPLEIN

Museum voor
Schone Kunsten

JANSSENSLAAN

Post
Office

Tourist
Office

GROENTEMARKT

WITTENONNEN

LEOPOLD II LAAN

Leopold
Park

KAPELLESTR.

KERKSTR.

KAAISTR.

HENDRIK SERRUYSLAAN

VISSERS KAAI

Montgomery Dok

SINT-PAULUSSTRAAT

STOCKHOLMSTR.

JOSEF II STR.

St. Petrus
en Pauluskerk

Ferry
Terminal

Museum of
Modern Art

VINDICTIVELAAN

Harbour

Mercator

LEOPOLD III LAAN

Railway Station
& Local Buses

Coastal Tram
Station

VERENIGDE NATIESLAAN

Voorhaven

DE NAEYER
LAAN

H.M.S. Vindictive
Memorial

The Town

There's precious little left of medieval Ostend, and today's town centre spreads out from beside the train station – a series of narrow, straight streets edged by the beach to the north, Leopold II Laan, the site of the old walls, to the west, and the marina, the former harbour, to the south. Across the Visserskaai from the station, **Sint Petrus en Sint Pieterkerk** looks old but in fact dates from the early twentieth century. Next to the church, the last remnant of its predecessor is a massive sixteenth-century tower with a canopied, morbid shrine of the Crucifixion at its base. From here, Kerkstraat leads to the main square, **Wapenplein**, where the **Museum voor Schone Kunsten** (daily except Tues 10am–noon & 2–5pm) is divided into two sections. There are modest temporary exhibitions of local history in the **Museum De Plate** on the first floor, and several well-displayed rooms of nineteenth- and twentieth-century paintings on the second. Apart from the harsh surrealism of Paul Delvaux's *De Ijzertijd*, pride of place goes to the canvases of James Ensor, who was born in Ostend in 1860 to an English father and Flemish mother. Barely noticed until the 1920s, Ensor spent nearly all his 89 years working in his home town, and is nowadays considered a pioneer of Expressionism. His first paintings were rather sombre portraits and landscapes, but in the early 1880s he switched to brilliantly contrasting colours, most familiar in his *Self-portrait of the Artist in a Flowered Hat*, a deliberate variation on Rubens' famous self-portraits. Less well-known is *Portrait of a Dead Mother*, a fine, rather fierce example of his preoccupation with the grim and macabre.

A couple of minutes' walk north of the Wapenplein, the **James Ensorhuis**, Vlaanderenstraat 27 (June–Sept daily except Tues 10am–noon & 2–5pm), was the artist's first home, and has been restored to its former state. On the ground floor there's the old shell and souvenir shop of his uncle and aunt, and up above are the painter's sitting room and studio, though none of the works on display are originals. James Ensor is further remembered immediately to the west of Wapenplein, in the **Museum voor Religieuze Kunst**, Sint Sebastiaanstraat 41 (July–Sept daily except Tues and Wed 3–6pm), sited in a disused chapel, which has several more paintings by the artist along with a mundane collection of eighteenth- and nineteenth-century religious pictures and sculpture. Just to the north of Sint Sebastiaanstraat, the **Casino-Kursaal** was built in 1953 as a successor to the first casino of 1852. Most of the town's classical concerts are performed here and one of the gambling rooms is decorated with murals by Paul Delvaux.

On either side of the Casino is Ostend's main attraction, a strip of sandy **beach** which extends east to the harbour and west as far as De Panne. On summer days thousands drive into town to soak up the sun, swim and amble along the sea-front **Promenade**, which runs along the top of the sea wall. Part sea-defence and part royal ostentation, the Promenade was once the main route from the town centre to the Wellington racecourse 2km to the west, an intentionally grand walkway designed to please the pretensions of Leopold II, whose imperial statue still stands in the middle of a long line of stone columns. Added in the 1930s, the adjoining **Thermae Palace Hotel** is similarly regal, but spoils the lines of the original walkway.

Heading east from the Casino, Albert I Promenade leads into the Visserskaai, where the **Aquarium** (April–Sept daily 10am–noon & 2–5pm), housed in the former shrimp market on the east side of the street, holds a series of displays on North Sea fish, crustacea, flora and fauna. To the south in the marina, the sailing ship **Mercator** (June–Sept daily 9am–noon & 1–6pm; March–May & Oct Sat &

Sun 10am–noon & 1–5pm; Nov–Feb Sun 10am–noon & 1–4pm; F60) is the old training boat of the Belgian merchant navy, converted into a marine museum holding an enormous collection of items accumulated during her worldwide voyages.

A few minutes' walk south of the railway station, in a sunken garden at the end of Westkaai, is the bow of the **HMS Vindictive**. On the night of May 9, 1918, the British made a desperate attempt to block Ostend's harbour. The sacrificial ships were manned by volunteers and the *Vindictive* was successfully sunk at the port entrance. After the war the bows were retrieved and kept as a memorial to the sailors who lost their lives. This was one of the most audacious operations of the war, but tragically it was based on false intelligence: German submarines hardly ever used the harbour.

East of Ostend

Trams leave from beside Ostend train station for the journey east to Knokke-Heist every ten minutes in summer and every thirty minutes in winter. Clearing the town's shabby suburbs, they shoot through a series of ugly tourist developments that disfigure the sand dunes as far as **DE HAAN**, an oasis of restraint amid the predominant high-rise construction, which has never been allowed here. Established at the end of the nineteenth century, De Haan was carefully conceived as an exclusive seaside village in a rustic Gothic Revival style – *style Normand*. The building plots were irregularly dispersed between the tram station and the sea around a pattern of winding streets reminiscent of – and influenced by – contemporaneous English suburbs like Liverpool's Sefton Park. The only formality was provided by a central circus around a casino (demolished in 1929). De Haan has survived pretty much intact, a welcome relief from the surrounding ugliness, and, flanked by empty sand dunes, it's now a popular family resort, with a good beach and pleasant seafront cafés.

The **tourist office** (April–Sept daily 9am–noon & 2–6pm; ☎050/23 57 23) is next to the tram stop named De Haan Preventorium and will help with **rooms** – available for about F700 per person per night. There are no less than 21 **hotels** in or near the village centre, including the convenient, reasonably priced *Des Brasseurs* (☎059/23 52 94), with rooms from F800 per person per night, and the *Belle Vue* (☎059/23 34 39), which has singles from F650, at Koninklijk Plein 1 and 5, a couple of minutes' walk from the tram stop towards the sea. In the opposite direction, the *'t Bosje* (☎059/23 42 72) and the *'t Nestje* (☎059/23 41 57) charge F950 for a double; they're at Wenduinesteenweg 55 and 55a, a left turn off Stationsstraat, five minutes' walk south of the tram stop. *Camping 54* is the nearest of a chain of **campsites**, a further five minutes along Wenduinesteenweg at no. 67.

Blankenberge

Nine kilometres east of De Haan, **BLANKENBERGE** is one of the busiest places on the coast, but it has precious little to recommend it. Hopelessly overcrowded during the summer, it's the archetypal "kiss-me-quick" seaside town, with a Victorian pier, a tiled Art Deco casino and dozens of guesthouses and fast food bars pumping out high-energy singalongs. The **tourist office** (June–Aug daily 9am–9pm; Sept–May Mon–Sat 9am–12.30pm & 2–6pm, Sun 9am–12.30pm; ☎050/ 41 29 21) is at the end of the main street, next to the tram stop.

Zeebrugge

A few kilometres beyond Blankenberge, work began on a brand new seaport and harbour next to the tiny village of **ZEEBRUGGE** in 1895. The key to the project was a crescent-shaped **Mole** some two and a half kilometres long and one hundred metres wide that stuck out from the shore, protecting incoming and outgoing shipping from the vagaries of the North Sea. Connected to the rail and canal systems, the harbour was an ambitious attempt to improve Belgium's coastal facilities and provide easy access to the sea from Bruges via the Boudewijnkanaal. Completed in 1907, it was a great commercial success, though two world wars badly damaged its prospects. During World War I, the Allies were convinced that Zeebrugge was a German submarine base, and in conjunction with the assault on Ostend attempted to obstruct the harbour in April 1918. Block ships, crewed by volunteers, were taken to strategic positions and sunk with heavy casualties and only partial success. There's a **monument** to the dead sailors and a map of the action at the base of the Mole, restored after it was destroyed during the German occupation. World War II saw the same job done rather more proficiently, but it didn't stop further bombing raids and the demolition of the port by the retreating Germans in 1944. The last of the block ships (the *Thetis*) was finally cleared and the harbour reopened in 1957.

Spreading out along the coast amongst the series of giant docks, Zeebrugge divides into sections, each with its own tram stop. On the west side, a couple of minutes' walk from Zeebrugge Pier tram stop, is the small beach resort. There's nothing much to come here for, but, pushed up against the base of the Mole to the east and edged by sand dunes to the west, it's a surprisingly pleasant place to stay if you're catching an early ferry, with two reasonably priced **hotels**, the *Strandhotel*, Zeedijk 14 (☎050/54 40 55), with doubles from F1450, and the cheaper *De Pier*, Zeedijk 4 (☎050/54 44 83), which has doubles from F970. The **tourist office** (July–Aug daily 10am–1pm & 2–6pm) is in a small kiosk on the seafront and can provide up-to-date details of the irregular **bus** service to Bruges rail station (#791, 2 daily, 6 in July and Aug; 30min) and of **ferries** to England. *P&O* operate services to Dover and Felixstowe from their office about 500m along the Mole; *North Sea Ferries* have sailings to Hull from the terminal building another

---

THE ZEEBRUGGE DISASTER

On Friday March 6, 1987, the 7pm ferry from Zeebrugge to Dover sank shortly after departure in the icy waters of the harbour, in sight of land. The boat, *Townsend Thoresen*'s *Herald of Free Enterprise*, was a roll-on, roll-off car ferry with an open car deck that filled with water once the ship left its moorings because the bow doors had not been closed. The crew made a desperate last-minute effort to close the doors, but it was too late, and within minutes the ship keeled over, drowning and crushing over 150 people. The cause of disaster was obvious enough, though the reasons for it have been variously attributed to poor communications between bridge and deck, human error and crew fatigue as a result of the tight schedule of sailings. The biggest controversy has been around the underlying limitations of this sort of open-deck car ferry, and many have argued that if the ferries were fitted with bulk heads on the car decks then they would be far safer. However, the ferry companies themselves remain unconvinced, not least because bulk heads decrease capacity and therefore profits.

500m to the north. Tickets are only available direct from the ferry operators on the Mole.

A twenty-minute walk east of the beach resort, or a couple of minutes from tram stop Vaart, Zeebrugge **railway station** (for Bruges, hourly; 15min) is surrounded by several rows of terraced houses that were built for harbour workers at the start of this century. The ferry companies run a free bus service from the station to coincide with sailings. A further 1km to the east, the third and oldest part of Zeebrugge fans out north from the tram line to the original fishing harbour, now part of the general dock complex.

Knokke-Heist

Generally regarded as Belgium's most sophisticated resort, **KNOKKE-HEIST** is the collective name for five villages whose individual identities have disappeared in a welter of development that stretches for some 6km along the coast as far as the Dutch frontier. Jam-packed in summer, the sophistication is hard to pick out among the confusion of high-rise apartment blocks and expensive second homes hidden away in their leafy, exclusive suburbs. To increase its popularity, a lot of effort goes into planning Knokke-Heist's varied special events programme, notably an annual **sand castle building competition** and the **International Cartoon Festival**, with 800 entries selected by an international panel shown every year in the **Humorhall**, just to the west of Duinbergen, south of the tram line. Up-to-date details on all events are available from the tourist office.

The most agreeable part of this giant resort is at the east end around **KNOKKE**, which is well connected to Ostend by **tram** and to Bruges by **bus** (#788 every 30min; 70min) and **train** (2 hourly; 15min). Tram, train and bus stations are grouped together at the south end of the long and featureless main street, the Lippenslaan, an inconvenient 2km south of the seafront, where the **tourist office**, Zeedijk 660 (daily 10am–noon & 2–5.30pm; July & Aug daily 10am–1pm & 2–7pm; ☎050/60 16 16), will ring around to make a reservation in any of Knokke's seven **hotels**. Two of the cheaper alternatives are on the Lippenslaan, where the *Prince De Liège*, no. 34 (☎050/60 49 21), has singles at F540, doubles from F950, and *Prince's*, no. 171 (☎050/60 11 11), has doubles from F1100. The nearest **campsite**, *Camping Nr.1*, is 3km to the west at Duinbergenlaan 17, the road heading north from Duinbergen train station.

Knokke itself has all the usual attractions of a busy beach resort, including an excellent range of sporting facilities, but it's distinguished by its desire to cater for the rich, who congregate in the expensive boutiques and private art galleries, where many of the big names of modern Dutch art come to exhibit and sell their work. Near the seafront, the centre of all the cultural activity is the sumptuous **Casino** (gambling daily from 3pm), which has an international reputation for its showings of modern art and is decorated with canvases by Paul Delvaux in the lobby and René Magritte's *Le Domaine Enchanté* in the gaming room.

Heading east along the sea dyke from Knokke, past the wealthy adjoining resort of HET ZOUTE, it's about 4km to the start of the **Het Zwin** nature reserve (April–Sept daily 9am–7pm; Oct–March 9am–5pm, closed Wed), a 150-hectare expanse of salt marsh that extends to the Dutch border. It's a beautiful spot with some unusual flora and fauna nourished by a combination of the river and occasional seawater flooding. Two-hour guided visits can be arranged by written request, three weeks in advance, to Het Zwin, Ooievaarslaan 8, 8300 Knokke-Heist (☎050/60 70 86). On foot, the best approach from Knokke is either straight along the shoreline, or along Kustlaan and subsequently Zwinlaan, a block behind the seafront. Strange as it seems today, this quiet area was once one of the busiest waterways in the world, connecting Bruges with the North Sea until the river Zwin silted up in the sixteenth century. In 1340, it was also the site of one of the largest naval engagements of the century, when Edward III sailed up the estuary with his Flemish allies to destroy a French fleet gathered for a projected invasion of England.

West of Ostend

West of Ostend, a series of dreary resorts spreads along the sea dunes beside the beach, an unappealing mixture of apartment blocks and seaside villas that occupies almost every inch of the coast. The tram line hugs the shore until it cuts inland to round the estuary of the river Ijzer (Yser) at the small town of **NIEUWPOORT** (tram stop Nieuwpoort Stad) – not to be confused with the crass high-rise development of NIEUWPOORT-AAN-ZEE just up the road. Nieuwpoort hasn't had much luck. Founded in the twelfth century, it was besieged nine times in the following six hundred years, but this was nothing compared to its misfortune in World War I. In 1914, the first German campaign reached the Ijzer before the Belgians opened the sluices along the Noordvaart canal, just to the south of the town. The water stopped the invaders in their tracks and permanently separated the armies, but it also put Nieuwpoort on the front line, where it remained for the rest of the war. Every day volunteers had to sacrifice the safety of their bunkers to operate the ring of sluice gates near the town centre – without this the water would either have drained away or risen to flood the Belgian trenches. Across the bridge near the tram stop, you can still see the ring of sluice gates, dotted with war memorials to the hundreds of men who died.

Four years of shelling reduced the town to a ruin, and what you see now is the result of a meticulous restoration that lasted well into the 1920s. There's nothing remarkable and the town is only worth a brief visit, though the neo-Renaissance **Stadhuis** and the adjoining **Halle** in the Marktplein give some indication of more prosperous days. The **tourist office** (Mon–Fri 8am–noon & 1.30–5pm, Sat 8am–noon; ☎058/23 55 94), Marktplein 7, has a list of cheap private **rooms** from F600 per person per night. The nearest **campsite** is southeast of town at Brugsesteenweg 49; take P. Dezwartelaan at the island on the near side of the bridge, first left across the canal and first right. In July and August, **boat trips** (Mon–Fri twice a day, 4 days a week; return fare F400, single F250) leave from the landing stage on P. Dezwartelaan for the journey south along the Ijzer to Dijksmuide, following the path of the front line of World War I. There's also a twice weekly excursion to Veurne (single F200, return F300). Further details from the tourist office.

De Panne

Some 7km west of Nieuwpoort, **OOSTDUINKERKE-BAD** has a particularly fine beach, from which local fishermen used to ride into the sea on horseback to sweep the ocean for shrimps. It's still done, but these days more usually for the benefit of tourists. Further west, **DE PANNE**, 2km from the French frontier, is now one of the largest settlements on the Belgian coast, though as late as the 1880s it was a tiny fishing village of low white cottages, nestling in a slight wooded hollow ("panne") from which it takes its name. Most of the villagers had their own fishing boats and a plot of land surrounded by trees and hedges. The peace and quiet ended with the arrival of surveyors and architects who reinforced the sea dyke, and laid out paths and roads in preparation for the rapid construction of lines of villas and holiday homes. However, with the exception of the buildings on the seafront, the contours of the land were respected and the houses of much of today's resort perch prettily among the dunes to the south of the beach.

Equipped with all the usual amenities of a seaside town, De Panne tends to be overcrowded in season, and its centre is distinctly unprepossessing. There's a **tourist information kiosk** (June to mid-Sept daily 10am–noon & 2–5pm; ☎058/ 41 29 63) on the promenade by the beach, and a main office in the **Gemeentehuis** (Mon–Fri 9am–noon & 1.30–5.30pm; ☎058/41 13 04), south from behind the kiosk at Zeelaan 21. Both offices have lists of **pensions** and private **rooms** and will ring around to find vacancies, providing they aren't too busy. Alternatively, there's a cluster of pensions along Nieuwpoortlaan, one block south of the sea-front near its junction with Zeelaan. These include *L'Avenue*, no. 56 (☎058/41 13 70) and *Phoebus*, no. 48 (☎058/41 11 73), with singles from F600 per night; the nearby **hotel** *Le Gai Sejour*, at no. 42 (☎058/41 13 03), which has doubles from F1800; and *Des Princes*, at no. 46 (☎058/41 10 91) – slightly cheaper with doubles from F1450.

There's little to see as such in De Panne, though the rather grand **monument** at the west end of Zeedijk marks the spot where King Leopold first set foot on Belgian soil in 1831. Otherwise, the town achieved passing fame in World War I, when it was part of the tiny triangle of Belgian territory that the German army failed to occupy, becoming the home of King Albert's government from 1914 to 1918. Some thirty years later, the retreating British army managed to reach the beaches between De Panne and Dunkirk, 15km to the west, just in time for the miraculous evacuation back to England.

The sand dunes southwest of De Panne form the **Westhoek Nature Reserve**, an expanse of wild, unspoilt coastline criss-crossed by signposted footpaths. The tourist office sells detailed maps and illustrated guides of local flora and fauna. Otherwise, if you're **heading for Veurne** (see below), 6km inland, it's a good 25-minute walk south from the beach down Zeelaan and then Kerkstraat to De Panne railway station, where trains make the ten-minute journey hourly; if you don't fancy the walk, buses leave for the station from near the junction of Nieuwpoortlaan and Zeeland every half-hour.

Veurne

Founded in the ninth century, **VEURNE** was part of a chain of fortresses built to defend Flanders from the raids of the Vikings, but without much success. By the eleventh century, Veurne had a modest livelihood, but all changed when Robert II of Flanders returned from the Crusades in 1099 with a piece of the True Cross. His ship was caught by a gale and in desperation he vowed to offer the relic to the first church he saw if he survived. The church was St Walburga at Veurne, and the annual procession that commemorated the gift made the town an important centre of medieval worship for some three hundred years. These days Veurne is one of the most popular day-trip destinations in West Flanders, but it's a rather drab town on the whole, its only real pull being its Grote Markt, which ranks as one of the best preserved town squares in Belgium.

The Town

Most of the main town sights are on or nearby the **Grote Markt**. At the north-west corner, the **Stadhuis** is a mixture of Gothic and Renaissance styles built between 1596 and 1612, with a fine, blue and gold decorated stone loggia project-ing from the original brick facade. Inside, a **museum** (April–Sept guided tours 6 times daily; F40) displays items of unexceptional interest, the best of which are a set of leather wall coverings made in Cordoba. The Stadhuis connects with the more austere classicism of the **Gerechtshof**, with its symmetrical pillars and rectangular windows, which once housed the offices of Inquisition. The attached tiered **belfry** remains closed to visitors, although you can visit the church of **St Walburga** behind (Easter–Sept daily 10am–noon & 3–6pm), the venue of the medieval pilgrimages, an enormous buttressed and gargoyled affair with weather-beaten brick walls dating from the thirteenth century.

On the northeast corner of the Grote Markt, at the end of Ooststraat, the **Spaans Paviljoen** (Spanish Pavilion) was built as the town hall in the middle of the fifteenth century, but takes its name from its later adaptation as the officers' quarters of the Hapsburg garrison. It's a self-confident building, whose long windows and fluted parapet contrast with the Flemish shutters and gables of the **Vleeshuis** directly opposite. On the south side of the square, the seventeenth-century **Hoge Wacht** originally served as the quarters of the town watch. Immediately to the east, just off the Grote Markt, the Appelmarkt is edged by **Sint Niklaaskerk**, whose thirteenth-century detached **tower** (mid-June to mid-Sept 10am–noon & 2–5pm; F30) gives spectacular views of the countryside around.

THE PENITENTS' PROCESSION

In 1650 a young soldier named Mannaert was on garrison duty in Veurne, when he was persuaded to commit a mortal sin by his best friend. After he had received the consecrated wafer during Communion, he took it out of his mouth, wrapped it in a cloth and returned to his lodgings where he fried it over a fire, under the delusion that by reducing it to powder he would make himself invulnerable to injury. The news got out, and he was later arrested, tried and executed, his friend suffering the same fate a few weeks later. Fearful of the consequences of this sacrilege in their town, the people of Veurne resolved that something must be done, deciding on a procession to commemorate the Passion of Christ. This survives as the **Penitents' Procession** (Boetprocessie), held on the last Sunday in July – an odd and distinctly macabre reminder of a remote past. Trailing through the streets, the leading figures dress in the brown cowls of the Capuchins and carry wooden crosses that weigh anything up to fifty kilos.

Practical details

Buses to Veurne drop passengers a couple of minutes' walk from the Grote Markt; the town **railway station** is a ten-minute stroll to the east of the centre – right out of the station building, first left along Stationsstraat and over the canal straight down Ooststraat. **Accommodation** is a problem. The **tourist office**, Grote Markt 29 (Mon–Fri 10am–noon & 1.30–5pm; ☎058/31 21 54), has details of a couple of private **rooms** from F600 per night, but they're often full. The only alternative is the town's one **hotel**, *'t Belfort*, Grote Markt 26 (☎058/31 11 55), with doubles from F1500 per night. Ring ahead in summer to make sure of a bed. For **food**, the Grote Markt is lined with snack bars and restaurants: try *De Vette Os*, at no. 21, or *De Kroon*, at no. 8, where you can sample the local delicacy, *potjesvlees* – veal, chicken and rabbit pies, best washed down with the Trappist ale of nearby Westvleteren. In July and August, **carillon concerts** are performed in the belfry of the Gerechtshof every Wednesday morning (10.30–11.30am) and Sunday evening (8–9pm). **Boat trips** leave from the quay beside the train station for Nieuwpoort once weekly (F200); exact dates and times from the tourist office.

Around Veurne: Beauvoorde, Lo and Dijksmuide

Veurne is the capital of the **Veurne-Ambacht**, an agricultural area of quiet and unremarkable villages that stretches south and west of the town, sandwiched between the French border and the river Ijzer. It's best seen by bike (cycles can be hired at Veurne railway station): maps of cycle routes are available from the tourist office. The region's prime attraction is the Renaissance castle of **Beauvoorde** (June–Sept daily except Mon, guided tours at 2, 3 & 4pm; F50; no buses), accessible from the signposted turning some 9km south of Veurne on the main road to Ieper – follow the turning west for about 3km into the village of WULVERINGEM, and it's a block to the north at Wulveringemstraat 10. Built in the early seventeenth century, the castle's angular gables sit prettily behind a narrow moat and the interior has displays of ceramics, silverware and glass.

The most agreeable village in the district is LO, 12km southeast of Veurne, on the bus route between Ieper and Veurne (7 daily; 30min). It was here that Julius Caesar is supposed to have tethered his horse to a yew by the Westpoort on his way across Gaul. Less apocryphally, the village once prospered under the patronage of its Augustinian abbey, founded in the twelfth century and suppressed by the French at the time of the Revolution. Only the dovecot of the abbey survives, but Lo is a classically picturesque village, with a cosy whitewashed church, gabled town hall, wooden windmill, and the fragmented remains of an old stone gate, the Westpoort. There's one **hotel**, *the Stadhuis*, Markt 1 (☎058/28 80 16), with doubles at F1100 per night.

Ten minutes from Veurne, the hourly train to Ghent passes the **Ijzertoren**, a massive, sombre war memorial that dominates the western approaches to the small town of **DIKSMUIDE**, which was so extensively shelled in World War I that by 1918 its location could only be identified from a map. It owed its destruction to its position to the immediate east of the river Ijzer, which formed the front line from October 1914. Rebuilt, the town is of little appeal, but for a closer look at the memorial and the adjacent **war museum** (March, April, Sept & Oct Mon–Fri 9am–5pm, Sat & Sun 10am–noon & 1–5pm; May–Aug daily 9am–7pm), follow the signs for the fifteen-minute walk from the town centre.

Ieper (Ypres)

Readily reached by train from Kortrijk and by bus from Veurne, **IEPER** (YPRES) is another Flanders town that prospered from the medieval cloth trade, its thirteenth-century population of 200,000 sharing economic control of the region with their rivals in Ghent and Bruges. The most precariously sited of the great Flemish cities, Ypres, as it was then known, was too near the French frontier for comfort, and too strategically important to be ignored by any of the armies whose campaigns criss-crossed the town's environs with depressing frequency. The city governors kept disaster at bay by reinforcing their defences and switching alliances whenever necessary, fighting against the French at the Battle of the Golden Spurs in 1302, and with them forty years later at Roosebeke, where the popular Ghent leader, Philip van Artevelde, was killed.

The first major misjudgement came in 1383 when Henry Spencer, Bishop of Norwich, landed at Calais under the pretext of supporting the armies of Pope Urban VI, who occupied the Vatican, against his rival Clement VII, who was installed in Avignon. The burghers of Ghent and Bruges flocked to Spencer's standard and the allies had little difficulty in agreeing on an attack against Ypres, which had decided to champion Clement and trust in the French for support. The ensuing siege lasted for two months before a French army appeared to save the day, and all of Ypres celebrated the victory. In fact, the town was ruined, its trade never recovered, and, unable to challenge its two main competitors again, many of the major weavers migrated. The process of depopulation proved irreversible and by the sixteenth century the town had shrunk to a mere 5000 inhabitants.

In World War I, the first German thrust of 1914 left a bulge in the Allied line to the immediate east of Ypres, and for the next four years a series of futile offensives attempted to use the bulge – or **Salient** – as a base to break through the enemy's front line. This had disastrous consequences for Ypres, which served as the Allied communications centre. Comfortably within the range of German artillery, the whole population was evacuated in 1915, and by the end of the war Ypres had literally been shelled to smithereens. The town was rebuilt in the 1920s and 1930s, its most prominent medieval buildings, the cloth hall and cathedral, being carefully reconstructed from the originals. The end result, however, can't help but seem a little antiseptic – old-style edifices but with no signs of decay or erosion.

The Town

A monument to the power and wealth of the medieval guilds, the **Cloth Hall**, on the **Grote Markt**, was built in the thirteenth century alongside the river Ieperlee, which now flows underground. Too long to be pretty and too square to be elegant, it's nothing special to look at, but it was meant to be practical. No less than 58 doors gave access from the street to the old selling halls, while boats sailed in and out of the gate on the west wing under the watchful eyes of its massive square belfry. During winter, wool was stored on the upper floor and cats were brought in to keep the mice down. The cats may have had a good time in winter, but they couldn't have relished the prospect of spring when they were thrown out of the windows to a hostile crowd below as part of the **Kattestoet** (Cats' Death) festival. The festival ran right up until 1817, and was revived in 1938, when the cats were replaced by cloth imitations, and it's since become Ieper's main shindig, held on the second Sunday in May, complete with processions and parades, dancers and bands and some of the biggest models and puppets imaginable.

The east end of the cloth hall is attached to the old **Stadhuis**, whose flamboyant Renaissance facade rises above an elegant arcaded gallery. Inside, on the first floor, the **Salient Museum** (April to mid-Nov daily 9.30am–noon & 1.30–5.30pm) outlines the course and effects of World War I on Ieper. Though a little self-conscious in its efforts to remain neutral, it is, at times, powerful stuff. There's a modest collection of personal memorabilia including the pipe, binoculars, ink pot, boots and revolver of one Major John Tucket; a number of helmets and rifles; and a pristine "Princess Mary" gift box, one of thousands sent out to British troops for Christmas 1914. Along the walls, some excellent photographs trace the development of the war from the packed British cavalry formations in Ieper on October 13, 1914, to smiling soldiers digging trenches, the pathetic casualties of a gas attack, flyblown corpses in the mud and panoramas of a destroyed Flemish countryside.

Around the back of the cloth hall, the **Sint Maartens Kathedraal**, built in 1930, is a copy of the thirteenth-century Gothic original, given over to a variety of memorials to the soldiers of World War I. The rose window above the main door is a fine tribute to King Albert I, its yellow, red and blue stained-glass panes the gift of the British armed forces. A few metres northwest, at the near end of Elverdingestraat, the **Saint George's English Memorial Church** was finished in 1929, a further celebration of military sacrifice, with a font cover dedicated to Sir John French, commander-in-chief of the British army from 1914 to 1915.

A few minutes' walk away, on the far side of the Grote Markt, the **Menin Gate** war memorial was built on the site of the old Menenpoort that served as the main route for British soldiers heading for the front. Of all the memorials to the carnage, this is the most moving, a simple brooding monument that towers over the

THE YPRES SALIENT

World War I was a catastrophe for Ieper. But it was entirely accidental. When the German army launched the war in the west by invading Belgium, they were following the principles – if not the details – laid down by an earlier Chief of the German General Staff, Von Schlieffen, who had died just eight years before. The idea was simple: to avoid fighting a war on two fronts, the German army would outflank the French and capture Paris by attacking through Belgium, well before the Russians had assembled on the eastern frontier. It didn't work, with the result that there were two lines of opposing trenches that stretched from the North Sea to Switzerland. No one knew quite what to do, but attention focused on the two main bulges – or salients – in the line, one at Ieper, the other at Verdun, on the Franco-German frontier just to the south of Luxembourg. To the Allied generals, the bulge at Ieper – the **Ypres Salient** – seemed a good place to break through the German lines and roll up their front from the north; to the Germans it represented an ideal opportunity to break the deadlock by attacking the enemy from several sides at the same time. No one disagreed with these ideas because contemporary military doctrine on both sides taught that the best way to win a war was to destroy the enemy's strongest forces first. In retrospect this may seem strange, but the generals of the day were schooled in cavalry tactics, where a charge that broke the enemy's key formations was guaranteed to spread disorder and confusion amongst the rest, paving the way for victory. The consequence of this tactical similitude was that the salients attracted armies like magnets, even though technological changes had shifted the balance of war in favour of defence – machine guns were more efficient, barbed wire more effective and, most important of all, the railways could shift defensive reserves far faster than an advancing army could march. Another problem was supply. Great efforts had been made to raise vast armies but they couldn't be fed off the land, and once they advanced much beyond the reach of the railways, the supply problems were enormous. As A.J.P. Taylor put it, "Defence was mechanised; attack was not".

Seemingly incapable of rethinking military strategy, the generals had no answer to the stalemate except an amazing profligacy with people's lives. Their tactical innovations were limited, and two of the new techniques – gas attack and a heavy prelimi-

edge of the town, its walls covered with the names of those 50,000 British and Commonwealth troops who died in the Ypres Salient but have no grave. The simple inscription above the lists of dead has none of the arrogance of the victor, but rather a sense of great loss:

> *To the armies of the British Empire who stood here from 1914 to 1918 and to those of their dead who have no known grave.*

The Last Post is sounded beneath the gate every evening at about 8pm. Oddly enough, the seventeenth-century town ramparts on either side of the Menin Gate were well enough constructed to survive World War I intact – the vaults even served as some of the safest bunkers on the front.

Around Ieper: Poperinge and the World War I battlefields

It's surprisingly difficult to find anything within the old World War I **Salient**, to the east of Ieper, which gives any real impression of the scale and nature of the

nary bombardment – actually made matters worse. The shells forewarned the enemy of an offensive and churned the trenches into a giant muddy quagmire where men, horses and machinery simply sunk without trace; the gas was as dangerous to the advancing soldiers as the retiring enemy. Tanks could have broken the impasse, but their development was never a high priority.

Naturally enough, the soldiers of all the armies involved lost confidence in their generals, and by 1917 – despite the court martials and the firing squads – the sheer futility of the endless round of failed offensives made desertion commonplace, and threatened to bring mass mutiny to the western front. It is true that few of the military commanders of the day showed much understanding of how to break the deadlock, and they have been bitterly criticised for their failures. However, some of the blame must be apportioned to the politicians who demanded assault rather than defence, and continued to call for a general "victory" even after it had become obvious that each useless attack cost literally thousands of lives.

Every government concerned had believed that a clear victor would emerge by Christmas 1914, and none of them was able to adjust to the new situation – there were no moves for a negotiated settlement, because no one was quite sure what they would settle for – a lack of clarity that contrasted starkly with the jingoistic sentiments stirred up to help sustain the conflict, which demanded victory or at least military success. In this context, how could a general recommend a defensive strategy or a politician propose a compromise? Those who did were dismissed.

This was the background to the four years of war that raged in and around the Ypres salient. There were four major battles. The first, in October and November of 1914, settled the lines of the bulge as both armies tried to outflank each other; the second was a German attack in the following spring that moved the trenches a couple of miles west. The third, launched by British Empire soldiers in July 1917, was even more futile, thousands of men dying for an advance of only a few kilometres. It's frequently called the Battle of Passchendaele, but Lloyd George more accurately referred to it as the "battle of the mud", a disaster that cost 250,000 British lives. The fourth and final battle of Ypres, in April 1918, was another German attack inspired by Ludendorff's desire to break the British army. Instead it broke his own and led to the Armistice of November 11.

conflict. The exception – and it's hardly spectacular – is the **Sanctuary Wood Museum** (daily, usually open daylight hours but check with the tourist office; F70), 6km southeast of town, signposted off the Ieper–Menen road, near the Canadian memorial on "Hill 62". Inside, the museum holds a ragbag of shells, rifles, bayonets, bully cans and incidental artefacts. Outside, things have been left much as they were the day the war ended, with some primitive zig-zags of sand-bagged trench, shell craters and a few shattered trees that give an idea – but not much – of what it was like. If you haven't got your own transport, taking a taxi is the easiest way to get here (F400 each way).

The museum is included in the **'14–'18 Route**, a forty-kilometre signposted car or bike trip around the northeast section of the Ypres Salient, detailed in a brochure sold by Ieper tourist office. The route passes through the villages of Poelkapelle, Passendale and Zonnebeke, around which the dips and sloping ridges signify what were then vitally important vantage points, many of which cost thousands of lives to capture. However, it's difficult to imagine what it was actually like, and the most resonant reminders of the blood-letting are the British **cemeteries**, immaculately maintained by the Commonwealth War Graves Commission. Each cemetery has a Cross of Sacrifice in white Portland stone, and the graves line up at precisely spaced intervals. Every headstone bears the individual's name, rank, number, age, date of decease and the badge of the service or corps, or a national emblem, plus an appropriate religious symbol and, at the base, an inscription chosen by relatives. The largest cemetery, **Tyne Cot**, 2km east of Zonnebeke on the road to Passendale (Passchendaele), contains 11,924 graves and a memorial to a further 35,000 whose bodies were never found. Some 10km west of Ieper, at the centre of a hop-growing area of undulating hills topped by trim circular woods, **POPERINGE** was a forward base for soldiers heading in and out of the Ypres Salient. It was here that the Reverend Philip Clayton opened the *Everyman's Club* at Talbot House, Gasthuisstraat 43, where everyone, regardless of rank, was able to come and rest or seek spiritual help. Clayton went on to found **Toc H**, the world-wide Christian fellowship that took its name from the army signallers' code for Talbot House. The original building is still run as a charity and offers simple, reasonable **accommodation** – though little remains to remind you of its history.

Practical details

Ieper's **rail** and **bus stations** stand on the western edge of the town centre, a ten-minute walk from the Grote Markt, straight down G. de Stuersstraat. The **tourist office** on the Grote Markt (April–Sept daily 9am–noon & 1–5.30pm; Oct–March daily 9am–noon & 1–4.30pm; ☎057/20 26 26) has good town maps and details of suggested car and cycle routes around the battlefields, cemeteries and monuments that dot the countryside to the east of town, marking the shifting perimeters of the Salient.

For **accommodation**, there are no pensions or private rooms and almost all of Ieper's **hotels** are on or very near the Grote Markt. These include the *'t Zweerd*, at no. 2 (☎057/20 04 75), with doubles for F980; the *Old Tom*, no. 8 (☎057/20 15 41), where doubles cost F1500; and the *Sultan*, no. 33 (☎057/20 01 93), with doubles for F1900. The *Hostellerie Sint Nicolas*, G de Stuersstraat 6 (☎057/20 06 22), charges F1500 for a double. For **food**, the Grote Markt is lined with cafés and restaurants; try the snacks of *De Trompet*, at no. 28, or those of the *De Kollebloeme*, at no. 24. *Old Tom*, at Grote Markt no. 8, is a good place for a full meal.

Kortrijk and around

From Ieper, hourly trains slip south to Comines past a string of spruce **war cemeteries** around the village of ZILLEBEKE, scene of some of the most bloody fighting of World War I. **COMINES** is a French-speaking town at the centre of a tiny enclave of the province of Hainaut, a sliver of land backing onto the river Leie, the frontier with France. From here, trains travel on to MENEN, the terminus of the infamous "Menin" road from Ypres, which cut across the Front for almost all the war, crowded with marching armies at night and swept by shrapnel all day.

Just 7km from the French border, **KORTRIJK** (Courtrai) is the largest town and main rail junction in this part of West Flanders, tracing its origins to a Roman settlement by the name of *Cortracum*. In the Middle Ages, its fortunes paralleled those of Ypres, but although it became an important centre of the cloth trade, it was also far too near France for comfort. Time and again Kortrijk was embroiled in the wars that swept across Flanders, right up to the two German occupations of this century.

The Town

Heavily bombed during World War II, the **Grote Markt**, at the centre of Kortrijk, is a pretty dire mixture of bits of the old and a lot of the new, surrounding the forlorn, turretted **Belfort** – all that remains of the medieval cloth hall. The rather grand **war memorial** at its base is still tended with much care and attention. At the northwest corner of the Grote Markt, the **Stadhuis** (Mon–Fri 9am–noon & 2–5pm) is a dreary edifice with modern statues of the counts of Flanders on the facade, above and beside two lines of ugly windows. Inside, there are two fine sixteenth-century chimneypieces: one in the old Aldermen's Hall (*Schepenzaal*) on the ground floor, a delicate, intricate work decorated with coats of arms and carvings of the seventeenth-century king and queen of Spain, Albert and Isabella; the other, in the first-floor Council Chamber, a more didactic work, ornamented by three rows of precise statuettes, representing, from top to bottom, the Virtues, Vices and the punishments of Hell.

Opposite, by the southeast corner of the Grote Markt, the giant tower of **Sint Maartenskerk** (closed) is swathed in scaffolding, its fifteenth-century white-stone exterior slowly reappearing from beneath the accumulated grime. There are plans to reopen the main body of the church in 1991, worth a peek for a look at the gilded stone tabernacle, the work of Hendrik Maes in 1585. Immediately to the north, the **Begijnhof**, founded in 1238 by Joanna of Constantinople, preserves the cosy informality of its seventeenth-century houses, overlooked from Groeningestraat, a couple of minutes away, by the **Onze Lieve Vrouwekerk** (normally 10am–noon & 2–6pm). This pushes into the street, a muscular grey structure that once doubled as part of the city's fortifications. In July 1302, the nave of the church was crammed with hundreds of spurs, ripped off the feet of dead and dying French knights – the pathetic remains of the army Philip the Fair had sent to avenge the slaughter of the Bruges Matins earlier that year – at what has become known as the Battle of the Golden Spurs. The two armies, Philip's heavily armoured cavalry and the lightly armed Flemish weavers, had met outside Kortrijk on marshy ground, which the Flemings had disguised with brushwood. Despising their lowly-born adversaries, the French knights made no reconnaissance and fell into the trap, milling around in the mud like cumbersome dinosaurs. They were massacred, victims of their own arrogance, and the battle was a military landmark, the first time an amateur civilian army had defeated professional mail-clad knights. The spurs disappeared long ago and today much of the inside of the church is in a predictable Baroque style, though the Counts' Chapel has an unusual series of rather crude late medieval portraits painted into the wall niches. Nearby, Van Dyck's *Raising of the Cross* was one of the artist's last paintings before he went to England.

From the church, an alley cuts through to the river Leie, where the squat twin towers, the **Broeltorens**, are all that remains of the old town walls. On the other side of the bridge, the **Stedelijk Museum**, Broelkaai 6 (Mon–Thurs & Sat 10am–noon & 2–5pm, Sun 10am–1pm & 3–5pm; free), houses a good selection of locally made lace and damask, a fine sample of eighteenth-century Delftware, and several paintings by a local sixteenth-century artist, Roelandt Savery. His favourite subjects were religious and mythical – a romantic classicism much favoured by his mainly German patrons and represented here by vivid variations on these themes.

Practical details

The town's **railway station** is a five-minute walk south of the Grote Markt; take the second road on the right out of Stationsplein. Before you reach the Grote Markt, the **tourist office** on Schouwburgplein (Mon–Fri 8.30am–noon & 2–5pm; July–Aug also Sat 9.30am–12.30pm & 1.30–4pm, Sun 9.30am–12.30pm; ☎056/20 25 00) has an **accommodation** list and will make bookings on your behalf at no charge. Otherwise, there are three reasonably priced places with doubles from F1550 – the *Groeninge*, near the Onze Lieve Vrouwekerk at Groeningestraat 1a (☎056/22 60 00); the *'t Belfort*, Grote Markt 52 (☎056/22 15 63); and the *'t Kopke*, Grote Markt 53 (☎056/22 15 63). There's a **youth hostel** fifteen minutes' walk north of the station at Passionistenlaan 1a (☎056/20 14 42).

For **food**, there's the vegetarian restaurant *Nektar* on Sint Janslaan, as well as several snack bars on the Grote Markt, including the *Grand Café*, at no. 8, and the *Savoyard* at no. 51. More expensively, there's a swish restaurant in the swanky *Hotel Damier* at Grote Markt 41 – worth trying if you can afford it.

Oudenaarde and around

Some 25km east across the Flanders plain from Kortrijk, the small town of **OUDENAARDE**, literally "old landing place", sits tightly around the river Scheldt as it twists its way towards Ghent, 30km to the north. Granted a charter in 1193, the town concentrated on cloth manufacture until the early fifteenth century when its weavers switched to tapestry-making, an industry that made its burghers rich and the town famous, the best products the prized possessions of the kings of France and Spain. Oudenaarde was a key military objective during the religious and dynastic wars of the sixteenth to the eighteenth centuries; time and again it was attacked and besieged, perhaps most famously in July 1708 when the Duke of Marlborough came to the rescue and won a spectacular victory here against the French in the War of the Spanish Succession. With the demise of the tapestry industry in the middle of the eighteenth century, the town became an insignificant backwater, a stagnant place in one of the poorest districts of Flanders. In the last few years, things have improved considerably due to its skilful use of regional development funds, and today's town makes for an interesting and pleasant day out.

The Town

Heading into Oudenaarde along Stationsstraat, the middle of the **Tacambaroplein** is taken up by a romantic war memorial that commemorates those who were daft or unscrupulous enough to volunteer to go to Mexico and fight for Maximilian, son-in-law of Leopold I. Unwanted and unloved, Maximilian was imposed on the Mexicans by a French army provided by Napoleon III, who wished to take advantage of the American Civil War to develop a western empire. It was all too fanciful and the occupation rapidly turned into a fiasco, though Maximilian paid for the adventure with his life in 1867 and few of his soldiers made the return trip.

The Markt: Stadhuis and Halle

Further south, the wide open space of the **Markt** is edged by one of the finest examples of Flamboyant Gothic in the country, an exquisite **Stadhuis** built around 1525. The subject of a long and expensive restoration that will last until the end of the century, work on the front was finished in 1989, revealing an elegantly symmetrical facade, spread out on either side of the extravagant tiers, balconies and parapets of a slender central tower, topped by the gilded figure of a knight, *Hanske de Krijge* (Little John the Warrior). Underneath the knight, the cupola is in the shape of a crown, a theme reinforced by the two groups of cherubs on the triangular windows below, who lovingly clutch at the royal insignia. To the rear of the Stadhuis, the dour and gloomy exterior of the adjoining Romanesque **Halle** dates from the thirteenth century. **Guided tours** of the Halle and Stadhuis start from the tourist office by the main entrance, but although the schedule is clear (April–Oct Mon–Thurs at 9am, 10am, 11am, 2pm, 3pm & 4pm; Fri 9am, 10am & 11am, Sat & Sun 10am, 11am, 2pm, 3pm, 4pm & 5pm; 1hr duration; F60), timings can in fact be erratic and only certain tours are in English – double-check the details first.

It's well worth the effort. The oak **doorway** that forms the entrance to the old Alderman's Hall is a magnificent, stylistically influential piece of 1531, the work of a certain Paulwel Vander Schelden. It consists of an intricate sequence of carvings, surmounted by miniature cherubs who frolic above three coats of arms and a 28-panel door, each rectangle a masterpiece of precise execution. Inside are many other interesting items, including seals and coins, local archaeological finds, a whole range of incidental guild memorabilia, and a couple of paintings by Adriaen Brouwer, who was a native of Oudenaarde – principally a typically ogrish encounter in *Amongst Drunkards*. On the walls of the Halle there are several well-preserved **tapestries**. *Susanna and the Two Elders* is a classic pictorial tapestry of the sixteenth century, its figures rather clumsily filling the central arbour, whose water fountain provides a sense of movement. By comparison, the seventeenth-century *Large Verdure with Two Pheasants* has a more intricate design of trees and plants, framing the outline of a distant castle. The *Return from Market* dates from the same period, but its trees are in shades of blue and green, edged by sky and bare earth – a composition directly reminiscent of Dutch landscape painters.

THE OUDENAARDE TAPESTRY INDUSTRY

Tapestry manufacture in Oudenaarde began in the middle of the fifteenth century, an embryonic industry that soon came to be based on a dual workshop and outworker system, the one with paid employees, the other with payment by results. From the beginning, the town authorities took a keen interest in the business, ensuring its success by a rigorous system of quality control that soon gave the town an international reputation for consistently well-made tapestries. The other side of this interventionist policy was less palatable: wages were kept down and the Guild of the Masters cleverly took over the running of the Guild of Weavers in 1501. To make matters worse, tapestries were by definition a luxury item, and workers were hardly ever able to accumulate enough capital to buy either their own looms or even raw materials.

The first great period of Oudenaarde tapestry-making lasted until the middle of the sixteenth century, when religious conflict overwhelmed the town, its Protestant-inclined weavers coming into direct conflict with their Catholic rulers, and many of them migrating north to the rival workshops in Antwerp and Ghent. In 1582, Oudenaarde was finally incorporated into the Spanish Netherlands, precipitating a revival of tapestry production, which entered its second great period, with a clearly defined luxury market around the king and queen of Spain, who were keen to support the industry and passed draconian laws banning the movement of weavers. Later, however, French occupation and the shrinking of the Spanish market led to the contraction of production, and the industry hung on only in much diminished form until 1772.

The technique applied to the production of tapestries was a cross between embroidery and ordinary weaving. It consisted of interlacing a wool weft above and below the strings of a vertical linen "chain", a process similar to weaving. However, the weaver had to stop to change colour, requiring as many shuttles for the weft as he had colours, as in embroidery. The appearance of a tapestry was entirely determined by the weft, the design taken from a painting to which the weaver made constant reference. Standard-size Oudenaarde tapestries took six months to make and were produced exclusively for the very wealthy, the most important of whom would, on occasion, insist on the use of gold and silver thread and the employment of the most famous artists of the day for the preparatory painting – Rubens, Jacob Jordaens and David Teniers all had tapestry commissions. There were only two significant types of tapestry: **decorative**, principally *verdures*, showing scenes of foliage in an almost abstract way (the Oudenaarde speciality), and **pictorial** – usually variations on the same basic themes, particularly rural life, knights, hunting parties and religious scenes. Over the centuries, changes in style were strictly limited, though the early part of the seventeenth century saw an increased use of elaborate woven borders, an appreciation of perspective and the use of a far brighter, more varied range of colours – the consequences of changes in the work of the painters. Oudenaarde tapestries are normally in yellow, brown, pale blue and shades of green, with an occasional splash of red.

The rest of the centre

Immediately southwest of the Markt, a couple of minutes' walk from the Stadhuis, the **Sint Walburgakerk** (visits by prior arrangement with the tourist office) is a decaying mass of masonry desperately in need of restoration, its powerful tower starting to crack and lean precariously. Inside there's a monument to four Catholic priests who in 1572 were thrown into the Scheldt from the windows of Oudenaarde's castle (since demolished). Across the road opposite the church, a group of ancient mansions follow the bend in what was once the line of the town wall, leading around towards the southern end of the Markt, where Burgstraat, and subsequently Kasteelstraat, head south past a trim seventeenth-century **portal** – all that remains of the Begijnhof. On the first left turn over the bridge, the **Huis de Lalaing**, Bourgondiestraat 9 (Mon–Fri 9am–4pm, Sat & Sun groups only, by appointment; ☎055/31 48 63), is home to the municipal tapestry repair workshops and occasionally shows paintings by local artists.

Practical details

A ten-minute walk north of the town centre down Nederstraat amd Stationsstraat, the Gothic **railway station**, with its chandelier in the hallway and coat of arms on the facade, is scheduled for restoration once work has finished on the new fast line from Brussels, whose concrete bridges and raised track look down on this side of town. The **tourist office**, in the Stadhuis (Mon–Fri 8.30am–noon & 1.30–5.30pm; June–Aug also Sat & Sun 10am–noon & 2–5pm; ☎055/31 14 91), has an **accommodation** list, but there are no private rooms and only four central **hotels**. The cheapest is the *Tijl*, Stationsstraat 62 (☎055/31 82 90), with doubles from F800. The pleasant *De Zalm*, on the northwest corner of the Markt at Hoogstraat 4 (☎055/31 13 14), has doubles at F1500, the *La Pomme d'Or*, close by at Markt 62 (☎055/31 19 00), at F1225. The nearest **campsite** is in the holiday complex *Vlaamse Ardennen*, some 2km west of the station: walk north over the railway lines beside the station building, away from town and along Beverestraat; turn left down Kortrijkstraat and it's at no. 342.

For **food**, try *The Bridge*, near the Huis de Lalaing on Bourgondiestraat, or any one of the restaurants on the Markt, including the *Poeskaffe* snack bar on the south side, next door but one to the swish *Crombé* restaurant.

Around Oudenaarde: Ronse

Some 15km south of Oudenaarde, the flattened fields of the Flanders plain give way to a ridge of low hills that make up the southwest corner of the province of East Flanders. From high points on some of the hills dotted around the road southeast from Kerkhove there are good views to north and west, but the sobriquet **Vlaamse Ardennen** (Flemish Ardennes), used by local tourist offices, is desperately optimistic.

In the middle of these hills lies the tiny textile town of **RONSE**, whose main claim to fame is the **Sint Hermeskerk**, a late-Gothic edifice situated just to the north of the main town square. The church takes its name from a Roman martyr, Hermes, who was recognised for his skills as an exorcist. His relics presented to Ronse during the ninth century and became the object of pilgrimages, the "possessed" dragged here from all over the Low Countries in the hope of a miraculous cure. Today, the rusted iron rings in a bench near the altar are reminders of the times when those considered insane were chained up waiting for exorcism, while the reliquary of Saint Hermes is in the chapel on the south side of the choir.

Bruges and around

"Somewhere within the dingy casing lay the ancient city," wrote Graham Greene of **BRUGES**, "like a notorious jewel, too stared at, talked of, trafficked over," And it's true that Bruges' (justified) reputation as one of the most perfectly preserved medieval cities in western Europe has made it the most popular tourist destination in Belgium, packed with visitors throughout the summer season. Inevitably, the crowds overwhelm the town's charms, but you would be mad to come to Flanders and miss the place: its museums, to name just one attraction, hold some of the country's finest collections of Flemish art; and its intimate, winding streets, woven round a pattern of narrow canals and lined with gorgeous ancient buildings, live up to even the most inflated tourist hype. See it out of season, or in the early morning before the hordes have descended, and it can be memorable.

Some history

Bruges originated from a ninth-century fortress built by the warlike first Count of Flanders, Baldwin Iron Arm, designed to defend the Flemish coast from Norman attack. The settlement prospered, and by the fourteenth century it shared effective control of the cloth trade with its two great rivals, Ghent and Ypres, turning high-quality English wool into thousands of items of clothing that were exported all over the known world. It was an immensely profitable business, and made the city a centre of international trade: at its height, the town was a key member of – and showcase for – the products of the Hanseatic League, the most powerful economic alliance in medieval Europe. Through the harbours and quays of Bruges, Flemish cloth and Hansa goods were exchanged for pigs from Denmark, spices from Venice, hides from Ireland, wax from Russia, gold and silver from Poland and furs from Bulgaria. The business of these foreign traders was protected by no less than 21 consulates, and the city developed a wide range of support services, including banking, money-changing, maritime insurance and an elementary shipping code, known as the *Roles de Damme*.

Despite – or perhaps because of – this lucrative state of affairs, Bruges was dogged by war. Its weavers and merchants were dependent on the goodwill of the kings of England for the proper functioning of the wool trade, but their feudal overlords, the Counts of Flanders and their successors the Dukes of Burgundy, were vassals of the king of France. Although some of the dukes and counts were strong enough to defy their king, most felt obliged to obey his orders, and thus take his side against the English when the two countries were at war. This conflict was compounded by the designs the French kings had on the independence of Bruges itself, leading to a series of disturbances in the city, the most famous of which, at the beginning of the fourteenth century, took place when Philip the Fair of France attempted to incorporate the towns of west Flanders into his kingdom. He and his wife, Joanna of Navarre, held a grand reception in Bruges, but both clearly felt uneasy in the face of the city's splendour: "I thought," said Joanna, "that I alone was Queen; but here in this place I have six hundred rivals." Their misgivings were confirmed a few weeks later when the town's guildsmen flatly refused to pay a new round of taxes. Enraged, Philip dispatched an army to restore order and garrison the town, but at dawn on Friday, May 18, 1302, a rebellious force of Flemings crept into the city and massacred Philip's sleepy army – an occasion later known as the **Bruges Matins**. Anyone who couldn't correctly pronounce the Flemish shibboleth *schild en vriend* ("shield and friend") was put to the sword.

By the end of the fifteenth century, Bruges was in decline, partly because of a general recession in the cloth trade, but principally because of the silting of the Zwin river – the city's trading lifeblood. By the 1490s, the stretch of water between Sluis and Damme was only navigable by smaller ships, and by the 1530s the town's sea trade had collapsed completely. Bruges simply withered away, its houses deserted, its canals empty, and its money shifted north with the merchants.

Frozen in time, Georges Rodenbach's novel *Bruges-la-Morte* alerted wealthy nineteenth-century Europeans to its aged, quiet charms, and Bruges escaped damage in both world wars to emerge a perfect tourist attraction.

> The Bruges area telephone code is ☎050

Arrival, accommodation, information and getting around

Bruges **railway station** adjoins the **bus station** about 2km south of the town centre. Inside the station, there's a **hotel reservation** service (April–Sept Mon–Sat 2.45–9pm; Oct to mid-Nov Mon–Sat 1.45–8pm), which will make bookings on your behalf at no charge, though they do require a deposit of F400 – deducted from your final bill. If you don't fancy the twenty-minute walk into town, most of the local buses that leave from outside the station building head into the Markt, bang in the centre, where the **tourist office**, a couple of minutes' walk from the Markt at Burg 11 (April–Sept Mon–Fri 9.30am–6.30pm, Sat & Sun 10am–noon & 2–6.30pm; Oct–March Mon–Sat 9.30am–12.45pm & 2–5.45pm; ☎44 86 86), provides a similar accommodation service and has maps, leaflets and other information, including suggestions for cycle trips in the countryside around town, and a useful, complimentary *Agenda Brugge*, which contains details of all current events and performances. Local bus timetables are pinned to the walls near the entrance.

There are several conveniently situated **unofficial youth hostels** with dormitory beds at about F400 per person per night, most of which also have a limited supply of smaller rooms at about F900 for a double per night. These include the *Bauhaus International Youth Hotel*, east of the Burg at Langestraat 135 (☎34 10 93); *Kilroy's Garden*, west of the Markt at Singel 12 (☎38 93 82); *Bruno's Passage*, on the same side of town at Dweersstraat 26 (☎34 02 32); and the excellent *Snuffel Travellers Inn*, a couple of minutes north of the Markt at Ezelstraat 49 (☎33 31 33), where the café serves cheap food and dangerously strong beer. There's an official **youth hostel** 2km south of the centre at Baron Ruzettelaan 143 (☎35 26 79) – bus #2 goes right there. The nearest **campsite**, *St Michiel*, is near the motorway 3km southwest of the train station at Tillegemstraat 55 (☎38 08 19): take bus #7 and get off at the junction of St Michielslaan and Rijselstraat; head west from here along Jagerstraat and take the left turn under the highway, which brings you onto Tillegemstraat.

Bruges has very few **pensions**, but there are a cluster to the west of the Markt, along 't Zand, among them the *Die Roya*, at no. 5 (☎34 32 84), the *Speelmanshuys*, at no. 3 (☎33 95 52), and the *Roosterhuys*, at no. 13 (☎33 3 0 35), all of which have double rooms for around F1000. Nearby, the *Lybeer* at Korte Vulderstraat 31 (☎33 43 55) has doubles from F1350, the *Pension Imperial* at Dweersstraat 29 (☎33 90 14) from F1100.

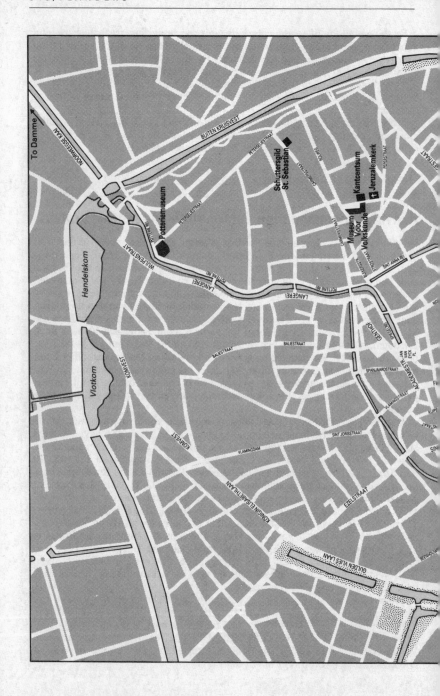

BRUGES

500 m

0

To the Youth Hostel

BARON RUZETTELAAN

BUITEN KAZERNEVEST

BUITEN BONINVEST

COUPURE

COUPURE

Koningin
Astridpark

Groeningemuseum

Brangwijnmuseum

NIEUWE GENTWEG

OUDE GENTWEG

KATELINE STRAAT

BUITEN KATELIJNE VEST

Minnewater
Park

Tourist
Office

Brugge
Vrije

Vismarkt

Stadhuis

Post
Office

Halle en
Belfort

PHILIPSTOCKSTRAAT

MARKT

Grauthuse
museum

O.L.
Vrouwekerk

MARIA STRAAT

WALPLEIN

Minnewater

St Jans Hospital

Memlingmuseum

OOSTMEERS

WESTMEERS

REGENWEG

Begijnhof

BUITEN BEGIJNENVEST

Sint-Salvator
Kathedraal

STEENSTRAAT

NOORDZAND STRAAT

GELMUNSTRAAT

JACOBSSTRAAT

KONING ALBERTLAAN

Bus Station

Railway
Station

HOFFLIZER LAAN

HENDRIK CONSCIENCELAAN

SINGEL

To Camping
St. Michiel

BOAT TRIPS

Half hour **boat trips** around the **city's canals** leave from a number of jetties along the waterway south of the Burg, daily from March to November (10am–6pm; F130). As for **trips out of town**, excursions to **Damme** start at the Noorweegse Kaai, 2km north of the town centre (bus #4 from the Markt), 5 times daily between April and September and once daily in October. Boats leave Damme for Bruges on a similar schedule; the journey takes about an hour and a single fare costs F100, a return F160. Trips to **Ghent** leave in July and August once weekly from the Bargeweg, near the Minnewater (F250).

Conveniently, the more reasonably-priced **hotels** cluster around the two central squares, Markt and Burg. You can get a double room in the *Aarendshuis*, an elegant old mansion at Hoogstraat 18 (☎33 78 89), for F1600–1900. There's also the plain *Central*, Markt 30 (☎33 18 05), the cosy *Cordoeanier*, Cordoeanierstraat 18 (☎33 90 51), the *De Sneeuwberg*, Hallestraat 2 (☎33 35 72), and the agreeably situated *Van Eyck*, Korte Zilverstraat 7 (☎33 52 67) – all of which charge under F2000. A little higher up the price scale, the *Koffieboontje*, Hallestraat 4 (☎33 80 27), has doubles for a little over F2000, as do the *Tassche*, Oude Burg 11 (☎33 03 19), the *Voermanshuys*, Oude Burg 14 (☎34 13 96), and the *Uilenspiegel*, Langestraat 2 (☎33 85 06). With a little more money still, you might try the *Hotel Adornes*, Sint Annarei 26 (☎34 13 36), sited in one of the most charming and least crowded parts of Bruges, along the canal east of Jan van Eyckplein, with double rooms starting at F2300 per night.

The only really practicable way to **explore the town** is on foot or by bike, available at standard rates from the railway station. **Mopeds and bikes** can also be hired from the *Koffieboontje* hotel, behind the belfry at Hallestraat 4 (☎33 80 27).

The City Centre

In 1896 Arnold Bennett moaned "The difference between Bruges and other cities is that in the latter you look about for the picturesque, while in Bruges, assailed on every side by the picturesque, you look curiously for the unpicturesque, and don't find it easily." Perhaps so, but a fair slice of Bruges is not quite what it seems, the pretty little bridge beside the Onze Lieve Vrouwekerk is nineteenth-century; the carved wood facades behind the Halle are from the 1950s; and the Beguines are Benedictine nuns in fancy costume. Bruges has spent time and money preserving its image, and although the bulk of the buildings are genuine enough, sometimes it can resemble nothing so much as a medieval theme park.

The Markt

A twenty-minute walk northeast of the main rail and bus stations, the older sections of Bruges fan out from two interlocking central squares, the Markt and the Burg. Of the two, the **Markt**, edged on three sides by rows of inconsequential buildings and packed with parked cars, is something of a disappointment, its mediocrity only redeemed by the **Belfry** (daily 9.30am–12.30pm & 1.30–5pm; F80) which lies on its south side. Built in the thirteenth century when the town was at its richest and most extravagant, the belfry is a potent symbol of civic pride and municipal independence, its distinctive octagonal lantern top visible for miles across the surrounding polders. Inside, the belfry staircase passes the room where the town charters were locked for safe-keeping, and an eighteenth-century carillon, before emerging onto the roof. It's well worth the haul up for the view, especially in the late afternoon when the warm colours of the town are at their deepest. At the foot of the belfry, the **Halle** is a much restored edifice dating from the thirteenth century, its style and structure modelled on the cloth hall at Ieper. In the middle, a rectangular courtyard is overlooked by a line of long galleries and was the location of the town's principal market, its cobbled space once crammed with merchants and their wares.

A few metres away, at the centre of the Markt, there's a late nineteenth-century **monument** to the leaders of the Bruges Matins, Peter de Coninck of the Guild of Weavers, and John Breidel, Dean of the Guild of Butchers. Standing close together, they clutch the hilt of the same sword, their faces turned to the west in slightly absurd poses of heroic determination. There's no other building of note on the Markt, but the *Craenenburg* café, on the corner of Sint Amandsstraat at Markt 16, is built on the site of the medieval mansion in which the Hapsburg heir, Archduke Maximilian, was imprisoned by the burghers of Bruges for three months in 1488. The reason for the argument was the archduke's efforts to limit the city's privileges, but whatever the justice of their cause, the burghers made a big mistake. Maximilian became emperor in 1493, and although he never actually attacked the town, he never forgave its people either, doing his best to push trade north to their great rival, Antwerp.

The Burg

From beside the neo-Gothic post office on the Markt, Breidelstraat leads through to the **Burg**, whose southern half is fringed by the city's finest group of buildings. One of the best of these is the **Heilig Bloed Basiliek** (Basilica of the Holy Blood; April–Sept daily 9.30am–noon & 2–6pm; Oct–March daily 10am–noon & 2–4pm; free) on the right, named after the holy relic that found its way here in 1150. The church divides into two parts. Tucked away in a corner, the **Lower Chapel** is a shadowy, crypt-like affair, originally built at the beginning of the twelfth century to house another relic, that of Saint Basil, one of the great figures of the early Greek church. The chapel's heavy, simple Romanesque lines are decorated with just one carved relief, set above an interior doorway – a representation of the baptism of Basil, a strange giant bird depicting the Holy Spirit, soaring above a pool of water. Next door, approached by a wide staircase, the **Upper Chapel** was built at the same time but has been renovated so frequently that it's impossible to make out the original structure, while the inside has been spoilt by excessively rich nineteenth-century decoration. In a side chapel, the rock-crystal phial of the Holy Blood is stored within a grandiose silver **tabernacle**, the gift of the King and Queen of Spain, Albert and Isabella, in 1611. One of the holiest relics in medieval Europe, the phial purports to contain a few drops of blood and water washed from the body of Christ by Joseph of Arimathea, and was the gift of Thierry d'Alsace, a Flemish knight who distinguished himself by his bravery during the Second Crusade and was given the phial by a grateful Patriarch of Jerusalem. After several weeks in Bruges, the relic was found to be dry, but soon after it proceeded to liquefy every Friday at 6pm until 1325, a miracle attested by all sorts of church dignitaries, including Pope Clement V. The Holy Blood is still venerated in the Upper Chapel on Fridays at 6pm, and despite modern scepticism, reverence for it remains strong, not least on Ascension Day when it is carried through the town in a colourful but solemn procession, the *Helig-Bloedprocessie*.

The tiny **Treasury** (April–Sept 9.30am–noon & 2–6pm; Oct–March 10am–noon & 2–4pm; F20) is home to an extravagant gold and silver reliquary that holds the Holy Blood during the procession. Near the entrance, the faded strands of a seventeenth-century, locally-woven tapestry depict Saint Augustine's funeral, the sea of helmeted heads and pikes that surround the monks and abbots very much a Catholic view of a muscular state supporting a holy church.

Just to the left of the basilica, the **Stadhuis** has a beautiful, turretted sandstone facade, a much-copied exterior that dates from 1376 – though its sequence of painted statues (of the counts and countesses of Flanders) is a 1960s replacement of one destroyed by the occupying French army in 1792. Inside on the first floor, the Gothic Hall of 1400 (daily 9.30am–noon & 2–5pm; F40) was the magnificent setting for the first meeting of the States General in 1464. The ceiling has been restored in a vibrant mixture of maroon, dark brown, black and gold, dripping pendant arches like decorated stalactites. The ribs of the arches converge in twelve tiny circular vault-keys, picturing scenes from the New Testament, while below they're supported by sixteen gilded corbels, representing the months and elements. The paintings round the walls were commissioned in 1895 to illustrate the history of the town, and an adjoining room has a modest display of incidental artefacts, including coins, seals and information on the modernisation of the town's harbour facilities at the turn of the century.

Next door to the Stadhuis, the **Oude Griffie** (closed) was built to house the municipal records office in 1537, its elegant facade decorated with Renaissance columns and friezes superimposed on the Gothic lines of the gables below. To the immediate left, the **Bruges Vrije Museum** (daily 10am–noon & 1.30–5pm; F20) has only one exhibit, an enormous marble and oak **chimneypiece** located in the province's old Schepenzaal (Magistrates' Hall), the only room to have survived from the original fifteenth-century palace. A fine example of Renaissance carving, the chimneypiece was completed in 1531 under the direction of Lancelot Blondeel, to celebrate the defeat of the French at Pavia in 1525 and the advantageous Treaty of Cambrai that followed. A paean of praise to the Hapsburgs, the work is dominated by figures of the Emperor Charles V and his Austrian and Spanish relatives, each person identified by the labelled diagram in front of the chimneypiece, although the most obvious features are the three large codpieces. Adjoining the Bruges Vrije, the drab courtyard complex of the **Gerechtshof** (Law Courts) dates from 1722 and houses the tourist office, while just north of here the new Bruges *Holiday Inn* is under construction – replacing the Cathedral of St Donatian which occupied the site until its destruction at the end of the eighteenth century, again by the French.

Along the Dijver

From the arch beside the Oude Griffie, Blinde Ezelstraat (Blind Donkey street) leads south across the canal to the eighteenth-century Doric colonnades of the **Vismarkt**, beyond which the huddle of picturesque houses that make up the **Huidevettersplaat** hold some of the most popular drinking and eating places in town. Close by, the **Dijver** passes the bridge at the bottom of Wollestraat, which is overseen by a statue of the patron saint of bridges, **St John Nepomuk**, who is reputed to have been thrown into a Bohemian river for refusing to reveal the confessional secrets of the wife of King Wenceslas IV. From here, the busy food and knick-knack stalls of the Dijver line the canal as far as Nieuwestraat, passing opposite the path to the first of the city's main museums, the Groeninge.

A combination ticket for Bruges' central museums, the Groeninge, Brangwyn, Gruuthuse and Memling, is available from any of the four and costs F250.

The Groeninge Museum

The **Groeninge Museum** at Dijver 12 (April–Sept daily 9.30am–6pm; Oct–March daily 9.30am–noon & 2–5pm; F100) houses the city's art collection, a superb sample of Flemish paintings from the fourteenth to the twentieth century. The exhibits are well-displayed in a series of small, interlocking rooms, and although the collection is labelled exclusively in Flemish, further information is available in the multi-lingual pamphlets on sale at reception for F5; there are also clear plans of the place laid out by the entrance. The Groeninge doesn't have enough room to display all its paintings at any one time, so lesser works are rotated, though the kernel of the collection, the early paintings in rooms 1–6, remains fairly constant.

The museum's best section is without question that holding **early Flemish paintings**, among which there are several by Jan van Eyck, who lived and worked in Bruges from 1430 until his death eleven years later. Arguably the greatest of the early Flemish masters, he was a key figure in the development of oil painting, modulating its tones to create paintings of extraordinary clarity and realism, good examples being the fine, tiny *Portrait of Margareta Van Eyck* and his *Madonna with Canon George van der Paele*, a glowing and richly analytical work with three figures surrounding the Madonna: the kneeling Canon, Saint George, his patron saint, and Saint Donatian, to whom he is being presented. Though the work is full of symbolic minutiae it's the luminous, fastidious detail that impresses; to those who saw it in the fifteenth century the portraiture must have seemed miraculous, the Virgin as real as the palpably human Canon. In Saint George's armour you can just make out the reflection of a man, presumably van Eyck himself, observing the scene, a similar statement of presence to the mirror reflection in his famous *Arnolfini Marriage* in London.

Close by, there are two fascinating matching panels of *The Legend of St Ursula*, completed in the middle of the fifteenth century by an unknown artist known as the "Master of the Ursula Legend", probably inspired by the discovery in Cologne a couple of centuries earlier of the supposed bones of the nuns massacred with Saint Ursula – a medieval sensation that would certainly have been known about in Bruges. Look also at the *Judgement of Cambyses*, a painting by Gerard David on two oak panels that was hung in the town hall by the city burghers as a sort of public apology for the imprisonment of Archduke Maximilian here in 1488. The painting is based on a story told of the Persian court by Herodotus, and in the first panel the corrupt judge, Sisamnes, is sentenced to be flayed alive; in the gruesome second panel the judgement is carried out by the king's servants, who apply themselves to the task with a scientific neutrality. Nearby, the *Baptism of Christ* is a later work by the same artist, depicting a boyish, partly bearded Christ as part of the Holy Trinity, which forms the symmetrical heart of the painting.

There's also work by Hieronymus Bosch, his *Last Judgement*, a trio of oak panels crammed with mysterious beasts, microscopic mutants and scenes of awful cruelty – men boiled in a pit or cut in half by a giant knife. It looks like unbridled fantasy, but the fact is that the scenes were read as symbols, each tiny cameo understood as a sort of strip cartoon of legend, proverb and tradition. Indeed Bosch's religious orthodoxy is confirmed by the appeal his work had for the most Catholic of Spanish kings, Philip II.

There's more grim symbolism in Jan Provost's striking *The Miser and Death*, the merchant with his money on one panel, trying desperately to pass a promisory note to the grinning skeleton on the next. Other highlights include the knockabout violence of the unattributed *Scenes of the Legend of St George*; the *Moreel Triptych* by Hans Memling, the general formality of the scene offset by some gentle individual acts – the priest stroking the fawn, the knight's hand on a neighbouring shoulder; and two paintings in imitation of lost works by Rogier van der Weyden, a tiny *Portrait of Philip the Good*, the sombre cloak balanced by the brightness of the hatpin and necklace, and the almost impudent smile of the baby Christ in *St Luke painting the Virgin*.

The museum's selection of **seventeenth-century paintings** is far more modest, though there's a delightfully naturalistic *Peasant Lawyer* after Pieter Brueghel the Younger; a couple of muted riverscapes by Jan van Goyen; and a *Country Scene* by Aelbert Cuyp. The **modern paintings**, too, aren't exactly engaging, but look out for Jean Delville's enormous and weird *De Godmens*, a repulsively fascinating picture of writhing bodies striving for Christ's salvation; the harsh surrealism of Paul Delvaux's *Serenity*; a lively *Birdspark* painted in 1918 by James Ensor; and the charcoal on paper *Angelus* by Constant Permeke – a typically dark and earthy representation of Belgian peasant life dated 1934.

The Brangwyn and Gruuthuse Museums

Further along Dijver, at no. 17, the **Gruuthuse Museum** (daily 9.30am–noon & 2–5pm; F100) is sited in a rambling fifteenth-century mansion, a fine example of civil Gothic architecture which takes its name from the owners' historical right to tax the *gruut*, the fermented barley used in beer brewing. The mansion's ancient beams and chimney pieces frame a varied collection of fine and applied art, well laid out in a series of clearly numbered rooms. The exhibits are only labelled in Flemish, but, if you're feeling flush, a detailed guidebook is available at reception for F595. Of the range of material on display, there are good samples of old Flemish lace, musical instruments, sixteenth- and seventeenth-century pictorial tapestries and many different types of furniture. Most intriguing of all is an oak-panelled chapel of 1472, which juts out from the first floor of the museum to oversee the high altar of the cathedral next door. A curiously intimate room, the low, rounded ceiling is partly decorated with simple floral tracery, its corbels cut in the form of tiny angels.

Just up the road from the Gruuthuse, the **Brangwyn Museum**, Dijver 16 (same times; F60), has a dull display of paintings, plates, pots and pewter, but is worth visiting if you're interested in the work of Sir Frank Brangwyn, a Welsh artist born in Bruges who donated this sample of his work to the town in 1936. A specialist in giant murals (the best of which you can see in the Royal Exchange and Lloyd's Registry in London), there's a large collection of his moody etchings, studies and paintings here.

The Onze Lieve Vrouwekerk

Back down the Dijver, next door to the Gruuthuse, the **Onze Lieve Vrouwekerk** (April–Sept Mon–Sat 10–11.30am & 2.30–5pm, Sun 2.30–5pm; Oct–March Mon–Sat 10–11.30am & 3–4.30pm, Sun 2.30–4.30pm; free) is a massive shambles of a building of different dates and different styles, whose bleak spire is the tallest in Holland and Belgium. Of the accumulated treasures inside, the most famous is a delicate marble *Madonna and Child* by Michelangelo, an early work which seems sadly out of place at the centre of an eighteenth-century altar, beneath the cold stone walls of the south aisle. Brought from Tuscany by a Flemish merchant living in Bruges, it was the only work to leave Italy during the artist's lifetime and had a significant influence on the painters working here at the beginning of the sixteenth century.

There's a charge of F30 to enter the choir and ambulatory, where the **mausoleums** of Charles the Bold and his daughter Mary of Burgundy are fine illustrations of Renaissance carving, the panels decorated with coats of arms connected by the most intricate of floral designs. On top, the royal figures are enhanced by tiny details which give a sense of familiarity, from the helmet and gloves placed gracefully by the side of Charles to the pair of dogs by Mary's feet. The earth beneath the mausoleums has been dug up and a couple of mirrors now reveal the original frescoes, painted on the tomb walls at the start of the sixteenth century. Both Mary and Charles died in unfortunate circumstances, she from a riding accident in 1482, when she was only 25, Charles during the siege of Nancy in 1477 – indeed there is some argument as to whether this is the body of Charles at all, since identification was, apparently, difficult. The body was buried in Nancy, but eighty years later Charles V had it exhumed for a more suitable burial here in Bruges.

Sint Jans Hospitaal: the Memling collection

Opposite the entrance to the Onze Lieve Vrouwekerk, the **St Jans Hospitaal** (daily 9.30am–noon & 2–5pm; F100) is a 600-year-old complex that was used as an infirmary until the nineteenth century. Inside, there's a well-preserved fifteenth-century dispensary, a neat little chapel and a number of partly furnished meeting rooms and old wards, but most visitors head straight for the small and important **Hans Memling** collection. Born near Frankfurt in 1433, Memling spent most of his working life in Bruges, where he was taught by Rogier van der Weyden – whose themes he often borrowed. Of the six works on display, the *Mystical Marriage of St Catherine* forms the middle panel of an altarpiece painted for the Hospital church between 1475 and 1479. Graceful and warmly coloured, its gently formal symmetry is in the Eyckian realist tradition. Close by, the *Reliquary of St Ursula* is an unusual and lovely piece of work, a miniature wooden Gothic church painted with the story of Saint Ursula and the 11,000 martyred virgins. Memling accepted the rather unpopular theory that the number of virgins had been erroneously multiplied by a thousand somewhere along the line, and his six panels show Ursula and ten companions on their way to Rome, only to be massacred on their return to Germany. It's the mass of incidental detail that makes the reliquary so enchanting – the tiny ships, figures and churches in the background exhaustively depicting the late medieval world.

The Kathedraal Sint Salvator

Just to the north of the entrance to St Jans Hospitaal, Heilige Geeststraat heads northwest to the **Kathedraal Sint Salvator** (April–Sept Mon–Sat 10am–noon & 2–5pm, Sun 3–5pm; Oct–March 2–5pm; free, museum F20), a replacement for the city centre cathedral that was destroyed by the French in the eighteenth century. Its spartan undecorated interior is similar to that of the Onze Lieve Vrouwekerk, though its graceful Gothic proportions are more appealing. The thirteenth-century choir is the oldest part of the interior, worth a quick glance for its stalls, whose misericords are decorated with delightful scenes of everyday life. Many of the city centre cathedral's treasures were moved here following its destruction, some of which are on display in the cathedral **museum**, notably a vividly realistic triptych by Dieric Bouts and Hugo van der Goes entitled *The Martyrdom of St Hippolytus*.

South of the city centre

From outside the Onze Lieve Vrouwekerk, Mariastraat runs south past sign-posted turnings to the **Begijnhof** (daily 9am–6pm), a rough circle of low, white-washed houses that surround a tidy green. The best time to visit is in spring, when a carpet of daffodils springs up between the wispy elms, creating one of the most photographed sights in Bruges. The streets around the Begijnhof have kept their seventeenth-century design, but the simple terraces now house dozens of restaurants and bars. To the immediate south of the Begijnhof, the picturesque **Minnewater** is another popular spot, edged by a fifteenth-century Lock Gate, a reminder of the lake's earlier use as a town harbour.

North and east of the city centre

A five-minute walk northeast of the belfry, **Jan van Eyckplaats** stands at the western edge of a canal that once ran as far as the Markt. This was at one time Bruges' busiest harbour, the trade missions of some 21 countries and towns spread out around the Spiegelrei, and today the series of uncrowded streets south of the Spiegelrei canal and around nearby Sint Annarei are some of the most charming in Bruges, classically picturesque terraced housing dating from the town's golden age. The square itself is edged by the elegant facade of the fourteenth-century **Poorters Loge**, where the most powerful of the town's merchants met, opposite the slim fifteenth-century **Tolhuis**, decorated with the coat of arms of the Dukes of Luxembourg, who levied tolls here. Next door is the tiny, old **guild house** of the stevedores. Further afield, to the east, the **Jeruzalemkerk**, on Balstraat (Mon–Sat 9am–noon & 2–6pm; free), is not the grandest but is perhaps the most likeable of the town's churches, built by the Adornes family in the fifteenth century as a copy of the church of the Holy Sepulchre in Jerusalem. Anselm Adornes, son of the church's founder, was executed in Scotland for spying, but his heart was returned to Bruges and buried here. You can see his portrait in the windows of the church, which was until very recently still owned by his descendants. A few metres to the north, the **Kantcentrum** (Lace Centre; same times) is situated in the almshouses sponsored by the same family. Inside, there's a modest display of different sorts of traditional Belgian lace and a couple of workshops. The **Museum voor Volkskunde** (daily 9.30am–noon & 2–5pm; F60), around the corner at Rolweg 40, has more lace, a sequence of period interiors and a miscellany of everyday objects.

Further east still, the **Schuttersgild St Sebastian**, Carmersstraat 174 (Archers' guild house; Mon–Fri 10am–noon & 2–6pm; F20), dates from the middle of the sixteenth century and has records of the guild alongside precious gold and silver trophies. The **De Potterie Museum**, at the northeastern end of Pottererei (daily 9.30am–noon & 2–5pm; F60), consists of a chapel and a small museum in an old people's home. The main highlights are some delightful fifteenth- and sixteenth-century pictorial tapestries hung in the chapel aisles.

Eating and drinking

Most of the **restaurants** in Bruges are geared up for the tourist industry and tend to be pricey. However, you can get cheap meals at most of the youth accommodations, best of which are the *Snuffel Travellers Inn*, Ezelstraat 49, and the *Bauhaus International Youth Hotel*, Langestraat 135. Also reasonably priced are the restaurant in the *Koffieboontje* hotel, Hallestraat 4, the self-service dishes at *Selfi*, Steenstraat 58, the mussels and herring at *Koetse*, Oude Burg 31, and *Malpertuus*, Eiermarkt 9, which serves a fine *waterzooi*. Check out also the scallops of the *Uilenspiegel* hotel restaurant, Langestraat 2, the snacks of the agreeable *Diligentie*, just off the Burg on Hoogstraat, and the steaks and smoked fish at *Vivaldi*, near the Begijnhof at Wijngaardstraat 24. Vegetarians should head for *Zen*, a five-minute walk west of the centre at Beenhouwersstraat 117.

At the more expensive end of the market, *Huidevettershuis*, Huidenvettersplein 11, serves a wide array of Belgian regional dishes; there's excellent seafood to be had at *De Visscherie*, Vismarkt 8 (closed Tues); classy surroundings at the *'t Beguntje* on the Walplein; and haute cuisine at *Karmeliet*, Jeruzalemstraat 1.

Most visitors seem to drink where they eat, but there are lots of lively **bars** in and around the town centre. The *'t Mozarthuys*, Huidenvettersplein 1, has background classical music, the *Oud Huis Achiel van Acker*, St Annarei 23, an interesting antique interior, while *Bauhaus* at Langestraat 135 plays rock music and serves bar snacks. *De Versteende Nacht*, Langestraat 11 (closed Mon), bills itself as a "Jazz Café"; while the *Uilenspiegel*, opposite, is a pleasant place to drink in the early evening, with its terrace overlooking the main canal.

Listings

Books A good range of English titles at *De Reyghere*, Markt 12.

Hospital St Franciscus-Xavieruskliniek, Spaanse Loskaai (☎33 98 01).

Left luggage At the station, daily 5am–midnight.

Medical emergencies ☎100. Weekend doctors (Fri 8pm–Mon 8am) ☎81 38 99.

Music Details of concerts and performances in *Agenda Brugge*, a free handout from the tourist office.

Police ☎101

Post office Markt 5 (Mon–Fri 9am–5pm, Sat 9am–noon).

Public transport Bus and train details on ☎38 23 82.

Taxis From the Markt (☎33 44 44) and Stationsplein (☎38 46 60).

Around Bruges: Damme

Originally the main city port, the trim village of **DAMME** was once a hectic, fortified harbour by the banks of the river Zwin, which gave direct access to the sea until it silted up in the late fifteenth century. At its height, the town had a population of some 10,000: it was the site of the marriage of Charles the Bold and Margaret of York, and the scene of a famous naval engagement on June 24, 1340. In the summer of that year, a French fleet assembled in the estuary of the Zwin to prepare for an invasion of England. To combat the threat, the English king, Edward III, sailed across the Channel and attacked at dawn. Although they were outnumbered three to one, Edward's fleet won an extraordinary victory, his bowmen causing chaos by bombarding the French ships with arrows at what was (for them) a safe distance. A foretaste of the battle of Crecy, there was so little left of the French force that no one dared tell King Philip of France, until finally the court jester took matters into his own hands: "Oh! The English cowards! They had not the courage to jump into the sea as our noble Frenchmen did." Philip's reply is not recorded.

Today Damme spreads out prettily beside the canal, its one major street, Kerkstraat, edged by what remains of the medieval town. Funded by a special tax on barrels of herrings, the fifteenth-century **Stadhuis** has an elegant, symmetrical facade balanced by the graceful lines of its exterior stairway. Just down the street, the **Museum Sint Jans Hospitaal** (April–Sept daily 9am–noon & 2–5pm) contains a number of partly furnished period rooms, while a couple of minutes further south there's an early thirteenth-century church tower, surrounded by the gaunt ruins of the **Onze Lieve Vrouwekerk** – abandoned for the past two hundred years.

The best way to visit **DAMME**, 7km northeast of town, is by boat along the poplar-lined canal from Bruges' Noorwegse Kaai (April–Sept 5 times daily each way; single fare F100, return F160). The mundane alternative is by **bus**, either #799 (Sept–June 3 or 4 daily; 25min) or #788 (July & Aug; every 2hr), which both leave from the Markt in the town centre. If you decide to **stay**, there are about a dozen private houses that offer double **rooms** for around F800 a night – just follow the signs on Kerkstraat. Otherwise, Damme has one **hotel**, the *De Gulden Kogge* (☎35 42 17), by the canal at Damse Vaart Zuid 12, with doubles from F1200 – though it's necessary to book ahead in summer. Damme's **tourist office**, Jacob van Maerlantstraat 3 (April–Sept Mon–Fri 9am–5pm; ☎35 33 19), will help to find you a bed if you're in difficulties. As for **food**, Kerkstraat is lined with expensive **restaurants**, mainly aimed at the town's many day-trippers; try the seafood specialities of the *'t Vylekotje*.

Ghent and around

The seat of the Counts of Flanders and the largest town in Western Europe during the thirteenth and fourteenth centuries, **GHENT** was at the heart of the Flemish cloth trade. By 1350, the city boasted a population of 50,000, of whom no less than 5000 were directly involved in the industry, a prodigious concentration of labour in a predominantly rural Europe. Like Bruges, Ghent prospered throughout the Middle Ages, but it also suffered from the endemic disputes between the nobles (who supported France) and the cloth-reliant citizens (to whom friendship with England was vital).

The relative decline of the cloth trade in the early sixteenth century did little to ease the underlying tension, the people of Ghent still resentful of their ruling class, from whom they were now separated by language – French against Flemish – and religion – Catholic against Protestant. Adapting to the new economic situation, the town's merchants switched from industry to trade, exporting surplus grain from France, only to find their efforts frustrated by another long series of wars. The catalyst was taxation: long before the Revolt of the Netherlands Ghent's citizens found it hard to stomach the financial dictates of their kings, and time and again they rose in revolt and were punished. In 1540 the Holy Roman Emperor, Charles V, lost patience and stormed the town, abolishing its privileges, filling in the moat, and building a new secure castle at the city's expense. Later, captured by Philip II's armies in 1584, Ghent was too far south to be included in the United Provinces and was reluctantly pressed into the Spanish Netherlands. Many of its citizens fled north, and those who didn't may well have regretted their decision when the Dutch forced the Hapsburgs to close the Scheldt as the price of peace in 1648.

In the centuries that followed, Ghent slipped into a slow decline from which it has only recently re-emerged, the result of a concerted campaign to attract new business into the area. It's a larger, more sprawling and less immediately picturesque city than Bruges, which may be to its advantage; it has also benefited from a comprehensive clean-up and restoration programme that has been taking place over the last decade. Certainly if you're put off by the tourists or tweeness of Bruges, or you simply can't find a room, it's a good alternative base.

> The Ghent area telephone code is ☎091.

Arrival, information, accommodation and getting around

Ghent has three **railway stations**, but the only one of much use is **St Pieters**, which adjoins the main **bus station**, some 2km south of the city centre. From outside the train station, **trams** #1, #2, #10, #11 and #12 connect with the centre every few minutes, most services passing along Nederkouter and continuing through to the Korenmarkt*. A couple of minutes' walk east of the Korenmarkt, the **tourist office**, in the crypt of the Stadhuis (April–Oct daily 9.30am–6.30pm; Nov–March daily 9.30am–4.30pm; ☎25 36 41), has a comprehensive range of information, including a full list of **accommodation**, which they will book on your behalf at no charge. A lot of what's on offer is at the expensive end of the market, but there are a variety of cheap alternatives, though you'll be lucky to get anything at all during the city's main festival – a boozy affair held in mid to late July.

There's a cluster of convenient, reasonably-priced **hotels** and **guesthouses** around St Pieters station, including several on Koningin Maria Hendrikaplein. Try the *Rambler* at no. 3 (☎21 88 77), or the *Castel*, at no. 9 (☎20 23 54), both of which have double rooms for around F1200. There's another, slightly cheaper group of hotels along neighbouring Prinses Clementinalaan – *La Paix* at no. 2 (☎22 27 79), and *Le Richelieu*, no. 134 (☎21 86 44), both have doubles for F500– 600; *La Lanterne*, at no. 140 (☎20 13 18), charges F900. Failing that, there are a few inexpensive options in the livelier centre of town: the *De Fonteyne*, Goudenleeuwplein 7 (☎25 48 71), with doubles from F700, is about as central as you can get, as is the *Du Progrès*, around the corner at Korenmarkt 10 (☎25 17 16; closed mid-Aug), with doubles at F750. The *Flandria*, off Nederpolder just east of

---

* In early 1990, extensive road works began on the Nederkouter and Kortrijksepoortstraat, making **tram connections between Ghent St Pieters station and the city centre** more awkward. The repairs will take at least a year to complete, and in the meantime you should take tram #21 or #22 from outside the station and ask the driver to put you off at Veldstraat, which is the nearest you'll get to the centre for the moment.

BOAT TRIPS

Between March and November **boat trips** around Ghent's inner waterways depart from the Korenlei and Graslei daily between 10am and 7pm. Trips last 45 minutes, cost F120 and leave roughly once every 15 minutes, though the wait can be longer as they'll only go when reasonably full. In winter, services are more irregular, ask for details at either the tourist office or at the jetty itself.

There are also other possible excursions which leave from the Ketelbrug, behind the Recollettenlei (Law Courts), at the west end of Zonnestraat. They include trips on the Lys, by day (June–Aug 3 or 4 times weekly 1.30–6.30pm; F220) or at night (July & Aug, Sat 8pm to Sun 1am; F220), and day trips to Bruges (July & Aug Thurs 9am–8pm; F300) – though this isn't as good a deal as it sounds: food and drink are very expensive and long sections of the canal are too deep to see over the banks. If you're after countryside, the excursion to the village of St Maartens (July 4 times weekly 3–6.20pm; F180) is far better.

the cathedal at Barrestraat 3 (☎23 06 26), is also handy, and does double rooms for upwards of F1000. If you're flush, the best place to stay is without doubt the *Gravensteen*, a lovely small hotel in an old Baroque mansion overlooking the Castle of the Counts at Jan Breydelstraat 35 (☎25 11 50); doubles cost F3600.

During the summer, between mid-July and the end of September, there's another option, cheaper than using a hotel, when over one thousand **student rooms** are let to visitors for F400 per person per night including breakfast. The rooms are dotted around the south of town in a number of complexes; ask at the tourist office for further details or enquire direct at *Home Vermeylen*, Stalhof 6 (☎22 09 11). Those **camping** should proceed to *Camping Blaarmeersen*, Zuiderlaan 12 (☎215 399; March to mid-Oct), at the water sports centre to the west of town. Buses #51, #52 and #53 run direct from Ghent St Pieters station.

The best way of seeing the sights is on foot, but Ghent is a large city and you may find you have to use a **tram** or **bus** at some point. This is easy enough: standard single fares cost F30, an eight-strip *Rittenkaart* F138, and a 24-hour unlimited tourist city travel pass F140. Single tickets can be bought direct from the driver; *Rittenkaarts* are sold at shops and kiosks all over town; and the pass, along with maps of the public transport system (*Netplan* – F50), is available at the **kiosk** by the tram stop on the Korenmarkt (Mon–Sat 8–11.30am & 1.30–5pm).

The City

The shape and structure of today's city centre reflects Ghent's ancient class and linguistic divide. The streets to the south of the Korenmarkt tend to be straight and wide, lined with elegant old mansions, the former habitations of the wealthier, French-speaking classes; while to the north, Flemish Ghent is all twisting alleys and low brick houses. They meet at the somewhat confusing sequence of large squares that surround the town's principal buildings, spreading out to the immediate east of Korenmarkt.

St Baaf's Cathedral

The best place to start an exploration of the city centre is the mainly Gothic **St Baaf's Cathedral**, squeezed into the eastern corner of St Baafsplein (April–Sept Mon–Sat 9.30am–noon & 2–6pm, Sun 1–6pm; Oct–March Mon–Sat 10am–noon &

2.30–4pm, Sun 2–5pm; free). St Baaf's tidy nave, begun in the fifteenth century, is supported by tall, slender columns that give the whole interior a cheerful sense of lightness, though the seventeenth-century marble screens rather spoil the effect by darkening the choir. In a small ambulatory chapel is the cathedral's – and Ghent's – greatest treasure, an **altarpiece** known as *The Adoration of the Mystic Lamb*, a seminal work of the early fifteenth century, though of dubious authorship. Since the discovery of a Latin verse on its frame in the nineteenth century, academics have been arguing about who actually painted the masterpiece. The inscription reads that Hubert van Eyck "than whom none was greater" began, and Jan van Eyck "second in art" completed the work, but as almost nothing is known of Hubert, some art historians doubt his existence. They argue that the citizens of Ghent invented "Hubert" to counter Jan's fame in the rival city of Bruges. No one knows for sure, but what is certain is that in their manipulation of the technique of oil painting the artists were able to capture a needle-sharp realism that must have seemed revolutionary to their contemporaries.

Certainly it's a complex work, an explanation of which (with its rich structure and symbolism) could fill volumes. The cover screens display a beautiful Annunciation scene with the archangel Gabriel's wings reaching up to the timbered ceiling of a Flemish house, the streets of a town visible through the windows. In a brilliant coup of lighting, the frames of the shutters throw their shadows into the room, emphasising the reality of the apparition. Below, the donor and his wife kneel piously alongside statues of the saints. But the restrained exterior painting is but a foretaste of what's within, a stunning visionary interior that was only revealed when the shutters were opened on Sundays and feast days. On the upper level sit God the Father, the Virgin and John the Baptist in gleaming clarity; on the left is a group of singing angels who strain to read their music. (Van Mander, writing in the sixteenth century, thought they were so artfully painted you could discern the different pitches of their voices.) In the lower panel the Lamb, the symbol of Christ's sacrifice, is approached by bishops, saintly virgins and Old and New Testament figures in a heavenly paradise – "the first evolved landscape in European painting" thought Kenneth Clarke, seen as a sort of idealised Low Countries. Look closely and you can see the cathedrals of Bruges, Utrecht and Maastricht surrounded by flora so fastidiously detailed they have been used in college reference books.

Tucked away in the small chapel, it's actually remarkable that the altarpiece has survived at all. Not surprisingly, the Calvinists wanted to destroy it; Philip II of Spain tried to acquire it; the Emperor Joseph II disapproved of the painting so violently that he replaced the nude Adam and Eve with a clothed version of 1784 (exhibited today just inside the church entrance); while a few years later the Germans stole it and hid it in an Austrian salt mine until the end of World War II. It'll cost you F50 to see the altarpiece, and you'd be crazy to miss it.

By comparison to the altarpiece, the **Crypt** (F50) of the cathedral is a bit of an anticlimax. Dating from the twelfth century, it preserves features of the earlier Romanesque church of St John, along with murals painted between 1480 and 1540 but only rediscovered in 1936. Crammed full of religious bric-a-brac, one or two of the reliquaries are worth a second look, but the prime exhibit is Justus van Gent's fifteenth-century **triptych**, *The Crucifixion of Christ* – with the crucified Christ flanked on the right by Moses and the bronze serpent that cured poisoned Israelites on sight, and on the left by Moses purifying the waters of Mara with wood.

GHENT

To
Dampoort Railway
Station (100 m)

Leie

Sint
Baafsabdij

St.-Baaf's
Cathedral

Stadhuis &
Tourist Office

Lakenhalle

Mad Meg

Toreken

St.-
Niklaas

Post
Office

PATERSHOL

Museum voor
Volkskunde

Gravensteen

City Boat Trips

St.-Michielsbrug

GEWAD

Museum voor
Sierkunst

Museum of Industrial
Archaeology & Textiles

Rabot

Ketelbrug

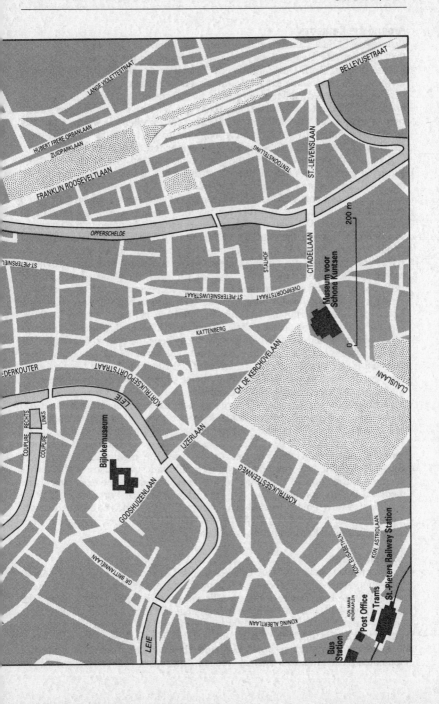

Around the Cathedral

Just west of St Baaf's, the fifteenth-century **Lakenhalle** or Cloth Hall is little more than an empty shell with a dreary audiovisual display on the first floor (Tues–Sun 9.30am–4.30pm, April–Oct until 6pm; F60) and an equally dismal restaurant in the basement. Accessible from the same first-floor entrance, the adjoining **Belfry** is a much amended edifice dating from the fourteenth century. Once a store-house of important civic documents, today the interior is a rather bare, dusty ruin. A glass-sided lift climbs up to the roof for excellent views over the city centre. In summer, there are usually long queues for the belfry's guided tours (daily every 30min, 10am–4.30pm; F100 per person for tours, otherwise F60).

Access to the **Stadhuis** across the street is also limited (May–Oct Mon–Thurs afternoon guided tours only; F40), and of the series of halls open to the public, the most interesting is the *Pacificatiezaal*, the site of the signing of the Pacification of Ghent in 1576. This was an agreement which momentarily bound north and south Flanders together against the Hapsburgs, with the promise of religious freedom. The tiled floor is, curiously enough, designed in the form of a sort of maze. Outside, the entrance to the tourist office is framed by a section of facade whose severity is a good example of post-Reformation architecture, in stark contrast to the wild, curling patterns of the section to the immediate north, carved in the Flamboyant Gothic style at the turn of the sixteenth century. Designed by Rombout Keldermans, each ornate niche holds a statuette – detailed carvings of the powerful and famous in characteristic poses, including Keldermans himself rubbing his chin and studying his plans for the Stadhuis. The last of this central cluster of buildings is **St Niklaaskerk** (April–Oct daily 2–5pm; F50), an architectural hybrid that's recently been restored from a dangerous state of dilapidation. The interior is bare, and once again it's the shape and structure that please most. Dodging the trams of the Korenmarkt and heading west, you pass the main **post office building**, whose carved heads represent the kings who came to Ghent for the World Exhibition of 1913. A few yards away, the St Michielsbrug bridge overlooks the city's oldest harbour, the **Tussen Bruggen** (Between the Bridges), where **boats** leave for trips round the neighbouring canals roughly once every fifteen minutes throughout the summer months (F120; 45min – see above). The **Korenlei**, the western side of the harbour, is home to a series of stolid merchants' houses dating from the eighteenth century; the **Graslei**, opposite, has the squat, gabled guild- and warehouses of the town's boatmen and grainweighers. Some of these are particularly fine examples of late medieval design, specifically no. 14, the *Gildehuis van de Vrije Schippers* (Free Boatmen), whose golden sandstone is decorated with scenes of boatmen weighing anchor; close by, the tiny *Tolhuisje* was built 150 years later, a delightful illustration of Flemish Renaissance composition.

's Gravensteen

A few minutes' walk north of Graslei, the **'s Gravensteen** (daily Oct–March 9am–4pm; April–Sept 9am–6pm; F40), or Castle of the Counts, looks sinister enough to be in a Bosch painting. Cold and cruel, its dark walls and angular turrets were built in 1180 as much to intimidate the town's unruly citizens as to protect them. Considering the castle has been used for all sorts of purposes (it was even a textile mill in the nineteenth century), it's survived remarkably intact, its gateway a deep-arched tunnel leading to the courtyard, framed by protective battlements complete with ancient wooden flaps, arrow slits and boiling oil and water holes. In the middle of the courtyard stand the castle's two main buildings, the Donjon on the right and the Count's Residence on the left, riddled with narrow, inter-connected staircases set within the thickness of the walls. A self-explanatory, numbered tour guides visitors through this labyrinth, and highlights include an assembly room with a magnificent stone fireplace, a gruesome collection of instruments of torture with a few illustrations of their use, and a couple of particularly dank oubliettes.

The rest of the centre

On the opposite side of the square from the castle entrance, at the junction of the two main canals, are the battered remains of the old **Vismarkt**, whose facade is dominated by a grand, but grubby relief of Neptune. It's in a terrible state, scheduled for restoration but for the moment used as a bowling alley and car park. Crossing the bridge immediately to the west, turn first left for the **Museum voor Sierkunst**, Jan Breydelstraat 5 (Tues–Sun 9am–12.30pm & 1.30–5.30pm; F40), which has a pleasant sequence of period rooms, ornamented by a number of fine examples of early Dutch and Chinese porcelain. Back at the bridge, turn right down Gewad for the **Museum voor Industriele Archeologie en Textiel**, at no. 13 (Tues–Sun 9am–12.30pm & 1.30–5.30pm; free), with its modest collection of looms and old textile materials. Opposite, Braderijstraat heads east to the **Lievekaai**, Ghent's second harbour, by the side of the old canal to Bruges. Closed and partly filled in during the nineteenth century, the Lievekaai originally extended right up to the front of the old merchants' houses that now flank what remains of the waterway from behind a cobbled pavement. To the northwest, a mixture of tumbledown and renovated seventeenth- and eighteenth-century properties line the sides of the canal as far as the **Rabot**, a fortified medieval sluice that today marks the end of the canal. The Rabot was crucial to the defence of old Ghent: the water level behind the sluice was higher than the water level outside and in emergencies the gates could be opened and the surrounding fields flooded, keeping the enemy at a safe distance.

Retracing your steps to the 's Gravensteen and continuing east across St Veerleplein onto the Kraanlei, you'll come to one of Ghent's better museums, the **Museum voor Volkskunde**, Kraanlei 65 (April–Oct Tues–Sun 9am–12.30pm & 1.30–5.30pm; Nov–March 10am–noon & 1.30–5pm; F40). Housed in a series of restored almshouses surrounding a central courtyard, this is made up of a delightful chain of period rooms depicting local life and work in the eighteenth and nineteenth centuries. A good detailed guide is available at reception (F30), and the reconstructed grocery and cooper's workshop are especially interesting. The most curious exhibits are the two wooden "goliaths" in the church: of obscure origin, goliaths are a common feature of Belgian street processions and festivals.

Behind the Kraanlei are the lanes and alleys of the **Patershol**, a web of terraced houses dating from the seventeenth century. Once the heart of the old Flemish working-class city, this thriving residential quarter had, by the 1970s, become a slum threatened with demolition. The area was preserved and a process of gentrification began that has dotted the streets with good bars and expensive bistros. The process isn't complete, and the fringes of the Patershol remain a rough and ready assortment of decay and restoration, including the old **Carmelite Monastery** on Vrouwebroerstraat, which is a good example of how things used to be – part ruin, part squat, it's an odd rabbit-warren of a place that feels unsafe at night.

Back on the Kraanlei, a new canal walkway opposite the Folklore Museum has replaced part of the original towpath and heads off northeast past gabled facades and nineteenth-century textile factories to re-emerge at the eastern end of the Patershol. Alternatively, the bridge adjacent to the start of the walkway leads into the **Vrijdagmarkt**, the old political centre of Ghent and the site of public meetings and executions. By the bridge, there's a fifteenth-century cannon that proved more dangerous to the gunners than the enemy, hence its name, *Mad Meg*, while the slim turret at the other end of the square, the **Toreken**, was once the Tanners' Guild House. Adjoining the Vrijdagmarkt is the crowded **Bij St Jacobs**, and there's nothing gentrified about the bars round here.

East of the centre

East of the Bij St Jacobs, Ghent's eighteenth- and nineteenth-century industrial suburbs stretch out towards the Dampoort railway station. A mish-mash of terrace, factory and canal, these suburbs were spawned by the sea-canals that were dug to replace the obsolete, narrow waterways of the city centre. Right next to the station, the large water-filled hole on **Oktrooiplein** is the link between the old and the new systems. One of the area's more interesting parts is sandwiched between the river Leie and the railway lines just north of Gandastraat, on and opposite **Stierstraat** – housing that dates from the very earliest days of the Industrial Revolution, including courtyard dwellings and a dilapidated urban terrace that incorporates some of the features of the rural workers' cottages that the terraces were beginning to replace. Nearby, at the west end of Gandastraat, are the scant remains of the church of **St Baafsabdij** (daily 9am–noon & 2–5pm; F40), the birthplace of John of Gaunt and the site of a small lapidary **museum** in the thirteenth-century refectory.

South of the centre

Ghent's main shopping street, **Veldstraat**, leads south from the city centre parallel with the course of the river to a couple more of Ghent's top-rung museums. The first, the **Bijlokemuseum** at Godhuizenlaan 2 (daily 9am–12.15pm & 1.30–5.15pm; F40), isn't especially remarkable, and the labelling of the exhibits – mainly art and applied art pertaining to the Ghent region – is chaotic. But the old abbey buildings in which the museum is housed are some of the prettiest in the city, and the guild room, in the old dormitory, is splendid.

Ten minutes' walk away to the southeast, the **Museum voor Schone Kunsten** (same times and price), on the edge of the park at Nicolaas de Liemaeckereplein 3, is rather better, though, once again, the layout and presentation are confusing. There are two main collections here, a fairly small display of modern art concentrated on the first floor and in the rooms to the left of the entrance, and older masters on the ground floor to the right. Of the latter (which is the more interesting part), highlights include a fourteenth-century *Head of Christ* and a finely detailed, unattributed panel of a triptych, *The Taking of Jerusalem by Titus*. Close by are Bosch's *Carrying of the Cross*, showing Christ mocked by some of the most grotesque and deformed characters Bosch ever painted, and the smaller, less well-known *St Jerome at Prayer*. There's also work by Pieter Brueghel the Younger, who inherited his father's interest in the landscape and those who worked and lived on it, as seen in his *Wedding Feast* and *Peasant Wedding*. Later paintings include several canvases by Jacob Jordaens, the *Men's Heads* and *Mythological Scene* mimicking the robust romanticism of his friend Rubens – who is poorly represented by several sketches for proposed paintings in Antwerp and Brussels – the muscular romance of Anthony van Dyck's *Jupiter and Antione*, and an earnest Frans Hals simply entitled *Elderly Lady*.

Food, drink and nightlife

Ghent's cheapest **eating** place is the university canteen, the *Overpoort* (Mon–Fri 11.30am–5pm), on Overpoortstraat near the Museum voor Schone Kunsten, where meals of reasonable quality cost F150 (though ISICs are sometimes requested). Otherwise, on and around the Korenmarkt, there's an excellent Italian restaurant, *Da Cesare*, above the *Twilight* bar at Korenmarkt 35; good basic fare at the busy *Du Progres*, Korenmarkt 10; old-style Flemish specialities at the *'t Marmietje*, on the Korenlei; and cheap snacks and meals until late at *Pascalino*, opposite the Stadhuis at Botermarkt 11. Vegetarians should try the tasty dishes at *Buddhasbelly*, Hoogpoortstraat 30 (Mon–Sat noon–2pm & 6–9pm).

If you're not so bothered about budget you should try the more upscale restaurants and bistros of the Patershol district, including the popular bar/restaurant *Amadeus* at Plotersgracht 8; *Pier Fagels* at Plotersgracht 6 is a good second choice. With money to burn, visit the pricey *De Hel* (Wed–Sat only), at Kraanlei 51, whose facade is extravagantly decorated with a sequence of classically-inspired red stone reliefs.

Like all Belgian cities, Ghent has some wonderful **bars**. Try the dark and mysterious *De Tap en de Tepel* (Tap and Nipple) on Gewad; the *Amadeus* on Plotersgracht (see above); or the rough-and-ready *Taverne in den Karmeliet* on Cordouwaniersstraat. The *Het Waterhuis*, near the castle at Groentenmarkt 9, serves over one hundred sorts of beer in pleasant surroundings, including a delicious local brew, *Stropken* (literally "noose"), named after the time in 1453 when the victorious Philip the Good compelled the city burghers to parade outside the town gate with ropes around their necks.

Listings

Airport There's a regular bus service (five times daily) from Ghent St Pieters train station and from outside the *Sabena* office, Kouter 151 (Mon–Fri 8.30am–3pm; ☎23 31 32), to the city's nearest airport, Brussels Nationaal. Price F300.

Bookshop *Fnac* at Veldstraat 88, close to the junction with Zonnerstraat, has a good selection of English titles.

Car hire *Avis*, Kortrijksesteenweg 676 (☎22 00 53); *Garage Gantois*, Kortrijksesteenweg 200 (☎22 10 22); *Hertz*, Einde Were 51 (☎24 04 06).

Festivals Ghent's main festivals are the Flanders Spring Fair in early April, the *Gentse Feesten* or town fair (held in mid to late July for ten days, always including July 21), the Patershol celebrations in mid-Aug, and the Flanders Music Festival at the end of Aug.

Left luggage Office at Ghent St Pieters station (6am–midnight); lockers in the station concourse.

Markets There's a flower market daily on the Kouter, although Sun is best (7am–1pm). There are also flea markets ("prondelmarkt") on Beverhoutplein and Bij St Jacobs (Fri–Sun 7am–1pm).

Police ☎101

Post office Main post office at Korenmarkt 15 (Mon–Fri 9am–6pm, Sat 9am–noon).

Travel agents *JEST*, Overpoortstraat 47 (☎21 21 47); *Divantoura*, Bagattenstraat 176 (☎23 00 69).

Around Ghent

The flat and dreary countryside that encircles Ghent and its untidy suburbs is without much interest, except for the moated and turreted castle of **Laarne** (Feb–Christmas Tues–Sun 10am–noon & 2–6pm; F100), which lies some 12km east of the city. Founded in the twelfth century, most of today's building is medieval, a picturesque mixture of towers and steeples that hides a magnificent collection of old silver and several beautifully preserved Brussels tapestries. The castle is accessible by bus #688 from St Pieters bus station (Mon–Sat every 1–2hr, 4 on Sun; 30min).

East of Ghent: Sint Niklaas, Dendermonde and Aalst

To the northeast of Gent lies the agricultural region of the **Waasland**, its sand and clay soils sandwiched between the Dutch border to the north, the Ghent–Terneuzen canal to the west, and the river Scheldt to the east. Once an isolated area of swamp and undrained forest, the lands of the Waasland were first cultivated by pioneering religious communities who cleared the trees and built the dykes. The soil was poor and conditions were hard until Ghent's demand for wool encouraged local landowners to introduce the sheep that produced the district's first cash crop and provided some degree of prosperity. Today, the area is popular with tourists seeking the quiet of the countryside.

Sint Niklaas

Some 40km east of Ghent, **SINT NIKLAAS** is the only settlement of any size in the Waasland, an unremarkable town whose principal feature is its Grote Markt, the largest in Belgium. It's edged by a motley combination of old and new buildings, including an attractively symmetrical **Stadhuis** from the nineteenth century, and the seventeenth-century **Sint Niklaaskerk**, which has a later Baroque interior. The only real surprise in town is the tiny old castle, **Kasteel Walburg** (no admission), a couple of minutes from the tourist office on Walburgstraat. Built of reddish brick in the middle of the sixteenth century, the castle is in the Flemish Renaissance style and was clearly made for comfort rather than defence. Part of an attractively wooded city park and encircled by a slender moat, it's classically picturesque – or at least it will be when the repairs are finished in 1991.

The municipal **museum** (Tues–Sat 2–5pm, Sun 10am–5pm; F30 ticket valid for both town museums), back towards the train station at Zamanstraat 49, consists of a predictable display of local artefacts saved from mediocrity by a wing dedicated to the maps, atlases and a couple of globes made by the Flemish cartographer Mercator, who was born in the neighbouring village of Rupelmonde in 1512. It's Mercator's projection of the spherical surface of the world onto a two-dimensional map that is now accepted as the usual view of the earth's surface, and it was originally an invaluable aid to navigation – though the view it gives of the world is to some extent a misleading one, distorting the relative size of the continents at the expense of the southern hemisphere: Europe simply isn't that big and neither is Greenland, while the surface area of Africa is in fact much larger. The other "trick" is the layout, with the colonial nations of Europe at the centre of the world.

Continuing up Zamanstraat, the first junction brings you to Regentiestraat, and, at no. 65 in the "Exlibris Centrum", Sint Nikolaas' other museum, the **Barbers' Museum** (Barbierama; Tues–Sat 2–5pm, Sun 10am–5pm) – an original and varied presentation that features some early electrical hairdressing appliances that look like sci-fi props from early *Flash Gordon* films.

Practical details

If you decide to stay in Sint Niklaas, the **tourist office**, Grote Markt 45 (Mon–Fri 8am–5pm; June–Aug also Sat & Sun 10am–4pm; ☎03/777 26 81), will provide a list of **campsites** and **hotels** in the town and surrounding area. There are two cheap and central **hotels**: the *De Spiegel*, near the station at Stationsstraat 1 (☎03/776 34 37), with doubles from F950, and the *De Arend*, in the centre at Onze Lieve Vrouweplein 8 (☎03/777 11 73) – doubles from F1315. The tourist office also has details of cycle tours and walks in the Waasland.

Dendermonde

Southeast of Ghent, the river Scheldt twists its way across the industrial heartland of East Flanders, its towns home to the host of factories that sprang up in the nineteenth century as Belgium was transformed from a predominantly agricultural society to – briefly – the fourth greatest industrial power in the world. Some 25km from Ghent, **DENDERMONDE**, at the confluence of the rivers Scheldt and Dender, shared in the industrial boom, just as previously its strategic location had seen it suffer its share of siege and assault. Badly damaged by the Germans in 1914, today's town centre is rather drab, but there are several medieval buildings of note spread out around the trim **Stadhuis**, whose fourteenth-century shape and structure was restored in the 1920s. Close by, the turreted **Vleeshalle** has a somewhat sombre facade dating from 1460, and to the rear, Kerkstraat leads west to the stolid **Onze Lieve Vrouwekerk**, housing the town's prime exhibits: a *Crucifixion* and *Adoration of the Shepherds* by Anthony van Dyck – two early canvases that are typical of the painter's romantic approach.

Dendermonde is, however, best known for its **carnival**, an extraordinary attempt to re-enact the medieval story of the *Steed Bayard* – a medieval tale of knights and honour, loyalty and friendship, dynastic quarrels and disputes. Picaresque in form, the story doesn't seem to make much sense – though the whole thing revolves around the trials and tribulations of the horse, represented by a giant prefabricated model, and its masters, the four brothers who perch on top. The clearest part of the story is the end, where the redoubtable steed repeatedly breaks free from the millstones tied round its neck and refuses to drown. The third time he comes to the surface, one of his masters walks away, unable to stand and watch the agonies of his horse any longer. The horse assumes he's been abandoned, cries out and only then does he drown. The carnival is held every few years at the end of May, but there are plans to make it an annual event. Further details are available at most Belgian tourist offices.

If you're staying over, there's one cheap **hotel**, *Wets*, Hoofdstraat 41a (☎052/ 211 407), with doubles from F900. The **tourist office** is in the Stadhuis (Mon–Fri 8.30am–noon & 1–5pm; May–Sept also Sat & Sun 10am–noon & 1.30–4.30pm; ☎052/21 39 56).

Aalst

About 20km south of Dendermonde, the ancient town of **AALST** was first fortified in the eleventh century and became a settlement of some importance as a seat of the Counts of Flanders, at the point where the Bruges to Cologne trade route crossed the river Dender. Later on Aalst became a key industrial centre, producing beer and textiles, and renowned for some of the worst slum and factory conditions in the country. Cleaned up in the 1950s, the town has one outstanding building, the fifteenth-century **Belfry**, a slender, balconied turret that rises elegantly from the Grote Markt, adorned by the statues of a knight and an armed citizen, symbols of municipal power and individual freedom. The belfry is attached to the **Schepenhuis** (Aldermen's House), a somewhat incoherent jangle of bits and pieces shoved together over the centuries, with a delicate Flamboyant Gothic **gallery** pushing out into the square from the main body of the building. Inside the belfry there's a small town **museum** (Mon–Fri 10am–noon & 2–5pm), commemorating the work of a local nineteenth-century radical Catholic priest, Adolf Daens, who campaigned to improve the pay and conditions of local workers. It's a modest collection, but an engaging one, sepia photographs illustrating the work of the priest, the organisation of a local Catholic-led trade union, and the harsh poverty of the period.

Just to the east of the Grote Markt lurks the massive hulk of the **Sint Martinuskerk** (normally daily 8am–noon & 2–6pm), a gloomy church that hides Aalst's only famous painting, the clumsily-named *St Roch Receiving from Christ the Gift of Healing Victims of the Plague* by Rubens. Commissioned by the guild of beer brewers and hop growers in 1623, the painting has faded quite badly, but it's still possible to make out the artist's fluent, exuberant lines, displayed within the original carved wooden frame. Close by, an ornate **Tabernacle** fills out the space between two of the church's arches, an extravagant mixture of columns and statuettes in several different sorts of marble, the work of Jeroom du Quesnoy in 1604.

Scheduled for relocation, Aalst **tourist office** (Oct–May Mon–Fri 10am–noon & 1–5pm; June–Sept Mon–Fri 10am–noon & 2–6pm, Sat 2–6pm, Sun 10am–12.30pm & 2–6pm; ☎053/77 11 11) is at present in the belfry. The town has two affordable **hotels**, the *De Lange Muur*, near the station at Stationsplein 13 (☎053/77 37 46), with doubles from F1000, and the arcaded eighteenth-century *Borse van Amsterdam*, opposite the belfry at Grote Markt 26 (☎053/21 15 81) – something of a bargain at F930 a double, although the elegance of the facade contrasts with the simplicity of the rooms behind.

travel details

Trains

From Bruges to Ghent/Brussels (3 hourly; 25/65min); Ostend (3 hourly; 15min).

From Ghent to Sint Niklaas/Antwerp Centraal (2 hourly; 25/45min); Kortrijk (2 hourly; 30min); Oudenaarde (1 hourly; 35min); Veurne/De Panne (1 hourly; 70/80min); Dendermonde/Mechelen (2 hourly; 30/65min); Aalst (3 hourly; 25min).

From Kortrijk to Ieper (hourly; 30min); Oudenaarde (hourly; 20min); Ghent (2 hourly; 25min); Lille (France) (hourly; 30min).

From Ostend to Bruges (3 hourly; 15min); Ghent/Brussels (3/4 hourly; 40/80min).

From Veurne to De Panne (hourly; 10min); Dijksmuide (hourly; 10min); Ghent (hourly; 70min).

From Ieper to Kortrijk (hourly; 30min).

Buses

From Ieper to Lo/Veurne (7 daily; 33/60min).
From Ostend to Nieuwpoort/Veurne (Mon–Sat 8 daily, Sun 3 daily; 35/75min).
From Veurne to Nieuwpoort (Mon–Sat 8 daily, Sun 3 daily; 40min), Ieper (7 daily; 1hr); Ostend (Mon–Sat 8 daily, Sun 3 daily; 75min).

Trams

From Ostend to De Panne (every 10min in summer & 30min in winter; 1hr 4min); Knokke (same frequency; 1hr).

CHAPTER NINE

ANTWERP AND THE NORTH

T he Flemish-speaking provinces of Antwerp and Limburg form the north-eastern rim of Belgium, stretching from the city of Antwerp in the west to the river Maas in the east, which forms the border with Holland. It's dull countryside on the whole, heralding the flat landscapes of Holland further north, and the main attraction is inevitably **Antwerp** – a large old port that is defi-nitely worth a stopover if you're travelling to or from Amsterdam. It's a sprawling and intriguing place, the international centre of the diamond trade and in part still a seedy dock city; it also has many reminders of its sixteenth-century golden age, before it was usurped by Amsterdam as the prime commercial centre of the region, from splendid medieval churches and guild houses to as fine a set of museums as you'll find anywhere in the Low Countries – Rubens spent most of his career in the city and produced much of his best work here. Outside of the city, **Antwerp province** has two other ancient towns that are worth a visit – the old centre of **Lier** and the ecclesiastical capital of the country, **Mechelen**.

The province of **Limburg**, to the east, is, unlike Antwerp, seldom visited by tourists, and to be honest its low-key mixture of small industrial towns and tran-quil farmland doesn't have terrific appeal. The capital, **Hasselt**, is of no particular interest but it does have a bustling, lively centre; and the nearby **Bokrijk** estate holds one of the best open-air museums in the country, primarily dedicated to the rural traditions of Flemish Belgium. Of the smaller towns, **Tongeren**, on the edge of the linguistic divide, is most worth a visit, known as the oldest town in the country. Across the border in Flemish **Brabant, Sint Truiden**, too, is a reward-ing stop, primarily for its bus connections to the village of **Zoutleeuw** with its spectacular fourteenth-century church – the only one in Belgium that managed to entirely avoid the attentions of Protestants, iconoclasts and invading armies.

Antwerp

About 30km north of Brussels, Belgium's second city, **ANTWERP**, fans out care-lessly from the east bank of the Scheldt, its grimy centre a rough polygon formed by its enclosing boulevards and the river. Most people prefer it to the capital: though not an immediately likeable place, it has a denser concentration of things to see, not least some fine churches and a varied selection of distinguished museums – reminders of its auspicious past as centre of a wide trading empire. It has a more clearly defined character too, less a dull location of political life, more a lively cultural centre, with a colourful, spirited nightlife. On the surface it's not a wealthy city – the area around the docks especially is run-down and seedy – but

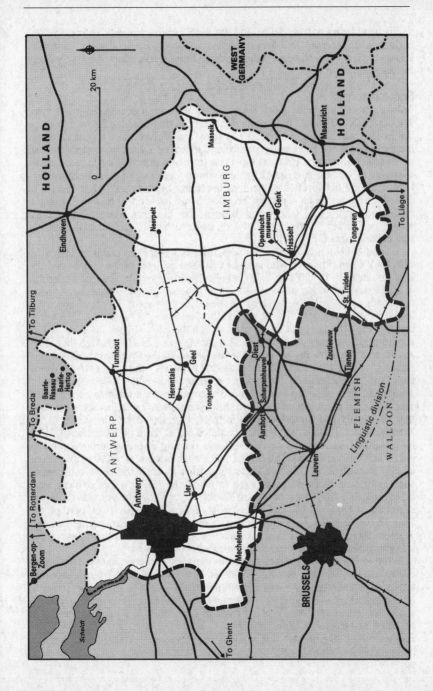

its diamond industry (centred behind the dusty facades around Centraal Station) is the world's largest. On a less contemporary note there is also the enormous legacy of Pieter Paul Rubens, some of whose finest works adorn Antwerp's many galleries and churches.

Some history

Antwerp wasn't originally much sought-after: although it occupied a prime river site, it was too far east to be important in the cloth trade and too far west to be on the major trade routes connecting Germany and Holland. But a general movement of trade to the west, and in particular the decline of Bruges, towards the end of the fifteenth century, led to its rapid rise from obscurity: within 25 years, many of the great trading families of western Europe had moved their headquarters here, the tiny old fortified settlement becoming overwhelmed by a deluge of splendid new mansions and churches, docks and harbours. Frustrated with the turbulent burghers of Ghent and Bruges, the Emperor Maximilian and his successor Charles V patronised Antwerp, underwriting its success as the leading port of their expanding empire.

Antwerp's golden age lasted for less than 100 years, prematurely stifled by Charles V's son, Philip II, who inherited the Spanish part of the empire and the Low Countries in 1555. Fanatically Catholic, Philip viewed the Reformist stirrings of his Flemish-speaking subjects with horror, encouraging the Inquisition to send thousands to the gallows. Antwerp seethed with discontent, its population swollen by religious refugees. The spark was the *Ommegang* of August 18, 1566, when priests carted the image of the Virgin through the city's streets, insisting that all should bend the knee as it passed. The parade was peaceful enough, but afterwards, with the battle cry of "Long live the beggars", the Protestant guildsmen of Antwerp smashed the inside of the cathedral to pieces – the most extreme example of the "iconoclastic fury" that was sweeping the region. Philip responded by sending an army of occupation, intended to overawe and intimidate from a brand new citadel on the south side of town. Nine years later, it was this same garrison that sat unpaid and underfed in its fortress, surrounded by the wealth of the "heretical" city. Philip's mercenaries mutinied and at dawn on November 4, 1576, they stormed Antwerp, for three long days running riot, plundering Antwerp's public buildings and private mansions, and slaughtering some 8000 of its citizens in the "Spanish fury". It was a catastrophe that finished the city's commercial supremacy, and more disasters were to follow. In 1577, Philip's soldiers were driven out, but they were back outside the city walls eight years later, laying siege for seven months, and afterwards confirming Antwerp as part of the Spanish Netherlands. Under the terms of the capitulation, Protestants had two years to leave town and a flood of skilled workers poured north to the relative safety of Holland, further weakening the city's economy.

In the early sixteenth century there was a modest recovery, but the Dutch now controlled the seaways of the Scheldt and determined that no neighbouring Catholic-controlled port would threaten their trade – in 1648, under the Treaty of Munster, they closed the river to all non-Dutch shipping. Antwerp was ruined, and remained so until the French arrived in 1797, when Napoleon declared it to be "little better than a heap of ruins . . . scarcely like a European city." The French rebuilt the docks and revived the city, and Antwerp later became independent Belgium's largest port, a position it has maintained until the present day.

The Antwerp area telephone code is ☎03.

Arrival, getting around and finding a place to stay

Antwerp has two main **railway stations**, Berchem and Centraal. International trains stop at Berchem (except those from Paris and Amsterdam), 4km south of town, and the rest at Centraal – far more conveniently placed on the edge of the city centre about 2km east of the Grote Markt. Connections between the two stations are frequent and fast (10 hourly; 3min). Inside the **Centraal Station** complex, an **information office** (Mon–Sat 8am–10pm, Sun 9am–5pm; ☎233 70 15) has international and domestic rail timetables along with details of special bargains and tariffs. Most long-distance **buses** arrive at the bus station on Franklin Rooseveltplaats, a five-minute walk northwest of Centraal Station. The **information kiosk** here (Mon–Fri 7am–7pm, Sat 10am–5pm) deals with bus services throughout the province of Antwerp.

Antwerp's tiny **airport** is in the suburb of DEURNE, about 6km east of the city centre, connected by occasional *Sabena* bus to the airline's office close by Centraal Station. Failing that, ordinary city buses leave from the main road straight ahead of the airport building once hourly (9am–6pm) for Pelikaanstraat, also by Antwerp Centraal. Taxis to Antwerp Centraal cost about F350.

A useful **tram** and **bus** system serves the city and its suburbs from a number of points around Centraal Station, especially from bus stops along Pelikaanstraat and in Koningin Astridplein. Tram services from Centraal station to the city centre (#2 or #15 to Groenplaats) go underground. A city transport **information office** (Mon–Fri 8am–noon & 1–4pm), in the underground station beside Antwerp Centraal, sells tickets and maps of bus and tram routes for F40. A standard single fare costs F40, an 8-strip *Rittenkaart* F154, a 24-hour unlimited travel tourist card F140.

Information and accommodation

Antwerp has two **tourist information offices**, one in front of Centraal Station in Koningin Astridplein (Mon–Fri 8.30am–8pm, Sat 9am–7pm, Sun 9am–5pm; ☎233 05 70), the other in the town centre at Grote Markt 15 (Mon–Fri 8.30am–6pm, Sat & Sun 9am–5pm; ☎232 01 03). Both offices have a comprehensive range of information on the city and its sights, including a map of the city and its suburbs for F30, leaflets for F5 detailing where to see the works of Rubens, and an extensive **accommodation** list. The tourist office will also make reservations on your behalf at no cost, charging only a F200 deposit that is subtracted from your final bill.

Otherwise, there are a number of places around town offering **dormitory accommodation**. The two cheapest are the *Boomerang*, south of the city centre, near the Museum voor Schone Kunsten at Volkstraat 58 (☎238 47 82; tram #8 from Groenplaats), with beds for F300 and double rooms at F750, and, for a few francs more, the *New International Youth Pension*, Provinciestraat 256 (☎230 05 22) – a ten-minute walk from Centraal Station: head south down Pelikaanstraat, turn left along Plantin en Moretuslei, and take the second right. Two other possibilities are the *Square Sleep-Inn*, 2km south of the city centre down Nationalestraat at Bolivarplaats 1 (☎237 37 48; tram #8 from Groenplaats), which has triple-bedded rooms for F1700 and doubles at F850, and the *International*

Seamen's House, a ten-minute walk north of the Grote Markt at Falconrui 21 (☎232 16 09) – doubles from F1080. The **youth hostel** is 3km south of the centre at Eric Sasselaan 2 (☎238 02 73), just to the west of the nearest **campsite**, *Vogelzang*, on Vogelzanglaan behind the Bouwcentrum (☎238 57 17; April–Sept). You can get to both places from Centraal Station by tram #2, direction Hoboken.

Strangely enough, there's only one **hotel** in the city centre, the comfortable *Cammerpoorte*, at Steenhouwersvest 55 (☎231 97 36), with doubles for F1900. This is by far the most convenient place to stay, though it's advisable to book ahead in summer. Most of Antwerp's other hotels are located near Centraal Station, cheapest of which are two rather grim hotels on Koningin Astridplein, the *Oud Dijksterhuis* at no. 22 (☎233 08 00), and the *Billard Palace* at no. 40 (☎233 44 55), which both have doubles for around F1000. Other reasonably priced but also rather seedy alternatives include the *Tourist*, Pelikaanstraat 22 (☎232 58 77), the *Florida*, De Keyserlei 59 (☎232 14 43), and the *Monico*, Koningin Astridplein 34 (☎225 00 93), all of which have double rooms for F1200–1400. Slightly pricier are the *Drugstore Inn*, Koningin Astridplein 43 (☎231 21 21), with doubles from F1650, and the *Terminus*, Franklin Rooseveltplaats 9 (☎231 47 95), which has doubles from F1500. If you're after more than the most basic of rooms, try the *Colombus*, on the edge of Franklin Rooseveltplaats at Frankrijklei 4 (☎233 03 90), with doubles from F1850, or the *Arcadel*, behind the Rubenshuis at Meistraat 39 (☎231 88 30), which charges F2200.

BOAT TRIPS

There are a number of **boat trips** to be made in and around Antwerp. Cruises down the **Scheldt** leave from the landing stage beside the Steen fortress from April to September. Hour-long trips cost F180 (April 5 daily; May & June Mon–Fri every 30min, 10am–4.30pm), 90-minute trips F240 (April Sat & Sun 8 daily; July & Aug daily every 30min, 10am–4.30pm; Sept 4–6 daily). Tours also take in the city's port area, leaving from Quay 13 (by Londenbrug at the end of Italielei on the left-hand side) and costing F320 per person for the two-and-a-half-hour trip (April–early May Sun only at 2.30pm; mid–May to June Mon, Tues, Thurs & Fri 10.30am & 2.30pm; June–Aug Mon–Fri 10.30am & 2.30pm; Sept Fri–Sun 2.30pm). A special bus leaves for Quay 13 from beside the Steen fortress 20min before each departure.

Day-long excursions to **Bruges** are also possible, via Zeebrugge. They leave from beside the Steen once or twice monthly in July and August, departing at 8.30am and returning by 9.30pm. The fare is F1700 per person and advance booking is essential.

Further information, including details of extra summer season sailings to other cities in Flanders, from the tourist office or the operators themselves, *Flandria*, Steenplein (☎231 31 00).

The City Centre

The centre of Antwerp is the **Grote Markt**, at the heart of which stands the **Brabo Fountain**, a haphazard pile of roughly sculpted rocks surmounted by a bronze of Silvius Brabo, depicted flinging the hand of the giant Antigonus into the Scheldt. Legend says that Antigonus extracted tolls from all passing ships, cutting off the arms of those who refused to pay. He was eventually beaten by the valiant Brabo, who tore off his hand and threw it into the river, giving rise to the name of the city, whch means literally "hand-throw". There are more realistic theories to explain the city's name, but this is the most colourful, and it certainly reflects Antwerp's early success at freeing the river from the innumerable taxes levied on shipping by neighbouring landowners.

The north side of the Grote Markt is lined with daintily restored **Guild Houses**, their sixteenth-century facades decorated with appropriate reliefs and topped by finely cast gilded figures basking in the afterglow of the city's Renaissance lustre. No. 5, the *Coopers' House*, with its barrel motifs, is the tallest and most distinctive, next door to the house of the *Crossbowmen*, with its figures of Saint George and the Dragon. They are overshadowed though, by the **Stadhuis**, completed in 1566 to an innovative design by Cornelis Floris (Mon 9am–noon, Tues–Thurs 9am–3pm, Fri noon–3pm, Sat 9am–4pm; F20; guided tours only; entry from a side door on the right on Zilversmidstraat from Mon–Fri; from Suikerrui, on the left, on Sat). The building's pagoda-like roof gives it a faintly oriental appearance, but apart from the central gable it's quite plain, with a long pilastered facade of short and rather shallow Doric and Ionic columns, which, along with the windows, lend a simple elegance, in contrast to the purely decorative gable (there's no roof behind it) – added at a time when a tower would have been considered old-fashioned. The niches at the top contribute to the self-congratulatory aspect of the building, with statues of Justice and Wisdom proclaiming virtues the city burghers reckoned they had in plenty. Inside, by way of the Zilversmidstraat entrance, the staircase of the high main hall used to be an open courtyard and was only covered in the late nineteenth century, accounting for the monumental gallery on all four sides. The paintings which take the place of windows represent aspects of commerce and the arts – a balance which Antwerp has long been conscious of, and is now anxious to preserve. Among the other rooms you can see are the Leys Room, named after Baron Hendrik Leys, who painted the frescoes in the 1860s, and the Wedding Room, which has a chimneypiece from the original town hall, decorated with two caryatids by Floris himself, who was also a master sculptor.

The Cathedral

Leaving the Grote Markt by its southeast corner, the triangular **Handschoenmarkt** is bordered by more elegant old facades, its tiny stone well adorned with an iron canopy bearing the legend "It was love connubial taught the smith to paint" – a reference to the fifteenth-century painter Quentin Matsys, who learnt his craft in order to successfully woo the daughter of a local artist (at the time marriage was discouraged between families of different guilds). The Handschoenmarkt is the most westerly of a sequence of somewhat confusing pedestrianised squares that occupy the area around the **Onze Lieve Vrouwe Cathedral** (Mon–Fri 10am–5pm, Sat 10am–3pm, Sun 1–4pm; F30), one of the finest Gothic churches in Belgium, mostly the work of Jan and Pieter Appelmans in the middle of the fifteenth century. A forceful and self-confident structure, the cathedral dominated the skyline of medieval Antwerp with a graceful spire that was finally completed in 1518. Long a source of fascination to travellers, William Beckford, fresh from spending a million pounds on his own house in Wiltshire at the start of the nineteenth century, was still impressed enough to write he "longed to ascend it that instant, to stretch myself out upon its summit and calculate, from so sublime an elevation, the influence of the planets". Over the centuries the building weathered badly, and in 1969 a long-term restoration project

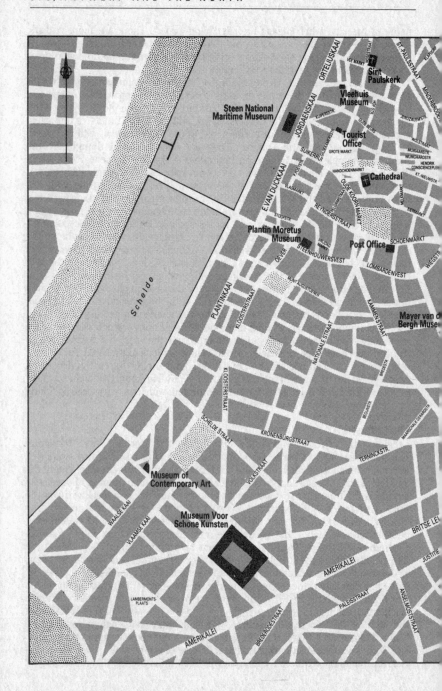

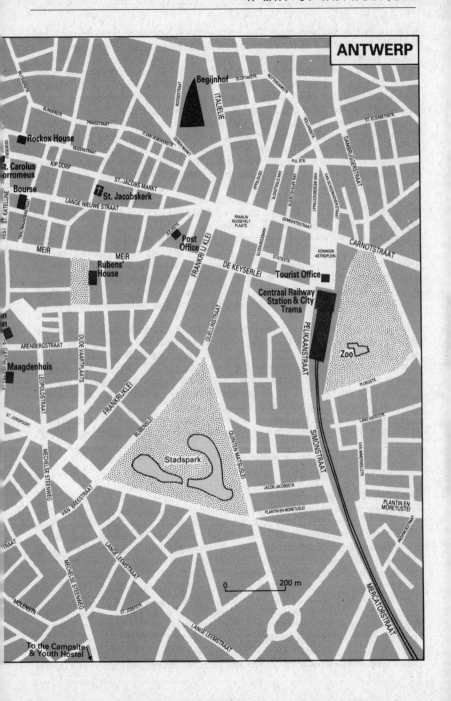

ANTWERP

Begijnhof

Rockox House

St. Carolus orromeus

Bourse

St. Jacobskerk

ST. KATELINE

MEIR

MEIR

Rubens' House

Post Office

FRANKRIJ KLEI

DE KEYSERLEI

Tourist Office

Centraal Railway Station & City Trams

CARNOTSTRAAT

KONINGIN ASTRIDPLEIN

Arenbergstraat

OUDE VAARTPLAATS

Maagdenhuis

LEOPOLDSTRAAT

FRANKRIJKLEI

RUBENSLEI

PELIKAANSTRAAT

Zoo

PLOEGSTR.

LANG KIEVITSTR.

ST. JORISPOORT

QUELLINSTRAAT

QUINTEN MATSIJSLEI

Stadspark

VAN IMMERSEELSTR.

SIMONSTRAAT

JACOB JACOBSSTR.

PLANTIN EN MORETUSLEI

PLANTIN EN MORETUSLEI

MECHELSE STEENWEG

VAN BREESTRAAT

LANGE LEEMSTRAAT

MECHELSE STEENWEG

ST. ROZESTR.

MOLENSTR.

LANGE LEEMSTRAAT

MERCATORSTRAAT

0   200 m

To the Campsite & Youth Hostel

began with the roof and nave. The front sections have now been finished, but work on the choir and ambulatory is scheduled to take another fifteen years.

The triple-aisled nave is in itself breathtaking, if only because of its sense of space, an impression that's reinforced by the rather antiseptic restoration. A fire of 1533, the Iconoclastic Fury of 1566, and the fact that the church briefly became Protestant later that century have ensured that no Gothic decoration remains, and what you see today are a number of subsequent Baroque embellishments, notably three early paintings by Rubens which for the moment hang in the nave. Of these, the *Descent from the Cross*, just to the right of the temporary high altar on the wall that closes off the choir, is without doubt the most beautiful, a triptych painted after the artist's return from Italy that displays an uncharacteristically restrained and moving realism, derived from Caravaggio. Christ languishes in the centre in glowing white, surrounded by mourners or figures who are tenderly struggling to lower him. As was normal, with commissions pouring in from everywhere, students in Rubens' studio worked on the painting, among them the young Van Dyck, who repaired the face of the Virgin and the arm of Mary Magdalen. His work was so masterful that Rubens is supposed to have declared it an improvement on his own, though this story appears to originate from Van Dyck himself. Oddly enough, the painting was commissioned by the Guild of Arquebusiers, who asked for a picture of Saint Christopher, their patron saint; Rubens' painting was not at all what they had in mind, and they promptly threatened him with legal action unless he added a picture of the saint to the wings.

To the left of the nave, in the treasury, there's another Rubens triptych, the *Resurrection*, painted in 1612 for the tomb of his friend, the printer Jan Moretus, and showing a strident, militaristic Christ carrying a red, furled banner. There's also a third triptych, variously titled the *Assumption* or *The Raising of the Cross*, to the left of the cathedral entrance, displayed behind glass panels during restoration work. Painted in 1610, it's the earliest of the three paintings, a grandiloquent Baroque canvas full of muscular soldiers and saints.

A free leaflet with a diagram of the church and a numbered list of exhibits is available either at the entrance or from the cathedral shop adjoining the exit. However, the only other highlight is Maarten de Vos's *Marriage at Cana*, hung near the *Assumption*, a typically mannered work completed towards the end of the artist's life in 1597.

The Plantin-Moretus Museum

Leaving the cathedral, you emerge on **Groenplaats**, a dreary open square that was once the town graveyard and now holds a mucky statue of Rubens. From here, it takes about five minutes to thread your way west to **Vrijdagmarkt**, where the **Plantin-Moretus Museum** (daily 10am–5pm; F75) is housed in the old mansion of the printer Christopher Plantin, who rose to fame and fortune here in the second half of the sixteenth century. Born in Tours in 1514, Plantin moved to Antwerp when he was 34 to set up a small bookbinding business, but in 1555 he was forced to give up all heavy work when, in a case of mistaken identity, he was wounded by revellers returning from carnival. Paid to keep quiet about his injuries, Plantin used the money to start a printing business. He was phenomenally successful, his fortune assured when Philip II granted him the monopoly of printing missals and breviaries for the whole of the Spanish Empire. On Plantin's death, the business passed to his talented son-in-law, Jan Moerentorf, who changed his name, in accordance with the fashion of the day, to Moretus; he in turn was succeeded by his son Balthasar, a close friend of Rubens. The family donated their mansion to the city in 1876.

From the entrance, a clearly labelled route takes visitors through most of the rooms of the house, set around a compact central courtyard. The mansion is worth seeing in itself and the museum as a whole provides a marvellous insight into how Plantin and his offspring conducted their business. A detailed booklet is available at reception for F40, and highlights include several well-preserved pictorial tapestries in room 1; a delightful seventeenth-century bookshop, equipped with a list of prohibited books, the *Librorium Prohibitorum*, along with a money-balance to help identify clipped and debased coins in room 4; and the old print room, with seven ancient presses, in room 14; not to mention dozens of intriguing, precise woodcuts and copper plates in room 27, the best of an enormous number that were used by several centuries of print workers. There are also a number of examples of the work of Christopher Plantin, including the *Biblia Polyglotta*, an annotated, five-language text produced on vellum for King Philip in 1572, as well as sketches by Rubens, who occasionally worked for the family as an illustrator, and a portrait of *Seneca* by the same artist.

The National Maritime Museum

Head east across Vrijdagmarkt from the museum, turn left and left again, and the first turning on the right is **Pelgrimstraat**, which has one of the best views of the cathedral, a tumble of sloping, uneven roofs set against the majestic lines of the church behind. On the left, by no. 8, an ancient alley called the **Vlaeykensgang** (Pie Lane) twists its way down to **Oude Koornmarkt**, a surviving fragment of the honeycomb of narrow streets that made up medieval Antwerp. From the end of the alley, Oude Koornmarkt and subsequently Suikkerui lead west to the banks of the Scheldt, clearly separated from the town since Napoleon razed the riverside slums and constructed proper quaysides in the early 1800s. Jutting out into the river at the end of Suikkerui, the scant remains of the Steen fortress are approached past a giant statue of **Lange Wapper**, a somewhat confusing local folklore figure – part practical trickster, part peeping Tom – who, despite a fondness for children, exploited his height by spying on people's bedrooms.

The **Steen** marks the site of the ninth-century fortification from which the rest of the town spread, later the location of an impressive medieval stronghold, successively reinforced and remodelled to keep the turbulent guildsmen of Antwerp in check. The gatehouse and front section are all that have survived, and today they house the **National Maritime Museum** (daily 10am–5pm; F75), whose cramped rooms feature exhibits illustrating a whole range of shipping activity from inland navigation to life on the waterfront and shipbuilding. Clearly laid out and labelled, with multi-lingual details on all the major displays, the museum is a delight, an appealing mixture of the personal and the public. The high points include some charming British scrimshaws and whale tooth engraving in room 1, an intriguing fifth-century nautical totem in the form of a snake's head in room 3, and several fine ship models in room 9. You should also look out for a model of the Italianate barge that was built for Napoleon's second visit to Antwerp, and peek into the old council chamber, decorated by two large canvases of the docks in the seventeenth century. Behind the Steen, the museum has an open-air section with a long line of tugs and barges packed in under a rickety corrugated roof.

The Vleeshuis

Crossing Jordaenskaai from beside the Steen, it's a couple of minutes' walk east along Palinburg to the tall, turreted gables of the **Vleeshuis** (Tues–Sun 10am–5pm; F75), built for the Guild of Butchers in 1503. With its alternating layers of red brick and stonework, the outside has often been likened to streaky bacon, but it's still an impressive building, the suitably grand headquarters of one of the most powerful of the medieval guilds. It was here in 1585, with the Spanish army approaching, that the butchers made the fateful decision to oppose the opening of the dykes along the Scheldt – a defensive ploy strongly recommended by William the Silent because it would have made it impossible for the Spaniards to mount a blockade of the river from its banks. However, the butchers were more worried about the safety of their flocks which grazed the threatened meadows, and so sent a deputation to the city magistrates to object. The magistrates gave way, and the consequences were disastrous – the Spaniards were able to close the Scheldt and force the town to surrender, a defeat that placed Antwerp firmly within the Spanish Netherlands.

Today, the enormous brick halls of the interior are used to display a large but rather incoherent collection of applied arts, in particular several fine fifteenth-century wood carvings on the ground floor and a good set of seventeenth- to eighteenth-century musical instruments on the uppermost level. The exhibits are labelled exclusively in Flemish although an English guide is available for F30, but it's the setting rather than the displays that pleases most.

North to the Falconplein and the St Pauluskerk

The streets around the Vleeshuis were badly damaged by wartime bombing, leaving a string of bare, open spaces edged by some of the worst of the city's slums. The whole area is scheduled for redevelopment, but progress is slow and few of the crumbling terraces have yet been restored, though several of the gaps have been filled by solid modern houses whose pinkish stone facades imitate the style of what went before. Cosy and respectable, these new buildings are in stark contrast to the dilapidated **red light area** all around, a sequence of grotty little streets with sporadic tattoo parlours and bored faces at the windows. It's a soulless district, a sure sign that you're approaching Antwerp's tough dockland area just to the north.

From the entrance to the Vleeshuis, it's a couple of minutes' walk north along Vleeshouwersstraat to Veemarkt, where an extravagant Baroque portal leads through to the precincts of the **St Pauluskerk** (May–Sept daily 2–5pm, F30; Oct–April daily 9am–noon, free), a dignified late Gothic church of 1571. The most prominent feature of the interior is the extraordinary wood carving of the confessionals and choir stalls, their snake-like, almost arabesque pillars the work of P. Verbrugghen the Elder in the mid-seventeenth century. Rubens' *Disputation on the Holy Sacrament*, an early work of 1609, hangs in an altar in the south transept, opposite a long series of paintings that line the north aisle, including works by Rubens (the *Scourging* of 1617), Van Dyck and Jordaens – though they're not at their best in the gloomy church light. Outside, near the entranceway, the **Calvaryberg** is an artificial grotto of 1697–1747 that clings to the buttresses of the south transept, eerily adorned with statues of Christ and other figures in a rather tawdry representation of the Crucifixion. Writing in the nineteenth century, the traveller Charles Tennant described it as "exhibiting a more striking instance of religious fanaticism than good taste", and he wasn't far wrong.

Five minutes northeast of the church, Klapdorp leads to **Falconplein**, at the heart of a solid working-class district just to the south of the docks. A far cry from the tourist trimmings of Grote Markt, it's here that Slav and Jewish minorities have set up their textile and domestic appliance shops, advertising their goods in Cyrillic for the benefit of those Soviet sailors whose ships are in port.

South to the Huis Rockox Museum and Hendrik Conscienceplein

From Falconplein, Mutsaertstraat leads south to Keizerstraat, where the **Huis Rockox Museum** at no. 12 (Tues–Sun 10am–5pm; free) is housed in the splendidly restored seventeenth-century town house of Nicolaas Rockox, friend and patron of Rubens. Inside, a sequence of rooms has been crammed with period furnishings and art work, based on an inventory taken after the owner's death in 1640. Of particular interest is Pieter Bruegel the Younger's *Netherlandish Proverbs*, one of several canvases he did on the subject. It's a mass of finely drawn detail, frenetically mixing the observed and imagined.

At the western end of Keizerstraat, **Hendrik Conscienceplein** takes its name from a local nineteenth-century novelist whose work concentrated on the life of the traditional Flemish peasantry. One of the most agreeable places in central Antwerp, the square is fringed by the church of **Sint Carolus Borromeus** (Mon & Wed–Fri 9.30am–1pm, Sat 9.30am–noon & 3–6pm; F20), whose finely contrived facade is claimed to have been based on designs by Rubens. Much of the interior was destroyed by fire at the beginning of the eighteenth century, but to the right of the entrance, the so-called Lady's Chapel survived, its streaky, coloured marble a key feature of the original church, here serving as a background for a series of tiny pictures.

From Hendrik Conscienceplein, walk west to the end of Wijngaardstraat, where a left and then a right turn takes you into the series of tiny squares that front the northern side of the cathedral. Here, the **Het Elfde Gebod** (The Eleventh Commandment) is one of the most unusual bars in the city, jam-packed with a bizarre assortment of religious statues.

South of the City Centre

South of Groenplaats spread Antwerp's older residential areas, bounded by the Amerikalei and Britselei boulevards, which mark part of the course of a circle of city fortifications finished in the early years of this century. Enormously expensive and supposedly impregnable, the design was a disaster, depending on a series of raised gun emplacements that were sitting targets for the German artillery in September 1914. The Allies had expected Antwerp to hold out for months, but in the event the city surrendered after a two-week siege, forcing Churchill and his party of marines into a hurried evacuation just two days after their arrival.

The Mayer van den Bergh Museum

Five minutes' walk southeast of Groenplaats, the delightful **Mayer van den Bergh Museum**, at Lange Gasthuisstraat 19 (Tues–Sun 10am–5pm; F75), consists of the private art collection of the wealthy merchant family of the same name, given to the city in 1920. Very much a connoisseur's collection, there are fine examples of many different branches of applied arts, from tapestries to ceramics, silverware, illuminated manuscripts and furniture, all crowded into a reconstruction of a sixteenth-century town house. There are also a number of excellent paintings, including a *Crucifixion* triptych by Quentin Matsys in room 4, the unidentified donors painted on the wings alongside a curious picture of the woman's patron saint, Mary of Egypt – a repentant prostitute who spent her last years in the desert miraculously sustained by three little loaves. Room 6 holds an early fourteenth-century carving of *St John on the Breast of Jesus*, and three tiny panels from a fifteenth-century polyptych that once decorated a fanciful travelling altar, the rest of which is on display in the United States. On each panel, the formality of the religious scene is in contrast to the informality of the detail – Saint Christopher crosses a stream full of fish and Joseph cuts up his socks for use as swaddling clothes for the infant Jesus. The next room holds another picture of *St Christopher*, the work of Jan Mostaert, its bold tones influenced by his long stay in Italy, while room 9 is home to the museum's best-known work, Bruegel's *Dulle Griet* or "Mad Meg", one of his most Bosch-like paintings, a rather misogynistic allegory in which a woman, loaded down with possessions, stalks the gates of Hell, a surrealist landscape of monsters and pervasive horror. The title refers to the archetypal shrewish woman, who, according to Flemish proverb "could plunder in front of hell and remain unscathed". Nearby, Bruegel's *Twelve Proverbs* is a less intense vision of the world, a sequence of miniatures illustrating popular Flemish aphorisms.

The Maagdenhuis

Down the street from the Van den Bergh Museum, the **Maagdenhuis**, at Lange Gasthuisstraat 33 (daily except Tues 10am–5pm; F75), was formerly a home for poor children but is now occupied by the city's social security offices and a small museum. Founded in the middle of the sixteenth century, the orphanage was run on the strictest of lines, its complex rules enforced by draconian punishments. At the same time, those children who were left here were fed, and taught a skill, and desperate parents felt that they could at least retrieve their children if their circumstances improved. To make sure their offspring could be identified, they were left with tokens, usually irregularly cut playing cards or images of saints – one part left with the child, the other kept by the parent. If the city fathers didn't actually encourage this practice, they certainly accepted it, and several buildings even had specially carved alcoves on their facades where temporarily unwanted babies could be abandoned under shelter, sure to be taken in come the morning.

Entrance to the museum is through an ornamental archway decorated with figures representing some of the first girls to be admitted to the orphanage set beside a tidy classroom scene, so finely chiselled that you can make out the tiny bookshelves. Inside, six ground-floor rooms, a chapel and a courtyard display a varied but modest collection of art include a touching *Portrait of an Orphan Girl* by Cornelius de Vos, an overpowering *Descent from the Cross* by Jordaens and an Italianate *Adoration of the Shepherds* by Jan van Scorel. There's also an assembly of some fifty colourful late medieval porridge bowls, the largest collection of its sort in Belgium, and a sealed certificate confirming the election of Charles V as Holy Roman Emperor in 1519. The exhibits are labelled exclusively in Flemish, but an English guidebook is available at reception for F30.

The Museum voor Schone Kunsten

Fifteen minutes' walk southwest of the Maagdenhuis (tram #8 from Groenplaats), the **Museum voor Schone Kunsten** (Tues–Sun 10am–5pm) occupies an immense neo-Classical edifice. It's normally free, though charges are sometimes made during temporary exhibitions. Of the permanent collection, downstairs displays relatively modern works, while upstairs shows older pieces, from Flemish Primitives to seventeenth-century masters. Everything is a little mixed up, including most of the signs, and it's difficult to plan a chronological route, but a lighting-up plan in the first room gives you some idea of where each painter is. Or you can buy a rough diagram of the museum's layout at reception for F10.

The **early Flemish** section isn't as comprehensive as you might expect from a major museum, but the collection includes two fine works by Jan van Eyck, a *Madonna at the Fountain* and a tiny *St Barbara*, where the usual symbol of the saint's imprisonment, a miniature tower held in the palm of her hand, has been replaced by a palm and prayer book, to represent her faith and self-sacrifice. Behind, a full-scale Gothic tower looms over her, a more powerful indication of her imprisonment. Hans Memling's *Portrait of Giovanni de Candida* and his *Angels Singing and Playing Instruments* are not among his most distinguished works, but they have a finely textured quality for which he is famous, while the angels are clearly copies of figures that had already appeared in his *Reliquary of St Ursula*, kept in Bruges. Rogier van der Weyden's *Triptych of the Seven Sacraments* was painted for the Bishop of Tournai in 1445, its inventive frame merging with the lines of the Gothic architecture inside; his *Portrait of Philippe de Croy* blends a dark background into the lines of his subject's cloak, a simple technique to emphasise the shape of the nobleman's angular face and his slender hands. Nearby, Jean Fouquet, the most influential French artist of the fifteenth century, has one canvas on display, a *Madonna and Child*, with remarkable, orange-red angels surrounding a chubby Jesus who looks away from a pale, bared breast. Look out also for Quentin Matsys's triptych of the *Lamentation*. Commissioned for the carpenter's chapel of Antwerp Cathedral in 1511, it's a profound and moving work, a dishevelled Christ pressed tightly into the foreground by crowds of mocking, twisted faces.

Rubens has two large rooms to himself, in which one very large canvas stands out: the *Adoration of the Magi*, a beautifully free and very human work, painted in 1624. Rubens apparently finished it in a fortnight, no doubt with the help of his studio, the major figures of which – Van Dyck and Jordaens – are represented in the rooms that follow, the latter by an especially skilled *Day and Night*.

Highlights of a small group of **Dutch paintings** from the late sixteenth and seventeenth centuries include Frans Hals' prim *Fisher Boy*; two genre paintings by Joachim Beuckelaer, *The Fish Market* and *The Vegetable Market*; and, fittingly placed in the same room, raucous scenes of peasant life by Adriaen Brouwer and David Teniers. Born in Flanders, apprenticed to Frans Hals in Haarlem and very much influenced by Bruegel, Brouwer bridges the gap between Flemish and Dutch art. When he was imprisoned in 1633, the prison baker, Joos van Craesbeek, became his pupil, and his pictures are here too, sometimes excelling even Brouwer in their violence.

The museum also has a comprehensive collection of **modern Belgian art**, supplemented by a smattering of works by well-known foreign artists. However, there's not enough room to show all the collection at any one time and an ambitious exhibitions programme means that paintings are regularly rotated, so it's difficult to give precise directions. That said, you should be able to see the work of James Ensor, whose subdued, conservative beginnings, such as *Afternoon at Ostend*, 1881, contrast with his piercing later works – *Skeletons Fighting for the*

Body of a Hanged Man. Also likely to be on show are paintings by Paul Delvaux, whose *Red Bow* shows a classical city in the process of disintegration, and the Impressionistic Rik Wouters – the latter's *Woman Ironing* a sensitive picture of his wife completed in 1912.

East of the City Centre

From the northeast corner of Groenplaats, Eiermarkt curves round to **Meir**, Antwerp's main shopping street, which connects the centre of town with Centraal Station, some fifteen minutes' walk to the east. At the start of Meir, near its junction with St Katelijnevest, the short Twaalfmaandenstraat ends in the **Beurs** (Mon–Fri 7.30am–5pm; free), the recently restored late nineteenth-century stock exchange, built as a rough copy of its medieval original which was burnt to the ground in 1868. Gloomy and deserted, it's still a splendid extravagance, a high glass-paned roof supported by spindly iron beams above the coats of arms of the maritime nations, with walls showing a giant map of the world.

The Rubenshuis

Back on the Meir, it's a five-minute walk east to Wapper, a dreary pedestrianised square, where the **Rubenshuis** at no. 9 (daily 10am–5pm; F75) attracts tourists in droves. Arguably the greatest northern Baroque painter, and certainly Antwerp's most celebrated, his house was only acquired by the town in 1937, by which time it was little more than a shell. Skilfully restored, it opened as a museum in 1946. It's not so much a house as a mansion, splitting into two parts – on the left the traditional, gabled Flemish house, and on the right the classical Italian studio, where Rubens worked, taught and entertained the artistic and cultural elite of Europe. He had an enviably successful career, spending the first eight years of the seventeenth century studying the Renaissance masters in Italy, and settling in this house in 1608. Soon after, he painted the Antwerp Cathedral series and his fame spread, both as a painter and diplomat, working for Charles I in England, and receiving commissions from all over Europe.

Unfortunately, there are only one or two of his more undistinguished paintings here, and very little to represent the works of those other artists he collected so avidly throughout his life. The restoration of the rooms is convincing though, and a clearly arrowed tour twists its way through a pleasant series of domestic interiors, neatly panelled and attractively furnished. In contrast to the cramped living quarters, the spacious **art gallery** was where Rubens once displayed his favourite pictures to his friends, in a scene comparable to that portrayed in Willem van Haecht's *The Gallery of Cornelis van der Geest*, which is now on display here in the main gallery, a suitable illustration of Rubens' grand lifestyle. Behind the house, the garden is laid out in the formal style of his day, as it appears in Rubens' *Amidst Honeysuckle*, now in Munich. The Baroque portico might also be familiar from the artist's Medici series, on display in the Louvre.

The St Jacobskerk

Rubens died in 1640 and was buried in the **St Jacobskerk**, just to the north of the Wapper at Lange Nieuwstraat 73 (April–Oct Mon–Sat 2–5pm; Nov–March Mon–Sat 9am–noon; F30). Very much the church of the Antwerp nobles, who queued up to be interred in its vaults and chapels, the church is a Gothic structure begun in 1491 but not finally finished until 1659, a delay that means much of its Gothic splendour is hidden by an over-decorous Baroque interior, the soaring heights of the nave broken and flattened by the heavy black altars. Seven chapels radiate from the ambulatory, including the **Rubens Chapel**, directly behind the high altar, where the artist and his immediate family are buried beneath a tomb-stone in the floor whose lengthy Latin inscription gives details of his life. The chapel's altar was the gift of Helene Fourment, Rubens's second wife, and shows one of his last works, *Our Lady Surrounded by Saints*, in which he painted himself as Saint George, his wives as Martha and Mary, and his father as Saint Jerome. It's as if he knew this was to be his epitaph; indeed, he is said to have asked for his burial chapel to be adorned with nothing more than a painting of the Virgin Mary with Jesus in her arms, encircled by various saints.

The rest of the church is crammed with the chapels and tombs of the rich and powerful, who kept the city's artists busy with a string of commissions destined to hang above their earthly remains. Most is only of moderate interest, but the chapel next to the tomb of Rubens is worth a peek for its clumsily titled *Saint Carolus Borromeus Pleading with the Virgin on Behalf of those Stricken by the Plague*, completed by Jacob Jordaens in 1655. It's a broad, sweeping canvas, not without its ironies: Borromeus, archbishop of Milan, was a savage reactionary and leader of the Counter-Reformation, while the artist was a committed Protestant. In the north aisle of the nave, there's the chapel of the Rockox family (see above) who are pictured on the panels of the triptych above the altar by Jan Sanders, and in a chapel in the south aisle, a flamboyant *St George and the Dragon* by Van Dyck.

East to Centraal Station

Meir heads east from the Rubenshuis past its junction with Jezusstraat, where the carved relief on the building on the corner is a tribute to **Lodewijk van Berckem**, who introduced the skill of diamond-cutting to the city in 1476. From here, Leystraat, a continuation of Meir, lined by a sweeping facade ending in a pair of high turreted gables, whose gilt figures and cupolas formed the impressive main entrance to the nineteenth-century town. Dead ahead, the magnificent neo-Baroque **Centraal Station** was finished in 1905, a confusion of spires and balconies, glass domes and classical pillars designed by Louis Delacenserie, who had made his reputation as a restorer of Gothic buildings in Bruges. It's an extraordinary edifice, a well-considered blend of earlier architectural styles and fashions – particularly the Gothic lines of the main body of the building and the ticket hall, which has all the darkened mystery of a medieval church – yet displaying all the self-confidence of the new age of industrial progress. Sadly, the station is also the victim of one of the greatest cock-ups in Belgium: the construction of the underground tram tunnels by its side disturbed the water table so that the oak pillars supporting the station have dried out, threatening it with collapse. No one knows quite what to do and the scaffolding around the front of the station is likely to be there for years.

The Diamond District

The discreet shabbiness of the streets just to the southwest of Centraal Station is home to the largest **diamond** market in the world. Behind these indifferent facades precious stones pour in from every continent to be cut or re-cut, polished and sold. There's no show of wealth, no grand bazaar, and no tax collector could ever keep track of the myriad deals that make the business hum.

The trade is largely controlled by Orthodox Jews, many of whom came here from eastern Europe towards the end of the last century and are often the only obvious sign that the business exists at all. They make most of their money as middlemen in a chain that starts in South Africa, where eighty percent of the world's diamonds are mined. As a form of price-fixing, the rate of production and the speed of distribution are strictly controlled by an all-powerful South African cartel led by the *De Beers* company, who organise ten "showings" in London every year. Guests are there by invitation only, and although the quality of the assortment of diamonds in each lot is controlled by the producers, if potential purchasers fail to buy on three occasions they aren't invited again.

In the heart of the diamond district, the **Provinciaal Diamantmuseum** at Lange Herentalsestraat 31 (daily 10am–5pm; free) deals with the geology, history, mining and cutting of diamonds in a long series of clearly labelled displays. The photographs of early prospectors and examples of most of the major types of diamond are of particular interest, but it's all a bit of a public relations job, glossing over, for example, the lucrative trade in stolen gems, mine conditions in South Africa itself, or the devious way the Soviets sell their thousands of diamonds without lowering the price fixed by the *De Beers*.

Antwerp's other museums

Though none are essential by any means, Antwerp has a number of other, more **specialist museums** that are either shrines of arcane interest or good places to shelter on rainy afternoons. The following is a more or less comprehensive (alphabetical) round-up.

Museum van Hedendaagse Kunst, Leuvenstraat 32 (Tues–Sun 10am–5pm; F50). Museum of contemporary art mounting lively, imaginative exhibitions in a 1920s Art Deco grain silo.

Museum voor Fotografie, Waalsekaai 47 (Tues–Sun 10am–5pm; free). Has an excellent collection of photograhs of old Antwerp.

National Zoo & Natural History Museum, by the train station at Koningin Astridplein 26 (daily 8.30am–5pm, later on summer evenings; F280). Standard zoo with a museum section that concentrates on Belgian fauna.

Open-Air Museum of Modern Sculpture, Middelheim Park, 5km south of the centre (daily 10am–5pm; free). Has over 300 exhibits, including pieces by Henry Moore and Auguste Rodin.

De Pelgrom, Pelgrimstraat 15 (daily from 11am by request; F60). A restored sixteenth-century merchant's house of which the cellars and ground floor have been converted to a restaurant, while upstairs there's a tiny privately owned museum, decked out with some period furniture.

Provinciaal Sterckshof Museum, Hooftvunderlei 160, Deurne (March–Oct Tues–Thurs 10am–5pm, Sat & Sun 10am–5pm; free). Period rooms and a large collection of silver.

Ridder Smidt van Gelder Museum, Belgielei 91 (Tues–Sun 10am–5pm; F75, but closed at least until 1991). A collection of art and applied art donated to the city by an aristocratic patron of the same name. The Japanese and Chinese porcelain is especially fine.

Volkskundemuseum, Gildekamersstraat 2–6 (Tues–Sun 10am–5pm; F75). Folklore museum that provides a survey of Flemish popular life, with a particular emphasis on puppets and devotional objects.

Eating and drinking

It's not difficult to **eat** cheaply and well in Antwerp, and there are bars serving decent food all over the city centre. These include *Het Elfde Gebod*, on the north side of the cathedral, with its odd statue-filled interior; the lively cellars though rather predictable fare of the *De Pelgrom*, on Pelgrimstraat; and the excellent food of the delightful *Den Yzeren Pot*, on Hendrik Conscienceplein. Cheaper, plainer **meals** are available in several bars in the student streets around Prinsstraat and St Jacobsmarkt, including the *Bistrot de Jezuiet*, on the corner of Venusstraat and Blindestraat. Up a notch in price, regular **restaurants** include the horsemeat specialities at *De Peerdestal*, off Hendrik Conscienceplein at Wijngaardstraat 8, and the good Italian food and cheap pizzas at *Pizzeria Tony*, on the corner of the Grote Markt at Suikerrui. Vegetarians should try *Elixir*, Steenhouwersvest 57. The *Cammerpoorte*, Steenhouwersvest 55, does fine seafood, while both the *Zeven Schaken*, Braderijstraat 24, and *De Wingerd*, Grote Markt 22, are good places to eat excellent French food, assuming you can afford it.

As for drinking, the city sports many **bars**. Try the agreeable *Den Engel*, on the northwest corner of the Grote Markt, the *De Herk*, Reyndersstraat 33, or the elegant *De Grote Witte Arend*, in the courtyard beside Reyndersstraat 18. *Het Groene Ongenoegen*, Jeruzalemstraat 9, is perhaps the country's most renowned specialist beer bar, with – it's claimed – some 1100 different beers; another place to try speciality beers is the *Kulminator*, Vleminckveld 32–34, with around 500 different brews. More interesting for the clientele than the drink are the offbeat charms of *Den Artist*, near the Museum voor Schone Kunsten, at Museumstraat 45, and the wild and wonderful *Café Pelikaan*, on the north side of the cathedral.

Listings

Airlines *Sabena*, De Keyserlei 74 (☎231 68 25); *Air Europe* (☎230 12 37).

Airport enquiries ☎218 12 11.

Books English books are available from *Standaard*, Huidevetterstraat 57, and *Fnac*, Groenplaats 31.

Buses and trams City transport enquiries at Terniersplaats in tram station Opera (Mon–Fri 8am–6pm, Sat 9am–noon) and at tram station Diamant, by Centraal Station (Mon–Fri 8am–noon & 1–4pm). Details of bus services in the province of Antwerp from the kiosk on Franklin Rooseveltplaats (Mon–Fri 7am–7pm, Sat 10am–5pm).

Bikes Can be hired at Centraal Station; standard rates.

Car Hire *All-Car-Rent*, Mechelsesteenweg 141 (☎230 81 00); *Avis*, Plantin en Moretuslei 62 (☎218 94 96), and at the airport (☎218 94 96); *Hertz*, Mechelsesteenweg 43 (☎233 29 92), and at the airport (☎230 16 41).

Cinema Good programme of films at *Cartoons*, Kaastraat 4–6 (☎232 9632). Mon evening price reductions May–Sept.

Consulates UK, Korte Klarenstraat 7 (☎232 6940); USA, Rubens Centre, Nationalestraat 5 (☎225 00 72);

Doctors List of 24hr doctors' service from the tourist office.

Emergencies Police ☎101; Fire/ambulance ☎100.

Gay scene There's a small grouping of gay bars behind Centraal Station in Van Schoonhovenstraat and Dambruggestraat.

Hospital 24hr service, St Elizabeth Hospital, Leopoldstraat 26 (☎234 41 11).

Left luggage There's an office (daily 6am–midnight) and coin-operated lockers at Centraal Station.

Lost property Police, Oudaan 5. Railway, Centraal Station. City bus and trams, Grote Hondstraat 58.

Markets Second-hand goods, including some great bargains if your Flemish is up to it, Wed and Fri mornings on Vrijdagmarkt. General and bric-a-brac market, Sun mornings on Theaterplein. Flowers, plants and birds, every Sun morning on Vogelmarkt. During the summer there are Sat antique markets on either Groenplaats or Lijnwaadmarkt, near the cathedral.

Pharmacies Details of 24hr pharmacies are available from the tourist office and in weekend copies of local newspapers.

Post office Main office at Groenplaats 42 (Mon–Fri 9am–6pm; Sat 9am–noon).

Student antics Look out for the riotous processions in October, when the students take to the streets to initiate the first-year intake.

Telephones International direct dialling and operator connected calls at Jezusstraat 1 (daily 8am–8pm).

Train enquiries Centraal Station (Mon–Sat 8am–10pm, Sun 9am–5pm; ☎233 70 15).

Travel agents *JEST*, Pieter van Hobokenstraat 20 (☎232 55 52), are good for discount flights, student cards, etc.

North and east of Antwerp: the Kempen

North of Antwerp the flat, sandy moorlands of the **Kempen** stretch east as far as the river Maas: a once barren wasteland, punctuated by tracts of heath, bog and deciduous woodland and dotted with the poorest of agricultural communities, its more hospitable parts were first cultivated and planted with pine by pioneering religious communities in the twelfth century. The monks helped develop and sustain a strong regional identity and dialect, though today the area's towns and villages are drab and suburban, formless modern settlements with little to attract the visitor. The principal exception is **Geel**, with a couple of interesting medieval relics and a strong sense of its own long and unusual history.

Herentals and Geel

Some 20km east of Antwerp, dreary **HERENTALS** became the principal town of the Kempen in the fourteenth century and made a living by supplying Antwerp's brewers with fresh water, by barge along the river Nete. Industrialised towards the end of the nineteenth century, the only building of any real interest is the medieval **St Waldetrudiskerk**, home to an intricate retable carved by Pieter Borremans in the sixteenth century.

Seven kilometres east of Herentals, **GEEL** has an international reputation for its care of the mentally ill, who have been boarded out in the community here for hundreds of years, though the system was only placed under orthodox medical control in the middle of the nineteenth century. The system has its origins in the tragedy of Saint Dimpna, a thirteenth-century Irish princess who fled her home and hid near Geel as a result of her father's incestuous advances. The king tracked her down and beheaded her, an act that could only have been committed, it was felt at the time, by a madman, and Dimpna's tomb became a centre of pilgrimage for those seeking a cure for mental sickness. The **Sint Dimpnaskerk** (Fri 10am–noon & 1–7pm, Sun 4–6pm), five minutes' walk east of the Markt along

Nieuwstraat, supposedly marks the spot where she was interred, its striped four-teenth-century brickwork home to several fine examples of medieval craftsman-ship. Framed by the slender pillars of the nave, these include a typically intricate mausoleum by Cornelis Floris (the architect of Antwerp's town hall) and several fine retables, one illustrating the Passion, the other the story of Saint Dimpna, carved with extraordinary attention to detail in the fourteenth and fifteenth centuries. Opposite the entrance to the church, the **Dimpna en Gasthuismuseum**, Gasthuisstraat 3 (April–Sept Wed, Thurs & Sun 2–5.30pm; F30), has a modest display of various aspects of local history.

Geel: practical details

Geel **tourist office** (Mon–Fri 8am–3.30pm, May to mid-Sept also Sat & Sun 10am–3pm; ☎014/57 09 55), in the town centre at Markt 1, has a list of private **rooms**, from F900 for a double, which they'll book for you at no charge. The *Sportwarande*, Markt 91 (☎014/58 80 19), is the only conveniently situated **hotel**, with doubles from F1300. As far as **eating** goes, try the prim and proper restaurant *Het Lam*, Markt 53, or *Taverne Toerist*, Markt 93, for cheaper snacks and meals.

Tongerlo Abbey

From Geel bus station, twice hourly buses make the fifteen-minute trip south to a bus stop that's a five-minute walk from the low brown buildings of **Tongerlo Abbey**. Founded in 1130, the abbey played a key role in the district's agricultural development until it was forcibly dissolved by the French in 1796. Reopened in 1840, it's become a flourishing farmstead once again, a hive of activity where the **Da Vinci Museum** (May–Sept Mon–Thurs & Sat, 2–5pm) houses a copy of the great man's *Last Supper*, by his pupil, a certain Andrea del Solario.

Turnhout

Readily accessible by train from Herentals and bus from Geel, **TURNHOUT** is typical of the industrialised towns of the northern Kempen, a careless, untidy sprawl fanning out into the surrounding countryside. The only conceivable object of interest is the **St Pieterskerk**, a giant, originally medieval brown-stone edifice that towers over the Grote Markt, its interior attractively Baroque in style. There's also a tiny **Museum van de Speelkaart** close by, with an exhibition of playing cards through the ages – the product the town is famous for. Turnhout's **tourist office** is at Grote Markt 36 (Mon–Fri 9am–noon & 1.30–3.30pm, May–Sept also Sat 10am–noon & 1–4pm; ☎014/41 89 96) .

South of Antwerp: Lier and Mechelen

South and west of the city of Antwerp, the boundary between the provinces of East Flanders and Antwerp follows the line of the Scheldt as it meanders its way to the tiny villages just to the east of Dendermonde; here it meets the northern edge of the province of Brabant, whose boundary heads off east cutting between Mechelen and Brussels. Criss-crossed by rivers and canals, this western sector of the province of Antwerp is densely populated, a string of industrial townships dotted round the ancient cities of **Mechelen** and **Lier**.

Lier

Seventeen kilometres southeast of Antwerp, **LIER** has an air of smug suburban comfort that is unusual for Belgium but seems appropriate for what is basically the prosperous annexe of a big city. Founded in the eighth century, Lier has always lived in the shadow of its larger neighbour, though Felix Timmermans, one of Belgium's best-known Flemish writers, did add a certain sparkle when he lived here from 1886 to 1947. The sparkle was needed – other Belgians once referred to the citizens of Lier as "sheepheads", a reference to their reputation for stubbornness and stupidity.

The Town

Lier spreads out from a large, rectangular **Grote Markt**, encircled and bisected by waterways that mark the course of its old harbours and moats. At the centre of Grote Markt, the turreted fourteenth-century **belfry** is incongruously attached to the plain and stolid **Stadhuis**, built to replace the medieval cloth hall in 1740. The **Municipal Museum Wuyts** (April–Oct daily except Wed & Fri, 10am–noon & 1.30–5.30pm; Nov–March Sun only 10am–noon; F30) is just off the northwest corner of the Grote Markt at Florent van Cauwenberghstraat 14. Its collection of paintings is surprisingly varied and includes several works by David Teniers the Younger, who made a small fortune from his rough-and-ready peasant scenes, as represented by *The Alchemist* and *The Jealous Woman*. There's also a cruelly drawn *Brawling Peasants* by Jan Steen and a pious portrait of *St Theresa*, by Rubens, as well as several works by Jan and Pieter Bruegel the Younger. There's also a laughable, pseudo-religious painting by local artist Isidore Opsomer (see below) entitled *Christ Preaches to Lier*. A list of all the exhibits is available from reception for F5, though only in Flemish.

From the southwest corner of the Grote Markt, Eikelstraat leads to the **Gevangenenpoort**, a strongly fortified medieval gate which served as the town's prison for many years. Opposite, the curious **Zimmertoren** (9am–noon & 2–4pm in winter, 1–7pm in summer; F40) is an old section of the ramparts that now houses the remarkable clocks and astronomic studio of one Lodewijk Zimmer (1888–1970). A wealthy city merchant, Zimmer made his clocks and dials in a determined effort to dispel superstition and show his fellow townspeople how the cosmos worked. An exercise in mathematical and pictorial precision, Zimmer's *Centenary Clock* co-ordinates the phases of the moon, the zodiac, the tides of Lier and just about everything else you can think of, with a similar bevy of rotating dials in the studio above. The *Wonder Clock*, in the pavilion next door, is just as detailed and was exhibited at the World Fairs of Brussels and New York in the 1930s. A detailed guide explaining the internal workings of the clocks and the meaning of all the dials is available in English.

From beside the Zimmertoren, Schapekoppenstraat leads southwest to a side-gate into the **Begijnhof**, a mixture of cosy cottage and cramped terrace that edges towards the site of the old city walls. Founded in the thirteenth century, most of the surviving buildings date from the seventeenth century, including an elegant Baroque chapel whose gentle, curving lines are badly in need of restoration.

Immediately southeast of the Zimmertoren, a narrow road crosses over an arm of the river Nete as it gracefully slices Lier into two. To the left, **Werf** was once the main city dock; to the right the **Timmermans-Opsomerhuis** (April–Oct daily except Wed & Fri 10am–noon & 1.30–5.30pm; Nov–March Sun only 10am–

noon & 1.30–4.30pm; F30) celebrates the town's two most famous inhabitants, the writer Felix Timmermans and the painter Isidore Opsomer. Timmermans and Opsomer were good friends, and thought of themselves as leading artistic custodians of Flemish culture, the one writing of traditional village life, most memorably in the earthy humour of his *Pallieter*, the other proud of his sea and townscapes and of his influence on contemporary Belgian painters. Inside, the spacious rooms of the ground floor contain a comprehensive selection of Opsomer's work, including a whole batch of heavy, rather pretentious portraits, and, of more immediate appeal, a number of rural scenes, such as the Expressionistic *Middelburg*. An adjoining room is devoted to the work of their friend, the sculptor Lodewijk van Boeckel, whose old forge is surrounded by examples of his intricate, profoundly black – and somewhat agressive – ironwork. Upstairs, there's a collection of writings by Timmermans, supplemented by several first editions together with general details of his life and times, all in Flemish.

Heading northeast along the Werf from here, the third turning on the right, Rechtestraat, leads to the **St Gummaruskerk**, which takes its name from a courtier of King Pepin of France, who settled here as a hermit in the middle of the eighth century. Built in Flamboyant Gothic style in the fifteenth century, and painstakingly restored in the 1970s, the immense buttresses of the church, surmounted by a tiered and parapeted tower, dominate the surrounding streets. On the inside, majestic pillars rise up to support a vaulted roof, whose simplicity contrasts with the swirling, twisting embellishments of the **rood-loft** below, a decoration which frames a passionate bas-relief cartoon strip of Calvary and the Resurrection. Behind, the high altar is topped by a second fine carving, a wooden altarpiece of the fourteenth century whose inside panels are alive with a mass of finely observed detail, from the folds of the bed linen to the pile of faggots underneath Abraham's son. The church's **stained-glass windows** are reckoned to be some of the finest in Belgium, the five elongated windows above the high altar presented to the town by Emperor Maximilian in 1516, a contrast to the more finely balanced yellows, reds and blues of the windows overlooking the first section of the left-hand side of the choir, partly the work of Rombout Keldermans in 1475. Close by, the wings of the triptych in the first ambulatory chapel on the left have pictures of *St Clare* and *St Francis* by Rubens – though this is closed until 1991.

Practical details

It takes just fifteen minutes for the twice-hourly train from Antwerp Centraal to reach Lier **railway station**, which adjoins the **bus station**, ten minutes' walk north of Grote Markt; veer left out of the train station building, turn right at the main road and carry straight on. The **tourist office**, in the basement on the south side of the Stadhuis in the Grote Markt (Mon–Fri 8.30am–12.30pm & 1.30–5pm; May–Aug also Sat & Sun same times; ☎03/489 11 11), can provide town maps and up-to-date **accommodation** details, though at present the options are limited: there are no private rooms and only one **hotel**, the reasonably priced *Handelshof*, opposite the station at Leopoldplein 39, where doubles cost F1300 per night. For **food**, most day-trippers stick to the mundane snacks of the series of bars and restaurants in front of the Zimmertoren – the *'t Zimmerke*, at no. 8, and the *Pallieter*, at no. 11, are your best bets. Alternatively, the *De Werf*, Werf 16, serves a wider range of meals for about F450 a throw.

Mechelen

Home of the Primate of Belgium and the country's ecclesiastical capital, **MECHELEN** was converted to Christianity by the itinerant eighth-century evangelist Saint Rombout. By the thirteenth century it had become one of the more powerful cities of medieval Flanders and entered a brief golden age when the Burgundian prince Charles the Bold decided to base his administration here in 1473. Impetuous and intemperate, Charles used the wealth of the Flemish towns to fund a series of campaigns that ended with his death on the battlefield in 1477. His widow, Margaret of York, and his son's regent, the remarkable Margaret of Austria, stayed in Mechelen and formed one of the most famous courts of the day. Artists and scholars were drawn here from all over Flanders, attracted by the Renaissance pomp and ceremony, with enormous feasts in fancy clothes in fancy buildings – a glamorous facade that camouflaged a serious political motive. Surrounded by wealthy, independent merchants and powerful, well-organised guilds, the dukes and duchesses of Burgundy realised that they had to impress and overawe as a condition of their survival.

Margaret of Austria died in 1530, the capital moved to Brussels and Mechelen was never quite the same. The Baedeker of 1900 described the town as a "dull place . . . totally destitute of the brisk traffic which enlivens most of the principal Belgian towns". Things aren't so bad today, but considering Mechelen's proximity to Antwerp and Brussels, it has a surprisingly provincial atmosphere supplemented by a disappointing range of sights.

The Town

The centre of town is, as ever, **Grote Markt**, marked by a modest statue of Margaret of Austria and flanked on the eastern side by the **Stadhuis**, whose bizarre and incoherent appearance was partly her responsibility. In 1526, she had the left-hand side of the original building demolished and replaced by what you see today, an ornate arched loggia backing onto a fluted, angular facade, to a design by Rombout Keldermans. The plan was to demolish and rebuild the rest of the building in stages, but after her death in 1530 the work was simply abandoned, leaving Keldermans' extravagance firmly glued to the plain stonework and the simple gables of the fourteenth-century section on the right. The interior of the later section (occasional opening; ask at the tourist office) is just as jumbled as the exterior, though there are a couple of interesting paintings – principally Coussaert's *A Sitting of the Parliament of Charles the Bold* and a fine sixteenth-century tapestry of the *Battle of Tunis*.

A little way west of the Grote Markt, the **Cathedral of St Rombout** (April–Sept Mon–Sat 7.30am–7.30pm, Sun 2–7pm; Oct–March Mon–Sat 7.30am–4pm, Sun 2–4pm) dominates the centre of Mechelen just as it was originally supposed to. A gigantic, buttressed church attached to a great square tower, work began with the draining of the surrounding marshes in 1217, though the money ran out before the tower was built, and the initial design had to be shelved for over 200 years. In 1451, the Pope provided the extra funds when he put St Rombout on a list of specified churches where pilgrims could seek absolution for their sins without visiting Rome. Pilgrims and money rolled in to Mechelen, and the present tower was completed by 1546. The problem today is that the structure is literally breaking up as it sinks unevenly into its foundations. A long-term effort to hold the church together began in 1963 and is still far from finished, encasing the building in almost permanent scaffolding.

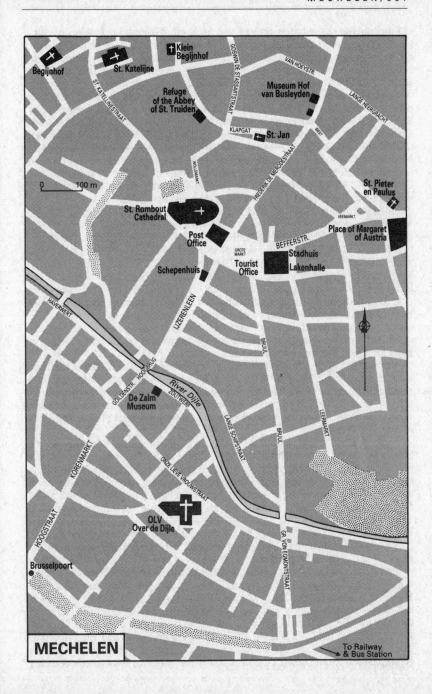

Begijnhof

St. Katelijne

Klein Begijnhof

Refuge of the Abbey of St. Truiden

Museum Hof van Busleyden

VAN HOEYSTR.

GOSWIN DE STASSARTSTRAAT

ST. KATELIJNESTRAAT

KLAPGAT

St. Jan

LANGE HEERGRACHT

BEST

FREDERIK DE MERODESTRAAT

VOLLEMARKT

St. Pieter en Paulus

0   100 m

St. Rombout Cathedral

Post Office

Schepenhuis

GROTE MARKT

Tourist Office

BEFFERSTR.

Stadhuis Lakenhalle

VEEMARKT.

Place of Margaret of Austria

IJZERENLEEN

HAVERWERT

BRUUL

HOOGBRUG

GOUDENSTR.

ZOUTWERF

River Dijle

De Zalm Museum

LANGE SCHIPSTRAAT

BRUUL

LEERMARKT

KORENMARKT

ONZE LIEVE VROUWSTRAAT

HOOGSTRAAT

OLV Over de Dijle

Brusselpoort

GR. VON EGMONTSTRAAT

To Railway & Bus Station

MECHELEN

Entry to the cathedral is around the back off Wollemarkt. Inside, the thir-teenth-century nave has all the cloistered elegance of the Brabantine Gothic style, although the original lines are spoilt by an unfortunate series of seventeenth-century statues of the apostles. Between the arches lurks an extraordinary Baroque **pulpit**, a playful mass of twisted and curled oak dotted with carefully camouflaged animal carvings. Nearby, one of the **chapels** on the north aisle contains the tomb of Cardinal Mercier of Mechelen and a plaque, presented by the Church of England, commemorating his part in co-ordinating the Mechelen Conversations. These ran from 1921 up to the time of his death in 1926 and inves-tigated the possibility of reuniting the two churches – although in Belgium Mercier is more often remembered for his staunch opposition to the German occupation of World War I. His pastoral letters, notably "Patriotism and Endurance", proclaimed loyalty to the Belgian king, paid tribute to the soldiers at the front and condemned the invasion as illegal and un-Christian.

The most distinguished painting in the church is in the south transept, where Van Dyck's muscular *Crucifixion* stands above a tidy eighteenth-century altar. To the west, the nine chapels of the **ambulatory** are rather dreary, with the excep-tion of the Chapel of the Relics, dedicated to a group of monks and priests who were slaughtered by Protestants near Dordrecht in 1572. Their supposed remains are stored in a number of gilt caskets, surrounded by the coats of arms of the Knights of the Golden Fleece, a Burgundian order established by Philip the Good in 1430. The elaborate doors at the rear of the high altar hide the remains of Saint Rombout himself, and are opened on major religious festivals only, when the reli-quary is paraded round the town centre. Curiously enough, many of the columns in and around the ambulatory are made of wood painted as marble, a sleight of hand for which Mechelen was famous.

Attached to the church, the cathedral tower contains Belgium's finest **carillon**, a fifteenth-century affair of 49 bells. There are concerts throughout the year, and regular performances on Monday evenings between June and September at 8.30pm. Guided tours of the tower leave from outside the tourist office through-out the summer (Easter–Sept Sat & Sun at 2.15pm; June–Sept Mon at 7pm; July & Aug daily 2.15pm).

From the cathedral entrance, Wollemarkt leads north into Goswin de Stassartstraat, where the **Refuge of the Abbey of St Truiden** (no entry) sits prettily by an old weed-choked canal, its picturesque gables once home to the destitute. Opposite, an alley called Klapgat leads to the weathered sandstone of the church of **St Jan** (Sat 2.30–3.30pm; June–Sept also Sun 2–5pm), worth a visit for the beautiful setting it provides for an altar triptych by Rubens, painted in 1619. A fine example of the artist's use of variegated lighting, the central panel depicts the *Adoration of the Magi,* with Rubens' first wife portrayed as the Virgin.

A few metres further east along St Jansstraat, Mechelen's **Carillon School** (no entry) is one of the most prestigious institutions of its sort in the world, attracting students from as far away as Japan and helping the town to sustain its interna-tional reputation for carillon playing. Next door, the **Museum Hof van Busleyden** (daily except Tues 10am–noon & 2–5pm; F50) is housed in a splen-did early sixteenth-century mansion built in high Gothic style with Renaissance touches for Hieronymus Busleyden, a prominent member of Margaret's court. It's a confusing, poorly organised affair, but a reorganisation and English guide-book are promised. The collection includes a display of miscellaneous bells, a room devoted to Mechelen's guilds and a whole range of local artefacts dating from the Gallo-Roman period. There's also an unusual assortment of unattributed paintings, including a seventeenth-century picture of the Groot Begijnhof supplemented by 46 miniatures of the Beguines at work, along with a graphic series of sixteen panels portraying the multiple sufferings of Saint Victor, painted for a local convent in around 1510.

The grotesque wooden doll by the museum entrance is **Op Signoorke**, whose festival is held every year on the second Sunday in September. Once a generalised symbol of male irresponsibility, the doll and its forebears had a variety of names – *vuilen bras* (unfaithful drunkard), *sotscop* (fool) and *vuilen bruidegom* (disloyal bridegroom) – until the events of 1775 redefined its identity. Every year it was customary for the dummy to be paraded through the streets and tossed up and down in a sheet. In 1775, however, a young man from Antwerp attempted to steal the doll and was badly beaten, the people of Mechelen convinced he was part of an Antwerp plot to rob them of their cherished mascot. The two cities were already great commercial rivals and the incident soured relations even further. Indeed, when news of the beating reached Antwerp, there was sporadic rioting and calls for the city burghers to take some sort of revenge. Refusing to be intimidated, the people of Mechelen derisively renamed the doll after their old nickname for the people of Antwerp – "Op Signoorke", from "Signor", a reference to that city's favoured status under earlier Spanish kings. Today, although the doll has kept its nickname, the intense rivalry between the two towns has disappeared, and the festival is just a good excuse for a long drinking session.

From opposite the Carillon School, Biest leads southeast to the Veemarkt where the church of **St Pieter en St Paulus** (May–Sept Mon–Fri 9.30am–noon & 2.30–7pm, Sun 10–11am & 2.30–7pm; Oct–April Mon–Fri 9.30am–noon, Sun 10–11am) was built for the Jesuits in the seventeenth century. The interior has an oak pulpit that pays tribute to the order's missionary work, carved in 1701 by Hendrik Verbruggen, with a globe near its base attached to representations of the four continents that were known about at the time.

There's not much else, but if you've the inclination, the **Begijnhof** is to the northwest of town and makes for a pleasant stroll, while to the south of the Grote Markt some intriguing sixteenth-century **facades** overlook the river Dijle from the Haverwerf. The most striking is the Devil's House, presumably named after the pagan-looking satyrs that adorn the windows. From here, it's a couple of minutes' walk southeast to the **Onze Lieve Vrouw over de Dijle**, on Onze Lieve Vrouwstraat (May–Sept Sat 2–5pm; July & Aug also Wed 2–5pm), begun in the fifteenth century, but only completed 200 years later. Inside, Rubens's exquisite *Miraculous Draught of Fishes* was a triptych painted for the Fishmongers' Guild in 1618, the year when the artist confided to a friend "I am so overburdened with public and private tasks, and already committed for the future, that for the next few years I cannot even be master of my own person". Five minutes' walk away, on the southern edge of town, the **Brusselpoort** is the only survivor of Mechelen's twelve fourteenth-century gates.

Practical details

Mechelen's **rail** and adjoining **bus stations** are about fifteen minutes' walk south of the town centre, straight ahead down Hendrik Consciencestraat. The **tourist office**, in the Stadhuis on the east side of the Grote Markt (April–Sept Mon–Fri 8am–6pm, Sat & Sun 9.30am–5pm; Oct–March Mon–Fri 8am–5pm, Sat 10am–

5pm; ☎015/21 18 73), has a handful of private **rooms** at a standard rate of F1600 per double, which they will book on your behalf at no extra charge. Alternatively, the town has several centrally sited **hotels**, of which the cheapest is the *Hotel Claes*, on the south side of town at Onze Lieve Vrouwstraat 51 (☎015/41 28 66; closed Dec–March), with doubles at F1800; the *Hotel Egmont*, near the station at Oude Brusselstraat 50 (☎015/413 498), has doubles from F2400.

There are plenty of places to **eat** around Grote Markt and along the main streets that lead off to the south – principally Bruul and Ijzerenleen. Here you'll find two of Mechelen's better snack bars, the *Cheers* on Korenmarkt and the self-service food bar of the *INNO* department store on Bruul. For **restaurants**, try the seafood delicacies of the *De Gouden Vis*, by the river Dilje, off Ijzerenleen on Nauwstraat, or the good-value Spanish food at the *Madrid*, overlooking the Dilje at Lange Schipstraat 4, or *La Riera*, Veemarkt 24. **Bars** worth trying include the lively *Lord Nelson* and *Arms of York*, on Wollemarkt, the earthy *Yser* and *Salvator* on the western side of Grote Markt. Mechelen is famous for its **beers**, including *Toison d'Or* and *Gouden Carolus* – as recommended by Emperor Charles V.

Hasselt and around

Capital of the province of Limburg, **HASSELT** is a busy, modern town that acts as the administrative centre for the surrounding industrial region. A pleasant but unremarkable place, the roughly circular city centre fans out from a series of small interlocking squares, with surprisingly few buildings to indicate its medieval foundation. To compensate for this lack of appeal and to attract foreign investment, the local authority has spent millions of francs on lavish and imaginative prestige projects, from an excellent range of indoor and outdoor sports facilities to a massive culture complex that aims to draw some of the world's finest artists. But perhaps more than anything else, Hasselt is associated with the open-air museum of Bokrijk which lies some 8km east of town – an extraordinarily comprehensive reconstruction of traditional Belgian village life.

In Hasselt itself, there's nothing special to look at, although the **Gerechtshof** on Havermarkt, just off Grote Markt, is housed in the town's one surprise – a trim Art Deco building, whose flamboyant interior of brown tiles, statuettes and lamps is in pristine condition. There are four modest municipal **museums** each charging F60 for entry, or you can buy a combined ticket from the tourist office for F120. Of them, the **Nationaal Jenevermuseum**, north from the Grote Markt down Hoogstraat/Demerstraat at Witte Nonnenstraat 19 (Tues–Fri 10am–5pm, Sat & Sun 2–6pm; closed Jan), is probably the most interesting, sited in a restored nineteenth-century distillery and detailing the history of local jenever production. The **Stadsmuseum**, nearby at Thonissenlaan 73 (same times), has displays on the history of fashion, while the **Stellingwerff-Waerdenhof Museum**, five minutes east of the Grote Markt at Maastrichterstraat 85 (same times), has some interesting Art Nouveau ceramics and possesses the oldest surviving monstrance in the world. Dating from 1297, it's reputed to bleed if subjected to sacrilege. Lastly, the **Beiaardmuseum** (June–Sept Sat & Sun 2–6pm), in the tower of the St Quintinus cathedral on Vismarkt, covers the development and workings of carillons.

Ten minutes' walk east of the adjoining **rail** and **bus stations** – along Stationsplein and keep straight ahead – the Hasselt **tourist office** is right in the centre of town at Lombaardstraat 3 (Mon–Fri 9am–5pm, also April–Oct Sat

10am–4pm; ☎011/22 22 35) and has free maps and information. There are no private rooms in town, and the cheapest place to **stay** is the *Hotel Schoofs*, by the railway station at Stationsplein 7 (☎011/22 31 88), which has doubles from F1000. Failing that, the handy *Hotel Pax*, Grote Markt 16 (☎011/22 38 75), costs F1900 for a double. **Eating** in Hasselt is easy: there are any number of cheap bars and restaurants on and around Grote Markt and Botermarkt and adjoining Zuivelmarkt. The popular *Majestic*, Grote Markt 2, is a good place for snacks; the *Martenshuys*, Zuivelmarkt 18, serves both light meals and more substantial dishes. The *De Karakol*, Zuivelmarkt 16 (closed Mon), is a more expensive restaurant, with a varied menu including vegetarian dishes. The *De Levensboom*, a couple of minutes' walk south of the Grote Markt at Leopoldplein 44 (closed Mon), is entirely vegetarian.

The Bokrijk park and museum

The **Open Air Museum of Bokrijk** (Openluchtmuseum; April–Sept daily 10am–6pm; Oct daily 9am–5pm; F150) is one of the best of its type in the country, a series of reconstructed buildings and villages from various parts of Flemish Belgium spread out within an enormous park of rolling fields and forest. Each village has been meticulously restructured, each building thoroughly researched, and although the emphasis is still very much on rural life, it's a bias partly balanced by the reconstruction of a small medieval cityscape in one corner of the park. Perhaps inevitably it gives a rather idealised picture, and certainly the assembled artefacts sometimes feel out of context and rather antiseptic. But the museum is tremendously popular and some of the individual displays outstanding. An excellent English guidebook, costing F295, provides a wealth of detail about every exhibit, and the whole museum is clearly labelled and signposted.

The museum's collection is divided into five sections, each with their own colour code. The most extensive range of buildings is in the **yellow** sector, where there are a number of Kempen farmhouses, from the long gables of a building from Helchteren to a series of compound (all-inclusive) farms that come from all over the provinces of Antwerp and Limburg. Other highlights include a lovely half-timbered smith's workshop from the village of Neeroeteren, a bakehouse from Oostmalle, a fully operational oil-press from Ellikom, an entire eleventh-century church from Erpekom and a peat-storage barn from Kalmthout. One particular curiosity is the skittle-alley and pall-mall. Throughout the Middle Ages, skittles was a popular pastime among all social classes, played in tavern and monastery alike. The original game had nine targets arranged in a diamond pattern until some time in the sixteenth century, when it was banned because the pattern was associated with gambling, and replaced by the more familiar ten-skittle game. Pall-mall, where heavy balls are driven through an iron ring with a mallet, was popular throughout Europe in the seventeenth and eighteenth centuries, but is now confined to some of the more remote villages of Limburg.

The open-air museum occupies most of the western half of the **Bokrijk estate**, whose other signposted attractions include a herb garden, a fine arboretum with over 3000 identified shrubs and trees, an animal park, a nature reserve and a rose garden. These spread out east of the museum section from beside the park's administrative building, the nineteenth-century **Kasteel Bokrijk**, which adjoins an information centre. The park is open daily during daylight hours throughout the year and entrance is free.

Practical details

There are two easy ways of reaching Bokrijk from Hasselt: **buses** #1 and #46 leave from the town's bus station every thirty minutes and pass the museum entrance (F50); **trains** leave hourly, take ten minutes, cost twice as much and drop you a five-minute walk from the gates. For **food**, the *St Gummarus* restaurant, straight ahead of the main museum entrance, serves reasonable food at affordable rates. If you want to **stay** near here, camping is not allowed in the Bokrijk estate, but there is a **youth hostel** (☎011/35 62 20; closed Nov–Feb), reachable through the park some 2km north of Bokrijk railway station – just follow the signs from the information centre.

Diest

Some 20km west of Hasselt, the small and ancient town of **DIEST** lies just south of the river Demer, its cramped and quiet centre still partly surrounded by the remnants of the town's once mighty fortifications, built to guard the eastern approaches to Brussels.

Its centre, **Grote Markt**, a ten-minute walk from the train station towards the southern end of the old town, is a wide open, irregularly shaped area, edged by trim seventeenth- and eighteenth-century facades. The somewhat spartan Stadhuis houses the municipal **museum** (April–Oct Mon–Fri 10am–noon & 1–5pm; Nov–March Sun only 10am–noon & 2–5pm; free), stashed away in the old vaulted cellars, whose prime exhibits are some seventeenth-century silver suits of armour and a fearful anonymous *Last Judgement* from about 1430. More interesting is the **Begijnhof**, a five-minute walk along Koning Albertstraat, and one of the best preserved in this part of Belgium, founded in the thirteenth century and retaining much of its medieval shape and atmosphere. The original main entrance is at the far northeast end of Begijnenstraat, an extravagant Baroque portal with a niche that frames a statue of the Virgin above a text that reads "Come in my garden, my sister and bride". Nearby, the weathered fourteenth-century Gothic chapel has an elegant Rococo interior.

The oldest part of the Begijnhof is the site of **Gasthof 1618**, on Kerkstraat, a restaurant that serves excellent, traditional Flemish food at high prices. While you're here, either of the local brews – *Gildebier* or *Diesterse* – are worth tasting, or you can try old-fashioned sweeties made in the traditional way at the "museum" on Engelen Conventstraat (July & Aug daily 2–5pm; otherwise Sat & Sun only) .

For devotees of nineteenth-century municipal fortifications, the **Schaffensepoort**, five minutes east of the station, is a dramatic defile through concentric lines of ramparts and across the river Demer. Heavy, studded oak gates indicate an enthusiasm for defence that was superseded by the development of more effective artillery.

Practical details

Diest **tourist office**, just off the Grote Markt at Zoutstraat 6 (daily 8.30am–12.30pm & 1.30–4pm; ☎013/31 21 21), has a useful and free town booklet, and – although it's unlikely you'll want to stay – a handful of private **rooms** for about F1200 for a double per night. There's also a **youth hostel** at St Jansstraat 2 (☎013/31 37 21), ten minutes' walk northeast of the Grote Markt, overlooking the city park – take Berchmansstraat/Botermarkt from the Grote Markt, turn left along

Wolvenstraat and keep going until you reach the park at the end, then turn right. For **eating**, try the solid snacks of the *De Haan*, Grote Markt 19, or the *De Keizer*, nearby at no. 24; or the pricey Flemish food of *Gasthuis 1618* (see above).

Genk

About 15km east of Hasselt, approaching the Dutch frontier, the gritty industrial town of **GENK** was a tiny, inconsequential village until the discovery of coal and the development of the Limburg coalfield at the start of the century. Bolstered by the mines, its economy – and the region – prospered until the 1960s, when the enforced contraction of coal-mining led to periods of intense labour unrest and steep rises in unemployment, both in Genk and the surrounding pit villages. This situation has been complicated by the composition of the workforce, which, in contrast to British mines, includes a high percentage of immigrant workers. Desperate efforts have been made to diversify the local economy, notably with the establishment of a giant Ford car plant, but the pressures for various forms of repatriation have been strong.

South of Hasselt: Tongeren and Sint Truiden

South of Hasselt, the Kempen gives way to the **Haspengouw**, a fertile expanse of gently undulating land that fills out the southern part of the province of Limburg, its soils especially suited to fruit-growing. Frankly, the scenery is equally dreary though, even at blossom time, and the area's tiny towns and villages spread carelessly along the sides of the roads without much charm or style. That said, the ancient towns of **Sint Truiden** and more particularly **Tongeren** are well worth a visit for their wide range of historic monuments.

Tongeren

Twenty kilometres southeast of Hasselt, tiny **TONGEREN** is the oldest town in Belgium, built on the site of a Roman camp on the important route to Cologne. Destroyed by the Franks and razed by the Vikings, its early history was plagued by misfortune, though it became a prosperous dependency of the bishops of Liège during the Middle Ages. Nowadays, it's a small market town with an old-fashioned, countrified appearance on the border of Belgium's language divide.

Five minutes' walk west of the railway station, the haughty statue of Ambiorix, in the Grote Markt, is supposed to commemorate a local chieftain who defeated the Romans here in 54 BC – a "noble savage" inspired more by mid-nineteenth-century Belgian nationalism than historical accuracy. Directly opposite, the **Onze Lieve Vrouwekerk** (daily 7am–noon & 2–7pm) towers over the city centre, with an impressive, symmetrical elegance that belies its piecemeal construction: it's the eleventh- to sixteenth-century outcome of an original fourth-century foundation that was the first church to be dedicated to the Virgin north of the Alps. Still very much in use, the dark tomb-like interior has preserved the feel of Catholic mystery with a bedecked medieval walnut statue of "Our Lady of Tongeren" in the north transept, surrounded by candles and overhung by a gaudy canopy. Above the altar, an intricately carved retable shows scenes from the life of the Virgin and just outside are the columns of the cloister. The church **treasury** (May–Sept daily 9am–noon & 2–5pm; F20) is crammed with reliquaries, monstrances and reliquary shrines from as early as the tenth century. Bones and bits of body poke at you from every corner, but best are a beautiful sixth-century Merovingian buckle, a pious and passive *Head of Christ* and an eleventh-century *Shrine of the Martyrs of Trier*.

On the right-hand side of the church, a small section of the second **Roman city wall** has been carefully excavated, though unfortunately it's underground and access is by a short flight of steps more reminiscent of a urinal than an archaeological site. Close by, on the southern side of the Grote Markt, the eight-eenth-century **Stadhuis** houses an unremarkable municipal **museum** (daily 10am–noon & 2–4.30pm; F30), whose exhibits illustrate the town's history. Tongeren's main museum, the **Gallo-Romeins** (Tues–Sat 9am–noon & 2–5pm, Sun 2–5pm; F20), is a couple of minutes' walk east of here along Groendreef, at Kielenstraat 15, and features a miscellany of prehistoric and Roman bric-a-brac that's really only of interest to the specialist. The **Moerenpoort** (May–Aug Sat & Sun 10am–4pm) was one of Tongeren's six medieval gates and is now home to a small military museum.

Practical details

Tongeren's **rail** and adjoining **bus stations** are ten minutes' walk east of the Grote Markt, along Stationslaan and Maastrichterstraat. For **accommodation**, the town's **tourist office**, in the Stadhuis (May–Sept Mon–Fri 8am–noon & 1–4.30pm, Sat & Sun 10am–noon & 2–5pm; Oct–April Mon–Fri 9am–noon & 1–4.30pm; ☎012/23 29 61), has the details of a handful of private **rooms**, for about F900 for a double per night, and will ring ahead to make a reservation. There are also three conveniently situated **hotels**, of which the *Chemin de Fer*, at Stationslaan 44 (☎012/23 31 05), and *Lido*, Grote Markt 19 (☎012/23 19 48), are cheapest, with doubles from about F1000. There's a **camping** complex, *Pliniusbron*, a twenty-minute walk north of the Grote Markt; take Sint Truiderstraat west from the Grote Markt, turn right down Beukenbergweg, the third road along, and keep straight down past the eighteenth-century Castle Betho. For **food**, the *'t Vrijthof*, by the Onze Lieve Vrouwekerk at Graanmarkt 5, serves excellent fish dishes, the *Au Phare*, Grote Markt 21, is good for snacks, and the *Etna*, Grote Markt 23, serves cheap pizzas.

Sint Truiden

Around 20km west of Tongeren, the small market town of **SINT TRUIDEN** grew up around an abbey founded by Saint Trudo in the seventh century and is today surrounded by the orchards of the Haspengouw. Known for the variety, if not the excellence, of its ancient churches, Sint Truiden is only of moderate interest, but it is the best place to catch the bus to the spectacular church at the village of Zoutleeuw.

The town's Grote Markt is edged by an elegant eighteenth-century **Stadhuis**, attached to an older **Belfry** – the middle of three sturdy towers that push against each other on the east side of the square. On the right, the spire of the **Onze**

Lieve Vrouwekerk has had a particularly chequered history: built in the eleventh century, it's been dogged by misfortune and in 1668 gave everyone a shock when it simply dropped off; it wasn't replaced for 200 years. On the left, the untidy, truncated **Abdijtoren** dates from the eleventh century, a massive remnant of the original religious complex that once dominated the medieval town. The abbey has been replaced by a dull and forbidding seminary that spreads out from the tower, though the ornate **gateway** does break the monotony – a carved relief showing the cruel, misogynistic legend attached to the abbey's foundation. The story goes that every time Saint Trudo tried to build a church, it was pulled down by an interfering woman. Not to be thwarted, Trudo prayed fervently and the woman was struck with paralysis.

The pick of Sint Truiden's many other churches are **St Gangulfus**, just west of the Grote Markt down Diesterstraat (daily 9am–5pm), and **St Pieters** (same times), south along Naamsesteenweg. Extensively renovated and built in the eleventh and twelfth centuries respectively, both these churches are classically Romanesque mixtures of cubic and square forms. For its period, the ribless cross-vaulting of St Pieters was experimental; the architect balanced the risk by deciding not to put windows in the upper walls.

Practical details

Sint Truiden's **tourist office**, in the Stadhuis (Mon–Sat 8am–noon & 1–5pm, April–Sept also Sun 10.30am–12.30pm & 1.30–4.30pm; ☎011/68 68 72), has brochures with details of cycle routes in the countryside around town, but no private rooms. The **hotel** *Cicindria*, just north of the Grote Markt at Abdijstraat 6 (☎011/68 13 44), has doubles for F2000. The coffee bar *Rimini*, Grote Markt 40, serves good, cheap snacks. Buses leave Sint Truiden for Zoutleeuw from beside the railway station (Mon–Fri 2 hourly 8am–6pm; Sat & Sun once every two hours).

Eastern Brabant: Zoutleeuw and Tienen

Just inside the eastern boundary of the province of Brabant, the tiny village of **ZOUTLEEUW**, well connected by bus both to Sint Truiden, 8km to the east, and Tienen, 14km west, was prosperous from the thirteenth to the fifteenth century, though it's been in economic decline ever since. Its rambling, irregularly turreted and towered church, **St Leonardus** (mid-April to Sept daily except Mon 2–5pm; F30), has a magnificently intact pre-Reformation interior that's among the most impressive in the country. Clearly labelled in English, it's crammed with the accumulated treasures – paintings, statues, sculptures – of several hundred years, its dark and mysterious naves and chapels redolent of medieval superstition. There's a wrought-iron sixteenth-century double-sided image of the virgin high in the nave, a fifteenth-century wooden cross hanging in the choir arch, an intricate altar and retable of Saint Anna, and, in the south transept, a fifteenth-century chapel dedicated to Saint Leonard, whose life is outlined in a gorgeous, naive altarpiece by Arnold de Maeler. Pride of place goes to the huge stone tabernacle carved in almost miraculous perspective by Cornelis Floris, architect of Antwerp's town hall, in 1550–52. Opposite the church, the sixteenth-century **Stadhuis** was designed by Rombout Keldermans and now houses the **tourist office** (April–Sept daily except Mon 10am–noon & 1–4pm; Oct–March Tues–Fri 2–4pm).

Tienen

The sugar-beet centre of Belgium, the undistinguished town of **TIENEN** spirals out from a pleasant, open main square that's fringed by a tidy nineteenth-century **Stadhuis** and the solemn late medieval bulk of the church of **Onze Lieve den Poel**. The interior of the church is predictably Baroque, but it's unusual in that it has no nave. Directly behind the Stadhuis and up on the hill, the church of **St Germanus** is a ninth-century foundation that's been repeatedly rebuilt and reshaped. The western facade is imposing and inside there are some particularly theatrical statues dating from the sixteenth and seventeenth centuries. The *Au Nouveau Monde* hotel, opposite the station, is a convenient place to stay, should you want to, with doubles from F1600. The **tourist office** is in the Stadhuis (☎016/81 61 37).

travel details

Trains

From Antwerp to Bruges (hourly; 1hr 10min); Lier/Diest/Hasselt (2 hourly; 15/50/70min); Mechelen/Brussels (3 hourly; 20/40min) for Brussels–Paris (7 daily; 3hr); Amsterdam (hourly; 2hr 15min); Geel (hourly; 40min).

From Turnhout to Herentals (hourly; 15min).

From Tongeren to Liège (hourly; 30min); Hasselt (hourly; 20min).

From Hasselt to Sint Truiden (1 or 2 hourly; 15min); Bokrijk (hourly; 15min); Tongeren (hourly;

20min); Diest (2 hourly; 15min); Liège (hourly; 55min).

From Diest to Leuven (hourly; 45min).

From Tienen to Brussels (hourly; 40min).

Buses

From Geel to Turnhout (2 hourly; 40min).

From Sint Truiden to Zoutleeuw (Mon–Fri 2 hourly, Sat & Sun 1 every 2hr; 10min).

From Tienen to Zoutleeuw (Mon–Fri 2 hourly, Sat & Sun 1 every 2 hours; 20min).

CHAPTER TEN

HAINAUT

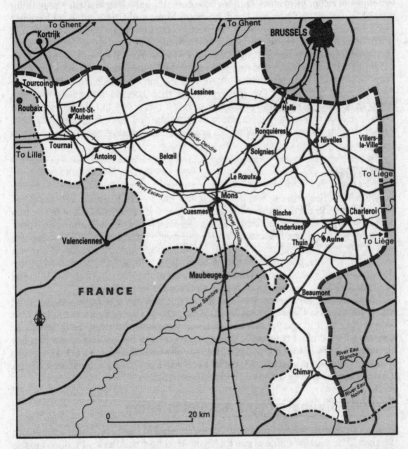

S outhwest of Brussels, the central portion of Wallonia is given over mainly to the province of **Hainaut**, a rolling agricultural area in its western reaches, but in the east home to one of Belgium's severest belts of industry between Mons and Charleroi. The highlight of Hainaut is **Tournai** in the western part of the province, close to the French border. Once part of France, it's a relaxing, rather genteel place, with a number of decent museums and the finest Romanesque-Gothic cathedral in the country. East of Tournai, the two large cities of **Mons** and the industrial and engineering city of **Charleroi** – the provincial capital – are less interesting, although you may have to use one or the other as a base for seeing some of Hainaut's more scattered attractions, especially if you're travelling by public transport. Mons is sited in the coal-mining area of the **Borinage**, home to many castles and stately homes, of which **Beloeil** is the grandest, while the countryside around Charleroi holds several abbeys, notably that of **Villers-la-Ville** – outstanding in size if nothing else. To the north, **Soignies** and **Nivelles**, the latter the principal town of French-speaking Brabant, contain superb examples of religious Romanesque architecture, though otherwise they're nothing special. **Binche**, on the other hand, between Mons and Charleroi, is a charming place, ancient and evocative, with ramparts to explore and a renowned carnival. South of Binche, the **Botte de Hainaut** is actually an extension of the Ardennes, so named for its position jutting deep into France from Hainaut's southeastern corner and growing hillier and more beautiful the further south you go. Half of the "boot" is officially Namur province but for touring purposes it's included here. Like the Ardennes proper, it's the scenery rather than specific attractions that you come for. **Chimay**, the main town, merits a visit for its castle and old alleys, though **Couvin**, a little way east, is nicer, more picturesque and more friendly. Outside of Couvin or Chimay, accommodation is a problem unless you've got a tent.

Tournai

TOURNAI is the nearest Southern Belgium has to the Flemish "art towns" of Flanders and the north: prosperous and bourgeois, it's a pleasant place to spend a couple of days. Along with Tongeren it's the oldest town in Belgium: Clovis, the Merovingian king, was born here in 465 and made it the capital of his kingdom; later it became the first capital of the Frankish kingdom, remaining in French hands for a large part of its history, and staying loyal to France during the Hundred Years' War. Tournai fell into the hands of the French kings in 1187, was incorporated in the Netherlands in 1521 and retaken by Louis XIV in 1667, who left his mark on the physiognomy of the town with a number of buildings, some of which survive, mostly along quai Notre-Dame and rue St-Nicholas. Louis was also responsible for the quay walls and houses that flank the river. Sadly much of Tournai's beautifully preserved old centre was destroyed by Allied bombing, but the town does *feel* old, and its cathedral is renowned as perhaps the finest in the country. The town is also easy to reach, just 25km from Lille in France, which is on the main route network of the *TGV* high-speed train.

Arrival, information and accommodation

Tournai's **railway station** is on the northern edge of the town about 400m from the river. The **tourist office** at rue du Vieux Marché-aux-Poteries 14, opposite the Belfry (☎069/22 20 45), has a list of **hotels**, the cheapest of which are in the streets on the far side of the Grand Place. *Aux Armes de Tournai* on place de Lille 24, the square at the end of rue Dorez Maux, leading away from the Grand Place (☎069/22 67 23), is the best bet, charging F500–800 for a single. *Tour St-Georges*, behind the Halle de Draps at place de Nedonchel 2 (☎069/22 53 00), is more expensive at F800–1000 for a single. There's a centrally placed **youth hostel** halfway along rue St-Martin at no. 64 (☎069/21 61 36). The nearest **campsite** is *Camping de l'Orient*, about 500m east of the ring road along rue Vieux Chemin de Mons.

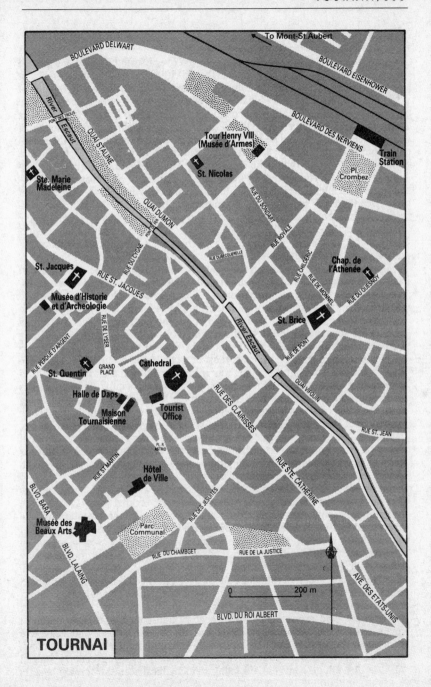

BOULEVARD DELWART

To Mont-St-Aubert

BOULEVARD EISENHOWER

River Escaut

QUAI ST ALINE

PONT DES TROUS

BOULEVARD DES NERVIENS

Tour Henry VIII
(Musée d'Armes)

Train
Station

QUAI DUMON

St. Nicolas

Pl.
Crombez

Ste. Marie
Madeleine

RUE DU SONDART

RUE ROYALE

RUE DUBECQUERELLE

St. Jacques

RUE DU CYGNE

RUE ST. JACQUES

RUE CHILDERIC

Chap. de
l'Athenée

Musée d'Historie
et d'Archeologie

RUE DE MONNEL

RUE DU QUESNOY

RUE DE L'YSER

River Escaut

St. Brice

RUE PERDUE D'ARGENT

RUE DE PONT

St. Quentin

GRAND
PLACE

Cathedral

QUAI VIFQUIN

Halle de Draps

RUE DES CLAIRISSES

RUE ST. JEAN

Maison
Tournaisienne

Tourist
Office

PL R
ASTRO

RUE ST MARTIN

Hôtel
de Ville

RUE STE CATHERINE

BLVD. BARA

RUE DES JESUITES

Musée des
Beaux Arts

Parc
Communal

BLVD. LALAING

RUE DU CHAMBGET

RUE DE LA JUSTICE

0   200 m

AVE. DES ETATS-UNIS

BLVD. DU ROI ALBERT

TOURNAI

The Town

The town centre is split down the middle by the river Escaut (Scheldt) and girdled by a ring road that follows the course of the old city ramparts – the only remaining part of which is the thirteenth-century **Pont des Trous**, on the northern edge of the centre. Most of Tournai's buildings show a clear French style, especially those left by Louis XIV, but curiously enough the town was also English for five years from 1513 to 1518, after Henry VIII seized it in a war against France, though all that remains of the citadel he built is a tower, also on the station side of the river – the **Tour Henri VIII**. A cylindrical keep, with walls over six metres wide and a conical brick-vaulted roof, it holds Tournai's **Musée d'Armes** (April–Oct daily except Tues 10am–noon & 2–5.30pm; Nov–March Sat & Sun 10am–noon & 2–6pm) with an interesting display on the Belgian Resistance. On the same side of the river there are two restored **Romanesque houses** (1172–1200) in rue St-Brice – said to be the oldest examples of bourgeois dwellings in Western Europe. Sadly you can't go inside, though their precarious, leaning appearance is convincing enough. Just along the street is a **Gothic house** (thirteenth- to fifteenth-century), which illustrates the development of the same style.

Most things of interest are on the opposite, southern side of the river, grouped around or within easy walking distance of the main hub, the **Grand Place**, a ten-minute walk from the station. Dominating the skyline with its distinctive five towers is Tournai's Romanesque **Cathédrale Notre-Dame**, built with the wealth of the flourishing wool and stone trades out of the local slate-coloured Tournai marble – a stone which led to a school of architecture and sculpture developing here whose influence was felt throughout the Scheldt valley. The present structure is the third church on this site, most of it completed in the latter half of the twelfth century – though the choir was reconstructed in the middle of the thirteenth. Apart from the spired towers, the most unusual feature of the exterior is the west facade on place de l'Evêche, which has three tiers of sculptures dating from the fourteenth to seventeenth centuries. The oldest, along the bottom, were carved from local stone and (oddly) are better preserved than the later works, narrating scenes from the story of Adam and Eve among other things. Around the corner, the northern Porte Mantile sports earlier sculpture, much of which is contemporary with the church – slightly decrepit morality scenes of Virtue fighting Vice, Avarice and Satan and the like.

Inside the cathedral, the choir is – unexpectedly – virtually the same length as the nave. The nave is part of the original structure, erected in 1171, as are the wonderfully carved capitals, but the vaulted roof is eighteenth-century. A side chapel holds a painting of the *Crucifixion* by Jordaens. The choir was the first manifestation of the Gothic style in Belgium (where it appeared later than in France), and its too-slender columns had to be reinforced later at the base – the whole still leans slightly to the side due to the unstable soil beneath. Communication galleries run along the inside, evidence of a Norman influence, while inside a chapel on the right is an over-restored painting by Rubens, a characteristically bold canvas entitled *Purgatory*.

The ample and majestic late twelfth-century transepts are probably the most impressive – and most beautiful – feature of the cathedral. Apsed and aisled to a very unusual plan, they impart a lovely diffuse light through the many windows, some of which (in the south transept) hold superb sixteenth-century stained glass by Arnoult de Nimegue, depicting semi-mythical scenes from way back in

Tournai's history. The side chapels of the north transept have a number of twelfth-century wall paintings, among the finest in Belgium, showing Byzantine influence in their scenes of the martyrdom of Saint Margaret. Be sure also to see the **Treasury** before you leave (closed noon–2pm; F25), which houses two important gilt reliquaries: the Romanesque-Gothic *châsse de Notre-Dame* (1207) by Nicolas de Verdun, with its fluidly carved robes and expressive faces, and medallions on the top evoking the life of Christ; and the *châsse de Saint Eleuthère* (1247), the first bishop of Tournai – a richer and more ostentatious but less elegant work. There is also a Byzantine Cross and a thirteenth-century ivory Virgin, as well as a tapestry sewn in Arras showing the lives of Saint Piat and Saint Eleuthère. Dated to the end of the fourteenth century, it's apparently the only Arras tapestry of the period which can be certified as authentic. You can see a selection of the cathedral's treasures carried around the town each year in the *Procession de Notre-Dame* – held on the second Sunday in September.

Across the way from the cathedral, the **Belfry** is the oldest such structure in Belgium, its lower portion dating from 1200. The bottom level held room for a prison cell, while higher up there's a mini-balcony from which public proclamations were made, and above that, a carillon, dating from the ˙ixteenth to the nineteenth centuries. You can go inside and climb to the top for a view over the town (daily 10am–noon & 2–5pm, closed Tues; F20).

A little way west from here, on the Grand Place itself, the fine seventeenth-century **Halle de Draps** maintains its original facade, although the inside has been rebuilt after destruction in the wartime bombing. Almost next door, back towards the Grand Place, the **Musée de Folklore**, housed in the so-called Maison Tournaisienne (same times; free), has several floors detailing old Tournai trades and daily life around 1850, with reconstructions of various workshops and domestic rooms. Make sure you go all the way to the top (fourth floor) to see a 1701 model of the town as it looked in Louis XIV's day, the original of which is in Paris. In the same room are prints of the town and various buildings at different times. At the far end of the square, the church of **St-Quentin** is also impressive from the outside, another building with its original (thirteenth-century) facade, but it has a disappointing, partially rebuilt interior. Continuing west, the church of **St-Jacques** is more interesting, with a twelfth-century tower and slightly later nave. Just up from here, behind a discreet brown door, the combined **Musée d'Histoire et d'Archeologie** contains – as well as an attached prehistorical museum – rooms devoted to the development of Tournai sculpture and a collection of pewterware, although its most appealing section is the display of tapestries upstairs. Tournai was among the most important pictorial tapestry centres in Belgium in the fifteenth and sixteenth centuries, producing characteristically huge works, juxtaposing many characters and several episodes of history, and leaving no empty space – a stylised design without borders. Major themes included history, heraldry and mythology, and although several of the best surviving Tournai tapestries are in Brussels, there are one or two good examples here, not least the tapestry of *Hercules* – an excellent and still richly coloured instance of the tendency to cram the picture with life and wry observation. Tournai also had a porcelain factory from 1751 onwards and the museum houses a large collection of chinaware, mostly Chinese-influenced work.

On the other side of the Grand Place, the **Hôtel de Ville** is an eighteenth-century building, part of which now houses a small natural history museum; it was renovated following a hefty bombardment during the last war. The building occupies the site of the former abbey palace of Saint Martin, the ruins of which are around the side, though they're barely recognisable. Almost next door, the **Musée des Beaux Arts** (daily 10am–noon and 2–5.30pm, closed Tues; free) is housed in a late Twenties building by Victor Horta, and has an impressive collection of mainly Belgian painting from the Flemish primitives to the twentieth century. There's work by Roger van der Weyden, a native of Tournai, including a *Virgin and Child*, and seventeenth-century paintings by Jordaens and Rubens. More modern galleries take in paintings by James Ensor, Henri de Braeckeleer and a number of French Impressionists – of which two large canvases by Manet, *Argenteuil* and *Chez le Père Lathuile*, stand out.

Eating, drinking and nightlife

Tournai has few genuinely cheap **eating** options. Opposite the train station, *La Belle Vue* has filling, cheap, standard food. *La Rochette friture* on place de Lille has the usual chips, plus pasta dishes and other meals, and there's a *Superfrite* on the corner of Grand Place. In the **evenings** there isn't much life, but what there is, is of a cliquey nature – everyone goes to the same place for a year or so, then the venue changes and they all move accordingly. At the time of writing the in place was *Bar Declic* on the Grand Place, almost opposite the Halle de Draps, which is in any case the only place open really late. Across the square, the *Au Trois Lys* is more sedate, as is the self-consciously elegant piano bar, *3 Pommes d'Orange*, near the Belfry.

Out of Tournai: Mont-St-Aubert and Antoing

There's not much to see around Tournai, but the countryside around the hamlet of **MONT-ST-AUBERT**, 7km out of town, is nice for gentle hikes, though you really need a car to get there. Otherwise, take bus #U from outside the train station to KAIN, from where it's a fifteen-minute walk uphill. Helpfully, suggested walks are marked on a board near the village church; the Tournai tourist office also produces a leaflet called *Le Petit Livre Vert du Tournaisis*. Beware on summer weekends, though, when Mont–St–Aubert and environs can be packed with escaping townies.

Otherwise the only real thing to see near Tournai is the neo-Gothic castle of the princes of Ligne at **ANTOING**, 5km south of the town. Originally twelfth-century, it was the site of some of the first stirrings of rebellion against the Spanish in the mid-sixteenth century, though most of it – aside from the twelfth-century double walls and a sixteenth-century tower – is a nineteenth-century reconstruction. The slow train to Mons stops here but the castle is only open on Sundays, when there are tours at 3pm, 3.30pm, 4.30pm, 5pm and 5.30pm.

Mons and around

About half an hour by train from Tournai, the name of **MONS** may be familiar for its military associations. It was the site of battles that for Britain marked the beginning and end of World War I, and in 1944 it was the location of the first big American victory on Belgian soil in the liberation campaign. It has also been a key military base since the last war: SHAPE (Supreme Headquarters Allied Powers in Europe) has its headquarters at Maisières, just outside, providing employment for thousands of Americans and other NATO nationalities – something which gives the town a lively, cosmopolitan feel. However, Mons itself is undergoing something of a slump, and although by no means unappealing, beyond a few surrounding attractions it doesn't have much that will hold you for long.

Arrival, accommodation and other details

The **train station** is on the western edge of the town centre, on place Leopold, a short walk up the hill from the central Grand Place, where at no. 20 you'll find the **tourist office** (☎065/33 55 80), with information on the town and around, as well as leaflets detailing the major battlefield sites. There's also a Hainaut regional office at rue des Clercs 31 (☎065/36 04 64).

Don't waste your time checking out the **hotels** in the scruffy street opposite the station: they may look cheap but they're not especially for what you get. Better to use the more conveniently situated *St Georges*, rue des Clercs 15 (☎065/31 16 29), which has doubles for about F1400. There's no youth hostel, but the **Infor-Jeunes** office (Mon–Wed & Fri 10am–6pm, Thurs & Sat 1–4pm), in a big building on the corner of rue des Tuileries (turn left out of the tourist office and take a right turning 100m along) runs a special *Service Hebergement Vacances* for travellers (Mon–Fri 10am–noon & 2–7pm, Sat 1–4pm) in July and August. They have a file of studios and rooms to let with prices at around F600 for a single room, about F1000 for a double. The tourist office also has details of privately owned rooms and studios for rent, though often again only in July and August, for prices starting at F500 per person. **Campers** should head for *Camping Communal*, which isn't far out, near Waux Hall gardens at avenue St-Pierre 17 – handy for the shops. Take avenue Reine Astrid out of town in the direction of Binche/Charleroi.

The Town

The **Grand Place** is the centre of most Mons life and activity, its terrace cafés a nice place for a drink in the early evening, though pricey. Dominating the square, the fifteenth-century **Hôtel de Ville** is a much altered building, its tower dating from the early eighteenth century. Some of the rooms inside are open to the public, and hold the odd fancy chimneypiece, tapestries and paintings. Outside the building, next to the front porch, there's a fifteenth-century brass monkey that brings good luck to all who stroke him, and has a bald, polished crown as a result.

Around the back of the Hôtel de Ville, through the arched porch and the Jardin du Mayeur beyond, the **Musées du Centenaire** (daily 10am–12.30pm & 2–6pm, in summer until 5pm on Fri, in winter until 5pm on Sun; closed Mon; F60 for all four, F30 for one) is a complex of four museums under one roof, displaying artefacts relating to a variety of subjects, from ceramics to coins and medals. There's a chinaware collection spanning the seventeenth- to twentieth-century, including over 400 pieces from Delft; there's also, on the ground floor, one of the most complete displays in Europe on World War I and the various nationalities involved, as well as a third-floor display on the Americans in 1940–45. Items include battlefield relics, regimental drums, weapons and uniforms. Other exhibits record life in Mons during the German occupations of both wars, during the second of which (after the French withdrawal in 1940) Mons was virtually deserted by its inhabitants, 2000 remaining out of 28,000. The further two museums are of more fringe interest – one of some 18,000 coins and medals, the other of prehistoric artefacts.

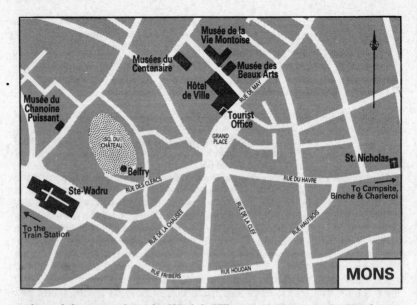

Around the corner from the Hôtel de Ville, on rue Neuve, is the **Musée des Beaux Arts** (same times; F30), whose collection of paintings ranges from the sixteenth century to the present day. It's not as heavyweight a museum as the one in Tournai, and its permanent collection is in any case only shown in rotation, much of the museum's space being given over to (often excellent) temporary exhibitions. But among the things you might be able to view are paintings by Jan Gossaert and Cornelis de Vos, later Dutch seventeeth-century work, and more modern canvases by Paul Delvaux and others. There's also a rotating collection of modern sculpture. Further along the street is another museum, though again of rather limited appeal, the **Musée de la Vie Montoise** (same times; F30), which has paintings through the ages by local artists, and displays on the customs and folklore of the region.

South from the Grand Place, the pedestrianised **rue de la Chaussée** is Mons' main shopping street, home to the main chain stores and the like; there is more interesting shopping to be had off to the left down rue des Fripiers and rue de la Coupe. Check out also rue des Gades and rue Cronque, off the Grand Place's southwest corner, at the foot of the Baroque Belfry, which are among the town's best preserved medieval streets. A little way past the Belfry, down rue des Clercs, the **Collégiale Ste-Waudru** (daily 2–5pm, closed Mon; F20) is a good example of late Gothic, a massive church which displays an unusual uniformity of style. There is much to see inside, most importantly the Renaissance works of the local sculptor Jacques du Broeucq, whose alabaster rood loft (1535–39) was broken up in the Revolution, and is now spread around different parts of the church. Look out for the reliefs in the transepts, chapels, and on the high altar, as well as his alabaster statues in the choir, notably the graceful figures of the Virtues. The treasury, too, is of interest, with goldsmiths' work from the thirteenth to nine-teenth centuries.

Behind the church at the foot of rue Notre Dame Debonnaire, the **Musée Chanoine Puissant** occupies a sixteenth-century house known as the *Vieux Logis*. It's made up of the private collection of an eponymous canon, who died in 1934 bequeathing an eclectic mix of chimneypieces, furniture, wrought-iron wares and drawings from different periods, though mostly sixteenth- and seventeenth-century. The most impressive item is in the first room – a 1531 wooden ceiling (upright against the back wall) beautifully carved in Renaissance style, taken from a pavilion in town.

MONS IN THE WARS

Mons has figured highly in both world wars. During **World War I**, in the latter part of August 1914, the British forces here found themselves outnumbered by the Germans by something like twenty to one. The subsequent Battle of Mons began on August 26, and the British – in spite of great heroics (the first two Victoria Crosses were awarded at Mons) – were inevitably defeated and forced into retreat. The casualties might have been greater. But according to a newspaper article written soon after the battle by the horror-story writer, Arthur Machen, the troops were spared by a host of bow-touting angels – the so-called **Angels of Mons** – hovering overhead, just at the point when the Germans were about to launch their final attack, causing them to fall back in fear and amazement. Machen later admitted that he had made the whole thing up, but at the time the story took on the status of legend, giving rise to any number of spin-offs, and soldiers (those that were lucky enough) returning home with similar stories of supernatural happenings on the battlefield. The tale also undoubtedly had a morale-boosting effect (and perhaps purpose), giving brief respite at home from the horrible casualty figures that were more normally reported from the front. There's a painting of the event, by one Marcel Gilis, in the Mons Hôtel de Ville.

The town remained in German hands until it was liberated by the Canadians in November 1918. Mons was, however, at the centre of the fighting again during **World War II**. It was occupied by the French on May 10, 1940, but, after a long and vicious German bombardment that went on for nine days, they were forced to withdraw. By the time the Nazis entered the town it had almost entirely been abandoned. Four years later, on September 2, 1944, the Allies took Mons again after more fierce fighting, this time from the air.

Around Mons

Mons is usually visited for its surrounding attractions. The nearest and most obvious of these is the **Vincent van Gogh house** just south of the city in the suburb of Cuesmes. But there are others besides, notably the castles of **Beloeil** and **Attre** about 15km to the northwest.

Vincent van Gogh and the Borinage

The region immediately south of Mons is known as the **Borinage**, a poor, thickly populated mining area that in the latter half of the nineteenth century was home to Vincent van Gogh for a time. After entering a Protestant school in Brussels, in 1878 he was sent on probation here as a missionary, living in acute poverty and helping the villagers in their fight for social justice – behaviour which so appalled the church authorities that he was forced to leave. He returned the following year and lived in **CUESMES**, on the southern outskirts of Mons – a fact that is, inevitably, opportunistically promoted but although the connection is important in terms of van Gogh's career – it was here he first started drawing seriously – there's very little to see. Inspiration to draw came from the hard life of the miners: "J'aime tellement ce triste pays du Borinage qui toujours me sera inoubliable ... C'est en somme dans le Borinage que j'ai, pour la première fois, commencé a travailler sur nature". The **house** van Gogh occupied (daily 10am–6pm, closed Mon; free) has recently been restored but it really is a major disappointment, with just two standard rooms containing prints of his study-drawings of the period and later famous paintings. Not even "the room as he left it" or a reconstruction of how it was, and no original work. If you are determined on a rewardless pilgrimage, take bus #1 or #2 from outside Mons station (every 15min); it's a ten-minute walk to the van Gogh house from the bus stop.

Beloeil and Attre

Further out of Mons, the château of **Beloeil** (April–Sept Mon–Fri 10am–6pm; Oct daily; F300 combined ticket for park and château, F100 château only; park daily 9am–8pm) is known as the Versailles of Belgium, an inflated tag that – whatever your views on Louis XIV's palace – is bound to cause disappointment. Built for the aristocratic Ligne family in the late seventeenth century, it's a stately building no question, but the main body was rebuilt after a fire in 1900 and the interior, though lavish enough, with tapestries, paintings and furniture, is standard-issue extravagance, the collected indulgencies of various generations of Lignes, who have lived at Beloeil since the fourteenth century. Best parts are the library, which contains 20,000 volumes, many ancient and beautifully bound, and the eighteenth-century formal gardens outside, the largest in the country, designed by Parisian architect and decorator, Jean Michel Chevotet – though even these are unkempt around the edges and dotted with stagnant ponds. Their grandeur is further diminished by the recreation area and model village in the far corner.

The nearest train station to Beloeil is at ATH, connected by hourly train to Mons every hour, a thirty-minute journey; buses leave from outside the station to Beloeil (another half-hour). Allow plenty of time because the buses are fairly irregular. From the stop in the village it's a 100-metre walk to the château.

If you want to make a day of it you can visit the château at ATTRE too. It's on the Mons–Ath rail line, or you can take a bus from Ath and save yourself a walk at the other end. The **Château d'Attre** (Easter–Oct Sat, Sun and holidays; July & August daily 10am–noon & 2–6pm, closed Wed; F100, park only F50) is much smaller than Beloeil, more like a country house than a castle. But it has a charm that Beloeil lacks, with a more lived-in, human feel, in part induced by the arrangements of freshly picked flowers chosen to enhance the character of each room. The different styles of the rooms mark not only the passing of time but also the decreasing fortunes of the family that lived here – something that's also explained well on the (obligatory) guided tours. A neo-Classical structure completed in 1752 on the site of a distinctly less comfortable medieval fortress, the house was a frequent residence of the Archduchess Marie-Christine of Austria and her husband, the Governors General of the Southern Netherlands during the reign of Joseph II, and it is filled with their carefully selected furniture.

Some of the walls are still covered with the original hand-painted wallpaper (the designs often Chinese in inspiration), some of which is 200 hundred years old but no less brightly coloured for that. The rooms themselves hold collections of porcelain and silver, as well as paintings by Watteau and other artists of the time. Outside, the grounds hold some deliberately wild "English Gardens", a Romantic "ruin" built at the bottom of the park as a folly, a purpose-built hill topped with a mock-Swiss chalet, and the remains of a tenth-century tower that is said to have been the refuge of a local villain.

Soignies and Ronquières

About 20km north of Mons, **SOIGNIES** is easy to reach from Mons by train, although there's nothing much to bring you here apart from the town's Romanesque church, the **Collégiale St-Vincent** – in the centre of town by the tourist office. Dedicated to one Saint Vincent Madelgar, the husband of Saint Waudru of Mons, who died here in 677 after founding a monastery, the church was begun in 965 and built over the ensuing three centuries. A squat and severe edifice with two heavy towers, it is sombrely decorated within, with a nave similar to that of Tournai, with Lombardian arches. The transept is eleventh-century but now has seventeenth-century vaulting. The oldest section is the huge cavernous choir, dating from 960 and containing one of the church's most outstanding features, a set of Renaissance choir stalls from 1576. Look out also for the fifteenth-century terracotta entombment on the south side of the choir, and the fourteenth-century polychrome Virgin close by.

A little way north of the church, down a little side road (rue Henry Leroy), is an ancient cemetery with a chapel even older than the church. It contains an archaeological museum open only on Sunday afternoon.

North of Soignies, **RONQUIÈRES** is perhaps more interesting, if only because of its one attraction, a curious "lift" or sloping lock for boats travelling on the Charleroi–Brussels canal. When the device was built in 1963 it cut the journey time between Charleroi and Brussels by some seven hours. It consists of two huge water tanks, each 91m long, which shift barges up or down 70m (depending on the change of water level) over a distance of 1500m. A neighbouring tower gives a birds-eye view of the proceedings, and also provides an audiovisual display on the area (May–Aug 10am–6pm; F70). Sadly, though, Ronqières isn't easy to reach from Soignies: you need to take a train to BRAINE-LE-COMTE 8km away – a five-minute journey – and a bus from there (direction Nivelles).

In the opposite direction are more castles, though they're of limited interest and one of them is difficult to reach on public transport. Bus #134 leaves Soignies station every hour and takes fifteen minutes to reach the château of **Le Roeulx** (April–Sept daily 10am–noon & 1.30–6pm, closed Wed; F50 castle and park), an originally fifteenth-century fortress with an eighteenth-century facade. A little way north, parts of the fortified castle of **Ecaussinnes Lalaing** (April–Oct 10am–noon & 2–4pm, closed Tues & Wed; F50) date from the twelfth century but the rest has been altered over the centuries up to the eighteenth century. In the hall and armoury there are early sixteenth-century chimneypieces; other rooms contain furniture, glass and Tournai porcelain, and a fifteenth-century kitchen stands as it would have looked then. Ecaussinnes Lalaing isn't easy to get to: again, trains run from Braine-le-Comte. From Mons, you can take a bus or train (the bus is slower) but only to ECAUSSINES, on the other side of the valley.

Binche

Halfway between Mons and Charleroi, **BINCHE** is in many ways a preferable centre to either of its larger neighbours, a pretty, quiet old town perched on a hill and – uniquely in Belgium – still surrounded almost entirely by ramparts. Even if you don't stay, it's worth half a day, and if you're here in February you may want to stop over longer, when the town erupts for several days with one of the best, and most renowned, of the country's **carnivals**.

Most things of interest are beyond the far end of the **Grand Place** – a spacious square lined with many cosy old bars and the **Hôtel de Ville** (which also holds the tourist office), built in 1555 by Jacques Du Broeucq to replace an earlier building destroyed during an invasion the previous year by Henry II of France. Beyond the Grand Place, to the south, stands a statue of a "Gille", one of the figures that dance through the city streets during carnival, close by the **Collégiale St-Ursmer**, whose interior holds a fifteenth-century oak *Pietà* and a rich treasury – though it's often only open to groups. Take the narrow street down behind the church for a good view of the **ramparts**, constructed between the twelfth and fourteenth centuries, and retaining 27 towers. On the other side of the church a park contains the ruins of another building by De Broeucq, the former palace of Mary of Hungary. But the high point of Binche is opposite the church, the **Musée International du Carnaval et du Masque** (Feb–March daily 2–6pm; April–Nov daily 10am–noon & 2–6pm; closed Fri; F100), which claims to be the only worldwide museum of carnivals in the world. True or not, its collection of masks and fancy dress from carnivals throughout Europe, Africa, Asia and seven Latin American countries is impressive, and is complemented by an audiovisual presentation on the Binche carnival, and temporary associated exhibitions.

Practical details . . . and the carnival

To get to Binche from Mons by train, change at LA LOUVIÈRE; failing that, bus #22 makes the forty-minute journey every half-hour from outside Mons train station. From Charleroi buses run every hour. The Binche **tourist office** is located in the town hall on the Grand Place (Mon–Thurs 8am–noon & 1–5pm, Fri 8am–noon; ☎064/33 41 77), though the only place to stay in town is a one-star **campsite** called *Binche Plage* in rue Balenfer.

Carnival has been celebrated in Binche since the fourteenth century. The festivities last for several days, getting under way in earnest on the Sunday before Shrove Tuesday, when thousands turn out in fancy dress, and leading up to the main events on Shrove Tuesday itself, when the traditional *Gilles* in clogs and embroidered costumes are out and about from dawn onwards. In the morning they wear "green-eyed" masks, dancing in the Grand Place carrying bunches of sticks to ward off bad spirits. Come the afternoon they don their plumes – a mammoth piece of headgear made of ostrich feathers – and throw oranges to the crowd (it used to be bread) as they pass through the town in procession.

Charleroi

CHARLEROI stinks. You can smell it on approach. Belching chimneys dot its horizon, beyond which rise grass-covered slag heaps. Glass works, coal mines and iron foundries have made the town the centre of one of Belgium's main industrial

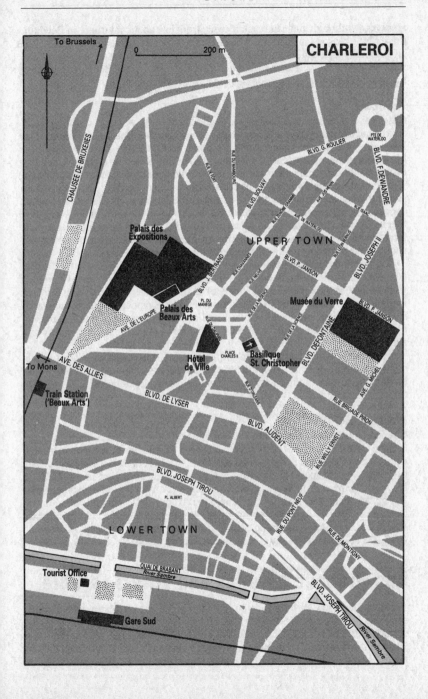

To Brussels

0   200 m

CHARLEROI

CHAUSSÉE DE BRUXELLES

PTE DE
WATERLOO

BLVD. G. ROULIER

BLVD. F. DEWANDRE

BLVD. SOLVAY

RUE DE MONTIGNY

RUE LEON BERNUS

AVE. DE WATERLOO

RUE ISAAC

AVE. DES CROMBE

UPPER TOWN

Palais des
Expositions

BLVD. J. BERTRAND

RUE CHAVANNES

RUE NEUVE

BLVD. P. JANSON

RUE LEON BERNUS

BLVD. JOSEPH II

Palais des
Beaux Arts

PL. DU
MANEGE

Musée du Verre

BLVD. P. JANSON

AVE. DE L'EUROPE

RUE DE LA REGENCE

RUE DE LA REGENCE

BLVD. DEFONTAINE

Hôtel
de Ville

PLACE
CHARLES II

Basilique
St. Christopher

To Mons

AVE. DES ALLIES

RUE DU DUC

AVE. DU MICHEL

Train Station
('Beaux Arts')

BLVD. DE LYSER

RUE BRIGADE PIRON

BLVD. AUDENT

RUE WILLY ERNST

BLVD. JOSEPH TIROU

PL. ALBERT

LOWER TOWN

RUE DU PONT NEUF

RUE DE MONTIGNY

Tourist Office

QUAI DE BRABANT
River Sambre

BLVD. JOSEPH TIROU

River Sambre

Gare Sud

areas, and, although you can reach it easily from just about anywhere in Belgium, there's little reason for doing so. It has a couple of decent museums, but these can just as easily be seen using Binche or Mons, or even Brussels, as a base. You might find yourself here in the course of travelling down to the Botte de Hainaut to the south, where the countryside is among the province's finest.

The Town

Charleroi divides into two distinct parts: the lower town, where you will probably arrive, and the upper town whose circular **place Charles II** is the city centre. The Hôtel de Ville, on the western side, is home to Charleroi's best museum, the **Musée de Beaux Arts** (daily 9am–5pm, closed Mon & holidays; free), which has excellent works by Hainaut artists and others who lived or worked in the province. There are the naturalistic works of Constanin Meunier depicting life in the mines and the factories, paintings by the Charleroi artist François Navez, and other canvases by local painters using the hard, brutal life of the surrounding area as a theme. By now the museum may have also added the collection of Jules Destrée, a local benefactor who donated furniture, paintings and historical items from the end of the eighteenth and the beginning of the nineteenth century.

Charleroi's other main museum, the **Musée du Verre**, is housed in the *Institut National du Verre* on boulevard Defontaine, on the far side of place Charles II (same times; free). A fascinating survey of all things glassy, the museum displays many beautiful glass items from different periods: Egyptian jewellery and vases from 5 BC, Roman and Venetian glass, and contemporary glass works, alongside displays dedicated to the material itself – what it is, how it is made, its history and suchlike. There's also a small archaeology museum in the basement.

The **Musée National de Photographie** (daily 10am–5pm, closed Mon & holidays) is just outside Charleroi, with 2000 square metres of floorspace given over to photos, the history of the camera and of photography. Take bus #70, #71 or #170 from the Gare du Sud to 11 avenue Paul Pasteur, Mont-sur-Marchienne.

Practical details

Charleroi has two **train stations**, the Gare du Sud, at which you're likely to arrive, and the Gare de Ouest, in the city centre. There's an **information kiosk** in front of Gare du Sud (Mon–Fri 8.30am–noon & 1–5pm; ☎071/31 82 18). If you have to stay overnight, the cheapest place is the *C.A.C.E.A.C.*, 7 rue Leon Bernus (☎071/31 31 86), near the Musée du Verre, a twenty-minute walk from the train station or take bus #2, #4, #7 or #22 – ask for the Monument stop; F250 per night plus a one-off payment of F140 for a sheet. Next up the scale, with doubles for F1400, is the **hotel** *Palais des Expositions* (near the Musée de Beaux Arts), avenue de l'Europe 24 (☎071/32 88 50), and the *Pim's Hotel*, place Buisset 13 (☎071/33 44 40), F1650.

Into Brabant: Nivelles and Villers-la-Ville

Travel far north of Charleroi and you cross the border into **Brabant**, whose southern French-speaking districts form a final band of countryside before you enter the sprawl of Brussels, beginning with the characterless splurge of Waterloo (see "Brussels and Around"). **Nivelles** is the area's main town, worth a stop on the way north and a short bike ride from the Cistercian abbey ruins at **Villers-la-Ville**.

Nivelles

NIVELLES grew up around its monastery, which was founded here in the seventh century and grew to become one of the most powerful religious orders hereabouts. Nowadays, most people visit the town for the remains of the former monastery, notably the enormous **Collégiale Ste-Gertrude**, a restored version of a tenth- to twelfth-century original badly damaged in World War II and sadly with little atmosphere or sense of age. It is, however, an interesting building architecturally, a good example of a Romanesque abbey church. Restoration began in 1948 and wasn't finished until 1984. The church is named after the first abbess of the monastery, the daughter of the woman who founded it. It was built in several stages from the tenth century onwards and some of its later additions show the influence of the Ottoman architecture of the period. It has two transepts and two choirs at opposite ends and is extremely simple inside, its original flat wooden roof now imitated in concrete. The pulpit in the east choir (the opposite end from which you enter) is by the eighteenth-century Belgian artist Laurent Delvaux. Near the main entrance door is a fifteenth-century wooden wagon which carried the shrine of Saint Gertrude in a procession through the surrounding fields once a year. Restored in 1987, it has 24 oak panels along the bottom and 16 along the top, illustrating the life of Gertrude and the miracles she performed. Unfortunately, the original thirteenth-century shrine was destroyed in 1940 and only fragments remain, but a modern replacement has been made and the autumn procession recently revived.

It's worth visiting the church on a guided tour even if you don't understand French, as these take you around parts of the church otherwise out of bounds (for an English tour you have to ring the tourist office ahead). Tours leave roughly every hour, between 10am and 4pm, with a break at lunch (F50, F30 students), and take you first upstairs to the large *Salle Imperial* over the west choir. There are vague plans to house a museum here to contain the thirteenth-century shrine and the wagon panels, among other related miscellany. En route you get a lovely view down over the church from the end gallery. You then pass through the huge Romanesque crypt to visit the interesting **sous-sol archéologique** (excavations), where the foundations of a Merovingian chapel and church (seventh-century) and three Carolingian churches (ninth- and tenth-century) have been discovered, as well as the tombs of Saint Gertrude and her relations.

After visiting the church don't miss the **Musée Communal d'Archéologie, d'Art et d'Histoire**, in an ivy-clad house at the end of rue de Bruxelles (daily 9.30am–12.30pm & 2.30–5pm, closed Tues; F40), which shows items from the end of the Middle Ages to the eighteenth century charting the history of Nivelles – collegiate church, town and region. Much of the material on display has actually come from the church, like the four fifteenth-century Brabantine Gothic statues of the Apostles, from the former rood loft, and the Baroque terracotta sculptures by Delvaux. There are also rooms on prehistory and the Gallo-Roman period.

Practical details

Nivelles' **train station** is ten minutes' walk from the centre of town at the Grand Place, down rue de Namur. The **tourist office** is on the opposite side of the Grand Place to the church, in the corner (Mon–Fri 9am–noon & 1–5pm, Sat 9am–

noon; ☎067/21 54 13), though with Brussels so near it's not really worth staying. For **food**, a few doors up from the museum, in the middle of rue Bruxelles, *Le Prevert* bistro is a good place for lunch, with an interesting and varied menu of pasta dishes, *tartines* and salads, and is reasonably priced and popular. Try the *salade wallonie*.

Villers-la-Ville

Some 12km east of Nivelles, accessible by train from Charleroi, the ruined Cistercian abbey of **VILLERS-LA-VILLE** (May–Aug daily 10am–8pm; Sept daily 10am–6pm; mid-March to April daily 10am–6pm; winter Sat & Sun 11am–5pm; F50) is one of the most haunting and evocative sights in the area. The first monastic community settled here in 1146, consisting of just one abbot and twelve monks. Later the abbey became a powerful local landowner, managing a domain of about 24,700 acres, with numbers that had risen to about 100 monks and 300 lay brothers, bringing in a healthy annual income which funded the construction, from 1200 onwards, of most of what you see now. The monastic edifices were erected wholly in the thirteenth century; less austere buildings, like the Abbot's Palace, went up in the seventeenth and eighteenth century. In 1796 the monastery was ransacked by French revolutionaries, and later on a railway was ploughed through the grounds.

It's an enormous complex comprising a church, sleeping quarters, refectory, parlour, warming room and workshops. Romanesque, Gothic and Renaissance features remain, with some inevitable nineteenth-century modifications. The buildings are pretty much a ruin, and the site is wild and overgrown, but some kind of mental reconstruction is possible using the numbers on the site and the guidebook available at the entrance.

From the entrance a path crosses the courtyard of honour of the Abbot's Palace to the warming room (27). This was the only place in the monastery where a fire was kept going all winter and it still has its original chimney. It's next to the monks' workroom, so they could keep warm while reading and studying. On the other side is the huge Romanesque-Gothic refectory (26), lit by ribbed twin windows topped with a rose window. It was formerly divided into two naves by vaults, of which you can see the remains of the pillars. Nearby is the kitchen (24) with the main drainage system to the river and a chimney for airing the room. The pantry (22) still has a complete vault intact on a single column. Crossing the court you come to the brewery (14) on the edge of the complex, one of the biggest and oldest buildings in the abbey, in transitional style, with groined vaults, despite its completion at the end of the thirteenth century.

The most spectacular building here, however, is the church, more like a cathedral than a Cistercian church, with pure lines and elegant proportions, and displaying the change from Romanesque to Gothic; indeed, the transept and choir are the first known examples of Gothic in the Brabantine area. It's 90m long, 40m wide and 23m tall at the highest point, with a majestic nave that was supported on strong cylindrical columns. An original feature is the series of bull's-eye windows which light the transepts. Of the original twelfth-century cloister only a pair of twin windows remain (rebuilt in Gothic style from the fourteenth to the sixteenth centuries). Around its edges are tombstones and the tomb of the crusader Gibert d'Aspremont.

Practical details

There is no public **transport** between Nivelles and Villers, though it's an easy and pleasant enough journey by bike. Trains run direct from Charleroi once hourly; from Brussels you have to change at OTTIGNIES. From Villers station follow the road which crosses the track in the Monticelli direction and turn right onto the main road. It's a good 20- to 25-minute walk to the abbey.

The **tourist office** is situated in the "Gate of Brussels", a little building to the side which was originally the main entrance. For a good view over the whole area of the abbey complex, take a look from the "bridge" outside the tourist office. If you want to make a day of it, there are fifteen signposted **walks** in the vicinity of the abbey. The tourist office or abbey itself has a booklet describing them. There's also a pamphlet (F30, French only) detailing three of the walks. Both publications include map sections. In summer the cloister is used for amateur theatre productions.

South of Charleroi: the Botte de Hainaut

There are a couple of other ruined abbeys immediately southwest of Charleroi, though to be honest they're difficult to get to and not really worth the bother unless you've got your own transport. The eighteenth-century abbey at **AULNES**, for example, is in part given over to an old people's home and the rest is very ruined – only the plan and doorway remain of the Romanesque church, with a sixteenth-century apse (summer daily 9am–noon & 1.30–6pm; winter daily except Mon 1.30–4pm; F30). The only way of getting there from Charleroi is to take a train to LANDELIES and walk for 35 minutes from there. The ruins of the abbey at **LOBBES**, further south, are similarly sparse, only the church remaining. The Thuin train from Charleroi takes you to Lobbes station, some 5km to the south, or you can catch tram #90 to ANDERLUES, and from there bus #91.

You'd do far better to head straight for the **Botte de Hainaut** (Boot of Hainaut), a tongue of land which reaches south into France, shared between the provinces of Hainaut and Namur. A natural extension of the Ardennes range further east, though a little flatter and less wooded, it's good walking country, and you visit more for the scenery than for any specific sights.

Beaumont and Walcourt

Accessible direct by bus from Charleroi, **BEAUMONT** is an old small town on a hill, with parts of its fortifications intact, most notably the **Tour Salamandre** which is now a museum of regional history (May–Sept 9am–noon & 2–7pm). A little further on are the **Barrages de l'Eau d'Heure** – a series of five reservoir lakes (Easter–Sept 9am–6pm) that have been turned into a recreation area with boating, windsurfing, etc, and campsites. If you're after water sports it's fine, but they are not especially attractive in themselves.

The main rail line from Charleroi heads south into the Botte as far as Couvin. **WALCOURT**, just across the border in Namur province, is the first town you reach on the rail line, a pleasant old place most interesting for its thirteenth- and fourteenth-century **Basilique St-Materne**. Entry is restricted to guided tours (call ☎071/61 13 66 for details), but if you have the time it's well worth it. Inside, the rood loft of 1531 is a marvellous piece of work in Flamboyant Gothic style, presented to Charles V on the occasion of a pilgrimage here to the tenth-century Virgin of Walcourt, a wooden statue coated in silver that stands in the transept. Believed to have been crafted in the tenth century, it's one of the oldest such figures in Belgium. The treasury, amongst other items, has a thirteenth-century cross-reliquary in the style of Hugo d'Oignies (see "Namur"), a native of Walcourt.

Chimay, Couvin and around

Further south down the train line from Walcourt there are two rough areas of interest – Chimay and the Virelles lake, and Couvin and the small villages to the east of it. The countryside around both towns is worth exploring, something you can do by way of the steam train, **Chemin de fer à vapeur des 3 Vallées**, which joins up Chimay, Couvin, Mariembourg and Treignes in the far east of the region along 14km of old track. You can buy a return for either of the two main sections – Mariembourg–Chimay or Mariembourg–Treignes – and get off en route wherever you want; trains stop at Nismes, Petigny and Olloy. At Mariembourg some of the trains also link up with trains to and from Charleroi Sud. The steam train runs from April to September and times are detailed in a very complicated leaflet available from train stations. Outside of these months Mariembourg and Couvin are connected by a regular train.

CHIMAY maintains an aristocratic air fitting to its history, its tiny centre piled on top of a hill, steep alleys leading down to the lower town below. Best known perhaps for the beer brewed in its local Trappist monastery (just outside town near the village of FORGES), which graces supermarket shelves nationwide, it was ruled through several centuries by members of the de Croy family, ever since Charles de Croy was made the first Prince of Chimay by the emperor Maximilian in 1486. At the centre of town the Grand Place has a **Monument des Princes** of 1852, an allegory representing the town with four members of the princely family. On the same square, the **Collégiale Saints Pierre et Paul** is a largely sixteenth-century church, with three bays of the choir remaining from an earlier thirteenth-century structure, that contains the sixteenth-century mauso-leum of Charles de Croy, a recumbent figure in alabaster. The **Château de Chimay** (April–Oct 10am–noon & 2–6pm; obligatory guided visits 10am, 11am, 2pm, 3pm & 5pm; F100) was the home of the de Croy family, situated on a rocky massif, the back of which plunges down to the Eau Blanche river, down a lane from the Grand Place. Originally built in the fifteenth century, it was severely damaged by fire in 1935, after it was reconstructed to Charles de Croy's original plans, and is now open to the public, its interior full of old family portraits and including a small private theatre. There is a good view from a terrace at the back over the river valley and surrounding woods.

Four kilometres away, the **Étang de Virelles** is the largest lake in Belgium, a nature reserve important for waterfowl, which have had special protection since 1985 (May–Sept daily 10am–6pm; Oct–April Sun only; F50; July & Aug guided visits 3pm; F40). A permanent exhibition details the area with the help of slides. Twelve kilometres north of Chimay, **RANCE** is famous for its red marble quar-ries, which have supplied buildings worldwide, from Versailles to St Peter's in Rome. It's a subject you can find out more about in the town's **National Marble Museum** (April–Oct Mon–Sat 9.30am–6pm, Sun 2pm–6pm; winter Mon–Sat 8.30am–5pm, closed Sun).

There is no cheap accommodation to be found in the Chimay area and hotels tend to be along country roads. Campers are best off with the **Camping Communal**, just outside Chimay in the Allée des Princes 1 (April–Oct), near a sports complex with swimming pool, shops, and with its own cafeteria. On the edge of town, the *Motel des Fagnes*, chaussée de Couvine 51c (☎060/21 27 89), has double rooms from about F1300. By the Virelles lake, the *Hostellerie Le Virelles*, rue du lac 28 (☎060/21 11 35), charges F950 for a double. For more information, the Chimay **tourist office** is in the Hôtel de Ville, opposite the church (☎060/21 18 46).

COUVIN makes a better base for seeing the best of the Botte de Hainaut, more geared to tourists and in a prettier setting along the Eau Noire river, the cliff face forming a backdrop to the town. There's not much to see in the town itself, its main feature being the **Cavernes de l'Abîme**, a series of caves that are now home to an exhibition and audiovisual display on prehistoric times (July & Aug daily 10am–noon & 2–6pm; Easter–Sept Sat & Sun only; combined ticket with *Grottes de Neptune*, 3km away). Just along from the cave entrance, in the rue de la Falaise, is an information office (July & Aug only; ☎060/34 54 54). There's also a **tourist office** with information on the town and region, opposite the bus/train station at the end of rue de la Gare, close to which the *Hôtel de la Gare* (☎060/34 41 03) is a good place to **eat**, with a generous, cheapish menu. Accommodation here is full-board only, though reasonable at a little over F1000 per person. Other hotels are *La Sapinière*, Vieille Route de Rocroy 7 (☎060/34 43 81), and *Les Forges de Pernelle*, rue de Pernelle 19 (☎060/34 48 02), which have doubles for F1100–1500. Campers should use *Camping Communal*. The immediate area is probably more suited to cycling than walking (there's a leaflet available with cycle routes), and bikes can be hired from *Daniel Davreux*, Grand Place.

Eight kilometres away, **NISMES** is neatly tucked into the end of a verdant valley on the banks of a river, the most picturesque of the villages that lie to the east of Couvin. It's possible to hire canoes and a there's a rather twee tourist train (April 1–end Sept; hourly; F100) that gives a fifty-minute ride through the surrounding area, passing through the **Viroin-Fagnes nature reserve**. There are several **campsites** – try *Camping Bourtembourg*, rue A. Gregoire, or *Le Sabot*, on rue de la Station – and a number of **hotels**, though none are particularly cheap; try *Auberge de l'Eau Noire*, rue Vielle Eglise 15 (☎060/31 10 22), *Auberge des 3 Vallees*, rue de la Station (☎060/31 11 24), or *La Bonne Auberge*, rue Bassidaine 29 (☎060/31 10 90), all of which have rooms for much the same kind of prices. For more information there's a **tourist office** on the riverfront (daily 9am–6pm; ☎060/31 16 35).

Closer to Couvin, **PETIGNY** is in more exposed countryside and is basically visited for the **Grottes de Neptune** caves (Easter–Sept daily 9.30am–noon & 1.30–6pm; Oct Sat & Sun only), a well-developed stop on tourist itineraries that includes a twenty-minute boat ride on a subterranean river, and a sound and light show – impressive, if rather slick, stuff. **OLLOY**, further along the same road, is, like Petigny, disturbed by the main road, but you can hire canoes for use on the swift river and there's a **campsite**, *Try des Baudets*, on rue de la Campagne. There's only one **hotel**, the *Rolinvaux*, rue de Fourcimont 46 (☎060/39 91 96), with doubles for F1200–1400.

travel details

Trains

From Tournai to Ath/Brussels (3 hourly; 20min/ 1hr).

From Mons to Ath (hourly; 30min); La Louvière/ Charleroi (hourly; 20min/1hr 10min).

From La Louvière to Binche (hourly; 10min); Charleroi (2 an hour; 45min).

From Charleroi to Nivelles/Brussels (hourly; 20min/50min); Walcourt/Mariembourg/Couvin (1–2 hourly; 30min/60min/65min); Namur (2 an hour; 30min); Thuin/Lobbes (2 an hour; 15min/ 20min); Ligny/Villers-la-Ville/Ottignies (hourly; 20min/30min/45min).

Buses

From Ath to Beloeil (4 daily; 30min).

From Soignies to Le Roeulx (hourly; 15min).

From Mons to Binche (2 an hour; 40min).

From Charleroi to Binche (hourly; 40min).

CHAPTER ELEVEN

THE ARDENNES

S ome people in the north say that Belgium ends at the Ardennes. And it's true that the region can seem a place apart from the industrial cities of the north and west of the country. It is sometimes painfully difficult to get around – a route that looks direct on the map may involve several changes by bus or train (sometimes both) – and even the major centres of Namur and Liège connect directly with only a few points of interest. Then again, poor communications is a fair guarantee of wild countryside, which is probably why you're here.

Geologically the Ardennes begins in France, enters Luxembourg and extends into Germany, and within Belgian territory is covered by the three provinces of **Namur** in the west, **Luxembourg** in the south and **Liège** in the east. The highest part of the Ardennes is the **Hohes Venns** (High Fens), in the German-speaking far east of the region, beyond which the range links up with the hills of Germany's (and Luxembourg's) Eifel area. But this is not the Ardennes' most attractive or popular corner, which lies further west, lent character and variety by the **rivers** which run through the area. Indeed it's the river valleys which form the real attraction, deep, wooded, winding canyons reaching up to high green peaks – at times sublimely, and inspiringly, beautiful. The Ardennes' **cave systems**, too, form a major focus, especially those in the Meuse, Ourthe and Lesse valleys, carved out by underground rivers that over the centuries have cut through and dissolved the chalk of the hills, leaving stalagmites and stalactites in their wake.

The obvious gateway to the region is **Namur**, strategically sited at the junction of the Sambre and Meuse rivers – worth a visit in its own right, with some decent museums, a huge citadel and (for the Ardennes) a lively night-scene. From Namur you can follow the Meuse by train down to **Dinant**, a scenic – and very popular – journey, going on to explore the **Meuse valley** south of Dinant by boat or taking a canoe up the narrower (and wilder) river **Lesse**. From here, routes lead east into the heart of the Ardennes, to **Han-sur-Lesse**, surrounded by undulating hills riddled with caves, **Rochefort** – also with caves – and **St-Hubert**, to the southeast, in the middle of some of the most savage scenery of the entire region. South, **Bouillon** is similarly picturesquely sited alongside the Semois river, like so many Ardennes towns topped by an ancient citadel. Further north, **La Roche-en-Ardennes** is a rustic, hardy kind of town, renowned for its smoked ham and game and seen as something of an Ardennes capital. North of here, big, grimy **Liège** is also a gateway city, a good stopover if you've come down to the region from Maastricht in Holland, to which it's connected by hourly train, and giving easy access to the area around the long-established resort of **Spa**, a little way south. The countryside around here is among the Ardennes' highest, though it's relatively flat and is crossed by major roads. Spa itself still pulls in the crowds, but it's out of curiosity mostly, and there's little, if anything, to see aside from the pretty nearby town of **Stavelot**, with its marvellous carnival.

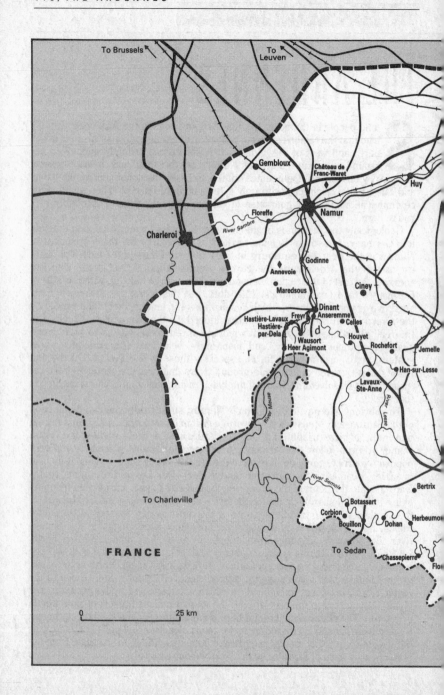

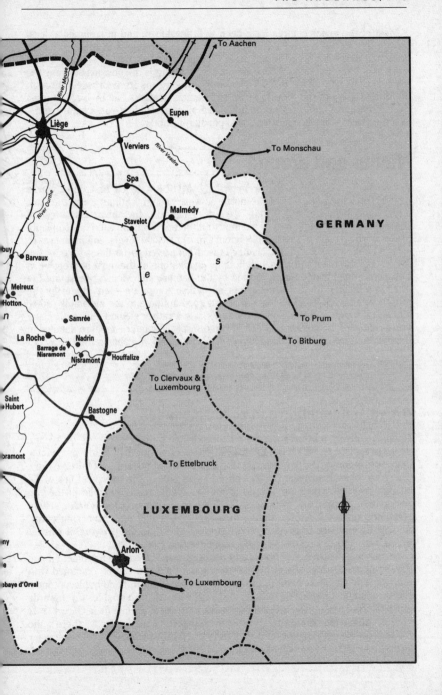

Most of the major centres have been well developed, and in summer at least resorts like La Roche and Bouillon can be full to bursting. But the crowds are never too oppressive, and in any case the appeal is less one of specific towns, more of outdoor pursuits. Wherever you are, **walking** is the obvious pastime; the really serious can follow the GR Namurois, which runs from Brussels through the three valleys of the Meuse, Lesse and Semois. **Kayaks** can be hired at most river settlements, and **mountain bikes** are often available. Cross-country and – in some places – on-piste **skiing** is also popular in winter.

Namur and around

Known as the "Gateway to the Ardennes", **NAMUR** is a logical first stop if you're heading into the region from the north or west, though without a car the dark forests and hills are still a long way off. That said, the town has a feel of somewhere refreshingly free of the industrial belt of Hainaut. There's also plenty to see in what is one of southern Belgium's most pleasant towns, and in an area of sparse public transport links, Namur is well connected to far-flung parts of the Ardennes. The town's principal sight is its citadel, one of the most impressive in Europe, wedged inside a fork formed by the Sambre and Meuse rivers, and the city has a handful of decent museums, as well as a nightlife – lent vigour by the presence of the city's university – that is a good antidote to the inevitably rather limited offerings of the region beyond. It's also a rather elegant city, with many fine old houses, a number of which, if you're especially interested, are detailed in the tourist office booklet, *Connaissance de Namur* (also available in English).

> The Namur area telephone code is ☎081

Arrival, information and accommodation

Namur's **railway station** is on the northern fringe of the city centre, on avenue de la Gare, close by which lies the **tourist office** (summer daily 9am–7pm; winter daily 9am–noon & 2–7pm; ☎22 28 59), in a chalet in square de l'Europe Unie. There are more information offices on the other side of the river, just below the citadel. Over the bridge on the tip of the "V" made by the junction of the two rivers (the *grognon* or "pig's snout"), there is an **information chalet** selling combined tickets for town sights, including the citadel and major museums. Across the car park from here, at rue Notre Dame 3, is the **provincial tourist office**, with information on the whole Namur region (☎22 29 98).

Namur has relatively few hotels and **accommodation** can be a problem if you haven't booked, especially in high season when the town can be crammed with tourists. The cheapest hotel in town is the *Queen Victoria*, handily placed opposite the station at avenue de la Gare 11–12 (☎22 29 71), with doubles for upwards of F1300. Also reasonable is the *Porte de Fer*, close by at avenue de la Gare 4 (☎22 49 65), which has rooms for a little over F1500. More centrally, there's the *L'Opera (Le Parisien)*, rue E. Cuvelier 16 (☎23 17 18) which has double rooms for as little as F1800 or as much as F3000.

The tourist office has a stock of private **rooms**, which may work out cheaper. Failing that, there's a **youth hostel** on the far edge of town at avenue F. Rops 8. ☎22 36 88), on the banks of the Meuse past the Casino. Take bus #3 or #4 from the stop opposite the station. There's no lock-out and the hostel has washing machines as well as many other facilities including a bar and decent restaurant. The nearest **campsite**, *Camping des 4 Fils Aymon*, is 10km away at chaussée de Liège 989, in the suburb of Lives-sur-Meuse (April–Sept).

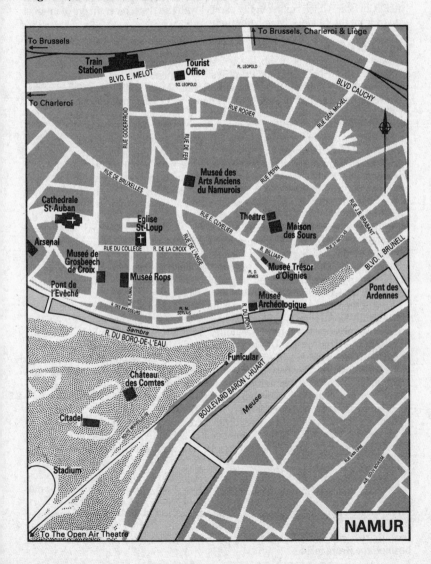

The Town

From the tourist office, rue de Fer leads south into **rue de l'Ange**, Namur's main shopping street, extending all the way down to the river Sambre, across which the **pont du Musée** connects the town centre proper with the citadel on the opposite side. The town's other main central artery, joining with the top end of rue de l'Ange, is a street variously named rue de Bruxelles, rue St-Jacques and rue E. Cuvelier, which runs roughly parallel with the river, most things of interest – apart from the citadel – lying below here.

The Town Centre

Halfway down rue de Fer, on the left at no. 24, one of the finest of Namur's mansions, the Hôtel de Gaiffier d'Hestroy, houses two of the town's best museums. One of these, the **Musée Felicien Rops** (daily 10am–5pm; closed Tues except during July & Aug; F50), is home to an important collection of work by the nineteenth-century Namur illustrator of the same name – paintings, drawings and engravings recording the development of his work. Rops settled in Paris in the 1870s, acquiring a reputation for his dabblings in the occult and debauched lifestyle and illustrating works by poets Mallarmé and Baudelaire. He was, apparently, greatly admired by the latter, but he is perhaps better known for his erotic drawings, which show an obsession with the macabre, skeletons and nuns and priests in oddly compromising poses characterising his later work. He also drew many satirical cartoons, savagely criticising the art establishment with whom he never had much of a rapport. The other museum, the **Musée des Arts du Namurois** (daily 10am–noon & 1.30–5pm; closed Tues & one week after Christmas), has displays of the work of Mosan goldsmiths and silversmiths of the eleventh to thirteenth centuries, though frankly the collections of the Oignie gallery (see below) are better. There are also wood and stone sculptures from the fourteenth to sixteenth centuries, paintings and reliquaries from the Collégiale de Walcourt, and a beautiful fourteenth-century ivory portable altarpiece.

West of the Gaiffier d'Hestroy house, on Place St-Aubain, Namur's neoclassical **Cathédrale St-Aubain** is brilliant white inside, with a triumphant, airy feel that forms a suitable backdrop to its paintings from the School of Rubens, including one from the hand of van Dyck. The attached **Musée Diocesain** (Easter–end Oct daily 10am–noon & 2.30–6pm; Nov–Easter daily 2.30–4pm; closed Mon), the cathedral treasury, displays objects from diocesan churches of Namur and Luxembourg provinces, including a golden crown reliquary with thorns from Christ's crown of thorns, a twelfth-century portable altar with eleventh-century ivory carvings, and a silver reliquary of Saint Blaise.

Walking down towards the river from here the **Musée de Groesbeeck de Croix**, at rue Saintrait 3 (daily 10am–noon & 2–5pm, visits on the hour, closed Tues), is another of Namur's luxury house museums, a luxurious Louis XV-style mansion containing seventeenth- and eighteenth-century art objects from the Namur region – clocks, marble fireplaces, furniture, ceramics and floor mosaics. A block from the river, **rue des Brasseurs** is lined with more restored seventeenth- and eighteenth-century houses – one of which was the home of Felicien Rops. In the opposite direction, on boulevard Frère Orban beside the river, the **Arsenal** was built at the end of the seventeenth century by Vauban. It was recently restored and is now a university building. You can go upstairs to see the beamed roof from inside.

Leaving place St-Aubain by way of rue du Collège, the Baroque **Église St-Loup** has a theatrical curved roof seen to best effect from the citadel; unfortunately you can no longer go inside. Further on lies perhaps Namur's most stunning museum, the **Trésor d'Oignies** (Mon–Sat 10am–noon & 2–5pm, Sun 2–5pm, closed Tues; F20), housed in the Maison des Soeurs de Notre-Dame at rue Julie Billiart 19 and administered by the nuns of the convent, most of whom speak some English. It's a unique collection consisting of examples of the exquisitely beautiful gold and silver work of the local craftsman Hugo d'Oignies, which were removed here from the abbey of Oignies in Hainaut when threatened by French revolutionary soldiers at the end of the eighteenth century. Hugo d'Oignies was the younger brother of the prior, and he produced these objects between 1230 and 1238. The Mosan gold and silver workers of the twelfth century were renowned, and form something of a transition between Romanesque and Gothic art. Hugo, for example, was open to French influences, and although he perfected Mosan decoration and techniques, he had his own unique style. He was an innovator in the art of filigree, raising the decoration from the background so that the tiny human figures and animals are seemingly suspended in space, giving depth to the narrative. He also used the technique of *niello* a lot – a black composition of sulphur or lead filling in engraved lines in the gold. Whatever his style, they're beautiful devotional pieces, most holding holy relics that were brought back from the Holy Land by one Jacques de Vitry, a Parisian ecclesiastic who joined the abbey in 1208. They are rich and elaborate pieces of work, studded with precious and semi-precious stones, and display an extraordinary level of craftsmanship, with an exquisite balance between ornament and form. The compositions themselves are lively and realistic, sometimes depicting minute hunting scenes, with animals leaping convincingly through delicate foliage, sometimes engraved with a Christian dedication, or a tiny picture of the artist offering up his art to God in worship. Other treasures on display include a Byzantine Cross, a mitre on illuminated parchment and another in gold thread.

Around the corner from the museum, the **Église Notre Dame** is a late eighteenth-century church with work by Laurent Delvaux. Close by also, by the pont du Musée, the former meat hall holds an **Archaeological Museum** (daily 10am–5pm; closed Tues), with a small, rather uninteresting display of prehistoric, Roman and later finds from the locality.

The Citadel

Across the bridge, Namur's **Citadel** (April–May & Sept 24–Oct 23 Sat & Sun only 1–5pm; June & Sept 23 daily 1–5pm; July & Aug daily 10am–6pm; F110) is, inevitably, the city's major attraction, and deservedly so, though it has only been open to the public since 1978. Namur's strategic position at the junction of the Sambre and Meuse rivers, plus the natural defence the sharp junction of the rivers afforded, led to its construction in medieval times, from which parts – those nearest the "V" – still survive. There are two main sections to the fortress: the fifteenth- and sixteenth-century Mediane constructions, which in 1640 were reinforced by the Spanish with the Terra Nova bastion. In successive centuries, the renowned military engineers Vauban and the Dutchman Coehorn further improved the structure, helping to make it into one of the most important strongholds in Europe.

The citadel is most easily accessible either by the *téléphérique* cable car (F120 return, F90 single) from the car park just over the Pont du Musée – a long and exhilarating ride – or by car, by taking route Merveilleuse from near the Casino on the Meuse bank. The entrance fee includes an audiovisual display on the history of the citadel, a miniature train ride around the grounds to see the various structures, and a guided visit of the deepest underground passages, as well as access to the fortress's museums. It's an immense complex, and you need two or three hours to cover it thoroughly. A booklet can be bought at the entrance office with the different parts of the site marked, but there are plenty of landmarks dotted around.

The main entrance leaves you in the part of the fortress known as the **Ouvrages à Cornes** – earthworks the shape of horns; turn left and walk around these to where an underground tunnel descends into the Terra Nova barracks – site of the audiovisual show and terminus of the mini-train. From here you can also visit – with a guide – the fortress's underground passages, the **Galeries Boufflers**, which extend for 300m and include a "War Office" used by Richelieu and Louis XIV. You can see the differences in the tunnels of different periods: ironically the oldest, built in typical Spanish style, are the dryest and best preserved because they were built with two layers of bricks. Of the citadel's museums, the **Musée de la Forêt** (April–Oct 9am–noon & 2–5pm) has displays pertaining to the wildlife of the Ardennes, in the shape of dioramas and the like, while the **Musée d'Armes et d'Histoire** (Easter–Sept daily 10am–6pm) has a large collection of artefacts relating to the military history of the area.

Eating and drinking

Namur has many **restaurants**. The best place to look is the area of streets around place Marché aux Legumes, especially rue Frippiers and rue de la Croix, which is packed with bistro-restaurants, several with tables outside. *Rapido Pat*, on rue du Pont, near the Archaeology Museum, serves very cheap, basic food – pasta, salads, soups, etc – and has very quick service; the *Maison de l'Ecologie* at rue Basse Marcelle 26, near the cathedral, has a wholefood shop downstairs selling snacks, and a vegetarian restaurant upstairs, *L'Allume Lune*, which is open every lunchtime except Sunday and on Friday evenings. For picnics use the shop *La Table de la Wallonie*, in rue de la Halle (off rue Brasseurs), which sells regional food.

The place Marché aux Legumes and around is also the best place to go in the **evening**. In one corner, the *Piano Bar* has live jazz Friday and Saturday evenings from about 10pm . On another corner is the *Ratin Tot*, the self-proclaimed oldest bar in town. If you're fed up with beer, go to *Les Brasseurs de la Dyle* on a corner of rue Marché; the owner of the bar has a vineyard in France.

Around Namur: Floreffe, a château, and south to Dinant

A few kilometres west of Namur, towards Charleroi, the attractively sited abbey of **FLOREFFE** is a possible stopoff on the way to or from Hainaut. Founded in 1121, little remains of the original complex – the domestic buildings are mainly eighteenth-century – but the **abbey church** is certainly worth the detour, principally for its carved oak choir stalls. The work of one man – Pierre Enderlin – who took sixteen years (1632–48) over them, they're a quite remarkable achievement, in a superb state of preservation and displaying a marvellous inventiveness and intricacy, carved with an array of figures – Biblical characters, eminent and holy persons, some 220 angels – of which each one is different. Many of the faces are obviously portraits, humorous, sometimes satirical, in tone, and include a self-portrait of the artist hidden amongst the rest. Also in the church is a wooden Virgin of Del Cour, carved in 1692, that has been the source, apparently, of many copies. It's an unusual vision of Mary, certainly, a very graceful figure, and the sculpting of her robes is extremely adept. In the restored Romanesque part of the church there is also a small museum, displaying various art objects, though since some were stolen viewing is only permitted on guided tours (10.30am, 11.30am, 1.30pm, 2.30pm, 4pm, 5pm & 6pm; F60). These are in French, but the guide speaks a little English. An audiovisual presentation also picks out the details of the stalls for you to study afterwards.

The abbey is also home to the Romanesque **Moulin Brasserie**, restored in 1972 and famous for three beers. The most distinctive, a dark, sweet ale, is sold here, though it's no longer brewed on the premises. If you're coming from or going to Charleroi by train, you can stop off at Floreffe (from the station it's a 25-minute walk), though a bus #10 from Namur bus station (8 daily) actually takes you nearer.

The Château de Franc-Waret
In the opposite direction, a short way northeast of Namur (bus #17; 5 daily), the **Château de Franc-Waret** (June–Sept Sat & Sun 2–5.30pm; F70) is another possible day excursion, a classical Louis XV building that was rebuilt in 1750 but sports two seventeenth-century towers. It houses period French and Dutch furniture, seventeenth-century Brussels tapestries and Flemish paintings.

South to Dinant
The river from Namur to Dinant is arguably the Meuse's best stretch, but even so it's too wide to be all that stunning. A boat makes the journey on Sundays but it's not a particularly good deal, and you're better off simply catching the train. On the way (and also reachable by bus from Namur – 4 daily, #21), **GODINNE** is a rather exclusive place, full of country villas, but there is a **gîte d'étape**, run by *Amis de Nature*, 6 rue Grande (☎082/61 15 36). From the pont de Godinne, you can walk over to **ANNEVOIE**, famous for its half-Classical, half-Romantic gardens in the grounds of an eighteenth-century château (April–Nov daily 9am–7pm; château F90, garden F135), created in 1775 by Charles Alexis de Montpellier. The gardens' most attractive feature are the many fountains and pools. You can also get here by bus from Dinant. Further on towards Dinant, though only accessible from Namur (also bus #21), **MAREDSOUS** has a Benedictine neo-Gothic abbey founded in 1872.

Dinant and the Meuse Valley

The centre of the Meuse valley tourist industry, **DINANT** has pretensions to being a very picturesque town, slung along the river beneath craggy green cliffs. But once here the cliffs hem in the town against the river, making it feel gloomy and oppressive, and, in summer at least, there are far too many visitors for a place of its size. There's also surprisingly little to see or do here, and although there are plenty of boat trips downriver and on the nearby Lesse (see below), transport connections to more interesting places are very limited. Basically, there are more beautiful destinations deeper in the Ardennes, and unless you're passing there's very little reason to stop.

The Town

The **Citadel**, visible from just about anywhere in town (summer daily 9.30am–6.30pm; winter daily 10am–4pm; F105 including *téléphérique*; tips expected by the guides), is the most obvious – indeed only – attraction in town, and even this is something of a letdown if you've already visited the fortress at Namur. It's reached either by way of the cable car or a flight of 400 or so steps, cut way back in 1577. The site was previously occupied by a fortified castle, but this was destroyed by the French in 1703 and the present structure was built by the Dutch from 1818 to 1821. The Germans occupied the place briefly in 1914, leading to a fierce battle during which they torched the town and executed hundreds of civilians. The Germans took the citadel again in 1940, and it was again the scene of bitter fighting in 1944 when the Allies took three days to remove them. The view from the top is good, while the inside has been turned over to what is essentially a historical museum, with models recreating particular battles and the Dutch occupation, and a military section with weapons from the Napoleonic era to the last war. You can also see the wooden beams which supported the first bridge in Dinant, built 900 years ago by monks and found again by accident in 1952, as well as prison cells and the kitchen and bakery of the Dutch stronghold.

Immediately below the citadel, Dinant's most distinctive landmark is the originally Gothic church of **Notre-Dame**, topped with the bulbous-spire which features on all the tourist brochures. There's not much to see inside – the church has been rebuilt several times – aside from a couple of paintings by Antoine Wiertz, who was born in the town.

After you've seen the church and citadel you've pretty much seen Dinant, though most people also take in the **Grotte La Merveilleuse** (April–Sept guided visits, in French and Flemish only, on the hour 10am–5pm; F140), across the bridge from the church down route de Philippeville. If you're into caves or haven't seen one before, it's worth going, although again there are better ones in the Ardennes proper (principally at Han-sur-Lesse). The caves' most unique feature is the whiteness of their rock formations.

Practical details

Dinant's train station is on the opposite side of the river to the town centre, just across the bridge by the church. The **tourist office** is on the main drag at rue Grande 37 (Mon–Fri 8.30am–12.30pm & 1–7.30pm, Sat & Sun 10am–noon & 1.30–5.30pm; ☎082/22 28 70) just before the casino. Budget **accommodation** is rather sparse. There is no hostel, although there are two **campsites** – *Camping Vilatoile*, beyond Anseremme by the Barrage de Pont-a-Lesse, and *Camping de Bouvignes sur Meuse,* 2km from the centre on the north side of town. The cheapest **hotels** are *Le Derby*, across the road from the station, and *Hostellerie Thermidor* (☎082/22 31 35), next door, which both have doubles for around F1000, and the *de L'Étoile*, rue St-Jacques 27 (☎082/22 22 60), which has doubles for F1100. The tourist office also has details of private **rooms**, although there are very few possibilities – one you might try direct is Mme Larue, 36 rue de Bonsecours (☎082/22 64 51). Opposite the *Derby*, the *Restaurant-Friterie Tour Eiffel* is popular and cheap, with good generous dishes. The most lively place in the **evening** is the *Bar Amical*, on the other side of the road from the tourist office, but don't expect too much.

The Meuse Valley

The stretches of the **Meuse** south of Dinant are not the river's most impressive, but the town's quayside is lined with leisure boats touting **cruises**. There are several different companies, each with boats leaving at different times, though the prices are the same whoever you go with. While the river is not especially picturesque, taking a boat is one way of moving on south if that's where you're headed. Destinations include Anseremme – the closest place, though it's not really worthwhile as it's cheaper and only takes a minute by train. Freyr and Heer Agimont on the French border, stopping at Waulsort and Hastière, are more rewarding trips, but even this far down the scenery is fairly tame, the river wide and gently curving.

If you actually want to have time to visit the above destinations on a day trip, you're better off getting the GIVET bus from outside Dinant station, which stops off at each of them, though you'll have to leave early in the morning to co-ordinate with the timetable. **FREYR** itself is home to an eighteenth-century château with a small but well-kept formal French-style garden. On the opposite side of the river, the sheer cliff face is used for training by climbers of the *Club Alpin* school. **WAULSOURT**, further along, also has a château, and is a resort with faded elegance and a yacht club. **HASTIÈRE** is the most interesting place to stop, a pretty village with a **gîte d'étape** (☎082/51 25 447) and a Romanesque-Gothic church over the river at **HASTIÈRE-PAR-DELÀ**. The church was built around 1035 and a Gothic choir added in the thirteenth century, though as a whole it's now much restored after destruction by Huguenots in 1568, and again by French revolutionaries two centuries later. It's a typical church of the Mosan Romanesque style, with a flat wooden roof, plain square pillars and Lombard arches, similar to the church at Celles. A faded painting on the triumphal arch dates from the original construction, but the crypt is the oldest surviving part, containing Merovingian sarcophagi. The wooden thirteenth-century stalls are about the oldest in Belgium, with original and unique carvings – some allegorical, some satirical and mocking – a number of which were, in 1443, replaced with a plain triangle since they were considered too disrespectful. An unusual German fifteenth-century calvary hangs above the altar, Christ, Mary and Saint John standing on a dragon. Near the baptismal font is a beautiful sixteenth-century statue of the Virgin, whose graceful posture has earned it a place in several national exhibitions.

The Lesse Valley

Exploring the valley of the **river Lesse**, which spears off the Meuse a little way south of Dinant, is perhaps the most exciting thing you can do in the area around the town – something most people do in reverse order travelling back upriver from Houyet by kayak. Three companies run trips, and again prices and options are fairly uniform, the standard trip beginning at Anseremme, where you buy a ticket and take a special morning bus to Houyet, where trips start; there are also trains (at 8.40am, 9.40am and 10.40am). Some companies have lockers and changing rooms at Anseremme, others at Houyet. From Houyet to Anseremme by kayak is 21km and takes about five hours. There are boats for one or two and also large steered "barges" for those who don't feel up to canoeing. There are places to stop for lunch along the way. Groups, by reservation, may leave from Gendron, from where the trip takes about two and a half hours.

The course is wild and winding, with great scenery, though be warned that sometimes it gets so packed there's a veritable traffic jam of kayaks. Get to Anseremme/Houyet as early as possible if you want to enjoy the river peacefully. For prior reservations ring ☎082/22 61 86 or ☎082/22 23 25 — though it's not usually necessary.

Halfway along to Anseremme you pass beneath the **Parc National de Furfooz**, (mid-March to mid-Nov daily 10am–two hours before sunset; F70), scenically the best part of the trip. Occupying a cliff promontory overlooking the Lesse, it's not a large park, and you should allow around ninety minutes to tour its marked circuit of three and a half kilometres. There's not actually a great deal to see, but a scattering of archaeological remains and geological formations give purpose to what is a pleasant walk – no more. There are reconstructed Roman baths, from where you can walk up to a high ridge overlooking the river. There are also foundations of an originally Roman fortress, converted in the Middle Ages and used many times since.

You can also visit the park by train from Dinant. Get off at Gendron-Celles (10min), turn left out of the station, make a sharp left before the bridge into the campsite and then a sharp right under the bridge. A path goes alongside the river for about twenty minutes to the park entrance (car drivers should use another signed entrance on the other side of the park).

From Gendron-Celles station it's a four-kilometre walk in the opposite direction to **CELLES**, where there's another Romanesque church, the **Église St-Hadelin**, with a huge tower and Lombard arches on the outside. Its thirteenth-century stalls are the oldest in the country along with those of Hastière-par-delà (see above).

At Houyet there's a **campsite** (☎082/66 61 00) and bikes can be hired from *La Bascule* (☎082/66 71 33). You can also make a kayak trip on another part of the river, up from Wanlin *to* Houyet. If you want to go to a more southern part of the Ardennes, the train from Dinant through Gendron-Celles and Houyet goes on to Bertrix and from there a bus goes to Libramont, a main train junction, with regular connections to Luxembourg, Namur and Virton.

Han, Rochefort and St-Hubert

A little way beyond the source of the Lesse river, to the south, lies one of the Ardennes' most beautiful regions, centring on the tourist resort of Han-sur-Lesse. It's a lovely area, but access is difficult from Dinant, and it's in fact easier to go back to Namur and take the train to Jemelle (direction Luxembourg), the nearest large train junction; trains also go to Jemelle from Libramont, Liège and Arlon. There are real crowd-pullers like the Han-sur-Lesse caves, the most spectacular in the country, and the odd castle, and the surrounding countryside is perfect for cycling.

As for **transport** in the area itself, apart from bikes, there are buses between Rochefort, Lessive and Han. There is also something called the GLT – **Guided Light Transit** – a tram/train/bus which automatically switches from electric to diesel as it travels between Jemelle station, Rochefort (stopping at the Cultural Centre), Han and the RTT at Lessive (see over). It's more expensive than a normal bus – 100F a head – but is, at least, environmentally sound. The GLT runs five times daily during the June to mid-September period and at weekends until October 2. The first one leaves Jemelle station at 10am, the last arrives back at

6.30pm. In July and August a special **tourist train** operates twice a day from Rochefort to Lavaux-Ste-Anne – a one-hour journey. It stops at Han and the RTT at Lessive but you must begin the journey from Rochefort. The adult fare is F120; details from Rochefort tourist office.

Han-sur-Lesse

Situated in the midst of some lovely countryside, **HAN-SUR-LESSE**, some 40km southeast of Dinant, is as good a centre for exploring the Ardennes as you'll find. It's not a particularly attractive place, but there's a youth hostel here, you can hire bikes, and it's well connected with the train station at Jemelle (where, incidentally, you can also hire bikes). It's best known for its caves, which are the most impressive in the Ardennes, and consequently it is in summer chock-a-block with tourists. But there are masses of hotels and, despite the small size of the town, it seems to absorb its visitors quite successfully.

Caves and Town

There's not much to actually see in Han apart from the **Grottes de Han** themselves, located outside the village a little way downriver (Easter–Aug trips daily every half-hour 9.30–11.30am & 1–5.30pm, 6pm in July & Aug; Sept & Oct daily every hour 9.30–11.30am & 1–5pm; Nov–Easter daily every 2 hours 9.30am–3.30pm, closed Jan & Feb; guided tours in English; F230). Not surprisingly there are enormous queues most of the time, and for the visit and return journey from the town (you're taken by special bus), you should allow about two hours; you return by special boat up the Lesse. The caves were discovered at the beginning of the nineteenth century, and measure about 8km in total, a series of limestone galleries carved out of the hills by the river Lesse millions of years ago. Tours only visit a small part of the total extent, taking in the so-called Salle du Trophée, site of the largest stalagmite, the Salle d'Armes, where the Lesse reappears after travelling underground for 1000m (it enters at the Belveux Gap), and the massive Salle du Dome – 145m long and 20m high – part of which holds a small lake.

To understand how the caves have formed, go to the **Musée du Monde Souterrain** (April to mid-Oct 10am–12.30pm & 1.30–6pm; F40) back in town at place Theo Lannoy 3, behind the tourist office, a section of which explains the process. Also in the museum are the findings of archaeological digs in the region – most was found where the Lesse surfaces again after travelling through the grottoes – among them flints, tools and bone ornaments from the neolithic period, as well as brilliant weapons and jewellery from the Bronze Age. Han's other attraction is a **wild animal reserve** (same hours as the caves; F150) just outside the town, an area of 620 acres containing animals which inhabited the Ardennes in prehistoric times – bison, bears and auroch (ancestor of present-day cattle), along with deer and wild boar. A special bus takes you round the area to seek them out, the whole thing lasting about an hour and a half. A combined ticket with the caves makes it cheaper.

Practical details

The cheapest place to stay in Han is the (unofficial) **youth hostel** at the far end of rue Gîte d'Étape (☎084/37 74 41; daily closed 10am–5pm), a friendly place that charges F190 a night, F70 for breakfast, F175 for a hot evening meal. There are two **campsites**, both by the river's edge: *Camping Le Pirot* (close to which you can hire kayaks) and *Camping de la Lesse*. Of the town's **hotels**, *Hôtel du Luxembourg*, rue d'Hamptay 61 (☎084/37 73 01), behind the caves office, is by far the cheapest, with some rooms going for as little as F750. The *Relais du Parc*, on rue Joseph Lamotte (☎084/37 70 72), charges F1200 for a double, F1500 a triple. *Hotel Henry IV*, on rue des Chasseurs Ardennais (☎084/37 72 21), has doubles for F1200. There are so many places to eat reasonably (though not wonderfully), there's little point in listing any here – though expect inflated prices pretty much everywhere.

Apart from the caves, Han has plenty of recreational amenities – tennis courts, *pétanque* lawns, and kayaks for hire. The **tourist office**, in a chalet opposite the caves office in the main street (daily 10am–5pm; ☎084/37 75 96), has a cycle tour leaflet *En Lesse et l'Homme* (40F), and a guide detailing walks in the area. **Kayaks** are available in the centre of town (☎084/37 72 30), and one possible trip is by boat to Lessive, returning by bike, a journey of two hours in all. You can hire boats between 10am and 6pm (last start at 4pm) and for a kayak and bike it costs around F500 for a two-seater, F350 for a one-seater (bike or tandem available). If you want to hire a **bike** independently, you can do so from the same place, by the hour, half-day or whole day. **Mountain bikes** can be hired from an office at the other end of town, *VTT*, at 19 rue des Grottes, opposite the *Hotel Central*: Costs are F150 an hour, F650 for a day, F1100 for a weekend.

Lessive and Lavaux-Ste-Anne

Five kilometres northwest of Han, **LESSIVE** is home to the Belgian space and satellite station or **RTT** (May–Sept daily 9.30am–5.30pm; F70; 1hr guided visit available). Topped with three huge antennae, it's something of a local tourist attraction, built here in a sheltered valley, far from wind and phone interference, and because the schist soil is very stable. Here they both broadcast TV programmes and receive and transmit information by satellite. There's an exhibition dedicated to its advanced technology and a museum demonstrating the first telephone and telegram services. You can also try out a video telephone.

A little way west of the centre, **LAVAUX-STE-ANNE** is home to an originally fourteenth-century **château** (daily 9am–noon & 1–6pm), surrrounded by a moat, with three fifteenth-century towers and one from the fourteenth century. The exterior has a medieval appearance and Renaissance buildings surround the sturdy interior courtyard. Inside, there's a **Museum of Nature and Hunting** and a **Museum of the Countryside and Folklore** – neither exactly vital stops, but a reasonable detour if you're in the area.

Rochefort and St-Hubert

The nearby town of **ROCHEFORT** is almost as popular a tourist centre as Han, home to the well-known Trappist beer and another **grotto** (Easter to mid-Sept 9.30am–5pm; F120), a colder and wilder affair than that of Han, though similar in type, with very large chambers. First discovered in 1865, its huge Salle du Sabbat is some 85m high. Close by the grotto is a feudal **castle**, transformed in the eighteenth century (visits 10am, 11am, 2pm, 3pm, 4pm & 5pm), but aside from that there's nothing much to see in the town. The **tourist office** at rue de Behogne 5 (☎084/21 25 37) has information on the town and details of accommodation possibilities.

ST-HUBERT, about 20km south of Rochefort, is another popular Ardennes resort, named after the patron saint of hunters who is said to have undergone his conversion in the woods nearby, afterwards becoming a monk at Stavelot abbey. Later, in the seventh century, an abbey was founded here, giving its name to the town that grew up around – these days one of the most remote of the Ardennes settlements, deep in the heart of one of the most thickly forested sections of the region. It's still a popular hunting centre, and a great base for some gentle hiking, though again the town itself is nothing to write home about. Its church, the **Basilique St-Hubert**, is a mid-sixteenth-century Flamboyant Gothic structure, parts of which (the crypt, for example) date back to the eleventh century. The interior is mainly eighteenth-century in style, the choir stalls illustrating the story of Saint Hubert, while nearby the retable has 24 Limoges enamels of 1560.

Outside the town is another wild animal park, **Parc à Gibier**, 2km to the north. Further north still (though easily within walking or cycling distance of the town), **Fourneau St-Michel** is a centre for ironworking, with an old forge and a museum showing old tools and the like. Close by there's a **Musée de la Vie Rurale en Wallonie** (Easter–Sept daily 9am–5pm), an open-air museum not unlike some of those you might have seen in Holland, with reconstructions of typical Walloon rural buildings set out by type.

The nearest **train station** to St-Hubert is at Poix-St-Hubert, from where you can either take a bus or hire a bike to the town, 5km away; there are also sporadic buses to Poix-St-Hubert from Libramont 15km south. In the town, the **tourist office** is at rue de la Liberté 18 (June–Sept daily 9.30am–noon & 1.30–5pm; ☎061/ 61 30 10) and has maps and copious information on walking routes in the surrounding district.

Southern Luxembourg Province: Bouillon, Orval and Arlon

Forty-odd kilometres southwest of St-Hubert, close to the French border, **BOUILLON** is a well-known holiday centre on the edge of the Ardennes, enclosed inside a loop of the Semois river and crowned by an outstanding castle. It's a relaxed and peaceful place, with a holiday feel about it, and it gives easy access to some lovely walking in the countryside around, which is gentler than that further north, but no less appealing for that.

The Town

The most distinctive feature of Bouillon is its **castle** (March, Oct & Nov daily 10am–5pm; April–June & Sept daily 10am–6pm; July & Aug daily 9.30am–7pm; F100 or combined ticket with musems F150), set up on a ridge which runs the length of the town. Access is from a road behind (rue du Château), or by a set of steep steps which climb up from rue du Moulin – the town's main street. The castle was originally held by a succession of independent counts who controlled most of the land around Bouillon. There were five of these, all called Godfrey, the fifth and last of which left on the First Crusade in 1096, selling his dominions (partly to raise the cash for his trip) to the prince-bishop of Liège. Later on, the castle was confiscated by Louis XIV, and Vauban, his military architect, was charged with modifying it – the results of which are in the main what you see now. It's an intriguing old place, and visits wind through most of its courtyards, along the battlements and towers, and through dungeons filled with weaponry and instruments of torture. A leaflet in English describes the various parts of the structure. The Salle Godefroy, hewn out of the rock and named after the Crusader leader, contains a statue of the last ruler of Bouillon and an ancient wooden cross in the floor that was only discovered in 1962. The so-called Chair of Godfrey is a lookout, also cut out of solid rock, and one of the oldest parts of the castle.

Down the ridge from the castle, the **Musée Ducal** (April, June, Sept & Oct daily 9.30am–5.30pm; July & Aug daily 9am–6.30pm; F80) displays material pertaining to Godfrey's crusades, most notably Eastern art (Byzantine ivory carvings, gold lacquer plates) and medieval items from various local churches, among them Limoges enamels from the thirteenth century. There's also a section of the museum concentrating on the folklore and history of the town and region, a tape recording guiding you from room to room and talking you through the exhibits, which range from a model of the town in 1690 to various period rooms – a weaving room, another devoted to hunting, etc.

Bouillon's **tourist office** is based at the ticket office of the castle (☎061/46 62 570), and in summer there's also an **information chalet** – Pavilion du Tourisme – (daily 10am–12.30pm & 1.30–7pm; ☎061/46 62 89) on the town side of the Porte de France (by the pont de France). For **accommodation**, there's a brand new **youth hostel** at Chemin du Christ 16, on the opposite hill from the castle (☎061/46 81 37); for a short cut, take the steps up from place St-Arnold, just across the pont de Liège, which lead there direct. There are a few rooms to let in **private homes**, details of which you can get from the tourist office; failing that, try Mme Gobin-Pierson, Vieille route de France 27 (☎061/46 72 13), or Mme Tussaint, Quai des Remparts (☎061/46 62 06). There are also a fair number of **hotels**, of which the *Central Duc de Bouillon*, rue des Hautes Voies 2–4, up the hill from the pont de Liège (☎061/46 63 20), is one of the cheapest, with double rooms for about F1000 – as is *La Tannerie*, on the waterfront near the pont de Liège at quai de la Tannerie 1 (☎061/46 62 27), a hotel-restaurant with rooms for F1000 and cheap menus too. *Hôtel au Vieux Moulin*, on porte de France (☎061/46 62 66), has rooms for around F1500, or, slightly cheaper, there's the nearby *Hôtel de France*, Faubourg de France (☎061/46 60 68), with doubles for F1400–1600. The nearest **campsite** is the *Halliru*, next to the river, just south of the town on the route de Corbion (April–Sept) – an easily walkable distance. There's a second campsite, *Moulin de la Falize*, at Vieille route de France 33, which is well-equipped with a restaurant, swimming pool, tennis courts, etc, and cross-country skiing in winter.

As for **eating**, you can either use the *Tannerie* restaurant (see above), or there's a pizzeria/taverna near place St-Arnould by the pont Liège. For **picnic food**, go to the *Unic* supermarket just next to the Porte de France on the river front. **Kayaks** can be hired from *Les Tritons* (☎061/46 63 91) on the Quai des Saulx near the Pont de Liège. The riverscape is gentle and sleepy, the Semois slow-moving and meandering; what's more you don't get the kind of canoe traffic jams that occur around, say, Dinant. **Bikes** can be hired from a Fiat garage a kilometre outside of town, although to enjoy the best of the scenery you should really be on foot . . .

On from Bouillon: some walking routes

The tourist office sells decent walking maps – *Cartes de Promenades de Grand Bouillon* – with many marked routes, though you shouldn't follow these too slavishly. As long as you have a map and can see where paths exist, you can improvise as you go along. One of the better marked routes is **Route 13**, which runs along the river edge, turning left out of the Porte de France and ascending for a great view over the valley from the **Rocher du Pendu** (Hanged Man's Rock). You can also simply carry on along the riverbank, though be warned that points that are sometimes marked as river crossings on the map can be no more than boulders or stepping stones, and may be difficult or even non-existent if the river is high (Moulin de l'Epine and one near the Tombeau du Géant are two like this). Whichever way you decide to go, a good place to make for is the village of **CORBION**, 4km west cross-country – nothing special in itself but with a campsite (on the Bouillon road), hotels and shops. If you've got time and energy, carry on to the village of **POUPEHAN**, which also has hotels and campsites. A great walk from here is the "tongue" of land you can see jutting out from Corbion on the map.

On the other side of the river, a nice walk is to the **Moulin de l'Epine** (where there's a café-restaurant), following the river from Bouillon. From there the high Route 93 offers a great view of the **Tombeau du Géant**, a conical land mass in a river loop. You could carry on to the village of BOTASSART. In the other direction from Bouillon, DOHAN (with a campsite) and BÛHAN are destinations for full-day walks.

South east of Bouillon, **Chiny**, **Chassepierre** and **Florenville** are promoted as tourist centres but the countryside is flatter, and although there are pretty corners, you need a car to find them. Of the three villages, **CHASSEPIERRE** is the prettiest (bus from Bouillon during the week only, 9.15am, returning 4.15pm). There's also a **youth hostel** (April–Oct) and **campsite** in the mountain village of **HERBEUMONT**, between Bouillon and Chiny, a tiny place with castle ruins and a twelfth-century church. The hostel's at rue de la Hulette 80 (☎061/41 13 68).

Virton and Orval

The area beyond Chiny and Herbeumont is known as the **Gaume**, effectively an extension of the Ardennes, hilly and thickly wooded, but less purely French-speaking, the region's closeness to the Luxembourg border being reflected in the local dialect. **VIRTON**, the main town, a minor stop on the railway line from Libramont, has a museum devoted to the customs and archaeology of the area, the **Musée Gaumais** (April–All Saints' Day daily 9.30am–noon & 2–6pm; F30), with ancient finds, art, religious sculpture, local ironwork (a regional speciality) and reconstructions of interiors. But otherwise the chief sight is the **Abbaye d'Orval**, 10km back towards Bouillon (Easter–Sept daily except Mon 9am–12.30pm & 1.30–6.30pm; rest of year daily except Mon 10am–12.30pm & 1.30–5pm; July & Aug, and weekends to end Sept, free guided tours; F60). Orval is a place of legendary beginnings. It was founded, the story goes, when Countess Mathilda of Tuscany lost a gold ring in a lake and a fish recovered it for her, prompting the countess to donate the land around to God for the construction of a monastery. A fish with a golden ring is still the emblem of the monastery, and can be seen gracing the bottles of beer for which the abbey is these days best known.

It's worth a visit if you've got transport, but is otherwise a tedious pilgrimage. Buses run from nearby Florenville, the nearest town on the rail network, but they're not at all frequent and you may find yourself having to change a lot. Bear in mind also that the abbey is by no means as complete or untouched as it might be. Originally a Benedictine structure, then Cistercian, it has always been first and foremost a working community, making beer, cheese and bread, but of the original twelfth- to thirteenth-century buildings, only the Romanesque-Gothic church of Notre-Dame is left, with its rose window and Romanesque capitals in the nave and transept. The rest was rebuilt in the eighteenth century to a design by Dewez, but most of this too was destroyed in the French Revolution, and the abbey was left abandoned until 1926, when the Trappist order acquired the property and built on the site to the seventeenth-century plans, creating an imposing new complex, complete with a monumental statue of the Virgin. You can wander around the ruins, but most of the new buildings are closed to the public, and the only part you can visit is the eighteenth-century cellars – all that is left of the buildings by Dewez – complete with a model of how the abbey looked in 1760.

Arlon

The chief town of Luxembourg province, **ARLON** is one of the oldest towns in Belgium, a trading centre for the Romans as far back as the second century AD. These days it's fairly undistinguished, a small, rather provincial place that has nothing in particular worth seeing, and is more a useful place to change trains or break a journey. There are some vestiges of the Roman period dotted around town, but none are especially exciting. There's a third-century Roman tower, the **Tour Romain**, part of the ramparts, on the corner of the Grand Place; ask for the keys from the bar next door (closed Sun and Mon; F10). Once decorated with reliefs, most have since found their way to the town museum, though there is one left, representing Neptune – climb down the iron ladder for a look. There are also some first-century **Thermes Romains** behind the old cemetery – though only the foundations remain and mental reconstruction demands a lot of imagination. If you're at all interested in the town's Roman era, it's better to head straight for the **Musée Luxembourgeois** in rue des Martyrs (Mon–Sat 9am–noon & 2–5pm; mid-June to mid-Sept daily 10am–noon & 2–5pm; F50), which holds the rest of the bas-reliefs from the tower and an outstanding collection of Gallo-Roman stones and sculptures from the town and region, some of which are wonderfully evocative of daily life during Roman times.

Arlon's **tourist office** is in place Leopold (Mon–Fri 8am–noon & 1–5pm, Sat & Sun 8am–noon; ☎063/21 63 60), and has maps and information on the town and accommodation, though a stay isn't recommended. If you do find yourself stuck, there are four **hotels**, cheapest of which is the *Hôtel des Druides*, rue de Neufchâteau 106–108 (☎063/22 04 89), which has double rooms for about F1300. But really you'd be better off crossing the border and putting up in Luxembourg city – no more expensive and only fifteen minutes away by fast train.

Bastogne

Immediately north of Arlon is the important road and rail junction of **BASTOGNE**, best-known for its heroic defence by the Americans in December 1944, who held out here against heavy bombardment from the surrounding

---

THE BATTLE OF THE BULGE

Though there's not a lot to see now beyond parked tanks and the odd war memorial, the Ardennes was the site of some of World War II's fiercest fighting during the **Battle of the Bulge**. The Allied campaign of the autumn of 1944 had concentrated on striking into Germany from Maastricht in the north and Alsace in the south, leaving a central section of lightly defended front line extending across the Ardennes from Malmédy to Luxembourg. In December 1944, Hitler embarked on a desperate plan to change the course of the war by breaking through this part of the front, seizing Antwerp and forcing the Allies to retreat. In command of the operation was one of his best generals, Von Rundstedt, who hoped to benefit from the wintery weather conditions which would limit Allied aircraft activity. Carefully prepared, Von Rundstedt's offensive began on December 16, 1944, and one week later had created a "bulge" in the Allied line that reached the outskirts of Dinant – though the American 101st Airborne Division held firm around Bastogne. The success of the operation depended on rapid results, however, and Von Rundstedt's inability to reach Antwerp meant failure. Montgomery's forces from the north and Patton's from the south launched a counter-attack, and by the end of January the Germans had been forced back to their original position.

Germans. A key engagement of the Battle of the Bulge (see above), the American commander in chief's response to the German demand for surrender – "Nuts!" – is one of the more quotable, if apocryphal, of World War II rallying cries. Otherwise there's not much to Bastogne, though, like Arlon to the south, it's a major stopping place for Luxembourg–Brussels trains. Don't, however, get stuck here if you can help it.

Not surprisingly the town and its surrounds are full of reminders of the battle. The main square is known as **place Macauliffe** and is the site of an American tank and a bust of the general. The story of the battle is told at the star-shaped **American Memorial**, about 2km outside Bastogne to the northeast, next door to which the **Bastogne Historical Center** (mid-Feb to May & Sept 9am–6pm; June–Aug daily 8.30am–6.30pm; Oct & Nov 10am–5pm) has film of the proceedings, collection of uniforms, vehicles, etc.

Northern Luxembourg Province: La Roche and around

The unofficial capital of the Ardennes, around 25km northeast of St-Hubert, **LA ROCHE-EN-ARDENNE** is amazingly picturesque, hidden by pressing hills until you're right upon it and topped by romantic castle ruins. It's a strange mixture: a hideaway place, geographically cut off from the rest of the world, yet it teems with people during summer, fulfilling its role as one of the region's major resorts. It is, however, surrounded by some of the wildest scenery in the Ardennes, and also has – by Ardennes standards – an animated night scene, with plenty of bars and late-opening restaurants.

The centre of La Roche squeezes into one bend in the river, its high street, winding between the two bridges, an unashamedly exploitative stretch of shops flogging Ardennes ham and camping gear. That, however, is about it as far as development goes, and the streets around are unspoilt and quiet. The only tangible thing to see is the grass-carpeted **castle** (daily 10am–noon & 2–5pm; F30), construction of which began in the ninth century and continued over 400 years. It was destroyed in the late eighteenth century and remains in ruins. To get there take the steps that lead up from the high street.

Once you've seen the castle, get out to the countryside and walk or canoe. It's possible to hire **kayaks** from *Zimmer Sports* opposite the church. The most scenic stretch on the river is from the Barrage de Nisramont, southeast of the town, and back to La Roche. Trips begin at 9am, stop for lunch at Mâboge and arrive back at 4pm. You can also hire **bikes** from M. Hennebert, place du Bronze, or from the *l'Escale* hotel on quai Gravier, but the area's very hilly – you're better off with a **mountain bike** (also from *l'Escale*). In winter there's cross-country skiing at nearby Samrée. You can buy a combined walking and cycling map (*Carte des Promenades Pedestres et Circuits Cyclotouristes*) from the tourist office in the high street (see below), who can also tell you about the guided walks that are arranged every Tuesday and Wednesday in July and August.

The **tourist office** is a little way down the main street on the left (daily 10am–noon & 2–6pm; ☎084/41 13 42) and has maps and booklets on the town and details of accommodation possibilities. There are loads of **places to stay**, but booking is advisable in season. The cheapest **hotel** is the *Royal*, rue de la Gare 1 (☎084/41 11 11), which has rooms for around F800 a double; there's also the *Luxembourg*, avenue du Hadja 1a (☎084/41 14 15), which charges F1000 a double, as does the *Hotel de Liège*, rue de la Gare 16 (☎084/41 11 64). The tourist office also has details of private **rooms**, among them ones at rue Clerue 24 (☎084/41 13 83), rue Châmont 18 (☎084/41 13 23), and rue du Chalet 47 and 35 (☎084/41 11 89 and 41 11 04). There are no less than ten **campsites** in the vicinity, most packed with caravans. Among the closest are *Camping de l'Ourthe* below Harzé, *Le Gourmet*, *Le Grillon* and *Benelux* – all in rue de Harzé, by the Ourthe.

There are lots of **restaurants** to choose from in the evening, mostly along the main street and around the car park-cum-main square at the southern entrance to the town centre. One of the best, *La Sapinière*, is just off here at rue Nulay 4 – great value classic Belgian country food: try the soup.

Around La Roche: some walks ... and moving on

Scenically, the most dramatic thickly forested countryside is southeast of La Roche, in the steep valley of the winding Ourthe. Near the village of **NADRIN**, in an area known as **Le Hérou** (reachable by way of the twice daily bus to Houffalize), is a belvedere from which you can see the Ourthe at six different points due to its looping course in and out of the tightly packed hills. There's another belvedere at **NISRAMONT**, from which you also get a good view over the river's dam. Carrying on to Houffalize you can pick up GR path #57, which follows the Ourthe right up to Liège – though the stretches north of La Roche are less spectacular. There are **campsites** at both Nadrin and Houffalize.

If you want a shorter walk, the route to BEAUSAINT, in open country and along hilltops, is easy. For a full day's walk the most varied is the one towards Mâboge, part through woods, part high up and in the open.

Moving on from La Roche, two or three buses a day go to MARLOIE, from where you can get a train to the busy junction of Libramont. Buses also run to Houffalize and MELREUX (6 daily), from where you can pick up trains to Jemelle and Liège. Nearby, **HOTTON** is an attractive small town on the Ourthe, with beautiful **grottoes** outside town. Two and a half kilometres from Melreux station (you can hire bikes there) is an *Auberge des Amis de la Nature* at route de Durbuy 140 (☎084/46 62 93). A little further north, also on the Ourthe, **DURBUY** is also very pleasant, a tranquil place with forest all around – reachable by taking a train to BARVAUX, 4km away. There are **campsites** at Barvaux, Durbuy and Melreux.

Huy

Midway between Namur and Liège, and easily accessible by train, **HUY** spreads across both sides of the Meuse – aside from Liège, the major centre of the northern Ardennes, and worth a stop even if you're only passing through on the way to Liège.

Most sights are on the opposite side of the river to the train station, principally the **Collégiale Notre-Dame**, an imposing Gothic church which occupies a prime site right by the water. Built between 1311 and 1536, it's a superb example of the style, its rose window – restored in 1973 – a dazzling conglomeration of reds and blues, the choir a huge structure, occupying a third of the total nave and cut with slender twenty-metre-high stained-glass windows. On the right side of the nave as you enter, stairs lead down to a Romanesque crypt of 1066, where the relics of Huy's patron saint, Saint Domitian, were once worshipped. His original twelfth-century shrine stands upstairs in the treasury under the rose window, along with three other large shrines from the twelfth and thirteenth centuries, crafted by the Mosan gold and silversmiths for which Huy was once famous – they're rather shabby affairs, but the beauty and skill of their execution still shines through.

On leaving the church, walk down the alleyway to the side which leads to the **Porte de Bethléhem**, above which is a mid-fourteenth-century central ogival arch decorated with scenes of the nativity. It's a short walk from here to the nominal centre of town at the **Grand Place**, with its bronze fountain of 1406 showing a representation of the town walls and surmounted by statues of the same saints commemorated in the church. The wrought-iron and stone vats were added in the eighteenth century. The square is flanked on the far side by the solid-looking eighteenth-century **Hôtel de Ville**, behind which place Verte gives way to rue des Frères Mineurs, on the corner of which (with rue de la Cloche) is the oldest house in Huy, the **Maison de la Tour** – an example of Gothic civil architecture of the late twelfth century, due to be restored.

At the top of rue des Frères Mineurs, the cloistered former monastery of the same name – late-seventeenth-century – houses the varied exhibits of the **Musée Communal** (April to mid-Oct Mon–Sat 2–6pm, Sun 10am–noon & 2–6pm; F30). There are old wine-making instruments, including a winepress of 1719 – wine was a major industry here from the seventh to the sixteenth centuries – alongside items of daily life, reconstructions of period rooms, and displays of ceramics, coins and religious paintings. The prize exhibit is a 1240 oak sculpture of Christ on the Cross, called the *Beau Dieu de Huy*, a typical Mosan thirteenth-century sculpture.

The last one of Huy's sights worth taking in is its **Citadel** (Easter–Sept daily 10am–6pm, until 7pm in July & Aug), accessible on foot by following chaussée Napoléon from the Quai de Namur and taking the path up to the left before the bridge, or by way of a cable car from avenue Batta on the other side of the river – cross over the pont Roi Badouin and turn left down the riverside Quai du Halage

438/THE ARDENNES

(F100 return). Huy's citadel is not actually all that old. Built in the early nineteenth century by the Dutch, the Nazis used it as a prison during World War II,
and it's now a kind of museum of that conflict, with prisoners' cells and the
Gestapo questioning room. You can carry on in the cable car to the Sarte plateau,
which gives good views over the top of the fort.

Practical details

Huy's **train station** is a short walk from the town centre on place Z. Gramme; walk
up rue des Jardins or the parallel avenue Albert 1 until you hit rue St-Pierre and
chaussée de Liège, where you should turn right on to place St-Germain and then
turn left. The **tourist office** is across the bridge on Quai de Namur (daily 10am–
6pm; ☎085/ 21 29 15). If you want to stay, the cheapest hotels are the *Renaissance*,
rue des Soeurs Grises 16–18 (☎085/21 28 45), and the *De La Collégiale* at rue de la
Collègiale 5 (☎085/23 06 11), both of which have doubles for just under F1000.
The *Hôtel du Fort*, at chaussée Napoleon 5–6 (☎085/23 04 04), is also not expensive at around F1500. There is an official **youth hostel** 3km out of town – next to a
campsite (April–end Sept) – at rue de la Paix 3 in nearby TIHANGE (☎085/23 10
51), though it's only open during the Easter holidays and in July and August.

Liège and around

Though the effective capital of the Ardennes, and of its own province, **LIÈGE** isn't
the most obvious stop on most travellers' itineraries. It's a large, grimy, industrial
city, with few notable sights and little immediate appeal. However, if you're heading down this way from Holland it is hard to avoid – trains on both routes to
Luxembourg, for example, pass through the city – and once you've got to grips
with its size, Liège even has a few surprises up its sleeve. Certainly, if you're over-
nighting, you'd be well advised to give it at least half a day before moving on.

Liège was actually independent for much of its history, from the tenth century
onward the seat of a line of so-called prince-bishops, who held sway here for
around 800 years. The last prince-bishop was expelled in 1794 by soldiers of revolutionary France, who also torched the cathedral, and Liège was later incorporated into the Belgian state, rising to prominence as an industrial city. The coal
and steel industries here actually date back to the twelfth century, but it was only
with the nineteenth century that real development of the city's position and natural resources took place – not least under one Charles Cockerill, a British entre-
preneur whose name you still see around town. However, the heavy industry
Cockerill bequeathed has been decimated of late, and the city is ringed by the
decaying remnants of industrial glories long past.

Arrival, information and accommodation

You're most likely to arrive in Liège at **Gare de Guillemins**, about 2km south of
the city centre. At the station there's a small information office where you can
pick up city maps, hotel lists, etc, though for more complete **information**, you're
best off going to the main **tourist office** at Feronstrée 92 (Mon–Fri 10am–6pm,

The Liège area telephone code is ☎041

Sat & Sun 10am–4pm; ☎22 24 56), where they also have maps and can advise on accommodation. There's also a **provincial tourist office** in the centre of town at Boulevard de la Sauvenière 77 (Mon–Sat 8.30am–6pm; ☎22 42 10), though they're not particularly helpful. All trains stop at the Guillemins station, but Liège also has two other stations – **Palais**, on rue de Bruxelles near place St-Lambert, and **Jonfosse**, on rue Stefany, not far from Boulevard de la Sauvenière – which handle local trains and connections to Verviers and Eupen to the east, Tournai, Mons and Charleroi in the west.

To get to the centre from the station, take bus #1 or #4 to place St-Lambert; the journey by taxi costs around F200. In general, **getting around** is most easily done on foot in the city centre, which is reasonably compact. However, Liège is a big, sprawling place, and to get from one side of town to the other, or to make a quick short hop, you'll need to take a **bus**. Tickets cost F30 for a journey of any length, either from the driver or one of the ticket booths located at major bus terminals like place St-Lambert, place de la Cathédrale or the railway station. These booths also sell eight-ride tickets for around F150, or tickets valid for 24 hours for F140.

Liège's low ranking as a tourist destination means it has relatively few **hotels**, but this also means they're rarely full, especially at weekends; the bulk of the city's visitors are businesspeople and some hotels even close up completely at weekends. The most economical choices are around the railway station, either on the station square itself or up rue des Guillemins. The *Couronne*, dead opposite the station (☎52 28 04), has doubles from F1500, not including breakfast; the *Univers*, on the corner of rue des Guillemins (☎52 21 68), has doubles from F1380, also not including breakfast, and three-bedded rooms too. You might also try the *Metropole*, at rue des Guillemins 141 (☎52 42 93), which is slightly cheaper at upwards of F1250 for a double. Slightly closer to the centre, the *Cygne d'Argent*, at rue Beekman 49 (☎23 70 01), has double rooms for F1400 up. For tighter budgets, the **Foyer Internationale des Etudiants**, on rue du Vertbois, near the church of St-Jacques, has dormitory beds for F150 per person, individual rooms for about F350 a head, though there's a three-night minimum stay and the place is a dump. The nearest youth hostel is 6km south of the city in TILFF (☎88 21 00), reachable by train – the site is five minutes' walk from Tilff train station. There are no **camp-sites** particularly convenient to Liège, the closest being *Camping de l'Allee Verte*, in VISÉ, fifteen minutes' to the north by hourly train (direction Maastricht) .

The City

Liège is a large city, and you'd be wise to concentrate your attentions on its reasonably compact centre. Situated on the west bank of the Meuse, this divides into two parts – the so-called **new town**, girdled by the traffic artery of boulevard de la Sauvenière, which curls around to the nominal centre of town at **place St-Lambert**; and the **older section**, north of here, with Feronstrée as its spine, hard below the steep heights which rise up to the former citadel. Most other places are without interest, though across the river the separate district of **Outremeuse**, on what is in effect an island in the Meuse, might be worth a visit for its tight grouping of bars and restaurants.

The main squares

The centre of the city is a bit of a mess really, the new and old sections meeting at **place de la République Française**, more of a roundabout than a square,

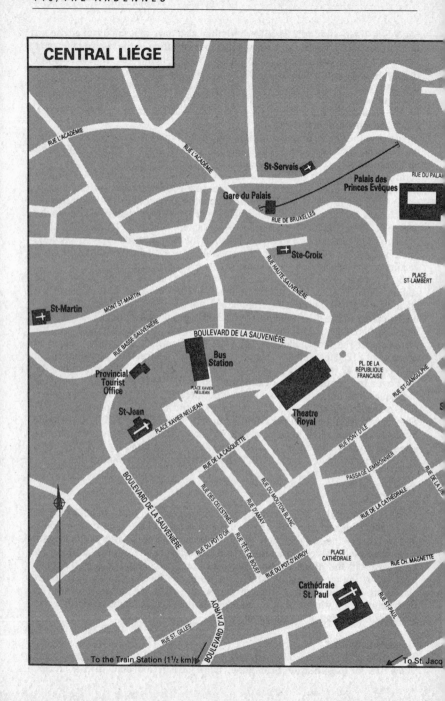

CENTRAL LIÉGE

RUE L'ACADÉMIE

RUE L'ACADÉMIE

St-Servais

RUE DU PALAI

Palais des
Princes Évêques

Gare du Palais

RUE DE BRUXELLES

Ste-Croix

RUE HAUTE-SAUVENIÈRE

PLACE
ST-LAMBERT

St-Martin

MONT ST-MARTIN

RUE BASSE-SAUVENIÈRE

BOULEVARD DE LA SAUVENIÈRE

Bus
Station

Provincial
Tourist
Office

PLACE XAVIER
NEUJEAN

PL. DE LA
RÉPUBLIQUE
FRANCAISE

RUE ST-GANGULPHE

St-Jean

PLACE XAVIER NEUJEAN

Theatre
Royal

S

RUE DE LA CASQUETTE

RUE PONT D'ILE

BOULEVARD DE LA SAUVENIÈRE

RUE DES CELESTINES

RUE D'AMAY

RUE DU MOUTON BLANC

PASSAGE LEMMONNIER

RUE DE LA U

RUE DE LA CATHÉDRALE

RUE DU POT D'OR

RUE TÊTE DE BŒUF

RUE DU POT-D'AVROY

PLACE
CATHÉDRALE

RUE CH. MAGNETTE

Cathédrale
St. Paul

RUE ST-PAUL

RUE ST. GILLES

BOULEVARD D'AVROY

To the Train Station (1½ km)

To St Jacq

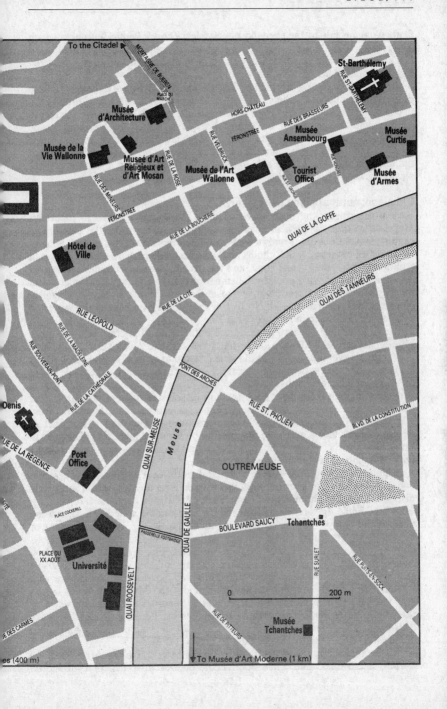

To the Citadel

MONTAGNE DE BUEREN

PLACE DU MARCHÉ

St-Barthélemy

RUE ST-BARTHÉLÉMY

Musée
d'Architecture

HORS-CHÂTEAU

RUE DES BRASSEURS

FÉRONSTRÉE

RUE VELBRUCK

Musée
Ansembourg

Musée
Curtis

Musée de la
Vie Wallonne

RUE DES MINEURS

Museé d'Art
Religieux et
d'Art Mosan

RUE DE LA ROSE

Musée de l'Art
Wallonne

Tourist
Office

RUE ST-GEORGE

RUE FÉRONCLÉ

Musée
d'Armes

FÉRONSTRÉE

RUE DE LA BOUCHERIE

QUAI DE LA GOFFE

Hôtel de
Ville

RUE DE LA CITÉ

QUAI DES TANNEURS

RUE LEOPOLD

RUE DE LA MADELEINE

RUE SOUVERAIN-PONT

RUE DE LA CATHÉDRALE

PONT DES ARCHES

QUAI SUR-MEUSE

Meuse

RUE ST. PHOLIEN

BLVD. DE LA CONSTITUTION

Denis

RUE DE LA REGENCE

Post
Office

OUTREMEUSE

PLACE COCKERILL

PASSERELLE FOOTBRIDGE

QUAI DE GAULLE

BOULEVARD SAUCY

Tchantches

PLACE DU
XX AOÛT

Université

QUAI ROOSEVELT

RUE SURLET

RUE PUITS-EN-SOCK

0   200 m

RUE DES CARMES

RUE DE PITTEURS

Musée
Tchantches

es (400 m)

▼To Musée d'Art Moderne (1 km)

flanked on one side by the shed-like neoclassical *Theatre Royale*, in front of which stands a statue of the Liège-born composer Andre Grétry (his heart is held in the urn just below). The square fades seamlessly into **place St-Lambert**, where the city is supposed to have begun – ironic considering its present-day role as a mixture of car park and bus stands. The **Palais des Princes Evêques** (Palace of the Prince-Bishops), behind, does its best to provide a stately backdrop to the mayhem of the square, but even its vast frontage, built in the early sixteenth century and reconstructed a century later, can't help but look tawdry by association. You can wander into its main courtyard during office hours, though there's not much to see beyond the carved grotesques on its pillars. Cut through the building and you may be able to get into its second court, a smaller, prettier square, planted with greenery.

Old Liège: north of place St-Lambert

East of the palace, the open space of place St-Lambert narrows to **place du Marché**, another car park in effect, its right side taken up by the eighteenth-century **Hôtel de Ville**. From here, **Feronstrée** leads east, the central spine of the so-called old town, which climbs up the sharp gradient to the citadel above. In reality this is a rather grimy affair, and the packed streets of the newer town on the other, southern side of place St-Lambert are more alluring. But the area has the city's densest concentration of museums, and there's a vigorous Sunday morning market, **La Batte**, which stretches along the riverfront all the way from the Quai de la Goffe to the corner of rue Hongrée.

The first turning off Feronstrée to the left, rue de Mineurs, leads up to the **Musée de la Vie Wallonne** (Tues–Sat 10am–noon & 2–5pm, Sun 10am–4pm; F50), one of several museums in the area devoted to aspects of Walloon culture. Housed in the reconstruction of a former Franciscan monastery, there are lots of photographs of nineteenth-century Walloon village life, a mock-up of a typical Ardennes kitchen from days gone by, and displays of tools of various trades, including those used in traditional Ardennes industries like glassblowing and "Dinanderie" or copper-working – once practiced in Huy and still a craft of Dinant. There's also a guillotine that used to be set up in place de la République Française. On the whole, though, it's a nostalgic collection, and adds little to understanding current tensions within Belgium.

Almost next door, the **Musée d'Art Religieux et d'Art Mosan** (Tues–Sun noon–5pm; F50) is another museum focusing on local themes, with a sensitively displayed, roughly chronological assortment of Christian carvings and paintings from the Middle Ages on from Liège and the surrounding area. In Liège, at least, many of the best pieces remain in the churches themselves, but there are one or two nice exhibits from outside the city, including some sixteenth-century poly-chrome wood carvings of Saint Lambert and Saint Hubert, the latter, the patron saint of hunting in the Ardennes, pictured with his emblem, a stag. There is also a seated Christ from 1240, and the so-called *Virgin of Berselius*, an exquisite carving in wood from 1530, cherubs stealing from under the Madonna's robes atop a serpent. Among the paintings is a *Virgin with St Donatrice and Mary Magdalen* by the Master of St Gudule, as well as landscapes by the early sixteenth-century Antwerp painter Joachim Patenier – lush canvases showing unfolding landscapes of hills and villages that are not unlike the scenes of Bruegel.

Just beyond the religious art museum, the **Musée d'Architecture** (Wed–Fri 3–7pm, Sat 3–8pm, Sun 11am–3pm; F50), housed in a beautifully restored convent, mounts regular temporary exhibitions on an architectural theme and incorporates the former studio of the local nineteenth-century violinist Eugene Ysaye. Just beyond, the 400 or so steps of the very steep **Montagne de Bueren** lead up to the **Citadel** – not much more than its ramparts these days, which enclose a modern hospital. The views, however, are immaculate, worth what is a genuinely lung-wrenching trek, looking right out over the city and the rolling countryside beyond. Afterwards you can follow an interesting route back into the centre of the city by way of rue du Pery and rue Volière, which brings you out behind Gare de Palais.

On the opposite side of Feronstrée, further down, is the third of the area's Walloon museums, the **Musée de l'Art Wallon**, Feronstreé 86 (Tues–Sat 1–6pm, Sun 11am–4.30pm; F50), housed in a modern building by the river. This is a small collection of some quality, comprising nineteenth- and twentieth-century work by French-speaking Belgian artists, and is much the best laid-out of all the museums here, arranged chronologically, starting at the top with seventeenth-century paintings and leading down in a circular movement. The nineteenth- and early twentieth-century sections are strongest, including a number of works by Constanin Meunier – the large *La Coulée a Ourgrée* is one – Antoine Wiertz's fleshy (and enormous) *Greeks and Romans in Dispute over the Body of Patrocle*, and the delicate paintings of women of Armand Rassenfosse. Look out, also, for the small group of works by Delvaux and Magritte, notably the former's wacky *L'homme de la Rue*, as well as more conventional earlier paintings by the same artist.

Further along Feronstrée, a little way past the tourist office, the **Musée d'Ansembourg** (Mon & Wed–Sat 10am–1pm & 2–5pm, Sun 10am–1pm; F50) has been recently renovated and hosts a sumptuous collection of eighteenth-century furniture and decorations in an authentic period setting. Almost opposite, set back from the road, the church of **St-Barthélemy** (Easter to mid-Oct Mon–Sat 10am–noon & 2–5pm, Sun 1–5pm; winter closed Mon & Sun afternoon) is a Romanesque structure on the outside, built at the end of the twelfth century, that has been pretty much spoilt inside by an insensitive eighteenth-century reconstruction. Its main item of interest, however, remains pristinely intact – a bronze baptismal font of 1118. The work of Renier de Huy, it rests on ten oxen and is decorated with a circular relief depicting various baptisms in progress. The figures are graceful and naturalistic, and the oxen bend their heads and necks as if under the weight of the great bowl.

On the riverfront, two further museums may command your interest before you turn around and head back towards the city centre proper – there's nothing else to see in this part of town. The **Musée d'Armes** (Tues–Sat 10am–12.30pm & 2–5pm, Sun 10am–2pm; F50) has, alongside an Ingres portrait of a young and dashing Napoleon, lots of beautifully engraved ornate pistols and rifles from the eighteenth to twentieth centuries – impressive if you're keen on such things – along with examples of military modelling, suits of armour and ancient swords, some dating back to the sixth century. Further along, the **Musée Curtius** is better (Mon & Wed–Sat 10am–1pm & 2–5pm, Sun 10am–1pm; F50). Housed in a turreted redbrick mansion from the early seventeenth century, it forms the sister collection to the Ansembourg, displaying decorative arts from the environs of Liège up to the nineteenth century, notably the late tenth-century Gospel Book of Bishop Notger, with a contemporary ivory frontispiece, and – in a separate section – a display of glasswork that is one of the world's finest, containing over 9000 exhibits ranging from European crystal to gorgeous medieval Islamic artefacts.

New Liège: south and west of place de la République Française

Walking in the opposite direction from place St-Lambert takes you into the heart of the **newer part of the city**, bordered roughly by the boulevard de la Sauvenière in the west, and the river and avenue Maurice Destenay to the south. It's in many ways a preferable area to the quarter around Feronstrée, partly pedestrianised, livelier and more engaging, with the bulk of the city's shops, bars, restaurants and nightlife. A short walk from rue Leopold, the church of **St-Denis**, on the square of the same name, is a curious mix of styles, the original, austere pillars of the nave and the brown brick of the base of the tower contrasting markedly with the later ornate stucco topping. At the end of the south aisle, the church's retable is by far its most remarkable feature – an early sixteenth-century work, carved in wood, that stands a good five metres high. The top – and principal – section has six panels showing the Passion of Christ, very Gothic in tone, full of drama, with assertively carved depictions of grieving, leering and abusing humanity. The bottom set of panels is later and gentler in style, with smaller figures, less sensationally observed, telling the story of Saint Denis from baptism to decapitation.

From St-Denis, rue de la Cathédrale leads down to the **Cathédrale St-Paul** (daily 7.30am–12.30pm & 2–6pm), the square in front of which is a busy spot to sit and watch the world go by. The church itself was actually only elevated to cathedral status in 1801, the replacement of an earlier, by all accounts more impressive building that was destroyed in 1794 by revolutionary French guards during the final days of the last prince-bishop. A fairly spartan structure, begun in the fourteenth century and not entirely finished off until the nineteenth, it has a couple of notable features, not least the swirling roof paintings of 1570 and a late thirteenth-century polychrome *Madonna and Child* by the high altar. But the **treasury** (F40) in the cloisters is of most interest, its small collection including a massive 90-kilogram bust reliquary of Saint Lambert, the work of a goldsmith from Aachen, dating from 1508–12. It contains the skull of the saint and depicts scenes from his life – the miracles he performed as a boy, his burial in Maastricht and the removal of his body from Maastricht to Liège by Saint Hubert, who succeeded him as bishop of the area. There are also some lovely examples of ivory work from the eleventh century, and a similarly dated missal, stained by the waters of a 1920s flood in the church.

South of the cathedral, just off avenue Maurice Destenay, the church of **St-Jacques** (Mon–Sat 8am–noon, May–Sept also 5–7pm) compares to the cathedral in size, and exhibits a transition in styles that varies from the Romanesque west front and pillar bases to the frilly, flamboyant Gothic of the rest of the church – note the lighter-coloured stone used in the upper levels of the building. The ornate stonework is impressive on its own, as is the painted vaulting of the nave. Look out also for a painted screen of 1598 showing the Resurrection, in the chapel to the left of the choir.

There's one other church you should see in the new town, that of **St-Jean** (daily 10am–noon & 2–5.15pm), on place X. Neujean, just off boulevard de la Sauvenière. This was originally a tenth-century church, modelled on Charlemagne's chapel in Aachen – hence the unusual shape – though only the tower remains from the first structure. Inside, behind glass, there's a beautifully carved statue of a Madonna and Child, thirteenth-century but still with its original gilt surface, next door to which are two polychrome figures of the Virgin and St John (press the button for lighting), again exquisitely carved and wonderfully preserved.

Over the river: Outremeuse and more museums

The district across the river from the centre of Liège, **Outremeuse**, is supposedly the city's most characteristic neighbourhood, a working-class quarter that's said to be the home of the true Liègois – it's sometimes known as the "free republic of Outremeuse". This is a slightly fake idea these days, not unlike the concept of the Cockney in London, but it is epitomised by the figure known as **Tchantchès** (Liège slang for Francis), the so-called "Prince of Outremeuse". Tchantchès is a character from Liège folklore, an earthy, independent-minded, brave but drunken figure who is said to have been born between two Outremeuse paving stones on August 25, 760; later, legend claims, he was, with the help of his enormous nose, instrumental in the campaigns of Charlemagne. Nowadays Tchantchès can be seen in action in traditional Liège puppet shows; he's also represented in a **statue** on place l'Yser, the traditional place of his death, carried as a symbol of freedom by a woman dressed as a coalminer.

There's a **museum** to Tchantchès nearby at rue Surlet 56 (Wed & Thurs 2–4pm), which displays various artefacts, costumes and other paraphernalia relating to the figure and his life as a puppet character. Though the opening times make it awkward, it's worth also considering a visit to the **Musée du Fer et du Charbon**, boulevard R. Poincaré 17 (Sat 2–5pm), where you can see displays of metalwork and a reconstituted forge from the eighteenth century. Further south, out of Outremeuse proper, there's another museum, the **Museum d'Art Moderne** in leafy Parc de Boverie, not far from the Palais de Congrès (Tues–Sat 1–6pm, Sun 11am–4.30pm), which displays a permanent collection of fairly minor works by recognised modern artists – Picasso, Chagal and Ensor among others – as well as mounting regular temporary exhibitions.

Eating, drinking and nightlife

As with anywhere in Belgium, Liège can be an excellent place to **eat**, and you don't always need to pay through the nose to do so. For lunch, at least, there are lots of places in the centre of town, especially around place de la République Française, offering plats du jour and cheap menus. *Le Tivoli*, across the road from the *Theatre Royale* on rue G. Clemenceau, has many dishes for under F200, and two-course daily specials for around F250. In the old town, *Le Cheval d'Or* on rue des Mineurs has menus at F395 and F625, as well as dishes (omelettes, etc) that for around F150 make for a good inexpensive lunch-stop between museums. Further up rue des Mineurs, on the corner, *Le Buffet du Hagar Dunor* serves a wide range of beers, well-priced snacks and light meals next door to its shop selling Belgian specialities.

Au Point de Vue, on place de la République Française, claims to be the oldest tavern in Liège, and its blend of homely bar atmosphere, a local crowd and cheap meals lunchtimes and evenings (around F200) are worth experiencing. Around the corner on boulevard de la Sauvenière, *La Louisane* is a good place to come of an evening if you can't decide what to eat: as well as regular Belgian food, it offers Italian, French and "Louisiana" menus, the latter incorporating much succulent seafood. Main courses run at F250–400, plats du jour for F300. Not far away, the popular *L'Ecailler du Café Robert*, rue des Dominicains 26, is also good for fish and seafood, though pricier, with main meals at F400–500.

If none of these suit, you'll find plenty more restaurants in the grid of streets that run north from rue Pont d'Avroy up to rue de la Casquette, which is the city's most popular area for **nightlife**, home to many good bars and clubs as well. Rue Pont d'Avroy itself has lots of **bars**, but they're mostly tacky places and the best establishments are on the narrower streets behind – though avoid the sleazy rue des Celestines. *L'Aquarelle*, on the corner of rue de Pot d'Or and rue Tête du Boeuf, is a youthful hang-out which plays good music, as does *La Papaya*, around the corner in rue Tête du Boeuf itself. *Le Seigneur d'Amay*, at rue d'Amay 10, is a more sedate, tiny bar, easy to miss, that has an odd baronial feel inside, with imposing wall paintings and impromptu performances at the piano. Five minutes' walk away, *Taverne St Paul*, behind the cathedral a little way down rue St-Paul, is a similarly well-established bar, cosy and friendly, with outside seating and bar snacks at lunchtime. You might also consider a trip across the river to **Outremeuse**, where rue Roture, a narrow street which spears right off the main shopping thoroughfare of rue Surlet, is entirely made up of restaurants and bars. *Pizzeria Comedia*, at no. 38, has pizzas from F150, the *Acropolis* Greek restaurant, at no. 72, offers main dishes for F300–400.

Listings

Books *Pax*, place Cockerill 4, has a small stock of English paperbacks.

Car hire *Avis*, boulevard d'Avroy 238b (☎52 55 00); *Europcar*, boulevard de la Sauvenière 37 (☎22 40 07); *Hertz*, boulevard d'Avroy 60 (☎22 42 73).

Exchange There's a 24-hour exchange office at Gare des Guillemins.

Newspapers English newspapers are available from the railway station bookstall, or in the centre of town from *Bellens*, rue de la Regence 6, or *Libro Plus*, on Feronstrée just before C&A.

Post office The main central post office is at rue de la Regence 61 (Mon–Fri 8.30am–6pm, Sat 8.30am–noon).

Telephones There's an office with booths at rue Université 32 (Mon–Fri 8am–8pm, Sat & Sun 10.15am–6pm).

Train enquiries ☎52 98 50

Travel agents *Nouvelles Frontières*, boulevard de la Sauvenière 32 (☎23 67 67); *Wasteels*, place X. Neujean 25 (☎23 70 26).

East of Liège: Verviers, Eupen and the Hohes Venn

East of Liège, the Vesdre river cuts through some lovely wooded countryside, sharp hills plunging down into deep wooded valleys as soon as you get free of the sprawl of Liège. **VERVIERS** is the main town of the Vesdre, a small place of around 50,000 people that is a good base for the area, though in itself it isn't the sort of place you make a beeline for; indeed you're far better off heading south into the Ardennes proper. However, if you're heading east into Germany and find yourself here at midday, you may want to stop off for lunch. In which case there are a couple of reasonable museums, together worth an hour or so of your time.

The centre of town, five to ten minutes' walk from the railway station, is **place Verte** and – a block away – **place des Martyrs**. Five minutes' walk from the latter, down rue de Collège and left onto rue Renier, is the **Musée des Beaux Arts** (Mon, Wed & Sat 2–5pm, Sun 3–6pm; free), worth visiting for its small, quality collection of paintings, which includes a number of canvases by Dutch artists. Notable among these are a small landscape by Jan van Goyen, a fine crowded *Adoration of the Magi* by Gerrit Dou, a portrait of a child by Cornelis de Vos, as well as later nineteenth-century works by Johan Barthold Jongkind, such as *The Skaters*. You should also look out for Jan Weenix's portrait of Admiral van Heemskerk, and a room entirely decorated with murals depicting views of the valley of the Vesdre (which runs alongside the museum) and parts of Malmédy by an unknown eighteenth-century artist.

Verviers' other museum, the **Musée d'Archeologie** (Tues & Thurs 2–5pm, Sat 9am–noon, Sun 10am–1pm; free), is of less interest, but it is close by at rue des Raines 42, so you may as well have a look. Expect a handful of rooms furnished in period style, some weaponry and artefacts pertaining to a local nine-teenth- century violinist, Henri Vieuxtemps, and a small collection of Roman coins and other local historical finds.

For maps of the town and other information, the **tourist office** is between place Verte and the station at rue Vieille-Xhavée 11 (Mon–Fri 9am–12.30pm & 1.30–5pm, Sat 9am–12.30pm & 1–4pm; ☎087/33 02 13). If you're **eating**, the *Brasserie de l'Europe* on the corner of place Verte is a busy, friendly place with good food and service, as is *Grand Café* on place des Martyrs, which offers cheap lunchtime menus.

Trains continue on to **EUPEN**, the landscape unfolding into a gentler affair of undulating pastureland. This again is pleasant enough, but has nothing especially to draw you other than its role as capital of the German-speaking part of Belgium. This area has been largely German since the early nineteenth century, when it was part of Prussia and a policy of enforced Germanisation was undertaken. The area was ceded to Belgium under the Treaty of Versailles in 1919, but German is the main language here, both spoken on the streets and used on signs, street-names and menus. Eupen certainly has a definite Teutonic feel, not least in the curvy twin towers of the eighteenth-century church of **St Nicholas** on the main Marktplatz, ten minutes' walk from the train station (five minutes' from the bus station), which sports some ornate Baroque altarpieces and an extravagant pulpit that could be straight out of provincial Bavaria.

Just outside the town, Eupen's main attraction is its **barrage**, a few kilometres to the east (reachable by bus from the bus station), the largest dam in Belgium, with a tower that gives marvellous views over the reservoir below and the area beyond. This is known as the **Hohes Venn** or "High Fens", the end of the Ardennes proper, sandwiched between the Eifel hills which stretch into Germany. The Hohes Venn are home to Belgium's highest peak, the **Signal de Botrange**, which rises to 694m a little way north of Malmédy. The rest of the area is boggy heath and woods, windswept and rather wild – excellent hiking country.

Spa and around

SPA was the world's first health resort, established as far back as the sixteenth century: Pliny the Elder knew of the healing properties of the waters here, and Henry VIII, of all people, was an early visitor. Since then it's lent its name to ther-mal resorts worldwide, reaching a height of popularity in the eighteenth and nine-teenth centuries, when it was visited by monarchs, statesmen, intellectuals and aristocrats from all over Europe. Later the town went into slow decline – when Matthew Arnold visited in 1860 he claimed it "astonished us by its insignificance" – and the years since have been no more kind, moneyed flashiness replacing glamour, with fast cars and big, pedigree dogs the order of the day. A waft of sophistication comes from the casino in the centre of town, but that's about it, and you'd do better to visit Spa for its access to the countryside around and its small towns, notably Stavelot.

The Town

There's nothing to do as such in Spa. The main thermal baths, the **Établisse-ment des Bains**, are bang in the centre of town on the main place Royale, next door to the casino (daily from 3pm), and provide a very grand venue for its arthri-tis- and high blood pressure-curing mud and water treatments. A little further along down rue Royale, off to the left, is the **Pouhan-Pierre-le-Grand** – the town's main mineral spring, named after Peter the Great who appreciated the therapeutic effects of its waters and visited often (Easter daily 10am–noon & 2–5pm; end Easter to mid-June Mon–Fri 2–5pm, Sat & Sun 10am–noon & 2–5pm; mid-June to mid-Sept daily 10am–noon & 2–5pm). For F10 you can get yourself a glass of the water, though it tastes disgusting even if it is very good for you. Spa's waters contain iron and bicarbonate of soda, useful for curing lung and heart ailments as well as rheumatism. There are **four other springs** around Spa: Tonnelet, Barisart, Géronstère and Sauvènière. A little tram-bus (called a *bala-deuse*) does the trip between them, but they don't normally let you off to drink and there's otherwise nothing to see. The buses are stationed around the main square, and trips cost about F90 – though there is a variety of itineraries. In town you can also visit the **Musée de la Ville d'Eau**, back towards the station, oppo-site rue de la Gare (mid-March to mid-June & Sept–Dec Sat & Sun only 2.30–5.30pm; Mid-June to mid-Sept daily 2.30–5.30pm; F40). This has posters and objects relating to the resort and its waters, in particular little painted wooden souvenir boxes and other such objects.

Practical details

The **train station** is west of the town centre, off to the left of avenue Reine Astrid. Coming out of the station, there are two cheap **hotels** – the *Chemin de Fer* (☎087/77 14 15) and *Hôtel de la Gare*, which have doubles for under F1000. There are also several places along avenue Reine Astrid, including *Pension Bij de Brabander* at no. 68 (☎087/77 12 21) and *Hôtel de l'Avenue* at no. 48 (☎087/77 20 67), which charge around F1000 a double. There are two **campsites** outside Spa, both in the same direction to the southeast of the centre, the nearer of which is *Camping Havette*, rue Chelui 21; follow rue Royale down to where it runs into rue de la Sauvenière, and rue Chelui is a turning off to the left a few hundred metres along. The other site, *Camping du Parc des Sources*, is further along on rue de la Sauvenière itself, at no. 141.

The **tourist office** at place Royale 3 (Whitsun to mid-Sept Mon–Fri 9am–12.30pm & 2–6pm, Sat & Sun 10am–12.30pm & 2–5pm; out of season same hours on weekdays but weekends mornings only; ☎087/77 25 10) is extremely well stocked with books, walking routes, cycle circuits and maps. Guided walks in the area are organised three or four times a week in July and August with a few during Easter holidays, either half-day tours of 8–11km or a full day of 14–18km, all free.

There are plenty of cheap **eateries** along avenue Reine Astrid, including *Restaurant Pic Nic*, which has a good inexpensive menu. Also good is *La Cortina* in place Royale opposite the casino, which serves well-priced spaghetti, pizza and steaks. Just along from here, the *Bidule* is a popular bar for evening **drinking**, especially at weekends. If it's hot, there are two Olympic-sized **swimming pools**, twenty minutes' walk from the centre, while just beyond lies the **Lac de Warfaaz**, with boating.

Around Spa: Stavelot, Malmédy and the Grottes de Remouchamps

The countryside around Spa is not really ideal for hiking – this is one of the highest parts of Belgium but it's on a flattish plateau crossed by lots of main roads, and without a car (or a bike – available from the station) there aren't many places to go. The most interesting trip out from Spa is to **STAVELOT** (bus #44), a half-hour journey away through Francorchamps, where Spa's Grand Prix racing circuit is. A small town set on a hill, Stavelot was fiercely fought over during the Ardennes campaign of the last war, and some of the Nazis' worst (in Belgium) atrocities were committed here, mostly by troops scared to death by the American counterattack. These days Stavelot is a pleasant old place with a former abbey that – with that of nearby Malmédy – was home to a line of powerful abbot-bishops who ran the area as an independent fiefdom from the seventh right up to the end of the eighteenth century. Most of the buildings are mainly eighteenth-century, but there's a sixteenth-century archway from the original abbey church. The abbey houses three museums, including the **Musée Regional d'Art Religieux et de l'Ancienne Abbaye** (April–Nov daily 10aı. 12.30pm & 2.30–5.30pm; F100 combined ticket for all abbey museums), which displays religious art of the Ardennes from the fourteenth to the nineteenth centuries – sculpture, silver and gold carvings and liturgical dress, and local history. Just over the courtyard and up some stairs is the **Musée Guillaume Apollinaire** (July & Aug daily 10.30am–12.30pm & 2–5.30pm), set up to remember the French writer, who spent the sumer of 1899 in the town and wrote many of his poems about Stavelot and the Ardennes. It contains newspaper articles, letters, poems, sketches and photos relating to the man who – despite a premature death – some claim was one of the most influential of early twentieth-century writers. In another wing of the abbey, the **Musée du Circuit de Spa-Francorchamps** contains racing cars and motorbikes from the nearby circuit (April–Oct daily 10am–12.30pm & 2.30–5.30pm; Nov–March daily 10am–noon & 2–4.30pm).

Above the abbey, the church of **St-Sebastien** contains a rich treasury, with an enormous thirteenth-century shrine of Saint Remacle, founder of Stavelot abbey in the seventh century; Mosan in style, it's of gilt and enamelled copper with filigree and silver statuettes. To see it you have to knock on a door opposite (address and times inside church door). Otherwise Stavelot is a nice place just to wander. The most picturesque road is rue Haute, at the foot of place St-Remacle, at the bottom of which are some eighteenth-century houses with exposed wooden beams.

If you can manage it, the best time to be in Stavelot is for its **carnival**, first celebrated here in 1502 and since the early 1900s a renowned annual event, held on the third weekend before Easter, Saturday to Monday evening. The main protagonists are the *Blancs Moussis*, figures with white hoods and long red noses. For more information, consult the **tourist office** in the abbey (daily 10am–12.30pm & 2–5.30pm; ☎080/86 23 39). Accommodation is difficult during carnival time, but otherwise the cheapest **hotel** is the *Mal Aime*, rue Neuve 12 (☎080/86 20 01) – doubles F900. There's also a **campsite**, *De Challes*, at route de Challes 25 (April–Nov).

Eight kilometres away, accessible by bus from Stavelot or direct from Spa, **MALMÉDY** also has a carnival, the *Cwarmê* (though it's less famous than Stavelot's), together with a **museum** on the subject (daily 2–5pm). However, that apart, there's nothing to see and the place is horribly overdeveloped, with tinny Germanic music playing over loudspeakers in the streets.

A few kilometres on the other side of Stavelot, the small resort of **COO** is the site of a rather feeble waterfall surrounded by lovely scenery that gives the excuse for a riot of amusements just off the main road – restaurants, cafés, go-karts, a deer park, and a two-person cable car that straddles the road up the mountain (F150 return). Fifteen kilometres or so northwest of here are more caves, the **Grottes de Remouchamps** (May–Aug daily 9am–6pm; April, Sept & Oct 9.30am–5pm; last departure one hour before closing; F300), where you can travel on the longest subterranean boat trip in the world (apparently) through beautiful coloured galleries of stalagmites and suchlike. **REMOUCHAMPS** itself is a resort on the Amblève river, though its nice position has been ruined by the presence of the nearby motorway to Liège. If you want to stay, **campsites** abound.

travel details

Trains
From Namur to Floreffe/Charleroi (1–2 an hour; 10min/50min); Godinne/Dinant (2 an hour; 20min/30min); Huy/Liège (2 an hour; 25min/45min); Jemelle/Libramont/Arlon/Luxembourg (hourly; 40min/1hr/1hr 20min/1hr 40min).
From Dinant to Anseremme/Gendron-Celles/Houyet/Bertix/Libramont (every 2hr; 10min/20min/25min/1hr 20min/1hr 40min).
From Libramont to Bertix/Florenville/Virton (every 2 hours; 10min/30min/50min); Bastogne (every 2hr; 45min); Poix-St-Hubert/Libramont (every 2hr; 18min/25min).
From Arlon to Libramont/Jemelle/Namur (6 daily; 30min/50min/1hr 30min); to Luxembourg (hourly; 20min).
From Liège to Huy/Namur (2 an hour; 20min/45min); Verviers/Cologne (hourly; 18min/1hr 50min), change at Verviers-Central for Eupen (hourly; 22min) and Spa (hourly; 30min); Jemelle

(every 2 hours; 1hr 20min); Tienen/Leuven/Brussels (hourly; 40min/50min/1hr 10min).
From Jemelle to Antwerp (hourly; 2hr).
From Rochefort to Lavaux-Ste-Anne (July & Aug 2 daily; 1hr).

Buses
From Dinant to Givet (France) (6 daily; 45min).
From Namur to Floreffe (8 daily; 30min).

Boats
From Dinant to Anseremme (every 20min; 45min round-trip); Freyr (1 daily; 1hr 30min round-trip); Heer Agimont (1 daily in July & Aug; 5hr round-trip); Namur (Sun only; 3hr 30min one-way).

Guided Light Transit
Jemelle–Rochefort–Han-sur-Lesse–Lessive (June to mid-Sept 5 times daily, mid-Sept to Oct 2 daily weekends only).

CHAPTER TWELVE

LUXEMBOURG

A cross the border from the Belgian province of Luxembourg (with which it has a closely entwined history), the **Grand Duchy of Luxembourg** is one of Europe's smallest sovereign states, a tiny independent principality with a total population of around 365,000, living in an area of just 2500 square kilometres. As a country it's relatively neglected by travellers, most people tending to write it off as a rather dull and expensive financial centre. This is a mistake. Compared to much of Europe, its attractions are fairly low-key, and it is pricey, but it has marvellous scenery in abundance: the green hills of the Ardennes spreading over the border to form a glorious heartland of deep wooded valleys spiked with sharp craggy hilltops crowned with castles.

In the more gentle landscape of the **south**, the capital of the country, **Luxembourg city**, is almost impossible to avoid if you're not travelling by car, most public transport connections emanating from here. It's worth spending time here – the dramatically situated city is perhaps the country's only genuinely urban environment, and something like a fifth of the population live there. But, with just 78,000 people, it's hardly a major metropolis, and you can exhaust its handful of sights and slightly groggy nightlife in two or three days. **Southwest** of the capital is the least interesting part of Luxembourg, carved with motorways heading south into France and home to most of the country's heavy industry around Esch-sur-Alzette. The **southeast**, on the other hand, is more of a tourist area, the vineyards of the Luxembourg bank of the Moselle river (which forms the border with Germany) evidence of Europe's smallest wine industry, and producing some very drinkable white and sparkling wines.

The **central** part of Luxembourg, reached by way of the spinal road and rail route through Ettelbruck up to Clervaux, is more spectacular, rucking up into rich green hills and valleys that reach their climax in the wooded hills of the **Luxembourg Ardennes**, in the narrowing **north** of the country. It's a lovely, richly scenic area, but there are few really feasible bases for seeing something of it without a car – **Echternach**, a tiny town dominated by its ancient abbey, nearby **Diekirch**, and **Vianden** to the north, surrounded by high green hills and crowned by a magnificent castle.

Wherever you decide to go, **getting around** by public transport isn't always easy. Despite (or perhaps because of) the country's size, everything tends to revolve around the capital, and while connections from there to most places (by train or, more usually, bus) are quite good, if not always especially frequent, travelling between the provincial towns and villages can be difficult, and involve several changes. Be patient, and try and see as much of the country as possible on day trips from the capital. This is quite feasible for many places – nowhere is more than a couple of hours' journey away – though for anywhere north of Echternach you're probably best off staying overnight.

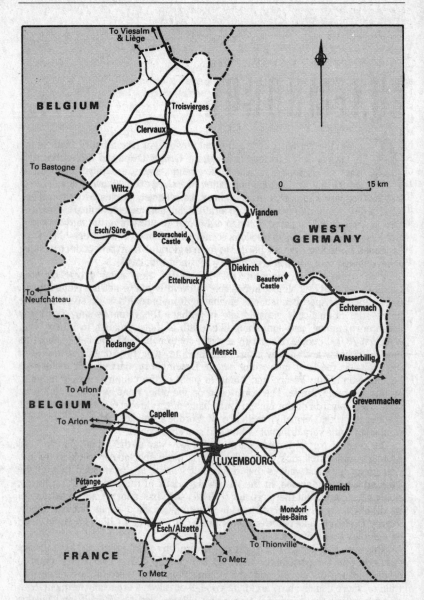

History, language . . . and modern Luxembourg

The **history** of Luxembourg is closely bound up with that of Belgium and – to a lesser extent – Holland. The city of Luxembourg came into being in **Roman times**, at the crucial strategic junction of the trading roads between Trier and Paris and Metz and Liège, and Roman camps were established in the countryside around. Its position at the top of the sheer gorges of the Pétrusse and Alzette rivers meant it could be easily defended – an advantage that was developed when one **Count Siegfried of Lorraine** fortified the place in 963, building the city's first citadel on the Bock cliff. Count Siegfried and his successors ruled the surrounding area from the town as a nominally independent fiefdom of the Holy Roman Empire. Later, in 1354, it became a **Duchy**, the first dukes – John the Blind and his son Wenceslas – extending its lands up to Limburg in the north and down to Metz in the south. In the **fifteenth century** Luxembourg became absorbed, like most of what is now Belgium, into the lands of the House of Burgundy, and its subsequent history mirrors that of its neighbour, becoming part of the Spanish, and later Austrian, Netherlands, and eventually falling for a short time under the suzerainty of Napoleon. The Congress of Vienna decided to create the **Grand Duchy of Luxembourg**, and though the country remained nominally independent, the throne was assumed by William I of the House of Orange-Nassau, the monarch of the new united kingdom of The Netherlands. At this time Luxembourg's borders included parts of what is now the Belgian Ardennes, now the *province* of Luxembourg – a situation which changed with the establishment of the Belgian state in **1830**, when this western area was handed over to Belgium and the smaller eastern section became what is the present country. More recently Luxembourg was the site of some of **World War II**'s fiercest fighting during the Ardennes campaign, when key engagements of the Battle of the Bulge, during the freezing winter of 1944–45, were decided here. Luxembourgers are keen to remember the period and you'll come across a number of museums honouring the (mainly American) dead.

Nowadays Luxembourg is a constitutional monarchy, ruled at present by the Grand Duke Jean, who came to the throne in 1964 and is married to the daughter of the previous Belgian king, Leopold II. The Grand Duke has a twelve-person cabinet of ministers, selected from a directly elected chamber of deputies. The country's capital is also one of the centres of the European community, as well as being among the continent's leading financial cities, lending the place a curiously international flavour – something which is enhanced by the fact that, although everyone speaks the indigenous language, Letzeburgesch (a dialect of German which sounds a bit like Dutch), most also speak French and German. Indeed French is the official **language** of the government and judiciary, the one you'll see on street signs and suchlike, and is the one people will most readily converse with you in. German is the language most used by the press, and is spoken with equal ease by all Luxembourgers. English, too, is widely understood and spoken.

LUXEMBOURG CITY

The city of **LUXEMBOURG** is one of the most spectacularly sited capitals in Europe. The valleys of the Alzette and Pétrusse rivers, which meet here, cut a green swathe through the city, their deep canyons lending it an almost perfect strategic location. It's a tiny place by capital city standards, and broadly divides into three distinct sections: the **old centre** on the northern side of the Pétrusse valley, high up on a tiny plateau no more than a few hundred metres across, is not noticeably very old, but its tight grid of streets, home to most of the city's real sights (such as they are), makes for a pleasant, lively area by day. Everything you might want to see is within easy walking distance and there are more than enough nooks and crannies to explore once you've seen these. On the opposite side of the Pétrusse, connected by two main bridges, the Pont Adolphe and Pasarelle, lies the **more modern part of the city** – less attractive, even slightly sleazy, and of no real interest beyond its location of the city's railway station and the majority of its cheap hotels. The **valleys** themselves, far below, are a curious mixture of huddles of houses, allotments and parkland, banking steeply up from the tame trickle of the city's two rivers to the massive bastions that secure the old centre. Between the two bridges is nothing but green, the natural landscaping providing a majestic – and welcome – city centre park. A little way east of the Pasarelle bridge, edging around to the jutting outcrop of the Bock bastion, the cluster of houses known as **Grund** is an almost villagey enclave, once the home of Luxembourg's working classes. To the east of Bock is the neighbourhood of **Clausen**, to the north **Pfaffenthal**, while on the far side of the Alzette valley is the **Kirchberg plateau**, home to the **Centre Européen**, and joined to the old centre by way of the imposing modern span of the Pont Grand-Duchesse Charlotte.

Arrival, information and getting around

Luxembourg's **airport**, *Findel*, is 6km east of the city on the road to Trier. There are a number of ways of getting into town. Bus #9 runs every twenty minutes between the airport and the stands to the right of the railway station; it takes thirty to forty minutes and costs a flat F25 (the price of an ordinary city bus ticket) plus an extra F25 for any large items of luggage. There are also *Luxair* buses to the same place, which are faster (fifteen minutes) but more irregular, about a dozen services a day connecting with major flight arrivals and departures; it costs F120 a head. If there are several of you and you're loaded up, it might be better to take a taxi; you'll pay about F400–500 to the station, F500–600 into the city centre.

The **railway station**, situated in the city's southern, modern quarter, 500m or so from the city centre proper, is a convenient place to find yourself: all of the city bus lines operate from here, and most of the more inexpensive hotels are located in the streets around; the station has an exchange office and left-luggage facilities (see "Listings").

Information

There are branches of the **national tourist office** at the airport (daily 10am–6.30pm; ☎40 08 08) and just outside the station on the right (daily 9am–noon & 2–6.30pm; ☎48 11 99). These have city maps, and can change money and advise on and book accommodation. There's also the busier **city tourist office**, in the centre on the place d'Armes (Mon–Sat 9am–1pm & 2–6pm; ☎22 809 or 27 565), which offers much the same facilities.

Getting around . . . and tours

Once installed, you're best off **getting around** the city **on foot**. There is a reasonable **public bus system**, but Luxembourg is such a small city, with such a compact centre, that the only time you'll need to take a bus is either between the centre and the station (though even this is easily walkable) and out to the airport

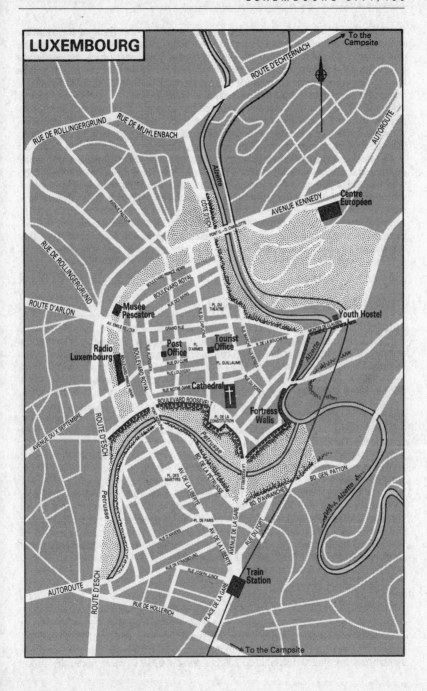

LUXEMBOURG

To the Campsite

ROUTE D'ECHTERNACH

AUTOROUTE

RUE DE ROLLINGERGRUND

RUE DE MUHLENBACH

Alzette

AVENUE KENNEDY

Centre Européen

CÔTE D'EICH

PONT G.—D. CHARLOTTE

RUE DE ROLLINGERGRUND

AVENUE PASTEUR

ROUTE D'ARLON

BOULEVARD PRINCE HENRI

BOULEVARD ROYAL

RUE DES BAINS

PL. DU THÉÂTRE

Musée Pescatore

AV. EMILE REUTER

RUE DU CAPUCINS

Youth Hostel

MONTÉE DE CLAUSEN

R. DE LA BOUCHERIE

Alzette

GRAND RUE

RUE ALDRINGEN

Post Office

PL. D'ARMES

Tourist Office

R. MÉ GENIE AU SEIGLE

Radio Luxembourg

BOULEVARD ROYAL

RUE DU CURE

PL. GUILLAUME

RUE LOUVIGNY

RUE DU FOSSE

BOULEVARD PRINCE HENRI

RUE NOTRE DAME

Cathedral †

BOULEVARD ROOSEVELT

Fortress Walls

PL. DE LA CONSTITUTION

AVENUE DU X SEPTEMBRE

ROUTE D'ESCH

Pétrusse

BD. GEN. PATTON

PL. DES MARTYRS

AV. DE LA PETRUSSE

BD. D'AVRANCHES

Alzette

Pétrusse

PL. DE PARIS

AVENUE DE LA LIBERTÉ

RUE D'ANVERS

AVENUE DE LA GARE

RUE DU FORT

RUE DE STRASBOURG

RUE JOSEPH JUNCK

Train Station

AUTOROUTE

ROUTE D'ESCH

PLACE DE LA GARE

RUE DE HOLLERICH

To the Campsite

or campsites. The main route hubs are the stands to the right of the railway station as you come out (the other side is for buses going outside the city limits), and place E. Hamilius in the city centre, by the main post office. Basically all buses from the railway station go to the city centre. Tickets on the buses cost a flat F25, however far you travel; day tickets are available for F100, from the main post office, though ten-ride tickets, available from the railway station, are better value for F175 – one of these could suffice for a couple of people staying in the city for two or three days. For getting down into the valleys, there are plenty of steps, and the city council has also built a **lift** connecting place St-Esprit with Grund – operating daily from 6.30am to 3.30am (free).

To orientate yourself you may want to take a **guided tour**. There are the usual coach tours, run by – among others – *Voyages H. Sales* (rue du Curé 26; ☎46 18 18), who will whisk you around the main city and suburban sites in a few hours, every morning between April and October, for F260 a head. There's also a **miniature train** – "Luxembourg Live" – which travels along the floor of the Pétrusse valley from the Pont Adolphe to Grund and up to the plateau du Rham, giving you a good view of the city fortifications. The train leaves at regular intervals throughout the day during summer from below the Pont Adolphe and costs F200 per person for a 45-minute tour. Buy tickets from place de Bruxelles, by the bridge at the top.

Finding a place to stay

Most of the city's cheaper **hotels** are close to the railway station, though, as with the rest of the country, you'll struggle to find anything ultra-affordable. There are a number of reasonable options down rue Joseph Junck, immediately opposite the station. The *Century*, at no. 6 (☎48 94 37), and the slightly nicer *Chemin de Fer*, next door at no. 4 (☎49 35 28), are fair bets – both charge around F1500 for a double room without private bath. Further down the street at no. 36, the *Zurich* (☎49 13 50) is slightly cheaper, at F1400 for a double, as is the *Axe*, across the road at no. 34 (☎49 09 53), which charges the same for doubles, and has triples for F2100. Other alternatives around the station include the *Red Lion*, five minutes away at rue Zithe 50 (☎48 17 89), a lively bar with double rooms starting at F1200, and the *Bristol* at rue de Strasbourg 11 (☎48 58 29) – though avoid the other hotels on this street as they (like the street) are decidedly seedy.

More upmarket choices include the *Italia*, opposite the *Red Lion* at rue d'Anvers 15–17 (☎48 66 27), which charges F2200 for singles and doubles with private bath, TV and phone, etc, and has an excellent (if slightly sniffy) Italian restaurant downstairs (see "Eating"). In the city centre there's also the *Français* – as central as you can get at place d'Armes 14 (☎47 45 34), for the comparatively reasonable cost of F2400 for a double room. A cheaper centrally placed hotel is the *San Remo*, place Guillaume 8–10 (☎47 25 68), which has doubles for F1600 upwards.

Hostels and camping

One of the best locations in town is enjoyed by the Luxembourg **youth hostel**, down below the Bock fortress on the Montée de Clausen at rue du Fort Olisy 2 (☎26 869), close by the Mousel brewery. Open all year, it's reachable from the station by taking bus #9 or #16; on foot it takes about 20 to 25 minutes from the station. Charges are the standard F250 per person, F210 if you're under 26.

Camping, there are several sites within reach of the city centre. The closest and most pleasant one is north of the centre on the edge of the Grungewald forest area, just past DOMMELDANGE off route d'Echternach; take bus #20 or it's a thirty- to forty-minute walk from the city centre. Dommeldange is also connected to the railway station by train (direction Ettelbruck). Another, less sheltered site, *Bon Accueil*, is south of the city in the suburb of ALZINGEN, to which there are three or four buses an hour from the stand to the left of the station as you walk outside. There's also a third site, *Kockelscheuer*, further out from the city to the southwest; again buses run fairly regularly from the railway station.

The City

The **centre** of Luxembourg isn't as ancient as you might expect – most of the medieval city was destroyed in a gunpowder explosion of 1554 and what you see now dates from a seventeenth-century remodelling. Most of the ramparts and bastions, too, were knocked down in 1867, the city centre's encircling boulevards being built on their foundations, although enough survives to give a clue to the city's awesome defensive capabilities.

The centre of Luxembourg is made up of two squares, the most important of which is **place d'Armes**, a shady oblong fringed with cafés and fast food restaurants and home to the city tourist office at its eastern end. Around the corner, the **Ratskeller** (summer Mon–Sat 10am–12.30pm & 2–6pm, closed Tues; F40) holds a model of the Luxembourg fortress and shows some slides, while to the north lie the city's principal shops, mainly along **Grand Rue**. On the southern side of rue du Curé a small alley cuts through to the much larger **place Guillaume**, the venue of Luxembourg's main general market on weekday mornings and flanked by the bland buildings of the city authorities. In the centre is a statue of William II and a memorial to the nineteenth-century Luxembourg poet Michel Rodange.

A block away from place Guillaume, the **Palais Grand-Ducal** (mid-July to early Sept tours daily except Wed & Sun; F100) was built originally as the town hall, a replacement for a previous Gothic structure that perished in the 1554 explosion, but was adopted by the Luxembourg royals as their residence in the nineteenth century. A Renaissance edifice, the left-hand side of which dates from the sixteenth century, its facade is oddly Moorish in style, turreted and lined with pilasters and arabesques. It's kept for state occasions only these days, but there's still a constant, rather self-important guard of honour maintaining an eye on things outside, only enhancing the slightly Ruritanian feel of things. If you're here at the right time, the tours are worth taking, winding through a set of sumptuous state apartments; outside those months, sadly, you'll have to content yourself with an outside view.

On the right of the palace, an extension of 1743 houses the Luxembourg chamber of deputies. Walk up in the opposite direction and turn right, and you're in the oldest part of the city, the **Rocher du Bock**, where in 963 Count Siegfried decided to build the fort that was to develop into the modern town – of which there are scanty remains. An ideal defensive position, it was subsequently expanded upon by just about every major European power, not least by Vauban for the French in 1648, who made Luxembourg into one of the most strongly defended cities in Europe. The streets here cling to the edge of the plateau, overlooking the sharp drop below, at the bottom of which nestle the slate-roofed houses of Grund.

Of the fortifications which remain in Luxembourg, the largest and most access-ible are the **Bock casemates** (March–Oct daily 10am–5pm; F40) – defensive positions carved out of the rock that it was impossible to demolish without remov-ing the base on which this part of town rests. Used as bomb shelters during World War II, their galleries honeycomb the long protrusion of the Bock, which slopes out into the valley. Actually they're a rather damp and draughty way to spend half an hour, and there's nothing much to see beyond a few rusty old cannons, but the views both ways, looking out over the spires and aqueducts of the city's green heart, are fine – across to the Kirchberg plateau to the northeast, south to the plateau du Rham and its Vauban-built barracks.

From the Bock casemates you can follow the pedestrian **promenade de la Corniche** to place St-Esprit and more fortifications, where the bastions of the **Citadelle du St-Esprit**, built in 1685 by Vauban, are now a grassy park with once again great views over the valley and the Passarelle bridge, which leads

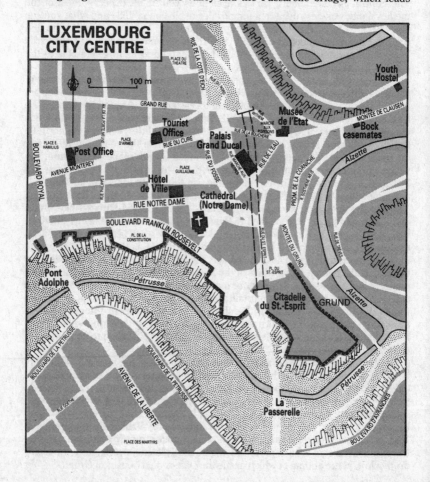

south towards the station from here. There are more casemates on the southern side of the city centre, the **Casemates de la Pétrusse** (Easter, Whitsun & July–Sept only; F40), hollowed out by the Spanish in 1674 and accessible by way of some steps off place de la Constitution. If you've already visited the Bock, however, you'd do better to give these a miss and pop your head around the door of the city's **Cathédrale Notre-Dame**, whose slender black spire dominates the city's puckered skyline. Actually it isn't a very interesting church, a rather perplexing building that went up in 1613–18 in a mixture of styles that varies from the Gothic vaulting of its interior, supported by massive pillars, to its eastern end Renaissance porchway. In the crypt you'll notice the tomb of John the Blind, who died at Crécy in 1346.

Back in the old part of town, the **Musée National** (Tues–Fri 10am–noon & 1–5pm, Sun 10am–noon & 2–6pm; free) occupies a number of converted patrician mansions on the left side of **Marché aux Poissons**, the main square of the old town. A large and rather rambling museum, it gives something of a lowdown on the city's – and country's – history. On the ground floor there are fragments of medieval sculpture, and, among many Roman archaeological exhibits, finds from – and models of – the palace at Echternach, including funerary monuments, bronze figurines, a weathered marble bust of Septimus Severus, and much else besides. Upstairs, on the second floor, you'll find rooms containing prehistoric and geological collections, arrays of fossils – dull stuff mainly, laid out in a deadening, schoolroom environment – and a popular and decorative arts section, with mock-ups of eighteenth- and nineteenth-century domestic rooms, including the inevitable apothecary's shop. The arms section has models of the city's fortifications, parts of which are much the same as they look now, many rifles, pistols and armour, and a room detailing the Luxembourg royal lineage. The third floor holds fine art, with an average set of mainly Netherlandish paintings ranging from the thirteenth to the nineteenth century, bolstered by the semi-permanent loan of the Bentinck-Thyssen collection. There are canvases by Cranach and Cornelisz van Haarlem, and Flemish paintings by Joos van Cleve and Quentin Matsys, notably a very expressive *Presenation in the Temple*. Later Dutch works include a soft *Young Girl on the Balcony* by Ferdinand Bol, a portrait by Hals, genre scenes by Jan Steen and Adrien van Ostade, and Brouwer's *Mussel Eater*. Finally, on the top floor of the museum there's a zoology collection, which – like the prehistoric material – has the distinct whiff of the science lab about it, with an unpleasant, rather archaic assortment of stuffed ostriches, owls, apes, wolves, deer, bison and just about anything that has ever swum, strolled, run or flown in the Luxembourg forests.

Cut behind the museum through the old seventeenth-century **Porte du Pfaffenthal** and follow the road around past the originally eleventh-century **Trois Tours** (on the right) up to Cote d'Eich, a little way down which is the **place du Theâtre**, a small square named after the old Capuchin convent here that has been converted to a theatre. It's home to a small flea market on the second and fourth Saturday of each month.

Over on the other side of the city centre from here, across boulevard Royale, home to most of the city's offshore banking businesses, is Luxembourg city's other main museum, the **Musée Pescatore** (Mon, Wed, Thurs & Fri 1–6pm, Sat & Sun 9am–noon & 3–7pm; free), housed in the nineteenth-century Villa Vauban, set back from the main road on the site of the old fortifications. It has a modest permanent collection of fine art, but this is only displayed during July and August and the rest of the time the building is turned over to temporary exhibitions. If you're here at the right time, it's worth the once-over but not much more, with a small array of paintings that takes in Dutch, Flemish and French artists from the seventeenth to the nineteenth century, including canvases by Dou, Danid Teniers and Courbet. What's more, labelling is virtually non-existent, forcing you to buy the F100 catalogue. Don't bother.

Outside of the city centre there's not much to see. Deep down in the valleys, the so-called "suburbs", old working-class communities gradually turning into yuppie enclaves, merit a stroll – they're very peaceful and hold some of the city's prettiest corners. Take the lift down to **GRUND** and either walk to the right to the park area, where you'll find the old fourteenth-century chapel of **St-Quirin**, or head in the other direction to **CLAUSEN**, from where it's possible to continue on back up out of the valley onto the plateau of Kirchberg, to the east, home to the main European institutions.

Eating, drinking and nightlife

Luxembourg city isn't a cheap place to **eat**, but it does have a much greater variety of restaurants than you'll find in the rest of the country. Many of the city's restaurants are located in the tawdry station area, but they're not particularly cheaper than places across the river, where the quality is likely to be better. For lunch, the *Brasserie Chimay*, rue de Chimay 15, just off place d'Armes, is central and unpretentious, serving up good quality filling *plats du jour* for about F270, and with plenty of dishes for less. *Chez Mami*, on the other side of the centre at rue des Bains 15, is also good and inexpensive, with omelettes, etc, for about F200, more substantial fare for F300. On the same street, at no. 23, the *Brasserie des Bains* is open evenings as well for its decent plates of pasta and wood-fired oven cooked pizzas, both under F200. *Um Dierfgen*, cote d'Eich 6, is also good, a bar and restaurant open both lunchtime and evening, and serving main courses for F400 or so, light meals and omelettes for about F200.

A little more expensively, the bar of *Club 5*, rue de Chimay 5, is one of the city centre's trendier hang-outs, with an excellent and not overpriced restaurant upstairs which serves good food for around F300–400 a main course; the house speciality is *carpaccio* – thin slices of raw beef served with chips and salad for F410. On the other side of the river, the restaurant of the *Hotel Italia* at rue d'Anvers 15–17 is a favourite with the city's professional classes, a pricey option but the best one if you're after a good value splurge; don't expect to pay much less than F1000 a head for two courses with drinks – but the service is impeccable and the surroundings reasonably unpretentious.

Luxembourg's nightlife is rather tame for a capital city, but it has a positive side in some convivial **bars**, all within easy walking distance of each other. The station area is home to sleazy nightclubs mainly and is again best avoided, but in the centre of the city, *Interview*, just up from the post office at rue Aldringen 21, and *Um Piquet*, around the corner at rue de la Poste 30, are two lively central watering-holes, popular with an under-thirties clientele. Close by, *Drive-in* is larger and younger in style, a dark, pseudo-Fifties brasserie with a giant video screen and menus at F300. Down in the valley, the **Grund** neighbourhood harbours a few good spots: *Bei der Infirmière*, on rue de Trèves, is an amicable little bar with a punky crowd; *Scotts*, by the bridge, is a pubby English bar that's the hang-out of Luxembourg's ex-pats – Guinness and bitter are available on draught and there's an upstairs restaurant serving Sunday brunch for F350 a head. If you're eating, you may need to book. Further east, **Clausen**, too, has a number of decent bars, notably *Malou*, rue de la Tour Jacob 57, and *Melusina*, on the same street at no. 145, which has live jazz and folk music most nights. *Casablanca*, on the station side of the valley at boulevard d'Avranches 36, has a basement bar with live music, usually jazz, an upstairs restaurant, and discos at weekends.

Listings

Airport enquiries ☎48 11 99 or ☎48 79 93.

Airlines *British Airways*, rue Notre Dame 15 (☎49 15 71); *Luxair*, place de la Gare (☎47 98 23 12); *Sabena*, Grand Rue 70 (☎21 212); *Icelandair* at Findel airport (☎47 98 24 70).

American Express, rue Origer 6–8 (☎49 60 41). Close to the railway station. Open Mon–Fri 9am–1pm & 2–5pm, Sat 9am–noon.

Car hire *Avis*, rue Duchscher 13 (☎48 95 95), and at the airport (☎43 51 71); *Budget*, at the airport (☎43 34 12); *Europcar*, route de Thionville 88 (☎48 76 84), and at the airport (☎43 45 88); *Hertz*, avenue de la Liberté 25 (48 54 85), and at the airport (☎43 46 45).

Car parks There are three central underground car parks, one off to the right of boulevard Royale near the post office, another on place du Theâtre, a third off rue Notre Dame, close to the corner with rue Chimay. Cost per hour F25, for eight hours about F185.

Doctor Dial ☎012 for details of English-speaking doctors.

Embassies Great Britain, boulevard Roosevelt 14 (☎ 29 864); Ireland, route d'Arlon 28 (☎45 06 10); USA, boulevard E. Servais 22 (☎46 01 23); Netherlands, rue C.M. Spoo 5 (☎27 570); Belgium, rue des Girondins (☎44 27 46).

Emergencies ☎012.

Exchange You can change money outside banking hours at the information office on place de la Gare (for times see "Arrival"), or at the office inside the station itself, though for poor rates (Mon–Sat 8.30am–9pm, Sun 9am–9pm).

Hospital The Clinique Ste-Elisabeth at avenue Emile Reuter 19 (☎45 05 81) is about the most central city hospital.

Launderette place de Strasbourg 3.

Left luggage There's a left-luggage office at the railway station, open daily 6am–10pm and charging F60 per item. There are also lockers (F40–60).

Newspapers English newspapers are available from the railway station bookstall the day after publication.

Pharmacy Dial ☎012 for details of late-opening pharmacies.

Police rue Glesener 58–60 (☎40 91 91).

Post office The main post office is on place Emile Hamilius (Mon–Fri 7am–8pm, Sat 7am–7pm). There's also an office opposite the railway station (daily 6am–8pm).

Swimming pools There's an Olympic-sized swimming pool out at Kirchberg, close to the Centre Européen. Open Mon noon–10pm, Tues–Fri 8am–6.30pm, Sun 9am–1.30pm. There's also the municipal *Bonnevoie* pool, beyond the railway station on rue des Ardennes. Open Mon–Sat 8am–8pm, Sun 8–11am. Closed Wed.

Telephones Both post offices have booths.

Train enquiries The office in the station is open daily 7am–8pm (☎49 24 24 or 499 05 72).

Travel agents *Wasteels*, place de la Gare 4 (☎48 63 63); *Nouvelles Frontières*, boulevard Royale (☎46 41 40); *Sotour*, place du Theâtre 15 (☎46 15 14 or 22 673).

THE GRAND DUCHY

Luxembourg is a city soon exhausted, and it's a good idea to spend some time while you're here seeing something of the **rest of the country**, about two-thirds of which is feasibly seen on day trips, especially if you have a car. Don't rush, however, if you can help it – some of the countryside is gorgeous and strictly deserves more time.

The Luxembourg **rail network** reaches up through the centre of the Grand Duchy, connecting the capital with Ettelbruck, Clervaux and Kautenbach in the north (branch lines run from Ettelbruck to Diekirch and from Kautenbach to Wiltz), and extending arms down to Esch-sur-Alzette in the south, and Wasserbillig on the Moselle – from which trains run on to Trier and Koblenz. You're bound at some point to have to take a **bus**, many of which are also run by *CFL* and supplement the sparse rail system.

Without a car, though, you're not going to be able to do much touring in a day. Better to select a centre and see as much on foot as is practical – no great hardship in the more scenic parts of the country.

In the south of the country, it's the **Moselle** which is of most interest, mainly for the vineyards of the Luxembourg wine industry. To the north, the first major rail junction is **Ettelbruck**, which, although not of interest in itself, gives access by bus to the first taste of the country's finest scenery, for which **Diekirch**, 5km down the road, is a possible base, home to the country's largest brewer and a decent museum remembering the Battle of the Bulge, much of which was fought in the surrounding area. Further east, **Echternach** is a pretty place best-known for its ancient abbey, around which the town is built, and is close to the rolling hiking country of the so-called **Petit Suisse** area. To the north **Vianden** lies in the heart of the Ardennes, and is one of Luxembourg's most important resorts, surrounded by craggy green hills and topped by a glowering newly restored castle. It's a possible centre for seeing the best of the countryside around – the castle of **Bourscheid** a little way southwest, the tiny settlement of **Esch-sur-Sûre**, clasped in the horseshoe bend of its river, the village of **Clervaux**, also with its castle – though this last is on the main rail line from Luxembourg and easily seen on a day trip.

Southern Luxembourg: the Moselle and industrial Southwest

The **south** of Luxembourg is the country's least appealing region, with relatively dull scenery and – southwest of Luxembourg city – much of its industry around the grim town of **Esch-sur-Alzette**. The western bank of the **Moselle river**, which for 25km or so forms the border between Luxembourg and Germany up as far as Wasserbillig (where it spears off towards Trier), is the sole highlight, its gentle slopes covered with vineyards which produce the grapes for Luxembourg's tiny **wine industry**. All of the wine produced is white, and most is good quality, varying from fruity Rieslings to delicate Pinot Blancs and flowery Gewurztraziners, as well as some excellent, underrated *méthode champenoise* sparkling wines. There are a number of producers, and their *caves* are open in season for tours and tasting – and buying if you're keen.

The southwestern corner is reasonably easily seen by train – there are regular connections to Esch – but for the Moselle you ideally need a car. Although buses and (in summer) boats run up and down the river, public transport links are infrequent and don't always tie in very conveniently with the sometimes awkward opening hours of the various *caves*.

The Luxembourg Moselle

If you are constrained by timetables, **REMICH** is probably the easiest place to reach from Luxembourg, and is as good a place as any to see something of the wine industry. It's also a major stop for the ferry boats that ply up and down the river during the summer, connecting Remich with Schengen to the south and Grevenmacher, Wormeldange and, eventually, Trier (Trèves) to the north (see "Travel Details" for the full picture on schedules).

There's not much to Remich in itself, which is a fairly typical border settlement, full of duty-free shops flogging cigarettes and booze to bargain-hunting Germans. But the town is headquarters of the Moselle wine industry, and the **Caves St Martin** (April–Oct daily 9–11.30am & 1.30–5.30pm; F60), a mainly sparkling wine producer, fifteen minutes' walk north from the centre of town on the left of the main road, offers one of the region's most interesting *caves* tours, taking in the minutiae of the *méthode champenoise* process, which at St Martin is still carried out in a fairly traditional way – the bottles, for example, are still turned by hand. The guides are informative and entertaining, and, like most of the wineries, there's a free tasting afterwards of the excellent St Martin product.

There's another chance for wine tasting in the other direction from the centre of Remich, where the village of **BECH-KLEINMACHER**, twenty minutes' walk away, is home to the **Musée A Possen** (mid-March to end Oct daily 2–7pm; F90), a small museum of wine and folklore, housed in the former home of a local vine-grower. Prefaced by a short slide show (in English) giving background on the industry, a number of authentically shabby rooms attempt to re-create life for wine growers in centuries past, with pin-neat bedrooms, a loom and spinning wheel, a kitchen with its walls blackened by cooking, and a mock-up bar and displays of winemaking equipment. Exit is through a real wine bar where you can sample (at a price) some of the local wine or eaux de vie.

Further upriver from Remich, the pretty village of **EHNEN** has another museum devoted to the wine industry, the **Musée du Vin** (April 1–Oct 31 daily except Mon 9.30–11.30am & 2–5pm; F60), on the main road. Housed in the rather less tatty mansion of another local wine baron, this is a rather more organised, less nostalgic affair than A Possen, with informative exhibits in the old fermenting cellar detailing various aspects of the wine-making process, past and present. **WORMELDANGE**, the next village along, strung along the river for a good kilometre, gives the opportunity to visit another working wine producer, the **Caves Cooperatives** (April 1–Oct 1 daily 9.30–11.30am & 1.30–5pm; F60), housed in the big pink building on the far side of the village.

GREVENMACHER, about 10km on from Wormeldange, is the capital of the Luxembourg Moselle and its most pleasant town, with a small but lively pedestrianised centre set up above the river. There are more wineries here, the most prominent of which is the **Caves Bernard Massard** (daily 9–11.30am & 2–5.30pm; F60), on the southern side of the town centre, bang next to the main road and river – follow rue de Trèves from the bus stop and turn left as if to go over the bridge. Like the St Martin *caves*, Bernard Massard are known for their sparkling, *methode champenoise* wine, though they are a much bigger concern, producing around four million bottles a year to St Martin's 800,000 or so. It shows in the production methods, which are far more automated, making for a less interesting – and shorter – tour (though it is preceded by a short slide show) and a less palatable product, sampling of which goes on in the slick hospitality suite afterwards.

The Bernard Massard organisation is also responsible for Grevenmacher's other attraction, the **Jardin des Papillons**, on the other side of town at the far end of route de Trèves (April 1–Oct 31 daily 9.30am–6pm; F200), where around forty species of butterfly are viewable in a specially created (28°C constant) hothouse. There's a lush array of flowers and plants, and at certain times of year you can watch the butterflies hatching, but it's clearly overpriced – although you do get another free glass of wine thrown in.

If you're basing yourself in the region, Grevenmacher is about the best place to **stay**, though it's not very easy to get to from Luxembourg city – basically you have to take a train to the next town north, WASSERBILLIG, and a bus from there (12 buses daily; 10min). There's a **campsite**, the *Route du Vin*, in Grevenmacher on the northern edge of town, next to the butterfly park, and a **youth hostel** a short walk up rue de Centenaire from the **bus stop** on route de Trèves (☎75 222). As for **hotels**, the *Mosellan*, at rue de Trèves 35 (☎75 157), has doubles for F1200.

The Southwest

The area immediately southwest of Luxembourg city is the country's least appealing, an iron ore mining region whose heavy industry and urban sprawls are best glimpsed from a train window on the way to somewhere else. **ESCH-SUR-ALZETTE** is the main centre, a large town, by Luxembourg standards, of around 25,000 people – the country's second biggest urban conglomeration. But there's no reason to come here except for the **Musée National des Mines**, devoted to the mining history of the area, in the nearby town of **RUMELANGE** (Easter–Oct 31 daily 2–6pm, Nov 1–Easter second Sat & Sun of each month 2–6pm; F100). Situated in a disused mine shaft, close on 1000m deep, guided tours of the museum last an hour and a half, and take in displays of ancient and modern tools, photos and charts, and assorted machinery from the nineteenth and twentieth centuries.

There are also one or two places you might want to visit if you're travelling with kids. Northeast of Esch, the **Parc Merveilleux** at nearby **BETTEMBOURG** (Easter–end Oct daily 9.30am–6pm; F80, children F60) is a very popular summer target of Luxembourg families, its large site containing a children's zoo, mini-train rides and lots of Disneylandish attractions. In the other direction, **RODANGE** is home to a contraption known as **Train 1900** (May 1–Sept 30 Sun 3pm, 4.20pm & 5.40pm; F120, children F60), a steam train that runs around the nearby Titelberg hill – the site of some scant traces of Roman occupation. Rodange is, like Esch, connected with Luxembourg by rail, and the steam train departs from a (signposted) point fifteen minutes' walk away from the rail station.

Central Luxembourg: Ettelbruck, Diekirch and Echternach

Heading north from the capital, Luxembourg's landscapes grow more spectacular, though you have to get some way out of the city before the scenery is anything but tame. The main road and rail lines run parallel, shadowing the course of the Alzette river. **MERSCH** is the first town that feels properly free of the sway of the capital, and the first real stop on the train line, though it's a rather unenticing place, with little to draw you beyond some rather thin remains of a **Roman villa**, southwest of the centre on rue des Romains. If you have your own transport, you might want to detour from here down to one of the country's most beautifully sited **youth hostels**, housed in the old castle of **Hollenfels**, 10km southwest of Mersch (☎30 70 37). Otherwise, push straight on to Ettelbruck.

Ettelbruck

Situated at the meeting point of the Alzette and Sûre river valleys, **ETTELBRUCK** is an important provincial centre, a town of around 6500 people that occupies a central position in the country and is an important road and rail junction. Again, there's not much to see in the town: Ettelbruck suffered heavy damage during the fighting of late 1944 and is pretty much without interest beyond a few mementoes of the war – a **memorial** in the shape of a parked US tank out on the Diekirch road, and a **Musée Patton** at the junction of Grand Rue and rue du Canal ((July 15–Sept 1 daily 1–6pm; F50). But you may find yourself here at least briefly. There's a **tourist office** in Ettelbruck's railway station (Mon–Fri 8.30am–noon & 1.30–5pm), though for **accommodation** you're better off staying in Diekirch (see below) unless you're hostelling. Ettelbruck's **youth hostel** is on rue Grand-Duchesse Josephine-Charlotte (☎82 269).

Diekirch

Five kilometres east, and accessible by bus or train from Ettelbruck station, **DIEKIRCH** is a more appealing place, though it too suffered during the 1944 fighting and is not immediately attractive. However, it is a good base for seeing some of the surrounding area (with a couple of good campsites) and it does have one or two things to see of mild interest.

One of these, the **Musée Historique**, 200m from the main square of place Guillaume, on the right up Montée de la Seitert (1 week before and 1 week after Easter & May 1–Oct 31 daily 10am–noon & 2–6pm; F80), provides an excellent historical survey of the Battle of the Bulge in Luxembourg, with a special, if rather adulatory, emphasis on the liberating US troops. The photographs on display steal the show, showing both sets of troops in action and at leisure, some recording the appalling freezing conditions of December 1944, others the horrific state of affairs inside the medics' tent. There's a variety of dioramas, many modelled diligently after actual photographs (which are often displayed alongside), along with a hoard of military paraphernalia – explosives, shells, weapons, and the bits and bobs dished out to both American and German soldiers (prayer books, rations, novellas, etc). There's also a display entitled "Veiner Miliz", which details the activities of the tiny Luxembourg resistance movement based in Vianden.

Diekirch's second museum, the **Musée Mosaiques Romaines**, is on the other side of the square (daily except Thurs 10am–noon & 2–6pm; F20) – two rooms basically, each holding a reasonably well preserved Roman floor mosaic, one from 150 AD, the other from around the third century, found on a site in the centre of Diekirch, just off rue Esplanade, together with a handful of other artefacts. The best mosaic is the one in the right-hand room, its design centring on a two-faced depiction of Medusa. Alongside it are a couple of skeletons, one still in its original wooden coffin, that were also found nearby.

There are more skeletons on the other side of the pedestrianised town centre, in the church of **St-Laurent** (daily 10am–noon & 2–6pm; free), 100m east of the other main square, place de la Liberation, at the top of the main shopping street of Grand Rue. A turreted church, some parts of which date back to the ninth century, you can climb down via a side door to an eerily lit set of medieval tombs that have been discovered under the floor.

Practical details

Diekirch's **bus and train station** is five to ten minutes' walk south of the centre of town on avenue de la Gare, next door to the Diekirch brewery – the country's largest beer producer. The **tourist office** is on the corner of place Guillaume (Mon–Fri 10am–noon & 2–7pm; ☎80 30 23), and can help with maps and accommodation needs. Of the town's **hotels**, the *Hotel de la Paix*, around the corner from the tourist office on place Guillaume, is the cheapest, with doubles for F1000, but it's pretty grotty. Rather nicer are two hotels opposite the bus station – the *Au Bon Accueil*, avenue de la Gare 77 (☎80 34 76), and the *De la Gare*, avenue de la Gare 73 (☎80 33 05), which both have double rooms from about F1400. The town's two **campsites** – *de la Sûre* and *Op de Sauer* – are handily placed a few minutes' walk from the centre by the river; follow the road 100m east from the *Hôtel Europe*, cross over the bridge and take the riverside path. There's also another site, the *Gritt*, a few minutes by bus towards Ettelbruck in INGLEDORF, which has a lovely location, also by the river. There isn't a huge amount of **eating** alternatives in Diekirch: you could try the pizzas and pasta served up for F180 upwards in the *Rialto*, at Grand Rue 15, or the more traditional Luxembourg fare at the excellent *Brasserie du Commerce*, at the top end of Grand Rue on place de la Liberation – main courses go for F300–400, omelettes etc F200.

Diekirch makes a good base for touring the surrounding area, either by car or by bike: you can hire **bikes** from the *de la Sûre* campsite, or from an office in the bus station, which charges F250 a day, F1250 a week. Between May and November the same office also hires out **kayaks** for travelling downriver to Dillingen or Echternach – an easy and safe but exciting trip. Two-seaters go for F900, one-seaters F600; reckon on about six hours to reach Echternach.

Echternach and around

Ten kilometres or so east of Diekirch, the Sûre becomes the border between Luxembourg and Germany, edging an area known – rather optimistically – as **Petit Suisse** or "Little Switzerland", for its thickly wooded hills and rocky valleys. **ECHTERNACH** is the main centre of this region, a town of around 4000 people that is one of Luxembourg's prime resorts. Echternach grew up around an abbey that was founded here in 698 by one Saint Willibrord, an English mission-ary monk who went on to become famous for curing epilepsy and cattle – skills which are commemorated by the renowned hour-long dancing procession around the saint's tomb and town centre, annually on Whit Tuesday.

The centre of town is the wedge-shaped **place du Marché**, an elegant conglomeration of ancient buildings, most notable among which is the fifteenth-century turreted old **town hall**, with its Gothic loggia of 1520. A short walk east of here there's a **Musée de Prehistorie** on the right-hand side of rue du Pont (daily except Mon 10am–noon & 2–5pm). But the town's real attraction is the **Abbey** itself, just off place du Marché to the north, signalled by the spires of its enormous **church**. This has had a long and rather chequered history. The origi-nal church of Saint Willibrord was a much smaller affair, but it was destroyed by fire in 1016 and a new structure erected later that century. Restored in 1862, it was later rebuilt to the former eleventh-century plan after sustaining heavy bomb damage during the Battle of the Bulge in 1944, and reconsecrated in 1952. It's a simple basilical structure with a Romanesque arched nave, and it can't help but feel very much a reconstruction. Downstairs the crypt is the only major part of Saint Willibrord's church to have survived. Dating from around 900, its white-washed walls are home to some unfinished frescoes and the primitive coffin of the saint himself, covered by an ornate canopy of 1906.

The huge abbey complex spreads out beyond the church to a set of formal gardens by the river, its mainly eighteenth-century buildings given over to a variety of secular activities these days. One houses the **Musée de l'Abbaye** (daily 10am–noon & 2–5pm; F40), which contains more fragments of Saint Willibrord's first convent and church – foundations mainly, along with some rather macabre eighth-century tombs complete with skeletons. The rest of the museum is well laid out and has some high quality exhibits, though sadly there's no English information. Highlights include a piece of mosaic flooring from Echternach's Roman villa (see below) and various examples of medieval calligra-phy and illumination, including the eleventh-century so-called *Codex Aureus* of Echternach, whose superb jewelled cover, from 990, was the work of a Trier craftsman.

Practical details

There's not much else to see in Echternach beyond the abbey, but like Diekirch it makes one of Luxembourg's best – and prettiest – countryside bases. The **bus station** is five minutes from the centre of town, down the long rue de la Gare, a lively street lined with tourist boutiques and hotels. The **tourist office** is opposite the abbey church (Mon–Fri 9am–noon & 1–5pm, Sat until 6pm, when closed go to *Hôtel Regine*; ☎72 230), and has maps of the town and information on **accom-modation**. Echternach has loads of **hotels**, many along rue de la Gare, among which there are a number of reasonable options: try the *Regine* at no. 53 (☎72 077) and the *Pavillon* at no. 2 (☎72 98 09), which both have double rooms for F1300; or the *Aigle Noir* at no. 54 (☎72 383), with rooms for as low as F1000. The *Postillon*, rue de Luxembourg 7 (☎72 188), has doubles for F1200. Failing that, the *Petite Poete* on place du Marché (☎72 072) is central and charges just F1150 for a double with shared bath. There's a **campsite** 300m beyond the bus station following the river out of town, and a **youth hostel** at rue André Deutscher 9 (☎72 158) – follow the road that runs south from the corner of place du Marché and rue de la Gare.

For **food**, the *Benelux* restaurant on the same corner is very reasonably priced, with most main courses going for F200–300. The *Hotel del'Abbaye* restaurant on rue la Gare is also affordable, with *plats du jour* and fixed-price menus – as is the *Hôtel du Commerce* on place du Marché, which serves a three-course special for F400. For snacks, or just a drink, use the *Bit Beim Dokter* bar, up by the tourist office, which serves sandwiches and light meals for under F200.

Around Echternach

About a kilometre south of Echternach, following the road to LAUTERBORN, a large artificial **lake** provides good, if crowded, distraction on hot summer afternoons. Close by lie the remains of a mainly second-century **Roman villa**, though these are very scant – more or less the foundations only.

Further afield, west into the heart of Petit Suisse, back towards Diekirch, the village of **BERDORF** is a popular climbing centre and a good starting-point for gentle hikes into the craggier reaches of the region – paths are marked out clearly and take you through some delightful spots. One destination might be the castle at **Beaufort**, about 6km west (April 1–Oct 25 daily 9am–6pm; F50), which enjoys a marvellous location overlooking the surrounding wooded hills. The site was originally a Roman encampment, and the oldest part of the castle dates from the mid-twelfth century; later parts were added in 1380 and 1500. It's no more than a ruin now but you can wander the site at will, enjoying the views and poking around the crumbling nooks and corners, which in fact simply fell into ruin through disuse and neglect – the building saw nothing of any kind of fighting, apparently, until hit by shells during the Battle of the Bulge.

There's a **youth hostel** in Beaufort village, a pleasant modern affair at rue de l'Auberge 6 (☎86 075). If you want a target for moving on, there's another castle at **LAROCHETTE**, a few kilometres south of Beaufort, poking out of the trees high above what is a very pretty little town. This one is a ruin too, but the later section has been restored and now retains its roof and turrets.

Northern Luxembourg: Vianden, Esch, Wiltz and Clervaux

The **northern** part of Luxembourg, within the narrowing neck of the country's triangle, is its most spectacular region, repeating the scenic highlights of the Belgian Ardennes. Again, transport connections are difficult without a car, and it's far enough from the capital to make day trips not nearly so feasible or enjoyable. Best to pick one centre as a base and see what you can do from there.

Vianden

Though it's not centrally placed, the best base for seeing the Luxembourg Ardennes is **VIANDEN**, close to the German border. A tiny place, not much more than a village really, Vianden is probably the most strikingly sited of all Luxembourg's provincial towns, and it consequently gets very crowded with tourists in summer. Confined by a bowl of green wooded hills, it spreads up the slope from the river Our, in part still surrounded by ramparts and totally dominated by the newly restored castle, which towers on the hill immediately above.

The main street curves down to the river, almost entirely lined by hotels and restaurants and finishing up at the bridge, on which a Rodin bust of **Victor Hugo** signals a **house** (in part now the tourist office) that was the part-time home of the French writer between 1862 and 1871. Hugo has since become Vianden's most famous adopted son, and his house has been turned over to a museum (April 1–Nov 1 daily 9.30am–noon & 2–6pm, closed Wed outside July & Aug; F25) commemorating his stay here, with many letters and copies of original poems and manuscripts, including his "Discourse on Vianden", written in 1871. There are also photographs of the town during the nineteenth century, and sketches by the great man of local places of interest – the castles at Beaufort and Larochette, for example. Sadly, though, there's no furniture left from Hugo's time, apart from his bedroom, complete with original bed.

There are **two other museums** in Vianden, one of Dinky toys at rue du Sanatorium 29 (April–Oct daily 2–6pm; F30), and another of so-called "Rustic Arts" at Grand Rue 98 (April–Oct daily 10am–noon & 2.30–6pm; F50). But Vianden's major sight is inevitably the **castle** itself (Jan & Feb Sat & Sun 10am–4pm; March daily 10am–4pm; April daily 10am–6pm; May–Aug daily 9am–7pm; Sept–Dec daily 10am–5pm; F100), recently open in its entirety following a very thorough restoration, before which much was in ruins. Originally a fifth-century structure, the present building dates mostly from the eleventh century and shows features from the Romanesque style to the Renaissance. It was the home of the Counts of Vianden, who ruled the town and much of the area around during the twelfth and thirteenth centuries until falling under the sway of the House of Luxembourg in 1264. Later, in 1417, the Nassau family took over the building, and it remains the property of the grand-ducal family. It forms a very large complex, the renovation sensitively done, though the crowds trooping through the pristine halls and galleries can't help but demean any atmosphere that might have been left. On display are the inevitable suits of armour and suchlike, but much has just been left empty, notably the long Byzantine Room, with its high trefoil windows open to the air, and the next door octagonal upper chapel, surrounded by a narrow defensive walkway. There are, too, exhibits on the development of the building, detailing its restoration, and on the history of the town, and some rooms that have been in part furnished in period style – the Banqueting Hall and the huge Counts' Hall, decorated with seventeenth-century tapestries – though the piped music is an odd (and unwelcome) accompaniment. For a more authentic mustiness, peek down the well just off the old kitchen, its murky darkness lit to reveal massive depths, and leave through the unrestored Gothic dungeon – perhaps the most evocative part of the entire building.

Beyond the castle it's the countryside around Vianden which beckons most positively – something you can survey from the hill above by taking the **Télésiège** or cable car to its 450-metre-high summit (Easter–Oct daily 10am–6pm; F140 return). This runs from a station on rue du Sanatorium, just off rue Victor Hugo on the western edge of the town centre. At the top there's a restaurant with a terrace; you can also walk down to the castle by way of a footpath.

Practical details

Buses to Vianden stop on the far eastern edge of town on the route de la Frontière, about five minutes' walk from the **tourist office** in the centre by the bridge (daily except Wed 9.30am–noon & 2–6pm; ☎84 257), which has copious information, maps, etc. **Accommodation** isn't too much of a problem – virtually every other building in Vianden is a **hotel** – though during the high season you'd be wise to book in advance. Among the cheaper alternatives on the castle side of the river are *Hôtel Collette*, Grand Rue 68–70 (☎84 004), *Hôtel Reunion*, Grand Rue 66 (☎84 155), and the *Café de la Poste*, Grand Rue 10 (☎84 209), all of which have double rooms starting at just over F1000, without private bath. On the other side of the river, the *Auberge de l'Our*, just over the bridge on the right at rue de la Gare 35 (☎84 675), also has rooms starting at F1000 (and a well-priced and popular restaurant too), and there are any number of other possibilities on both sides of the road as far as the bus station – the *Petry*, rue de la Gare 15 (☎84 122), has doubles for just under F1000. There's also a **youth hostel** nicely placed at the top of Grand Rue, hard beneath the ramparts of the castle at Montée du Chateau 3 (☎84 177). The nearest **campsite** is *Op dem Deich*, by the river near the bus station; there are also two other campsites further on down the road to Echternach – *De l'Our* and *Du Moulin* – though all are closed during the January to April period.

Most of the hotels have **restaurants**, and these form the bulk of the town's eating options. The *De l'Our* hotel by the bridge serves a good array of Luxembourg specialities, though its terrace by the river means it gets very crowded; its **bar** is also about the most convivial and cheap place to drink in Vianden. On the other side of the river, the *Café de la Poste* on Grand Rue offers menus for just F300, the *Hôtel Bingen*, further up, for a little more. If you're flush, you might try the rather swankier surroundings of the *Auberge de la Château* restaurant further up Grand Rue – though avoid the hotel itself, which is unfriendly and overpriced.

West from Vianden: Bourscheid, Esch and Wiltz

The only way to go from Vianden and remain in Luxembourg is **west**, a route which takes you through the best of the Ardennes scenery, though you'll need a car to do it comfortably – if at all. The castle at **Bourscheid** (March 1–Sept 30 daily 10am–7pm; F50) provides one of the most spectacular stops if you do have wheels: perching high above the surrounding wooded hills, it's without question the most superbly sited of all Luxembourg's castles. The first proper fortification was erected here around the year 1000, when a stone wall was substituted for a previous wooden structure, though nothing much is left of this period and most of the later building you see now went up during the fourteenth century. It's entirely ruin these days, and there's not much to see beyond the shape of the walls and the odd tower, and some dusty artefacts in the gabled late fourteenth-century Stolzembourg house. But the views, as you'd expect, are stunning.

Below the castle, the river Sûre winds a very picturesque route through its valley – a beauty spot you can take most advantage of from a couple of **campsites** situated right by the river in **BOURSCHEID MOULIN** – the *Moulin* and *Um Gritt*. In the opposite direction, the road continues up towards the village of **BOURSCHEID** proper, on the way to which there's another **campsite**. From here, you can follow the Sûre to **ESCH-SUR-SÛRE**, a small village of just 300 people with a fame out of all proportion to its size, mainly due to its gorgeous site within an ox-bow loop in the river. Once here, there's nothing to see in particular, and Esch itself, once you get into its few streets, is not even especially attractive. But the location is a fine one, surrounded by a high wall of green in its sheltered position at the bottom of the valley. The castle above, perched on two, entirely separate crags, each part of which you can wander around, dates from the tenth century and has been ruined for a couple of hundred years now – and it shows. The *Hôtel du Moulin* is about the least expensive **place to stay**, with double rooms for F1000, and it offers three-course **menus** for F450 that include some intriguing local specialities. Failing that, the *Hôtel des Ardennes*, up by the bridge, has a cheap self-service restaurant and snack bar.

About 10km north of Esch, **WILTZ** is one of the larger but not one of the Grand Duchy's most appealing centres, much of it a sprawl of unchecked settlement. But its upper town, high on the hill above, holds one or two items of mild interest around its **château**, a largely seventeenth-century building now, though built on a twelfth-century base. High above the wooded valley, the somewhat over-zealously restored château, looking like a transplant from the Loire valley, is home to the Wiltz **tourist office** (summer daily 2–6pm; ☎95 74 44) and **two museums**, one yet another rather tired display devoted to the **Battle of the Bulge**, the other – much better – a **Musée Arts et Metiers** (Whitsun–Sept 15 daily 10am–noon & 1.30–5pm; F30), with ceramics, agricultural tools, basketwork, and a huge still. Part of the château gardens are laid out for performances of the town's **music festival** during July and August – a nice setting – while **paths** lead down into the wooded grounds below.

It's not really worth **stopping over** in Wiltz, which is a fairly dead place at the best of times, though there is a **campsite** 200m up Grand Rue on the left (July–Aug only). For **food**, the *Zumm Treffpunkt*, on Grand Rue close to the château, is good and cheap, with most dishes from around F250, pizzas for less.

Clervaux

About 15km from Wiltz, in the far north of Luxembourg, **CLERVAUX** is another small town topped with a castle and built around a loop in the river. Clervaux's castle dates from the twelfth century but was rebuilt in the seventeenth century and after considerable damage in the last war, as is recounted in a tokenistic and rather unimaginative **Battle of the Bulge museum** across the atmospheric, cobbled, ivy-swathed castle courtyard (daily 10am–5pm; F40). Another part of the castle holds a **museum of models** (same times and price), with dusty maquettes of all the castles of Luxembourg in a series of large echoing rooms.

The castle is also home to the **tourist office** (daily except Sun 2–5pm; ☎92 072), which has details on accommodation in Clervaux – there are plenty of **hotels** for a place of this size, of which the *Des Ardennes*, Grand Rue 22 (☎92 254), is the cheapest and most central, with doubles for F1400. There's also a **campsite**, *Reillerweiller*, about 2km out of town on the Vianden road, beside the river. The best place **to eat** in a town of pricey restaurants is the *Splendid*, Grand Rue 32.

travel details

Trains

From Luxembourg to Wasserbillig/Trier/Koblenz (8 daily; 30min/45min/2hr); Ettelbruck/Clervaux (hourly; 35min/1hr 5min); Liège (for Maastricht) (7 daily; 2hr 30min); Diekirch (change at Ettelbruck) (8 daily; 40min); Kautenbach (hourly; 1hr); Wiltz (change at Kautenbach) (8 daily; 1hr 10min); Arlon/Namur/Brussels (for Amsterdam) (11 daily; 20min/1hr 45min/2hr 30min).

Buses

From Luxembourg to Mondorf/Remich (hourly; 30min/45min); Echternach (12 daily; 1hr 10min);

Diekirch (8 daily; 1hr 20min); Vianden (2 daily; 55min).

From Wiltz to Esch-sur-Sûre (4 daily; 25min).

From Remich to Wormeldange/Grevenmacher/ Wasserbillig (5 daily; 15min/30min/40min).

From Grevenmacher/Wasserbillig to Echternach (12 daily; 40min/30min).

From Ettelbruck to Diekirch (6 an hour; 10min); Vianden (12 daily; 30min); Echternach (10 daily; 45min); Clervaux (2 daily; 1hr); Esch-sur-Sûre (4 daily; 40min).

From Diekirch to Vianden (hourly; 20min); Echternach (10 daily; 35min).

Boats
Schengen–Remich–Wormeldange– Grevenmacher–Wasserbillig–Trier (mid-April to end Sept roughly 6 weekly). For full time-table details of the Moselle ferry boats, contact *Navigation Touristique de l'Entente de la Moselle Luxembourgeoise*, route de Thionville 32, Grevenmacher (☎75 82 75).

PART FOUR

THE

CONTEXTS

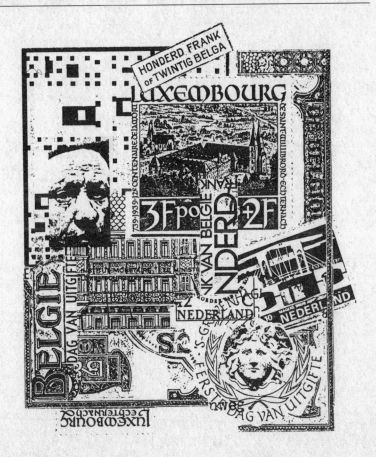

THE HISTORICAL FRAMEWORK

What are now known as the countries of Belgium, Luxembourg and the Netherlands didn't reach their present delimitations until 1830. Until then their borders were continually being redrawn following battles, treaties and alliances, and, inevitably, what follows is an outline of the history of the whole region, rather than an individual country-by-country guide. The term "Holland" refers to the province – not the country – throughout.

BEGINNINGS

Little is known of the prehistoric settlers of the Low Countries, their visible remains largely confined to the far north of the Netherlands. Here, mounds known as *terpen* were built to keep the sea at bay in Friesland and Groningen, and in Drenthe megalithic tombs, *hunebeds*, stretch scattered across a low ridge of hills, the *hondsrug*, north of Emmen.

Clearer details of the Low Countries emerge at the time of Julius Caesar's conquest of Gaul in 57 to 50 BC. He found three tribal groupings living in the region: the mainly Celtic **Belgae** (hence the nineteenth-century term "Belgium") settled by the Rhine, Maas and Waal to the south; the Germanic **Frisians** living on the marshy coastal strip north of the Scheldt; and the **Batavi**, another Germanic people, inhabiting the swampy river banks of what is now the southern Netherlands. The Belgae were conquered and their lands incorporated into the imperial province of **Gallia Belgica**, but the territory of the Batavi and Frisians was not considered worthy of colonisation, and these tribes were granted the status of allies, a source of recruitment for the Roman legions and curiosity for imperial travellers. In 50 AD Pliny observed "Here a wretched race is found, inhabiting either the more elevated spots or artificial mounds . . . When the waves cover the surrounding area they are like so many mariners on board a ship, and when again the tide recedes their condition is that of so many shipwrecked men".

The **Roman occupation** continued for 500 years until the legions were pulled back to protect the heartlands of a crumbling empire. But despite the length of their stay, there's precious little left to indicate their presence, with the notable exception of the odd stretch of city wall around Tongeren and the beautiful baths at Heerlen in Limburg, one of the main Roman settlements. As the empire collapsed in chaos and confusion, the Germanic **Franks**, who had been settling within Gallia Belgica from the third century, filled the power vacuum to the south, along with their allies the Belgae, and established a **Merovingian** kingdom based around their capital in Tournai. A great swathe of forest extending from the Scheldt to the Ardennes separated the Frankish kingdom from the more confused situation to the north and east, where other tribes of Franks settled along the Scheldt and Leie, Saxons occupied parts of Overijssel and Gelderland, and the Frisans clung to the shore.

Towards the end of the fifth century, the Merovingians extended their control over much of the rest of what is now north and central France, and in 496 their king, Clovis, was converted to Christianity, a faith which slowly filtered north, spread by energetic missionaries like Saint Willibrord, first bishop of Utrecht from about 710, and Saint Boniface, who was killed by the Frisians in 754 in a final act of pagan resistance before they too were converted. United by faith, the whole region was soon to be united in a single kingdom under **Charlemagne**, son of Pepin III and king of the west Franks from 768.

In a dazzling series of campaigns, Charlemagne extended his empire south into Italy, west to the Pyrenees, north to Denmark and east to the Oder, his secular authority bolstered by his coronation as the first Holy Roman Emperor in 800, a title bestowed on him by the Pope in order to legitimise his claim as the successor to the emperors of Imperial Rome.

The strength and stability of Charlemagne's court at Aachen spread to the Low Countries, bringing a flurry of building of superb Romanesque churches like Maastricht's St Servaas, and a trading boom, utilising the region's principal rivers. However, unlike his Roman predecessors, Charlemagne was subject to the divisive inheritance laws of the Salian tribe of Franks, and after his death in 814, his kingdom was divided between his grandsons into three roughly parallel strips of territory, the precursors of France, the Low Countries and Germany.

THE GROWTH OF THE TOWNS

The tripartite division of Charlemagne's empire placed the Low Countries between the emergent French- and German-speaking nations, a dangerous location which was subsequently to decide much of its history, though this was not apparent in the cobweb of local alliances that made up early feudal western Europe in the ninth and tenth centuries. During this period, French kings and German emperors exercised a general authority over the region, but power was effectively in the hands of local lords who, remote from central control, brought a degree of local stability. From the twelfth century, feudalism slipped into a gradual decline, the intricate pattern of localised allegiances undermined by the increasing strength of certain lords, whose power and wealth often exceeded that of their nominal sovereign. Preoccupied by territorial squabbles, this streamlined nobility was usually willing to assist the growth of towns by granting charters which permitted a certain amount of autonomy in exchange for tax revenues, and military and labour services. The first major cities were the **cloth towns** of Flanders, particularly Ghent, Bruges and Ieper, which grew rich from the manufacture of cloth, their garments exported far and wide and their economies dependent on a continuous supply of good-quality wool from England. Meanwhile,

their smaller northern neighbours concentrated on trade, exploiting their strategic position at the junction of several of the major waterways and trade routes of the day.

Predictably, the economic interests of the merchants and guildsmen of the cities often clashed with those of the local lord. This was especially true in Flanders, where the towns were anxious to preserve a good relationship with the king of England, who controlled the wool supply, whereas their count, a vassal of the king of France, was often embroiled in the dynastic conflicts between the two monarchs. As a result, the history of thirteenth- and fourteenth-century Flanders is punctuated by sporadic fighting, the fortunes of war oscillating between the cities and the nobility.

BURGUNDIAN RULE

By the late fourteenth century the political situation in the Low Countries was fairly clear: five lords controlled most of the region, paying only nominal homage to their French or German overlords. In 1419 **Philip the Good** of Burgundy succeeded to the countship of Flanders and by a series of adroit political moves gained control over Holland, Zeeland, Brabant and Limburg to the north, and Antwerp, Namur and Luxembourg to the south. He consolidated his power by establishing a strong central administration in Bruges and restricting the privileges granted in the towns' charters. During his reign **Bruges** became an emporium for the Hanseatic League, a mainly German association of towns who acted as a trading group and protected their interests by an exclusive system of trading tariffs. The wealth of Bruges was legendary, and the Burgundian court patronised the early and seminal Nederlandish painters like Jan van Eyck and Hans Memling, whose works are displayed in Ghent and Bruges today.

Philip died in 1467 to be succeeded by his son, Charles the Bold, who was killed in battle ten years later, plunging his carefully crafted domain into turmoil. The French seized the opportunity to take back Arras and Burgundy and before the people of Flanders would agree to fight the French they kidnapped Charles's daughter, Mary, and forced her to sign a charter that restored the civic privileges removed by her grandfather Philip.

THE HABSBURGS

After her release, Mary married the **Hapsburg** Maximilian of Austria, who was forced to assume sole authority when Mary was killed in a riding accident in 1482. Today, her tomb stands beside that of her father in the Onze Lieve Vrouwekerk in Bruges. Maximilian continued to rule until 1494, when he became Holy Roman Emperor and transferred control of the Low Countries to his son, Philip the Handsome, and subsequently to his grandson **Charles V**, who in turn became King of Spain and Holy Roman Emperor in 1516 and 1519 respectively. Charles was suspicious of the turbulent burghers of Flanders and, following in Maximilian's footsteps, favoured Antwerp at their expense. Indeed, the great Flemish towns of Ghent and Bruges were in decline, their economies undermined by England's cloth-manufacturing success and Bruges suffering from the devastating effects of the silting of the river Zwin, whose estuary connected the town to the sea. **Antwerp** became the greatest port in the empire, part of a general movement of trade and prosperity away from Flanders to the cities to the north.

Charles was keen to assert Hapsburg authority over the merchant cities of the Low Countries, but regardless of his display of force, a spiritual trend was emerging that would question not only the rights of the Emperor but the power of the Church itself.

STIRRINGS OF THE REFORMATION

An alliance of church and state had dominated the medieval world: pope and bishops, kings and counts were supposedly the representatives of God on earth, and crushed religious dissent wherever it appeared. Much of their authority depended on the ignorance of the population, who were entirely dependent on their priests for the interpretation of the scriptures, their view of the world carefully controlled.

There were many complex reasons for the **Reformation**, the stirring of religious revolt that stood sixteenth-century Europe on its head, but certainly the **development of typography** was a key. For the first time, printers were able to produce relatively cheap Bibles in quantity, and the religious texts were

no longer the exclusive property of the church. A welter of debate spread across much of western Europe, led initially by theologians who wished to cleanse the Catholic church of its corruptions, superstitions and extravagant ceremony; only later did many of these same thinkers decide to support a breakaway church. Humanists like **Erasmus of Rotterdam** (1465–1536) saw man as the crowning of creation rather than the sinful creature of the Fall; and, most importantly, in 1517 **Martin Luther** produced his 95 theses against indulgences, rejecting among other things Christ's presence in the sacrament of the Eucharist, and denying the Church's monopoly on the interpretation of the Bible. His works and Bible translations were printed in the Netherlands and his ideas gained a following in a group known as the Sacramentarians. They, and other reforming groups branded as **Lutheran** by the Church, were persecuted and escaped the towns to form fugitive communes where the doctrines of another reformer, **John Calvin** (1509–64), became popular. Luther stated that the Church's political power was subservient to that of the state; Calvin emphasised the importance of individual conscience and the need for redemption through the grace of Christ rather than the confessional. The seeds of Protestantism fell on fertile ground among the merchants of the cities of the Low Countries, whose wealth and independence could not easily be accommodated within a rigid caste society; similarly, their employees, the guildsmen and their apprentices, had a long history of opposing royal authority, and many were soon convinced of the need to reform an autocratic, venal church. In 1555, Charles V abdicated, transferring his German lands to his brother Ferdinand, and his Italian, Spanish and Low Countries territories to his son, the fanatically Catholic **Philip II**. The scene was set for a massive confrontation.

THE REVOLT OF THE NETHERLANDS

On his father's abdication, Philip decided to teach his heretical subjects a lesson. He garrisoned the towns of the Low Countries with Spanish mercenaries, imported the Inquisition and passed a series of anti-Protestant edicts. The opposition to these measures was, however, so widespread that he was pushed into a tactical withdrawal, recalling his soldiers and transferring control to his sister Margaret in 1559. Based in Brussels, the equally resolute Margaret implemented the policies of her brother with gusto. In 1561 she reorganised the church and created fourteen new bishoprics, a move that was construed as a wresting of power from civil authority, and an attempt to destroy the local aristocracy's powers of religious patronage. Protestantism and Protestant sympathies spread to the nobility, who petitioned Philip for moderation but were dismissed out of hand. In 1565 a harvest failure caused a winter famine among the workers, and in many towns, particularly Antwerp, they ran riot in the churches, sacking them of their wealth and destroying their rich decoration in the **Iconoclastic Fury**.

The ferocity of this outbreak shocked the higher classes into renewed support for Spain, and Margaret regained the allegiance of most nobles – with the principal exception of the country's greatest landowner, Prince William of Orange-Nassau, known as **William the Silent** (though William the Taciturn is a better translation). Of Germanic descent, he was raised a Catholic but the excesses and rigidity of Philip had caused him to side with the Protestant movement. A firm believer in individual freedom and religious tolerance, William became – and for the Dutch remains – a symbol of liberty; but after the Fury had revitalised the pro-Spanish party, he prudently slipped away to his estates in Germany.

Philip II saw himself as responsible to God for the salvation of his subjects and therefore obliged to protect them from heresy. In 1567, keen to take advantage of the opportunity provided by the increased support for Margaret, he appointed the **Duke of Alva**, with an army of 10,000 men, to enter the Netherlands and suppress his religious opponents absolutely. Alva's first act was to set up the **Council of Blood**, which tried and condemned 12,000 of those who had taken part in the rioting of the year before. The policy briefly worked: when William attempted an invasion from Germany in 1568 the towns, garrisoned by the Spanish, offered no support. William waited and conceived other means of defeating Alva. In April 1572 a band of privateers entered Brielle on the Maas and captured it from the Spanish. Known as *Waterguezen* or sea-beggars, these

commando-style units initially operated from England, but it was soon possible for them to secure bases in the Netherlands, whose citizens had grown to loathe Alva and his Spaniards.

The revolt spread rapidly: by June the rebels controlled the province of Holland and William was able to take command of his troops from Delft. Alva and his son Frederick fought back, taking Gelder, Overijssel and the towns of Zutphen and Naarden, and in June 1573 Haarlem, massacring the Calvinist ministers and most of the garrison. But the Netherlanders retaliated: utilising their superior naval power the dykes were cut and the Spanish forces, unpaid and threatened with destruction, were forced to withdraw. Frustrated, Philip replaced Alva with Luis de Resquesens, who initially had some success in the south, where the Catholic majority were more willing to compromise with Spanish rule than their northern neighbours.

William's triumphant relief of Leiden in 1574 increased the pride of the rebel forces, and when de Resquesens died in 1576, his unpaid garrison in Antwerp mutinied and attacked the town, slaughtering some 8000 of its people in what was known as the **Spanish Fury**. Though Spain still held several towns, the massacre alienated the south and pushed its peoples into the arms of William, whose troops now controlled most of the Low Countries. Momentarily, it seemed possible for the whole region to unite behind William, and the various provinces signed the **Pacification of Ghent** in 1576, an agreement that guaranteed freedom of religious belief. However, differences between Protestant north and Catholic south proved irreconcilable, with many Walloons and Flemings suspicious both of William's ambitions and his Calvinist cronies. Consequently, when another army arrived from Spain, under the command of Alexander Farnese, Duke of Parma, the south was reoccupied without much difficulty, beginning a separation that would lead, after many changes, to the creation of two modern countries.

In 1579 seven provinces (Holland, Zeeland, Utrecht, Groningen, Friesland, Overijssel and Gelderland) signed the **Union of Utrecht**, an alliance against Spain that was to be the first unification of the Netherlands as an identifiable country – the **United Provinces**. The agreement stipulated freedom of belief in the provinces, an important step since the struggle against Spain wasn't simply a religious one: many Catholics disliked the Spanish occupation and William did not wish to alienate this possible source of support. This liberalism did not, however, extend to freedom of worship, although a blind eye was turned to the celebration of Mass if it was done privately and inconspicuously, giving rise to the "hidden churches" found throughout the country.

THE SPANISH NETHERLANDS (1579–1713)

In 1579, representatives of the southern provinces of Hainaut, Artois and Douai signed the **Union of Arras**, a Catholic-led agreement that declared loyalty to Philip II and counterbalanced the Union of Utrecht in the north. Subsequently, Alexander Farnese used this area as a base to reconquer the cities of Flanders, recapturing Antwerp after a long siege in 1585. He could go no further north – his enemies were too strong, and the shape of the **Spanish Netherlands**, roughly today's Belgium and Luxembourg, was decided, ruled by a Hapsburg governor in Brussels. Although the Spanish were prepared to permit some degree of economic and political autonomy, they were determined to eradicate Protestantism, and in the last years of the sixteenth century thousands of weavers, apprentices and skilled workers – the bedrock of Calvinism – were obliged to leave, moving north to fuel the economic boom in the province of Holland. It took a while for this migration to take effect, and for several years the Spanish Netherlands had all the trappings – if not, increasingly, the substance – of success, the successors of Philip II, the Archdukes Isabella and Albert, presiding over a brief artistic flourish centred on **Rubens** and his elite circle of friends in Antwerp.

The Spaniards resumed their campaign against the Protestant north in 1621, part of a general conflict, the **Thirty Years' War**, that devastated much of Europe. It was a military disaster and the victorious Dutch were strong enough to insist on the closure of the Scheldt to sea traffic from Antwerp in the **Peace of Westphalia** of 1648. The city was ruined and simply withered away, while the southern provinces as a whole had suffered terribly for their loyalty to the Hapsburgs: highwaymen infested the roads, trade had almost disappeared, the population had been halved in Brabant, and

acres of fertile farmland lay uncultivated. But the ruling families seemed proud to appear to the world as the defenders and martyrs of the Catholic faith – and those who disagreed left.

Politically dependent on a decaying Spain, economically ruined and deprived of most of its more independent-minded citizens, the country turned in on itself, sustained by the fanatical Catholicism of the Counter-Reformation. Religious worship became strict and magnificent, medieval carnivals were transformed into exercises in piety, and penitential flagellation became popular, all of which was encouraged by the Jesuits.

The number of **Jesuits** was extraordinary. France as a whole only had 2000, the Spanish Netherlands 1600, and it was here they wrote their most important works, exercised their greatest influence and owned vast tracts of land. Supported by draconian laws that barred known Protestants from public appointments, declared their marriages illegal and forbade them municipal assistance, the Catholic priests overwhelmed the religious opposition and in half a century transformed this part of the Low Countries into an introverted world shaped by a mystical faith, where Christians were redeemed by the ecstasy of suffering.

The visible signs of the change were all around, from extravagant Baroque churches to crosses, calvaries and shrines scattered across the countryside. Literature disappeared, the sciences vegetated and religious orders multiplied, all at the time the Dutch were building the greatest fleet in the world. In painting, artists – such as Rubens – were used to confirm the ecclesiastical orthodoxies, their canvases full of muscular saints and angels, reflecting a religious faith of mystery and hierarchy; others, such as David Teniers and the later Bruegels, retreated into minutely observed realism.

The Peace of Westphalia freed the king of France from fear of Germany, and the political and military history of the Spanish Netherlands after 1648 was dominated by the efforts of Louis XIV to add the region to his territories. Fearful of an over-powerful France, the United Provinces, England and Sweden, amongst others, determinedly resisted French designs, fighting a long series of campaigns which began with the **War of Devolution** in 1667 and ended with the **War of the Spanish Succession** from 1702 to 1713. At one time or another, all of the region's major cities were besieged and badly damaged, and only with the **Treaty of Utrecht** in 1713 did the French abandon their attempt to conquer the Spanish Netherlands, which now passed under the control of Emperor Charles VI of Austria.

THE UNITED PROVINCES (1579–1713)

In order to follow the developments of the sixteenth and seventeenth centuries in what is today the Netherlands, it's necessary to have an idea of the organisation of the **United Provinces**. Holland, comprising North and South Holland, was by far the dominant province economically and politically. The provinces maintained a decentralised independence, but as far as the United Provinces as a whole were concerned, what Holland said, went.

The assembly of the provinces was known as the **States General**, and met at The Hague; it had no domestic legislative authority, and could only carry out foreign policy by unanimous decision. The role of **Stadholder** was the most important in each province, roughly equivalent to that of governor, though the same person could occupy this position in any number of provinces. The Council Pensionary was another major post and in both cases the man who held the title in Holland was a powerful statesman.

In 1584 a French Catholic tricked his way into William's court in Delft and shot him, his family receiving the reward Philip II had promised for such an assassination. As William's son **Maurice** was only 17, control of the United Provinces was handed to **Johan van Oldenbarneveldt**, later Council Pensionary of Holland. Things were going badly in the fight against the Spanish: Nijmegen had fallen and Henry III of France refused help even with the offer of sovereignty. In desperation the United Provinces turned to Elizabeth I of England, who offered the Earl of Leicester as govenor general. He was accepted but completely mishandled the situation militarily, alienating the Dutch into the bargain. Oldenbarneveldt and Maurice took over and had great success in routing the Spanish from much of the country. By 1609 the English had defeated the Spanish Armada and Philip II was dead; the **Twelve Year Truce** was signed and the United Provinces were consolidated.

THE EARLY SEVENTEENTH CENTURY: INTERNAL DISCORD AND FURTHER FIGHTING

In the breathing space created by the truce, the long-standing differences between Maurice and Oldenbarneveldt polarised. An obscure argument within the Calvinist church on predestination proved the catalyst of Oldenbarneveldt's downfall.

The quarrel, between two Leiden theologians, began in 1612: Armenius argued that God gave man the choice of accepting or rejecting faith; Gomarus, his opponent, that predestination was absolute – to the degree that God chooses who will be saved and who damned with man powerless in the decision. This row between the two groups (known respectively as Remonstrants and counter-Remonstrants) became closely linked to the political divisions of the early seventeenth century. When a synod was arranged at Dordrecht to resolve the matter, the State of Holland, led by Oldenbarneveldt, refused to attend, insisting on Holland's right to decide its own religious orthodoxies. He and his fellow deputies supported the provincial independence favoured by Remonstrant sympathisers, whereas Maurice sided with the counter-Remonstrants who favoured a strong central authority. The counter-Remonstrants won at Dordrecht: Maurice, with his troops behind him, quickly overcame his opponents and had Oldenbarneveldt arrested. In May 1619 he was executed in The Hague "for having conspired to dismember the states of the Netherlands and greatly troubled God's church".

With the end of the Twelve Year Truce in 1621, fighting with Spain once more broke out, this time part of the more general **Thirty Years' War** (1618–48), a largely religious-based conflict between Catholic and Protestant countries that involved most of western Europe. In the Low Countries, the Spanish were initially successful, but they were weakened by war with France and by the fresh attacks of Maurice's successor, his brother Frederick Henry. From 1625, the Spaniards suffered a series of defeats on land and sea that forced them out of what is today the southern part of the Netherlands, and in 1648 they were compelled to accept the humiliating terms of the **Peace of Westphalia**. This was a general treaty that ended the Thirty Years' War, whose terms recognised the independence of the United Provinces and closed the Scheldt estuary, an action designed to destroy the trade and prosperity of Antwerp. The commercial expansion and pre-eminence of Amsterdam was assured, and the Golden Age began.

THE GOLDEN AGE

The brilliance of **Amsterdam**'s explosion on the European scene is as difficult to underestimate as it is to detail. The size of its merchant fleet had long been considerable, bringing masses of Baltic grain into Europe. Even the determined Spaniards had been unable to undermine Dutch naval power, and following the effective removal of Antwerp as a competitor, Amsterdam became the emporium for the products of north and south Europe and the new colonies in the East and West Indies. Amsterdam didn't only prosper from its markets – her own ships carried the produce, a cargo trade that greatly increased the city's wealth. Dutch banking and investment brought further prosperity, and by the mid-seventeenth century Amsterdam's wealth was spectacular. The Calvinist bourgeoisie indulged themselves gently in fine canal houses and commissioned their reflections in group portraits. Civic pride burgeoned, and if some were hungry, few starved, with the poor cared for in municipal almshouses. The arts flourished and religious tolerance stretched even to the traditional scapegoats, the Jews, many of whom quickly became enterprising merchants. Huguenot refugees from France were drawn to the city, along with Protestants escaping persecution in the Catholic south.

One organisation that kept the country's coffers brimming throughout the Golden Age was the **East India Company**. Formed by the newly powerful Dutch Republic in 1602, the Amsterdam-controlled enterprise sent ships to Asia, Indonesia, and as far as China to bring back spices, woods and other assorted plunder. Given a trading monopoly in all lands east of the Cape of Good Hope, it had unlimited military powers over the lands it controlled, and was effectively the occupying government in Malaya, Ceylon and Malacca. Twenty years later the **West Indies Company** was inaugurated to protect new Dutch interests in the Americas and Africa. Expending most of its energies in waging war on Spanish and

Portuguese colonies from a base in Surinam, it never achieved the success of the East India Company, and was dismantled in 1674, ten years after its small colony of New Amsterdam had been captured by the British – and renamed New York. Elsewhere, the Netherlands held on to its colonies for as long as possible – **Java** and **Sumatra** were still under Dutch control after World War II.

A constant problem in the seventeenth century was the conflict between central authority and provincial autonomy. Although the **House of Orange** had established its royal credentials, many of Holland's leading citizens were reluctant to accept its right to power. On William II's death in 1650 the state of Holland used the fact that his heir was still an infant to force through measures abolishing the position of Stadholder, thereby reducing the powers of the Orangists and increasing those of the provinces, chiefly Holland itself.

Holland's foremost figure in these years was **Johan de Witt**, Council Pensionary to the States General. He guided the country through wars with England and Sweden, concluding a triple alliance between the two countries and the United Provinces in 1678. This didn't succeed, however, and when France and England marched on the Provinces two years later, the republic was in trouble. The previous victories had been at sea, and the army, weak and disorganised, could not withstand an attack. The country turned to **William III of Orange** for leadership and Johan de Witt was brutally murdered by a mob of Orangist sympathisers in The Hague. By 1678 William had defeated the French and made peace with the English – and was rewarded (along with his wife Mary) with the English crown ten years later.

THE AUSTRIAN NETHERLANDS (1713–1794)

The transfer of the country from Spanish to Austrian control made little appreciable difference: there were more wars and more invasions – principally the **War of the Austrian Succession** in the 1740s – and a remote central authority continued to operate through Brussels. The strength of the region lay in its agriculture, which easily survived the various armed incursions, though the country remained vitrified and stagnant – only three percent of the population were literate, workers were forbidden to change towns or jobs without obtaining permission from the municipal authorities, and skills and crafts were tied to particular families.

This sorry state of affairs began to change in 1753 with the arrival of a new governor, the Count of Cobenzl, who was determined to shake the country from its torpor. He initiated an ambitious programme of public works, including extensive road and canal construction, organised financial incentives to industry, and took a firm line with his clerical opponents, who tried to encourage the population to thwart him in his aims.

In 1780, Emperor **Joseph II** came to the throne, determined to organise further reforms himself. Authoritarian and impulsive, his efforts to "root out silly old prejudices", as he put it, resulted in a deluge of edicts and decrees that managed to offend most of the country's major groups – from peasants to nobility, bureaucrats to traders. Pandemonium ensued, and opposition crystallised around the Flemish lawyer Francois Vonck, whose liberal-minded **Vonckists** were countered by the conservative **Statists**. The latter, with the assistance of the priests, raised the peasantry to arms and encouraged them to attack the Vonckists, who were killed in their hundreds. The country was in turmoil and when Emperor Joseph died in 1790, his successor, Leopold, was quick to withdraw many of the reforming acts and send in his troops to restore order.

THE UNITED PROVINCES IN THE EIGHTEENTH CENTURY

Though King William had defeated the French, Louis XIV retained designs on the United Provinces. When William's grandson inherited the Spanish throne and control of the Spanish Netherlands in 1700, Louis forced him to hand the latter over to French control. This threatened the balance of power in Europe, and the Provinces, England and Austria formed an alliance against the French and so began the **War of the Spanish Succession**, a haphazard series of campaigns distinguished by the spectacular victories of the Duke of Marlborough – Blenheim, Ramillies, Malplaquet – that dragged on till 1713 and the **Treaty of Utrecht**.

The fighting drained the United Provinces' riches and a slow economic and political decline began, accelerated by a mood of unadventurous conservatism that reflected the development of an increasingly socially static society, with power and wealth concentrated within a small elite.

Effectively freed from the threat of foreign conquest by the treaty of 1713, the next decades were marred by internal fighting between the Orangists and the pro-French ruling families (who called themselves "patriots"). The situation deteriorated even further in the latter half of the century and the last few years of the United Provinces were dogged by interminable rivalry and conflict.

In 1795 the French, aided by the Patriots, invaded, setting up the **Batavian Republic** and dissolving the United Provinces and much of the control of the rich Dutch merchants. Effectively part of the Napoleonic empire, the Netherlands were obliged to wage unenthusiastic war with England, and in 1806 Napoleon appointed his brother Louis as their king in an attempt to create a commercial gulf between the country and England. Louis, however, wasn't willing to allow the Netherlands to become a simple satellite of France; he ignored Napoleon's directives and after just four years of rule was forced to abdicate. The country was then formally incorporated into the French Empire, and for three gloomy years suffered occupation and heavy taxation to finance French military adventures.

Following Napoleon's disastrous retreat from Moscow, the Orangist faction once more surfaced to exploit weakening French control. In 1813, Frederick William, son of the exiled William V, returned to the country and eight months later, under the terms of the **Congress of Vienna**, was crowned King William I of the United Kingdom of the Netherlands, incorporating both the old United Provinces and the Spanish (Austrian) Netherlands. A strong-willed man, he spent much of the later part of his life trying to control his disparate kingdom, but he failed primarily because of the north's attempt to dominate the south. The southern provinces revolted against his rule and in 1830 the **Kingdom of Belgium** was proclaimed.

THE AUSTRIAN NETHERLANDS (1794–1909)

Occupied by French Republican armies in 1794, the Austrian Netherlands were annexed the following year, an annexation that was to last until 1814. The **French** imposed radical reforms: the Catholic church was stripped of much of its worldly wealth, feudal privileges were abolished, a consistent legal system was formulated and, most unpopular of all, conscription was introduced, provoking a brutally repressed Peasants' Revolt in 1798. Napoleon, in control from 1799, also rebuilt the docks of Antwerp and forced the Dutch to accept the reopening of the Scheldt, but, with the exception of a radical minority, the French occupation remained unpopular.

Following the battle of Waterloo, the great powers decided to give William I's German lands to Prussia and in return presented him with the newly independent **Grand-Duchy of Luxembourg**. This was a somewhat confused arrangement, as the Duchy was detached from the rest of the Low Countries constitutionally and pushed into the German Confederation at the same time as it shared the same king with the old United Provinces and Austrian Netherlands.

Indeed, the main concern of the great powers was to create a buffer state against any possible future plans the French might have to expand to the north. With scant regard to the feelings of those affected, they therefore decided to establish the **United Kingdom of the Netherlands** under the control of William I. But the king failed to calm the anxieties of his southern subjects and in 1830 **revolution** broke out in Brussels. Aided by the French, the revolutionaries managed to resist Dutch invasion and in January 1831 the **Conference of London** reluctantly agreed to recognise Belgium's independence, insisting it be classified a "neutral" state, ceding to it the western segments of Luxembourg, and digging out the uncle of Queen Victoria, Leopold of Saxe-Coburg, to present with the crown.

Shrewd and capable, **Leopold I** (1830–65) was careful to maintain his country's neutrality and encouraged an industrial boom that saw coal mines developed, iron-making factories established and the rapid expansion of the railway system. Politically, a strictly limited fran- chise ensured the domination of the middle classes, who divided into two loose groups, the one attempting to undermine Catholic influence and control over such areas as education, the other profoundly conservative in its desire to maintain the status quo.

Leopold II's (1865–1909) long reign was dominated by similar themes, and saw the emergence of Belgium as a major industrial power. However, the 1860s and 1870s also witnessed the first stirrings of a type of **Flemish nationalism**, which felt little enthusiasm for the unitary status of Belgium, divided as it was between a French-speaking majority in the south of the country – the **Walloons**, – and the Dutch-speakers of Flanders, Antwerp and Limburg in the north. Then in the early 1900s the king's personal ownership of the Belgian Congo led to a scandal when the level of exploitation, slavery and atrocity became too great to ignore. The Belgian state took over the administration of Leopold's fiefdom in 1908.

THE NETHERLANDS: 1830 TO THE PRESENT DAY

A final invasion of Belgium in 1839 gave William most of Limburg, and all but ended centuries of changes to borders and territory. The Netherlands benefited from this new stability, the trade surplus picked up and canal building opened Rotterdam and Amsterdam to the North Sea. The outstanding political figure of the times, **J. R. Thorbecke**, formed three ruling cabinets (1849–53, 1862–66 and 1872, in the year of his death) and steered the Netherlands through a profound change. The political parties of the late eighteenth century had wished to resurrect the power and prestige of the seventeenth-century Netherlands; Thorbecke and his allies resigned themselves to the country's reduced status of a small power and eulogised its advantages. For the first time, from about 1850, liberty was seen as a luxury made possible by the country's very lack of power, and the malaise which had long disturbed public life gave way to a positive appreciation of the narrowness of its national existence. One of the results of Thorbecke's liberalism was a gradual extension of the fran- chise, culminating in the Act of Universal Suffrage in 1917.

At the outbreak of **World War I** the Netherlands remained neutral, but suffered privations as a result of the Allied blockade of ports through which Germany might be supplied. Similar attempts to remain neutral in **World War II** soon failed: the Germans invaded on May 10, 1940, destroying Rotterdam four days later. The Dutch were quickly overwhelmed, Queen Wilhelmina fled to London, and opposition to Nazi occupation was continued by the Resistance. Instrumental in destroying German supplies and munitions, they also helped many downed airmen escape back to England. A heavy price was paid for their contribution to the war effort: 23,000 resistance fighters were killed in the war years. In Amsterdam, the old Jewish community, swollen by those who had fled Germany to escape the persecution of the 1930s, was obliterated, leaving only the deserted Jodenhoek and the diary of **Anne Frank** as testament to the horrors.

Liberation began in autumn 1944 with **Operation Market Garden**. This was a British plan to finish the war quickly by creating a corridor stretching from Eindhoven to Arnhem, gaining control of the three main rivers en route, isolating the occupying forces to the west in the Netherlands and pushing straight into Germany. It was a gamble, but if successful would hasten the end of hostilities. On September 17 the 1st Airborne Division parachuted into the countryside around Oosterbeek, a small village near the most northerly target of the operation, the bridge at **Arnhem**. German opposition was much stronger than expected, and after heavy fighting the Allied forces could only take the northern end of the bridge. The advancing British army was unable to break through fast enough, and after four days the decimated battalion defending the bridge was forced to withdraw.

With the failure of Operation Market Garden, the Allies were obliged to resort to more orthodox military tactics to clear the south and east Netherlands of the Germans, a slow process that took all the winter and spring of 1945. As the assault was concentrated on Germany itself, the coastal provinces of the country were left alone, but they suffered terribly from lack of food and fuel. Finally, on April 5, 1945, the German army surrendered to the Canadians at Wageningen.

The postwar years were spent patching up the damage of occupation. Rotterdam was rapidly rebuilt, and the dykes blown in the war to slow the German advance repaired. Two events were to mar the late 1940s and early 1950s: the former Dutch colonies of Java and Sumatra, taken by the Japanese at the outbreak of the war, were now run by a nationalist Republican government in Java that refused to recognise Dutch sovereignty. Following the failure of talks on Dutch control the troops were sent in; world opposition to this was strong, and after much condemnation and pressure the Dutch reluctantly handed over their colonies .

Back at home, tragedy struck on February 1 1953 when an unusually high tide was pushed over Zeeland's sea defences by a westerly wind, flooding 40,000 acres of land and drowning over 1800 people. The response was to secure the area with the **Delta Project**, closing off the western part of the Scheldt and Maas estuaries with massive sea dykes. A brilliant and graceful piece of engineering, the main storm surge barrier on the Oosterschelde was finally completed in 1986.

Elsewhere rebuilding continued; in Amsterdam all the land projected in 1947 for use by the year 2000 was in fact used up by the "garden cities" of the dormitory suburbs by 1970, and the polder towns on the reclaimed stretches of Flevoland also expanded. But growth wasn't only physical: the social consciousness and radicalism of the 1960s reached the country early, and the word of the psychedelic revolution was quick to catch on. It was quick to fade, too, replaced by the cynicism of the 1970s, but one manifestation of the spread of radical thinking that had some tangible positive results was the **squatting movement**, which precipitated major riots in Amsterdam and other cities throughout the late 1960s and early 1970s. The squatters and other activists won considerable success in attempting to prevent the wholesale destruction of low cost urban housing, a move that would have turned the country's city centres into places where only the rich could afford to live.

Today, the country's finely balanced system of proportional representation forces almost continuous political compromise and debate, but brings little rapid change, politics and politicking seeming a bland business conducted between the three main parties, the

Protestant-Catholic **CDA coalition**, the **Liberal VVD** and the **Socialist PvdA**.

A governmental system that has so effectively incorporated the disparate elements of a modern and diverse state – Catholic and Protestant, management and union, city and country, socialist and conservative – has earned the Netherlands a well-deserved reputation for comfortable complacency, and outbreaks of opposition, when they do appear, on such items as eco-issues, housing and racism, provoke a mad rush to the bargaining table.

BELGIUM AND LUXEMBOURG IN THE TWENTIETH CENTURY

King Leopold died in 1909, to be succeeded by his nephew **Albert**, whose reign was dominated by **World War I**. Indifferent to Belgium's proclaimed neutrality, the German invasion of 1914 extended over almost all of the country, the exception a narrow strip of territory around De Panne, where Albert was forced to move to continue his administration. For four years, the northern stretches of the lines of trenches which separated the opposing armies from the North Sea to Switzerland crossed Belgium, following roughly the path of the river Yser and the Yserkanaal, through Nieuwpoort, Diksmuide and Ieper. The violation of Belgian neutrality and Albert's spirited resistance attracted worldwide sympathy and admiration. The principal engagements on Belgian soil took place in the bulge in the line around Ieper, where a series of futile, bloody battles came to epitomise the pointlessness of the war and the tactical stupidity of its generals.

After the war, Belgium received extensive reparations from Germany including the slice of land around Eupen. In November 1919, King Albert addressed parliament to announce a package of radical reforms that included universal suffrage and equal rights for the two national languages. Perhaps surprisingly, this proclamation sharpened the embryonic tensions between the Walloon and Flemish sections of the population – for although the Flemings had accepted the domination of the French-speakers without much protest for several centuries, as their province became more prosperous, so they grew in self-confidence, becoming increasingly unhappy with their social and political subordination.

In the 1930s, **Fascism** drew some ten percent of the vote in both the Walloon and Flemish communities, though for very different reasons: the former for its appeal to a nationalist bourgeoisie, the latter for its assertion of "racial" pride amongst an oppressed group.

In May 1940, the **Germans** launched their sudden, surprise attack on the Netherlands and Belgium. This time there was no heroic resistance by the Belgian king, who to many seemed only too prepared to surrender – and subsequently collaborate – and the entire country was occupied within three weeks. As in the Netherlands, it took time for the Belgians to adjust to the new situation, but by 1941 a Resistance movement was organising acts of sabotage against the occupying forces. The **liberation** came some four years later, in the autumn of 1944, and, with the exception of the Battle of the Ardennes (the Bulge) and damage to the port of Antwerp, went relatively smoothly.

After the liberation, the Belgians set about the task of economic reconstruction, helped by aid from the United States, but hindered by a divisive controversy over the **wartime activities of King Leopold**. Many felt his prompt surrender to the Germans was cowardly and his subsequent willingness to work with them treacherous; others pointed out his efforts to increase the country's food rations and his negotiations to secure the release of Belgian prisoners. Inevitably, the complex shadings of collaboration and forced co-operation were hard to disentangle, and the debate continued until 1950 when a referendum narrowly recommended his return from exile as king. Leopold considered this insufficient recommendation and abdicated in favour of his son, the present king, **Baudouin**.

The development of the postwar Belgian economy follows the pattern of most of western Europe – reconstruction in the 1950s; boom in the 1960s; recession in the 1970s; and retrenchment in the 1980s. Significant events have included an ugly, disorganised and hasty evacuation of the Belgian Congo in 1960; the transformation of Brussels from one of the more insignificant European capitals into the home of the EC and NATO; and acute labour unrest in the Limburg coalfield in the early 1980s, following plans to close most of the remaining pits. But, above all, the postwar period has been dominated by the increasing **tension between the Walloon and Flemish communities**. Every facet of Belgian life is now dogged by the prerequisites of bilingualism – speeches in parliament have to be delivered in both languages, and every instance of the written word, from road signs to yellow pages, have to be bilingual too. Politically, the parties reflect three broad ranges of opinion – conservative, liberal and socialist – but they are also divided into Flemish- and French-speaking sections, further complicating the structure of national administrations from an already complex system of proportional representation. In 1962 the Linguistic Divide (or Language Frontier) was formally delineated and in 1980 central government was partially regionalised, with major areas of administration transferred to regional councils. In many ways, therefore, Belgium is a divided society, the two linguistic groups viewing each other with suspicion punctuated by hostility.

LUXEMBOURG

The second half of the nineteenth century had seen Luxembourg's poor, agricultural economy transformed by the discovery and mining of **iron ore deposits**, and by 1939 the Grand Duchy was the world's seventh largest producer of steel. Occupied in both world wars, the Luxembourgers put up a stubborn resistance, leading to many brave acts of defiance and considerable loss of life. The Battle of the Ardennes (the Bulge) was a major disaster, and in 1945 one third of the country's farmland lay uncultivated, the public transportation system in ruins, and some 60,000 people homeless.

In the **postwar years**, reconstruction was rapid and the government wisely pursued a policy of industrial diversification that has made the country one of the most prosperous parts of Europe. Disappointed by the results of neutrality, Luxembourg also joined the EC and NATO and is now home to many major Community departments. The present Grand-Duke and Grand-Duchess are Jean and Josephine Charlotte of Nassau.

AN INTRODUCTION TO DUTCH AND BELGIAN ART

The following piece is the very briefest of introductions to the subject, designed to serve only as a quick reference on your way round the major galleries. For more in-depth and academic studies, see the recommendations in the "Books" listings, p.499. For where to find the paintings themselves, turn to the hit list at the end.

THE EARLY FLEMISH MASTERS

Until the sixteenth century the area now known as the Low Countries was in effect one country, the most artistically productive part of which was Flanders in modern Belgium, and it was there that the solid realist base of later Dutch painting developed. Today the works of these early Flemish painters, known as the **Flemish Primitives**, are relatively sparse in the Low Countries, and even in Belgium few collections are as complete as they might be – indeed, many ended up as the property of the ruling Hapsburgs and were removed to Spain. Most major galleries do, however, have a few examples.

Jan van Eyck (1385–1441) is generally regarded as the originator of Low Countries painting, and has even been credited with the invention of oil painting itself – though it seems more likely that he simply perfected a new technique by thinning his paint with the recently discovered turpentine, thus making it more flexible. His fame partially stems from the fact that he was one of the first artists to sign his work – an action that indicates how highly his talent was regarded in his own time. Van Eyck's most famous work is still in the Low Countries, the altarpiece of St Baaf's Cathedral in Ghent, known as the *Adoration of the Mystic Lamb*. It was debatably painted with the help of his lesser-known brother, Hubert, and was revolutionary in its realism, for the first time using elements of native landscape in depicting Biblical themes. His work was also rich in a complex symbolism, whereby everyday objects take on a disguised, usually religious meaning, the nature of which has generated analysis and discussion ever since. Van Eyck's style and technique were to influence several generations of subsequent Low Countries artists.

Firmly in this Eyckian tradition were the **Master of Flemalle** (1387–1444) and **Rogier van der Weyden** (1400–64). The Flemalle master is a shadowy figure: some believe he was the teacher of van der Weyden, others that the two artists were in fact the same person. There are differences between the two, however: the Flemalle master's paintings are close to van Eyck's, whereas van der Weyden shows a more emotional and religious intensity; few of his more important paintings remain in Belgium. Van der Weyden influenced such painters as **Dieric Bouts** (1415–75), who was born in Haarlem but was active in Leuven (where his *Altarpiece of the Sacrament* remains in the St Pieterskerk) and is recognisable by his stiff, rather elongated figures and horrific subject matter against carefully drawn landscapes. **Petrus Christus** (d.1472), a contemporary of Bouts, was also influenced by van der Weyden and van Eyck: he was the next painter of importance to work in Bruges after van Eyck, and may have been his pupil. His portraits have a directness and simple clarity, but with the exception of a *Lamentation* in the Musée d'Art Ancien, Brussels, most of his masterpieces are now outside the Low Countries. **Hugo van der Goes** (d.1482) was the next Ghent master after van Eyck, most famous for the *Portinari Altarpiece* in Florence's Uffizi. After a short painting career, he died insane, and his late works have strong hints of his impending madness in their subversive use of space and implict acceptance of the viewer's presence. Few doubt that **Hans Memling** (1440–94) was a pupil of van der Weyden. Active in Bruges throughout his life, he is best remembered for the pastoral charm of his landscapes and the quality of his portraiture, much of which survives on the rescued side panels of triptychs. The museum named after him in Bruges has an excellent survey of his work. **Gerhard David** (d.1523) moved to Bruges in 1484, and was the last of the great painters to work in that city, before it was overtaken in prosperity by Antwerp – which itself became the focus of a more Italianate school of art in the sixteenth century.

Hieronymus Bosch (1450–1516) lived for most of his life in Holland, though his style is linked to that of the Flanders painters (see below). His frequently reprinted religious allegories are filled with macabre visions of tortured people and grotesque beasts, and appear at first faintly unhinged, though it's now thought that these are visual representations of contemporary sayings, idioms and parables. While their interpretation is far from resolved, Bosch's paintings draw strongly on subconscious fears and archetypes, giving them a lasting, haunting fascination.

THE SIXTEENTH CENTURY

Meanwhile, there were movements to the north of Flanders. **Geertgen tot Sint Jans** ("Little Gerard of the Brotherhood of St John") (d.1490), a student of **Albert van Ouwater**, had been working in **Haarlem**, initiating – in a strangely naive style – an artistic tradition in the city that would prevail throughout the seventeenth century. **Jan Mostaert** (1475–1555) took over after Geertgen's death, and continued to develop a style that diverged more and more from that of the southern provinces. **Lucas van Leyden** (1489–1533) was the first painter to effect real changes in northern painting. Born in Leiden, his bright colours and narrative technique were refreshingly new at the time, and he introduced a novel dynamism into what had become a rigidly formal treatment of devotional subjects. There was rivalry, of course. Eager to publicise Haarlem as the artistic capital of the northern Netherlands, Carel van Mander (see

below) claimed Haarlem native **Jan van Scorel** (1495–1562) as the better painter, complaining, too, of Lucas's dandyish ways.

Certainly van Scorel's influence should not be underestimated. At this time every painter was expected to travel to Italy to view the works of Renaissance artists. When the Bishop of Utrecht became Pope Hadrian VI, he took van Scorel with him as court painter, giving him the opportunity to introduce Italian styles into what had been a completely independent tradition. Hadrian died soon after, and van Scorel returned north, combining the ideas he had picked up in Italy with Haarlem realism and passing them on to **Maerten van Heemskerck** (1498–1574), who later went off to Italy himself in 1532, staying there five years before returning to Haarlem.

Bruges' pre-eminence in the medieval Low Countries gradually began to give way to Antwerp, and the artists who worked there at the beginning of the sixteenth century combined the influence of the Italian painters with the domestic Flemish tradition. **Quinten Metsys** (1464–1530) introduced florid classical architectural detail and intricate landscape backgrounds to his works, influenced perhaps by the work of Leonardo da Vinci. As well as religious works, he painted portraits and genre scenes, all of which have recognisably Italian facets, and paved the way for the Dutch genre painters of later years. His follower, **Joos van Cleve** (c.1485–1540/1), painted in a similarly refined and realistic manner. **Jan Gossaert** (d. c.1523) made the pilgrimage to Italy, and his dynamic works are packed with detail, especially finely drawn classical architectural backdrops. He was the first Low Countries artist to introduce the subjects of classical mythology into his works, part of a steady trend through the period towards secular subject matter, which can also be seen in the work of **Joachim Patinir** (d.c.1524), who painted small landscapes of fantastic scenery.

The latter part of the sixteenth century was dominated by the work of **Pieter Bruegel the Elder** (c.1525–69), whose gruesome allegories and innovative interpretations of religious subjects are firmly placed in Low Countries settings. Most famous are his paintings of peasant lowlife, though he himself was well connected in court circles in Antwerp and, later, Brussels. **Pieter Aertsen** (c.1508–75) also worked in the peasant genre, adding aspects of the still life: his paintings often show a detailed kitchen scene in the foreground, with a religious episode going on behind. Towards the latter half of the century the stylised Italianate portrait was much in vogue, its chief exponents being **Adrien Key**, **Anthonis Mor** and **Frans Pourbus**.

RUBENS AND HIS FOLLOWERS

Pieter Paul Rubens (1577–1640) was the most influential Low Countries artist of the early seventeenth century and the most important exponent of Baroque painting in northern Europe. Born in Siegen, Westphalia, his parents returned to their native Antwerp when Rubens was a child. He entered the Antwerp Guild in 1598, became court painter to the Duke of Mantua in 1600, and until 1608 travelled extensively in Italy, absorbing the art of the High Renaissance and classical architecture. By the time of his return to Antwerp in 1608 he had acquired an enormous artistic vocabulary: the paintings of Caravaggio in particular were to influence his work strongly. His first major success was *The Raising of the Cross*, painted in 1610 and kept today in Antwerp cathedral. A large, dynamic work, it caused a sensation at the time, establishing Rubens reputation and leading to a string of commissions that enabled him to set up his own studio. The *Descent from the Cross*, his next major.work (also in the cathedral), consolidated this success: equally Baroque, it is nevertheless quieter and more restrained.

The division of labour in Rubens' studio, and the talent of the artists working there (who included Antony van Dyck and Jacob Jordaens) ensured a high output of excellent work. The degree to which Rubens personally worked on a canvas would vary – and would determine its price. From the early 1620s onwards he turned his hand to a plethora of themes and subjects – religious works, portraits, tapestry designs, landscapes, mythological scenes, ceiling paintings (including that of the Banqueting Hall in Whitehall, London – a commission for Charles I, by whom he was knighted) – each of which was handled with supreme vitality and virtuosity. From his Flemish antecedents he inherited an acute sense of light, and used it not to dramatise his subjects (a technique favoured by

Caravaggio and other Italian artists), but in organic association with colour and form. The drama in his works comes from the tremendous animation of his characters. His large-scale allegorical works, especially, are packed with heaving, writhing figures that appear to tumble out from the canvas.

The energy of Rubens' paintings was reflected in his private life. In addition to his career as an artist, he also undertook diplomatic missions to Spain and England on behalf of the governors of Holland, and used the opportunities to study the works of other artists and – as in the case of Velázquez – to meet them personally. In the 1630s, gout began to hamper his activities, and from this time his painting became more domestic and meditative. Hélène Fourment, his second wife, was the subject of many portraits and served as a model for characters in his allegorical paintings, her figure epitomising the buxom, well-rounded women found throughout his work.

Rubens' influence on the artists of the period was enormous. The huge output of his studio meant that his works were universally seen, and widely disseminated by the engravers he employed to copy his work. Chief among his followers was the portraitist **Antony van Dyck** (1599–1641), who worked in Rubens' studio from 1618, often taking on the depiction of religious figures in his master's works that required particular sensitivity and pathos. Like Rubens, he was born in Antwerp and travelled widely in Italy, though his initial work was influenced less by the Italian artists than by Rubens himself. Eventually van Dyck developed his own distinct style and technique, establishing himself as court painter to Charles I in England, and creating portraits of a nervous elegance that would influence the genre there for the next hundred and fifty years. Most of his great portraiture remains in England, though his best religious works – such as the *Crucifixion* in Mechelen cathedral and a *Lamentation* in Antwerp's Museum voor Schone Kunsten – can be found in Belgium.

Jacob Jordaens (1593–1678) was also an Antwerp native who studied under Rubens. Although he was commissioned to complete several works left unfinished by Rubens at the time of his death, his robustly naturalistic works have an earthy – and sensuous – realism that's quite distinct in style and technique.

Other artists working this part of the Low Countries during the early seventeenth century were also, understandably, greatly influenced by the output of Rubens' studio. **Gerhard Seghers** (1591–1651) specialised in painting flowers, usually around portraits or devotional figures painted by other artists, including Rubens himself.

Theodor Rombouts (1579–1637) was strongly influenced by Caravaggio following a trip to Italy, but changed his style to fall in line with that of Rubens when he returned to Antwerp from Holland. **Jacob van Oost the Elder** chose to live and work in Bruges: his delicate work embraces Dutch and Italian elements. **Frans Snyders** (1579–1657) took up the genre of the still life where Aertsen left off, amplifying his subject – food and drink – to even larger, more sumptuous canvases. He too was part of the Rubens art machine, painting animals and still life sections for the master's works.

THE DUTCH GOLDEN AGE

Carel van Mander (1548–1606) had a tremendous impact in Holland at the beginning of the sixteenth century. A Haarlem painter, art impresario, and one of the few chroniclers of the art of the Low Countries, his *Schilderboek* of 1604 put Flemish and Dutch traditions into context for the first time and specified the rules of fine painting. Examples of his own work are rare, but his followers were many, among them **Cornelius Cornelisz van Haarlem** (1562–1638), who produced elegant renditions of Biblical and mythical themes; and **Hendrik Goltzius** (1558–1616), who was a skilled engraver and an integral member of van Mander's Haarlem academy. These painters' enthusiasm for Italian art, combined with the influence of a late revival of Gothicism, resulted in works that combined Mannerist and classical elements. An interest in realism was also felt, and, for them, the subject became less important than the way in which it was depicted: Biblical stories became merely a vehicle whereby artists could apply their skills in painting the human body, landscapes, or copious displays of food – all of which served to break religion's stranglehold on art, and make legitimate a whole range of everyday subjects for the painter.

In Holland (and this was where the north and the south finally diverged) this break with tradition was compounded by the **Reformation**: the austere Calvinism that had supplanted the Catholic faith in the northern provinces had no use for images or symbols of devotion in its churches. Instead, painters catered to the public, and no longer visited Italy to learn their craft; the real giants of the seventeenth century – Hals, Rembrandt, Vermeer – stayed in the Low Countries all their lives. Another departure was that painting split into more distinct categories – genre, portrait, landscape, etc – and artists tended (with notable exceptions) to confine themselves to one field throughout their careers. So began the greatest age of Dutch art.

HISTORICAL AND RELIGIOUS PAINTING

If Italy continued to hold sway in the Low Countries it was not through the Renaissance painters but rather via the fashionable new realism of Caravaggio. Many artists – Rembrandt for one – continued to portray classic subjects, but in a way that was totally at odds with the Mannerists' stylish flights of imagination. Though a solid Mannerist throughout his career, the Utrecht artist **Abraham Bloemaert** (1564–1651) encouraged these new ideas, and his students – **Gerard van Honthorst** (1590–1656), **Hendrik Terbrugghen** (1588–1629), and **Dirck van Baburen** (1590–1624) – formed the nucleus of the influential **Utrecht School**, which followed Caravaggio almost to the point of slavishness. Honthorst was perhaps the leading figure, learning his craft from Bloemaert and travelling to Rome, where he was nicknamed "Gerardo delle Notti" for his ingenious handling of light and shade. This was, however, to become in his later paintings more routine technique than inspired invention, and though a supremely competent artist, Honthorst remains somewhat discredited among critics today. Terbrugghen's reputation seems to have aged rather better: he soon forgot Caravaggio and developed a more personal style, his lighter, later work having a great impact on the young Vermeer. After the obligatory jaunt to Rome, Baburen shared a studio with Terbrugghen and produced some fairly original work – work which also had some influence on Vermeer – but few of his paintings survive today, and he is the least studied member of the group.

But it's **Rembrandt** who was considered the most original historical artist of the seventeenth century, painting religious scenes throughout his life. In the 1630s, the poet and statesman Constantijn Huygens procured for him his greatest commission – a series of five paintings of the Passion, beautifully composed and uncompromisingly realistic. Later, however, Rembrandt received fewer and fewer commissions, since his treatment of Biblical and historical subjects was far less dramatic than that of his contemporaries. It's significant that while the more conventional Jordaens, Honthorst and van Everdingen were busy decorating the Huis ten Bosch near The Hague for patron Stadholder Frederick Henry, Rembrandt was having his monumental *Conspiracy of Claudius Civilis* (completed for the new Amsterdam town hall) rejected – probably because it was thought too pagan an interpretation of what was an important symbolic event in Dutch history. **Aert van Gelder** (1645–1727), Rembrandt's last pupil and probably the only one to concentrate on historical painting, followed the style of his master closely, producing shimmering Biblical scenes well into the eighteenth century.

GENRE PAINTING

The term **genre** refers to scenes from everyday life, a subject that, with the decline of the church as patron, became popular in Holland by the mid-seventeenth century. Many painters devoted themselves solely to such work. Some genre paintings were simply non-idealised portrayals of common scenes, while others, by means of symbols or carefully disguised details, made moral entreaties to the viewer.

Among early seventeenth-century painters, **Hendrik Terbrugghen** and **Gerard Honthorst** spent much of their time on religious subjects, but also adapted the realism and strong chiaroscuro learned from Caravaggio to a number of tableaux of everyday life. **Frans Hals**, too, is better known as a portraitist, but his early genre paintings no doubt influenced his pupil, **Adriaen Brouwer** (1605–38), whose riotous tavern scenes were well received in their day and collected by, among others, Rubens and Rembrandt. Brouwer spent only a couple of years in Haarlem under Hals before returning to his native Flanders to influence the younger **David Teniers** (1610–90), who worked in Antwerp, later in Brussels. His earlier paintings are Brouwer-like peasant scenes, his later work more delicate and diverse, including *Kortegaardje* – guardroom scenes that show soldiers carousing. Like Brouwer, **Adriaen van Ostade** (1610–85) studied under Hals but chose to remain in Haarlem, skilfully painting groups of peasants and tavern brawls – though his later acceptance by the establishment led him to water down the realism he had learnt from Brouwer. He was teacher to his brother **Isaak** (1621–49), who produced a large number of open-air peasant scenes, subtle combinations of genre and landscape work.

The English critic E. V. Lucas dubbed Teniers, Brouwer and Ostade "coarse and boorish" compared with **Jan Steen** (1625–79), who, along with Vermeer, is probably the most admired Dutch genre painter. You can see what he had in mind: Steen's paintings offer the same Rabelaisian peasantry in full fling, but they go their debauched ways in broad daylight, and nowhere do you see the filthy rogues in shadowy hovels favoured by Brouwer and Ostade. Steen offers more humour, too, as well as more moralising, identifying with the hedonistic mob and reproaching them at the same time. Indeed, many of his pictures are illustrations of well-known proverbs of the time – popular epithets on the evils of drink or the transience of human existence that were supposed to teach as well as entertain.

Gerrit Dou (1613–75) was Rembrandt's Leiden contemporary and one of his first pupils. It's difficult to detect any trace of the master's influence in his work, however, Dou instead initiating a style of his own – tiny, minutely realised, and beautifully finished views of a kind of ordinary life that was decidedly more genteel than Brouwer's, or even Steen's for that matter. He was esteemed, above all, for his painstaking attention to detail: he would, it was said, sit in his studio for hours waiting for the dust to settle before starting work. Among his students, **Frans van Mieris** (1635–81) continued to produce highly finished portrayals of the Dutch bourgeoisie, as did **Gabriel Metsu** (1629–67) – perhaps Dou's greatest pupil – whose pictures often convey an overtly moral message. Another pupil of Rembrandt's, though a much later one, was **Nicholaes Maes** (1629–93), whose early paintings were almost entirely genre paintings, sensitively executed and again with a moralising message. His later work shows the influence of a more refined style of portrait, which he had picked up in France.

As a native of Zwolle, **Gerard ter Borch** (1619–81) found himself far from all these Leiden/Rembrandt connections, and despite trips abroad to most of the artistic capitals of Europe, he remained very much a provincial painter all his life, depicting Holland's merchant class at play and becoming renowned for his curious doll-like figures and his enormous ability to capture the textures of different cloths. His domestic scenes were not unlike those of **Pieter de Hooch** (1629–after 1684), whose simple depictions of everyday life are deliberately unsentimental, and, for the first time, have little or no moral commentary. De Hooch's favourite trick was to paint darkened rooms with an open door leading through to a sunlit courtyard, a practice that, along with his trademark rusty red colour, makes his work easy to identify – and, at its best, exquisite. That said, his later pictures reflect the encroaching decadence of the Dutch republic: the rooms are more richly decorated, the arrangements more contrived and the subjects far less homely.

It was, however, **Jan Vermeer** (1632–75) who brought the most sophisticated methods to painting interiors, depicting the play of natural light on indoor surfaces with superlative skill; it's for this and the curious peace and intimacy of his pictures that he is best known. Another recorder of the better-heeled Dutch households, and, like de Hooch, without any overt moral tone, he is regarded (with Hals and Rembrandt) as one of the big three Dutch painters – though, he was, it seems, a slow worker, and only about forty small paintings can be attributed to him with any certainty. Living all his life in Delft, Vermeer is perhaps the epitome of the seventeenth-century Dutch painter – rejecting the pomp and ostentation of the High Renaissance to quietly record his contemporaries at home, painting for a public that demanded no more than that.

PORTRAITURE

Naturally, the ruling bourgeoisie of Holland's flourishing mercantile society wanted to put their success on record, and it's little wonder that portraiture was the best way for a young painter to make a living. **Michiel Jansz**

Miereveld (1567–1641), court painter to Frederick Henry in The Hague, was the first real portraitist of the Dutch Republic, but it wasn't long before his stiff and rather conservative figures were superseded by the more spontaneous renderings of **Frans Hals** (1585–1666). Hals is perhaps best known for his "corporation-pictures" – portraits of the members of the Dutch civil guard regiments that had been formed in most larger towns while the threat of invasion by the Spanish was still imminent. These large group pieces demanded superlative technique, since the painter had to create a collection of individual portraits while retaining a sense of the group, and accord prominence based on the importance of the sitter and the size of the payment each had made. Hals was particularly good at this, using innovative lighting effects, arranging his sitters subtly, and putting all the elements together in a fluid and dynamic composition. He also painted many individual portraits, making the ability to capture fleeting and telling expressions his trademark; his pictures of children are particularly sensitive. Later in life, his work became darker and more akin to that of Rembrandt.

Jan Cornelisz Verspronck (1597–1662) and **Bartholomeus van der Helst** (1613–70) were the other great Haarlem portraitists after Frans Hals – Verspronck recognisable by the smooth, shiny glow he always gave to his sitters' faces, van der Helst by a competent but unadventurous style. Of the two, van der Helst was the more popular, influencing a number of later painters and leaving Haarlem while still young to begin a solidly successful career as portrait painter to Amsterdam's burghers.

The reputation of **Rembrandt van Rijn** (1606–69) is still relatively recent – nineteenth-century connoisseurs preferred Gerrit Dou – but he is now justly regarded as one of the greatest and most versatile painters of all time. Born in Leiden, the son of a miller, he was apprenticed at an early age to **Jacob van Swanenburgh** – a then quite important, though uninventive, local artist. He shared a studio with **Jan Lievens**, a promising painter and something of a rival for a while (now all but forgotten), before going up to Amsterdam to study under the fashionable **Pieter Lastman**. Soon he was painting commissions for the city elite and an accepted member of their circle. The poet and statesman Constantijn Huygens acted as his agent, pulling strings to obtain all of Rembrandt's more lucrative jobs, and in 1634 he married Saskia van Ulenborch, daughter of the burgomeister of Leeuwarden and quite a catch for the still relatively humble artist. His self-portraits at the time show the confident face of security – on top of things and quite sure of where he's going.

Rembrandt would not always be the darling of the Amsterdam smart set, but his fall from grace was still some way off when he painted the *Night Watch* – a group portrait often associated with the artist's decline in popularity. Although Rembrandt's fluent arrangement of his subjects was totally original, there's no evidence that the military company who commissioned the painting were anything but pleased with the result. More likely culprits are the artist's later pieces, whose obscure lighting and psychological insight took the conservative Amsterdam burghers by surprise. His patrons were certainly not sufficiently enthusiastic about his work to support his taste for art collecting and his expensive house on Jodenbreestraat, and in 1656 possibly the most brilliant artist the city would ever know was declared bankrupt, dying thirteen years later, as his last self-portraits show, a broken and embittered old man. Throughout his career Rembrandt maintained a large studio, and his influence pervaded the next generation of Dutch painters. Some – Dou, Maes – more famous for their genre work, have already been mentioned. Others turned to portraiture. **Govert Flinck** (1615–60) was perhaps Rembrandt's most faithful follower, and he was, ironically, given the job of decorating Amsterdam's new town hall after his teacher had been passed over. He died before he could execute his designs, and Rembrandt was one of several artists commissioned to paint them – though his contribution was removed shortly afterwards. The work of **Ferdinand Bol** (1616–80) was so heavily influenced by Rembrandt that for a long time art historians couldn't tell the two apart. Most of the pitifully slim extant work of **Carel Fabritius** (1622–54) was portraiture, but he too died young, before he could properly realise his promise as perhaps the most gifted of all Rembrandt's students. Generally regarded as the teacher of Vermeer, he forms a link between the two

masters, combining Rembrandt's technique with his own practice of painting figures against a dark background, prefiguring the lighting and colouring of the Delft painter.

LANDSCAPES

Aside from Bruegel, whose depictions of his native surroundings make him the first true Low Countries landscape painter, **Gillis van Coninxloo** (1544–1607) stands out as the earliest Dutch landscapist. He imbued the native scenery with elements of fantasy, painting the richly wooded views he had seen on his travels around Europe as backdrops to Biblical scenes. In the early seventeenth century, **Hercules Seghers** (1590–1638), apprenticed to Coninxloo, carried on his mentor's style of depicting forested and mountainous landscapes, some real, others not: his work is scarce but is believed to have had considerable impact on the landscape work of Rembrandt. **Esaias van der Velde**'s (1591–1632) quaint and unpretentious scenes show the first real affinity with the Dutch countryside, but – though his influence, too, was great – he was soon overtaken in stature by his pupil **Jan van Goyen** (1596–1656), a remarkable painter who belongs to the so-called "tonal phase" of Dutch landscape painting. Van Goyen's early pictures were highly coloured and close to those of his teacher, but it didn't take him long to develop a markedly personal touch, using tones of greens, browns and greys to lend everything a characteristic translucent haze. His paintings are, above all, of nature, and if he included figures it was merely for the sake of scale. Neglected until a little over a century ago, his fluid and rapid brushwork became more acceptable as the Impressionists rose in stature.

Another "tonal" painter and a native of Haarlem, **Salomon van Ruisdael** (1600–70) was also directly affected by van der Velde, and his simple, atmospheric, though not terribly adventurous, landscapes were for a long time consistently confused with those of van Goyen. More esteemed is his nephew, **Jacob van Ruisdael** (1628–82), generally considered the greatest of all Dutch landscapists, whose fastidiously observed views of quiet flatlands dominated by stormy skies were to influence European painters' impressions of nature right up to the nineteenth century. (Constable, certainly, acknowledged a debt to him.)

Ruisdael's foremost pupil was **Meindert Hobbema** (1638–1709), who followed the master faithfully, sometimes even painting the same views (his *Avenue at Middelharnis* may be familiar).

Nicholas Berchem (1620–83) and **Jan Both** (1618–52) were the "Italianisers" of Dutch landscapes. They studied in Rome and were influenced by Claude, taking back to Holland rich, golden views of the world, full of steep gorges and hills, picturesque ruins and wandering shepherds. **Allart van Everdingen** (1621–75) had a similar approach, but his subject matter stemmed from travels in Scandinavia, which, after his return to Holland, he reproduced in all its mountainous glory.

Aelbert Cuyp (1620–91), on the other hand, stayed in Dordrecht all his life, painting what was probably the favourite city skyline of Dutch landscapists. He inherited the warm tones of the Italianisers, and his pictures are always suffused with a deep, golden glow.

Of a number of **specialist seventeenth-century painters** who can be included here, **Paulus Potter** (1625–54) is rated as the best painter of **domestic animals**. He produced a fair amount of work in a short lifetime, most reputed being his lovingly executed pictures of cows and horses. The accurate rendering of **architectural features** also became a specialised field, of which **Pieter Saenredam** (1597–1665), with his finely realised paintings of Dutch church interiors, is the most widely known exponent. **Emanuel de Witte** (1616–92) continued in the same vein, though his churches lack the spartan crispness of those of Saenredam. **Gerrit Berckheyde** (1638–98) worked in Haarlem soon after, but limited his views to the outside of buildings, producing variations on the same scenes around town.

In the seventeenth century another thriving category of painting was the **still life**, in which objects were gathered together to remind the viewer of the transience of human life and the meaninglessness of all worldly pursuits: often a skull would be joined by a book, a pipe or a goblet, and some half-eaten food. Again, two Haarlem painters dominated this field: **Pieter Claesz** (1598–1660) and **Willem Heda** (1594–1680), who confined themselves almost entirely to these carefully arranged groups of objects.

THE EIGHTEENTH CENTURY

With the demise of Holland's economic boom, the quality – and originality – of Dutch painting began to decline. The delicacy of some of the classical seventeenth-century painters was replaced by finicky still lifes and minute studies of flowers, or finely finished portraiture and religious scenes, as in the work of **Adrian van der Werff** (1659–1722). Of the era's big names, **Gerard de Lairesse** (1640–1711) spent most of his time decorating the splendid civic halls and palaces that were going up all over the place, and, like the buildings he worked on, his style and influences were French. **Jacob de Wit** (1695–1754) continued where Lairesse left off, receiving more church commissions as Catholicism was allowed out of the closet. The period's only painter of any true renown was **Cornelis Troost** (1697–1750), who, although he didn't produce anything really new, painted competent portraits and some neat, faintly satirical pieces that have since earned him the title of "The Dutch Hogarth". Cosy interiors also continued to prove popular, and the Haarlem painter **Wybrand Hendriks** (1744–1831) satisfied demand with proficient examples.

French influence was dominant in the area that was to become Belgium. Artists such as **Jan Joseph Horemans I** and **Balthasar van den Bossche** took the Flemish genre painting of the previous century and made it palatable for Parisian tastes. Towards the end of the century neo-Classicism became the vogue, and the entire period was marked by the weakening of domestic tradition in favour of external influences. **Laurent Delvaux** (1696–1778) was also an important figure during this period, a Flemish sculptor who produced a large number of works for Belgian churches, including the pulpit of Ghent's cathedral and other pieces in Brussels.

THE NINETEENTH CENTURY

HOLLAND

Johann Barthold Jongkind (1819–91) was the first great artist to emerge from nineteenth-century Holland, painting landscapes and seascapes that were to influence Monet and the early Impressionists. He spent most of his life in France and his work was exhibited in Paris with the Barbizon painters, though he owed less to them than to the landscapes of van Goyen and the seventeenth-century "tonal" artists.

Jongkind's work was a logical precursor to the art of the **Hague School**, a group of painters based in and around that city between 1870 and 1900 who tried to re-establish a characteristically Dutch national school of painting. They produced atmospheric studies of the dunes and polderlands around The Hague, pictures that are characterised by grey, rain-filled skies, windswept seas, and silvery, flat beaches – and that, for some, verge on the sentimental. **J. H. Weissenbruch** (1824–1903) was a founding member, a specialist in low, flat beach scenes dotted with stranded boats. The banker-turned-artist **H. W. Mesdag** (1831–1915) did the same but with more skill than imagination, while **Jacob Maris** (1837–99), one of three artist brothers, was perhaps the most typical Hague School painter, with his rural and sea scenes dominated by gloomy chasing skies. His brother, **Matthijs** (1839–1917), was less predictable, ultimately tiring of his colleagues' interest in straight observation and going to London to design windows, while **Willem** (1844–1910), the youngest, is best known for his small, unpretentious studies of nature.

Anton Mauve (1838–88) is a better known artist, an exponent of soft, pastel landscapes and an early teacher of van Gogh. Profoundly influenced by the French Barbizon painters – Corot, Millet *et al* – he went to Hilversum in 1885 to set up his own group, which became known as the "Dutch Barbizon". **Jozef Israëls** (1826–1911) has often been likened to Millet, though it's generally agreed that he had more in common with the Impressionists, and his best pictures are his melancholy portraits and interiors. Lastly, **Johan Bosboom**'s (1817–91) church interiors may be said to sum up the nostalgia of the Hague School – shadowy works, populated by figures in seventeenth-century dress, that seem to yearn for Holland's Golden Age.

Vincent van Gogh (1853–90) was one of the least "Dutch" of Dutch artists, and he lived out most of his relatively short painting career in Belgium and France. After countless studies of peasant life in his native North Brabant – studies which culminated in the sombre *Potato Eaters* – and a spell in the industrial Borinage area of southern Belgium, he went to live in Paris with his art-dealer brother, Theo. There, under the influence of the Impressionists, he lightened his palette, following the pointillist work of Seurat and "trying to render intense colour and not a grey harmony". Two years later he went south to Arles, the "land of blue tones and gay colours", and, struck by the harsh Mediterranean light, his characteristic style began to develop. A disastrous attempt to live with Gauguin, and the much-publicised episode when he cut off part of his ear and presented it to a woman in a nearby brothel, led eventually to committal to an asylum at St-Remy, where he produced some of his most famous, and most Expressionistic, canvases – strongly coloured and with the paint thickly, almost frantically, applied.

Like van Gogh, **Jan Toorop** (1858–1928) went through multiple artistic changes, though he didn't need to travel the world to do so; he radically adapted his technique from a fairly conventional pointillism through a tired Expressionism to Symbolism with an Art Nouveau feel. Roughly contemporary, **G. H. Breitner** (1857–1923) was a better painter, and one who refined his style rather than changed it. His snapshot-like impressions of his beloved Amsterdam figure among his best work and offered a promising start to the new century.

BELGIUM

Until the coming of the Kingdom of Belgium in 1830, French styles of painting remained the most significant – neo-Classicist painting, chiefly that derived from Jacques Louis David, was particularly popular in first part of the century. David's pupil, **François Joseph Navez** (1787–1869), was the most important of his followers working in Belgium, furthering the influence of neo-Classicism via his position as director of the Brussels academy. With independence from Holland, came, as might be expected, a rise in nationalism – artists such as **Gustave Wappers** (1807–74) leading a movement that favoured a romantic interpretation of historical events, idealising both recent and medieval history. **Antoine Wiertz** (1806–65) was celebrated for his grandiose romantic canvases, and **Henri de Braekeleer** (1840–88) for his Dutch-inspired interiors and landscapes. Indeed landscape painting underwent a resurgence of popularity throughout Europe in the mid-nineteenth century, and Belgian artists once again reflected the tastes and movements of France, with artists like **Théodor Fourmois** and **Eugène Huberti** involved with the Barbizon group, and **Emile Claus** (1849–1924) adapting French Impressionist ideas into an individual style known as Luminism. **Paul-Jean Clays** (1819–1900), **Louis Artan** (1837–90) and **Theodoor Baron** (1840–99) also took their lead from the Impressionists, but retained a distinctive local approach.

One artist who stands out during this period is **Constantin Meunier** (1831–1905), a painter and sculptor whose naturalistic paintings and sculptures of brawny workers and mining scenes were the perfect mirror of a fast-industrialising Europe – and Belgium. Much of Meunier's work depicts life in the industrial parts of Hainaut, notably the Borinage, and there are good collections of it all over Belgium, not least in Brussels.

Perhaps the best known Belgian artist of the late nineteenth century is **James Ensor** (1860–1949). Ensor, who lived in Ostend for most of his life, painted macabre, disturbing works, whose haunted style can be traced back to Bosch and Bruegel and which was itself a precursor of Expressionism. He was active in a group known as **Les XX** (*Les Vingt*), which organised exhibitions of new styles of art from abroad, and greatly influenced his contemporary Belgian painters.

THE TWENTIETH CENTURY

HOLLAND

Most of the trends in the visual arts of the early twentieth century found their way to Holland at one time or another: of many minor names, **Jan Sluyters** (1881–1957) was the Dutch pioneer of Cubism. But only one movement was specifically Dutch – **de Stijl** (literally "the Style").

Piet Mondrian (1872–1944) was de Stijl's leading figure, developing the realism he had learned from the Hague School painters – via Cubism, which he criticised for being too cowardly to depart totally from representation – into a complete abstraction of form which he called **neo-plasticism**. He was something of a mystic, and this was to some extent responsible for the direction that de Stijl – and his paintings – took: canvases painted with grids of lines and blocks made up of the three primary colours and white, black and grey. Mondrian believed this freed the work of art from the vagaries of personal perception, and made it possible to obtain what he called "a true vision of reality".

De Stijl took other forms, too: there was a magazine of the same name, and the movement introduced new concepts into every aspect of design, from painting to interior design to architecture. But in all these media lines were kept simple, colours bold and clear. **Theo van Doesburg** (1883–1931) was a de Stijl co-founder and major theorist: his work is similar to that of Mondrian except for the noticeable absence of thick, black borders and the diagonals that he introduced into his work, calling his paintings "contra-compositions" – which, he said, were both more dynamic and more in touch with twentieth-century life. **Bart van der Leck** (1876–1958) was the third member of the circle, identifiable by white canvases covered by seemingly randomly placed interlocking coloured triangles.

Mondrian split with de Stijl in 1925, going on to attain new artistic extremes of clarity and soberness before moving to New York in the 1940s and producing atypically exuberant works such as *Victory Boogie Woogie* – so named because of the artist's love of jazz.

During and after de Stijl, a number of other movements flourished, though their impact was not so great and their influence largely confined to the Low Countries. The Expressionist **Bergen School** was probably the most localised, its best-known exponent **Charley Toorop** (1891–1955), daughter of Jan, who developed a distinctively glaring but strangely sensitive realism. **De Ploeg** (The Plough), centred in Groningen, was headed by **Jan Wiegers** (1893–1959) and influenced by Kirchner and the German Expressionists; the group's artists set out to capture the uninviting landscapes around their native town, and produced violently coloured canvases that hark back to van Gogh. Another group, known as the **Magic Realists**, surfaced in the 1930s, painting quasi-surrealistic scenes that, according to their leading light, **Carel Willinck** (b.1900), reveal "a world stranger and more dreadful in its haughty impenetrability than the most terrifying nightmare".

Postwar Dutch art began with **CoBrA**: a loose grouping of like-minded painters from Denmark, Belgium and Holland, whose name derives from the initial letters of their respective capital cities. Their first exhibition, at Amsterdam's Stedelijk Museum in 1949, provoked a huge uproar, at the centre of which was **Karel Appel** (b.1921), whose brutal Abstract Expressionist pieces, plastered with paint inches thick, were, he maintained, necessary for the era – indeed, inevitable reflections of it. "I paint like a barbarian in a barbarous age," he claimed. In the graphic arts the most famous twentieth-century figure is **M. C. Escher** (1898–1970).

As for **today**, there's as vibrant an art scene as there ever was, best exemplified in Amsterdam by the rotating exhibitions of the Stedelijk or the nearby Overholland Museum, and some of the numerous private Amsterdam galleries. Of contemporary Dutch artists, look out for the abstract work of **Edgar Fernhout** and **Ad Dekkers**; the reliefs of **Jan Schoonhoven**; the multi-media productions of **Jan Dibbets**; the glowering realism of **Marlene Dumas**; the imprecisely coloured

LOW COUNTRIES GALLERIES: A HIT LIST

HOLLAND

In **Amsterdam**, the *Rijksmuseum* gives a complete overview of Dutch art up to the end of the nineteenth century, in particular the work of Rembrandt, Hals, and the major artists of the Golden Age; the *Van Gogh Museum* is best for the Impressionists and, of course, van Gogh; and, for twentieth-century and contemporary Dutch art, there's the *Stedelijk*. Within easy reach of the city, the *Frans Hals Museum* in **Haarlem** holds some of the best work of Hals and the Haarlem School; also in Haarlem, the *Teyler's Museum* is strong on eighteenth- and nineteenth-century Dutch works. In **Leiden**, the *Lakenhal* has by, among others, local artists Dou and Rembrandt, and the *Centraal* in **Utrecht** has paintings by van Scorel and the Utrecht School. Also in Utrecht, the *Catherine Convent Museum* boasts an excellent collection of works by Flemish artists and by Hals and Rembrandt.

Further afield, **The Hague**'s *Gemeente Museum* owns the country's largest set of Mondrians, and its *Mauritshuis* collection contains works by Rembrandt, Vermeer and others of the era. The *Boymans van Beuningen Museum* in **Rotterdam** has a weighty stock of Flemish primitives and surrealists, as well as works by Rembrandt and other seventeenth-century artists; and nearby **Dordrecht**'s *Municipal Museum* offers an assortment of seventeenth-century paintings that includes work by Aelbert Cuyp, and later canvases by the Hague School and Breitner.

The *Kroller-Muller Museum*, just outside **Arnhem**, is probably the country's finest modern art collection, and has a superb collection of van Goghs; a little further east, **Enschede**'s *Rijksmuseum Twenthe* has quality works from the Golden Age to the twentieth century.

BELGIUM & LUXEMBOURG

Brussels' *Musées Royaux des Beaux Arts* together comprise an excellent survey of Low Countries painting: the Flemish Primitives, Bruegel and Rubens in the *Musée d'Art Ancien*, Ensor, Magritte and Delvaux in the *Musée d'Art Moderne*. **Antwerp's** *Museum voor Schone Kunsten* has everything from Flemish Primitives to nineteenth-century masters, with all the great names – van Eyck, van der Weyden, Rubens, van Dyck, Jordaens, Brouwer, Teniers, Ensor and Delvaux – getting a look in. The *Mayer van den Burgh* museum has work by Quentin Matsys and Bruegel, and the *Onze Lieve* cathedral two of Rubens' seminal works. The *Memling Museum* in

Bruges has some of the artist's best works, housed in a magnificent medieval hospice; the *Groeninge Museum* also has work by the Flemish Primitives: van der Weyden, van der Goes, Gerhard David and an important van Eyck. Van Eyck's greatest work, *The Adoration of the Mystic Lamb* is housed in St Baaf's Cathedral in **Ghent**.

Luxembourg isn't well served in terms of great collections, although the *Musée National* in Luxembourg city has recently taken custody (for seven years) of the Bentick-Thyssen collection of mainly Dutch and Flemish art – a marvellous coup for a museum whose own array of art is fairly mediocre.

geometric designs of **Rob van Koningsbruggen**; the smeary Expressionism of **Toon Verhoef**; and the exuberant figures of **Rene Daniels** – to name only the most important figures.

BELGIUM

As in Holland, each of the major modern movements had its followers in Belgium, and each was diluted or altered according to local taste. **Expressionism** was manifest in a local group of artists established in Laethem St Marten in Flanders, most eye-catching of which was the work of **Constant Permeke** (1886–1952), whose bold, deeply coloured canvases can be found in many Belgian galleries. **Surrealism** also caught on in a big way, perhaps because of the Flemish penchant for the bizarre and grotesque. **René Magritte** (1898–1967), one of the leading lights of the movement, was born and trained in Belgium and returned there after being involved in the movement's birth in 1927. His Surrealism is gentle compared to the work of Dalí or de Chirico: ordinary images are used in a dreamlike way, often playing on the distinction between a word and its meaning. His most famous motif was the man in the bowler hat, whose face was always hidden from view. **Paul Delvaux** (1897–1989) adopted his own rather salacious interpretation of the movement – a sort of "What-the-butler-saw" Surrealism.

Most of the interwar artists were influenced by van Doesburg and de Stijl in Holland, though none figured highly in the movement. The abstract geometrical works of **Victor Severanckx** (1897–1965) owed much to de Stijl, and he in turn inspired the postwar group known as **La Jeune Peinture**, who along with CoBrA (see above) were the most notable artists working in the country, the antecedents of the Abstract Expressionists of the 1950s. While none of the CoBrA artists achieved the fame of Karel Appel, **Pierre Aleckinsky** is perhaps the best known among the Belgians.

Contemporary Belgian painting seems to have turned away from "movements" in favour of individualism and community art, a trend underlined by the fact that there are separate Flemish amd Walloon ministries of culture. Even so, the country has produced few artists of recent note, and it seems left to Holland to remain at the vanguard of the contemporary Low Countries art scene.

BOOKS

HISTORY

Pieter Geyl *The Revolt of The Netherlands 1555–1609*; and *The Netherlands in the Seventeenth Century 1609–1648* (Cassell £6.95 each). Geyl's two volumes of history present a concise account of the Netherlands during its formative years, chronicling the uprising against the Spanish and the formation of the United Provinces. Without doubt the definitive books on the period.

Geoffrey Parker *The Dutch Revolt* (Penguin £5.95). Compelling account of the struggle between the Netherlands and Spain. Perhaps the best work of its kind.

J.H. Huizinga *Dutch Civilisation in the Seventeenth Century* (Collins o/p). Analysis of life and culture in the Dutch Republic by the late, widely respected historian.

J.L. Price *Culture and Society in the Dutch Republic in the Seventeenth Century* (Batsford o/p). An accurate, intelligent account of the Golden Age.

Simon Schama *The Embarrassment of Riches: An Interpretation of Dutch Culture in the Golden Age* (Collins £12.95). The most recent – and one of the most accessible – works on the Golden Age, drawing on a huge variety of archive sources. Justifiably the biggest selling book on Dutch history ever written.

Sir William Temple *Observations upon the United Provinces of The Netherlands* (OUP £20). Written by a seventeenth-century English diplomat, and a good, evocative account of the country at the time.

Dedalo Carasso *A Short History of Amsterdam* (Amsterdam Historical Museum f17.50). Brief account written from a left-wing perspective, well illustrated with photos of artefacts from the Amsterdam Historical Museum.

Geoffrey Cotterell *Amsterdam* (Saxon House o/p). Popularised, offbeat history giving a highly readable account of the city up to the late 1960s.

E.H. Kossmann *The Low Countries 1780–1940* (OUP £30). Gritty, technically detailed but ultimately rather turgid narrative of the Low Countries from the Austrian era to World War II. Concentrates on the narrow arena of party politics.

A de Meeüs *History of the Belgians* (o/p). Entertaining if rather confused attempt at an exhaustive history of the Belgians, from "prehistoric dawns" to modern times. Good on incidental detail.

Michael Glover *A New Guide to the Battlefields of Northern France and the Low Countries* (Michael Joseph £14.95). Battlefields guide that is not entirely devoted to the Low Countries but has substantial sections on the conflicts at Bastogne, Arnhem, Ypres and Waterloo. Deliberately readable, well illustrated, and an essential handbook if you're exploring the region.

ART AND ARCHITECTURE

Max J. Friedlander *From Van Eyck to Bruegel* (Phaidon £6.50). Definitive and learned account of the early Flemish masters, though stylistically and factually (in the light of modern research) beginning to show its age.

Walter S. Gibson *Bosch* (Thames & Hudson £5.95). Standard introductory work on the late fifteenth-century painter.

Gregory Martin *Bruegel* (Thames & Hudson £5.95). Good introduction to the religious paintings and genre scenes of Pieter, the most well-known and influential of the Bruegel s.

Eugene Fromentin *The Masters of Past Time: Dutch and Flemish Painting from Van Eyck to Rembrandt* (Phaidon £6.50). Entertaining essays on the major Dutch and Flemish painters.

R. H. Fuchs *Dutch Painting* (Thames & Hudson £5.95). As complete an introduction to the subject – from Flemish origins to the present day – as you could wish for in a couple of hundred pages.

Jacob Rosenberg et al. _Dutch Art and Architecture 1600–1800_ (Penguin £18.95). Full and erudite anthology of essays on the art and buildings of the Golden Age and after. Strictly for dedicated Dutch art fans.

Christopher White _Rembrandt_ (Thames & Hudson £4.95). The most widely available – and wide-ranging – study of the painter and his work.

Svetlana Alpers _Rembrandt's Enterprise_ (Thames & Hudson £20). Intriguing study of Rembrandt, positing the theory – in line with the recent findings of the Leiden-based Rembrandt Research Project – that many previously accepted works are not by Rembrandt at all but merely the products of his studio.

Pierre Cabanne _Van Gogh_ (Thames & Hudson £4.95). Standard mix of art criticism and biography, drawing heavily on the artist's own letters, which are published by Flamingo at £3.50.

Irving Stone _Lust for Life_ (Methuen £2.95). Everything you ever wanted to know about Vincent van Gogh in a pop genius-is-pain biography.

Wolfgang Stechow _Dutch Landscape Painting of the Seventeenth Century_ (Phaidon £7.50). All-encompassing rundown on the many and varied landscapists of the Dutch Golden Age.

Alastair Smart _The Renaissance and Mannerism outside Italy_ (Thames & Hudson o/p). A very readable survey that includes lengthy chapters on van Eyck and his contemporaries, their successors, Bosch and Bruegel, and the later, more Mannerist-inclined painters of the Low Countries. A fine introduction to a lengthy period.

H.L.C. Jaffe _De Stijl: Visions of Utopia_ (Phaidon £15.95). A good, informed introduction to the movement and its philosophical and social influences.

Christopher White _Peter Paul Rubens: Man and Artist_ (Yale UP £50). A beautifully illustrated introduction to both Rubens' work and social milieu.

Kenneth Clark _Civilisation_ (Penguin £3.95). This includes a warm and scholarly rundown on the Golden Age, with illuminating insights on the way in which the art reflected the period.

SPECIFIC GUIDES

Peter Glencross (ed.) _Top Guide to Amsterdam_ (Excellent Publications). The definitive gay guide to the city, by a Rough Guide contributor.

Guus Kemme (ed.) _Amsterdam Architecture: A Guide_ (Thoth f29.50). Illustrated guide to the architecture of Amsterdam, with potted accounts of the major buildings.

Christian Rheinwald _Amsterdam Art Guide_ (Art Guide Pubs £5.95). Comprehensive guide to the city's galleries, shops and contact points for both artists and those wanting to tour the art scene.

Jan Stoutenbeek et al. _A Guide to Jewish Amsterdam_ (De Haan £9.50). Fascinating, though perhaps over-detailed, guide to just about every Jewish monument in the city. Purchase a copy before you leave from the _Netherlands Board of Tourism_, or in better Amsterdam bookshops.

LITERATURE

Jerome Brouwers _Sunken Red_ (Peter Owen £12.95). A best-selling novel in Holland that tells a bleak tale of a child's imprisonment in Japan during World War II.

Simon Carmiggelt _Kronkels_ (De Arbeiderspers o/p). Simon Carmiggelt wrote these short pieces, usually concise, wry anecdotes concerning everyday Dutch life, for _Het Parool_, an Amsterdam daily newspaper he helped to found. This is the second collection of what he termed his "slight adventures".

Hugo Claus _The Sorrow of Belgium_ (Viking £12.99). One of the Dutch language's foremost novelists, and another concerned with the subject of the effects of World War II in the region, charting the growing maturity of a young boy living in Flanders under the Nazi occupation. A huge book, it gets to grips well with the guilt, bigotry and mistrust of the period, causing an uproar when first published seven years ago.

Anne Frank _The Diary of a Young Girl_ (Pan £1.95). Lucid and moving, the most revealing thing you can read on the plight of Amsterdam's Jews during the war years.

Nicolas Freeling *A City Solitary, Love in Amsterdam; Cold Iron; Strike Out Where Not Applicable* (all published by Penguin at £2.25-2.50). Freeling writes detective novels, and his most famous creation is the rebel cop, van der Valk, around whom a successful British TV series was made. Light, carefully crafted tales, with just the right amount of twists to make them classic cops 'n' robbers reading – and with some good Dutch and Belgian locations.

Etty Hillesum *Etty: An Interrupted Life* (Granada £2.50). Diary of a young Jewish woman uprooted from her life in Amsterdam and taken to Auschwitz, where she died. As with Anne Frank's more famous journal, penetratingly written – though on the whole much less readable.

Margo Minco *The Glass Bridge* and *An Empty House* (Peter Owen £9.95, £12.95). An atmospheric novel, describing the plight of Dutch Jews during the last war, *The Glass Bridge* sold half a million copies in Holland. Its sequel follows the main character back to Amsterdam, where she tries to pick up the pieces of her life. A later novel, *The Fall*, is also published by Peter Owen (£10.95).

Harry Mulisch *The Assault* (Penguin £2.50). Set part in Haarlem, part in Amsterdam, *The Assault* traces the story of a young boy who loses his family in a Nazi reprisal-raid. A powerful tale, made into an excellent and effective film. Mulisch's later novel, *Last Call*, is a more introspective, less specifically Dutch work, more concerned with metaphysical questions concerning the nature of reality and fiction.

Multatuli *Max Havelaar: or the Coffee Auctions of the Dutch Trading Company* (Penguin £4.50). Classic nineteenth-century Dutch satire of colonial life in the East Indies. Eloquent and, at times, amusing.

Cees Noteboom *Rituals* (Penguin £2.95). An absorbing, sparsely written novel, mapping the empty existence of a rich Amsterdammer who dabbles in antiques. The later *In the Dutch Mountains* (Viking £10.95) is similarly aloof in style, and not directly about Holland, but it is nonetheless compelling at times, casting up offbeat philosophical musings like pearls.

Jona Oberski *Childhood* (Hodder & Stoughton £5.95). First published in 1978, this is a Jewish child's eye-witness account of the war years, the camps and executions. Written with feeling and precision.

Janwillem van de Wetering *Hard Rain* (Gollancz £9.95). An offbeat detective tale set in Amsterdam and provincial Holland. Like van de Wetering's other stories (sadly only available in the US), it's a humane, quirky and humorous story, worth reading for characters and locations as much as for inventive narrative.

Jan Wolkers *Turkish Delight* (Marion Boyars £3.95). Wolkers is one of the Netherlands' best-known artists and writers, and this is one of his early novels, examining closely a relationship between a bitter, working-class sculptor and his young, middle-class wife. It's not one of his best books by any means, but at times shows flashes of Wolkers' typically sardonic wit.

LANGUAGE

Throughout **Holland**, and in the **northern part of Belgium** (chiefly the provinces of Flanders, Antwerp and Limburg), the principal language is **Dutch**. Most Dutch-speakers, particularly in the main towns of Holland and in the tourist industry, speak English to varying degrees of excellence. The Dutch have a seemingly natural talent for languages, and your attempts at speaking theirs may be met with bewilderment.

Though around sixty percent of Belgians speak Dutch, the other forty percent speak a **dialect of French** known as **Walloon**, and live in Brussels and the country's southern provinces, known logically enough as Wallonia. Walloon is almost identical to French, and if you've any previous knowlege of the language, you'll be readily understood.

French is also the most widely spoken language of **Luxembourg**, along with German – although most Luxembourgers also speak their indigenous language of **Letzeburgesch**, a dialect of German.

DUTCH

Dutch is a Germanic language – the word "Dutch" itself is a corruption of *Deutsche*, a label inaccurately given by English sailors in the seventeenth century. Though the Dutch are at pains to stress the differences between the two languages, if you know any German you'll spot many similarities. As noted above, English is very widely spoken, but in smaller towns and in the countryside, where things aren't quite as cosmopolitan, the notes that follow will prove handy; they can be supplemented with the detailed "Food Glossary" on p.28.

Of the **phrase books and dictionaries** available, *Dutch at your Fingertips* (Routledge £3.95) is the most up-to-date and useful companion. To continue your studies, take a look at *Colloquial Dutch* (Routledge £3.95).

PRONUNCIATION

Dutch is pronounced much the same as English. However, there are a few Dutch sounds that don't exist in English, which can be difficult to pronounce without practice.

Consonants

v is like the English f in **f**ar

w like the v in **v**at

j like the initial sound of **y**ellow

ch and *g* are considerably harder than in English, enunciated much further back in the throat; in Amsterdam at least, where the pronunciation is particularly coarse, there's no real English equivalent. They become softer the further south you go, where they're more like the Scottish lo**ch.**

ng is as in bri**ng**

nj as in o**ni**on

Otherwise double consonants keep their separate sounds – *kn*, for example, is never like the English "knight".

Vowels and Dipthongs

Doubling the letter lengthens the vowel sound:

a is like the English **a**pple

aa like c**a**rt

e like l**e**t

ee like l**a**te

o as in p**o**p

oo in p**o**pe

u is like the French t**u** if preceded but not followed by a consonant (eg *nu*); it's like w**oo**d if followed by a consonant (eg *bus*).

uu the French t**u**

au and *ou* like h**o**w

ei and *ij* as in f**i**ne, though this varies strongly from region to region; sometimes it can sound more like l**a**ne.

oe as in s**oo**n

eu is like the dipthong in the French l**eu**r

ui is the hardest Dutch dipthong of all, pronounced like h**o**w but much further forward in the mouth, with lips pursed (as if to say "oo").

DUTCH WORDS AND PHRASES

Basics and Greetings

yes	*ja*	do you speak English?	*spreekt u Engels?*
no	*nee*	I don't understand	*Ik begrijp het niet*
please	*alstublieft*	women/men	*vrouwen/mannen*
(no) thank you	*[nee] dank u* or *bedankt*	children	*kinderen*
hello	*hallo* or *dag*	when?	*wanneer?*
good morning	*goede morgen*	I want	*ik wil*
good afternoon	*goedemiddag*	I don't want	*Ik wil niet. . .(+verb)*
good evening	*goedenavond*		*ik wil geen. . .(+noun)*
goodbye	*tot ziens*	how much is. . .?	*wat kost. . .?*
see you later	*tot straks*		

Finding the way

how do I get to. . .?	*hoe kom ik in. . .?*	left/right	*links/rechts*
where is. . .?	*waar is. . .?*	straight ahead	*recht uit gaan*
how far is it to. . .?	*hoe ver is het rnaar. . .?*	platform	*spoor* or *perron*
far/near	*ver/dichtbij*		

Money

post office	*postkantoor*	cashier	*kassa*
stamp(s)	*postzegel(s)*	ticket office	*loket*
money exchange	*wisselkantoor*		

Useful Words

good/bad	*goed/slecht*	cheap/expensive	*goedkoop/duur*
big/small	*groot/klein*	hot/cold	*heet/koud*
open/shut	*open/gesloten*	with/without	*met/zonder*
push/pull	*duwen/trekken*	here/there	*hier/daar*
new/old	*nieuw/oud*	men's/women's toilets	*heren/damen* s

Days and Times

Sunday	*Zondag*	Saturday	*Zaterdag*	minute	*minuut*
Monday	*Maandag*	yesterday	*gisteren*	hour	*uur*
Tuesday	*Dinsdag*	today	*vandaag*	day	*dag*
Wednesday	*Woensdag*	tomorrow	*morgen*	week	*week*
Thursday	*Donderdag*	tomorrow	*morgenochtend*	month	*maand*
Friday	*Vrijdag*	morning		year	*jaar*

Numbers

When saying a number, the Dutch generally transpose the last two digits: e.g., *drie gulden vijf en twintig* is f3.25.

0	*nul*	9	*negen*	18	*achttien*	80	*tachtig*
1	*een*	10	*tien*	19	*negentien*	90	*negentig*
2	*twee*	11	*elf*	20	*twintig*	100	*honderd*
3	*drie*	12	*twaalf*	21	*een en twintig*	101	*honderd een*
4	*vier*	13	*dertien*	30	*dertig*	200	*twee honderd*
5	*vijf*	14	*veertien*	40	*veertig*	201	*twee honderd een*
6	*zes*	15	*vijftien*	50	*vijftig*	500	*vijf honderd*
7	*zeven*	16	*zestien*	60	*zestig*	1000	*duizend*
8	*acht*	17	*zeventien*	70	*zeventig*		

FRENCH

French – or, more properly, the Walloon dialect of French spoken in Belgium's south – isn't language, despite the number of words shared with English, but learning the bare essentials is not difficult and makes all the difference. Even just saying "*Bonjour Madame/Monsieur*" when you go into a shop and then pointing will usually get you a smile and helpful service. People working in hotels, restaurants, etc, almost always speak some English and tend to use it if you're struggling – be grateful, not amused.

Differentiating words is the initial problem in understanding spoken French – it's very hard to get people to slow down. If, as a last resort, you get them to write it down, you'll probably find you know half the words anyway. See also French "Food Glossary", p264.

Of the available **phrase books and dictionaries**, *Harrap's French Phrase Book* (Harrap, £1.95) is a good pocket reference book, with useful contemporary phrases and a 5000 word dictionary of terms. *Harrap's Mini French Dictionary* (£1.95) has a brief grammar and pronunciation guide.

PRONUNCIATION

One easy rule to remember is that **consonants** at the ends of words are usually silent. *Pas plus tard* (not later) is thus pronounced pa-plu-tarr. But when the following word begins with a vowel, you run the two together: *pas après* (not after) thus becomes "pazapre'.

Consonants

Much as in English, except that: *ch* is always sh, *c* is s, *h* is silent, *th* is the same as t, *ll* is like the y in yes, *w* is v, and r is growled (or rolled).

Vowels

These are the hardest sounds to get right. Roughly:

a as in h**a**t
e as in g**e**t
é between g**e**t and g**a**te
è between g**e**t and g**u**t
eu like the **u** in h**u**rt
i as in mach**i**ne
o as in h**o**t
o, au as in **o**ver
ou as in f**oo**d
u as in a pursed-lip version of **u**se

More awkward are the **combinations** in/im, en/em, an/am, on/om, un/um at the ends of words, or followed by consonants other than n or m. Again, roughly:

in/im like the **an** in **an**xious
an/am, en/em like the d**on** in D**on**caster when said with a nasal accent
on/om like the d**on** in D**on**caster said by someone with a heavy cold
un/um like the **u** in **u**nderstand

FRENCH WORDS AND PHRASES

Useful Words and Phrases

Excuse me	pardon	good morning/ afternoon	bonjour
Do you speak English?	Vous parlez anglais?	good evening	bonsoir
yes	oui	good night	bonne nuit
no	non	How are you?	Comment allez-vous?/ Ça va?
I understand	Je comprends		
I don't understand	Je ne comprends pas	Sorry	Pardon, Madame/ je m'excuse
OK/agreed	d'accord		
please	s'il vous plaît	Leave me alone (aggressive)	Fichez-moi la paix!
thank you	merci		
hello	bonjour	Please help me	Aidez-moi, s'il vous plaît
goodbye	au revoir		

Finding the way

how do I get to...?	Comment est-ce que je peux arriver à . . ?	far	loin
		left	à gauche
where is . . .?	Où est . . .?	right	à droite
how far is it to . . .?	Combien y a-t-il jusqu' à	straight on	tout droit
near	près/pas loin	behind	derrière

Basics and Greetings

now	maintenant	big	grand
later	plus tard	small	petit
man	un homme	a lot	beaucoup
woman	une femme	good	bon
here	ici	bad	mauvais
there	là	hot	chaud
open	ouvert	cold	froid
closed	fermé		

Days and Dates

Sunday	dimanche	Friday	vendredi	tomorrow morning	aujourd'hui matin
Monday	lundi	Saturday	samedi	hour	heure
Tuesday	mardi	today	aujourd'hui	day	jour
Wednesday	mercredi	yesterday	hier	week	semaine
Thursday	jeudi	tomorrow	demain	month	mois

Numbers

1	un	11	onze	21	vingt-et-un	95	quatre-vingt-quinze
2	deux	12	douze	22	vingt-deux	100	cent
3	trois	13	treize	30	trente	101	cent-et-un
4	quatre	14	quatorze	40	quarante	200	deux cents
5	cinq	15	quinze	50	cinquante	300	trois cents
6	six	16	seize	60	soixante	500	cinq cents
7	sept	17	dix-sept	70	soixante-dix	1000	mille
8	huit	18	dix-huit	75	soixante-quinze	1,000,000	un million
9	neuf	19	dix-neuf	80	quatre-vingts		
10	dix	20	vingt	90	quatre-vingt-dix		

GLOSSARIES

DUTCH TERMS

ABDIJ Abbey or group of monastic buildings.

AMSTERDAMMERTJE Phallic-shaped objects placed alongside Amsterdam streets to keep drivers off pavements and out of canals.

BEIAARD Carillon chimes.

BEGIJNHOF Similar to a *hofje* but occupied by Catholic women (*Begijns*) who led semi-religious lives without taking full vows.

BELFORT Belfry.

BURGHER Member of the upper or mercantile classes of a town in the fifteenth to eighteenth centuries, usually with certain civic powers.

FIETSPAD Bicycle path.

GASTHUIS Hospice for the sick or infirm.

GEMEENTE Municipal: eg *Gemeentehuis* – town hall.

GEVEL Gable. The only decoration practical on the narrow-fronted canal house was on its gables. Initially fairly simple, they developed into an ostentatious riot of individualism in the late seventeenth century before turning to a more restrained classicism in the eighteenth and nineteenth centuries.

GILD Guild.

GERECHTSHOF Law Courts.

GRACHT Canal.

HALLE Hall.

HIJSBALK Pulley beam, often decorated, fixed to the top of a gable to lift goods, furniture etc. Essential in canal houses whose staircases were narrow and steep, *hijsbalken* are still very much in use today.

HOF Courtyard.

HOFJE Almshouse, usually for elderly women who could look after themselves but needed small charities such as food and fuel; usually a number of buildings centred around a small, peaceful courtyard.

HUIS House.

JEUGDHERBERG Youth hostel.

KERK Church; eg *Grote Kerk* – the principal church of the town; *Onze Lieve Vrouwe kerk* –

church dedicated to the Virgin Mary.

KONINKLIJK Royal.

LAKENHAL Cloth hall. The building in medieval weaving towns where cloth would be weighed, graded and sold.

LUCHTHAVEN Airport.

MARKT Central town square and the heart of most Dutch communities, normally still the site of weekly markets.

OMMEGANG Procession.

POLDER An area of land reclaimed from the sea.

POSTBUS Post office box.

PLEIN A square or open space.

RAADHUIS Town hall.

RANDSTAD Literally "rim-town", this refers to the urban conurbation that makes up much of North and South Holland, stretching from Amsterdam in the north down to Rotterdam and Dordrecht in the south.

RIJKS State.

SCHEPENZAAL Alderman's Hall.

SCHOUWBURG Theatre.

SIERKUNST Decorative arts.

SCHONE KUNSTEN Fine arts.

SPIONNETJE Small mirror on canal house enabling occupant to see who is at the door without descending stairs.

SPOOR Platform (on a train station).

STADHUIS The most common word for a town hall.

STICHTING Institute or foundation.

STEDELIJK Civic, municipal.

STEEN Fortress.

VOLKSKUNDE Folklore.

VVV Dutch tourist information office

WAAG Old public weighing-house, a common feature of most towns – usually found on the Markt.

FRENCH TERMS

ABBAYE Abbey.

AUBERGE DE LA JEUNESSE Youth hostel.

BEAUX ARTS Fine arts.

CHÂTEAU Mansion, country house, or castle.

COUVENT Convent, monastery.

DEGUSTATION Tasting (wine or food).

DONJON Castle keep.

ÉGLISE Church.

ENTRÉE Entrance.

FERMETURE Closing period.

FOUILLES Archaeological excavations.

GALLO-ROMAIN Period of Roman occupation of Gaul, from the first to fourth century AD.

GARE Station.

GÎTE D'ÉTAPE Basic hostel accommodation, primarily for walkers.

GOBELINS Most famous tapestry manufacturer, based in Paris, whose most renowned period was in the reign of Louis XIV.

HALLES Covered market.

HÔTEL DE VILLE Town hall.

JOURS FERIÉS Public holidays.

MARCHÉ Market.

PLACE Square.

PORTE Gateway.

PTT Post office.

QUARTIER District of a town.

SORTIE Exit.

SYNDICAT D'INITIATIVE Tourist office.

TOUR Tower.

ARCHITECTURAL TERMS

AMBULATORY Covered passage around the outer edge of the choir of a church.

APSE Semicircular protrusion at (usually) the east end of a church.

ART DECO Geometrical style of art and architecture popular in the 1930s.

ART NOUVEAU Style of art, architecture and design based on highly stylised vegetal forms. Popular in the early part of the twentieth century.

BAROQUE High Renaissance period of art and architecture, distinguished by extreme ornateness, exuberance and complex spatial arrangement of interiors.

CABINET-PIECE Small, finely detailed painting of a domestic scene.

CARILLON A set of tuned church bells, either operated by an automatic mechanism or played by a keyboard.

CARYATID A sculptured female figure used as a column.

CAROLINGIAN Dynasty founded by Charlemagne; late eighth to early tenth century. Also refers to art, etc, of the time.

CLASSICAL Architectural style incorporating Greek and Roman elements – pillars, domes, colonnades etc – at its height in the seventeenth century and revived, as **Neoclassical**, in the nineteenth century.

CLERESTORY Upper story of a church, incorporating the windows.

FLAMBOYANT Florid form of Gothic (see below).

FRESCO Wall painting – durable through application to wet plaster.

GABLE The triangular upper portion of a wall – decorative or supporting a roof. See *Gevel*, above.

GOTHIC Architectural style of the thirteenth to sixteenth centuries, characterised by pointed arches, rib vaulting, flying buttresses and a general emphasis on verticality.

MEROVINGIAN Dynasty ruling France and parts of Germany from sixth to mid-eighth centuries. Refers also to art, etc, of the period.

MISERICORD Ledge on choir stall on which occupant can be supported while standing; often carved with secular subjects (bottoms were not thought worthy of religious ones).

NAVE Main body of a church.

NEOCLASSICAL Architectural style derived from Greek and Roman elements – pillars, domes, colonnades, etc – popular in the Low Countries during French rule in the early nineteenth century.

ROCOCO Highly florid, light and graceful eighteenth-century style of architecture, painting and interior design, forming the last phase of Baroque.

RENAISSANCE Movement in art and architecture developed in fifteenth-century Italy.

RETABLE Altarpiece.

ROMANESQUE Early medieval architecture distinguished by squat forms, rounded arches and naive sculpture.

STUCCO Plastic used to embellish ceilings, etc.

TRANSEPT Arms of a cross-shaped church, placed at ninety degrees to nave and chancel.

TRIPTYCH Carved or painted work on three panels. Often used as an altarpiece.

TYMPANUM Sculpted panel above a church door.

VAUBAN Seventeenth-century military architect – his fortresses still stand all over Europe and the Low Countries.

VAULT An arched ceiling or roof.

INDEX